SAḤĪḤ MUSLIM

BEING TRADITIONS OF THE SAYINGS AND DOINGS OF THE PROPHET MUḤAMMAD AS NARRATED BY HIS COMPANIONS AND COMPILED UNDER THE TITLE *AL-JĀMI'-UṢ-ṢAḤĪḤ*

BY IMĀM MUSLIM

Rendered into English by

'ABDUL ḤAMĪD ṢIDDĪQĪ

With Explanatory Notes and Brief Biographical Sketches of Major Narrators

VOL. I—Containing

(1) Kitāb al-Īmān
(2) Kitāb al-Ṭahārah
(3) Kitāb al-Ḥaiḍ
(4) Kitāb al-Ṣalāt (Contd.)

SH. MUHAMMAD ASHRAF
PUBLISHERS & BOOKSELLERS
7-Aibak Road (New Anarkali) LAHORE-7 (Pak.)

ISBN No. 969—432 –092-5

Reprinted 1990.

Published by Sh. Shahzad Riaz for Sh. Muhammad Ashraf, Publishers and Booksellers, Lahore, Pakistan, Printed and bound in Pakistan at Ashraf Printing Press, 7-Aibak Road, Lahore.

S.M.A.-I.E.A. NWP 90 - Q. II . .

INTRODUCTION

Muḥammad (may peace be upon him) and the Holy Qur'ān are, no doubt, two separate entities but they are both so closely allied that we cannot conceive of their independent existence. It is through Muḥammad (may peace be upon him) that the Holy Qur'ān has been vouchsafed to us and it is in his august personality that we find its visible expression.

> He it is Who sent His Messenger with Guidance and the Religion of Truth, that He may cause it to prevail over all religions (ix. 34).

The verse bears clear testimony to the fact that the fountain-head of True Guidance and True Religion is the Prophet of Allah (may peace be upon him) since he has been entrusted with the responsibility of showing to the people the path of Righteousness and the path of Salvation, as desired by the Lord. He is the trusted Messenger of Allah on earth and it is through him that mankind has been able to know His Will with all its major and minor implications.

We have been told in clear terms that the Holy Prophet (may peace be upon him) neither said anything nor did anything of his own accord; whatever he said and whatever he did emanated from the Lord:

> He does not speak of his own desire (liii. 8).
>
> Say: I follow only that which is revealed to me from my Lord (vii. 203).

All the utterances and deeds of the Holy Prophet (may peace be upon him) are thus divinely inspired, and in them alone can one find the true meaning and the real significance of the Will of Allah.

Mere transmission of the Book of Allah to the people faithfully and sincerely does not exhaust the Prophet's duties. On him also lies the responsibility of explaining the real purport of the Qur'ānic teachings and then giving them a visible shape so that mankind may see, along with the injunctions of Allah, the process of their transformation into reality and the outward forms in which they are to be crystallised. Words alone, however powerful and however pointed, cannot be fully comprehended unless these conjure before our minds definite forms and shapes. Similarly, precepts, however valuable, can be best understood only when these are supported by living examples.

It is indeed a boundless favour of Allah to humanity that, along with His message, He also sent to us His Messengers to elaborate and elucidate it, and then transmute it into practical reality under His direct guidance.

> And We have sent unto thee the Admonition that thou mayest expound unto mankind that which hath been revealed towards them (xvi. 44).

As a final dispenser of the Message of Allah, the Prophet alone is best fitted and, therefore, divinely authorised to determine the meanings of the Holy Qur'ān, to unfold before humanity the deep wisdom contained in it, and then, on the basis of this wisdom, to purify the souls of the people and elevate them to the highest pinnacle of morality and God-consciousness.

> Assuredly Allah conferred a favour on the believers when He raised unto them an Apostle from among themselves, reciting to them His revelations and purifying them, and teaching them the Book and the wisdom (iii. 163).

Reciting Lord's revelations, purifying the souls of the people, teaching the Book and the wisdom lying in it—these are the different aspects of the prophetic ministry and nothing falls outside the orbit of Allah's revelation.

> Whatever the Apostle commands you, accept; and whatever he forbids you, avoid (lix. 7).

What this verse implies is that the commands and prohibitions of the Prophet are not to be treated in the spirit in which are taken the wise sayings of sages or philosophers or the verdicts of rulers. The words and the deeds of the Prophet are, indeed, the perfect expressions of the highest wisdom ever conceivable; but this alone does not completely fulfil the demands of belief in prophethood. The basic point in this belief is that one should affirm with full confidence that it is Allah Who speaks through the Prophet whatever he utters by way of spiritual guidance or practical legislation, and thus follow him in every walk of life with a view to achieving the love of the Lord and salvation in this world and the world to come. The Prophet is no doubt human, but his leadership is divinely inspired and none can be called a Muslim who does not accept this basic doctrine of the Holy Qur'ān.

> Say (O Muḥammad): If you love Allah, follow me and Allah will love you and forgive you your sins: for Allah is Forgiving, a Dispenser of Mercy (iii. 31).

It is by following Muḥammad (may peace be upon him) that we can achieve the cherished goal of winning Allah's favour.

The question arises: Did the Holy Prophet (may peace be upon him) utter not a word besides what was revealed to him by the Lord in the form of the Qur'ān? The answer obviously is: No. He did also explain the contents of the Divine revelations. He gave practical demonstration of their significance by leading his life according to them, and was thus instrumental in moulding the lives of his Companions after his own pattern of life. He did all this, of course, under Divine inspiration.

This is why the Holy Qur'ān has been declared as a Guide and a Light and the Prophet's sacred life as a model pattern for the Muslims:

> Indeed, there has come to you from Allah a Light and a Book Luminous (v. 15).

> Verily in the Apostle of Allah you have the best example for everyone who looks forward towards Allah and the Day of Judgment (xxxiii. 21).

It is only from the Holy Qur'ān and the authentic record of the Aḥādīth that we can obtain full view of this model pattern. Thus, next to the Holy Qur'ān the Ḥadīth is the second source of the Islamic law of social and personal behaviour, because the commandments of the Holy Prophet are as binding on the believers as the Commands of Allah.

> Whenever Allah and the Apostle have decided a matter it is not for a faithful man or woman to follow a course of their own choice (xxxiii. 36).

Some of the misguided people suggest that the commands of the Holy Prophet (may peace be upon him) were valid only during his lifetime, and that now when he is no more amongst us, we need follow only the injunctions of the Holy Qur'ān and treat the Ḥadīth as an account of the past which has some allusions to the life of the Holy Prophet (may peace be upon him), having no practical value as a code of life. These so-called pseudo-reformers little realise that a denial of the eternal validity of the Sunnah amounts to a denial of the Holy Qur'ān's claim that the prophethood of Muḥammad (may peace be upon him) is not time-bound; it is universal and the Prophet's words and deeds are the timeless expressions of the Will of Allah.

> Say: O mankind! surely I am the Messenger of Allah to you all, of Him Whose is the Kingdom of the heavens and the earth. There is no god but He: so believe in Allah and His Messenger, the *ummī* Prophet, who believes in Allah and His words, and follow him so that you may be guided aright (vii. 158).

Muḥammad (may peace be upon him) is the Messenger of Allah for the whole of mankind; no new prophet is to be raised after him. His prophethood is thus both universal and eternal. It is, therefore, an integral part of one's faith in the prophethood of Muḥammad (may peace be upon him) that his words and deeds should always be taken as one of the two most reliable sources of right guidance. The Code of Divine Guidance which does not regard Muḥammad (may peace be upon him) as the supreme guide from the Lord cannot in any way be relied upon in Islam. One could seek this guidance directly from the Holy Prophet during his lifetime, but now it is the authentic traditions that serve this purpose admirably well.

Right from the time of the Companions down to this day, there has been consensus of opinion among the Muslims that whatever is transmitted to us from the Holy Prophet (may peace be upon him) on the authority of reliable transmitters of Aḥādīth is the valid explanation and enunciation of Allah's Commands and the opinion of anyone else is subservient to it. It is acceptable only if it conforms to the sayings or the deeds of the Holy Prophet (may peace be upon him), but if it conflicts with a ḥādīth, it must be outright rejected.

The Ḥadīth, which in the religious sense stands for the report of the actions or approval or disapproval of the Prophet, has always been a subject of keen interest for the Muslims since the time of the Holy Prophet (may peace be upon him). His Companions (may Allah be pleased with them), who were mostly Arabs, had wonderful memory and could immaculately retain whatever they saw in the Prophet's life or whatever they heard from him. Some of them even put these down in *Ṣaḥīfahs* which were later on read by them to their students. They left for us a large number of *Ṣaḥīfahs*, for example the *Ṣaḥīfah Ṣādiqah* compiled by Ḥaḍrat 'Abdullah b. 'Amr b. al-'Āṣ, *Ṣaḥīfah* of Ḥaḍrat 'Alī, Ḥadīth collection of Ḥaḍrat Rāfi' b. Khadīj, Ḥaḍrat Jābir b. 'Abdullah, Ḥaḍrat Samūrah b. Jundab, Ḥaḍrat Abū Huraira, Ḥaḍrat 'Abdullah b. 'Abbās, Ḥaḍrat 'Abdullah b. Mas'ūd, and *Ṣaḥīfah* of Ḥammām bin Munabbih (may Allah be pleased with all of them). These are the blessed names of some of those Companions who kept a record of the Prophet's utterances and addresses, judgments and verdicts on different issues and his actions and deeds in all sets of circumstances.

The study of the records of the Aḥādīth and the life-history of those who maintained them proves beyond any shadow of doubt that the preservation of the Ḥadīth was not an after-thought, conceived long after the death of the Holy Prophet (may peace be upon him). It started right during his lifetime and was continued immediately after him with full earnestness and religious fervour, because it had to serve eternally as the fountain-head of right guidance.

Sprenger, who claims to have been the first to submit the sources of the life of Muḥammad to a critical scrutiny, says:

> It is generally believed that the ṭraditions were preserved during the first century of the Hijrah solely by memory. European scholars, under the erroneous impression that *haddathana* (he informed us) is the term by which the traditions are usually introduced, are of the opinion that none of the traditions contained in the collection of al-Bukhari had been written down before him. . . . This appears to be an error. Ibn 'Amr and other companions of Muhammad [may peace be upon him] committed his sayings to writing and their example was followed by many of the Tabi'un.[1]

Side by side with the collection of Aḥādīth was initiated their critical scrutiny so that the genuine traditions may be sifted from the concocted ones. "The fact that there are numberless spurious ahadith did not in the least escape the attention of the Muhaddithun, as European critics naively seem to suppose. On the contrary, the critical science of hadith was initiated by the necessity of discerning between authentic and spurious, and the very Imams Bukhari and Muslim, not to mention the lesser Traditionists, are direct products of this critical attitude. The existence, therefore, of false ahadiṭh does not prove anything against the system of hadith as a whole—no more than a fanciful tale from the *Arabian Nights* could be regarded as an argument against the authenticity of any historical report of the corresponding period."[2]

The traditionists and the jurists have formulated sound principles in the light of which the genuineness of the Ḥadīth can be fully established. These principles relate to both parts of the Ḥadīth: *Isnād* (chain of transmission) and *Matn* (text). The trustworthiness of those through whom the Ḥadīth is transmitted, i.e. *Isnād*, can be reliably judged with the help of *Asmā' al-Rijāl,* a science which critically scrutinises the lives of the narrators of the Aḥādīth. Those who understood this work showed perfect impartiality and honesty, thoroughness and minuteness and objectivity in recording the details of their life. Similarly, laws were also framed to test the genuineness of the text. The reliability of a narrator may be taken as an external evidence and criticism of the text may be treated as an internal evidence for establishing the authenticity of a ḥadīth. A ḥadīth which admirably stands this thorough search and scrutiny and is proved to be authentic is a part and parcel of Divine injunctions and is binding on a believer.

These Aḥādīth have been compiled in different books amongst which *Ṣaḥīḥ Bukhārī*, *Ṣaḥīḥ Muslim*, *Sunan* of Abū Dāwūd, Tirmidhī, Ibn Mājah, al-Nasā'ī, *Muwaṭṭā* of Imām Mālik, *Musnad* of Imām Aḥmad bin Ḥanbal, *Musnad* of Abū Dāwūd al-Ṭayālīsī are important. The first six of these compilations are known as *Ṣiḥāḥ Sittah*, the six *Ṣaḥīḥs*, i.e.

1. *Journal of the Asiatic Society of Bengal*, Calcutta, Vol. XXV, p. 303.
2. Asad, *Islam at the Crossroads*, pp. 127-8.

the correct reliable collections. The collections by Bukhārī and Muslim are particularly held in high esteem. They are known as the two *Ṣaḥīḥs* (*al-Ṣaḥīḥain*). The Aḥādīth which are recognised as absolutely authentic are included in these two marvellous compilations.

Even of these two, Bukhārī's occupies a higher position in comparison to Muslim's.

One may pertinently ask why it is that Muslim's rather than Bukhārī's *Ṣaḥīḥ* has been selected by me for translation into English.

I fully subscribe to the view of the Muḥaddithīn that, after the Holy Qur'ān, Bukhārī's *Ṣaḥīḥ* is the most reliable Book of Islamic Sharī'ah. Muslim's *Ṣaḥīḥ* comes after it. However, in certain respects the latter is considered superior to the former. Imām Muslim strictly observed many principles of the science of Ḥadīth which had been slightly ignored by his great teacher Imām Bukhārī (may Allah have mercy on both of them). Imām Muslim considered only such traditions to be genuine and authentic as had been transmitted to him by an unbroken chain of reliable authorities and were in perfect conformity with what had been related by other narrators whose trustworthiness was unanimously accepted and who were free from all defects.

Moreover, Imām Bukhārī, while describing the chain of narrators, sometimes mentions their *kunya* and sometimes gives their names. This is particularly true in case of the narrators of Syria. This creates a sort of confusion. Imām Muslim has avoided this.

Imām Muslim takes particular care in recording the exact words of the narrators and points out even the minutest difference in the wording of their reports.

Imām Muslim has also constantly kept in view the difference between the two well-known modes of narration, *Ḥaddathana* (he narrated to us) and *Akhbarana* (he informed us). He is of the opinion that the first mode is used only when the teacher is narrating the Ḥadīth and the student is listening to it, while the second mode of expression implies that the student is reading the Ḥadīth before the teacher. This reflects his utmost care in the transmission of a ḥadīth.

Imām Muslim has taken great pains in connecting the chain of narrators. He has recorded only that ḥadīth which, at least, two reliable tābi'īn (successors) had heard from two Companions and this principle is observed throughout the subsequent chain of narrators.

All these considerations are there, but the reason of my choice for the translation of Muslim's *Ṣaḥīḥ* is that Bukhārī's is a difficult book in that the different portions of Aḥādīth are fragmented into parts and these are put down under different headings according to their importance from the point of view of Fiqh. Unless one has thorough grounding in the study of Ḥadīth and has a strong background of religious knowledge, one is not likely to grasp fully and appreciate the compilation of Imām Bukhārī.

Imām Muslim has, on the other hand, recorded the Aḥādīth in their integrated forms. This is quite essential and highly useful for those who have a meagre knowledge of the Ḥadīth or who have just started its study.

The full name of Imām Muslim is Abu'l-Ḥusain 'Asākir-ud-Dīn Muslim b. Ḥajjāj al-Qushayrī al-Naisābūrī. "Muslim" as his *nasba* shows that he belonged to the Qushayrī tribe of the Arabs, an offshoot of the great clan of Rabī'a. He was born in Naisābūr (Nīshāpūr) in 202/817 or 206/821. His parents were religiously devoted persons and as such he was brought up in a pious atmosphere. This left such an indelible impression on his mind that he spent the whole of his life as a God-fearing person and always adhered to the path of Righteousness. He was in fact a saint of high calibre. His excellent moral character can be well judged from the simple fact that he never indulged in backbiting, a very common human failing.

Imām Muslim travelled widely to collect traditions in Arabia, Egypt, Syria and Iraq where he attended the lectures of some of the prominent Traditionists of his time: Isḥāq b. Rahwaih, Aḥmad b. Ḥanbal, 'Ubaydullah al-Qawārīrī, Qutaiba b. Sa'īd, 'Abdullah b. Maslama, Ḥarmalah b. Yaḥyā, and others.

Having finished his studies, he settled down at Nīshāpūr. There he came into contact with Imām Bukhārī and was so much impressed by his vast knowledge of Ḥadīth and his deep insight into it that he kept himself attached to him up to the end of his life. He was an ardent admirer of another great teacher of Ḥadīth, Muḥammad b. Yaḥyā al-Dhuhlī and attended his lectures regularly, but when the difference of opinion between Muḥammad b. Yaḥyā and Imām Bukhārī, on the issue of the creation of the Holy Qur'ān, sharpened into hostility, Imām Muslim sided with Imām Bukhārī and abandoned Muḥammad b. Yaḥyā altogether. He was thus a true disciple of Imām Bukhārī.

He wrote many books and treatises on Ḥadīth but the most important of his work is the collection (*Jami'*) of his *Ṣaḥīḥ*. Some of the commentators of Aḥādīth are of the opinion that in certain respects it is the best and most authentic work on the subject. Imām Muslim took great pains in collecting 300,000 Traditions and then after a thorough examination of them retained only 4000, the genuineness of which is fully established.[3]

He prefixed to his compilation a very illuminating introduction in which he specified some of the principles which he had followed in the choice of his material.

Imām Muslim has to his credit many other valuable contributions to different branches of Ḥadīth literature and most of them retain their eminence even to the present day. Amongst these *Kitāb al-Musnad al-Kabīr 'Alā al-Rijāl, Jāmi' Kabīr, Kitāb al-Asmā' wa'l-Kuna, Kitāb al-'Ilal, Kitāb al-Wijdān* are very important.

Imām Muslim had a very wide circle of students who learnt Ḥadīth from him. Some of them occupy a very prominent position in Islamic history, e.g. Abū Ḥātim Rāzī, Mūsā b. Hārūn, Aḥmad b. Salama, Abū 'Īsā Tirmidhī, Abū Bakr b. Khuzaima, Abū 'Awāna, and Ḥāfiẓ Dhahabī.

Imām Muslim lived for fifty-five years in this mortal world. Of this short span of

3. It is essential to remove one of the serious misgivings under which so many Orientalists and westernised Muslim scholars are labouring. When they are told that Imām Muslim selected 4000 Aḥādīth out of a total collection of 300,000, they think that since quite a large number of aḥādīth were unreliable, therefore, these were rejected, and then jump to the conclusion that the whole stock of Ḥadīth is unauthentic and should be rejected outright. This betrays utter ignorance of the critics even about the elementary knowledge of Ḥadīth. *Matn* (text) is not the basis on which is calculated the number of Aḥādīth. Ḥadīth is counted on the chain of transmission. Thus when we say that Imām Muslim collected 300,000 Aḥādīth and included only 4000 in his compilation, it does not imply that he rejected the rest of the whole lot of the Prophet's sayings, being unreliable. What it means is that the words and deeds of the Holy Prophet (may peace be upon him) were transmitted to Imām Muslim through so many chains of transmission out of which he selected 4000 chains as most authentic and narrated the text on their authority. A text (*Matn*) which is transmitted through one hundred *Isnāds* is in Ḥadīth literature treated as one hundred traditions. For example, the text of the first Aḥādīth in Bukhārī (The Actions Are Based on Intention) is counted as a selection of one out of 700 Aḥādīth since it has been transmitted through such a large number of *Isnāds*.

his life he spent most of his time in learning Ḥadīth, in its compilation, in its teaching and transmission. He always remained absorbed in this single pursuit and nothing could distract his attention from this sacred task. He died in 261/875 and was buried in the suburbs of Nīshāpūr.

A few words may be said about the translation of this marvellous book which comprises the sayings and traditions of the Holy Prophet (may peace be upon him). Translation is itself a very difficult task, and it becomes still more difficult when difference in the genius of two languages is immeasurably vast. The Arabic language is rich, colourful and vigorous, and is best fitted to express thoughts and concepts with more conciseness than the Aryan languages, because of the extraordinary flexibility of its verbs and nouns. English, on the other hand, is essentially a language of under-statement. Moreover, every language is a framework of symbols expressing its people's particular sense of life-values and the particular way of their perception of Reality. No good translation can, therefore, be successfully attempted unless the translator is able to produce within himself the conceptual symbolism of the language in question. Mere translation of words conveys no more than the outer shell and thus misses the original beauty of the words translated. The problem becomes insurmountably difficult when we take into consideration the fact that it is not the matter of translating a book of Arabic into English but translating the words of the Holy Prophet (may peace be upon him). He was divinely inspired and was thus gifted with a very chaste mode of expression, the like of which is not to be found in human history. The translation of his words and expressions is, therefore, bound to remain but a distant and faulty echo of the original meaning and spirit.

I do not claim for myself competence in either of the two languages, Arabic or English, the one translated from and the other translated into. The lamentable fact that not even one complete book out of the whole lot of *Ṣiḥāḥ Sittah* has been translated into English tempted me to take this great responsibility on my not-competent shoulders, with the hope that more competent scholars would take the lead and, with their better knowledge and acumen, render into English other Hadīth collections, and thus wash the blame of gross negligence on the part of the Muslim society.

While translating *Ṣaḥīḥ Muslim* it has been my constant endeavour to give as literal and as faithful a rendering as is consistent with tolerable English. Accuracy, rather than literary embellishment, has been my aim throughout.

A word may be added about the Notes. I have as far as possible avoided theological discussions and tried to explain the meaning of the Ḥadīth in the light of the expositions made by eminent Muḥaddithīn. I have taken great care to follow them both in letter and spirit, since, I believe, they are alone competent to speak with authority on this subject.

I have, at every step, cited the authority so that anyone interested in the detailed study of the point at issue can look into it. Wherever it is found that a ḥadīth is capable of interpretation, its interpretation is given, but that too on the authority of an eminent scholar of Ḥadīth literature. Interpretations are there, but at no point have these been made an apology to the Western thought and Western mind; that would have been a distortion of the sayings of the Holy Prophet (may peace be upon him), and is a highly dangerous and objectionable trend. It undermines the very basis of belief in Allah and His Prophet (may peace be upon him).

The outcome of my humble labour is before Allah and man. If there is any merit discernible in it, it is absolutely due to the unbounded Grace and Mercy of the Merciful Allah, but for all acts of omission and commission I alone am responsible.

ACKNOWLEDGMENTS

I am highly indebted to Malik Ghulām 'Ali, an eminent scholar of Ḥadīth and Fiqh who, on my humble request, agreed to revise the whole of the manuscript. His guidance has been of so great help to me that no words can adequately express my feelings of indebtedness to him. I am also obliged to Maulānā Sayyid Abu'l-A'lā Maudūdī who always helped and guided me in this heavy task. Dr 'Ābid Aḥmad 'Alī also helped me in the revision of translation for which I am highly obliged to him.

I have undertaken this work in the capacity of a Fellow of the Islamic Research Academy, Karachi. The Academy had assigned to me some other projects, but when I requested its Directors to permit me to undertake translation of the *Ṣaḥīḥ Muslim*, they readily agreed. I am in this connection very much obliged to Professor Khurshīd Aḥmad and late Ch. Ghulām Muḥammad. Both these gentlemen treated me with generosity and evinced keen interest in the progress of this work.

Sayyid 'Aṭā' Ḥusain, Manager of Sh. Muhammad Ashraf, has been a constant source of help and encouragement to me. It is due to his selfless efforts that this work is seeing the light of the day.

To Mr Mohammad Ashraf Darr I am particularly indebted for his very keen interest in the project and for his active collaboration in not only seeing the publication through the press, but also critically examining the manuscript and giving me valuable suggestions at every step, which have gone far in giving this book the look and shape that it bears.

Ch. 'Abdur Raḥmān typed the manuscript with great skill and interest and I am obliged to him for this valuable service.

The staff of the Punjab Public Library, Lahore, deserve my special thanks for their willing co-operation in providing me books and other facilities.

Last but not least I owe a debt of gratitude to my publisher, Shaikh Muḥammad Ashraf, who, in spite of his heavy responsibilities, agreed to undertake such a big project and took keen personal interest in its publication.

March, 1971 'Abdul Ḥamīd Ṣiddīqi.

SOME TERMS EXPLAINED

(1) *Ḥadīth and Sunnah :*

In the religious literature of Islam these two terms are considered to be synonymous with each other. There is, however, a slight difference in them. The word ***Sunnah*** means precedent and custom. In the technical sense it implies the doings and practices of Muḥammad (may peace be upon him) only. Sunnah is thus a concrete implementation, a tangible form and the actual embodiment of the Will of Allah in the form of Muḥammd's deeds.

Ḥadīth originally means a piece of news, a tale, a story or a report relating to a present or past event. In the technical sense it stands for the report of the words and deeds, approval or disapproval of the Holy Prophet (may peace be upon him).

(2) *Classification of Aḥādīth :*

(*a*) *Ṣaḥīḥ* (Sound). This name is given to the utterly faultless ḥadīth in which there is no weakness either in the chain of transmission (*Isnād*) or in the text (*Matn*) and in which there is no tendency to contradict any established belief of Islam.

(*b*) *Ḥasan* (Approved) is like a *Ṣaḥīḥ* tradition except for the fact that some of its narrators are found to have a defective memory in comparison to the narrators of *Ṣaḥīḥ* Ḥadīth.

(*c*) *Ḍa'īf* tradition is that in which there is some defect either in the chain of transmission, or in proper understanding of the transmitter, or its contents are not in perfect agreement with Islamic beliefs and practices. It is in fact a tradition of weak or less reliable authority.

(*d*) ***Mutawātir*** (Continuous) is a tradition reported by a large number of people in different times, so as to make it impossible for any falsehood to creep into it.

(*e*) ***Mashhūr*** is a tradition which is handed down by at least three different reliable authorities, or, according to another view, a tradition which, although widely disseminated later, was originally transmitted by one person in the first generation.

(*f*) *Mauḍū'* (Forged) ḥadīth is that which a liar fabricates and then attributes it to the Holy Prophet (may peace be upon him).

(*g*) *Muttafaq 'Alaih* (Agreed upon). A tradition accepted both by Imām Bukhārī and Imām Muslim and included in their respective collections.

BOOKS MAINLY DEPENDED UPON AND FREQUENTLY QUOTED

(1) *Minhāj al-Ṭālibīn* by Muḥyī al-Dın Abū Zakariya Yaḥyā al-Ḥiẓāmī al-Dimashqī al-Nawawī (commentary on *Ṣaḥīḥ Muslim*).

(2) *Fatḥ al-Mulḥim* (Commentary on *Ṣaḥīḥ Muslim*) by Maulānā Shabbīr Aḥmad 'Uthmānī.

(3) *Fatḥ al-Bārī* (Commentary on *Ṣaḥīḥ Bukhārī*) by Ḥāfiẓ Ibn Ḥajr 'Asqalānī.

(4) *'Umdat al-Qārī* (Commentary on *Ṣaḥīḥ Bukhārī*) by Badr al-Dīn 'Ainī.

(5) *Faiḍ al-Bārī* (Commentary on *Ṣaḥīḥ Bukhārī*) by Maulānā Anwar Shāh Kāshmīrī.

(6) *Al-Sirāj al-Wahhāj* by Nawāb Ṣiddīq Ḥasan.

(7) *Mirqāt al-Mafātīḥ* by 'Alī b. Sulṭān Muḥammad Qārī (popularly known as Mulla 'Alī Qārī).

(8) *Ẓād al-Ma'ād* by Ḥāfiẓ Ibn Qayyim.

SOURCES ON THE LIFE OF THE NARRATORS

(1) *Tahdhīb-ul-Tahdhīb* by Ḥāfiẓ Ibn Ḥajar 'Asqalānī.

(2) *Kitāb al-Ṭabaqāt al-Kabīr* by Muḥammad b. Sa'd.

(3) *Tadhkirat al-Ḥuffāẓ* by Shams al-Dīn Abū 'Abdullah Muḥammad b. Aḥmad al-Dhahabī.

(4) *Mīzān al-I'tidāl fī Naqd al-Rijāl* by Shams al-Dīn al-Dhahabī.

TRANSLITERATION OF ARABIC WORDS AND NAMES

ا ء	Consonantal sound	a	ط		ṭ
ا	Long vowel	ā	ظ		ẓ
ب		b	ع		' inverted apostrophe
ت		t	غ		gh
ث		th	ف		f
ج		j	ق		q
ح		ḥ	ک		k
خ		kh	ل		l
د		d	م		m
ذ		dh	ن		n
ر		r	ه		h
ز		z	و	consonant	w
س		s	و	long vowel	ū
ش		sh	و	diphthong	au
ص		ṣ	ی	consonant	y
ض		ḍ	ی	long vowel	ī
			ی	diphthong	ai

CONTENTS

Book I.—KITĀB AL-IMĀN
(The Book of Faith)

Chapter

BOOK II.—KITĀB AL-ṬAHĀRAH
(The Book of Purification)

BOOK III.—KITĀB AL-ḤAIḌ (Menstruation)

بِسْمِ اللهِ الرَّحْمٰنِ الرَّحِيْمِ

KITAB AL-IMAN[1]

THE BOOK OF FAITH

Chapter I

(1) It is narrated on the authority of Yaḥya[2] b. Ya'mar that the first man who discussed about *Qadr*[3] (Divine Decree) in Baṣra was Ma'bad al-Juhanī. I along with Ḥumaid b. 'Abdur-Raḥmān Ḥimyarī set out for pilgrimage or for *'Umrah*[4] and said :

1. Faith (*Īmān*) has two aspects—cognitive and volitional. It is at once an affirmation of truth from the depth of one's heart and a surrender to the truth affirmed. When the volitional aspect is emphasised, we have the notion commonly denoted by the word ''trust'' ; when the cognitive aspect is stressed, we have belief. The word *īmān* signifies originally conviction of the heart, while Islām signifies originally submission and hence primarily action.

2. His name was Yaḥya and his *kunyah* was Abū Sulaimān. He belonged to the tribe of Laith. He was a famous Tābi'ī, and a profound scholar of the Qur'ān, Ḥadīth, Islamic law, Arabic language and literature. He transmitted so many traditions of the Holy Prophet on the authority of eminent Companions (may Allah be pleased with them) like 'Uthmān b. 'Affān, 'Alī b. Abī Ṭālib, 'Ammār b. Yāsir, Abū Dharr Ghifārī, Abū Huraira, Abū Mūsā Ash'arī, Abū Sa'īd Khudrī, Ibn 'Abbās and 'Ā'ishah Ṣiddīqah. His greatest achievement was that he was the first to put diacritical points on the Holy Qur'ān and thus made its correct recitation quite easy. He died in 119 or 120 н.

3. *Qadr* and *Taqdir*, according to Imām Rāghib, mean the making manifest of the measure (*kamiyyah*) of a thing, or simply measure. In the words of the same authority, Allah manifests *Taqdir* in two ways : by granting *qudrah*, i.e. power, or by making them in a particular measure and in a particular manner as His infinite wisdom requires. *Taqdir* is, therefore, the law or measure which is working throughout the whole of creation. For example, the Qur'ān states : "Glorify thou the name of thine Lord, the Most High, Who created, then proportioned, and Who made things according to a measure, then guided them to a goal" (lxxxvii. 1-3).

That the very first ḥadīth of *Ṣaḥīḥ Muslim* begins with *Taqdir* is a matter of great significance. It gives a clear concept of the universe and its Creator. What this ḥadīth implies is that this whole creation is not the incomplete handiwork of a whimsical Lord who was interested only in creating and not directing it to its proper end.

The basic concept which the word *Taqdir* furnishes and which is substantiated by the Qur'ān and the Sunnah is that this universe and everything contained therein is the outcome of a Planning Will of the Creator Who has created and fashioned it with His infinite wisdom and with a definite purpose and is not only supervising all that is going on in this universe, but is directing it to its destined end. What Islam really stresses is that the Lord is the supreme power of the universe and He creates and directs it with a rational will. His omnipotence is not arbitrary, but is one with the all-wise will, nor is His necessity blind but rational, and likewise identical with the all-wise will.

4. 'Umrah is the minor pilgrimage with fewer rites. Literally, a visit, or a visiting ; it is technically a religious visit to the sacred places at Mecca with the performance of a ceremony of circuiting round the Ka'bah and going to and fro between aṣ-Ṣafā' and al-Marwah with *al-iḥrām*. Ḥajj differs from 'Umrah inasmuch as it is at a particular time of the year and is not complete without halting at 'Arafāt on the day of 'Arafah.

should it so happen that we come into contact with the one among the Companions of the Messenger of Allah (may peace be upon him) we ask him about what is talked about *Taqdīr* (Divine Decree). Accidentally we came across 'Abdullah b. 'Umar b. al-Khaṭṭāb while he was entering the mosque. I and my companion surrounded him. One of us (stood) on his right side and the other one stood on his left side. I expected that my companion would authorise me to speak. I, therefore, said: Abū 'Abdur-Raḥmān! there have appeared some persons in our land who recite the Holy Qur'ān and pursue knowledge. And then after talking about their affairs added: They (such persons) claim that there is no such thing as Divine Decree and events are not predestined. He ('Abdullah b. 'Umar) said: When you happen to meet such persons tell them that I have nothing to do with them and they have nothing to do with me. And verily they are in no way responsible for my (belief). 'Abdullah b. 'Umar swore by Him (the Lord) (and said): If any one of them (who does not believe in the Divine Decree) had with him gold equal to the bulk of (the mountain) Uḥud and then he should spend it (in the way of Allah) Allah would not accept it unless he affirms his faith in Divine Decree, and further said: My father 'Umar b. al-Khaṭṭāb told me: One day we were sitting in the company of the Messenger of Allah (may peace be upon him) when there appeared before us a man dressed in extremely white clothes, his hair extraordinary black. There were no signs of (fatigue) of journey on him. None amongst us recognised him. At last he sat along with the Apostle (may peace be upon him). He leaned his knees before his knees and placed his palms on his thighs and said: Muḥammad, inform me about al-Islam. The Messenger of Allah (may peace be upon him) said: Al-Islam implies that you testify that there is no god but Allah and that Muḥammad is the messenger of Allah, and you establish prayer, pay Zakāt, observe the fast of Ramaḍān, and perform pilgrimage to the (House) if you are solvent enough (to bear the expense of) journey. He (the inquirer) said: You have told the truth. He ('Umar b. al-Khaṭṭāb) said: It amazed us that he would put the question and then he would himself verify the truth. He (the inquirer) said: Inform me about Īmān (faith). He (the Holy Prophet) replied: That you affirm your faith in Allah, in His angels, in His Books, in His Apostles, in the Day of Judgment, and you affirm your faith in the Divine Decree to good and evil.[5] He (the inquirer) said: You have told the truth. He (the inquirer) again said: Inform me about al-Iḥsān (performance of good deed). He (the Holy Prophet) said: That you worship Allah as if you are seeing Him, for though you don't see Him, He, verily, sees you. He (the inquirer) again said: Inform me about the hour (of the Doom). He (the Holy Prophet) remarked: One who is inquired knows no more than the one who is inquiring (about it). He (the inquirer) said: Tell me some of its indications. He (the Holy Prophet) said: That the slave-girl would give birth to her mistress and master, that you would find barefooted, destitute shepherds of goats vying with one another in the construction of magnificent buildings. He (the narrator, 'Umar b. al-Khaṭṭāb) said: Then he (the inquirer) made his way but I stayed with him (the Holy Prophet) for a long while. He, then, told me: 'Umar, do you know who this inquirer was? I replied:

5. It repudiates the Magian concept of Godhood that there are two creators, a creator of good and a creator of evil. The Holy Prophet declared this concept to be false and taught pure monotheism that God is one and He is Potent enough to create both good and evil. This concept strikes at the root of the dualistic doctrine of the Magian religion.

Allah and His Apostle know best. He (the Holy Prophet) remarked: He was Gabriel (the angel). He came to you in order to instruct you in matters of religion.

(2) It is narrated on the authority of Yaḥya b. Ya'mar that when Ma'bad discussed the problem pertaining to Divine Decree, we refuted that. He (the narrator) said: I and Ḥumaid b. 'Abdur-Raḥmān Ḥimyari argued. And they carried on the conversation about the purport of the ḥadīth related by Kahmas and its chain of transmission too, and there is some variation of words.

(3) It is narrated on the authority of Yaḥya b. Ya'mar and Ḥumaid b. 'Abdur-Raḥmān that they said: We met 'Abdullah b. 'Umar and we discussed about the Divine Decree, and what they talked about it and he narrated the ḥadīth that has been transmitted by 'Umar (may Allah be pleased with him) from the Apostle (may peace be upon him). There is slight variation in that.

Chapter II

WHAT IS ĪMĀN[6] AND WHAT ARE ITS CHARACTERISTICS

(4) Abū Huraira[7] reported: One day the Messenger of Allah (may peace be upon him) appeared before the public that a man came to him and said: Prophet of Allah, (tell me) what is Īmān. Upon this he (the Holy Prophet) replied: That you affirm your faith in Allah, His angels, His Books, His meeting,[8] His messengers and that you affirm your faith in Resurrection Hereafter. He (again) said: Messenger of Allah, (tell me) what does al-Islam signify. He (the Holy Prophet) replied: Al-Islam signifies that you worship Allah and do not associate anything with Him and you establish obligatory prayer and you pay the obligatory poor-due (Zakāt) and you observe the fast of Ramaḍān. He (the inquirer (again) said: Messenger of Allah, what does al-Iḥsān[9]

6. Īmān (faith) may be described as the mental state of assurance or conviction in which mind accepts and endorses its experience as corresponding with Reality—the Reality, assented to and endorsed in the case of religious belief, of course being of a far wider, far deeper and far more comprehensive nature than reality elsewhere. With faith or belief in this sense, there invariably emerges a sense of security, a feeling of satisfaction that the road to salvation has been found—a subsuming of oneself in the all-comprising Reality.

7. His full name is Abū Huraira al-Dāwasī al-Yamanī. Before embracing Islam he was called 'Abd Shams but when he became Muslim, his name was changed to 'Abd Allah or 'Abdul-Raḥmān. He was called Abū Huraira because while he herded his people's goats, he kept a kitten to play with. When he came to Medina, the Prophet was on the expedition to Khaybar (7/629). He was a devout Muslim and was one of the prominent members of Ahl al-Ṣuffa. He died in 58/678. He had no other business to attend to and no occupation to distract his attention but to listen to the words of the Holy Prophet. So long as the Prophet remained outside the four walls of his house, he stayed with him and listened to him very attentively. He had an extraordinary memory and nothing was blurred or effaced from his mind. The traditions of the Holy Prophet narrated on his authority are estimated at 3500.

8. Meeting with the Lord after the Doom.

9. Iḥsān means beneficence, performance of good deeds, but in the religious sense it implies the doing of good deeds over and above what is just and fair. It is indicative of the intense devotion of man to his Creator and Master and his enthusiasm for virtue and piety. What implies by the term *Taṣawwuf* in Islam is nothing but Iḥsān. The aim of Iḥsān is to create a sense of inner piety in man and to train his sensibilities in a way that all his thoughts and actions flow from the fountainhead of the love of God.

imply? He (the Holy Prophet) replied: That you worship Allah as if you are seeing Him and in case you fail to see Him then observe prayer (with this idea in your mind) that (at least) He is seeing you.[10] He (the inquirer) again said: Messenger of Allah, when would there be the hour of (Doom)? He (the Holy Prophet) replied: The one who is asked about it is no better informed than the inquirer. I, however, narrate some of its signs (and these are): when the maid-servant will give birth to her master,[11] when the naked, barefooted would become the chiefs of the people—these are some of the signs of (Doom). (Moreover) when the shepherds of the black (camels) would exalt themselves in buildings,[12]—this is one of the signs of (Doom). (Doom) is one of the five (happenings wrapped in the unseen) which no one knows but Allah. Then he (the Messenger of Allah) recited (the verse): Verily Allah! with Him alone is the knowledge of the hour and He it is Who sends down the rain and knows that which is in the wombs and no person knows whatsoever he shall earn tomorrow, and a person knows not in whatsoever land he shall die. Verily Allah is Knowing, Aware.[13] He (the narrator, Abū Huraira) said: Then the person turned back and went away. The Messenger of Allah (may peace be upon him) said: Bring that man back to me. They (the companions of the Holy Prophet present there) went to bring him back but they saw nothing there. Upon this the Messenger of Allah remarked: He was Gabriel who came to teach the people their religion.

(5) This ḥadīth is narrated to us on the authority of Muḥammad b. 'Abdullah b. Numair, on the authority of Muḥammad b. Bishr, on the authority of Abū Ḥayyān al-Taymī with the exception that in this narration (instead of the words اذا ولدت الأمة ربها, the words are) اذا ولدت الأمة بعلها, i.e. when slave-girl gives birth to her master.

(6) It is narrated on the authority of Abū Huraira that the Messenger of Allah (may peace be upon him) said: Ask me (about matters pertaining to religion), but they (the companions of the Holy Prophet) were too much overawed out of profound respect for him to ask him (anything). In the meanwhile a man came there and sat near his knees and said: Messenger of Allah, what al-Islam is?—to which he (the Holy Prophet)

10. The consciousness of the existence of an Omnipotent Lord Who is not only vigilant of man's deeds and actions, but Who is fully aware of all his thoughts and feelings is the basis of true piety. This attitude has been positively insisted upon by all the authorities of religion as the *sine qua non* of a successful contemplation of the higher divine truths. In fact, God-consciousness is the very breath and soul of religion.

11. This ḥadīth has been explained in different ways. We give below only two interpretations. (*a*) A time would come when the rulers would not observe the sanctity of marriage. They would bring into their household women without marrying them. This licentiousness would become so common that the majority of the children would be born of this wedlock and they would occupy thrones and positions of responsibility. This view is held by Imām Nawawī and is supported by Ḥāfiẓ Ibn Ḥajar 'Asqalānī.

(*b*) The children would become disobedient, defiant and unruly to their parents and especially mothers and they would treat them not with the respect and honour which the mothers rightly deserve, but would show an insolent behaviour towards them and would treat them on the level of maid-servants and slave-girls. (Ibn Ḥajar 'Asqalānī, *Fatḥ-ul-Bārī*, Egypt, 1378 H., Vol. I, p. 131.)

12. It signifies the fact that even the common men would be engrossed in material pleasures and would vie with one another in accumulating riches and then spending them lavishly on things of vain glory.

13. xxxi. 34.

replied: You must not associate anything with Allah, establish prayer,[14] pay the poor-due (Zakāt) and observe (the fasts) of Ramaḍān. He said: You (have) told the truth. He (again) said: Messenger of Allah, what al-Īmān (the faith) is? He (the Holy Prophet) said: That you affirm your faith in Allah, His angels, His Books, His meeting, His Apostles, and that you believe in Resurrection and that you believe in Qadr (Divine Decree) in all its entirety. He (the inquirer) said: You (have) told the truth. He (again) said: Messenger of Allah, what al-Iḥsān is? Upon this he (the Holy Prophet) said: (Al-Iḥsān implies) that you fear Allah as if you are seeing Him, and though you see Him not, verily He is seeing you. He (the inquirer) said: You (have) told the truth. He (the inquirer) said: When there would be the hour (of Doom)? (Upon this) he (the Holy Prophet) said: The one who is asked about it is no better informed than the inquirer himself. I, however, narrate some of its signs (and these are): when you see a slave (woman) giving birth to her master—that is one of the signs of (Doom); when you see barefooted, naked, deaf and dumb (ignorant and foolish persons) as the rulers of the earth—that is one of the signs of the Doom. And when you see the shepherds of black camels exalting in buildings—that is one of the signs of Doom. The (Doom) is one of the five things (wrapped) in the unseen. No one knows them except Allah. Then (the Holy Prophet) recited (the following verse): Verily Allah! with Him alone is the knowledge of the hour and He it is Who sends down the rain and knows that which is in the wombs and no person knows whatsoever he shall earn on morrow and a person knows not in whatsoever land he shall die. Verily Allah is Knowing, Aware.[15] He (the narrator, Abū Huraira) said: Then the person stood up and (made his way). The Messenger of Allah (may peace be upon him) said: Bring him back to me. He was searched, but they (the companions of the Holy Prophet) could not find him. The Messenger of Allah (may peace be upon him) thereupon said: He was Gabriel and he wanted to make you learn (things pertaining to religion) when you did not ask (them yourselves).

Chapter III

ON PRAYER (ṢALĀT) WHICH IS ONE OF THE PILLARS OF ISLAM

(7) It is reported on the authority of Ṭalḥa b. 'Ubaidullah[16] that a person with dishevelled hair, one among the people of Nejd, came to the Messenger of Allah (may

14. Prayer is the central phenomenon of religion, the very heartstone of all piety. Without prayer one cannot find God. It is the effective means by which we seek and find Him. Prayer is in fact the elementary and necessary expression of the religious life, and it is a test by which the religious sense of a man is tried and tested.

15. xxxi. 34.

16. Ṭalḥa b. 'Ubaidullah was surnamed Abū Muḥammad Quraishī and was one among the eight early converts to Islam. He was ruthlessly tortured, but he never wavered and remained a devoted Muslim to the end of his life. He showed remarkable devotion and sense of endurance in the battle of Uḥud and was severely wounded while defending the person of the Holy Prophet (may peace be upon him). In the battle of Camel he was shot by an arrow which ultimately proved fatal. He died of this wound at Baṣra at the age of sixty-four years.

peace be upon him). We heard the humming of his voice but could not fully discern what he had been saying, till he came nigh to the Messenger of Allah (may peace be upon him). It was then (disclosed to us) that he was asking questions pertaining to Islam. The Messenger of Allah (may peace be upon him) said: Five prayers during the day and the night. (Upon this) he said: Am I obliged to say any other (prayer) besides these? He (the Holy Prophet) said: No, but whatever you observe voluntarily, out of your own free will,[17] and the fasts of Ramaḍān. The inquirer said: Am I obliged to do anything else besides this? He (the Holy Prophet) said: No, but whatever you do out of your own free will. And the Messenger of Allah told him about the Zakāt (poor-due). The inquirer said: Am I obliged to pay anything else besides this? He (the Holy Prophet) said: No, but whatever you pay voluntarily out of your own free will. The man turned back and was saying: I would neither make any addition to this, nor will I decrease anything out of it. The Prophet remarked: He is successful if he is true to what he affirms.

(8) Another ḥadīth, the like of which has been narrated by Mālik (b. Anas) (and mentioned above) is also reported by Ṭalḥa b. 'Ubaidullah, with the only variation that the Holy Prophet remarked: By his father, he shall succeed if he were true (to what he professed), or: By his father,[18] he would enter heaven if he were true (to what he professed).

Chapter IV

PERTAINING TO FAITH IN ALLAH

(9) It is reported on the authority of Anas b. Mālik that[19] he said: We were

17. Five daily prayers, the fasts during the month of Ramaḍān, and the Zakāt are the obligatory acts of devotion to the Lord. If a man does not perform them, he is liable to be punished. The love of God and the keen sense of devotion to Him, however, demand that a true devotee of God should not content himself only with performing obligatory acts; he must endeavour to do good beyond what is incumbent on him.

18. There is apparently some contradiction between this ḥadīth and another in which the Muslims have been forbidden to swear by another name except that of Allah. The Holy Prophet (may peace be upon him) said: (*a*) He who takes an oath should swear by Allah; (*b*) Verily Allah has forbidden you that you swear by your fathers. Imām Nawawī is of the opinion that there is no contradiction in these aḥādīth. The Holy Prophet (may peace be upon him) did not use this phrase "by his father" in the sense of oath, but used it only to stress the importance of his assertion. It was a watchword of the Arabs and they frequently used it in their speech and conversation.

19. Anas b. Mālik was surnamed Abū Ḥamza, and was known among his companions as the servant of the Messenger of Allah. He belonged to an eminent tribe Najjār of Anṣār. He was born in Medina eight or ten years before the migration of the Holy Prophet. His mother Umm Sulaim was one of the earlier converts of Medina and was abandoned on this very reason by her husband. She married Abū Ṭalḥa, a devout Muslim. Anas was, therefore, brought up in a family which stood eminent in its devotion to Islam when the Holy Prophet settled in Medina. Abū Ṭalḥa came to the Holy Prophet along with his step-son Anas and requested him to take the promising boy under his care. The Prophet readily accepted the offer. Anas was always eager to live in the company of the Holy Prophet and, therefore, spent the whole day along with him, listening to his sacred words, watching his deeds and doing different jobs for him. The Holy Prophet was very much pleased with him and

forbidden[20] that we should ask anything (without the genuine need) from the Holy Prophet. It, therefore, pleased us that an intelligent person from the dwellers of the desert should come and ask him (the Holy Prophet) and we should listen to it. A man from the dwellers of the desert came (to the Holy Prophet) and said: Muḥammad, your messenger came to us and told us your assertion that verily Allah had sent you (as a prophet). He (the Holy Prophet) remarked: He told the truth. He (the bedouin) said: Who created the heaven? He (the Holy Prophet) replied: Allah. He (the bedouin again) said: Who created the earth? He (the Holy Prophet) replied: Allah. He (the bedouin again) said: Who raised these mountains and who created in them whatever is created there? He (the Holy Prophet) replied: Allah. Upon this he (the bedouin) remarked: By Him Who created the heaven and created the earth and raised mountains thereupon, has Allah (in fact) sent you? He (the Holy Prophet) said: Yes. He (the bedouin) said: Your messenger also told us that five prayers (had been made) obligatory for us during the day and the night. He (the Holy Prophet) remarked: He told you the truth. He (the bedouin) said: By Him Who sent you, is it Allah Who ordered you about this (i.e. prayers)? He (the Holy Prophet) said: Yes. He (the bedouin) said: Your messenger told us that Zakāt had been made obligatory in our riches. He (the Holy Prophet) said: He has told the truth. He (the bedouin) said: By Him Who sent you (as a prophet), is it Allah Who ordered you about it (Zakāt)? He (the Holy Prophet) said: Yes. He (the bedouin) said: Your messenger told us that it had been made obligatory for us to fast every year during the month of Ramaḍān. He (the Holy Prophet) said: He has told the truth. He (the bedouin) said: By Him Who sent you (as a prophet), is it Allah Who ordered you about it (the fasts of Ramaḍān)? He (the Holy Prophet) said: Yes. He (the bedouin) said: Your messenger also told us that pilgrimage (Ḥajj) to the House (of Ka'bah) had been made obligatory for him who is able to undertake the journey to it. He (the Holy Prophet) said: Yes. The narrator said that he (the bedouin) set off (at the conclusion of this answer, but at the time of his departure) remarked: By Him Who sent you with the Truth, I would

often visited his house and blessed him. He addressed him as son and on some occasions called him Unais. Anas was very much elated for the favours conferred on him by the Holy Prophet and said: I served the Messenger of Allah for full ten years, but he was never annoyed and never uttered a word of displeasure about me. He was the trusted friend of the four righteous Caliphs. 'Umar sent him to Baṣra for educating the people there. He died in 93 H. at the age of 103 in that city. He was the last of the companions of the Holy Prophet in Baṣra and with the honourable exception of Abū al-Ṭufail was the last of those blessed souls who had had the opportunity to live and see the Messenger of Allah as his devoted followers.

20. It refers to the verse of the Holy Qur'ān: O you who believe, ask not about things which, if made known to you, may annoy you (v. 101).

It is not the actual curiosity to know the teachings of Islam which is discouraged, but frivolous questioning and useless speculation have been looked down upon with displeasure. Allah does not encourage hair-splitting on those abstruse issues which have no bearing on practical life. Moreover, in the comprehensive scheme of life as envisaged by Islam a good deal had to be left to the individual will and the circumstances to meet the exigencies of time and place. The Holy Prophet, therefore, did not like the idea that he should be pressed to decide the issues on which Allah wanted him to remain silent, because if his decision was solicited it must have been the final say as "he does not speak of his own desire" (liii. 3).

neither make any addition to them nor would I diminish anything out of them. Upon this the Holy Prophet remarked: If he were true (to what he said) he must enter Paradise.

(10) It is narrated on the authority of Thābit that Anas said: We were forbidden in the Holy Qur'ān that we should ask about anything from the Messenger of Allah (may peace be upon him) and then Anas reported the ḥadīth in similar words.

Chapter V

CONCERNING ĪMĀN BY WHICH A PERSON WOULD ENTER HEAVEN

(11) It is narrated on the authority of Abū Ayyūb[21] Anṣārī that once during the journey of the Holy Prophet (may peace of Allah be upon him) a bedouin appeared before him and caught hold of the nosestring of his she-camel and then said: Messenger of Allah (or Muḥammad), inform me about that which takes me near to Paradise and draws me away from the Fire (of Hell). He (the narrator) said: The Prophet (may peace be upon him) stopped for a while and cast a glance upon his companions and then said: He was afforded a good opportunity (or he had been guided well). He (the Holy Prophet) addressing the bedouin said: (Repeat) whatever you uttered. He (the bedouin) repeated that. Upon this the Apostle (may peace be upon him) remarked: The deed which can draw you near to Paradise and take you away from Hell is, that you worship Allah and associate none with Him, and you establish prayer and pay Zakāt, and do good to your kin. After having uttered these words, the Holy Prophet asked the bedouin to release the nosestring of his she-camel.

(12) This ḥadīth is transmitted by Muḥammad b. Ḥātim on the authority of Abū Ayyūb Anṣārī.

(13) It is narrated on the authority of Abū Ayyūb that a man came to the Prophet (may peace be upon him) and said: Direct me to a deed which draws me near to Paradise and takes me away from the Fire (of Hell). Upon this he (the Holy Prophet) said: You worship Allah and never associate anything with Him, establish prayer, and pay Zakāt, and do good to your kin. When he turned his back, the Messenger of Allah (may peace be upon him) remarked: If he adhered to what he had been ordered to do, he would enter Paradise.

21. Abū Ayyūb. His name was Khālid b. Zaid b. Kulayb. He was a prominent member of the family of Najjār, an important family of the tribe of Khazraj. He was one among those fortunate Anṣār who embraced Islam at the hand of the Holy Prophet in the valley of 'Aqaba before he migrated to Medina. He had had the privilege of staying the Holy Prophet in his house before his own house was built. He took part in all the battles of early Islam and served under the command of 'Amr b. al-'Āṣ during the conquest of Egypt. Later he was appointed by 'Alī (may Allah be pleased with him) to the governorship of Medina. During the reign of Mu'āwiya he took part in the invasion of Cyprus and the expedition led against Constantinople. During the siege of the Byzantine capital an epidemic broke out which took a heavy toll of human life. Abū Ayyūb (may Allah be pleased with him) fell victim to it in the year 50 or 51 H. and was buried under the walls of Constantinople. (The Byzantines respected it and made pilgrimage to it in the time of draught to pray there for rain.)

(14) It is reported on the authority of Abū Huraira that a bedouin came to the Messenger of Allah (may peace be upon him) and said: Messenger of Allah, direct me to a deed by which I may be entitled to enter Paradise. Upon this he (the Holy Prophet) remarked: You worship Allah and never associate anything with Him, establish the obligatory prayer, and pay the Zakāt which is incumbent upon you, and observe the fast of Ramaḍān. He (the bedouin) said: By Him in Whose hand is my life, I will never add anything to it, nor will I diminish anything from it. When he (the bedouin) turned his back, the Prophet (may peace be upon him) said: He who is pleased to see a man from the dwellers of Paradise should catch a glimpse of him.

(15) It is narrated on the authority of Jābir[22] that Nu'mān b. Qaufal came to the Holy Prophet (may peace be upon him) and said: Would I enter Paradise if I say the obligatory prayers and deny myself that which is forbidden and treat that as lawful what has been made permissible (by the Sharī'ah). The Holy Prophet (may peace be upon him) replied in the affirmative.

(16) A similar ḥadīth is narrated on Jābir's authority in which the following words are added: I will do nothing more.

(17) It is narrated on the authority of Jābir that a man once said to the Messenger of Allah (may peace be upon him): Would I enter Paradise in case I say the obligatory prayers, observe the (fasts) of Ramaḍān and treat that as lawful what has been made permissible (by the Sharī'ah) and deny myself that what is forbidden, and make no addition to it. He (the Holy Prophet) replied in the affirmative. He (the inquirer) said: By Allah, I would add nothing to it.

Chapter VI

CONCERNING THE SAYING OF THE APOSTLE: ISLAM IS FOUNDED ON FIVE (FUNDAMENTS)

(18) It is narrated on the authority of ('Abdullah)[23] son of 'Umar (may Allah be pleased with them) that the Holy Prophet (may peace of Allah be upon him) said:

22. His name was Jābir and was surnamed Abū 'Abdullah and was counted amongst the prominent personalities of Khazraj. He was born twenty years before the migration of the Holy Prophet and embraced Islam along with his father on the occasion of the second pledge of 'Aqaba, when he was eighteen years old. His father was a devoted follower of Islam and fell martyr in the battle of Uḥud. Jābir filled the void created in the Muslim army by the death of his father and took part in almost all the battles which were fought during his lifetime. He was one among those companions of the Holy Prophet who suffered torture at the hands of Ḥajjāj b. Yusūf. He was too old and infirm to bear this hardship and died in 74 H. at the age of ninety-four.

Jābir (may Allah be pleased with him) had an ardent desire to collect aḥādīth and travelled hundreds of miles for this purpose. The traditions narrated on his authority are estimated to be 1540. He exercised utmost care in the transmission of aḥadīth.

23. His name was 'Abdullah and *kunyah* was Abū 'Abdur-Raḥmān. He was the illustrious son of the illustrious father 'Umar b. al-Khaṭṭāb. He is one of the most prominent personalities of the first generation of the Muslims, and of the authorities most frequently quoted for traditions. He derived his reputation not only from being a son of the Caliph, but because of his high moral qualities and his keen insight into the teachings of Islam. He was a devoted Muslim and followed the precepts of Islam with such scrupulous obedience and sagacity that his contemporaries and the subsequent gene-

(The superstructure of) al-Islam is raised on five (pillars),[24] i.e. the oneness of Allah, the establishment of prayer, payment of Zakāt, the fast of Ramaḍān, Pilgrimage (to Mecca).

A person said (to 'Abdullah b. 'Umar, the narrator) : Which of the two precedes the other—Pilgrimage or the fasts of Ramaḍān ? Upon this he (the narrator) replied : No (it is not the Pilgrimage first) but the fasts of Ramaḍān precede the Pilgrimage.

(19) It is narrated on the authority of ('Abdullah) son of 'Umar, that the Holy Prophet (may peace of Allah be upon him) said : (The superstructure of) al-Islam is raised on five (pillars), i.e. Allah (alone) should be worshipped, and (all other gods) besides Him should be (categorically) denied. Establishment of prayer, the payment of Zakāt, Pilgrimage to the House, and the fast of Ramaḍān (are the other obligatory acts besides the belief in the oneness of Allah and denial of all other gods).

(20) It is narrated on the authority of 'Abdullah son of 'Umar that the Messenger of Allah (may peace be upon him) said : (The superstructure of) al-Islam is raised on five (pillars), testifying (the fact) that there is no god but Allah, that Muḥammad is His bondsman and messenger, and the establishment of prayer, payment of Zakāt, Pilgrimage to the House (Ka'ba) and the fast of Ramaḍān.

(21) It is reported on the authority of Ṭā'ūs[25] that a man said to 'Abdullah son of 'Umar (may Allah be pleased with him) : Why don't you carry out a military expedition ?[26] Upon which he replied : I heard the Messenger of Allah (may peace be upon

rations always looked up to him for guidance. As transmitter of traditions, he is regarded as one of the most reliable authorities and is well known for his accuracy (both in letter and spirit) of narration. He was born before Hijra, but the exact date of his birth is not known. It is, however, established that when Ḥaḍrat 'Umar accepted Islam, 'Abdullah was five years old.

Ibn 'Umar died of septicaemia in 74 H. at the age of eighty-four, as the result of a wound in the foot inflicted by one of the soldiers of al-Ḥajjāj with the lower end of his lance, in the throng of pilgrims returning from 'Arafāt.

24. In this ḥadīth Islam is compared to a magnificent structure which rests on five pillars. The Muslims have, therefore, been exhorted to strengthen them since their weakness would undermine the very foundation of faith. This may be called the sum and substance of Islam.

25. Ṭā'ūs was a famous Tābi'ī. His *kunyah* was Abū 'Abdur-Raḥmān. He was a non-Arab and was the son of Kisān. 'Allāma Nawawī writes : Ṭā'ūs was an eminent scholar and was one of the famous successors of the companions. His greatness, depth of knowledge and superb memory are the facts over which there is no difference of opinion amongst the critics of ḥadīth and the jurists. He had had the opportunity of learning Ḥadīth from at least fifty leading companions of the Holy Prophet (may peace be upon him). He died in 106 H., a day before the Pilgrimage and was buried there in Mecca.

26. This ḥadīth has been debated amongst the traditionists. Jihād which implies an all-round struggle for the propagation and dominance of Islam is also regarded as one of the pillars of Islam. But the five pillars mentioned above are more important than this. It is because Jihād is not absolutely obligatory as the belief in the oneness of God, establishment of prayer, Zakāt, Pilgrimage and the fasts of Ramaḍān. It is a *farḍ-i-kifāya* which signifies that it is no doubt binding on every Muslim, but if some persons undertake this task, the whole of the Muslim society is absolved of its responsibility. It is essential for every believer to participate in the Jihād, but it is not necessary for everyone to join military expeditions. The weak, the infirm, the women and the children are exempted from this duty. In the ḥadīth under discussion 'Abdullah b. 'Umar was questioned as to why he did not carry out military expeditions. He had been enthusiastically participating in battles in his youth. He must have been avoiding it either on account of old age or due to the fact that the Muslims had drawn swords against one another and he did not consider it advisable to join either side.

him) say: Verily, al-Islam is founded on five (pillars): testifying the fact that there is no god but Allah, establishment of prayer, payment of Zakāt, fast of Ramaḍān and Pilgrimage to the House.

Chapter VII

RELATING TO THE COMMAND FOR BELIEF IN ALLAH AND HIS PROPHET AND THE LAWS OF ISLAM AND INVITING (PEOPLE TO) THEM

(22) It is narrated on the authority of Ibn 'Abbās that a delegation of 'Abdul-Qais[27] came to the Messenger of Allah (may peace be upon him) and said: Messenger of Allah, verily ours is a tribe of Rabī'a and there stand between you and us the unbelievers of Muḍar and we find no freedom to come to you except in the month of Ḥarām. Direct us to an act which we should ourselves perform and invite those who live beside us. Upon this the Prophet remarked: I command you to do four things and prohibit you against four acts. (The four deeds which you are commanded to do are): Faith in Allah, and then he explained it for them and said: Testifying the fact: that there is no god but Allah, that Muḥammad is the messenger of Allah, establishment of prayer, payment of Zakāt, that you pay *khums* (one-fifth) of the booty fallen to your lot, and I prohibit you to use round gourd,[28] wine jars,[29] wooden pots [30] or skins [31] for wine. Khalaf b. Hishām has made this addition in his narration: Testifying the fact that there is no god but Allah, and then he with his finger pointed out the oneness of the Lord.

27. 'Abdul-Qais was the name of an eminent Arab whose posterity was called Banī 'Abdul-Qais and it was one of the important branches of the famous Arab tribe Rabī'a. It is recorded that fourteen prominent men amongst Banū 'Abdul-Qais came to the Holy Prophet and told him that the men of Muḍar tribe who were unbelievers and lived between the habitations of Banū 'Abdul-Qais and Medina had barred their way to this city. So they could not frequently visit him and learn the commandments of Allah. It was only during the four months of Ḥarām (i.e. dhī-Qa'd, dhul-Ḥijjah, Muḥarram and Rajab) that they could come to him and learn things pertaining to Islam.

28. The background of the ḥadīth is indicative of the fact that the people of 'Abdul-Qais were given to drinking and had developed an art to prepare liquor and then preserve it. The Holy Prophet, keeping in view the nature of the vice which had become a second nature to them, gave them two types of commandments. The first type includes belief in the oneness of God, the prophethood of Muḥammad and the basic acts of virtue and piety which inculcate God-consciousness. The second type deals with the evil which had taken a firm root in their hearts and crept into the fibre of their society. The Holy Prophet struck at the very base of this vice and forbade them to use even jars and skins in which liquor was prepared. He wanted them to realise the fact that when the use of such utensils in which liquor was manufactured and preserved was strictly prohibited, what an enormous crime it would be to drink it.

29. *Ḥantam* is a wine jar glazed or varnished green which used to be carried to Medina with liquor in it. It was also used for preparing the *nabidh* (نبيذ). It quickly became potent in them by reason of glazing, or varnish, or as some say because they used to be made of clay kneaded with blood and hair (Lane's *Arabic-English Lexicon*).

30. *al-Naqqir*. It means a hollowed block of wood, or a stump or the lower part of a palm-tree, in which beverage called *nabidh* is made. It was a common custom with the Arabs to hollow out a block of wood or stump and then crush in it ripe dates and unripe dates and pour water upon them. It was then left until fermentation had taken place therein. The word is of the measure of *fa'il* (فعيل) in the sense of measure.

31. *Muqayyar*. It is a skin for preserving wine.

(23) Abū Jamra reported: I was an interpreter between Ibn 'Abbās and the people, that a woman happened to come there and asked about *nabīdh* or the pitcher wine.[32] He replied: A delegation of the people of 'Abdul-Qais came to the Messenger of Allah (may peace be upon him). He (the Holy Prophet) asked the delegation or the people (of the delegation about their identity). They replied that they belonged to the tribe of Rabī'a. He (the Holy Prophet) welcomed the people or the delegation which were neither humiliated nor put to shame.[33] They (the members of the delegation) said: Messenger of Allah, we come to you from a far-off distance and there lives between you and us a tribe of the unbelievers of Muḍar and, therefore, it is not possible for us to come to you except in the months of Ḥarām. Thus direct us to a clear command, about which we should inform people beside us and by which we may enter heaven. He (the Holy Prophet) replied: I command you to do four deeds and forbid you to do four (acts), and added: I direct you to affirm belief in Allah alone, and then asked them: Do you know what belief in Allah really implies? They said: Allah and His Messenger know best. The Prophet said: It implies testimony to the fact that there is no god but Allah, and that Muḥammad is the messenger of Allah, establishment of prayer, payment of Zakāt, fast of Ramaḍān, that you pay one-fifth of the booty (fallen to your lot) and I forbid you to use gourd, wine jar, or a receptacle[34] for wine. Shu'ba sometimes narrated the word *naqīr* (نقير=wooden pot) and sometimes narrated it as *muqayyar* (مقير). The Holy Prophet also said: Keep it in your mind and inform those who have been left behind.

(24) There is another ḥadīth narrated on the authority of Ibn 'Abbās[35] (the contents of which are similar to the one) narrated by Shu'ba in which the Holy Prophet (may peace be upon him) said: I forbid you to prepare *nabīdh* (نبيذ) in a gourd, hollowed block of wood, a varnished jar or receptacle. Ibn Mu'ādh made this addition on the authority of his father that the Messenger of Allah said to Ashajj,[36] of the tribe of 'Abdul-Qais: You possess two qualities which are liked by Allah: insight and

32. The woman came to Ibn 'Abbās, the cousin of the Holy Prophet and a highly talented and trustworthy scholar of the Qur'ān and the Sunnah, to find out whether it was permitted to use those pitchers in which wine was previously prepared and preserved. Ibn 'Abbās narrated to her the directives given by the Holy Prophet to the delegate of 'Abdul-Qais concerning the use of such receptacles.

33. It means that the delegation represented the tribe whose members did not come to a clash with the Holy Prophet and accepted Islam cheerfully of their own sweet will.

34. *Muzaffat* is a vessel or receptacle for wine.

35. 'Abdullah b. al-'Abbās (frequently Ibn 'Abbās) is considered one of the greatest, if not the greatest, scholars of the past generations of Muslims. He was born three years before the Hijrah when the Hāshimite family was living shut up in the Ravine (al-Sha'b). It was from his childhood that he showed a strong inclination towards accurate scholarly research and gathered full information about the Holy Prophet by questioning his companions. While still young he became a master mind around whom thronged people desirous to learn. Besides retaining knowledge in his memory he made a large collection of written notes. Not only the common Muslims but even eminent scholars sought his advice in matters relating to religion. He was especially expert in explaining the implications of the Qur'ānic verses and in solving judicial questions.

He was the first to lay the foundation of Islamic jurisprudence in Mecca and his legal decisions were collected by Abū Bakr Muḥammad Mūsā in twenty volumes. He died in 68 H. at Ṭā'if.

36. He was one of the prominent figures of 'Abdul-Qais. His real name was Mundhar b. 'Aiyid. The Prophet called him Ashajj because he had the scar of a wound on his forehead.

deliberateness.[37]

(25) It is reported on the authority of Qatāda[38] that one among the delegates of the 'Abdul-Qais tribe narrated this tradition to him. Sa'īd said that Qatāda had mentioned the name of Abū Naḍra on the authority of Abū Sa'īd Khudrī who narrated this tradition: That people from the tribe of 'Abdul-Qais came to the Messenger of Allah (may peace be upon him) and said: Messenger of Allah, we belong to the tribe of Rabī'a and there live between you and us the unbelievers of Muḍar tribe and we find it impossible to come to you except in the months of Ḥarām; direct us to a deed which we must communicate to those who have been left behind us and by doing which we may enter heaven. Upon this the Messenger of Allah (peace be upon him) said: I enjoin upon you four (things) and forbid you to do four (things): worship Allah and associate none with Him, establish prayer, pay Zakāt, and observe the fast of Ramaḍān, and pay the fifth part out of the booty. And I prohibit you from four (things): dry gourds, green-coloured jars, hollowed stumps of palm-trees, and receptacles. They (the members of the delegation) said: Do you know what *al-naqīr* is? He replied: Yes, it is a stump which you hollow out and in which you throw small dates.[39] Sa'īd said: He (the Holy Prophet) used the word *tamar* (تمر = dates). (The Holy Prophet then added): Then you sprinkle water over it and when its ebullition subsides, you drink it (and you are so intoxicated) that one amongst you, or one amongst them (the other members of your tribe, who were not present there) strikes his cousin with the sword.[40] He (the narrator) said: There was a man amongst us who had sustained injury on this very account due to (intoxication) and he told that he tried to conceal it out of shame from the Messenger of Allah (may peace be upon him). I, however, inquired from the Messenger of Allah (if we discard those utensils which you have forbidden us to use), then what type of vessels should be used for drink? He (the Holy Prophet) replied: In the water-skin the mouths of which are tied (with a rope). They (again) said: Prophet of Allah, our land abounds in rats and water-skins cannot remain preserved. The Holy Prophet of Allah (may peace be upon him) said: (Drink in water-skins) even if these are

37. This ḥadīth throws a good deal of light on the mental and moral qualities which Islam wants to develop in its followers. The first quality is that of deep insight into the affairs of things and not their superficial survey. The second quality is that of deliberateness, that nothing should be done in hot-haste. Whatever is to be done should be deliberated upon and it should be undertaken after having fully considered all its aspects.

38. His name was Qatāda and *kunyah* was Abū 'Umar. He came of the family Ẓafar, an important group of the Anas tribe. His father's name was Nu'mān b. Zaid. His mother Anīsa bint Qais was a talented lady of the tribe of Najjār and was the mother of the famous narrator Abū Sa'īd al-Khudrī. Qatāda embraced Islam at the hand of the Holy Prophet in the second pledge of 'Aqaba and remained a devoted and pious Muslim throughout his life. He died in 23 H. during the caliphate of 'Umar.

39. The original word is *Quṭi'ā'* (قطيعاء). Imām Nawawī has given the meaning of this word as "small dates" which are also known as *al-shahrīr*.

40. Here the Holy Prophet explained to them one of the gravest evils of using liquor, i.e. it clouds the intellect and renders a man incapable of judging his actions and ascertaining what is right and what is wrong. He, therefore, strictly prohibited its use because intoxication and God-consciousness cannot go together. It should, however, be remembered that when a beverage becomes intoxicant, even a small quantity of it that cannot intoxicate is not allowed: that of which alarge quantity intoxicates, even a small quantity of it is prohibited (Abū Dāwūd).

nibbled by rats.[41] And then (addressing) al-Ashajj of 'Abdul-Qais he said: Verily, you possess two such qualities which Allah loves: insight and deliberateness.

(26) It is narrated on the authority of Abū Sa'īd[42] al-Khudrī that when the delegation of the tribe of 'Abdul-Qais came to the Prophet of Allah (may peace be upon him), (its members) said: Apostle of Allah, may God enable us to lay down our lives for you, which beverage is good for us? He (the Prophet) said: (Not to speak of beverages, I would lay stress) that you should not drink in the wine jars. They said: Apostle of Allah, may God enable us to lay down our lives for you, do you know what *al-naqīr* is? He (the Holy Prophet) replied: Yes, it is a stump which you hollow out in the middle, and added: Do not use gourd or receptacle (for drink). Use water-skin the mouth of which is tied with rope (for this purpose).

Chapter VIII

CALLING PEOPLE TO TESTIFICATIONS AND THE CANONS OF ISLAM

(27) It is reported on the authority of Ibn 'Abbās that Mu'ādh[43] said: The Messenger of Allah sent me (as a governor of Yemen) and (at the time of departure) instructed me thus: You will soon find yourself in a community one among the people

41. These words have been repeated in order to emphasise the enormity of the crime of drinking. The Holy Prophet stressed this point to make them realise that whatever might be their difficulties they could not be allowed to use wine jars since these could revive their associations with this evil habit. The Holy Prophet in fact wanted that they should completely break away from this vice and no connecting link should be left which could take them back to this evil practice. This gives us an idea of the deep understanding of the Holy Prophet about the psychology of human mind.

42. His name was Sa'd. Abū Sa'īd was his *kunyah*. He belonged to the eminent tribe o Khadra. His father's name was Mālik b. Sanān and his mother was Anīsa daughter of Abī Ḥāritha. Abū Sa'īd was born in a family where both father and mother were devoted Muslims. He participated in the construction of the mosque in Medina and joined the battle of Uḥud. The Holy Prophet was reluctant to enlist him in the Muslim army but when his father Mālik requested him not to reject him, he yielded to his demand. Subsequently Abū Sa'īd participated in almost all major expeditions of the Muslim army.

Abū Sa'īd was one of the famous jurists of the early days of Islam. The traditions narrated on his authority number 1170. He died in 74 H. at the age of eighty-six.

43. Mu'ādh was one of the eminent companions of the Holy Prophet. He was the son of Jabal belonging to the tribe of Khazraj. He embraced Islam in his early childhood and was one among those noble souls who gave allegiance to the Messenger of Allah at 'Aqaba for the first time. Mu'ādh was a highly talented young man and Muḥammad (may peace of Allah be upon him) took special care to give him training in different spheres of Islamic learning. He always showed full devotion to Islam and the Prophet and spared no pains in carrying the light of Islam to all those corners where he could possibly reach. The Holy Prophet and his companions always trusted him and sought his advice on all important issues. He was entrusted with multifarious duties on different occasions. As a governor, as an envoy, as a military officer, as a preacher, as an orator, as a jurist, and as a commentator of the Holy Qur'ān he showed marvellous intelligence and practical wisdom.

It was during the caliphate of 'Umar that there broke out plague in Syria where Mu'ādh had been staying. Abū 'Ubaida who was the commander of the Muslim army there died of this epidemic. Mu'ādh son of 'Abdur-Raḥmān and his two wives shared the same fate and then Mu'ādh himself fell a victim to this scourge. He died in 18 H. when he was hardly thirty-six years old.

of the Book, so first call them to testify that there is no god but Allah,[44] that I (Muḥammad) am the messenger of Allah[45] and if they accept this, then tell them that Allah has enjoined upon them five prayers during the day and the night and if they accept it, then tell them that Allah has made Zakāt obligatory for them that it should be collected from the rich and distributed among the poor,[46] and if they agree to it, don't pick up (as a share of Zakāt) the best of their wealths.[47] Beware of the supplication of the oppressed for there is no barrier[48] between him and Allah.

(28) It is narrated on the authority of Ibn 'Abbās that when the Messenger of Allah (may peace be upon him) sent Mu'ādh towards Yemen (as governor) he said to him: Verily you would reach a community of the people of the Book, the very first thing to which you should call them is the worship of Allah, may His Glory be Magnificent, and when they become fully aware of Allah, instruct them that He had enjoined five prayers on them during the day and the night, and when they begin observing it, then instruct them that verily Allah had made Zakāt obligatory for them, which would be collected from the wealthy amongst them and distributed to their have-nots, and when they submit to it, then collect it from them and avoid (the temptation) of selecting the best (items) of their riches.

Chapter IX

COMMAND FOR FIGHTING AGAINST THE PEOPLE SO LONG AS THEY DO NOT PROFESS THAT THERE IS NO GOD BUT ALLAH AND MUḤAMMAD IS HIS MESSENGER

(29) It is narrated on the authority of Abū Huraira that when the Messenger of Allah (may peace be upon him) breathed his last and Abū Bakr was appointed as his

44. Imām Nawawī says that this part of the narration clearly shows that mere faith in God is not enough, because the people of the Book never denied the existence of God, but as their belief in God was not correct, it was alloyed with so many wrong conceptions and mistaken notions; therefore, the Holy Prophet asked Mu'ādh to call the people of the Book to testify God as is directed by Islam. It should be *Tauḥid* pure and simple, and nothing should be associated with Him in His Godhood.

45. Calling to the prophethood of Muḥammad is indicative of the fact that belief in his prophethood is an integral part of the faith.

46. This explains the nature and purpose of Zakāt: it is meant to bring about economic justice in society.

47. This ḥadīth throws a good deal of light on the practical wisdom with which the Divine Faith should be preached amongst people. They should not, at one and the same time, be burdened with all sorts of beliefs and religious practices. Firstly, the preacher should winnow out the mistaken notions which had taken a firm root in their minds, and correct beliefs about God, apostlehood, should be instilled in their minds. Then on the basis of God-consciousness the religious practices should be enjoined upon the people. On the negative side, attempt should be made to weed out all those evils which undermine God-consciousness in man and thus hamper his spiritual and moral growth.

48. Mu'ādh was especially instructed to be aware of the feelings of the oppressed. He was sent as a governor and it was his bounden duty to see that no man in society became victim of high-handedness. This is one of the fundamental duties of an Islamic State. In the *Musnad* of Aḥmad it is narrated on the authority of Abū Huraira that supplication of an oppressed is granted even though he is profligate, his profligacy rebounds on him (*Fatḥ-ul-Bāri*). There is another ḥadīth in the *Musnad* of Aḥmad narrated on the authority of Ḥaḍrat Anas: The supplication of the oppressed is granted even though he is an unbeliever. There is no barrier between it and (the Lord) (*vide 'Umdat-ul-Qāri*).

successor (Caliph) after him, those amongst the Arabs who wanted to become apostates became apostates.[49] 'Umar b. Khaṭṭāb said to Abū Bakr: Why would you fight against the people when the Messenger of Allah declared: I have been directed to fight against people so long as they do not say: There is no god but Allah, and he who professed it was granted full protection of his property and life on my behalf except for a right.[50] His (other) affairs rest with Allah.[51] Upon this Abū Bakr said: By Allah, I would definitely fight against him who severed prayer from Zakāt,[52] for it is the obligation upon the rich. By Allah, I would fight against them even to secure the cord (used for hobbling the feet of camel) which they used to give to the Messenger of Allah (as Zakāt) but now they have withheld it. 'Umar b. Khaṭṭāb remarked: By Allah, I found nothing but the fact that Allah had opened the heart of Abū Bakr for (perceiving the justification of) fighting (against those who refused to pay Zakāt) and I fully recognised that the (stand of Abū Bakr) was right.[53]

(30) It is reported on the authority of Abū Huraira that the Messenger of Allah said: I have been commanded to fight against people so long as they do not declare that there is no god but Allah,[54] and he who professed it was guaranteed the protection of

49. Al-Ṭībī is of the opinion that most of the apostates belonged to the tribes of Ghaṭafān and Sulaim. Qāḍī 'Iyāḍ says that the apostates formed three distinctive groups. One group consisted of those people who returned to idolatry after the demise of the Holy Prophet; the second group was that which accepted the liars Musailima and Aswad 'Ansī as prophets; and the third comprised of those persons who refused to pay Zakāt on the false pretext that it was obligatory only during the lifetime of the Holy Prophet and after his death no one had the right to force them for its payment (*Fatḥ al-Mulhim* by Maulānā Shabbīr Aḥmad 'Uthmānī). It should be borne in mind that this command for fighting against people refers to a particular group, i.e. apostates. Some of the Western critics have wrongly concluded on the basis of these aḥādīth that Islam exhorts its followers to fight against all those who do not profess this religion. This is sheer ignorance. Non-Muslims had been living in the Islamic State and they were guaranteed full protection of their lives, property and honour. If they were not forced to accept Islam as their faith, how could other people be pressed to do so at the point of the sword? This command of fighting against people till they profess the oneness of Allah, and establish prayer and pay Zakāt, pertains to the apostates. The very first ḥadīth of this chapter makes this point explicitly clear. In an Islamic State apostasy signifies the same threat as high treason in other States and, therefore, it is not to be tolerated.

50. His life and property are fully protected, but if he commits a cognizable offence, he would be punished for that.

51. If a man makes a verbal profession of Islam, he must be treated as a Muslim. If he is a hypocrite and is not sincere in his faith, let his affair be decided by Allah Himself Who is Well Aware and All-Knowing.

52. Islam is one organic whole; it cannot be fragmented into pieces. Zakāt like prayer is an integral part of Islam and, therefore, its followers can under no stress of circumstances, or on the basis of ostensible advantages, be allowed to adopt a defiant attitude towards any commandment of Islam. That the two commandments, prayer and payment of Zakāt, go together can be seen in numerous verses of the Holy Qur'ān. In Sūrah lxxiii., which is undoubtedly one of the earliest revelations we have: And keep up prayer and pay the Zakāt and offer to Allah a goodly gift (verse 20). And they are not enjoined anything except that they should serve Allah, being sincere to Him in obedience, be upright and keep up prayer, and pay the Zakāt, and that is the right religion (xcviii. 5).

53. This ḥadīth abundantly reflects the deep insight of Haḍrat Abū Bakr in understanding the teachings of Islam and his courage to handle the situation.

54. This ḥadīth has been made the target of criticism by the hostile critics of Islam. They wrongly assert that it is by sheer force that people are converted to Islam. But there is not an iota of truth in it. They do not look into the words used by the Holy Peophet. Here the verb قاتل is highly

his property and life on my behalf except for the right, and his affairs rest with Allah.

(31) It is reported on the authority of Abū Huraira that he heard the Messenger of Allah say: I have been commanded to fight against people till they testify the fact that there is no god but Allah, and believe in me (that) I am the messenger (from the Lord) and in all that I have brought.[55] And when they do it, their blood and riches are guaranteed protection on my behalf except where it is justified by law, and their affairs rest with Allah.

(32) It is narrated on the authority of Jābir that the Messenger of Allah said: I have been commanded that I should fight against people till they declare that there is no god but Allah and when they profess it that there is no god but Allah, their blood and riches are guaranteed protection on my behalf except where it is justified by law, and their affairs rest with Allah, and then he (the Holy Prophet) recited (this verse of the Holy Qur'ān): "Thou art not over them a warden" [56] (lxxxviii. 22).

(33) It has been narrated on the authority of 'Abdullah b. 'Umar that the Messenger of Allah said: I have been commanded to fight against people till they testify that there is no god but Allah, that Muḥammad is the messenger of Allah, and they establish prayer, and pay Zakāt and if they do it, their blood and property are guaranteed protection on my behalf except when justified by law, and their affairs rest with Allah.

(34) It is narrated on the authority of Abū Mālik: I heard the Messenger of Allah (may peace be upon him) say: He who professed that there is no god but Allah and made a denial of everything which the people worship besides Allah, his property and blood became inviolable, and their affairs rest with Allah.

(35) Abū Mālik narrated on the authority of his father that he heard the Apostle (may peace be upon him) say: He who held belief in the oneness of Allah, and then narrated what has been stated above.

meaningful. A person who is conversant even with the rudiments of Arabic grammar knows fully well that it is from the *bāb* مفاعلة which implies that it is not a one-sided action but a participation of both sides. Thus according to the *bāb* of the verb used, it becomes clear that the Holy Prophet exhorted to fight against those who had raised arms against the Muslims. This command is not directed against every non-Muslim.

55. This ḥadīth substantiates the fact that a man becomes a Muslim only when he sincerely believes in the Lord, in the apostlehood of Muḥammad and in all that is revealed to him. It repudiates the claim of those who think that belief in the oneness of Allah is enough to make them Muslims.

Maulānā Shabbīr Aḥmad has rightly pointed out that this ḥadīth explicitly speaks of the basic importance of the Sunnah as an integral part of faith, and believing in all that has authentically come down from the Holy Prophet (*Fatḥ-ul-Mulhim*, Vol. I, p. 194).

56. Imām Rāghib has explained this word مصيطر as derived from the root سطر ، صطر which means "he wrote". This word, according to its derivation, denotes one who writes the destiny. The Holy Prophet was told that he was not مصيطر meaning thereby that it was not his duty to force his will upon them and change their destiny.

Chapter X

HE WHO ACCEPTS ISLAM AT THE DEATH-BED, BEFORE THE ACTUAL AGONY OF DEATH, IS A MUSLIM. IT IS FORBIDDEN TO SUPPLICATE BLESSINGS FOR THE POLYTHEISTS. HE WHO DIES AS A POLYTHEIST IS ONE AMONG THE DENIZENS OF HELL AND NO MEANS WOULD BE EFFECTIVE ENOUGH TO TAKE HIM OUT OF THAT

(36) It is reported by Sa'id b. Musayyib who narrated it on the authority of his father (Musayyib b. Ḥazm) that when Abū Ṭālib was about to die, the Messenger of Allah (may peace be upon him) came to him and found with him Abū Jahl ('Amr b. Hishām) and 'Abdullah b. Abī Umayya ibn al-Mughīrah. The Messenger of Allah (may peace be upon him) said: My uncle, you just make a profession that there is no god but Allah, and I will bear testimony before Allah (of your being a believer). Abū Jahl and 'Abdullah b. Abī Umayya addressing him said: Abū Ṭālib, do you abandon the religion of 'Abdul-Muṭṭalib? The Messenger of Allah (may peace be upon him) constantly requested him (to accept his offer), and (on the other hand) was repeated the same statement (of Abū Jahl and 'Abdullah b. Abī Umayya) till Abū Ṭālib gave his final decision and he stuck to the religion of 'Abdul-Muṭṭalib and refused to profess that there is no god but Allah. Upon this the Messenger of Allah remarked: By Allah, I will persistently beg pardon for you till I am forbidden to do so[57] (by God). It was then that Allah, the Magnificent and the Glorious, revealed this verse:

> It is not meant for the Prophet and for those who believe that they should beg pardon for the polytheists even though they were their kith and kin, after it had been made known to them that they were the denizens of Hell[58] (ix. 113).

And it was said to the Messenger of Allah (may peace be upon him):

> Verily thou canst not guide to the right path whom thou lovest. And it is Allah Who guideth whom He will, and He knoweth best who are the guided (xxviii. 56).

(37) It is narrated on the authority of Abū Huraira that the Messenger of Allah said to his uncle at the time of his death: Make a profession of it that there is no god

57. This ḥadīth shows how immensely did the Holy Prophet love his uncle and how anxious he was to bring him to the path of righteousness and piety. It also reflects that the Holy Prophet, in spite of his eminence as a messenger of Allah and as a dispenser of the final message of God, was His bondsman and did not dictate his will in the universe; he rather submitted himself cheerfully before the will of his Master. The prophets are Allah's bondsmen and their duty is to propagate His message with full wisdom and devotion. The outcome of their efforts rests with Allah. This is pure monotheism of Islam which distinguishes it from other religions.

58. It should be noted that this verse does not prohibit praying for the guidance of the disbelievers in general, but only in case of such disbelievers about whom it became clear that they were doomed to the Fire.

The commentators are of the opinion that either a revelation from Allah with regard to a person or his death in disbelief or idolatry alone settles the point. So long as a man is alive, however hard he may be in his disbelief, it is not forbidden to pray for his guidance.

but Allah and I will bear testimony (of your being a Muslim) on the Day of Judgment. But he (Abū Ṭālib) refused to do so. Then Allah revealed this verse:

> Verily thou canst not guide to the right path whom thou lovest. And it is Allah Who guideth whom He will and He knoweth best who are the guided (xxviii. 56).

(38) It is narrated on the authority of Abū Huraira that the Messenger of Allah said to his uncle (at the time of his death): Make a profession of it that there is no god but Allah and I will bear testimony (of your being a Muslim) on the Day of Judgment. He (Abū Ṭālib) said: Were it not the fear of the Quraysh blaming me (and) saying that it was the fear of (approaching death) that induced me to do so,[59] I would have certainly delighted your eyes. It was then that Allah revealed:

> Verily thou canst not guide to the right path whom thou lovest. And it is Allah Who guideth whom He will and He knoweth best who are the guided (xxviii. 56).

Chapter XI

HE WHO MEETS HIS LORD WITH IMPLICIT FAITH WOULD ENTER HEAVEN AND FIRE WOULD BE FORBIDDEN TO HARM HIM

(39) It is narrated on the authority of 'Uthmān[60] that the Messenger of Allah (may peace be upon him) said: He who died knowing (fully well) that there is no god but Allah entered Paradise.[61]

59. The words of Abū Ṭālib give us one of the clues why some people in spite of knowing the Truth do not affirm it. It is the fear of public opinion that stands in their way. This is also a kind of idolatry in which, instead of worshipping the idols of stones and clay, man submits before public pressure, however wrong it may be. Monotheism not only inculcates true love for and devotion to one God, but also fosters an attitude of disregard for everything which comes into conflict with the commandments of God.

60. 'Uthmān b. 'Affān, the third caliph, was born in Mecca forty-seven years before Hijra. He was closely related to the Holy Prophet from the side of his mother 'Urwa. He was a rich merchant and was a highly accomplished man and was regarded as a model of modesty and piety. He was amongst the earlier converts to Islam and remained devoted to it till the end of his life. He took part in the two migrations to Abyssinia and then joined the Holy Proph t in Medina. The Holy Prophet loved him very dearly and offered the hand of his daughter Ruqayyah to him and after her death renewed this affinity by offering him his second daughter Umm Kulthūm. He played a very important role during the life of the Holy Prophet and during the caliphate of his two renowned successors, Abū Bakr and 'Umar. He was elected as the third caliph and tried to conduct the affairs of the State according to the Qur'ān and the Sunnah. It was indeed unfortunate that during his caliphate there arose some disturbances which were the outcome of some highly complex and complicated factors. 'Uthmān tried to meet the situation with wisdom but avoided force and ultimately became victim of the high-handedness of the rebels. He was reciting the Holy Qur'ān when he was attacked by Kanāba b. Bishr and he fell as a martyr.

The whole of his life is an example of devotion, piety, selflessness and intense love for Allah and His Prophet, but the greatest service that he rendered to the cause of Islam is the preparation of the official and standard copy of the Qur'ān and then its wide distribution in the various lands where Muslims had settled.

61. Some persons ask whether it is enough for a man that he should recite these words and enter heaven. A little bit of penetration into the words of the ḥadīth would reveal the fact that mere expres-

(40) It is narrated on the authority of Ḥumrān that he heard 'Uthmān saying this: I heard the Messenger of Allah (may peace be upon him) uttering these words (as stated above).

(41) It is narrated on the authority of Abū Huraira: We were accompanying the Apostle (may peace be upon him) in a march (towards Tabūk). He (the narrator) said: The provisions with the people were almost depleted. He (the narrator) said: (And the situation became so critical) that they (the men of the army) decided to slaughter some of their camels. He (the narrator) said: Upon this 'Umar said: Messenger of Allah, I wish that you should pool together what has been left out of the provisions with the people and then invoke (the blessings of) Allah upon it. He (the narrator) said: He (the Holy Prophet) did it accordingly. He (the narrator) said: The one who had wheat in his possession came there with wheat. He who had dates with him came there with dates.[62] And Mujāhid said: He who possessed stones of dates came there with stones. I (the narrator) said: What did they do with the date-stones. They said: They (the people) sucked them and then drank water over them. He (the narrator said): He (the Holy Prophet) invoked the blessings (of Allah) upon them (provisions). He (the narrator) said: (And there was such a miraculous increase in the stocks) that the people replenished their provisions fully.[63] He (the narrator) said: At that time he (the Holy Prophet) said: I bear testimony to the fact that there is no god but Allah, and I am His messenger. The bondsman who would meet Allah without entertaining any doubt about these (two fundamentals) would enter heaven.

(42) It is narrated either on the authority of Abū Huraira or that of Abū Sa'īd Khudrī. The narrator A'mash has narrated this ḥadīth with a little bit of doubt (about the name of the very first narrator who was in direct contact with the Holy Prophet. He was either Abū Huraira or Abū Sa'īd Khudrī. Both are equally reliable transmitters of the traditions). He (the narrator) said: During the time of Tabūk expedition, the (provisions) ran short and the men (of the army) suffered starvation; they said: Messenger of Allah, would you permit us to slay our camels? We would eat them and use their fat. The Messenger of Allah (may peace be upon him) said: Do as you

sion of these words does not suffice. It implies that he who makes a sincere profession of the fact that there is no god but Allah deserves admittance to heavens. And this in turn entails heavy responsibilities. It means that the man is declaring in unequivocal terms that he believes in one God, and does not associate any other god with Him, whether those of stone and clay or heavenly bodies or human beings. The man who negates the existence of all false gods and affirms the existence of one God in fact makes a profession that he would submit to His command alone and would submit to nothing else except that which has been vouchsafed to him by the true Messenger of Allah. Thus the affirmation of this simple truth covers all the responsibilities, obligations and duties which fall upon the shoulders of a man after submitting his will to the will of the Lord and accepting Him as the sole object of worship.

62. This ḥadīth provides a justification for pooling the provisions of food, and then their fair distribution when, on account of acute shortage, it becomes a dire necessity. But this arrangement should not lead anyone to find justification for the regimentation of society which has become a common feature of communism. It was a temporary measure and that too was adopted at the time when the army had set out on an important expedition and it fell into the grip of acute shortage of food.

63. It was a miracle of the Holy Prophet that when he invoked the blessings of Allah, the provision of food increased adequately to meet the requirements of the army.

please. He (the narrator) said: Then 'Umar came there and said: Messenger of Allah, if you do that (if you give your consent and the men begin to slay their camels), the riding animals would become short. But (I would suggest you to) summon them along with the provisions left with them. Then invoke Allah's blessings on them (different items of the provisions). It is hoped Allah shall bless them. The Messenger of Allah replied in the affirmative. He (the narrator) said: He called for a leather mat to be used as a table cloth and spread it out. Then he called people along with the remaining portions of their provisions. He (the narrator) said: Someone was coming with a handful of mote, another was coming with a handful of dates, still another was coming with a portion of bread, till small quantities of these things were collected on the table cloth. He (the narrator said): Then the Messenger of Allah invoked blessings (on them) and said: Fill your utensils with these provisions. He (the narrator) said: They filled their vessels to the brim with them, and no one amongst the army (which comprised of 30,000 persons) was left even with a single empty vessel. He (the narrator) said: They ate to their fill, and there was still a surplus. Upon this the Messenger of Allah (may peace be upon him) remarked: I bear testimony that there is no god but Allah and I am the messenger of Allah. The man who meets his Lord without entertaining any doubt about these two (truths) would never be kept away from the Paradise.[64]

(43) It is narrated on the authority of 'Ubādah b. Ṣāmit that the Messenger of Allah (may peace be upon him) observed[65]: He who said: "There is no god but Allah, He is One and there is no associate with Him, that Muḥammad is His servant and His messenger, that Christ is His servant[66] and the son of His slave-girl and he (Christ) is

64. There is a very close connection between the first part of ḥadīth and the second. A miracle had been performed at the hand of the Holy Prophet which was one of the most effective means to awaken the consciousness of man to the fact that this universe is not being controlled by inexorable laws of Nature, but by a Power Who can, when He deems necessary, act freely according to His own will. At the time when the people had seen with their own eyes that the eatables had been miraculously increased on the Holy Prophet's invoking blessings on them, their minds had become keenly sensitive to the Great Truth that there reigns an Almighty Power in the universe. The Holy Prophet thought it an opportune moment to impress upon their hearts this fundamental truth and he preached to the audience the oneness of the Lord.

Secondly, a miracle had been performed at the hand of Muḥammad (may peace be upon him) and there was the likelihood that the new converts to Islam, whose minds had not been properly trained in Tauḥīd, might look upon the Holy Prophet as a demigod, who was powerful enough to change the laws of Nature. Thus after a belief in the oneness of God, it was also stressed that Muḥammad is neither God, nor a demigod, but an apostle, and the miracle performed at his hand is not the manifestation of his own power and authority, but it is the gift of the Lord, the Creator and Master of the universe.

65. Imām Nawawī is of the opinion that this ḥadīth is very important as regards the fundamentals of faith. It beautifully sums up the essentials of Īmān.

66. The word *'abd* has been used both for Muḥammad and Christ to show that none of them is a deity; both are the bondsmen of Allah. Then the ḥadīth also stresses the point that Christ is not the begotten son of God in the sense in which the Christians generally hold him, but he is the son of the mortal woman Mary. The epithet ابن مريم calls attention to, and emphasises the fact of his humanness. It is one of the miracles of the Qur'ān and of the Holy Prophet that in speaking of Jesus it refutes both the Jewish and the Christian misconceptions simultaneously and constantly uses a language that implies answers both to the Christian deification and to the Jewish denunciation of Jesus and his mother.

His word[67] which He communicated to Mary and is His spirit,[68] that Paradise is a fact and Hell is a fact," Allah would make him (he who affirms these truths) enter Paradise through one of its eight doors which he would like.

(44) It is narrated on the authority of 'Umair b. Hānī with the same chain of transmitters with the exception of these words: Allah would make him (he who affirms these truths) enter Paradise through one of the eight doors which he would like.

(45) It is narrated on the authority of Ṣunābiḥī[69] that he went to 'Ubāda b. Ṣāmit[70] when he was about to die. I burst into tears. Upon this he said to me: Allow me some time (so that I may talk with you). Why do you weep? By Allah, if I am asked to bear witness, I would certainly testify for you (that you are a believer). Should I be asked to intercede, I would certainly intercede for you, and if I have the power, I would certainly do good to you, and then observed: By Allah, never did I hear anything from the Messenger of Allah (may peace be upon him) which could have been a source of benefit to you and then not conveyed it to you except this single ḥadīth. That I intend to narrate to you today, since I am going to breathe my last. I heard the Messenger of Allah (may peace be upon him) say: He who testifies that there is no god but Allah and that Muḥammad is the messenger of Allah, Allah would prohibit the fire of Hell for him.

(46) It is narrated on the authority of Mu'ādh b. Jabal: I was riding behind the Prophet (may peace be upon him) and there was nothing between him and me but the rear part of the saddle, when he said: Mu'ādh b. Jabal! To which I replied: At your beck and call, and at your pleasure, Messenger of Allah! He moved along for a few

67. Jesus has been called a "word" which Allah communicated to Mary, signifying the fact that he was brought into existence by the Command of Allah, without the ordinary instrumentality of a father (Baiḍāwī). If the whole universe could be emerged into being by a single word of Allah and Adam could be created without the instrumentality of both father and mother, it is quite conceivable that a command of Allah can easily bring into being a man without the instrumentality of father.

68. The word "spirit" used for Jesus does not carry him a step beyond the limits of mortality, for Adam also it has been said: "I breathed My spirit into him" (Qur'ān, xv. 29). In fact, according to the Holy Qur'ān, the spirit of God is breathed into every man: "Then He made him complete and breathed into him of His spirit and gave you hearing and sight and hearts (xxxii. 9). The epithet, *rūḥ-um-minhū*, "a spirit from Him," does not imply that the soul of Allah has incarnated in Jesus; it only signifies the eminence of Christ as it has been explained by the famous commentators of the Holy Qur'ān, Ibn 'Abbās, Ibn Jarīr, Ibn Kathīr.

69. Ṣunābiḥī: His name was Abū 'Abdullah 'Abdur-Raḥmān b. Usaila and belonged to the family of Ṣunābaḥ, a famous branch of the well-known tribe Murād. According to Imām Nawawī, he was one amongst the eminent tābi'īn. He was proceeding to Medina in order to see the Holy Prophet. But unfortunately the Messenger of Allah left for his heavenly abode a week before his arrival there. He met the devoted Companions of the Holy Prophet. He died during the rule of 'Abdul-Malik.

70. His name was 'Ubāda b. Ṣāmit b. Qais and belonged to the tribe of Khazraj. His mother's name was Qurat-ul-'Ain and she was the daughter of 'Ubāda b. Nadla. He was one among the earlier Anṣār converts and had the privilege of owing allegiance at the famous "bai'at al-Riḍwān". The Holy Prophet trusted him and he was made the Collector of Zakāt. He was appointed as a Qāḍī of Palestine by the second caliph 'Umar.

'Ubāda b. Ṣāmit is counted amongst the famous Companions of the Holy Prophet. He was a Qārī and was one of those fortunate souls who committed the whole of the Qur'ān to memory. He was an enthusiastic preacher and disseminated the teachings of the Qur'ān and the Sunnah. He also devoted much of his time to impart instructions to the famous school of the Prophet "Aṣḥāb-i-Ṣuffa". He died in 34 H. in Syria.

minutes, when again he said: Mu'ādh b. Jabal! To which I replied: At your beck and call, and at your pleasure, Messenger of Allah! He then again moved along for a few minutes and said: Mu'ādh b. Jabal! To which I replied: At your beck and call, and at your pleasure, Messenger of Allah! He (the Holy Prophet) said: Do you know what right has Allah upon His servants? I said: Allah and His Messenger know best. He (the Holy Prophet) said: Verily the right of Allah over His servants is that they should worship[71] Him, not associating anything with Him. He (the Holy Prophet), with Mu'ādh behind him, moved along for a few minutes and said: Mu'ādh b. Jabal! To which I replied: At your beck and call, and at your pleasure, Messenger of Allah! He (the Holy Prophet) said: Do you know what rights have servants upon Allah in case they do it (i.e. they worship Allah without associating anything with Him)? I (Mu'ādh bin Jabal) replied: Allah and His Messenger know best. (Upon this) he (the Holy Prophet) remarked: That He would not torment them (with the fire of Hell).

(47) It is narrated on the authority of Mu'ādh b. Jabal that he observed: I was riding behind the Messenger of Allah (may peace be upon him) on an ass known as 'Ufair. He (Mu'ādh) observed: He (the Holy Prophet) said: Mu'ādh, do you know what right has Allah over His bondsmen and what right have His bondsmen over Him? Mu'ādh added: I replied: Allah and His Messenger know best. Upon this he (the Holy Prophet) remarked: The right of Allah over His bondsmen is that they should worship Allah and should not associate anything with Him, and the right of His bondsmen over Allah, Glorious and Sublime, is that He does not punish him who associates not anything with Him. He (Mu'ādh) added: I said to the Messenger of Allah: Should I then give the tidings to the people? He (the Holy Prophet) said: Do not tell them this good news, for they would trust[72] in it alone.

(48) It is narrated on the authority of Mu'ādh b. Jabal that the Messenger of Allah (may peace be upon him) said: Mu'ādh, do you know the right of Allah over His bondsmen? He (Mu'ādh) said: Allah and His Apostle know best. He (the Messenger of Allah) said: That Allah alone should be worshipped and nothing should be associated with Him. He (the Holy Prophet) said: What right have they (bondsmen) upon Him in case they do it. He (Mu'ādh) said: Allah and His Apostle know best. He (the Holy Prophet) said: That He would not punish them.

(49) It is narrated on the authority of Aswad b. Hilāl that he heard Mu'ādh say this: The Messenger of Allah (may peace be upon him) called me and I replied him. He (the Holy Prophet) said: Do you know the right of Allah upon the people, and then followed the ḥadīth (mentioned above.)

(50) It is reported on the authority of Abū Huraira: We were sitting around the

71. *'Abada*, which we have translated as "worship," conveys, in Islam, a much deeper meaning and covers a far wider field as compared with the English word "worship". It means complete submission to God in all aspects of life, whether devotional or worldly. It includes fundamentals of faith, religious practices, e.g. prayer, Zakāt, pilgrimage, fasts and all those laws which Allah has given to regulate the individual and collective life of the Muslims. There is no concept of no-man's land in Islam. Everything falls within the orbit of religion.

72. The Holy Prophet forbade him to give wide currency to the tidings for he felt that the people might not at that stage, when they had not fully imbibed the teachings of Islam, take the word "worship" in the narrow sense and conclude wrongly that a mere lip service to the Lord would entitle them to Paradise and may show negligence in all those commands which Allah has given to humanity,

Messenger of Allah (may peace and blessings be upon him). Abū Bakr and 'Umar were also there among the audience. In the meanwhile the Messenger of Allah got up and left us. He delayed in coming back to us, which caused consternation that he might be attacked by some enemy when we were not with him; so being alarmed we got up. I was the first to be alarmed. I, therefore, went out to look for the Messenger of Allah (may peace and blessings be upon him) and came to a garden belonging to the Banū an-Najjār, a section of the Anṣār. I went round it looking for a gate but failed to find one. Seeing a *rabī'* (i.e. streamlet) flowing into the garden from a well outside, I drew myself together, like a fox, and slinked into (the place) where God's Messenger was. He (the Holy Prophet) said: Is it Abū Huraira? I (Abū Huraira) replied: Yes, Messenger of Allah. He (the Holy Prophet) said: What is the matter with you? I replied: You were amongst us but got up and went away and delayed for a time, so fearing that you might be attacked by some enemy when we were not with you, we became alarmed. I was the first to be alarmed. So when I came to this garden, I drew myself together as a fox does, and these people are following me. He addressed me as Abū Huraira and gave me his sandals and said: Take away these sandals of mine, and when you meet anyone outside this garden who testifies that there is no god but Allah, being assured of it in his heart, gladden him by announcing that he shall go to Paradise. Now the first one I met was 'Umar. He asked: What are these sandals, Abū Huraira? I replied: These are the sandals of the Messenger of Allah with which he has sent me to gladden anyone I meet who testifies that there is no god but Allah, being assured of it in his heart, with the announcement that he would go to Paradise. Thereupon 'Umar struck me on the breast and I fell on my back. He then said: Go back, Abū Huraira. So I returned to the Messenger of Allah (may peace be upon him), and I was about to break into tears. 'Umar followed me closely and there he was behind me. The Messenger of Allah (may peace and blessings be on him) said: What is the matter with you, Abū Huraira? I said: I happened to meet 'Umar and conveyed him the message with which you sent me. He struck me on my breast which made me fall down upon my back and ordered me to go back. Upon this the Messenger of Allah (may peace be upon him) said: What prompted you to do this, 'Umar? He said: Messenger of Allah, my mother and father be sacrificed to thee, did you send Abū Huraira with your sandals to gladden anyone he met and who testified that there is no god but Allah, and being assured of it in his heart, with the tidings that he would go to Paradise? He said: Yes. 'Umar said: Please do it not, for I am afraid that people will trust in it alone; let them go on doing (good) deeds. The Messenger of Allah (may peace be upon him) said: Well, let them.[73]

73. This ḥadīth has been put to adverse criticism by so many hostile critics of Ḥadīth. They assert 'Umar had no right to interfere with the commands of the Prophet. But a little bit of thinking would make it clear that 'Umar was not doubting the fact told to Abū Huraira by the Holy Prophet. His only objection was that if it were given an unrestricted circulation, it might cool down the zeal of the people in carrying out the commands of Allah and His Prophet. There were not a few people who were new converts to Islam. They had not yet fully imbibed the true spirit of the faith and the great revolution which it aimed at bringing about in the individual and social life of the human beings. It required hard work and unceasing labour. Mere lip service to Allah was not enough. What 'Umar apprehended was that if this message was conveyed to all the Muslims, the raw minds who had not yet fully attuned themselves to Islam might rely on this and regard it as a

(51) It is reported on the authority of Anas b. Mālik that the Prophet of Allah (may peace and blessings be upon him) addressed Mu'ādh b. Jabal as he was riding behind him to which he replied : At thy beck and call, and at thy pleasure, Messenger of Allah. He again called out : Mu'ādh. To which he (again) replied : At thy beck and call, and at thy pleasure. He (the Holy Prophet) addressed him (again) : Mu'ādh, to which he replied : At thy beck and call, and at thy pleasure, Messenger of Allah. Upon this he (the Holy Prophet) observed : If anyone testifies (sincerely from his heart) that there is no god but Allah, and that Muḥammad is His bondsman and His messenger, Allah immuned him from Hell. He (Mu'ādh) said : Messenger of Allah, should I not then inform people of it, so that they may be of good cheer ? He replied : Then they would trust in it alone. Mu'ādh told about it at the time of his death, to avoid sinning.[74]

(52) It is narrated on the authority of 'Itbān b. Mālik[75] that he came to Medina and said : Something had gone wrong with my eyesight. I, therefore, sent (a message to the Holy Prophet) : Verily it is my ardent desire that you should kindly grace my house with your presence and observe prayer there so that I should make that corner a place of worship. He said : The Prophet (may peace be upon him) came there,

sure passport to Paradise. Affirmation in the oneness of God, without associating anything with Him, is certainly the golden rule to enter heavens, but it entails heavy responsibilities which the new converts could not fully appreciate and understand at that stage. This is why 'Umar objected to it. Moreover, what he did was perfectly in accordance with the wishes of the Holy Prophet as we find in Ḥadīth 47, that when Mu'ādh asked his permission to convey the tidings to the people, he did not agree on the ground that the people might begin relying on it alone.

74. This ḥadīth is very important in the sense that it throws a good deal of light on the superb method which the Holy Prophet employed in the propagation of Islam. He did not address people at random but as a keen observer of human psychology instructed them, keeping fully in view their mental level, their power of comprehension and understanding the implication of Islamic teachings, their possible response and reaction to them and finally their grounding in the faith. Now if this ḥadīth were related to a raw Muslim who had not received the training in the doctrines and practice of Islam, it could lead to indolence. But at the same time it was a narration which was also obligatory since it was not the word of only a wise man, but that of the Prophet who said or did nothing of his own accord, but uttered what he was asked to do by his Lord. "He does not speak out of his own desire" (liii. 3).

This ḥadīth also clarifies the point which is often raised in connection with the last ḥadīth in which Ḥaḍrat 'Umar forbade Abū Huraira to convey the tidings to the people. Its transmission was allowed by the Prophet but Ḥaḍrat 'Umar apprehended that if at that stage when the new converts were not fully conversant with the teachings of Islam, the tidings gained wide currency, they might become indolent. That is why when he put forward this plea before the Holy Prophet, he readily accepted that. This ḥadīth endorses the fact that the Messenger of Allah did not like its unrestricted transmission to every quarter at that stage when the new converts to Islam had not imbibed its real spirit ; he also wanted it to be definitely conveyed since it was divine inspiration and its dissemination was essential. Mu'ādh, therefore, informed people about it at the proper stage. For detailed discussion see *Fatḥ-ul-Mulhim*, Vol. I, p. 206.

75. 'Itbān b. Mālik belonged to the tribe of Sālim. He lived in Qubā' and was the chief of his tribe. He had embraced Islam before Migration. When the Holy Prophet created brotherhood between the Muhājirīn and the Anṣār, he was made the brother of 'Umar. He participated in the battle of Badr but then lost his eyesight and could not, therefore, join other battles. He led the prayers in the mosque of Banī Sālim to the end of his life. He died in 52 H. at Medina. He was an extremely pious and devoted Companion of the Holy Prophet.

and those amongst the Companions whom Allah willed also accompanied him. He entered (my place) and offered prayer at my residence and his Companions began to talk amongst themselves (and this conversation centred round hypocrites), and then the conspicuous one, Mālik b. Dukhshum[76] was made the target and they wished that he (the Holy Prophet) should curse him and he should die or he should meet some calamity. In the meanwhile the Messenger of Allah (may peace and blessings be upon him) completed his prayer and said : Does Mālik b. Dukhshum not testify the fact that there is no god but Allah and verily I am the messenger of Allah. They replied : He makes a profession of it (no doubt) but does not do it out of (sincere) heart. He (the Holy Prophet) said : He who testifies that there is no god but Allah and I am the messenger of Allah would not enter Hell or its (flames) would not consume him.[77] Anas said : This ḥadīth impressed me very much and I told my son to write it down.[78]

(53) It is narrated on the authority of Anas that 'Itbān b. Mālik told him that he became blind. He sent a message to the Messenger of Allah (may peace be upon him) that he should come and mark a place of worship for him. Thereupon came the Messenger of Allah (may peace be upon him) and his people and then there was a discussion[79] among them about a man who was known as Mālik b. Dukhshum, and subsequently the narrator described the ḥadīth of Sulaimān b. Mughīra as stated above.

Chapter XII

HE RELISHED THE FLAVOUR OF ĪMĀN WHO WAS PLEASED WITH ALLAH AS HIS LORD

(54) It is narrated on the authority of 'Abbās b. 'Abdul-Muṭṭalib[80] that he heard the Messenger of Allah saying : He relished the flavour of faith (Īmān) who became

76. Mālik b. Dukhshum who was labelled as a hypocrite by some of the enthusiastic Companions of the Holy Prophet had nothing positive against him except one thing that he had social relations with the hypocrites. He was in fact like Ḥāṭib b. Abī Balta'a under the stress of circumstances obliged to do so and was not doing it out of his free will. He participated in Badr and all the major battles with courage and devotion. His whole career was a proof of his sincerity to Islam.

77. This ḥadīth has an object lesson for the Muslims for their social solidarity. They have been dissuaded to bring a charge against any one of their brothers-in-faith unless there is a substantial proof to support it. It should be based on hard facts and not on mere whims.

78. This ḥadīth refutes the claim of those who assert that the aḥādīth were recorded three hundred years after the death of the Holy Prophet. Ḥadrat Anas was the eminent Companion and he ordered his son to put this ḥadīth in black and white.

79. In this text the Arabic word is نعت but in another text it is فتغيب which means "he was absent".

80. His *kunya* was Abu'l-Faḍl and was the half brother of the Prophet's father 'Abdullah, his mother being Nutayla bint Jannāb of al-Namīr. 'Abbās had been a silent admirer of Islam since its beginning and supported his nephew in this noble cause, but made an announcement of his conversion on the eve of the conquest of Mecca. He was held in high esteem by the Holy Prophet and his Companions and they sought his advice on all important matters. 'Abbās was very generous and always looked after the needs of his poor relations. He had an immense God-consciousness, and whenever he raised his hands in supplication, tears rolled out of his eyes. He died in 32 H. at the age of eighty-eight, during the caliphate of Ḥadrat 'Uthmān who led his funeral prayer and was lowered into the grave by his eminent son 'Abdullah.

pleased[81] with Allah as Lord, with al-Islam as the code of life[82] and with Muḥammad as the Messenger[83] (of Allah).

Chapter XIII

CONCERNING THE BRANCHES OF ĪMĀN

(55) It is narrated on the authority of Abū Huraira that the Prophet (may peace be upon him) said: Īmān has over seventy[84] branches, and modesty[85] is a branch of Īmān.

(56) It is narrated on the authority of Abū Huraira that the Messenger of Allah (may peace and blessings be upon him) said : Faith has over seventy branches or over sixty branches, the most excellent of which is the declaration that there is no god but Allah, and the humblest of which is the removal of what is injurious from the path : and modesty is the branch of faith.

(57) Sālim reported on the authority of his father that the Prophet (may peace

81. Sincere attachment to Allah, Islam and the Holy Prophet is the sum and substance of faith. Īmān is not something which can be thrusted from without. It is an attitude of mind which is formed by willing adherence to Allah, His Apostle and the code of life which He has given to the human race. It signifies that the spring of Īmān is love and not coercion. To be pleased with Allah as Lord means that the entire soul with all its powers and inclinations is gathered up into God and man looks upon His pleasure as the sole achievement of his life.

82. To be pleased with al-Islam as the code of life implies that whatever Islam has laid down for a believer by way of spiritual guidance or practical legislation should be looked upon as the timeless expression of God's will and should be willingly and cheerfully put into practice.

83. To be pleased with Muḥammad (may peace be upon him) as the Messenger of Allah is indicative of the fact that it is through Muḥammad that God's will has been made known to us. He is the bearer of revelation and is, therefore, best fitted and divinely authorised to tell the human race how Allah is to be loved and obeyed and how His pleasure can be rightly sought for and how His laws can be applied in practical life. Thus without showing obedience to Muhammad and following him sincerely and earnestly we cannot obey our Lord.

84. Here the figure seventy or sixty does not imply an exact number, but only their multiplicity. What it means is that Īmān is not an inert or lifeless thing but it is dynamic in the sense that it revolutionises the whole life and thought of man and brings into being numerous healthy changes.

Of all these changes the most important is that man does not worship any god but Allah and frees himself from the bondage of all other deities. And in the sphere of action the notable change is that he always works for the good of humanity, the most common expression of which is that he clears the roads of all those things which are injurious to the passers by.

85. It is very significant that modesty has been particularly stressed as a part of the faith. It is because modesty reflects a state of mental piety. Wāḥidī is of the opinion that both the words *ḥayā'* and *istiḥyā'* have been derived from *ḥayā'* which means life or life-blood. Thus *ḥayā'* is something which sustains a man spiritually and morally. Abū 'Alī Miskawaih is of the opinion that *ḥayā'* implies restraint from doing anything abominable. There is a ḥadīth in *Tirmidhī* which succinctly explains the significance of this quality. Once the Holy Prophet said to his Companions : Fight shy of Allah, it is His right. They replied : Praise be to Allah : we do fight shy. Upon this the Holy Prophet observed : That is not what *ḥayā'* really implies. To fight shy of Allah in fact means that you should fully guard your mind and all thought crowded in it and stomach and all that is contained in it against evil. And remember death and what would come after it in the grave. He who does it fights shy of Allah.

and blessi gs be upon him) heard a man instructing his brother about modesty. Upon this the Prophet remarked: Modesty is an ingredient of Īmān (faith).

(58) Zuhrī has narrated this ḥadīth with the addition of these words: He (the Holy Prophet) happened to pass by a man of Anṣār who was instructing his brother (about modesty).

(59) It is narrated on the authority of 'Imrān b. Ḥuṣain that the Prophet (may peace and blessings be upon him) said: Modesty brings forth nothing but goodness. Bushair b. Ka'b said: It is recorded in the books of wisdom, there lies sobriety in it and calmness of mind in it.[86] 'Imrān said: I am narrating to you the tradition[87] of the Messenger of Allah (may peace and blessings be upon him) and you ṭalk of your books.

(60) It is narrated on the authority of the Qatāda: We were sitting with 'Imrān b. Ḥuṣain in a company and Bushair ibn Ka'b was also amongst us. 'Imrān narrated to us that on a certain occasion the Messenger of Allah (may peace and blessings be upon him) said: Modesty is a goodness through and through, or said: Modesty is a goodness complete. Upon this Bushair ibn Ka'b said: Verily we find in certain books or books of (wisdom) that it is God-inspired peace of mind or sobriety for the sake of Allah and there is also a weakness in it.[88] 'Imrān was so much enraged that his eyes became red and he said: I am narrating to you the ḥadīth of the Messenger of Allah (may peace be upon him) and you are contradicting it. He (the narrator) said: 'Imrān reported the ḥadīth. He (the narrator) said: Bushair repeated (the same thing). 'Imrān was enraged. He (the narrator) said: We asserted: Verily Bushair is one amongst us, Abū Nujaid! There is nothing wrong with him (Bushair).

(61) Isḥāq b. Ibrāhīm narrates this ḥadīth of the Holy Prophet on the authority of 'Imrān b. Ḥuṣain, like the one narrated by Ḥammād b. Zaid.

Chapter XIV

CONCERNING THE COMPREHENSIVE ATTRIBUTES OF ISLAM

(62) It is narrated on the authority of Sufyān b. 'Abdullah al-Thaqafī that he said:

86. Sobriety and tranquillity of mind are closely related with each other. The man who is God-conscious and shuns evil would never be whimsical. Moreover, his would be a calm mind as it would not be disturbed by evil thoughts.

87. This ḥadīth explains the status of a prophet. The source of prophetic knowledge is divine; it is, therefore, perfect and free from all kinds of error. Human wisdom is based on observation, experience and inference and can, therefore, be never infallible. This is the reason why humanity has always been exhorted to follow the commands of the prophets and not those of philosophers. This ḥadīth also clearly brings into light the position of the Ḥadīth. It is a part of divine knowledge and, therefore, it should be accepted with the spirit of religicus devotion.

88. It should be remembered that this is not part of the ḥadīth, but it is the assertion of Bushair which he has made on the authority of some book. Here the weakness of modesty is explained—that it sometimes becomes a weakness when a man conceals the truth and fails to give a dispassionate verdict on the deeds and thoughts of man or a group. A man, either out of fear or misplaced courtesy, keeps silent and does not boldly condemn a wrong view or a wrong act. Such weakness is often shown when an act is done either by the ruler or by a friend or by one with whom we have certain interests to serve. This type of modesty is not encouraged by Islam.

I asked the Messenger of Allah to tell me about Islam a thing which may dispense with the necessity of my asking anybody after you. In the ḥadīth of Abū Usāma the (words) are: other than you. He (the Holy Prophet) remarked: Say I affirm my faith in Allah and then remain steadfast to it.[89]

Chapter XV

CONCERNING THE EMINENCE OF ISLAM AND OF THE AFFAIRS WHICH ARE EXCELLENT[90]

(63) It is narrated on the authority of 'Abdullah b. 'Amr[91] that a man asked the Messenger of Allah (may peace and blessings be upon him) which of the merits (is superior) in Islam. He (the Holy Prophet) remarked: That you provide food and pay salutations to one whom you know or do not know.

(64) 'Abdullah b. 'Amr b. al-'Āṣ is reported to have said: Verily a person asked the Messenger of Allah (may peace and blessings be upon him) who amongst the Muslims was better. Upon this (the Holy Prophet) remarked: From whose hand and tongue the Muslims[92] are safe.

89. This ḥadīth succinctly sums up the spirit of Islam and explains the verse of the Holy Qur'ān: "Verily those who say: Our Lord is Allah, and have thereafter stood fast by it" (xli. 30). To keep steadfastness in Tauḥīd is not an ordinary thing. It means that the concept of oneness of God has taken its root firmly in the minds of men and now no interest, however alluring, no pressure, however heavy, can deviate man from the right path. It is a test of man's faith in the Lord and is a clear proof of the fact that it is not under the influence of a whim or wayward emotion that man accepts Tauḥīd as the guiding principle of his life, but he has affirmed it after a careful deliberation and fully realising the heavy responsibilities that this affirmation entails.

90. In the previous aḥādīth the articles of faith have been clearly pointed out. In this chapter we have been told what changes does faith bring about in the behaviour of a man and in his daily routine of life. Two things are essential for cementing the social ties amongst men. One is that a man should be generous enough to serve food to the guests and the hungry and, secondly, he should be courteous to pay salutations to his fellowmen. As-Salāmu-'Alaikum (peace be upon you) is the epithet used for conveying salutations in the Muslim society. It means that a believer is a well-wisher and conveys the greetings of peace to everyone whom he meets. Peace is the most cherished goal of the Muslim society and the salutation as prescribed by Islam embodies it as a slogan and watchword.

91. 'Abdullah b. 'Amr b. al-'Āṣ: He accepted Islam before his illustrious father. He belonged to the tribe of Sālim, a branch of the Quraish. He was an extremely pious and God-fearing Companion of the Holy Prophet and was very much devoted to him. He recorded the traditions of the Messenger of Allah (may peace and blessings be upon him). There is a good deal of difference of opinion with regard to the date of his death: 63 or 73 H. at Mecca.

92. We have seen that the Holy Prophet in the foregoing aḥādīth stressed the importance of the generosity of mind, courtesy and the spirit of sacrifice, on the part of the Muslims. Now in this and subsequent aḥādīth he emphasises the fact that a Muslim can never be a tyrant. He is sympathetic and a protector of the life, honour and dignity of his fellowmen. This virtue is of utmost importance because no good society can be founded on tyranny and oppression. For a peaceful life it is essential that every human being should exercise full control over his evil passions and should refrain from doing anything which may be harmful to others. There are numerous forms of atrocities which are perpetrated on humanity. In these forms both hand and tongue have an important role to play. An individual by his superior physical strength can make weaker human beings the victims of his high-

(65) It is narrated on the authority of Jābir that he heard the (Holy Prophet) saying: A Muslim is he from whose hand and tongue the Muslims are safe.

(66) It is narrated on the authority of Abū Mūsā Ash'arī: I asked the Messenger of Allah which (attribute) of Islam is more excellent. Upon this he remarked: One in which the Muslims are safe, protected from the tongue and hand of (other Muslims). Ibrāhīm b. Sa'īd al-Jauharī has narrated this ḥadīth with the same words in addition to these. The Messenger of Allah (may peace and blessings be upon him) was asked as to who amongst the Muslims is better, and the rest of the ḥadīth was narrated like this.

Chapter XVI

CONCERNING THE ATTRIBUTES BY WHICH ONE GETS THE RELISH OF ĪMĀN

(67) It is reported on the authority of Anas that the Prophet of Allah (may peace and blessings be upon him) said: There are three qualities for which anyone who is characterised by them will relish the sweetness of faith: he to whom Allah and His Messenger are dearer than all else; he who loves a man for Allah's sake alone; and he who has as great an abhorrence of returning to unbelief after Allah has rescued him from it as he has of being cast into Hell.

(68) It is reported on the authority of Anas that the Messenger of Allah (may peace be upon him) said: There are three qualities for which anyone who is characterised by them will relish the savour of faith: that he loves man and he does not love him but for Allah's sake alone; he is to whom Allah and His Messenger are dearer than all else; he who prefers to be thrown into fire than to return to unbelief after Allah has rescued him out of it.[93]

(69) A similar ḥadīth has been reported on the authority of Anas (with another chain of transmitters) with the exception of these words: that he again becomes a Jew or a Christian.

handedness. He can also sling mud on others and malign and slander them. It should, however, be remembered that the ḥadīth covers a very wide field. Every act of high-handedness is condemned whether it is in the form of tyrannical rule or unjust social order or exploitation of the weak by the strong, or danger to the safety of the life, honour and property of the people. Similarly, every unjust word or verdict or decision which harms the human race or injurs the feelings of innocent human beings is an act of tyranny on the part of the tongue.

We find in a ḥadīth of Tirmidhī which is narrated on the authority of Ibn Ḥibbān, these words too: from whose hand and tongue, the people are safe, which means that not only Muslims but every human being should be respected and honoured.

93. This ḥadīth is in fact the explanation of what we have learnt before that. He who is well pleased with Allah as the Lord, with Islam as the religion and with Muḥammad as the messenger will relish the savour of faith. Īmān is a mental state of mind in which the love for God and that for His Prophet predominate every other attachment. The second part that he loves man for the sake of Allah is the natural outcome of the first principle. A believer's liking or disliking is not his own. He loves people for the sake of Allah and has no selfish motive or material consideration in it. Lastly, his love for Islam is immense and unbelief for him is as painful for his soul as the fire of Hell.

Chapter XVII

IT IS OBLIGATORY TO LOVE THE PROPHET MORE THAN THE MEMBERS OF ONE'S HOUSEHOLD: ONE'S CHILD, FATHER OR EVEN THE WHOLE OF HUMANITY

(70) It is reported on the authority of Anas that the Messenger of Allah (may peace be upon him) said: No bondsman believes, and, in the ḥadīth narrated by 'Abdul-Wārith, no person believes, till I am dearer to him, than the members of his household, his wealth and the whole of mankind.

(71) It is reported on the authority of Anas b. Mālik that the Messenger of Allah said: None of you is a believer till I am dearer to him than his child, his father and the whole of humanity.[94]

Chapter XVIII

CONCERNING THE FACT THAT IT IS ONE OF THE CHARACTERISTICS OF ĪMĀN THAT ONE SHOULD LIKE THE SAME THING FOR ONE'S BROTHER-IN-ISLAM AS ONE LIKES FOR ONE'S SELF

(72) It is narrated on the authority of Anas b. Mālik that the Prophet (may peace and blessings be upon him) observed: None amongst you believes (truly) till one likes for his brother or for his neighbour that which he loves for himself.

(73) It is narrated on the authority of Anas that the Prophet (may peace and blessings be upon him) observed: By Him in whose Hand is my life, no bondsman (truly) believes till he likes for his neighbour, or he (the Holy Prophet) said: for his brother, whatever he likes for himself.[95]

94. It is often asked why love for the Holy Prophet has been made as the test of a man's faith. The answer is quite simple. It is in his **august** personality that we can know the will of the Lord, His love for humanity and His view how man should live in this world. In him all those values which our Lord wanted us to uphold took flesh and blood without compromise and without alloy. He has been, therefore, made for us the focus of loyalty because it is through him that we have learnt the true concept of God, the real implication of Tauḥīd, the role of man, his accountability in the Hereafter—in fact the whole of the *dīn*. It is Muḥammad (may peace be upon him) who has shown us the way to love our Lord. He is the central figure in Islam: that is the reason why the Qur'ān says:

> Say: If you love Allah, follow me: Allah will love you, and will forgive your sins; and Allah is Forgiving, Merciful (iii. 30).

95. These three aḥādīth refer to two more qualities which are the natural outcome of Īmān. A true believer has a strong sense of fellow-feeling and inculcates love for his brother-in-Islam.

Then it has also been stressed that it is the bounden duty of every Muslim to refrain from saying anything or doing anything which may be a source of trouble to his neighbour. These aḥādīth along with such others give us an idea that Islam's approach to life is not non-social. Islam no doubt makes man stand in the presence of the Lord as an individual, but he is never isolated from other men. The distress which vexes him is not his own only, it is that of his brethren as well; the redemption for which he longs for is also the redemption of his people, his fellow believers, nay, the entire humanity. It is the duty of a Muslim not only to lead a peaceful life himself but also to create a social atmosphere where every man feels secure from the tyranny of the oppressors. It should also be

Chapter XIX

CONCERNING THE PROHIBITION TO HARM NEIGHBOUR

(74) It is narrated on the authority of Abū Huraira that the Messenger of Allah (may peace and blessings be upon him) observed: He will not enter Paradise whose neighbour is not secure from his wrongful (or injurious) conduct.[96]

Chapter XX

CONCERNING EXHORTATION TO ACCORD HONOUR AND RESPECT TO THE NEIGHBOUR AND THE GUEST AND OBLIGATION TO OBSERVE SILENCE EXCEPT IN GOODNESS, AND ALL THESE QUALITIES COME WITHIN THE ORBIT OF ĪMĀN

(75) It is reported on the authority of Abū Huraira that the Messenger of Allah (may peace be upon him) observed: He who believes in Allah and the Last Day should either utter good words or better keep silent[97]; and he who believes in Allah and the Last Day should treat his neighbour with kindness and he who believes in Allah and the Last Day should show hospitality to his guest.

(76) It is reported on the authority of Abū Huraira that the Messenger of Allah (may peace and blessings be upon him) observed: He who believes in Allah and the Last Day does not harm his neighbour, and he who believes in Allah and the Last Day shows hospitality to his guest and he who believes in Allah and the Last Day speaks good or remains quiet.

(77) Another ḥadīth similar to one narrated (above) by Abū Ḥaṣīn is also reported by Abū Huraira with the exception of these words: He (the Prophet) said: He should do good to the neighbour.

(78) It is narrated on the authority of Abū Shuraiḥ al-Khuzā'ī that the Prophet (may peace and blessings of Allah be upon him) observed: He who believes in Allah and the Last Day should do good to his neighbour and he who believes in Allah and the Last Day should show hospitality to the guest and he who believes in Allah and the Last Day should either speak good or better remain quiet.

remembered that the words لا يومن used in these aḥādīth do not mean the very negation of Īmān, but these imply the negation of the perfection and sublimity of Īmān. To put it differently it does not signify that such man is deprived of Īmān altogether, but it points out the fact that he has not become a believer in the true sense of the term.

96. The actual word used in the ḥadīth is بوائق (bawā'iq) which is the plural of بائقة (bā'iqa). It means misfortune or calamity. Lane in his *Lexicon* has given the following meanings:

> A calamity, misfortune, or disaster, a vehement evil or mischief, a trial that befalls a people, wrongful or injurious conduct, malevolent or mischievous dispositions.

97. The gift of speech is undoubtedly a great blessing of the Lord, which if properly used can do a lot of good, But the irresponsible use of tongue proves very harmful. That is why the Holy Prophet has exhorted the Muslims to keep a careful watch over this talent. They must use it only for the propagation of good, and refrain from indulging into idle or vulgar talk. The Holy Qur'ān observes: "He utters not a word, but there is by him a watcher at hand" (l. 18).

The famous saint Dhunnūn al-Miṣrī once remarked: The best guardian of one's self is the man who exercises maximum control on his tongue.

Chapter XXI

CONCERNING THE FACTS THAT INTERDICTION AGAINST ABOMINABLE IS A PART OF FAITH, THAT FAITH INCREASES AND DIMINISHES; ENJOINING THAT WHICH IS GOOD AND FORBIDDING THAT WHICH IS ABOMINABLE ARE OBLIGATORY (ACTS)

(79) It is narrated on the authority of Ṭāriq b. Shihāb[98]: It was Marwān who initiated (the practice) of delivering khuṭbah (address) before the prayer on the 'Īd day. A man stood up and said: Prayer should precede khuṭbah. He (Marwān) remarked: This (practice) has been done away with. Upon this Abū Sa'īd remarked: This man has performed (his duty) laid on him. I heard the Messenger of Allah saying: He who amongst you should see something abominable should modify it with the help of his hand; and if he has not strength enough to do it, then he should do it with his tongue, and if he has not strength enough to do it, (even) then he should (abhor it) from his heart, and that is the least of faith.[99]

(80) The same ḥadīth of the Holy Prophet (may peace and blessings be upon him) has been reported by Abū Sa'īd al-Khudrī in connection with the story of Marwān.

98. His *kunya* was 'Abū 'Abdullah. He belonged to Kūfah. He was fortunate enough to see the Holy Prophet but nothing has been transmitted directly from him. He took part in thirty-three battles during the caliphate of Ḥaḍrat Abū Bakr and 'Umar and died in 82 H.

99. This ḥadīth throws a good deal of light on how the society is to be kept safe and secure from evil and corruption. It has been made an obligatory act for every Muslim to see carefully that the moral health of the community does not deteriorate, and whenever there is any sign of decadence in any quarter it should be checked with determination. Islam does not allow its followers to lead the life of a silent spectator in the world; it has made them duty bound to eradicate evil, since once it is allowed to creep into the society, it corrodes it and the whole social structure crumbles down. It has, therefore, been enjoined upon the believers to take effective measures to fight against it. Those who have power enough to check it with force must do so, while others with the help of preaching and persuasion should try to sweep it out of effective existence, but if the circumstances become so adverse that even this becomes impossible then we should at least keep our hearts alive to the fact that it is an evil and should be strongly abhorred and wait for a suitable opportunity to drive it out completely.

It must be made clear in this connection that the commentators of the aḥādīth are of the view that forbidding with the help of hand implies the power of the State. That it is the duty of the State and society to check the evil in all its forms and shape and in case of necessity even the strictest measures may be adopted.

Imām Nawawī says there is a consensus of opinion that this act of bidding the people to do good and forbidding them to commit evil is obligatory on every believer.

Some people ask why the Holy Prophet has put forward three alternatives and those too in a descending order for fighting against the evil, whereas everyone can make use of his hand and tongue. The commentators have explained the reason of this. They observe that reckless use of force and tongue is not required. If by the use of hand the mischief can be nipped effectively, well and good. But if one feels that this force will give rise to greater mischief which it will not be possible for its user to control, then he should resort to the other measure, i.e. persuasion. Similarly, if its use creates the same type of critical situation, then the third alternative may be resorted to, i.e. abhorrance against evil.

(81) It is narrated on the authority of 'Abdullah b. Mas'ūd[100] that the Messenger of Allah (may peace and blessings be upon him) observed: Never a prophet had been sent before me by Allah towards his nation who had not among his people (his) disciples and companions who followed his ways and obeyed his command. Then there came after them their successors who said whatever they did not practise, and practised whatever they were not commanded to do. He who strove against them with his hand was a believer; he who strove against them with his tongue was a believer, and he who strove against them with his heart was a believer and beyond that there is no faith even to the extent of a mustard seed. Abū Rāfi' said: I narrated this ḥadīth to 'Abdullah b. 'Umar; he contradicted me. There happened to come 'Abdullah b. Mas'ūd who stayed at Qanāt, and 'Abdullah b. 'Umar wanted me to accompany him for visiting him (as 'Abdullah b. Mas'ūd was ailing), so I went along with him and as we sat (before him) I asked Ibn Mas'ūd about this ḥadīth. He narrated it in the same way as I narrated it to Ibn 'Umar.

(82) The same ḥadīth has been transmitted by another chain of narrators on the authority of 'Abdullah b. Mas'ūd who observed: Never was there one among the prophets who had had not disciples who followed his direction and followed his ways. The remaining part of the ḥadīth is like that as narrated by Ṣāliḥ, but the arrival of Ibn Mas'ūd and the meeting of Ibn 'Umar with him is not mentioned.

Chapter XXII

PRECEDENCE OF THE BELIEVERS OVER ONE ANOTHER AND THE SUPERIORITY OF THE PEOPLE OF YEMEN IN THIS RESPECT

(83) It is narrated on the authority of Ibn Mas'ūd that the Apostle of Allah (may peace and blessings be upon him) pointed towards Yemen[101] with his hand and said:

100. Ibn Mas'ūd: His name was 'Abdullah son of Mas'ūd, son of Ghafil, son of Ḥabīb, son of Shamkh, son of Fa'r, son of Makhzūm. His *kunya* was Abū 'Abdur-Raḥmān. As a young man he herded the cattle of 'Uqba b. Abī Mu'ait. 'Abdullah is regarded rightly as one of the first converts; he was fond of calling himself the sixth of six (Muslims); according to other traditions, he embraced Islam before the Prophet entered the house of Arqam or even before 'Umar. He is said to have been the first to recite the Holy Qur'ān openly in Mecca. He was put to severe torture by the Meccans, but he never wavered for a moment. He also migrated to Abyssinia.

'Abdullah was one of those ten fortunate souls to whom Paradise was promised by the Holy Prophet. He participated in the battles and fought bravely on all occasions. He was always trusted by the Messenger of Allah and then by his pious successors. 'Umar (may Allah be pleased with him) sent him to Kūfah as an administrator of public treasury and as a teacher of religion. He was highly respected by the people for his piety, God-consciousness and profound knowledge of the Qur'ān and the Sunnah. He is said to be the authority for 848 traditions. It was indeed a peculiar feature of his that while narrating the ḥadīth of the Holy Prophet, he trembled, the sweat often broke out on his forehead and he transmitted the words with extraordinary caution and exactness. His traditions are collected in *Musnad Aḥmad*. He died in 32 H. at the age of seventy. His funeral prayer was led by the third caliph Hadrat 'Uthmān and buried by the side of 'Uthmān b. Maz'ūn (may Allah be pleased with all of them).

101. The Holy Prophet praised the inhabitants of Yemen as they accepted Islam quite readily and showed no stubbornness in this respect.

Verily Īmān is towards this side, and harshness and callousness of the hearts is found amongst the rude owners of the camels[102] who drive them behind their tails (to the direction) where emerge the two horns of Satan,[103] they are the tribes of Rabī'a and Muḍar.

(84) It is narrated on the authority of Abū Huraira that the Messenger of Allah observed : There have come the people of Yemen ; they are tender of hearts, the belief is that of the Yemenites,[104] the understanding[105] (of the faith) is that of the Yemenites and sagacity[106] is that of the Yemenites.

(85) Abū Huraira reported the same ḥadīth which is transmitted to us by another chain of transmitters, e.g. Muḥammad b. al-Muthannā, Isḥāq b. Yūsuf Azraq, Ibn 'Aun, etc.

(86) Abū Huraira reported : The Messenger of Allah (may peace and blessings be upon him) observed : There came to you the people from Yemen ; they are tender of hearts and mild of feelings, the understanding is Yemenite, the sagacity is Yemenite.

(87) It is narrated on the authority of Abū Huraira that the Messenger of Allah (may peace and blessings be upon him) remarked : The summit of unbelief is towards the East[107] and the pride and conceitedness is found among the owners of horses and camels who are rude and uncivil, people of the tents,[108] and tranquillity[109] is found among those who rear goats and sheep.

102. فداد (faddād) which we have translated as the owner of the camel is a highly significant word which covers a very wide range of meanings. It means "a person having a strong or loud voice, rude, course and uncivil in speech, possessing camels in number from one hundred or two hundred to a thousand therewithal rude, coarse, or uncivil and proud" (Lane's *Arabic-English Lexicon*).

103. Various interpretations have been given with regard to the horns of Satan. According to one interpretation, it denotes the rise of the sun in the east as it was worshipped by many polytheist tribes living towards that direction (*Nawawi*).

104. It does not imply that the Muslims other than from Yemen were bereft of all these qualities. What the Holy Prophet has stressed was that the people belonging to Yemen embraced Islam without any reluctance. They produced eminent Muslims like Uwais al-Qaranī and Abū Muslim al-Khaulānī. Imām Nawawī has rightly pointed out that this laudation of the Yemenites refers to the Muslims of the Prophet's own time and not of all times.

105. The word *al-Fiqh* here does not mean Muslim jurisprudence, but it signifies correct understanding of Islam.

106. The word *Ḥikmah* which we have translated as sagacity or wisdom stands for knowledge by which is unfolded the mysteries of the Lord and His creation. It illuminates understanding and the self is properly trained.

107. It refers to the Magian unbelievers who lived in Persia and worshipped the fire. So haughty was their king Parvaiz that he tore into pieces the letter of the Holy Prophet. Some commentators are of the opinion that it refers to that part of Najd in which the fierce tribes of Rabī'a and Muḍar lived (*vide Fatḥ-ul-Mulḥim*, Vol. I, p. 229).

108. The original word is اهل الوبر (*ahl al-wabar*). *Wabar* means fur, or soft hair of the camel. They are in fact the people of the desert or rather the people of the tents, because they make their tents of the hair of the camels and goats.

109. According to Maulānā Shabbīr Aḥmad 'Uthmānī, it relates to the people of Yemen who reared goats and sheep and presented a striking contrast, both in temperament and devotion to Islam, to the hostile and haughty tribes of Rabī'a and Muḍar who owned horses and camels and were very proud of their riches. Ḥāfiẓ Ibn Qayyim in his book *Madārij-us-Sālikin* asserts that the occupation of a man goes a long way in shaping his behaviour and outlook. The goats and sheep are humble and meek and their rearing inculcates humility and politeness.

(88) It is narrated on the authority of Abū Huraira that the Messenger of Allah (may peace and blessings be upon him) observed : The belief is among the Yemenites, and the unbelief is towards the East, and tranquillity is among those who rear goats and sheep, and pride and simulation is among the uncivil and rude owners of horses and camels.

(89) It is reported on the authority of Abū Huraira : I heard the Messenger of Allah saying this : The pride and conceitedness is found among the uncivil owners of the camels and tranquillity is found among the owners of sheep and goats.

(90) The same ḥadīth has been narrated by Zuhrī with the same chain of authorities with the addition : The belief is among the Yemenites, the sagacity is that of the Yemenites.

(91) Abū Huraira said : I heard the Prophet (may peace and blessings be upon him) saying : There came the people of Yemen, they are tender of feelings and meek of hearts. The belief is that of the Yemenites, the sagacity is that of the Yemenites, the tranquillity is among the owners of goats and sheep, and pride and conceitedness is among the uncivil owners of the camels, the people of the tents in the direction of sunrise.

(92) It is reported on the authority of Abū Huraira that the Messenger of Allah (may peace and blessings be upon him) observed : There came to you the people of Yemen who are soft of hearts, tender in feelings ; the belief is that of the Yemenites, the sagacity is that of the Yemenites and the summit of unbelief is towards the East.

(93) Qutaiba b. Sa'īd and Zuhair b. Ḥarb say : Jarīr narrated this on the authority of A'mash[110] with the same chain of narrators (as mentioned above).

(94) Shu'ba narrated the ḥadīth as reported by Jarīr with the same chain of narrators with this addition : The pride and conceitedness is among the owners of the camels and tranquillity and sobriety is found amongst the owners of sheep.

(95) It is reported on the authority of Jābir b. 'Abdullah that the Messenger of Allah (may peace and blessings be upon him) observed : The callousness of heart and sternness is in the East and the belief is among the people of Ḥijāz.

110. A'mash : His name was Sulaimān and *kunya* Abū Muḥammad, but he was known by the title of A'mash. His father's name was Mihrān and he belonged to Persia. A'mash was a freed slave.

He was born on the 10th of Muḥarram in 61 H. He is counted as one of the great scholars of the Holy Qur'ān and the Sunnah. He was the follower of 'Abdullah b. Mas'ūd in recitation which was looked upon as a standard for others.

He was eminent in the knowledge of ḥadīth too. Ḥāfiẓ Dhahabī spoke highly of him and Ibn al-Madīnī counts him among one of those half a dozen scholars who preserved the ḥadīth literature. Thirteen hundred aḥadīth are believed to be transmitted on his authority. Some of the critics of Ḥadīth count this number as 4000. The traditions narrated by him are regarded authentic both in respect of letter and spirit. Ibn 'Ammār is of the view that A'mash is one of the most reliable of the traditionists. The bulk of aḥadīth narrated by him is based on authorities like 'Abdullah b. Mas'ūd, Anas b. Mālik.

A'mash was also a great jurist and people looked to him for help and guidance. He was a devoted Muslim and spent much of his time in meditation and prayer. Ḥāfiẓ Dhahabī is of the opinion that A'mash was the chief both in useful knowledge and good deeds. He was a contented pious Muslim who had no liking for the worldly riches. He was very humble and modest in behaviour. He died in 147 or 148 H.

Chapter XXIII

CONCERNING THE FACT THAT NO ONE WILL ENTER PARADISE EXCEPT BELIEVERS, THAT LOVE FOR BELIEVERS IS (A CHARACTERISTIC FEATURE OF) FAITH AND GIVING CURRENCY TO (THE PRACTICE OF PAYING SALUTATION BY SAYING) AS-SALĀMU 'ALAIKUM (PEACE BE UPON YOU) IS THE MEANS TO ACHIEVE IT (FAITH)

(96) Abū Huraira reported: The Messenger of Allah (may peace and blessings be upon him) observed: You shall not enter Paradise so long as you do not affirm belief (in all those things which are the articles of faith) and you will not believe as long as you do not love one another. Should I not direct you to a thing which, if you do, will foster love amongst you: (i.e.) give currency to (the practice of paying salutation to one another by saying) as-salamu 'ālaikum. [111]

(97) Zuhair b. Ḥarb said: Jarīr reported on the authority of A'mash with this chain of transmitters that the Messenger of Allah (may peace be upon him) observed: By Him in Whose hand is my life, you shall not enter Paradise unless you believe. The rest of the ḥadīth is the same as narrated by Abū Mu'āwiya and Wakī'.

Chapter XXIV

DĪN IS SINCERITY AND WELL-WISHING

(98) Ịt is narrated on the authority of Tamīm ad-Dārī [112] that the Apostle of Allah (may peace and blessings be upon him) observed: Al-Dīn is a name of sincerity and

111. Just as face is the index to the mind, in the same way the words of salutation are the bold indicator of the sentiments of a man. The expression used is highly significant as it reflects the very soul of religious and cultural pattern to which the man belongs.

Salām is a verbal noun from *salima*, to be well, uninjured, used as substantive in the meaning of peace, health. But salām is most frequently used in the Qur'ān as a form of salutation:

> And when those who believe in Our signs come unto them; say thou: peace be upon you (vi. 54).

Then it is also commanded to give a very enthusiastic response to the salutation.

> And when you are greeted with a greeting, greet with one better than it, or return it (iv. 86).

It implies that when a person is greeted by a person with *as-salāmu 'alaikum*, he should at least respond him with *wa 'alaikum-us-salām*, but it is better to extend it by the addition of the words *wa raḥamtu'llahi wa barakātuhū*. This greeting is a prayer for the good of one another. These gentle words of greeting: *as-salāmu 'alaikum*, epitomise the feeling of a Muslim, his aspiration in life. He blesses his brother with peace.

Moreover, it reflects the sense of equality in the Muslim society. These words of greeting are exchanged amongst the Muslims irrespective of their social status.

112. He was one of the famous Companions of the Holy Prophet. His *nisba* ad-Dārī is said to be derived from the clan of Bani'l-Dār. Al-Nawawī is, however, of the opinion that his *nisba* al-Dārī is derived from the convent (dair) in which he was a monk before his conversion to Islam. His geneaology was Tamīm b. Aus b. Khārija b. Sawād. He embraced Islam in 9 H. He is an authentic narrator and

well-wishing.[113] Upon this we said: For whom? He replied: for Allah,[114] His Book,[115] His Messenger[116] and for the leaders[117] and the general Muslims.[118]

(99) Muḥammad b. Ḥātim and others narrate the same ḥadīth of the Apostle (may peace and blessings be upon him) on the authority of Tamīm ad-Dārī.

(100) Umayya b. Bisṭām narrates the same ḥadīth of the Messenger of Allah (may peace and blessings be upon him) on the authoriny of Tamim ad-Dārī.

(101) It is narrated on the authority of Jarīr[119] that he observed: I gave pledge of allegience to the Messenger of Allah (may peace and blessings be upon him) on the observance of prayer, payment of Zakāt, and sincerity and well-wishing for every Muslim.

(102) Sufyān narrated on the authority of Ziyād b. 'Ilāqa that he heard Jarīr b. 'Abdullah saying: I pledged allegiance to the Apostle of Allah (may peace and blessings be upon him) on sincerity and well-wishing for every Muslim.

(103) It is narrated on the authority of Jarīr that he observed: I owed allegiance to the Apostle of Allah (may peace and blessings be upon him) on hearing (his commands) and obeying (them) and (the Prophet) instructed me (to act) as lay in my power, and sincerity and well-wishing for every Muslim.

the aḥādīth concerning the end of the world and the coming of al-Dajjāl are particularly transmitted by him. He left Medina after the martyrdom of Ḥaḍrat 'Uthmān in 35 H. and went to his native place Syria, where he died at the end of the caliphate of Ḥaḍrat 'Alī in 40 H.

113. The word نصيحة (*naṣiḥa*) is derived from the verb *naṣaḥa* which carries a wide range of meanings. Imām Abū Sulaimān Khaṭṭābī says: It is a very comprehensive term and it stands for all those virtues and deeds for which the counsel is given. Some are of the opinion that it originally means to sew the garment or to purify the honey as we have such expressions in Arabic as: نصح الرجل ثوبه — نصحت العسل Thus according to its derivation it would mean to make man's heart chaste and pure and to order his life according to Islam with sincere counsel or advice. نصيحة is the opposite of impurity aud alloy.

114. In the light of these meanings the *naṣiḥa* for Allah would imply that man's heart is cleansed from all impurities and alloys with regard to belief in Allah, i.e. one should believe in Him as the Sole Creator and Master with all His Attributes and with an earnest desire to obey all commands given by Him.

115. *Naṣiḥa* in the case of Allah's Book means that it should be sincerely believed as a revelation from the Lord and should be read and understood with the same zeal and enthusiasm in which the Divine Message is read, and all its commands must be carried out in a spirit of devotion.

116. *Naṣiḥa* for the Messenger signifies that his Apostlehood must be affirmed with perfect sincerity of heart and whatever he has vouchsafed to humanity should be respected as the Word and Will of God and he should be respectfully followed in all his precepts and examples and obeyed in all the commands given by him.

117. *Naṣiḥa* for the leaders and rulers implies that they should be respected, obeyed and given support in all those affairs which they conduct according to the Sharī'ah of Islam. But where they deviate from the path of righteousness they should be advised and admonished and sincere efforts made to bring them to the right path.

118. *Naṣiḥa* for the general Muslims is that they should be advised in all matters concerning the good of this world and the hereafter, their life, honour and dignity should be protected and sincere endeavour made to ameliorate their lot.

Naṣiḥa thus covers the whole field of religion and its scope is as wide as that of Islam itself. It applies both to words and deeds. It is a *farḍ-i-kifāya* and is essential to maintain the moral health of the society.

119. His *kunya* was Abū 'Amr. He embraced Islam forty days before the death of the Holy Prophet. He stayed in Kūfah for some time and then shifted to Qarqsiyād and died there in 51 H. A large number of traditionsts havs transmitted traditions on his authority.

Chapter XXV

CONCERNING DIMINUTION OF BELIEF DUE TO SINS AND ITS SEPARATION FROM THE SINNER: NEGATION OF THE EXCELLENCE OF ĪMĀN AT THE TIME OF COMMITTING SIN

(104) Abū Huraira reported that the Messenger of Allah observed: The fornicator who fornicates is not a believer so long as he commits it and no thief who steals is a believer as long as he commits theft, and no drunkard who drinks wine is a believer as long as he drinks it. 'Abdul-Malik b. Abī Bakr narrated this on the authority of Abū Bakr b. 'Abdur-Raḥmān b. Ḥārith and then said: Abū Huraira made this addition: No plunderer who plunders a valuable thing that attracts the attention of people is a believer so long as he commits this act.[120]

(105) 'Abdul-Malik b. Shu'aib narrated this ḥadīth on the authority of Abū Huraira that he observed: The Messenger of Allah said that a fornicator does not fornicate, and then narrated the ḥadīth like this, and he also made mention of plundering too, but did not mention of a thing having value. Ibn Shihāb said: Sa'īd b. al-Musayyib and Abū Salama narrated this ḥadīth on the authority of Abū Huraira a ḥadīth like that of Abū Bakr with the exception of (the mention) of plundering.

(106) Muḥammad b. Mihrān narrates this ḥadīth on the authority of Abū Huraira and made mention of plundering but did not talk of (a thing) having value.[121]

(107) Imām Muslim has reported this ḥadīth by Ḥasan b. 'Alī al-Ḥalwānī and other traditions.

(108) It is reported on the authority of Qutaiba b. Sa'īd who reported on the authority of Abū Huraira the ḥadīth like that narrated from Zuhrī with this exception that in the ḥadīth narrated by 'Alā' and Ṣafwān b. Sulaim there is no mention of: People raise their eyes towards him, and in the ḥadīth narrated by Hammām: The believers raise their eyes towards him, and such like words, so long as he plunders (is not) a believer, and these words were added: And no exploiter who makes an exploitation is a believer as long as he exploits it; therefore avoid and shun (these evils).[122]

120. Īmān, as we have explained before, is the name of intense God-consciousness. The true believer is he who always feels that he is living in the presence of an All-Knowing, Omnipresent and All-Powerful Lord and nothing is hidden from His ever-watchful eye. Such heinous crimes as fornication, plundering, theft and drinking are the very negation of faith. A man who commits them is bereft of God's consciousness even though for a short time, because if he were aware that he is being watched by the Lord and he shall be punished in the Hereafter for these misdeeds, he would never violate His commands and commit such evils.

This ḥadīth is also indicative of the fact that Īmān is not something static but dynamic. It increases and decreases and seldom remains constant. But it should be made clear that Īmān in this ḥadīth refers to the state of God's consciousness, inner piety and a sense of accountability of one's deeds, and not Īmān in the technical sense of the term, the negation of which makes one the eternal denizen of Hell.

121. Maulānā Shabbīr Aḥmad 'Uthmānī has translated the epithet ذات شرف as a thing having value. There is a delicate difference between a valuable thing and a thing having value. A valuable thing is precious, but a thing having value means one which is useful and thus desired by people.

122. This ḥadīth is found both in Bukhārī and Muslim on the authority of Ibn 'Abbās with the addition of these words: "No one who kills is a believer as long as he is engaged in the act of killing.

(109) It is narrated on the authority of Abū Huraira : A fornicator who fornicates is not a believer as long as he commits fornication, and no one who steals is a believer as long as he commits theft, and no one who drinks wine is a believer as long as he drinks it, and repentance[123] may be accepted after that.

(110) Muḥammad bin Rāfi', 'Abdur-Razzāq, Sufyān, A'mash narrated this ḥadīth like one narrated by Shu'ba, on the authority of Abū Huraira raising[124] it (right to the Holy Prophet).

Chapter XXVI

CONCERNING THE PECULIARITIES OF A HYPOCRITE

(111) It is narrated on the authority of 'Abdullah b. 'Amr that the Prophet observed: Four characteristics made anyone who possessed them, a sheer hypocrite; anyone who possessed one of them possessed a characteristic of hypocrisy till he abandons it; when he talked he lied, when he made a covenant he acted treacherously, and when he quarrelled he deviated from the truth.[125]

(112) It is reported on the authority of Abū Huraira that the Messenger of Allah (may peace and blessings be upon him) said: Three are the signs of a hypocrite: when he spoke he told lie, when he made promise he acted treacherously against it, when he was trusted he betrayed.

(113) Abū Huraira reported that the Messenger of Allah (may peace and blessings be upon him) observed: There are three characteristics of a hypocrite: When he spoke he told lie, when he made promise he acted treacherously, and when he was trusted he betrayed.

(114) 'Uqba b. Mukarram al-'Amī reported that he heard 'Alā' b. 'Abdur-Raḥmān narrating this ḥadīth with this chain of transmitters and he said: Three are the signs

123. التوبه (repentance), originally meaning return, is a verb noun derived from *tāba* (تاب); this verb is often used in the Qur'ān (iv. 17, 18; ix. 104; xlii. 25) either absolutely or with *ilā* (الى), of one who returns to God for repentance, and also with *'alā* (على) of God, who turns with forgiveness to tho penitent. He is "*Tawwāb-ur-Raḥīm,*" very Forgiving and Merciful (ii. 37). In religious terminology *tauba* stands for an act of the soul in breaking away from the past as a preliminary step to the work of ethical reform. It is in fact a form of self-judgment and purgation of the soul. It is, therefore, not peculiar to Islam only, but is implied in all the higher religions and systems of morality. The validity of *tauba* in Islam depends on three things :

(*a*) Confession of a sin means that a penitent should have the feeling of acknowledgment of sin or of wrong-doing.

(*b*) Remorse which denotes poignant sorrow for the wrong act done by a man. It is the root of the moral faculty.

(*c*) A firm resolution to abstain from sin in future (Ghazālī, *Iḥyā' 'Ulūm al-Din*, Book IV).

124. It is a type of ḥadīth which is known as *Marfū'*, meaning raised. It implies a tradition which reaches up to the Holy Prophet (may peace and blessings be upon him) without any defect in the transmission.

125. فجر (*fajara*) is generally translated in this ḥadīth as "he used abusive language," but Imām Nawawī and Maulānā Shabbīr Aḥmad 'Uthmānī have translated this as: مال عن الحق "he deviated from the truth".

of a hypocrite,[126] even if he observed fast and prayed and asserted that he was a Muslim.

(115) It is reported on the authority of Abū Huraira that the Messenger of Allah (may peace and blessings of Allah be upon him) made observations like them embodied in the ḥadīth narrated by Yaḥyā b. Muḥammad on the authority of 'Alā', and added to it: Even if he observed fast and prayed and asserted that he was a Muslim.

Chapter XXVII

THE CONDITION OF THE FAITH OF ONE WHO CALLS HIS BROTHER MUSLIM AS AN UNBELEIVER

(116) It is reported on the authority of Ibn 'Umar that the Apostle (may peace and blessings be upon him) observed: When a man calls his brother an unbeliever it returns (at least) to one of them.

(117) It is reported on the authority of Ibn 'Umar that the Messenger of Allah (may peace and blessings be upon him) said: Any person who called his brother: O unbeliever! (has in fact done an act by which this unbelief) would return to one of them. If it were so, as he asserted (then the unbelief of man was confirmed but if it was not true), then it returned to him (to the man who labelled it on his brother Muslim).[127]

Chapter XXVIII

THE CONDITION OF THE FAITH OF ONE WHO KNOWINGLY DENIES HIS TRUE FATHERHOOD

(118) It is reported on the authority of Abū Dharr[128] that he heard the Messenger

126. النفق from which *nifāq* and *munāfiq* are derived means a tunnel which has its both sides open. It is mentioned in the Qur'ān : "Then seek out if you can build a tunnel or a passway into the earth" (vi. 35).

In the religious terminology *nifāq* means to profess a thing and act contradictory to that. *Nifāq* is of two types (1) *nifāq fi'l-i'tiqād*, and (2) *nifāq fi'l-'amal. Nifāq fi'l-i'tiqād* is that one makes a declaration of one's Īmān in public and asserts that he is a Muslim, but does not affirm it in the heart of his heart. The second is *nifāq fi'l-'amal* which implies that whatever a man professes he does not put it into practice. In the words of Ḥasan Baṣrī, *nifāq fi'l-'amal* is the name of dissemblance between the inner and the outer life of man, i.e. his beliefs and his practices. This is a hypocrisy which undermines the moral fibres of human beings and that is why it has been condemned by the Prophet and the Holy Qur'ān.

127. This ḥadīth tells us that labelling others with unbelief is not an insignificant thing but a matter of vital importance, and one should use utmost care in passing these remarks on others. This ḥadīth also shows that whatever is said or done in the world is retained and preserved and nothing is lost. This point has been illustrated by a ḥadīth recorded in Abū Dāwūd and narrated on the authority of Abū Dardā'. The Holy Prophet observed: "When a person curses anyone, it goes directly towards the sky, but when it finds no path to Mercy, it comes down, then it moves right and left, but finding no place moves towards the man who was cursed, but if he does not deserve it, then it comes back to the one who has cursed the other one.

128. His full name was Jundub b. Junādah Ghifārī. He was one of the refugees and was a well-known Companion of the Holy Prophet. He was very pious, meek and humble, and spent most of his

of Allah (may peace and blessings be upon him) saying: No person who claimed knowingly anyone else as his father besides (his own) committed nothing but infidelity,[129] and he who made a claim of anything, which (in fact) did not belong to him, is not amongst us; he should make his abode in Fire, and he who labelled anyone with unbelief or called him as the enemy of Allah, and he was in fact not so, it rebounded on him.

(119) It is narrated on the authority of Abū Huraira that the Messenger of Allah (may peace and blessings be upon him) observed: Do not detest your fathers; he who detested his father committed infidelity.

(120) It is reported on the authority of Sa'd b. Abī Waqqāṣ[130]: Both of my ears heard the Messenger of Allah saying this: He who claimed the fatherhood of anyone else besides his real father knowingly (committed a great sin). Paradise is forbidden for him. Abū Bakra asserted that he too heard it from the Messenger of Allah (may peace be upon him).

(121) Sa'd and Abū Bakra[131] each one of them said: My ears heard and my hearing preserved it that Muḥammad (peace and blessings be upon him) observed: He who claimed for another one his fatherhood besides his own father knowingly that he was not his father—for him Paradise is forbidden.

time in meditation and prayer. Even before his conversion to Islam he was known as a man of ideal devotion and piety. He preached Islam among his tribesmen and lived at Damascus for a pretty long time but subsequently settled at Rabadha near Medina at the time of the third caliph, Ḥaḍrat 'Uthmān (may Allah be pleased with him). He died there on the 8th of dhil-Ḥijj in 32 H. Accidentally there came a party of pilgrims under the leadership of 'Abdullah b. Mas'ūd. The funeral prayer was led by this eminent Companion of the Holy Prophet and a great jurist of Islam.

129. Imām Nawawī is of the view that this word كفر has been used in the sense of كفران (infidelity). It is the height of ingratitude that one should attribute his fatherhood to another man than his own father. The Arabs did it only to excel their high birth. Islam gave a death-blow to them and told humanity that all these artificial distinctions are meaningless in the eye of Allah and carry no weight at all. It is, therefore, shameful for a man to claim anyone else as his father besides his real father.

130. Sa'd b. Abī Waqqāṣ: His *kunya* was Abū Isḥāq and his father's name was Mālik b. Wuhaib b. 'Abd Manāf b. Zuhra b. Kilāb b. Murra. The *kunya* of his father was Abū Waqqāṣ. The Holy Prophet was closely related to Sa'd from the side of his mother who belonged to the family of Zuhra. He embraced Islam at the age of seventeen and was one of the earliest Companions of the Holy Prophet. He was one of those ten fortunate souls who were promised Paradise during their lives. He took part not only in the Battles of Badr and Uḥud, but almost in all those campaigns which followed. He was a great military general, an eminent statesman and an able administrator.

Sa'd was regarded as one of the most reliable narrators of the aḥadīth of the Holy Prophet. Ḥaḍrat 'Umar would often say: When a ḥadīth is narrated on the authority of Sa'd it needs no further scrutiny.

He was a very pious and generous Muslim who spent much of his time in meditation and prayer. He was deeply attached to the Holy Prophet and always stood by him and cheerfully suffered all those hardships that mounted his way. He died in 55 H. at a place known as 'Aqab at a distance of ten miles from Medina.

131. Abū Bakra: His name was Nufay' b. al-Ḥārith b. Kalda Thaqafī. He was an Abyssinian slave who was absorbed in the tribe of al-Ḥārith. During the siege of Ṭā'if (the abode of the Thaqafī tribe) by the Holy Prophet in 8 H. Abū Bakra joined the Muslims by letting himself down by a pulley and was emancipated by Muḥammad (may peace and blessings be upon him). He was, therefore, the Maulā (freed slave) of the Holy Prophet.

Chapter XXIX

ABUSING A MUSLIM IS AN OUTRAGE[132] AND FIGHTING AGAINST HIM IS UNBELIEF

(122) It is narrated on the authority of 'Abdullah b. Mas'ūd that the Messenger of Allah (may peace and blessings be upon him) observed: Abusing a Muslim is an outrage and fighting against him is unbelief.[133] Zubaid said: I asked Abū Wā'il: Did you hear it from 'Abdullah narrating it from the Messenger of Allah (may peace and blessings be upon him)? He replied: Yes. But there is mention of the talk between Zubaid and Abū Wā'il in the ḥadīth narrated by Shu'ba.

(123) Abū Bakr b. Abū Shaiba narrated a ḥadīth like this from the Apostle (may peace and blessings be upon him) on the authority of 'Abdullah.

Chapter XXX

DON'T BECOME UNBELIEVERS AFTER ME BY STRIKING THE NECKS OF ONE ANOTHER

(124) It is narrated on the authority of Jarīr b. 'Abdullah that the Apostle of Allah (may peace and blessings be upon him) asked him on the occasion of Farewell Pilgrimage to make the people silent and then said: Do not return to unbelief after me by striking the necks of one another.

(125) 'Ubaidullah b. Mu'ādh narrated from the Apostle (may peace and blessings be upon him) a ḥadīth like this on the authority on Ibn 'Umar.

(126) It is narrated on the authority of 'Abdullah b. 'Umar that the Apostle (may peace and blessings be upon him) observed at the occasion of Farewell Pilgrimage: Woe unto you,[134] distress unto you! Don't turn back as unbelievers after me by striking the neck of one another.

(127) Ḥarmula b. Yaḥyā, 'Abdullah b. Wahb, 'Umar b. Muḥammad, Ibn 'Umar narrated like the ḥadīth reported by Shu'ba on the authority of Wāqid.

132. *Fusūq* originally means to deviate from the right course. Here it means deviation from the path shown by God and His Apostle.

133. The ḥadīth sheds a good deal of light on how much restraint a Muslim is required to exercise on his tongue and hand. It is indeed an enormous crime to use insulting language for a Muslim and a sort of unbelief to fight against him. One can read in these words of the Holy Prophet the importance of love, fellow feeling in the Muslim society and the horrors of those acts which undermine the solidarity of the *ummah*. It should, however, be remembered in this connection that these things are not permitted even against the non-Muslims. Their life and honour are also to be respected and honoured. This restraint has been stressed in case of Muslims simply because of the fact that it is a chapter of Īmān, and its importance as the foundation of the *ummah's* solidarity is being emphasised here. The aḥadīth which follow these will elucidate this point.

134. Both the epithets *waiḥakum* and *wailakum* can be interpreted differently. Qāḍī 'Iyāḍ is of the opinion that these are the expressions of exclamation. The famous grammarian Sībawaih asserts that these stand for destruction. It is reported from 'Umar b. Khaṭṭāb that *waiḥa* denotes mercy over the victims (*Fatḥ-ul-Mulḥim*, Vol. I, p. 238).

Chapter XXXI

THE USE OF THE WORD "UNBELIEF" IN CASE OF SLANDERING (ANYONE) OR ONE'S LINEAGE, AND LAMENTATION

(128) It is narrated on the authority of Abū Huraira that the Messenger of Allah (may peace and blessings be upon him) observed: Two (things) are found among men which are tantamount to unbelief: slandering one's lineage and lamentation on the dead.[135]

Chapter XXXII

CALLING THE FUGITIVE SLAVE AS INFIDEL

(129) It is narrated on the authority of Jarīr that he heard (the Holy Prophet) saying: The slave who fled from his master committed an act of infidelity as long as he would not return to him. Manṣūr observed: By God this ḥadīth was narrated from the Apostle (may peace and blessings be upon him), but I do dot like that this should be narrated on my authority here in Baṣra.[136]

(130) It is narrated on the authority of Jarīr that the Messenger of Allah (may peace and blessings be upon him) observed: The slave who fled from his master, responsibility[137] with regard to him was absolved.

(131) Jarīr b. 'Abdullah reported it from the Holy Prophet: When the slave runs away from his master, his prayer is not accepted.[138]

135. Imām Nawawi is of the view that these two practices don't make a man unbeliever in the technical sense of the term, but these are highly despised in Islam, since these are deeds of the Jāhiliya. The Arabs before Islam took pride in their high birth and slandered those who were born of poor parents and, secondly, they lamented over the dead by tearing their collars and beating their chests. The Holy Prophet has condemned both these acts as the practices of the Jāhiliya.

136. This ḥadīth very appropriately explains the use of the word *kufr* in context with different aḥadīth which have been given above. Here kufr does not imply that unbelief which makes a man unbeliever but here it signifies ingratitude or a grave offence. Why Manṣūr did not like this ḥadīth to be narrated on his behalf in Baṣra was due to the fact that here the Khwārij were dominating at that time and these people condemned every man as kāfir and treated him so who committed any sin. This ḥadīth also clarifies the point that a sinner is not an unbeliever.

137. There are several responsibilities which fall on the shoulder of a man with regard to his slave. The master is required to provide him with food which he himself eats, clothe him with the clothes he himself wears and assign him task according to his working capacity. Then his life and honour are also to be protected. The slave who runs from his master is deprived of all these guarantees and his master is absolved of all his responsibilities.

138. Running of the slave from his master without any reason is an act of ingratitude which is not liked by Allah and, therefore, the prayer is not accepted. Imām Nawawī, however, makes it clear that when a slave offers farḍ prayers, the farḍ is fulfilled.

Chapter XXXIII

THE UNBELIEF OF ONE WHO SAID: WE GOT RAINFALL BY THE MOVEMENT (OF THE STARS)

(132) It is narrated on the authority of Zaid b. Khālid al-Juhanī: The Messenger of Allah (may peace and blessings be upon him) led the morning prayer at Ḥudaybiya. There were some marks of the rainfall during the night. At the conclusion of prayer he turned towards people and observed: Do you know what your Lord has said? They replied: Allah and His Messenger know best. Upon this he (the Holy Prophet) remarked: He (Allah) said: Some of My bondsmen entered the morning as My believers and some as unbelievers. He who said: We have had a rainfall due to the Blessing and Mercy of Allah, he is My believer and a disbeliever of stars, and who said: We have had a rainfall due to the movement of such and such (star) disbelieved Me and affirmed his faith in the stars.[139]

(133) It is reported on the authority of Abū Huraira that the Messenger of Allah (may peace and blessings be upon him) said: Don't you know what your Lord said? He observed: I have never endowed My bondsmen with a favour, but a section amongst them disbelieved it and said: Stars, it was due to the stars.

(134) It is reported on the authority of Abū Huraira that the Messenger of Allah (may peace and blessing be upon him) observed: Allah does not shower His blessings from the heaven that in the morning a group of men disbelieve it (to be a blessing from Allah). Allah sends down rain, but they (the disbelievers) say: Such and such star (is responsible for that).

(135) It is reported on the authority of Ibn 'Abbās that there was (once) a downpour during the life of Apostle (may peace and blessings be upon him). Upon this the Apostle (may peace and blessings be upon him) observed: Some people entered the morning with gratitude and some with ingratitude (to Allah). Those who entered with gratitude said: This is the blessing of Allah, and those who entered with ingratitude said: Such and such asterism was right. It was upon this that the verse was revealed:

> I swear by the setting of the stars to the end and make your provision that you should disbelieve it[140] (lvi. 75-82).

139. نوء (nau') means a star or an asterism, verging or setting: or the setting of the stars. The Arabs of pre-Islamic Arabia like so many other nations of the world believed that the movements of particular stars control the rain. The ḥadīth declares such a belief to be kufr and makes it explicitly clear that the whole universe with its solar system is controlled by Allah and everything moves at His Command. It is He Who brings rainfall, glides stars according to a Plan.

140. Ibn 'Abbās in his commentary says it implies that you get provision out of the favour and blessing of Allah but you belie it and consider it as a favour of the star or other such deity.

Chapter XXXIV

THE LOVE OF ANṢĀR (HELPERS) AND 'ALĪ (MAY ALLAH BE PLEASED WITH ALL OF THEM) IS (AN INGREDIENT) OF ĪMĀN AND (ONE OF) ITS SIGNS, AND HATRED AGAINST THEM IS A SIGN OF DISSEMBLANCE

(136) It is reported on the authority of Anas that the Messenger of Allah (may peace and blessings be upon him) observed: The sign of a hypocrite is the hatred against the Anṣār and the sign of a believer is the love for the Anṣār.[141]

(137) It is narrated on the authority of Anas that the Apostle (may peace and blessings be upon him) said: The love of the Anṣār is the sign of Īmān and hatred against them is the sign of dissemblance.

(138) Al-Barā'[142] reported it from the Apostle (may peace and blessing be upon him) that he observed with regard to the Anṣār: None but the believer loves them, none but the hypocrite hates them. He who loved them loved Allah and he who hated them hated Allah. I (the narrator) said: Did you hear this ḥadīth from al-Bāra'? He said: To me, he narrated it.

(139) It is reported on the authority of Abū Huraira that the Messenger of Allah (may peace and blessings be upon him) said: A person who believes in Allah and the Last Day never nurses a grudge against the Anṣār.

(140) It is narrated on the authority of Abū Sa'īd Khudrī that the Messenger of Allah observed: The person who believes in Allah and the Last Day never nurses a grudge against the Anṣār.

(141) Zirr[143] reported: 'Alī observed: By Him Who split up the seed and created

141. Īmān makes a man realistic and purifies his heart of all grudges which he has nursed on his personal whims and out of his selfish interests. The Anṣār have always been a source of great strength to Islam since their first pledge to the Holy Prophet. They remained constantly devoted to Allah and showed no weakness on any occasion. The Holy Prophet along with his Companions was tortured in his home town; the Anṣār accepted his authority cheerfully. They treated their brethren-in-faith from Mecca in such a hospitable manner the like of which is not to be found in history. Allah and His Prophet fully appreciated their sincerity, their steadfastness in the cause of Allah and their tremendous sacrifices which they made for the sake of Islam.

142. Al-Barā' b. 'Āzib b. al-Ḥārith al-Aswī al-Anṣārī. His *kunya* was Abū 'Amāra. He embraced Islam at a very early age. His father 'Āzib was also the Companion of the Holy Prophet. He studied the Holy Qur'ān from the famous Companion Ibn Maktūm. He accompanied the Prophet of Allah in various expeditions and later took part in the war of conquest. He brought Rayy and Qizwīn under Muslim dominion. He later espoused the cause of 'Alī b. Abī Ṭālib and fought under his banner at the battle of the Camel, at Ṣiffīn and at al-Nahrawān.

Ḥaḍrat al-Barā' was one of the eminent Companions of the Holy Prophet and was a reliable traditionist. Three hundred and five aḥādīth have been transmitted on his authority. He narrated the ḥadīth with utmost care. At the end of his life he retired to Kūfah and died in 72. H. at the age of seventy-two.

143. His name was Zirr b. Ḥubaish and his *kunya* was Abū Maryam. He lived as a non-Muslim for sixty years and spent sixty years as a Muslim in the company of the famous Companions of the Holy Prophet. He did not embrace Islam during the lifetime of Muhammad (may peace and blessings be upon him) and, therefore, is counted among the Tābi'īn. Imām Nawawī regarded him as an eminent Tābi'ī. He was a great scholar and reciter of the Holy Qur'ān. Ibn Sa'd is of the view that he was one of the reliable narrators of ahadīth. He has transmitted traditions on the authority of the

something living,[144] the Apostle (may peace and blessing be upon him) gave me a promise that no one but a believer would love me, and none but a hypocrite would nurse grudge against me.[145]

Chapter XXXV

DIMINUTION OF ĪMĀN BY FAILING IN SUBMISSION AND THE USE OF THE WORD "KUFR" FOR THINGS BESIDES UNBELIEF OF ALLAH, FOR EXAMPLE UNGRATEFULNESS AND INGRATIUDE[146]

(142) It is narrated on the authority of 'Abdullah b. 'Umar that the Messenger of Allah observed: O womenfolk, you should give charity and ask much forgiveness for I saw you in bulk amongst the dwellers of Hell. A wise lady among them said: Why is it, Messenger of Allah, that our folk is in bulk in the Hell? Upon this the Holy Prophet observed: You curse too much and are ungrateful to your spouses. I have seen none

famous Companions of the Holy Prophet. There is difference of opinion about the date of his death. It is recorded as 81 H., 82 H. and even 83 H. His age was 122 at the time of his death.

144. An-nasama: It can be translated both as man or a soul. Nasama is in fact a soul and it stands for all those creatures which have a soul (*Fatḥ-ul-Mulhim*, Vol I, p. 243).

145. Here love of Ḥaḍrat 'Alī (may Allah be pleased with him) has been made as one of the criteria of a true believer. As I have discussed earlier, faith inculcates in man the spirit of true piety and purifies him of all prejudices. A Muslim nurses no ill-will against anyone, out of his own whim, but hates and loves according to the standard of Islam. All those personalities like Ḥaḍrat Abū Bakr, Ḥaḍrat 'Umar, Ḥaḍrat 'Uthmān and many others who served Islam with sincere conviction and earnest endeavour should be loved and respected. Ḥaḍrat 'Alī was one of these eminent souls who had done a great service to the cause of Truth and Righteousness and whose life was an example of true devotion to the Holy Prophet. He was hardly ten or eleven years old when he embraced Islam and was one of the first converts from among the young boys. He was fortunate enough to have the privilege of living in the house of the Holy Prophet and grow up under his kind care. The Messenger of Allah was very affectionate towards him, and trusted him in all matters. He was asked to occupy the Prophet's bed on the night when the latter left Mecca for Mèdina, and when the conspirators entered the house to kill Muḥammad, they were surprised to discover his young cousin sleeping there. After restoring to their owners the objects which the Holy Prophet was holding on trust, 'Alī joined him at Qubā'. He was married to the Prophet's daugt her Fāṭima. He was elected as the fourth caliph. He was an extremely pious man and always maintained a very high standard of morality and God-consciousness and always presented a fine example of a true believer. Enmity against such a devoted lover of Islam is in fact enmity against Allah and His Apostle.

These aḥādīth in which love of true believers and trusted Companions of the Holy Prophet has been described as the criteria of Īmān bring into prominence the fact that it is Islam alone which has produced such a large number of Muslims whose lives can be presented as perfect examples of Islam clothed in reality. It is from them that one can form an idea of the practical aspects of Islamic values.

146. This ḥadīth is clearly indicative of the fact that the word *kufr* used in the ḥadīth is not always synonymous with unbelief in the real sense of the term. It has its other implications too and is used in so many other senses, e.g. in case of ingratitude and ungratefulness.

lacking in common sense[147] and failing in religion[148] but (at the same time) robbing[149] the wisdom of the wise, besides you. Upon this the woman remarked: What is wrong with our common sense and with religion? He (the Holy Prophet) observed: Your lack of common sense (can be well judged from the fact) that the evidence of two women is equal to one man, that is a proof of the lack of common sense, and you spend some nights (and days) in which you do not offer prayer and in the month of Ramaḍān (during the days) you do not observe fast, that is a failing in religion. This ḥadīth has been narrated on the authority of Abū Ṭāhir with this chain of transmitters.

(143) A ḥadīth like this as narrated by Ibn 'Umar has also been transmitted by Abū Huraira.

Chapter XXXVI

APPLICATION OF THE WORD "KUFR" ON ONE WHO NEGLECTS PRAYER

(144) It is narrated on the authority of Abū Huraira that when the son of Adam recites the Āyat of Sajdah (prostration) and then falls down in prostration, the Satan goes into seclusion and weeps and says: Alas, and in the narration of Abū Kuraib the words are: Woe unto me, the son of Adam was Commanded to prostrate, and he prostrated and paradise was entitled to him and I was commanded to prostrate, but I refused and am doomed to Hell.[150]

(145) A'mash narrated this ḥadīth with the same chain of transmission, with this change of words that he (the Satan) said: I disobeyed and I am doomed to hell.

(146) It is narrated on the authority of Jābir that he heard the Apostle (may peace and blessings be upon him) saying: Verily between man and between polytheism and unbelief is the negligence of prayer.[151]

147. The Holy Prophet has supported his contention with reason. Women are generally shy, capricious and whimsical, and are easily carried off by their emotions and thus their study of the situation is hardly objective. That is the reason why the Sharī'ah has accepted the evidence of two women equal to one man and it is only in this sphere that they are declared to be inferior in wisdom as compared with men. But in their own sphere their evidence is considered to be most authentic, for example in *raḍā'* it is absolutely on their evidence that the case is decided.

148. Women are forbidden to pray and observe fasts during the days of menstruation. This fact has been narrated not as a wilful negligence on their part but to stress the importance of prayer and fasting in Islam (Imām Nawawī).

149. Woman has an art to play with the sentiments of man and she succeeds in forcing her will upon him.

150. This ḥadīth explains how one becomes a kāfir. Mere negligence in prayer does not make a man unbeliever, strictly in religious sense. It is no doubt a grave sin, because there is no idea of religion without prayer. But if a man shows some negligence he would not be treated as an apostate. The fault with Satan was that he refused to obey the Commands of Allah and flouted His authority. There is a good deal of difference between negligence or omission and a wilful deniel or refusal.

151. Religion and prayer always go together. It is by prayer, in fact, that the process of the religious life of man is governed. Take prayer out of the world and it is as you have torn asunder the delicate bond that binds humanity to God. We recognise our Lord through prayer and feel His indwelling in our life. A man who neglects prayer is religiously dead and he who denies it is, according to all schools of Muslim thought, an unbeliever, for he denies the most fundamental basis of religion.

(147) It is narrated on the authority of Abū Zubair that he heard Jābir b. 'Abdullah saying: I heard the Messenger of Allah (may peace and blessings be upon him) observing this: Between man and polytheism and unbelief is the abandonment of ṣalāt.

Chapter XXXVII

BELIEF IN ALLAH IS THE BEST OF DEEDS

(148) Abū Huraira reported: The Messenger of Allah was asked about the best of deeds. He observed: Belief in Allah. He (the inquirer) said: What next? He (the Holy Prophet) replied: Jihād (struggle to the utmost) in the cause of Allah. He (the inquirer) again said: What next? He (the Holy Prophet) replied: Pilgrimage accepted into the grace of the Lord. In the tradition narrated on the authority of Muḥammad b. Ja'far (the words are) that he (the Holy Prophet) said: Belief in Allah and His Messenger. Muḥammad b. Rāfi' and 'Abd b. Ḥumaid, 'Abdur-Razzāq and Ma'mar and Zuhrī have narrated a ḥadīth like this on the authority of the same chain of transmitters.

(149) Abū Dharr reported: I said: Messenger of Allah, which of the deeds is the best? He (the Holy Prophet) replied: Belief in Allah and Jihād in His cause. I again asked: Who is the slave whose emancipation is the best? He (the Holy Prophet) replied: One who is valuable for his master and whose price is high. I said: If I can't afford to do it? He (the Holy Prophet) replied: Help an artisan or make anything for the unskilled[152] (labourer). I (Abū Dharr) said: Messenger of Allah, you see that I am helpless in doing some of these deeds. He (the Holy Prophet) replied: Desist from doing mischief to the people. That is the charity of your person on your behalf.

(150) Muḥammad b. Abū Rāfi' narrated the ḥadīth on the authority of Abū Dharr with a slight difference.

(151) It is narrated on the authority of 'Abdullah b. Mas'ūd that he observed: I asked the Messenger of Allah (may peace be upon him) which deed was best. He (the Holy Prophet) replied: Prayer at its appointed hour. I (again) said: Then what? He (the Holy Prophet) replied: Kindness to the parents.[153] I (again) said: Then what? He replied: Earnest endeavour (Jihād) in the cause of Allah. And I would have not ceased asking more questions but out of regard (for his feelings).

(152) 'Abdullah b. Mas'ūd reported: I said: Messenger of Allah, which of the deeds (take one) nearer to Paradise? He (the Holy Prophet) replied: Prayer at its proper

152. اخرق (*akhraq*) is one who is deficient in intellect or understanding and does not know his handicraft. To help such a man has been pronounced as the best of the deeds. This ḥadīth speaks eloquently of the social responsibility of a Muslim. He is required to help his brother who is deficient and is unable to procure for himself a reasonable living by his own efforts.

153. Obedience to parents is one of the main duties of a Muslim. It has been placed next to the duty towards Allah, for among fellow beings, none has a greater claim upon a person than his parents. This duty has been stressed in the Qur'ān in the following verse:

> And thy Lord has decreed that you serve none but Him, and do good to parents. If either or both of them reach old age with thee, say not "fie" to them, nor chide them, and speak to them a generous word (xv. 23).

time. I said: What next, Messenger of Allah? He replied: Kindness to the parents. I said: What next? He replied: Jihād in the cause of Allah.

(153) It was heard from Abū 'Amr Shaibānī that, pointing towards the house of 'Abdullah, he said: The owner of this house told me that he asked the Messenger of Allah (may peace be upon him): Which of the deeds are liked by Allah? He (the Holy Prophet) observed: Prayer at its proper time. I (again) said: What next? He replied: Then goodness to the parents. I (again) said: What then? He replied: Then Jihād in the cause of Allah. He ('Abdullah) said: This is what I was told (by the Holy Prophet). Had I questioned further, he would have made additions for me.

(154) This ḥadīth has been transmitted by Muḥammad b. Bashshār, Muḥammad b. Ja'far, Shu'ba with this chain of narrators, with the addition that he pointed towards the house of 'Abdullah, but he did not mention his name for us.

(155) It is reported on the authority of 'Abdullah that the Apostle of Allah observed: The best of the deeds or deed is the (observance of) prayer at its proper time and kindness to the parents.

Chapter XXXVIII

POLYTHEISM IS THE MOST SHAMEFUL OF SINS AND THE MENTIONING OF THE GRAVEST SIN NEXT TO IT

(156) 'Abdullah reported: I asked the Messenger of Allah (may peace be upon him): Which sin is the gravest in the eye of Allah? He (the Holy Prophet) replied: That you associate partner with Allah (despite the fact) that He has created you.[154] He (the reporter) said: I told him (the Holy Prophet): Verily it is indeed grave. He (the reporter) said: I asked him what the next (gravest sin) was. He (the Holy Prophet) replied: That you kill your child out of fear that he shall join you in food.[155] He (the reporter)

154. Polytheism, that is, associating partner with Allah, is the most grievous offence in Islam. The Holy Qur'ān calls it as the most atrocious act on the part of man:

> And recall the time Luqmān said to his son, while he was exhorting him: O my son! associate not aught with Allah; verily this associating is surely a tremendous wrong (xxxi. 13).
>
> Verily Allah shall not forgive that aught be associated with Him, and He will forgive all else to whom He pleases. And whoever sets up a partner with Allah, he devises indeed a great sin (iv. 48).

Here in this ḥadīth the Holy Prophet has given one of the reasons why it is a grave sin. The reason is that man is created by Allah and it is the height of ingratitude on his part that he should associate other partners with his Creator. Moreover, this act also lowers his own dignity and status. He has been made the vicegerent of the Lord in this world, but he stoops himself low by bowing before other deities who are amongst the created things of Allah and humbler in rank as compared with man.

155. That is also a kind of *shirk* and height of selfishness on man's part. It is *shirk fi'l-Rubūbiyah*, i.e. man assumes the role of a nourisher and sustainer and thinks that he is responsible for the nourishment of his babes. The Qur'ān repudiates such a wrong belief and says:

> And kill not your children for fear of want—We provide for them and for you. Surely the killing of them is a great crime (xvii. 31).

said: I asked (him) what the next (gravest sin) was. He (the Holy Prophet) observed: Then (the next gravest sin) is that you commit adultery with the wife of your neighbour.[156]

(157) It is narrated on the authority of 'Abdullah b. Mas'ūd that a man said: Messenger of Allah, which offence is the most grievous in the eye of Allah? He (the Holy Prophet) replied: That you associate partner with Allah (despite the fact) that He created you. He (the man) said: What next? He (the Holy Prophet) replied: That you kill your child out of fear that he would join you in food. He (the inquirer) said (again): What next? He (the Holy Prophet) replied: That you commit adultery with the wife of your neighbour. And the Almighty and Exalted Lord testified it (with these verses):

> All those who call not unto another god along with Allah, and slay not any soul which Allah has forbidden, except in the cause of justice, nor commit fornication,[157] and he who does this shall meet a requital of sin (xxv. 68).

This practice of killing children, or of *coitus interruptus* and other methods of birth control, is in fact the denial of the *rubūbiyah* (the attribute of nourishing) of the Lord. The modern craze for birth control is based on a false concept of God that He is a tyrant and is playing havoc with humanity in the sense that the resources He has created to maintain humanity are far meagre as compared with their ever-increasing numbers. But experience has demonstrated absolute untenability of this very assumption. God is very Bountiful and Merciful and the means of subsistence that He has provided are far more vast and rich than the growth in population. Since the time of Malthus, the first modern promulgator of this theory of birth control, population has not outrun the means of subsistence, rather there has been a tremendous increase in the production of food and goods. Moreover, this practice of birth control reflects selfishness on the part of man which the Holy Prophet has described in his own prophetic style that "a man is afraid lest anyone else should come and share food with him". In other words, he looks upon marriage as the means of sensuous pleasure only, but is not prepared to make any sacrifice for his child which is the natural outcome of this wedlock. This is also an act of ingratitude.

156. Adultery in itself is a very grave offence but it is most shamefully grave when it is committed with the wife of a neighbour. A person has every right to expect fellow feeling and security from his neighbour and believe that his trust would not be violated. What enormous crime it is that this trust should be treacherously violated by a neighbour and he should go to the extent of committing adultery with his wife. This offence undermines the very trust of a man upon one who should be most reliable and trustworthy. One can well imagine the state of insecurity in a society given to such breach of trust.

There is a very close meaningful relation in the different sins described in the ḥadīth. Polytheism is an ingratitude through and through. Killing of children is also ungratefulness of the Bounties of the Lord and height of selfishness on the part of man. The third sin, i.e. committing adultery with the wife of a neighbour, is also an act of ingratitude and a denial of the Ever-Vigilant Eye of the Omnipresent Lord. It is easy to have a secret access to the wife of a neighbour without being known to the society. It is interesting to note that the Holy Prophet has very significantly used the verb تزانی (*tuzāni*) and not تزنی (*tazni*) in this connection. It implies that the offence of fornication is being committed with the common consent of both the parties and in such a case there is no fear of public criticism and intervention of the State. Under these circumstances when the offence can be safely hidden from the view of society, it is the consciousness of God and His Omnipresence that can restrain one from doing evil deeds.

157. The Arabic word زنی (*zinā*) is much more comprehensive than either "fornication," which is restricted to the illicit sexual intercourse of "unmarried persons," or "adultery" which denotes the sexual intercourse of two persons either of whom is married to a third person. Zinā is general. It denotes the sexual intercourse between any man and woman, whether married or not, who do not stand to each other in the relation of husband and wife.

Chapter XXXIX

MAJOR SINS[158] AND THE GRAVEST AMONG THESE

(158) It is narrated on the authority of 'Abdur-Raḥmān b. Abū Bakra that his father said: We were in the company of the Messenger of Allah (may peace be upon him) that he observed: Should I not inform you about the most grievous of the grave sins? (The Holy Prophet) repeated it three times, and then said: Associating anyone with Allah, disobedience to parents, false testimony or false utterance. The Holy Prophet was reclining, then he sat down, and he repeated it so many times that we wished if he should become silent.[159]

(159) Anas narrated from the Apostle (may peace be upon him) about the major sins. He (the Holy Prophet) observed: Associating anyone with Allah, disobedience to parents, killing a person and false utterance.

(160) 'Ubaidullah b. Abū Bakr said: I heard Anas b. Mālik saying: The Messenger of Allah (may peace be upon him) talked about the major sins, or he was asked about the major sins. Upon this he observed: Associating anyone with Allah, killing of a person,[160] disobedience to parents. He (the Holy Prophet further) said: Should I not inform you about the gravest of the major sins, and (in this connection) observed: False utterance or false testimony. Shu'ba said: It was most probably "false testimony".

(161) It is reported on the authority of Abū Huraira that the Messenger of Allah (may peace be upon him) observed: Avoid the seven noxious things. It was said (by the hearers): What are they, Messenger of Allah? He (the Holy Prophet) replied: Associating anything with Allah, magic, killing of one whom God has declared inviolate without a just cause, consuming the property of an orphan,[161] and consuming of usury,[162]

158. Some of the sins in Islam are very grave and these make a man either an unbeliever, or a *fāsiq*. These are known as the major sins (*kabā'ir*), whereas some sins are minor and these are washed off by daily prayers. It should, however, be remembered that when a minor sin is committed deliberately or is repeated without any qualm of conscience and one feels no remorse over it, it becomes a major sin. The Muslim scholars and saints are of the view that along with the nature of offence we should also see the attitude with which a man has committed it. The attitude of defiance makes a minor sin major.

159. The Holy Prophet (may peace be upon him) was repeating it only to stress the gravity and enormity of these sins and he was uttering these words with such an agony of heart that his followers wished him to keep silent.

160. It is killing without sufficient cause and without having proved one's guilt and affording one an opportunity of defence that is counted as the grave offence. The Holy Qur'ān says:

And kill not the soul which Allah has made sacred except in the course of justice (vi. 152).

161. The Qur'ān says:

And let those beware who, should they leave behind them weakly offspring, would fear on their account. Let them, therefore, fear Allah, and utter right words.

Those who swallow the property of the orphans unjustly, they swallow only fire into their bellies. And they will burn into blazing fire (iv. 9-10).

162. *Ribā* (literally, an excess or addition) means an addition over and above the principal sum that is lent (Imām Rāghib) and includes usury as well as interest. In the Holy Qur'ān the *ribā* is discussed immediately after charity (see ii. 275, 276) which implies that both these things stand in striking contrast to each other. Charity is the broad basis of human sympathy, usury annihilates all tender feelings and leads to the extreme of miserliness.

turning back when the army advances, and slandering chaste women[163] who are believers, but unwary.

(162) It is narrated on the authority of 'Abdullah b. 'Amr b. al 'Āṣ that the Messenger of Allah (may peace be upon him) observed: Abusing one's parents is one of the major sins. They (the hearers) said: Messenger of Allah, does a man abuse his parents too? He (the Holy Prophet) replied: Yes, one abuses the father of another man, who in turn abuses his father. One abuses his mother and he in turn abuses his (the former's) mother.

(163) This ḥadīth has also been transmitted on the authority of Sa'd b. Ibrāhīm with this chain of narrators.

Chapter XL

FORBIDDENCE OF PRIDE

(164) It is narrated on the authority of 'Abdullah b. Mas'ūd that the Apostle of of Allah (may peace be upon him) observed: He who has in his heart the weight of a grain of mustard seed of pride[164] shall not enter Paradise. A person (amongst his hearers) said: Verily a person loves that his dress should be fine, and his shoes should be fine. He (the Holy Prophet) remarked: Verily, Allah is Graceful and He loves Grace.[165] Pride is disdaining the truth[166] (out of self-conceitedness) and contempt for the people.[167]

163. In the ḥadīth the words are المحصنات الغافلات. That they are so noble and simple that they know nothing about the indecent and obscene acts and they are so absorbed in their own work that they know nothing about mud-slinging of the mischief-mongers (*Fatḥ-ul-Mulḥim*).

164. Pride is the offspring of self-conceitedness, and this is the very negation of faith. Pride and faith cannot thus go together. Īmān inculcates in man the spirit of humility and submission to Truth. Pride is the expression of vanity which is one of the greatest hurdles in the path of truth. The self-conceited man accepts nothing which does not satisfy his vanity and, therefore, he cannot be a true believer. He is a worshipper of his "own self".

165 Islam does not teach asceticism and, therefore, does not blunt the aesthetic sense of man. It is with Beauty and Grace that the Lord has created this universe, and man, by his very nature, has a love for these two qualities. Islam makes no attempt to deprive man of his natural urges but canalises his aesthetic sense to fruitful channels. It exhorts its followers not to lead a life of renunciation but to use the bounties of the Lord according to His Command. There is no idea of the depravity of human nature in Islam, because man is not born with a stigma and his natural instincts are not the mainsprings of vices. They are primarily good in themselves provided they are satisfied in accordance with the commands of God.

166. The Holy Qur'ān has mentioned at numerous places that it is vanity and self-conceit which stand in the way of man in accepting the Truth, e.g. it was out of pride that Iblīs refused to obey the command of Allah (ii. 34).

> Is it then that whenever there came to you a messenger with what your souls desired not, you were arrogant? And some of you belied and some of you slew (ii. 87).
>
> Those who belie Our Signs and turn away from them in arrogance, the doors of Heaven will not be opened for them, nor will they enter the Garden, until the camel pass through the eye of the needle. And thus do We reward the guilty (vii. 40).

167. The vain and self-conceited persons not only belie the truth, but they even look down upon the people who have ties of human brotherhood with them. They consider themselves to be superior beings marked off from the rest of mankind. The Qur'ān says:

(165) It is narrated on the authority of 'Abdullah b. Mas'ūd that the Messenger of Allah (may peace be upon him) observed: None shall enter the Fire (of Hell) who has in his heart the weight of a grain of mustard seed of Imān and none shall enter Paradise who has in his heart the weight of a grain of mustard seed of pride.

(166) It is narrated on the authority of 'Abdullah that the Apostle of Allah (may peace be upon him) observed: He who has in his heart the weight of a grain of mustard seed of pride shall not enter Paradise.

Chapter XLI

HE WHO DIES ASSOCIATING NONE WITH ALLAH WOULD ENTER PARADISE AND HE WHO DIES AS A POLYTHEIST WOULD ENTER THE FIRE OF HELL

(167) It is narrated on the authority of 'Abdullah b. Mas'ūd that Wakī' told (him) that the Messenger of Allah had observed and Ibn Numair asserted: I heard the Messenger of Allah (may peace be upon him) saying: He who dies associating anything with Allah would enter the Fire (of Hell). 'Abdullah b. Mas'ūd said: I say that he who died without associating anything with Allah entered Paradise.

(168) It is narrated on the authority of Jābir that a man came to the Apostle of Allah (may peace be upon him) and said: Messenger of Allah, what are the two things quite unavoidable? He replied: He who dies without associating anyone with Allah would (necessarily) enter Paradise and he who dies associating anything with Allah would enter the (Fire of) Hell.

(169) It is narrated on the authority of Jābir b. 'Abdullah: I heard the Messenger of Allah (may peace be upon him) saying: He who met Allah without associating anything with Allah entered Paradise and he who met Him associating (anything) with Him entered Fire.

(170) The same ḥadīth has been narrated by Isḥāq b. Manṣūr on the authority of Jābir with another chain of transmitters.

(171) I heard Abū Dharr narrating it from the Apostle (may peace be upon him) that he observed: Gabriel came to me and gave me the tidings: Verily he who died amongst your Ummah without associating anything with Allah would enter Paradise. I (the narrator) said: Even if he committed adultery and theft. He (the Holy Prophet) said: (Yes), even if he committed adultery and theft.[168]

(172) Abū Dharr reported: I came to the Apostle (may peace be upon him) and he was asleep with a white mantle over him. I again came; he was still asleep. I came again and he had awakened. I sat by his side and (the Holy Prophet) observed: There

And turn not thy face away from people in contempt, nor go about in the land exultingly. Surely Allah loves not any self-conceited boaster (xxxi. 18).

168. This ḥadīth supports the viewpoint of the *Ahl-i-Sunnah* that, except *shirk* and *kufr*, no misdeed, however serious, dooms man to the eternal fire. It repudiates the claim of the Khwārij that serious offences make a man infidel and a permanent denizen of Hell.

is none among the bondsmen who affirmed his faith in *Lā ilāha ill-Allah* (there is no god but Allah) and died in this state and did not enter Paradise. I (Abū Dharr) said: Even if he committed adultery and theft? He (the Holy Prophet) replied: (Yes) even though he committed adultery and theft. I (again said): Even if he committed adultery[169] and theft? He replied: (Yes) even though he committed adultery and theft. (The Holy Prophet repeated it three times) and said for the fourth time: In defiance of Abū Dharr.[170] Abū Dharr then went out and he repeated (these words): In defiance[171] of Abū Dharr.

Chapter XLII

PROHIBITION OF THE KILLING OF AN INFIDEL AFTER HE SAYS: "THERE IS NO GOD BUT ALLAH"

(173) It is narrated on the authority of Miqdād b. Aswad that he said: Messenger of Allah, you just see (here is a point): If I encountered a person amongst the infidels (in the battlefield) and he attacked me and struck me and cut off one of my hands with the sword. Then he (in order to protect himself from me) took shelter of a tree and said: I become Muslim for Allah's sake. Messenger of Allah, can I kill him after he had uttered this? The Messenger of Allah (may peace be upon him) said: Do not kill him. I (the narrator) said: Messenger of Allah, he cut off my hand and uttered this after amputating it; should I then kill him? The Messenger of Allah (may peace be upon him) said: Don't kill him, for if you kill him, verily he would be in a position where you had been before killing him and verily you would be in a position where he had been before uttering (*kalima*).[172]

169. It should be noted that, according to the Islamic Sharī'ah, adultery is the violation of the right of Allah and theft is the infringement of the right of man. These are both serious offences in Islam and there is a punishment for these both in this world and in the Hereafter but these do not doom the offender to the eternal Hell.

170. Abū Dharr was a very pious Companion of the Holy Prophet and, therefore, he could not, by any stretch of imagination, conceive that a Muslim can ever commit such heinous crimes. Allah and His Apostle have, on several occasions, stressed their enormity and given grim note of warning to the Muslims with regard to them. The words of the Holy Prophet in this ḥadīth: "even though he committed adultery and theft," too clearly indicate that the Holy Prophet held them to be grave offences in Islam. The point which he wanted to stress was that, although these are very serious crimes, yet not so serious as polytheism and infidelity. Allah may pardon them after some punishment, but association with the Lord is an unpardonable crime and the man who commits it is doomed to Hell.

171. *Raghima anfuhū* (رغم انفه) is a phrase, meaning "may his nose cleave to the earth or dust". In idiomatic sense it means "may he be abased, humbled or rendered submissive against his will." In this ḥadīth the meanings of this phrase are quite clear. A pious man like Abū Dharr could hardly believe that an adulterer or a thief could ever be admitted to Paradise. The Holy Prophet was giving verdict against his inclination. It was at this juncture that the Messenger of Allah said: It is so, despite the will of Abū Dharr. In other words, Abū Dharr was made submissive against his will in this matter.

172. This part of the ḥadīth has been interpreted differently by different authorities but, according to Imām Nawawī, the most appropriate meaning is given by Imām Shāfi'ī and Ibn Qassar:

(174) The same ḥadīth has been transmitted by the same chain of narrators. The ḥadīth transmitted by Auzā'ī and Ibn Juraij contains these words: I embraced Islam for Allah's sake, and in the ḥadīth narrated by Ma'mar the words are: I knelt down to kill him, that he said: There is no god but Allah.

(175) It is narrated by Miqdād, and he was an ally of B. Zuhra and was one amongst those who participated in the Battle of Badr along with the Messenger of Allah, that he said: Messenger of Allah, here is a point: If I happened to encounter a person amongst the infidels (in the battle). Then he narrated a ḥadīth similar to the one transmitted by Laith.

(176) It is narrated on the authority of Usāma b. Zaid[173] that the Messenger of Allah (may peace be upon him) sent us in a raiding party. We raided Ḥuraqāt of Juhaina in the morning. I cought hold of a man and he said: There is no god but Allah. I attacked him with a spear. It once occurred to me and I talked about it to the Apostle (may peace be upon him). The Messenger of Allah (may peace be upon him) said: Did he profess "There is no god but Allah," and even then you killed him? I said: Messenger of Allah, he made a profession of it out of the fear of the weapon. He (the Holy Prophet) observed: Did you tear his heart in order to find out whether it had professed or not, and he went on repeating it to me till I wished if I had embraced Islam that day.[174] Sa'd said: By Allah, I would never kill any Muslim so long as a person with a heavy belly,[175] i.e. Usāma, would not kill. Upon this a person remarked: Did Allah not say this: And fight them until there is no more mischief[176] and religion is wholly for Allah? Sa'd said: We fought so that there should be no mischief, but you and your companions wish to fight so that there should be mischief.

When he made a profession of *Lā ilāha ill-Allah* and embraced Islam he became a Muslim like you and his life was protected, and when you killed him you came to his position and the protection was withdrawn.

The point stressed in the ḥadīth is that when a man makes a profession of Islam, he should be treated as a Muslim and we should not try to probe his intention, because Allah alone knows what is there in the mind of a man.

173. Usāma b. Zaid b. Ḥāritha al-Kalbī al-Hāshimī, Abū Muḥammad son of the Abyssinian freed woman Baraka Umm Aiman and reckoned among the Prophet's freed men, was born in Mecca in the fourth year of the Call. He, like his father, was very much loved by the Holy Prophet (may peace be upon him). He fought in Khaibar and rode back with the Prophet into Mecca and entered the Ka'ba with him. He fought gallantly at Ḥunain. Muḥammad (may peace be upon him) put him in command of an expedition to avenge his father Zaid fallen at Mu'tah, but the expedition was detained due to the Prophet's death. He was again sent by the first Caliph and came victoriously to Medina. Usāma is regarded as one of the authentic transmitters of Ḥadīth. At the fag end of his life, he lived in retirement first in Wādī al-Qura, then in Medina. He died at the age of fifty-four and was buried there.

174. The Holy Prophet was very much perturbed over the act of Usāma and he repeated it in order to make him realise the seriousness of his act. Usāma realised it and wished that he should have embraced Islam that day so that his act of high-handedness must have been effaced by his conversion to the faith.

175. Usāma was called ذوالبطين (Dhu al-Buṭain), because he had a big belly. *Buṭain* is a diminutive noun of *Baṭn* which has been used in the sense of exaggeration.

176. This is a Qur'ānic verse (ii. 193) in which the aim of fighting in Islam is determined. The Muslims have been exhorted to fight neither for imperialistic designs nor for personal glory but to eradicate mischief from human society.

(177) It is narrated on the authority of Usāma b. Zaid: The Messenger of Allah (may peace be upon him) sent us to Ḥuraqāt, a tribe of Juhaina. We attacked that tribe early in the morning and defeated them and I and a man from the Anṣār caught hold of a person (of the defeated tribe). When we overcame him, he said: There is no god but Allah. At that moment the Anṣārī spared him but I attacked him with my spear and killed him. The news had already reached the Apostle (peace be upon him), so when we came back he (the Apostle) said to me: Usāma, did you kill him after he had made the profession: There is no god but Allah? I said: Messenger of Allah, he did it only as a shelter. The Holy Prophet oberved: Did you kill him after he had made the profession that there is no god but Allah? He (the Holy Prophet) went on repeating this to me till I wished I had not embraced Islam before this day.

(178) It is narrated by Ṣafwān b. Muḥriz that Jundab b. 'Abdullah al-Bajalī during the stormy days of Ibn Zubair sent a message to 'As'as b. Salāma: Gather some men of your family so that I should talk to them. He ('As'as) sent a messenger to them (to the members of his family). When they had assembled, Jundab came there with a yellow hooded cloak [177] on him. He said: Talk what you were busy in talking. The talk went on by turns, till there came his (Jundab's) turn. He took off the hooded cloak from his head and said: I have come to you with no other intention but to narrate to you a ḥadīth of your Apostle: Verily the Messenger of Allah (may peace be upon him) sent a squad of the Muslims to a tribe of the polytheists. Both the armies confronted one another. There was a man among the army of polytheists who (was so dashing that), whenever he intended to kill a man from among the Muslims, he killed him. Amongst the Muslims too was a man looking forward to (an opportunity of) his (the polytheist's) unmindfulness. He (the narrator) said: We talked that he was Usāma b. Zaid. When he raised his sword, he (the soldier of the polytheists) uttered: "There is no god but Allah," but he (Usāma b. Zaid) killed him. When the messenger of the glad tidings came to the Apostle (may peace be upon him) he asked him (about the events of the battle) and he informed him about the man (Usāma) and what he had done. He (the Prophet of Allah) called for him and asked him why he had killed him. He (Usāma) said: Messenger of Allah, he struck the Muslims and killed such and such of them. And he even named some of them. (He continued:) I attacked him and when he saw the sword he said: There is no god but Allah. The Messenger of Allah (may peace be upon him) said: Did you kill him? He (Usāma) replied in the affirmative. He (the Holy Prophet) remarked: What would you do with: "There is no god but Allah," when he would come (before you) on the Day of Judgment? He (Usāma) said: Messenger of Allah, beg pardon for me (from your Lord). He (the Holy Prophet) said: What would you do with: "There is no god but Allah" when he would come (before you) on the Day of Judgment? He (the Holy Prophet) added nothing to it but kept saying: What would you do with: "There is no god but Allah," when he would come (before you) on the Day of Judgment? [178]

177. برنس (*burnus*) is a long cap which the devotees used to wear in the early period of Islam. According to some authorities, it stands for any garment of which the headgear forms a part, being joined to it. It is applied in the present day to a hooded cloak mostly of white woollen stuff.

178. The ḥadīth has an object lesson for the Muslims how they should behave during the stormy days when there is dissension among the believers and they are out to strike the necks of one

Chapter XLIII

THE UTTERANCE OF THE APOSTLE (MAY PEACE BE UPON HIM): HE WHO TAKES UP ARMS AGAINST US IS NOT OF US (I.E. HE CEASES TO BE A MUSLIM)

(179) It is narrated on the authority of 'Abdullah b. 'Umar who narrates from the Prophet of Allah (may peace be upon him) who said: He who took up arms against us is not of us.

(180) Iyās b. Salama narrated from his father that the Apostle (may peace be upon him) observed: He who draws the sword against us is not of us.

(181) It is narrated on the authority of Abū Mūsā Ash'arī[179]: He who took up arms against us is not of us.

Chapter XLIV

THE UTTERANCE OF THE APOSTLE (PEACE BE UPON HIM): HE WHO ACTED DISHONESTLY TOWARDS US IS NOT OF US (I.E. HE IS NOT TO BE COUNTED AMONGST MUSLIMS)

(182) It is narrated on the authority of Abū Huraira that the Messenger of Allah (may peace be upon him) observed: He who took up arms against us is not of us and he who acted dishonestly towards us is not of us.

(183) It is narrated on the authority of Abū Huraira that the Messenger of Allah (may peace be upon him) happened to pass by a heap of eatables (corn). He thrust his hand in that (heap) and his fingers were moistened. He said to the owner of that heap of eatables (corn): What is this? He replied: Messenger of Allah, these have been drenched by rainfall. He (the Holy Prophet) remarked: Why did you not place this (the drenched part of the heap) over other eatables so that the people could see it? He who deceives is not of me (is not my follower).

another. We have been taught that they should, during these days, desist from doing harm to the other believers because killing of a Muslim is a grave offence in the sight of Allah.

179. His name was 'Abdullah; Abū Mūsā was his *kunya*. He was the son of Qais, son of Sālim. He belonged to Ash'ar, one of the famous tribes of Yemen. He embraced Islam along with other members of his tribe and set out for Medina by sea. Accidentally, there was a gale which drifted their boats to the Abyssinian shore. There they found the company of Ja'far and other Muslims who had migrated to this place on account of the atrocities of the haughty Meccans. When the Holy Prophet migrated to Medina, Ja'far and other Muslims set forth to join him in the new city. Abū Mūsā also accompanied them. The caravan reached there at the time when the Muslim army was coming victoriously from Khaibar. Abū Mūsā took part in the Battle of Ḥunain. He was also sent to the Yemen with Mu'ādh b. Jabal to spread Islam there. 'Umar (may Allah be pleased with him) appointed him Governor of Baṣrah, when he recalled Mughīra b. Shu'ba from that post in 17 H.

As Governor of Baṣrah, Abū Mūsā organised and carried out the occupation of Khuhistan of which he must be considered as the conqueror. He also took part in the conquest of Mesopotamia. Abū Mūsā was one of the arbitrators appointed at Ṣiffīn in 37 H. to settle the dispute between 'Alī and Mu'āwiya (may Allah be pleased with them). Abū Mūsā was highly thought of for his recitation and understanding of the Qur'ān and his deep insight into the Ḥadīth. He was one of the devoted Companions of the Holy Prophet and an enthusiastic preacher of Islam. He died in 44 H. at Mecca.

Chapter XLV

BEATING OF THE CHEEKS, TEARING OF THE FRONT OPENING OF THE SHIRT, AND CALLING THE CALLS OP THE JĀHILIYA (IGNORANCE) ARE FORBIDDEN

(184) It is narrated on the authority of ʻAbdullah b. Masʻūd that the Holy Prophet observed: He is not one of us (one among the Ummah of Islam) who beat the cheeks or tore the front opening of the shirt or uttered the slogans of (the days of) Jāhiliya (ignorance).[180] Ibn Numair and Abū Bakr said (instead of the word أَوْ or it is و [and] the words are) and tore and uttered (the slogans) of Jāhiliya without "alīf".

(185) This ḥadīth has been narrated by Aʻmash with the same chain of narrators and the transmittors said: He tore and called.

(186) It is narrated on the authority of Abū Burda b. Abū Mūsā that Abū Mūsā was afflicted with grave pain and he became unconscious and his head was in the lap of a lady of his household. One of the women of his household wailed. He (Abū Mūsā) was unable (because of weakness) to say anything to her. But when he was a bit recovered he said: I have no concern with one with whom the Messenger of Allah (may peace be upon him) had no concern. Verily the Messenger of Allah (may peace be upon him) has no concern with that woman who wails loudly, shaves her hair and tears (her garment in grief).

(187) It is narrated on the authority of Abū Burda that Abū Mūsā fell unconscious and his wife Umm ʻAbdullah came there and wailed loudly. When he felt relief he said: Don't you know?—and narrated to her: Verily the Messenger of Allah (may peace be upon him) said: I have no concern with one who shaved her hair, lamented loudly and tore (her clothes in grief).

(188) This ḥadīth is narrated on the authority of Abū Mūsā with this change only: That (the Holy Prophet) did not say that he had no concern but said: He is not one of us.

Chapter XLVI

SERIOUS PROHIBITION OF TALE-CARRYING

(189) It is reported from Ḥudhaifa that news reached him (the Holy Prophet) that a certain man carried tales. Upon this Ḥudhaifa remarked: I heard Allah's Messenger (may peace be upon him) saying: The tale-bearer[181] shall not enter Paradise.

180. Beating of the cheeks, tearing of the front opening of the shirt and uttering loudly the words of Jāhiliya were common features of the pre-Islamic Arabs. Whenever anyone among them died, they wailed and lamented in a boisterous manner. Islam has exhorted its followers to be moderate in grief. It should be noted that it is not weeping which is forbidden, but wailing and fulsome laudation has been prohibited.

181. The verb is نم (namma) which means "he betrayed, bespoke, he reported in a libelous manner". It also means "he embellished his speech with falsehold." نم الحديث would, therefore signify: he divulged, or made known in a malicious or mischievous manner so as to occasion discord, dissension or the like. The noun نميمة (namīma) (pl. نمائم = namā'im) means: slander, defamation, calumny, malicious and mischievous misrepresentation.

(190) It is reported on the authority of Hammām b. al-Ḥārith that a man used to carry tales to the governor. We were sitting in the mosque. The people said : He is one who carries tales to the governor. He (the narrator) said : Then he came and sat with us. Thereupon Ḥudhaifa remarked : I heard the Messenger of Allah (may peace be upon him) saying : The bearer of false tales would never enter heaven.[182]

(191) It is narrated on the authority of Hammām b. al-Ḥārith : We were sitting with Ḥudhaifa in the mosque. A man came and sat along with us. It was said to Ḥudhaifa that he was the man who carried tales to the ruler. Ḥudhaifa remarked with the intention of conveying to him : I have heard the Messenger of Allah (may peace be upon him) saying : The tale-bearer will not enter Paradise.

Chapter XLVII

SERIOUS PROHIBITION OF LETTING DOWN THE LOWER GARMENT, OF LAYING OBLIGATION, OF SELLING GOODS BY FALSE OATHS, AND DESCRIPTION OF THOSE THREE (PERSONS) WITH WHOM ALLAH WOULD NOT SPEAK ON THE DAY OF RESURRECTION, NOR WOULD HE SEE TOWARDS THEM NOR WOULD ABSOLVE THEM, AND FOR THEM IS A PAINFUL CHASTISEMENT

(192) It is narrated on the authority of Abū Dharr that the Messenger of Allah (may peace be upon him) observed : Three are the (persons) with whom Allah would neither speak on the Day of Resurrection, nor would look[183] at them nor would absolve[184] them, and there is a painful chastisement for them. The Messenger of Allah (may peace be upon him) repeated[185] it threc times. Abū Dharr remarked : They failed and they lost ; who are these persons, Messenger of Allah ? Upon this he (the Holy

182. Imām Nawawī has made it clear that carrying of tales is a grave sin in Islam, especially when it is done with a view to sowing dissension and discord amongst the different persons or group of persons. But in cases where informing is justified from the moral point of view it is essential and there is a great reward for it in the heaven. For example, if a man commits murder or rape and another man knows it, it is his moral duty to inform the authorities about the culprit, or if a man becomes the victim of high-handedness of a tyrant, he has every right to report to the governor of the harm done to him. Moreover, when a man finds that if correct information is not given to one who needs it, one may suffer loss, then it is the bounden duty of a man that he should faithfully appraise him of the situation and should withhold nothing from him. For example, a man intends to marry his daughter to another man and he asks about his conduct and behaviour from his friends and relatives ; in that case it becomes the moral obligation of these persons to give him the right information and hold nothing secret.

183. Look with an eye of mercy.

184. Would purify them of sins and send them to Paradise.

185. It refers to the following verse of the Holy Qur'ān :

Those who take a small price for the Covenant of Allah and their own oaths—they have no portion in the Hereafter, and Allah will not speak to them, nor will He look upon them on the Day ef Resurrection, nor will He purify them, and for them is a painful chastisement (iii. 76).

Prophet) observed : They are : the dragger of lower garment,[186] the recounter[187] of obligation, the seller of goods by false oath.

(193) It is narrated on the authority of Abū Dharr who narrates that the Prophet (may peace be upon him) observed : Three are the persons with whom Allah would not speak on the Day of Resurrection : the bestower of gift who does not give anything but by laying obligation on him, the seller of goods who sells them by taking false oath and one who hangs low his lower garment.

(194) Bishr b. Khālid has narrated this ḥadīth on the authority of Sulaimān with the same chain of transmitters with this addition : Allah shall neither speak nor look at nor absolve them, and there is a tormenting punishment for them.

(195) It is narrated on the authority of Abū Huraira that the Messenger of Allah (may peace be upon him) observed : Three (are the persons) with whom Allah would neither speak, nor would He absolve them on the Day of Resurrection. Abū Mu'āwiya added : He would not look at them and there is grievous torment for them : the aged adulterer, the liar king and the proud destitute.[188]

(196) Abū Huraira narrated on the authority of Abū Bakr that the Messenger of Allah (may peace be upon him) said : Three are the persons with whom Allah would neither speak on the Day of Resurrection, nor would He look towards them, nor would purify them (from sins), and there would be tormenting chastisement for them : a person who in the waterless desert has more water (than his need) and he refuses[189] to give it to the traveller and a person who sold a commodity to another person in the afternoon[190] and took an oath of Allah that he had bought it at such and such price and he (the buyer) accepted it to be true though it was not a fact, and a person who pledged allegiance to the Imām but for the sake of the world (material gains). And if the Imām bestowed on him (something) out of that (worldly riches) he stood by his

186. It is a sign of pride that people go about with their lower garment dragging on the earth. It should, however, be borne in mind that if one is obliged to do so, not actuated by pride and vanity, but due to other circumstances, e g. a heavy belly, there is no punishment for him.

187. It is a grave sin in Islam to lay obligations on those whom you have shown some favour and they are obliged to you :

O ye who believe ! make not your alms void by laying an obligation and by hurt (Qur'ān, ii. 264).

188. Adultery, telling of lies, pride and vanity are in themselves grave sins in Islam, but when these are committed by the above-mentioned persons, their enormity is enhanced. Qāḍī 'Iyāḍ is of the opinion that the committing of these sins by these persons reflects the attitude of denial of the teachings of Islam because they are in no way compelled to do so. The aged man is mature and his sexual lust is considerably abated. The king is a master and he is under no duress to tell lies and the destitute has nothing with him on which he can boast and take pride. It is by sheer arrogance or the love of committing offence for the sake of offence or the moral depravity of man and, above all, disregard of Allah which make a man so daring as to commit such heinous crimes.

189. According to Imām Nawawī, it is a serious offence and the person who commits it is devoid of all tenderly feelings. Not to talk of human beings it is a grave sin to withhold water even from the animals and the beasts. This type of selfishness reflects the callousness of a person who is completely deprived of mercy and fellow feeling.

190. The time of afternoon, according to Imām Nawawī, is a sacred time when the angels meet together.

allegiance and if he did not give him, he did not fulfil the allegiance.[191]

(197) The same ḥadīth has been transmitted by another chain of transmitters with the exception of these words : He offered for sale a commodity to another person.

(198) This ḥadīth has been narrated on the authority of Abū Huraira that he (the Apostle of Allah) observed : Three are the persons with whom Allah would neither speak (on the Day of Resurrection), nor would He look at them, and there would be a painful chastisement for them : a person who took an oath on the goods of a Muslim in the afternoon and then broke it. The rest of the ḥadīth is the same as narrated by A'mash.

Chapter XLVIII

SUICIDE IS THE GRAVEST SIN

(199) It is narrated on the authority of Abū Huraira that the Messenger of Allah (may peace be upon him) observed: He who killed himself with steel (weapon) would be the eternal denizen of the Fire of Hell and he would have that weapon in his hand and would be thrusting that in his stomach for ever and ever; he who drank poison and killed himself would sip that in the Fire of Hell where he is doomed for ever and ever; and he who killed himself by falling from (the top of) a mountain would constantly fall in the Fire of Hell and would live there for ever and ever.[192]

(200) This ḥadīth has been transmitted by another chain of transmitters.

(201) Thābit b. Ḍaḥḥāk reported that he pledged allegiance to the Messenger of Allah (may peace be upon him) under the Tree,[193] and verily the Messenger of Allah (may peace be upon him) observed: He who took an oath of a religion other than Islam,[194] in the state of being a liar,[195] would become so, as he professed. He who killed himself with a thing would be tormented on the Day of Resurrection with that very thing. One is not obliged to offer votive offering of a thing which is not in his possession.

(202) It is narrated on the authority of Thābit b. al-Ḍaḥḥāk[196] that the Apostle of

191. Such a person who pledges allegiance for the sake of worldly riches is completely deprived of religious sense, which stands for selflessness and spirit of sacrifice for the sake of Allah. A person who exploits spiritual allegiance for gaining worldly aims is bereft of God-consciousness and religious piety.

192. Suicide is one of the gravest sins in Islam because it is a flagrant breach of Allah's trust. The life of a person is a sacred trust of Allah and man has no right to do any harm to it or destroy it. His duty is to use it according to His Command and Will. The man who commits suicide usurps the right of Allah and betrays His Trust.

193. It refers to Bai'at-i-Riḍwān.

194. If he should take an oath like this : I shall be a Christian, or a Jew, or a Hindu, if I do this or that, etc.

195. Oath is generally taken of a thing which is held in high esteem by a person who takes an oath. In this case it means that he holds other religions far superior to Islam. This is a sheer falsehood and if a man in the heart of his hearts does not hold them so but only makes a public profession of it in order to befool people, he is a liar (see *Fatḥ-ul-Mulhim*, Vol. I, p. 266).

196. His name was Thābit and his *kunya* was Abū Zaid. He belonged to the tribe of Ish-hal. He was born in the third year of the Prophet's Call. The first battle in which he participated was that of

Allah (may peace be upon him) observes: None is obliged to give votive offering (of a thing) which is not in his possession, and the cursing of a believer is tantamount to killing him, and he who killed himself with a thing in this world would be tormented with that (very thing) on the Day of Resurrection, and he who made a false claim to increase (his wealth), Allah would make no addition but that of paucity, and he who perjured would earn the wrath of God.

(203) It is narrated on the authority of Thabit b. Ḍaḥḥāk that the Apostle of Allah (may peace be upon him) observed: He who took deliberately a false oath on a religion other than Islam would become that which he had professed. And he who killed himself with anything Allah would torment him with that in the Fire of Hell.

(204) In the ḥadīth narrated by Shu'ba the words are: Verily the Messenger of Allah (may peace be upon him) said: He who took an oath on a religion other than Islam as a liar would become so as he said, and he who slaughtered himself with a thing would be slaughtered with that on the Day of Resurrection.

(205) It is narrated on the authority of Abū Huraira: We participated in the Battle of Ḥunain along with the Messenger of Allah (may peace be upon him). He (the Holy Prophet) said about a man who claimed to be a Muslim that he was one of the denizens of the Fire (of Hell). When we were in the thick of the battle that man fought desperately and was wounded. It was said: Messenger of Allah, the person whom you at first called as the denizen of Fire fought desperately and died. Upon this the Apostle of Allah (may peace be upon him) remarked: He was doomed to the Fire (of Hell). Some men were on the verge of doubt[197] (about his fate) when it was said that he was not dead but fatally wounded. When it was night he could not stand the (pain of his) wound and killed himself. The Apostle (may peace be upon him) was informed of that. He (the Holy Prophet) observed: Allah is Great, I bear testimony to the fact that I am the servant of Allah and His messenger.[198] He then commanded Bilāl to anounce to the people that

Khandaq. He settled in Syria after the death of the Holy Prophet and stayed there till he died in 64 H. during the caliphate of 'Abullah b. Zubair. He was survived by a son whose name was Zaid. Fourteen aḥādīth have been transmitted on his authority.

197. They were not harbouring doubts in their minds about the truth of the Prophet's statement. They could not at that moment reconcile to themselves what they saw in the battlefield and what was said about him by the Messenger of Allah. The position was soon clarified on receiving the information of his suicide and their doubts were changed into implicit faith.

This ḥadīth also throws a good deal of light on the nature of the prophetic verdict. The utterances and the verdicts of the Prophet are above doubt as these are inspired by Allah. There is no haziness about them. That is why whatever messengers of Allah say, they say with perfect confidence.

198. The utterance of these words at this juncture is very significant. The Holy Prophet had given information on the basis of knowledge which he had received from Allah. This is the function of the Apostle that he informs us about those facts which are hidden from the view of men and which are beyond the realm of their knowledge. Their minds, however penetrative, and their intellects, however keen, cannot by their own efforts comprehend these Great Realities of the Unseen. It is meaningful to note that on this occasion when the Holy Prophet had made prophecies which came to be perfectly true to the amazement of the people, he did not try to glorify himself, but said the same thing which is a fundamental fact in Islam: that it is not his personal achievement but the favour of Allah, as he is His messenger. Then in order to safeguard that people might not, at this amazing information, take the Holy Prophet to be the demigod, he first stressed that he was the servant of Allah and then emphasised his apostleship.

none but a Muslim would enter Paradise. Verily Allah helps this faith even by a sinful person.

(206) It is reported on the authority of Sahl b. Sa'd al-Sā'idī that there was an encounter between the Messenger of Allah (may peace be upon him) and the polytheists, and they fought (against one another). At the conclusion of the battle the Messenger of Allah (may peace be upon him) bent his steps towards his army and they (the enemies) bent their steps towards their army. And there was a person (his name was Quzmān and he was one among the hypocrites) among the Companions of the Messenger of Allah (may peace be upon him) who did not spare a detached (fighter of the enemy) but pursued and killed him with the sword. They (the Companions of the Holy Prophet) said: None served us better today than this man. Upon this the Messenger of Allah (may peace be upon him) remarked: Verily he is one among the denizens of Fire. One among the people (Muslims) said: I will constantly shadow him. Then this man went out along with him. He halted whenever he halted, and ran along with him whenever he ran. He (the narrator) said: The man was seriously injured. He (could not stand the pain) and hastened his own death. He placed the blade of the sword on the ground with the tip between his chest and then pressed himself against the sword and killed himself. Then the man (following him) went to the Messenger of Allah (may peace be upon him) and said: I bear testimony that verily thou art the Messenger of Allah. He (the Holy Prophet) said: What is the matter? He replied: The person about whom you just mentioned that he was one among the denizens of Fire and the people were surprised (at this) and I said to them that I would bring (the news about him) and consequently I went out in search of him till I (found him) to be very seriously injured. He hastened his death. He placed the blade of the sword upon the ground and its tip between his chest and then pressed himself against that and killed himself. Thereupon the Messenger of Allah (may peace be upon him) remarked: A person performs the deeds which to the people appear to be the deeds befitting the dweller of Paradise, but he is in fact one among the denizens of Hell. And verily a person does an act which in the eyes of public is one which is done by the denizens of Hell, but the person is one among the dwellers of Paradise.[199]

(207) It is reported on the authority of Ḥasan: A person belonging to the people of the past suffered from a boil; when it pained him, he drew out an arrow from the quiver and pierced it.[200] And the bleeding did not stop till he died. Your Lord said: I forbade his entrance into the Paradise. Then he (Ḥasan) stretched his hand towards the mosque and said: By God, Jundab transmitted this ḥadīth to me from the Messenger of Allah (may peace be upon him) in this very mosque.

(208) It is reported on the authority of Ḥasan: Jundab b. 'Abdullah al-Bajalī narrated this hadīth in this mosque which we can neither forget and at the same time

199. This ḥadīth is clearly indicative of the fact that Īmān is something which concerns the heart of man. An action, however good but not actuated by a sincere heart, has no value in Islam. Similarly, an act which to a superficial observer seems to be an ordinary deed may be highly valued in Islam for its being rooted in sincerity and motivated by an unalloyed Love for Allah.

200. Maulānā Shabbīr Aḥmad 'Uthmānī has made it clear that it is not surgical operation which is forbidden in Islam, but a deliberate piercing of the wound with the intention of committing suicide (*Fatḥ-ul-Mulḥim*, Vol. I, p. 286).

we have no apprehension that Jundab could attribute a lie[201] to the Messenger of Allah (may peace be upon him). He (the Holy Prophet) observed : A person belonging to the people of the past suffered from a boil, and then the rest of the ḥadīth was narrated.

Chapter XLIX

STRICT FORBIDDANCE OF ACTING UNFAITHFULLY IN RELATION TO THE SPOILS OR BOOTY. THE BELIEVERS ALONE WOULD ENTER PARADISE

(209) It is narrated on the authority of 'Umar b. Khaṭṭāb that when it was the day of Khaybar a party of Companions of the Apostle (may peace be upon him) came there and said : So and so is a martyr,[202] till they happened to pass by a man and said: So and so is a martyr. Upon this the Messenger of Allah remarked: Nay, not so,[203] verily I have seen him in the Fire for the garment or cloak that he had stolen from the booty.[204] Then the Messenger of Allah (may peace be upon him) said : 'Umar son of Khaṭṭāb, go and announce to the people that none but the believers would enter Paradise. He ('Umar b. Khaṭṭāb) narrated : I went out and proclaimed : Verily none but the believers would enter Paradise.[205]

(210) It is narrated on the authority of Abū Huraira : We went to Khaybar along with the Apostle (may peace be upon him) and Allah granted us victory. We plundered neither gold nor silver but lay our hands on goods, corn and clothes, and then bent

201. Maulānā Shabbīr Aḥmad observes : This statement reveals the fact that the Companions of the Holy Prophet (may peace be upon him) were truthful, just and honest and were especially careful and cautious about attributing anything to the Holy Prophet.

202. The Arabic word used for martyr is Shahīd which literally means one who gives testimony or bears witness. So Shahīd in Islam is one who gives testimony to the truth of Islam even at the cost of his life. It means that that man gives an unshakable proof of his fidelity to Islam and, by sacrificing his life, proves that there is nothing more precious and dear to him than the faith of Allah.

203. The above discussion makes it clear that martyrdom is closely connected with sincere devotion to Islam and it is achieved when the intention is purely the love of Allah. Sincerity of purpose is something which is hidden from the view of men. God alone knows the true motive of a man. It is, therefore, forbidden to say definitely about a person that he is a martyr and is surely entitled to Paradise. The Muslims should make simple claims relying upon the outward behaviour of man, and should refrain from saying anything with perfect certainty.

204. The Muslims were calling that man to be a Shahīd but it was revealed to the Apostle of Allah that he was not so, because he had not fought the battle for the Glory of Allah, but for the spoils of war and, therefore, he acted treacherously in regard to them.

205. Apparently, the second part of the ḥadīth seems to have little connection with the first part. But a little penetration would reveal that there is a meaningful relation between the two. We have been told that only the believers would enter Paradise which implies that only those persons would be admitted to Paradise who sincerely and faithfully, without having any worldly end before them, believe in Allah and stand for Islam and then struggle for its cause. And those who claim themselves to be Muslims but who have other motives before them are not entitled to Paradise, because Islam is an unalloyed, single-minded devotion to Allah and His Prophet (may peace be upon him).

our steps to a valley; along with the Messenger of Allah (may peace be upon him) there was a slave who was presented to him by one Rifā'a b. Zaid of the family of Judhām, a tribe of Ḍubayb. When we got down into the valley the slave of the Messenger of Allah stood up and began to unpack the saddle-bag and was suddenly struck by a (stray) arrow which proved fatal. We said: There is a greeting for him, Messenger of Allah, as he is a martyr. Upon this the Messenger of Allah (may peace be upon him) remarked: Nay, not so. By Him in Whose hand is the life of Muḥammad, the small garment which he stole from the booty on the day of Khaybar but which did not (legitimately) fall to his lot is burning like the Fire (of hell) on him. The people were greatly perturbed (on hearing this). A person came there with a lace or two laces and said: Messenger of Allah, I found (them) on the day of Khaybar. He (the Holy Prophet) remarked: This is a lace of fire or two laces of fire.

Chapter L

ARGUMENT IN FAVOUR OF THE FACT THAT HE WHO KILLS HIMSELF DOES NOT BECOME UNBELIEVER

(211) It is narrated on the authority of Jābir that Ṭufail son of 'Amr al-Dausī[206] came to the Apostle (may peace be upon him) and said: Do you need strong, fortified protection? The tribe of Daus had a fort in the pre-Islamic days. The Apostle (may peace be upon him) declined this offer since it (the privilege of protecting the Holy Prophet) had already been reserved for the Anṣār.[207] When the Apostle (may peace be upon him) migrated to Medina, Ṭufail son of 'Amr also migrated to that place, and there also migrated along with him a man of his tribe. But the climate of Medina did not suit him, and he fell sick. He felt very uneasy. So he took hold of an iron head of an arrow and cut his finger-joints. The blood streamed forth from his hands, till he died. Ṭufail son of 'Amr saw him in the dream. His state was good and he saw him with his hands wrapped. He (Ṭufail) said to him: What treatment did your Allah accord to you? He replied: Allah granted me pardon for my migration to the Apostle[208] (may peace be

206. He embraced Islam at Mecca and then migrated to Medina and stayed there till the Prophet died. He fell a martyr at the Battle of Yamāma. He was counted as an eminent scholar of Ḥijāz. Jābir and Abū Huraira have narrated Aḥadīth on his authority.

207. Allah had entrusted the responsibility of protecting the life of the Prophet to the people of Anṣār.

208. Nawawī is of the view that this ḥadīth substantiates the belief of the Ahl-i-Sunnah that a believer does not become infidel how grave his sin may be. Moreover, this ḥadīth sheds a good deal of light on the fact that the sinners would be punished for their sins and it repudiates the claim of the Murji'a that no one with faith would be given any punishment in the next life. There is also a possibility that the man did not intend to kill himself. He might have done it in spite of himself under the effect of unbearable pain and affliction. This ḥadīth brings into light the great value of the act of migration for the sake of Islam.

A close analysis of this ḥadīth would reveal that it is an act of sin to effect any change in the healthy limbs of the body and thus hinder their normal working. The operation of both the male and the female for the sake of birth control can be held a condemnable and sinful act on the basis of this ḥadīth. The Companion of the Holy Prophet cut his joints for the unbearable physical pain. The operation for birth control is conducted for the fear and pain of poverty.

upon him). He (Ṭufail) again said : What is this that I see you wrapping up your hands? He replied : I was told (by Allah) : We would not set right anything of yours which you damaged yourself. Ṭufail narrated this (dream) to the Messenger of Allah (may peace be upon him). Upon this he prayed : O Allah ! grant pardon even to his hands.

Chapter LI

CONCERNING THE WIND WHICH WOULD BLOW NEAR THE DAY OF RESURRECTION AND WOULD CAUSE TO DIE ANYONE HAVING ANYTHING LIKE FAITH IN HIS HEART

(212) It is narrated on the authority of Abū Huraira that the Messenger of Allah (may peace be upon him) said : Verily Allah would make a wind to blow from the side of Yemen more delicate than silk and would spare none but cause him to die who, in the words of Abū 'Alqama, has faith equal to the weight of a grain ; while 'Abdul-'Azīz said : having faith equal to the weight of a dusṭ particle.[209]

Chapter LII

EXHORTATION TO BE PROMPT IN DOING GOOD DEEDS BEFORE THE APPEARANCE OF TURBULANCE

(213) It is narrated on the authority of Abū Huraira that the Messenger of Allah (may peace be upon him) observed : Be prompt in doing good deeds (before you are overtaken) by turbulance which would be like a part of the dark night. During (that stormy period) a man would be a Muslim in the morning and an unbeliever in the evening, or he would be a believer in the evening and an unbeliever in the morning, and would sell his faith for worldly goods.[210]

Chapter LIII

PERTAINING TO THE FEAR OF A BELIEVER LEST HIS DEEDS SHOULD BE LOST

(214) It is narrated on the authority of Anas b. Mālik that when this verse : "O ye who believe ! raise not your voices above the voice of the Prophet, nor shout loud unto

209. The world shall not come to an end so long as there is a grain of religious piety, truthfulness, belief in one God and an earnest desire to follow the footsteps of the Holy Prophet. But when these qualities are absolutely banished from the human race, its very existence would become useless and Allah would exterminate them from the world. It is the belief in Allah alone that makes human life meaningful but when this belief is lost, then there is no use to keep human beings on the earth, for without belief the man becomes a veritable brute.

210. There would be no stability in the faith of man. Faith would become cheaper as compared to the material benefits and would be freely bartered for worldly gains.

him in discourse, as ye shout loud unto one another, lest your deeds should become null, while you perceive not" (xlix. 2-5), was revealed Thābit b. Qais confined himself in his house and said : I am one among the denizens of Fire and he deliberately avoided coming to the Apostle (may peace be upou him). The Apostle (may peace be upon him) asked Sa'd b. Mu'ādh about him and said : Abū 'Amr, how is Thābit ? Has he fallen sick ? Sa'd said : He is my neighbour but I do not know of his illness. Sa'd came to him (Thābit) and conveyed to him the message of the Messenger of Allah (may peace be upon him). Upon this Thābit said : This verse was revealed, and you are well aware of the fact that, amongst all of you, mine is the voice louder than that of the Messenger of Allah, and so I am one amongst the denizens of Fire. Sa'd informed the Holy Prophet about it. Upon this the Messenger of Allah observed : (Nay, not so) but he (Thābit) is one among the dwellers of Paradise.[211]

(215) This ḥadīth has been narrated on the authority of Anas b. Mālik by another chain of transmitters in which these words are found : Thābit b. Qais was the orator of the Anṣār, when this verse was revealed : the rest of the ḥadīth is the same with the exception that there is no mention of Sa'd b. Mu'ādh in it. This ḥadīth is also transmitted by Aḥmad b. Sa'īd, Ḥabbān, Sulaimān b. Mughīra on the authority of Anas who said : When the verse was revealed : "Do not raise your voice louder than the voice of the Apostle," no mention was made of Sa'd b. Mu'ādh in it.

(216) This ḥadīth is narrated on the authority of Anas by another chain of transmitters in which there is no mention of Sa'd b. Mu'ādh, but these words are there : We observed a man, one among the dwellers of Paradise, walking about amongst us.

Chapter LIV

WOULD (PEOPLE) BE HELD RESPONSIBLE FOR THE DEEDS COMMITTED DURING THE STATE OF IGNORANCE?

(217) It is narrated on the authority of 'Abdullah b. Mas'ūd that some people said to the Messenger of Allah (may peace be upon him) : Messenger of Allah, would we be held responsible for our deeds committed in the state of ignorance (before embracing Islam) ? Upon this he (the Holy Prophet) remarked : He who amongst you performed good deeds in Islam, he would not be held responsible for them (misdeeds which he committed in ignorance) and he who committed evil[212] (even after embracing Islam) would be held responsible for his misdeeds that he committed in the state of ignorance

211. This ḥadīth is indicative of the fact that naturally heavy and loud voice is no sin. What is prohibited is that one should try to drown the voice of the Prophet by deliberately talking louder than him. It may be out of impertinence or the desire to become prominent or to carry one's point by demonstrating the strength of one's vocal chords. All these motives are enough to nullify the deeds of a Muslim, because the Prophet is to be obeyed and not led and dictated. Good manners demand that one should not speak loudly in the presence of one's superiors.

212. The two phrases من احسن فى الاسلام and من آساء فى الاسلام have been explained by Maulānā Shabbīr Aḥmad in the following words : ‹‹من احسن فى الاسلام›› means : He accepted Islam truly. There is no dissemblance or doubt in it. من آساء فى الاسلام signifies : He professed Islam as a hypocrite (*Fatḥ-al-Mulḥim*, Vol. I, p. 271).

as well as in that of Islam.[213]

(218) It is narrated on the authority of 'Abdullah b. Mas'ūd: We once said: Messenger of Allah, would we be held responsible for our deeds committed in the state of ignorance? He (the Holy Prophet) observed: He who did good deeds in Islam would not be held responsible for what he did in the state of ignorance, but he who committed evil (after having come within the fold of Islam) would be held responsible for his previous and later deeds.

(219) This ḥadīth has been transmitted by Minjāb b. al-Ḥārith Tamīmī with the same chain of transmitters.

Chapter LV

ISLAM EFFACES ALL THE PREVIOUS MISDEEDS AND SO DO MIGRATION AND PILGRIMAGE

(220) It is narrated on the authority of Ibn Shamāsa Mahrī that he said: We went to 'Amr b. al-'Āṣ[214] and he was about to die. He wept for a long time and turned his face towards the wall. His son[215] said: Did the Messenger of Allah (may peace be upon him) not give you tidings of this? Did the Messenger of Allah (may peace be upon him) not give you tidings of this? He (the narrator) said: He turned his face (towards the audience) and said: The best thing which we can count upon is the testimony that there is no god but Allah and that Muḥammad is the Apostle of Allah. Verily I have passed through three phases. (The first one) in which I found myself averse to none else more than I was averse to the Messenger of Allah (may peace be upon him) and there

213. This ḥadīth is highly meaningful and throws a good deal of light on the attitude of Islam towards good and evil. Islam is not a mere expression of a few words but a complete submission of one's life to Allah. It is a wholehearted change, both in thought and deed. Now if a man makes a profession of Islam but he brings about no change in his life, it means that he has not accepted Islam in the heart of his hearts. Faith is not something inert; it is dynamic in the sense that it revolutionises the whole life of a man. If one accepts Islam and then leads a virtuous and pious life in accordance with its teachings, all his previous misdeeds would be wiped off as he has proved that he sincerely wants a healthy change in his life and is prepared to put earnest efforts for his moral uplift. But if a man persists in the path of evil which he was treading before Islam, he shows his attachment to evil. He is, therefore, in no way entitled to any remission. This ḥadīth is an elucidation of the well-known verse of the Qur'ān: "Verily virtues wipe off vices" (xi. 114). The stand taken by Islam in regard to evil presents a striking contrast to all those religions which believe that an evil act once committed is like a fixed deposit in the balance sheet of a man's deeds or a permanent entry in his character roll and no amount of earnest desire or honest effort can wipe it out.

According to Islam, misdeeds can be effaced by good deeds as it does not close its door eternally to a man. Allah is Merciful, Compassionate and He is always ready to grant him pardon and admit him to His Grace provided he is prepared to change his attitude and behaviour.

214. 'Amr b. al-'Āṣ. His *kunya* was Abū 'Abdullah and Abū Muḥammad. His mother's name was Nābigha. He belonged to the tribe of Quraysh. Before his conversion to Islam he was the arch enemy of the Muslims and the Holy Prophet and perpetrated horrifying atrocities on them. He embraced Islam after the Battle of the Ditch and then participated in almost all the expeditions, but his real fame is due to his conquest of Egypt. In the rift between 'Alī and Mu'āwiya (may Allah be pleased with them) he associated himself wholeheartedly with the latter. He died in Egypt in 51 H.

215. 'Abdullah. He was a very pious man.

was no other desire stronger in me than the one that I should overpower him and kill him. Had I died in this state, I would have been definitely one among the denizens of Fire. When Allah instilled the love of Islam in my heart, I came to the Apostle (may peace be upon him) and said: Stretch out your right hand so that I pledge my allegiance to you. He stretched out his right hand. I withdrew my hand. He (the Holy Prophet) said: What has happened to you, O 'Amr? I replied: I intend to lay down some condition. He asked: What condition do you intend to put forward? I said: I should be granted pardon. He (the Holy Prophet) observed: Are you not aware of the fact that Islam wipes out all the previous (misdeeds)? Verily migration wipes out all the previous (misdeeds) and verily the pilgrimage wipes out all the (previous) misdeeds. And then no one was more dear to me than the Messenger of Allah and none was sublimer in my eyes than he. Never could I pluck courage to catch a full glimpse of his face due to its splendour. So if I am asked to describe his features, I cannot do that for I have not eyed him fully. Had I died in this state I had every reason to hope that I would have been among the dwellers of Paradise. Then we were responsible for certain things[216] (in the light of which) I am unable to know what is in store for me. When I die, let neither female mourner nor fire accompany me. When you bury me fill my grave well with earth, then stand around it for the time within which a camel is slaughtered and its meat is distributed so that I may enjoy your intimacy and (in your company) ascertain what answer I can give to the messengers (angels) of Allah.

(221) It is narrated on the authority of Ibn 'Abbās that some persons amongst the polytheists had committed a large number of murders and had excessively indulged in fornication. Then they came to Muḥammad (may peace be upon him) and said: Whatever you assert and whatever you call to is indeed good. But if you inform us that there is atonement of our past deeds (then we would embrace Islam). Then it was revealed:

> And those who call not unto another god along with Allah and slay not any soul which Allah has forbidden except in the cause of justice, nor commit fornication; and he who does this shall meet the requital of sin. Multiplied for him shall be the torment on the Day of Resurrection, and he shall therein abide disgraced, except him who repents and believes and does good deeds. Then these! for them Allah shall change their vices into virtues. Verily Allah is Ever Forgiving, Merciful (xxv. 68-70).
>
> Say thou: O my bondsmen who have committed extravagance against themselves, despair not of the Mercy of Allah! Verily Allah will forgive the sins altogether. He is indeed the Forgiving, the Merciful[217] (xxxix. 53).

216. This refers to those acts which he performed as an associate of Mu'āwiya or perhaps as governor of Egypt.

217. Western critics have time and again tried to give a wrong concept of God in Islam. They assert that the qualities of Justice and Power outweigh the quality of Mercy. This assertion is absolutely erroneous and baseless. The mercy of Allah predominates all other qualities. "And My Mercy encompasses all things" (vii. 156) is the verdict of the Holy Qur'ān. The Muslims have been exhorted not to feel despaired but to have perfect faith and confidence in the Mercy of Allah.

A little bit of penetration into the working of human mind will reveal that it is despair which incites people to commit grave offences. Whenever a man is convinced that the wrong done by him cannot be righted, he becomes desperate and throws himself utterly in the arms of vice, with no hope to get out of them.

Chapter LVI

PERTAINING TO THE VIRTUOUS ACT OF A MAN BEFORE EMBRACING ISLAM

(222) Ḥakīm b. Ḥizām reported to 'Urwa b. Zubair that he said to the Messenger of Allah : Do you think if there is anything for me (of the reward with the Lord) for the deeds of religious purification that I did in the state of ignorance ? Upon this he (the Apostle of Allah) said to him : You accepted Islam with all the previous virtues that you practised.[218]

(223) Ḥakīm b. Ḥizām reported it to 'Urwa b. Zubair that he said to the Messenger of Allah (may peace be upon him) : Messenger of Allah, do you think if there is any reward (of the Lord with me on the Day of Resurrection) for the deeds of religious purification that I performed in the state of ignorance, such as charity, freeing a slave, cementing of blood-relations ? Upon this he (the Apostle of Allah) said to him : You accepted Islam with all the previous virtues that you practised.[219]

(224) It is narrated on the authority of Ḥakīm b. Ḥizām : I said : Messenger of Allah, I did some of the deeds in the state of ignorance. (One of the transmitters) Hishām b. 'Urwa explained them as acts of piety.[220] Upon this the Messenger of Allah remarked : You embraced Islam with all the previous acts of virtue. I said : By God, I would leave nothing undone in Islam the like of which I did in the state of ignorance.[221]

(225) Hishām b. 'Urwa narrated it on the authority of his father : Ḥakīm b. Ḥizām[222] freed one hundred slaves and donated one hundred camels (for the sake of

218. The good deeds performed in the state of ignorance are indicative of the fact that a man is inclined towards piety. But to be truly pious and virtuous it is quite essential to have the correct understanding of the Will of God. This can be confidently known only through the prophets and is embodied in Islam. Thus without having faith in Islam we cannot serve our Master and Lord according to His Will. When we embrace Islam, we recognise Him, His virtues, His Love and Power, His Will and His Desire, how He wants us to behave and act. It is the conscious adherence to the path shown by Him which makes one a true Muslim. The acts of virtue may be good in their own way but it is by coming within the fold of Islam that these become significant and meaningful in the eyes of the Lord. When a man accepts Islam as his code of life, his previous acts of piety, which were dark and dreary for the lack of the light of faith, begin to glow with God-consciousness and true sense of religious piety which is developed only by true belief in Allah and sincere devotion to Him.

219. The virtues practised by him before embracing Islam would be credited to his account,

220. تبرر (*tabarrara*) means : he affected or endeavoured to characterise himself by piety. Maulānā Shabbīr Aḥmad 'Uthmānī has explained it as "an act of piety and that is obedience to Allah". Another commentator of ḥadīth has given the following meaning : "By this act he endeavoured to practise virtue and do good to the people and seek nearness of the Lord".

221. He would do all good deeds in Islam which he used to do in the state of ignorance and thus gather the maximum amount of virtue as a Muslim, because when a virtue is practised with full God-consciousness, its spiritual and moral value is immeasurably increased.

222. Imām Nawawī observes : The unrivalled distinction of Ḥakīm b. Ḥizām is that he was born in the Ka'bah. He lived for one hundred and twenty years. Half of his life was spent in the Jahiliya and half was devoted to the service of Islam. He embraced Islam at the conquest of Mecca and died in 54 H. in Medina. He was a very pious Companion of the Holy Prophet and was greatly devoted to him (Vol. I, p. 77).

Allah) during the state of ignorance. Then he freed one hundred slaves and donated one hundred camels (for the sake of Allah) after he had embraced Islam. He subsequently came to the Apostle (may peace be upon him). The remaining of the ḥadīth is the same as narrated above.

Chapter LVII

THE VERACITY OF FAITH AND ITS SINCERITY

(226) It is narrated on the authority of 'Abdullah (b. Mas'ūd) that when this verse was revealed : "It is those who believe and confound not their belief with wrong-doing" (vi. 82), the Companions of the Messenger of Allah were greatly perturbed.[223] They said : Who amongst us (is so fortunate) that he does not wrong himself ?[224] Upon this the Messenger of Allah (may peace be upon him) remarked : It does not mean that which you presume.[225] It implies that which Luqmān said to his son : O my son, do not associate anything with Allah, for indeed it is the gravest wrong-doing (xxxi. 13).

(227) This ḥadīth is narrated by another chain of transmitters, (namely), Isḥāq b. Ibrāhīm. Ibn Idrīs says : My father transmitted it from Abān b. Taghlib who heard it from A'mash ; then I heard it also from him (A'mash).[226]

223. This fact is an unchallengable proof of the high moral sense of the Companions of the Holy Prophet. Whenever there was any indication from the Lord, they searched their souls and tried to perceive if there was any failing on their part in any aspect of their lives. They were very sensitive on the point of obedience to Allah and were always on the look out to make their lofty character still more sublime.

224. The Companions of the Holy Prophet, although they occupied the highest pinnacle of moral sublimity, were yet very humble and modest and were always ready to confess their failings and faults. We do not find any trace of vanity in them for their noble deeds. Love for God had inculcated in them a spirit of humility.

225. This part of the ḥadīth is clearly indicative of the fact that the Ḥadīth is the indispensable key to the correct understanding of the Holy Qur'ān, because as the bearer of Revelation, the Holy Prophet was best fitted and, therefore, divinely authorised to interpret and explain the implications of the Holy Qur'ān. Allah says: And We have sent down unto thee the Admonition, that thou (O Muḥammad) mayest make clear to mankind what has been revealed for them (xvi. 44). It means that the responsibility of determining the true meaning and significance of the verses of the Holy Qur'ān lies with the Holy Prophet and it is he whose explanation is to be accepted as valid and final.

In this ḥadīth we find that when the noble Companions of the Holy Prophet heard the exhortation of the Holy Qur'ān in which they were asked not to confound their belief with wrong-doing, they were very much upset as they took the word *Zulm* (wrong-doing) in an ordinary sense. *Zulm* originally signifies : putting a thing in a place not its own ; putting it in a wrong place ; or misplacing it ; transgressing the proper limit much or little. Now when this word is taken in its literal sense, everyone is a *Ẓālim* (wrong-doer) in one way or the other. This is what disturbed the Companions of the Holy Prophet who told them that the word *Zulm* here refers to the heinous act of associating partners with Allah.

226. The point that Imām Muslim wants to stress is that in one case Ibn Idrīs heard it from his father and other narrators, and here the chain is not successive and it apparently reduces the ḥadīth to the level of *Munqaṭi'* (broken). But it is not so because Ibn Idrīs heard it directly from A'mash also and this elevates this ḥadīth to the position of *Muttaṣil* which means a tradition which has got unbroken links in the chain of transmission.

Chapter LVIII

CONCERNING THE WORDS OF ALLAH WHETHER YOU MANIFEST WHATEVER IS IN YOUR MIND OF HIDE IT

(228) It is reported on the authority of Abū Huraira that when it was revealed to the Messenger of Allah (may peace be upon him) : "To Allah belongs whatever is in the heavens and whatever is in the earth and whether you disclose that which is in your mind or conceal it, Allah will call you to account according to it.[227] Then He forgives whom He pleases and chastises whom He pleases ; and Allah is over everything Potent" (ii. 284), the Companions of the Messenger of Allah (may peace be upon him) felt it hard and severe and they came to the Messenger of Allah (may peace be upon him) and sat down on their knees and said : Messenger of Allah, we were assigned some duties which were within our power to perform, such as prayer, fasting, struggling (in the cause of Allah), charity. Then this (the above-mentioned) verse was revealed unto you and it is beyond our power to live up to it. The Messenger of Allah (may peace be upon him) said : Do you intend to say what the people of two books (Jews and Christians) said before you : "We hear and disobey"? You should rather say : "We hear and we obey, (we seek) Thy forgiveness, our Lord ! and unto Thee is the return." And they said : We hear and we obey, (we seek) Thy forgiveness, our Lord ! and unto Thee is the return." When the people recited it and it smoothly flowed on their tongues, then Allah revealed immediately afterwards : "The Apostle believes in that which is sent down unto him from his Lord, and so do the believers. Each one believes in Allah and His Angels and His Books and His Apostles, saying : We differentiate not between any of His Apostles and they say : We hearken and we obey : (we seek) Thy forgiveness, our Lord ! and unto Thee is the return" (ii. 285). When they did that, Allah abrogated[228] this (verse) and the Great, Majestic Allah revealed : "Allah burdens not a soul beyond its capacity. It gets every good that it earns and it suffers every ill that it earns. Our Lord, punish us not if we forget or make a mistake." (The Prophet[229] said :) Yes, our Lord ! do not lay on us a burden as Thou didst lay on those before us. (The Prophet said :) Yes, our Lord, impose not on us (burdens) which we have not the strength to bear. (The Prophet said :) Yes, and pardon us and grant us protection ! and have mercy

227. The Companions of the Holy Prophet were greatly perturbed because this verse gave them an indication that they would be called to account by Allah for what they do or profess or even hide in their minds. Now one can control one's tongue or can put a restraint upon one's deeds, but it is beyond the power of a man to completely safeguard himself against evil promptings, which invade human mind in spite of themselves. The worry of the Companions of the Holy Prophet was, therefore, quite natural. The Messenger of Allah (may peace be upon him) soothed and comforted them and exhorted them to adopt an attitude of submission rather than that of defiance. What he in fact wanted to stress upon them was that they should on their own behalf do their utmost to obey the Commands of Allah and then beg His mercy for all those acts of omission and commission which are done inadvertently. To err is human. No man can claim infallibility. The best way is to ask forgiveness from the Lord.

228. Some of the commentators of the Ḥadīth are of the opinion that here abrogation is not used in its technical sense, but it simply implies that their vexation was changed into comfort on the revelation of the verse : "Allah burdens not a soul beyond its capacity."

229. The Holy Prophet was instructed to utter these words by God Himself.

on us. Thou art our Patron, so grant us victory over the disbelieving people" (ii. 286). He (the Lord) said: Yes.

(229) It is narrated on the authority of Ibn 'Abbās: When this verse: "Whether you disclose that which is in your mind or conceal it, Allah will call you to account according to it" (ii. 284), there entered in their minds something (of that fear) such as had never entered their hearts (before). The Apostle (may peace be upon him) observed: Say: We have heard and obeyed and submitted ourselves. He (the reporter) said: Allah instilled faith in their hearts and He revealed this verse: "Allah burdens not a soul beyond its capacity. It gets every good that it earns and it suffers every ill that it earns. Our Lord, call us not to account if we forget or make a mistake. He the (Lord) said: I indeed did it. Our Lord! do not lay on us a burden as Thou didst lay on those before us. He (our Lord) said: I indeed did it. And pardon us, have mercy on us, Thou art our Protector" (ii. 286). He said: I indeed did it.

Chapter LIX

ALLAH DISREGARDS THE PREMONITION OR THE EVIL PROMPTINGS OF THE HEART SO LONG AS THEY DO NOT TAKE A FIRM ROOT

(230) It is narrated on the authority of Abū Huraira that the Messenger of Allah (may peace be upon him) observed: Verily Allah forgave my people the evil promptings which arise within their hearts as long as they did not speak about them or did not act upon them.

(231) It is narrated on the authority of Abū Huraira that the Messenger of Allah (may peace be upon him) observed: Verily the Great and Mighty Allah forgave my people the evil promptings arising in their minds, but they neither talked about them nor acted upon them.[230]

(232) The same ḥadīth has been narrated by Zuhair b. Ḥarb, Wakī', Isḥāq b. Manṣūr, Ḥusain b. 'Alī.

230. There is a good deal of controversy about this ḥadīth. Some scholars are of the opinion that the Holy Qur'ān and some of the Aḥādīth indicate that entertaining evil thoughts or wrong beliefs is a sin; for example, the Holy Qur'ān says: "Those who love that scandal should circulate respecting those who believe, for them is a grievous chastisement in this world and the Hereafter. And Allah knows while you know not" (xxiv. 19). Further: "O you who believe, avoid most of suspicion, for surely suspicion in some cases is sin" (xlix. 12). Then there are several Aḥādīth which condemn hatred, jealousy, looking down upon others and these, clearly, are evils of the mind. Moreover, unblief is something which concerns the heart of man. All these facts prove beyond any shadow of doubt that man would be punished for evil thoughts. But this ḥadīth shows that man will not be held responsible for the evil promptings of his mind. Apparently this conflicts with the views mentioned above. But a close study would reveal that there is no contradiction between the two views. The ḥadīth under discussion takes into consideration those wayward thoughts of evil which arise in our minds in spite of ourselves and we do not harbour them intentionally, and whenever we become conscious of them we make efforts to be relieved of them. Such thoughts are not punishable. But when we deliberately entertain evil thoughts and try to nurse them they are punishable. (For a detailed discussion, see Imām Nawawī, Vol. I, pp. 78-80, and *Fatḥ-ul-Mulhim*, Vol. I, pp. 277-9).

Chapter LX

WHENEVER A PERSON INTENDS TO DO A GOOD DEED, IT IS RECORDED, BUT WHENEVER HE INTENDS TO COMMIT EVIL, IT IS NOT WRITTEN

(233) It is narrated on the authority of Abū Huraira that the Messenger of Allah (may peace be upon him) said: The Great and the Glorious Lord said (to angels): Whenever My bondsman intends to commit an evil, do not record it against him, but if he actually commits it, then write it as one evil. And when he intends to do good but does not do it, then take it down as one act of goodness, but if he does it, then write down ten good deeds (in his record).

(234) It is narrated on the authority of Abū Huraira that the Messenger of Allah (may peace be upon him) observed: Allah, the Great and Glorious, said: Whenever my bondsman intends to do good, but does not do it, I write one good act for him, but if he puts it into practice I wrote from ten to seven hundred good deeds in favour of him. When he intends to commit an evil, but does not actually do it, I do not record it. But if he does it, I write only one evil.

(235) Abū Huraira reported that Muḥammad, the Messenger of Allah (may peace be upon him), said: When it occurs to my bondsman that he should do a good deed but he actually does not do it, I record one good for him, but if he puts it into practice, I make an entry of ten good acts in his favour. When it occurs to him to do evil, but he does not commit it, I forgive that. But if he commits it, I record one evil against his name. The Messenger of Allah (may peace be upon him) observed: The angels said: That bondsman of Yours intends to commit evil, though His Lord is more Vigilant than he. Upon this He (the Lord) said: Watch him; if he commits (evil), write it against his name, but if he refrains from doing it write one good deed for him, for he desisted from doing it for My sake. The Messenger of Allah said: He who amongst you is good of faith, all his good acts are multiplied from ten to seven hundred times (and are recorded in his name) and all the evils that he commits are recorded as such (i.e. without increase) till he meets Allah.

(236) It is narrated on the authority of Abū Huraira that the Messenger of Allah (may peace be upon him) observed: He who intended to do good, but did not do it, one good was recorded for him, and he who intended to do good and also did it, ten to seven hundred good deeds were recorded for him. And he who intended evil, but did not commit it, no entry was made against his name, but if he committed that it was recorded.

(237) It is narrated on the authority of Ibn 'Abbās that the Messenger of Allah (may peace be upon him) transmitted it from the Blessed and Great Lord: Verily Allah recorded the good and the evil and then made it clear that he who intended good but did not do it, Allah recorded one complete good in his favour, but if he intended it and also did it, the Glorious and Great Allah recorded ten to seven hundred virtues and even more to his credit. But if he intended evil, but did not commit it, Allah wrote down full one good in his favour. If he intended that and also committed it,

Allah made an entry of one evil against him.[231]

(238) This ḥadīth has been narrated with another chain of transmitters with the addition of these words: Allah would even wipe out (the evil committed by a man) and Allah does not put to destruction anyone except he who is doomed to destruction.[232]

Chapter LXI

PERTAINING TO EVIL SUGGESTION[233] OR PROMPTING IN FAITH AND WHAT SHOULD BE SAID WHEN IT OCCURS TO THE MIND OF A MAN

(239) It is narrated on the authority of **Abū Huraira** that some people from amongst the Companions of the Aposle (may peace be upon him) came to him and said: Verily we perceive in our minds that which everyone of us considers it too grave to express. He (the Holy Prophet) said: Do you really perceive it? They said: Yes. Upon this he remarked: That is the faith manifest.[234]

231. This ḥadīth succinctly sums up the meanings of all the Aḥadīth which have been recorded in this chapter. It has been made clear that if we make up our mind to do good, Allah would give us a reward for this, since this intention is also an act of religious piety. It is the intention and the determination which exhort people to do a certain act. Without good intention there can be no idea of good deeds. If a man puts his intention into practice, he in fact makes an advance in virtue, because transmuting of thought into practical reality is not something easy; it demands a good deal of sacrifice on the part of man. This is the reason why Allah in His infinite Mercy would multiply man's good deeds and credit them to his account.

On the other hand, when he intends to commit evil, but refrains from doing so for the fear of the Lord, he is rewarded by Allah with a good deed, for he has struggled hard to prevail upon his evil self. This fighting against the evil within his mind is an act of inner piety and one has to put in a good deal of effort in order to overcome evil promptings of one's mind. The evil thoughts provide opportunities to the believers to wage war against them.

232. Maulānā Shabbīr Aḥmad 'Uthmānī has explained its meaning in the following words: "None would be destroyed except one who is fit to be destroyed. And who can be that unfortunate soul?—one who deliberately persists on harbouring evil thoughts giving vent to them and committing evil deeds; he who purposely avoids goods, and does not make the slightest effort to entertain good thought, to give expression to good ideas or to do good deeds" (*Fatḥ-ul-Mulḥim*, Vol. I, p. 280).

233. وسوسة (*waswasa*, pl. وساوس = *wasāwis*) is derived from *waswas*, which means the low sound of the ornament, or low or faint sound of the hunter and the dogs or a faint sound (or rustling) of wind. It denotes speech or talk that is indistinct, low, faint and confused. In the religious sense it signifies evil prompting or suggestion, an evil and unprofitable thought or idea or imagination which bestirs itself in a man or occurs to his mind.

234. This ḥadīth speaks eloquently of the deep insight of the Holy Prophet in human psychology. The very fact that they perceived the stir of the evil, realised its gravity and tried to wipe it out of their minds bears unchallenging testimony to their deep-rooted love for faith. The evil thoughts occurred to them, not because their minds were polluted, but to goad them to struggle against them and thus strengthen their faith. The evil promptings have their value in life as they throw a challenge to the believer to fight against them. This is how the religious sensibilities of a man become active and strong enough to overcome evil. If there were no evil thoughts, minds would have become inert and dormant, for there would have been no impetus to struggle. The fidelity of one's belief is clearly borne out by the fact that evil thoughts come to his mind, but he never allows them to implant themselves in his soul. He gives them a tough fight and tries to uproot them and does not permit them to reside in the chambers of his heart.

(240) The same ḥadīth has been transmitted by Muḥammad b. ʻAmr, Abū Bakr b. Īsḥāq, Abu'l-Jawwāb, Aʻmash and Abū Huraira.

(241) It is narrated on the authority of ʻAbdullah b. Masʻūd that the Apostle (may peace be upon him) was asked about evil prompting, to which he replied: It is pure faith.[235]

(242) It is narrated on the authority of Abū Huraira that the Messenger of Allah (may peace be upon him) said: Men will continue to question one another till this is propounded: Allah created all things but who created Allah? He who found himself confronted with such a situation should say: I affirm my faith in Allah.[236]

(243) This ḥadīth has been transmitted by Maḥmūd b. Ghailān by another chain of transmitters (and the words are): The Messenger of Allah (may peace be upon him) said: The Satan will come to everyone of you and say: Who created the heaven, who created the earth? (And the man) replies: It is Allah. Then the remaining part of the ḥadīth was narrated as mentioned above and the words "His prophets" were added to it.

(244) It is narrated on the authority of Abū Huraira that the Messenger of Allah (may peace be upon him) observed: The Satan comes to everyone of you and says: Who created this and that?—till he questions: Who created your Lord? When he comes to that, one should seek refuge in Allah and keep away (from such idle thoughts).

(245) This ḥadīth is transmitted by ʻUrwa b. Zubair on the authority of Abū Huraira (and the words are): The Satan comes to the bondsman (of Allah) and says: Who created this and that? The remaining part of the ḥadīth is the same.

(246) It is narrated on the authority of Abū Huraira that the Apostle of Allah (may peace be upon him) observed: People will constantly ask you questions pertaining to knowledge till they would say: Allah created us, but who created Allah? He (the narrator) says: He (Abū Huraira) was (at the time of narrating this ḥadīth) catching hold of the hand of a man and he said: Allah and the Messenger told the truth. Two persons have already put me this question, and this is the third one, or he said: One man has put me this question and he is the second one.

(247) It is narrated on the authority of Abū Huraira that he said: The people will constantly ask, and the rest of the ḥadīth is the same as that transmitted by ʻAbdul-

235. When evil thought is not allowed to take its root and its position remains as a wayward idea, it is a clear proof of one's faith, as it reflects the mental struggle of a man against evil.

236. It is not rational and logical thinking that has been discouraged by the Holy Prophet, but the useless mental speculations which lead a man nowhere but to a trackless jungle of confusion. In this ḥadīth the Holy Prophet has pointed to a simple fallacy in human reasoning, i.e. the law of causality is made to apply to the metaphysical question. God is the universal essence of things, the real and abiding substrata of the universe, the subject as well as the object of man's consciousness, and, therefore, both the Primal and the Final Cause of things. We, therefore, do not need to start on a speculative journey in our effort to find God at the end of our quest, as a sort of goal or ***terminus ad quam*** (to which we are going). God has always been with us since the dim beginning of our consciousness and has remained throughout with us at every step—the Master Light of all our seeing. He is not reached at the close of our inquiry as a deduction from an assumed premise. He is recognised as the Infinite, Who is reflected in all finite beings and whose existence is implied in every existence of thought.

Wārith with the exception that there is no mention of the Apostle[237] of Allah in that, but he observed at the end of the ḥadīth: Allah and His Messenger told the truth.

(248) Abū Huraira reported: The Messenger of Allah (may peace be upon him) said to me: They (the people) will constantly ask you, Abū Huraira, (about different things pertaining to religion) till they would say: Well, there is Allah, but after all who created Allah? He (Abū Huraira) narrated: Once we were in the mosque that some of the Bedouins came there and said: Well, there is Allah, but who created Allah? He (the narrator) said: I took hold of the pebbles in my fist and flung at them and remarked: Stand up, stand up (go away), my friend (the Holy Prophet) told the truth.

(249) Yazīd b. al-Aṣamm said: I heard Abū Huraira saying that the Messenger of Allah (may peace be upon him) observed: People will certainly ask you about everything till they will propound: Allah created everything, but who created Allah?

(250) Anas b. Mālik transmitted it from the Messenger of Allah (may peace be upon him) that the Great and Glorious Allah said: Verily your people would constantly question about this and that[238] till they would say: Well, it is Allah Who created the creation, but who created Allah?

(251) This ḥadīth has been narrated by another chain of transmitters with the exception that Isḥāq made no mention of this: Allah said: Verily your people.

Chapter LXII

WARNING FOR ONE APPROPRIATING THE RIGHT OF A MUSLIM BY TAKING A FALSE OATH: THE FIRE (OF HELL) IS HIS CHASTISEMENT

(252) It is narrated on the authority of Abū Umāma that the Messenger of Allah (may peace be upon him) observed: He who appropriated the right of a Muslim by (swearing a false) oath, Allah would make Hell-fire necessary for him and would declare Paradise forbidden for him[239] A person said to him: Messenger of Allah, even if it is something insignificant? He (the Holy Prophet) replied: (Yes) even if it is the twig of the arāk tree.[240]

237. This type of ḥadīth is known as Mauqūf (retarded) which implies that the tradition reaches up to a Companion who uttered it.

238. Maulānā Shabbīr Aḥmad is of the opinion that the very words of the ḥadīth and style of expression indicate the fact that persistent questioning is not desirable because sometimes such illogical argumentation leads to mental confusion (*Fatḥ-ul-Mulhim*, Vol. I, p. 281).

239. For a Muslim nothing is so damaging as the fact that he should go to the extent of taking a false oath in the name of Allah and that too for some material benefit over which he has no legitimate claim. It implies that such a person has no fellow feeling, no respect for the Lord, and he is absolutely bereft of the sense of fairness and justice and is consumed by a lust for material possessions. Imām Nawawī has made it clear that it is wrong to infer on the basis of this ḥadīth that high-handedness is permissible in case of a non-Muslim. The right of a non-Muslim must also be respected, for Islam does not permit its infringement. Here in this ḥadīth the word "Muslim" has been stressed with a view to emphasising the fact that, apart from other considerations, the person has no regard even for the brotherhood of faith.

240. اراك (arāk). It is a kind of a tree well known in Arabia and bears what resembles the bunches of grapes and of which the sticks for cleaning the teeth are made and camels feed on its leaves. Its Latin name is *Salvadora Persica* and is known in Arabic as the Shajar al-Suwak (*vide Polyalottic Dictionary of Plant Names*).

(253) This ḥadīth has been transmitted by another chain of narrators: Abū Bakr b. Abī Shaiba, Isḥāq b. Ibrāhīm, Hārūn b. 'Abdullah, Abī Usāma, Walīd b. Kathīr, Muḥammad b. Ka'b, his brother 'Abdullah b. Ka'b and Abī Umāma.

(254) It is narrated on the authority of 'Abdullah (b. 'Umar) that the Messenger of Allah (may peace be upon him) observed: He who perjured with a view to appropriating the property of a Muslim, and he is in fact a liar, would meet Allah in a state that He would be angry with him. He (the narrator) said: There came Ash'ath b. Qais and said (to the people): What does 'Abu 'Abdur-Raḥmān (the *Kunya* of 'Abdullah b. 'Umar) narrate to you? They replied: So and so. Upon this he remarked: Abū 'Abdur-Raḥmān told the truth. This (command) has been revealed in my case. There was a piece of land in Yemen over which I and another person had a claim. I brought the dispute with him to the Apostle of Allah (to decide). He (the Holy Prophet) said: Can you produce an evidence (in your support)? I said: No. He (the Holy Prophet) observed: (Then the decision would be made) on his oath. I said: He would readily take an oath. Upon this the Messenger of Allah (may peace be upon him) remarked: He who perjured for appropriating the wealth of a Muslim, whereas he is a liar, would meet Allah while He would be angry with him. This verse was then revealed: "Verily those who barter Allah's covenant and their oaths at a small price . . ." (iii. 77).[241]

(255) It is narrated on the authority of 'Abdullah that he heard the Prophet saying: He who took an oath in order to entitle himself (to the possession) of a property, whereas he is a liar, would meet Allah in a state that He would be very much angry with him. Then the remaining part of the ḥadīth was narrated as transmitted by A'mash but with the exception of these words: There was a dispute between me and another person in regard to a well. We referred this dispute to the Messenger of Allah (may peace be upon him). Upon this he remarked: Either (you should produce) two witnesses (to support your contention) or his oath (would be accepted as valid).[242]

(256) Ibn Mas'ūd says: I heard the Messenger of Allah observing: He who took an oath on the property of a Muslim without legitimate right would meet Allah and He would be angry with him. Then the Messenger of Allah (may peace be upon him) in support of his contention recited the verse: "Verily those who barter Allah's covenant and their oaths at a small price. . . ."

(257) It is narrated on the authority of Wā'il that there came a person from Ḥaḍramaut and another one from Kinda to the Apostle (may peace be upon him). One who had come from Ḥaḍramaut said: Messenger of Allah, verily this man has appropriated my land which belonged to my father. The one who had come from Kinda contended: This is my land and is in my possession; I cultivate it. There is no right for him in it. The Messenger of Allah said to the Ḥaḍramite: Have you any evidence (to support you)? He replied in the negative. He (the Apostle of Allah) said: Then your

241. The complete verse is this: "Verily those who barter Allah's covenant and their oaths at a small price—no portion is theirs in the Hereafter, nor shall Allah speak unto them or look at them on the Day of Resurrection, nor shall He cleanse them and theirs shall be a grievous torment."

242. This ḥadīth throws a good deal of light on the judicial procedure of Islam. The responsibility of proving one's claim to be valid lies with the claimant. It is he who is required to support his contention on reliable evidence. If the claimant fails to provide evidence, then the case would be decided on the oath of the defendent.

case is to be decided on his oath. He (the Ḥaḍramite) said: Messenger of Allah, he is a liar and cares not what he swears and has no regard for anything. Upon this he (the Messenger of Allah) remarked: For you then there is no other help to it.[243] He (the man from Kinda) set out to take an oath. When he turned his back the Messenger of Allah (may peace be upon him) observed: If he took an oath on his property with a view to usurping it, he would certainly meet his Lord in a state that He would turn away from him.

(258) Wā'il reported it on the authority of his father Ḥujr: I was with the Messenger of Allah (may peace be upon him) that two men came there disputing over a piece of land. One of them said: Messenger of Allah, this men appropriated my land without justification in the days of ignorance. The (claimant) was Imru'l-Qais b. 'Ābis al-Kindī and his opponent was Rabī'a b. 'Ibān. He (the Holy Prophet) said (to the claimant): Have you evidence (to substantiate your claim)? He replied: I have no evidence. Upon this he (the Messenger of Allah) remarked: Then his (that is of the defendent) is the oath. He (the claimant) said: In this case he (the defendent) would appropriate this (the property). He (the Holy Prephet) said: There is then no other way left for you but this. He (the narrator) said: When he (the defendent) stood up to take oath, the Messenger of Allah (may peace be upon him) said: He who appropriated the land wrongfully would meet Allah in a state that He would be angry with him. Isḥāq in his narration mentions Rabī'a b. 'Aidān (instead of Rabī'a b. 'Ibdān).

Chapter LXIII

CONCERNING THE FACT THAT VIOLABLE IS THE BLOOD OF ONE WHO MAKES AN ATTEMPT TO TAKE POSSESSION OF THE PROPERTY OF ANOTHER WITHOUT ANY LEGITIMATE RIGHT. IF SUCH A MAN IS KILLED HIS ABODE IS FIRE AND HE WHO DIES IN PROTECTING HIS PROPERTY IS A MARTYR

(259) Abū Huraira reported: A person came to the Messenger of Allah (may peace be upon him) and said: Messenger of Allah, what do you think if a man comes to me in order to appropriate my possession? He (the Holy Prophet) said: Don't surrender your possession to him. He (the inquirer) said: If he fights me? He (the Holy Prophet) remarked: Then fight (with him). He (the inquirer) again said: What do you think if I am killed? He (the Holy Prophet) observed: You would be a martyr. He (the inquirer) said: What do you think of him (Messenger of Allah) if I kill him. He (the Holy Prophet) said: He would be in the Fire.[244]

243. What the Prophet wanted to impress upon him was the fact that justice must follow its natural course. If you cannot produce two witnesses, then the case would be decided on the oath of the defendent. There is no other way out.

244. This ḥadīth sheds a good deal of light on the fact that the right of ownership is held sacred in Islam and if one dies in safeguardiug this right, he is a martyr. However, on the basis of this ḥadīth it is wrong to justify modern capitalism which generates individualist self-interest and which leads

(260) It is narrated on the authority of Thābit, that when 'Abdullah b. 'Amr and 'Anbasa b. Abī Sufyān were about to fight against each other, Khālid b. 'Āṣ rode to 'Abdullah b. 'Amr and persuaded him (not to do so). Upon this 'Abdullah b. 'Amr said: Are you not aware that the Messenger of Allah (may peace be upon him) had observed: "He who died in protecting his property is a martyr." [245]

This ḥadīth has been narrated by Muḥammad b. Ḥātim, Muḥammad b. Bakr, Aḥmad b. 'Uthmān Naufalī, Abū 'Āṣim, Ibn Juraij.

Chapter LXIV

THE RULER WHO IS UNJUST TO HIS SUBJECTS DESERVES PUNISHMENT OF FIRE

(261) Ḥasan[246] reported: 'Ubaidullah b. Ziyād paid a visit to Ma'qil b. Yasār Muzanī[247] in his illness of which he (later on) died. (At this juncture) Ma'qil said: I am going to narrate to you a ḥadīth which I have heard from the Messenger of Allah (may peace be upon him) and which I would not have transmitted if I knew that I would survive. Verily I have heard the Messenger of Allah (may peace be upon him) say: There is none amongst the bondsmen who was entrusted with the affairs of his subjects and he died in such a state that he was dishonest in his dealings with those over whom he

to ruthless exploitation and gross injustice in society. In the capitalistic system the right of ownership implies that the possessor has every right to use his property or wealth in any way he likes, irrespective of its moral and social repercussions. Islam does not grant people such unrestricted and unlimited rights of ownership. The property, according to Islam, is the sacred trust of Allah and it has to be used with a sense of religious piety and not as a reveller and it is to be spent in the same noble cause as it is permitted in Islam.

Thus in the social order envisaged by Islam the ownership of property is not the means to satisfy the acquisitive instinct of a man or an instrument of exploitation but a means of achieving spiritual heights by sacrifice, fellow-feeling and resisting the wellnigh temptations of material wealth.

245. Imām Nawawī has made it clear that he would get the reward in the Hereafter like that of a Shahīd but he would not be treated as a martyr in this world, i.e. unlike a Shahīd in the technical sense (one who fights against the non-Muslim army and dies), who is buried unbathed and without coffin, he would be given a bath and buried with a coffin and funeral prayer would be offered over his dead body. The Muslim who dies in an accident, or by cholera or plague, would be treated as a martyr in the Hereafter but not in this world and the religious ceremonies would be performed in his case.

246. Ḥasan al-Baṣrī (*Kunya* Abū Sa'd) is a successor (tābi'ī) and an important figure of the first century of the Hijrah. His father's name was Yasār. He was born in 12 H. in the house of Umm Salama (wife of the Holy Prophet) as Baṣrī's mother served in her house. He was, therefore, brought up in a very sacred and pious atmosphere and he fully imbibed its spirit. After attaining the age of twenty-one he married and afterwards settled in Baṣra. There he won a great reputation for strength of character, piety, learning and devotion to Allah and love for the Holy Prophet. Ḥasan was fearless and he frankly expressed his disapproval when his opinion was sought about the succession of Yazīd. He was highly esteemed as a reliable transmitter of the Ḥadīth because he was believed to have met and seen a large number of the eminent Companions of the Holy Prophet. He exercised a lasting influence on the development of Ṣūfism by his piety. He died in 110 H. at Baṣra.

247. Ma'qil b. Yasār was a famous Companion. He was one of those who took the oath of allegiance at Hudaibiyah. He settled afterwards in Baṣra. He died in 60 H.

ruled that the Paradise is not forbidden for him.[248]

(262) Ḥasan reported: 'Ubaidullah b. Ziyād went to see Ma'qil b. Yasār and he was ailing. He ('Ubaidullah) inquired (about his health) to which he (Ma'qil) replied: I am narrating to you a ḥadīth which I avoided narrating to you (before). Verily the Messenger of Allah (may peace be upon him) observed: Allah does not entrust to his bondsman the responsibility of managing the affairs of his subjects and he dies as a dishonest (ruler) but Paradise is forbidden by Allah for such a (ruler). He (Ibn Ziyād) said: Why did you not narrate it to me before this day? He replied: I (in fact) did not narrate it to you as it was not (fit) for me to narrate that to you.[249]

(263) Ḥasan reported: We were with Ma'qil b. Yasār inquiring about his health that 'Ubaidullah b. Ziyād came there. Ma'qil said to him: Verily I am going to narrate to you a ḥadīth which I heard from the Messenger of Allah (may peace be upon him). Then he narrated the ḥadīth like those two (mentioned above).

(264). It is narrated on the authority of Abū Malīḥ that 'Ubaidullah b. Ziyād visited Ma'qil b. Yasār in his illness. Ma'qil said to him: I am narrating to you a ḥadīth which I would have never narrated to you had I not been in death-bed. I heard Allah's Apostle (may peace be upon him) say: A ruler who has been entrusted with the affairs of the Muslims, but he makes no endeavours (for the material and moral uplift) and does not sincerely mean (their welfare) would not enter Paradise along with them.[250]

Chapter LXV

REMOVAL OF TRUSTWORTHINESS AND FAITH FROM SOME HEARTS AND APPEARANCE OF DISCORD THEREIN

(265) Ḥudhaifa[251] reported: The Messenger of Allah (may peace be upon him)

248. Islam exhorts its followers to create a kingdom of heaven in their hearts but this kingdom of heart must be externalised in a just social, political and economic system. The ruler and the State have thus important responsibilities to shoulder. It is the bounden duty of the ruler to see that he acquits himself creditably of the responsibilities saddled on him. He should see that the life and honour of the people are protected. He should also see that no one falls victim to the high-handedness of another. He should also take care that none amongst his subjects is deprived of the basic needs of life and there is God-consciousness and piety amongst the people. In short, it is the duty of a Muslim ruler to ensure the welfare of the citizens, both material and moral.

249. 'Ubaidullah was the son of Ziyād who had shown cruelty to the grandson of the Holy Prophet. What Ma'qil wanted to say was that a person from whose hand the life and honour of such noble souls was not safe was not expected to show kindness to anybody. He, therefore, refrained from narrating this ḥadīth. But at the same time it was his responsibility to transmit it to others since it was a ḥadīth of the Holy Prophet and it was his religious duty to transmit it. Qāḍī 'Iyāḍ says that his reluctance in the transmission of this ḥadīth was not out of fear but due to the fact that it might create more dissension and bitterness in the society which was already torn by internal strife. He was, therefore, reluctant to narrate it at first, but when he looked to his religious duty, he narrated it boldly and that too before a person who was the target of this warning.

250. It is the moral and spiritual position of a man which determines his status in the Hereafter. The proud and haughty monarch would be thrown in the Hell while the religiously pious souls, having no worldly possession, would be admitted to the Paradise.

251. *Ḥudhaifa*: He was the son of Ḥusail with *Kunya* of al-Yamān. He was a trusted Companion of the Holy Prophet. A large number of prominent Companions and their successors like Ḥaḍrat

narrated to us two aḥādīth. I have seen one (crystallised into reality), and I am waiting for the other. He told us: Trustworthiness descended in the innermost (root) of the hearts of people.[252] Then the Qur'ān was revealed and they learnt from the Qur'ān and they learnt from the Sunnah.[253] Then he (the Holy Prophet) told us about the removal of trustworthiness.[254] He said: The man would have a wink of sleep[255] and trustworthiness would be taken away from his heart leaving the impression of a faint mark.[256] He would again sleep and trustworthiness would be taken away from his heart leaving an impression of a blister,[257] as if you rolled down an ember on your foot and it was vesicled. He would see a swelling having nothing in it.[258] He (the Holy Prophet) then took up a pebble and rolled it down over his foot and (said): The people would enter into transactions amongst one another and hardly a person would be left who would return (things) entrusted to him.[259] (And there would be so much paucity of honest persons) till it would be said: There in such a such tribe is a trustworthy man. And they would also say about a person: How prudent he is, how broad-minded he is and how intelligent he is, whereas in his heart there would not be faith even to the weight

'Umar, Ḥaḍrat 'Alī, Ḥaḍrat Abū Dardā' narrated on his authority. He died in 36 н. shortly after the martyrdom of Ḥaḍrat 'Uthmān in Medina and was buried there.

252. It means that the root of religious piety, God-consciousness, is the heart of man. It cannot be thrusted from without; it springs up from the recesses of the heart.

253. This part of the ḥadīth speaks of the fact that the Companions of the Holy Prophet not only learnt the Qur'ān but they also learnt the Sunnah of the Holy Prophet, since it is the key to the right understanding of the Book of Allah.

254. امانة (amāna), fidelity or trustworthiness, and Imān have a common root. Here amāna refers to the following verse of the Holy Qur'ān:

Verily We offered the trust unto the heavens and the earth and the mountains, but they refused to bear it and shrank thereof. And man bore it (xxxiii. 72).

There is difference of opinion amongst the scholars in regard to the word amāna (trust) in this verse. Some take it to be a moral responsibility which is the human sense of answerableness for all acts of thought and conduct, some take it to be a din, and some take it to be the obligations and duties enjoined upon man by al-Islām. If we look deeply into the matter we will find that there is little difference between these meanings. Faith is the acceptance of the moral trust reposed in man and affirmation of the fact that he would prove true to his salt and would undertake all the responsibilities saddled on him by Islam and would do nothing to betray that trust. Thus fidelity, integrity, inner piety and moral sense of responsibility are all the component parts of the faith.

255. Sleep is here used in the sense of forgetfulness (Fatḥ-ul-Mulḥim). It means that he would for some time become unconscious of his moral responsibility that faith puts on him. It may be due to his love for material wealth or due to bad company, but it would undermine God-consciousness in him.

256. The temporary phase of forgetfulness of God would benumb his moral sensibilities and only some faint impressions of faith would be left in his mind.

257. When this forgetfulness overtakes him for the second time and it is repeated again and again, the canker would grow which would eat into the vitals of his moral health.

258. According to Badr-ud-Din 'Aynī, it implies that nothing sacred and pious would be left in the heart of man and, just as in the blister there is only pus, similarly, in the heart not illuminated by the love of God, there would be nothing but the darkness of sin.

259. With the deterioration of faith there would be a deterioration of the sense of moral responsibility and man would become utterly untrustworthy. When there is lack of God-consciousness, there is also a lack of virtue, trustworthiness and inner piety.

of a mustard seed.[260] I have passed through a time in which I did not care with whom amongst you I entered into a transaction, for if he were a Muslim his faith would compel him to discharge his obligations to me[261] and if he were a Christian or a Jew, the ruler would compel him to discharge his obligations to me.[262] But today I would not enter into a transaction with you except so and so.

(266) This ḥadīth has been transmitted by another chain of transmitters: Ibn Numair, Wakī', Isḥāq b. Ibrāhīm, 'Īsā b. Yūnus on the authority of A'mash.

(267) It is narrated on the authority of Ḥudhaifa: We were sitting in the company of 'Umar and he said: Who amongst you has heard the Messenger of Allah (may peace be upon him) talking about the turmoil?[263] Some people said: It is we who heard it. Upon this he remarked: Perhaps by turmoil you presume the unrest of man in regard to his household or neighbour.[264] They replied: Yes. He ('Umar) observed: Such (an unrest) would be done away with by prayer, fasting and charity. But who amongst you has heard from the Apostle (may peace be upon him) describing that turmoil which would come like the wave of the ocean.[265] Ḥudhaifa said: The people hushed into silence. I replied: It is I. He ('Umar) said: Ye, well, your father was also very pious. Ḥudhaifa said: I heard the Messenger of Allah (may peace be upon him) observing: Temptations will be presented to men's hearts as reed mat is woven stick by stick[266]

260. The decline of faith would change the very angle of vision of the people and with this would change the values of life and the sense of right and wrong, just and unjust—in short, good and evil. The man who is corrupt, who is unscrupulous in his dealings, would be branded as a prudent and intelligent man and the honest people would be looked down upon as fools.

261. Faith would exhort him to be fair in his dealings with others and not to be dishonest.

262. The society permeated with a spirit of God-consciousness will have pious and just rulers who would see that no wrong is done to anyone and all people have a sense of security against any type of injustice, high-handedness or aggression.

263. Originally, the word فتنة (*fitna*) means burning of gold in a fire so as to purify it from the alloy. In common language it stands for a trial which tests the worth of a man or a temptation which induces a man to evil deeds, but which, when resisted, proves the strength of one's character. This word is also used for intrigue, sedition, riot, discord and dissension, commotion or turmoil.

264. Ḥadrat 'Umar (may Allah be pleased with him) was right in visualising that by *fitan* the people were presuming the ordinary discord or unrest which, according to the Holy Qur'ān, could be easily effaced by acts of virtue and piety, e.g. prayer, fasting and charity: "Verily virtues take away vices" (xi. 114).

265. This refers to the mounting wave of turmoil which would shake the very foundation of Muslim society. The commentators of Ḥadīth have tried to determine it. Some of them are of the opinion that this refers to the large-scale dissension amongst the Muslims which started at the fag end of the Caliphate of Ḥadrat 'Uthmān (may Allah be pleased with him) and then erupted in an armed conflict between Ḥadrat 'Alī and Amīr Mu'āwiya (may Allah be pleased with them) and which finally culminated in the martyrdom of Imām Ḥusain and his companions (may Allah shower His blessings on them).

266. This is read in three different ways:

(*a*) عُوداً عُوداً (*b*) عَوداً عَوداً (*c*) عَوذاً عوذاً

We have in the text translated the first expression which means that the temptations would come to the heart of a man one after another in quick succession just as in the weaving of the reed mat, one reed is joined to another.

The second expression means that the temptations would stick in the niche of a man's heart, just as the reed mat leaves deep marks on one who sleeps over it, and the temptations would

and any heart which is impregnated by them will have a black mark put into it, but any heart which rejects them will have a white mark put in it. The result is that there will become two types of hearts : one white like a white stone[267] which will not be harmed by any turmoil or temptation, so long as the heavens and the earth endure ; and the other black and dust-coloured like a vessel which is upset,[268] not recognising what is good or rejecting what is abominable, but being impregnated with passion. Ḥudhaifa said : I narrated to him ('Umar) : There is between you and that (turmoil) a closed door, but there is every likelihood of its being broken. 'Umar said : Would it be broken ? You have been rendered fatherless.[269] Had it been opened, it would have been perhaps closed also. I said : No, it would be broken, and I narrated to him : Verily that door implies a person who would be killed or die.[270] There is no mistake in this ḥadīth. Abū Khālid narrated : I said to Sa'd, O Abū Mālik, what do you mean by the term اسود مربادا (Uswad Murbadda) ? He replied : High degree of whiteness in blackness. I said : What is meant by الكوز مجخيا ? He replied : A vessel turned upside down.

(268) It is narrated on the authority of Rib'ī (b. Ḥirāsh) : When Ḥudhaifa came from 'Umar he sat down to narrate to us and said : Verily yesterday when I was sitting with the Commander of the believers he asked his companions : Who amongst you retains in his memory the utterance of the Messenger of Allah (may peace be upon him) with regard to the turmoil ?—and he cited the ḥadīth like the ḥadīth narrated on the authority of Abū Khālid, but he did not mention the exposition of his words مربادا (Murbāddan) and مجخيا (Mujakhiyyan).

(269) It is transmitted by Rib'ī b. Ḥirāsh who narrated it on the authority of Ḥudhaifa that verily 'Umar said : Who would narrate to us or who amongst you would narrate to us (and Ḥudhaifa was one amongst them) what the Messenger of Allah (may peace be upon him) had said about the turmoil ? Ḥudhaifa said : I will, and recited the ḥadīth like that transmitted by Abū Mālik on the authority of Rib'ī and he observed in connection with this ḥadīth that Ḥudhaifa remarked : I am narrating to you a ḥadīth and it has no mistake, and said : That it is transmitted from the Messenger of Allah (may peace be upon him).

come again and again.

Thirdly, the temptations would invade the hearts but would abide there like the marks of reed on the bare body of a man.

267. *Al-Ṣafā'* means the stone or smooth stone ; it is used for the purity of life and mind.

268. Dust-coloured vessel which is turned upside down is a highly meaningful simile. Dust-coloured implies that it would lose its lustre and its colour would be so dusty that one would not be able to discern dark spots on it. When the conscience is pure one can easily discern in oneself the marks of evil. But when the man is used to evil or sin, his conscience is blurred and then it fails to distinguish between right and wrong. Then the heart is compared to an upturned vessel with a view to indicating that just as a vessel in this position cannot contain anything, similarly a perverted heart cannot retain any goodness in it, and if it is ever inspired by noble sentiments, it is unable to perpetuate this healthy state and it soon reverts to its previous position.

269. It is a common expression in Arabic which is used with a view to exhorting a man to a noble deed. It implies if Ḥudhaifa had his father alive he must have joined him in mitigating his troubles, but now that there is none to offer him help and assistance he should try to stand on his own feet.

270. The commentators are of the view that the closed door implies Ḥaḍrat 'Umar, because his great personality exercised the most formidable check on the spread of evil.

Chapter LXVI

ISLAM WAS INITIATED AS SOMETHING STRANGE, AND IT WOULD REVERT TO ITS (OLD POSITION) OF BEING STRANGE, AND IT WOULD CONCENTRATE BETWEEN THE TWO MOSQUES

(270) It is narrated on the authority of Abū Huraira that the Messenger of Allah (may peace be upon him) said: Islam initiated as something strange, and it would revert to its (old position) of being strange, so good tidings for the strangers.[271]

(271) It is narrated on the authority of Ibn 'Umar ('Abdullah b. 'Umar) that the Messenger of Allah (may peace be upon him) observed: Verily Islam started as something strange and it would again revert (to its old position) of being strange just as it started, and it would recede between the two mosques[272] just as the serpent crawls back into its hole.

(272) It is narrated on the authority of Abū Huraira that the Messenger of Allah (may peace be upon him) said: Verily the faith would recede to Medina just as the serpent crawls back into its hole.

Chapter LXVII

THE EFFACING OF FAITH IN THE LATER AGE

(273) It is narrated on the authority of Anas that verily the Messenger of Allah (may peace be upon him) observed: The Hour (Resurrection) would not come so long as Allah is supplicated in the world.

271. This ḥadīth is generally translated: "Islam started from the poor..."; but it is not correct. What this ḥadīth implies is that, although the teachings of Islam are so akin to the nature of man, yet when these were preached the people shunned them as strange and unfamiliar things. Secondly, the preaching of Islam was started at Mecca, the birthplace of the Holy Prophet, but the atmosphere did not prove congenial to its growth and the Meccans treated the Holy Prophet as a stranger. He had to find a new abode in Medina—a place where he and Islam were both strangers, but it proved to be very congenial, for it made an amazing progress. The Holy Prophet became the central figure of Arabia, and won a large number of adherents. Islam became the most powerful religion and began to gain ascendancy even far beyond the frontiers of Arabia.

The second part of the ḥadīth is a prophecy, the truth of which can be seen by every man. The Muslims are so engrossed in other pursuits of life that a large majority of them seems to have not even a nodding acquaintance with Islam. Their ideals, their individual and social behaviour, their tastes and tendencies, their manners and habits, their political, economic and social systems are nothing but a blind imitation of un-Islamic values. These values have taken such a firm hold on the minds of the Muslims that Islamic values appear strange to them and those who uphold them are considered to be strangers in the modern society. To such noble souls who resolutely profess and practise Islam even in such untoward, rather hostile, circumstances, the tidings is given by the Holy Prophet. Every Muslim can see with his own eyes the truth of the prophecy made 1400 years ago by the Messenger of Allah (may peace be upon him).

272. This ḥadīth prophesies that Islam would not be completely swept out of existence but would become a spent-up force and recede to the place where it started its march, that is between the old mosques of Mecca and Medina.

(274) It is narrated on the authority of Anas that the Messenger of Allah (may peace be upon him) said: The Hour (Resurrection) would not come upon anyone so long as he supplicates Allah.[273]

Chapter LXVIII

PERMISSIBILITY OF CONCEALING THE FAITH OF ONE WHO FEARS

(275) Ḥudhaifa reported: We were in the company of the Messenger of Allah (may peace be upon him) when he said: Count[274] for me those who profess al-Islām. We said: Messenger of Allah, do you entertain any fear concerning us and we are (at this time) between six hundred and seven hundred (in strength).[275] He (the Holy Prophet) remarked: You don't perceive; you may be put to some trial. He (the narrator) said: We actually suffered trial so much so that some of our men were constrained to offer their prayers in concealment.[276]

Chapter LXIX

TO HABITUATE THE HEART WITH FAITH WHICH, DUE TO ITS WEAKNESS, IS SCARED AND THE FORBIDDANCE TO CALL POSITIVELY ONE A BELIEVER WITHOUT A DEFINITE PROOF

(276) Sa'd narrated it on the authority of his father (Abī Waqqāṣ) that he observed: The Messenger of Allah (may peace be upon him) distributed shares (of booty

273. What it means is that it is God's consciousness which endows human life with a meaning and thus makes it worth living. Human life is not a mere pastime in the world. It has a definite end before it and this end determines the nature of its struggle. The whole cosmos with all its wide and varied phenomena bears testimony to the fact that it is not mere accident, but the result of a Planning Will. So long as one is not in spiritual accord with that Will, there can be no harmony in the life of a man. The consciousness of this Planning Will is the basic need of human beings, because without this consciousness all those values which sustain social and moral life, e g. justice, selflessness, inner piety, love for humanity, would cease to exist. Without belief in God human life would be directed only by expediency and material interests. Humanity would thus become a large warring camp where everyone would be fighting against the other. All noble values of life and all higher strivings would suffer extinction and man would become a veritable beast. It is at this stage that the human race would be doomed to destruction because when the salt loses its savour, it is no use to preserve it any more. It must be thrown as a mere waste in the street.

274. This act of the Holy Prophet clearly indicates how realist he was and how much care did he take in assessing correctly his strength. It has an object lesson for those in whose hands are the affairs of the Muslims. They should very objectively assess the strength which they possess and then undertake any campaign.

275. This shows that the followers of Muḥammad, despite their meagre numerical strength, were neither dismayed nor obsessed with fear. The faith in Allah had made them fearless and they were sanguine enough to believe that with the help of God they could successfully meet any danger.

276. This refers to the hostilities which erupted in armed conflict between different sections of the Muslim society which started at the end of Ḥaḍrat 'Uthmān's (Allah be pleased with him) caliphate and ended the lives of so many noble and eminent personalities of Islam. That was not the end of the tragedy. It is in so many different periods of Muslim history that we see such sad happenings which made public prayer an impossible task.

amongst his Companions). I said: Messenger of Allah! give it to so and so, for verily he is a believer. Upon this the Apostle of Allah remarked: Or a Muslim?[277] I (the narrator) repeated it (the word "believer") thrice and he (the Holy Prophet) turned it back upon me (and substituted the word) "Muslim," and then observed: I bestow it (this share) to a man out of apprehension lest Allah should throw him prostrate into the fire (of Hell) whereas in fact the other man is dearer to me than he.[278]

(277) It is narrated on the authority of Sa'd that the Messenger of Allah (may peace be upon him) bestowed upon a group of persons (things), and Sa'd was sitting amongst them. Sa'd said: The Messenger of Allah (may peace be upon him) ignored some of them. And he who was ignored seemed to be more deserving in my eyes (as compared with others). I (Sa'd) said: Messenger of Allah! why is it that you did not give to such and such (man)? Verily I see him a believer. Upon this the Messenger of Allah (may peace be upon him) observed: Or a Muslim? I kept quiet for some time but I was again impelled (to express) what I knew about him. I said: Messenger of Allah! why is it that you did not give it to such and such (man)? Verily, by Allah, I see him a believer. Upon this the Messenger of Allah (may peace be upon him) remarked: (Nay, not a believer) but a Muslim. He (Sa'd) said: I again kept quiet for some time but what I knew about him again impelled me (to express my opinion) and I said: Why is it that you did not give (the share) to so and so? By Allah, verily I see him a believer. The Messenger of Allah (may peace be upon him) remarked: (Nay, not so) but a Muslim. Verily (at times) I give (a share) to a certain man apprehending that he may not be thrown prostrate in the Fire, whereas the other man (who is not given) is dearer to me (as compared with him).

(278) Sa'd reported: The Messenger of Allah (may peace be upon him) bestowed upon a group of persons (booty) and I was sitting with them. The remaining part of the

277. A Muslim is he who makes profession of Islam, but the believer is one who believes in Islam from the depth of his heart. Thus the believer is always a Muslim but a man who makes a mere verbal profession of Islam may not necessarily be a believer, for there is a possibility that he may not be assenting to the truth in the heart of his heart.

278. Belief is a complex process in which both heart and mind participate. In some cases it may be a sudden assent to truth with complete transformation of the soul. But in other cases it may be a very slow process of mental revolution. All these cases require proper nourishment and assistance at every step. The Holy Prophet has, therefore, by his personal example, exhorted us to treat such men with generosity so that the new converts overcome their failings and develop power enough to withstand the hardships of the new way of life. The assistance at the initial stages of Īmān helps a man strengthen his faith and ultimately dispense with the need of relying upon others except upon the never-failing help of God. The Western critics have made this assistance to the new converts as the target of criticism by telling people that it is a kind of bribery or a bait to induce persons to enter the fold of Islam. It is nothing but a sheer folly. The purpose of such a bestowal is to offer assistance to the new converts to Islam so that they may be able to rehabilitate themselves in the Muslim society. Islam awakens the Muslims to their social responsibilities and exhorts them not to leave their new brethren-in-faith to the strokes of untoward circumstances. This help and assistance is a token of cordial welcome and sincere heart with which the Muslim society receives his new brother who forsakes everything for the sake of Islam.

This ḥadīth also shows that the real Īmān is that which is above all material and monetary considerations and which makes the love of Allah and His pleasure as the highest achievement of human life.

ḥadīth is the same as mentioned (above) with the addition : I stood up and went to the Messenger of Allah (may peace be upon him) and whispered to him : Why did you omit such and such a man ?

(279) The same ḥadīth has been narrated on the authority of Muḥammad b. Sa'd and these words (are also there) : The Messenger of Allah (may peace be upon him) gave a stroke on my neck or between my two shoulders and said : Sa'd, do you fight with me simply because I gave (a share) to a man ?

Chapter LXX

THE HEART IS MORE SATISFIED ON SEEING EVIDENCE

(280) It is narrated on the authority of Abū Huraira that the Messenger of Allah (may peace be upon him) observed : We have more claim to doubt than Ibrāhīm (may peace be upon him)[279] when he said : My Lord ! show me how Thou wilt quicken the dead. He said : Believeth thou not ? He said : Yes ! But that my heart may rest at ease.[280] He (the Holy Prophet) observed : May Lord take mercy on Lot, that he wanted a strong support,[281] and had I stayed (in the prison) as long as Yūsuf stayed, I would

279. This part of the ḥadīth has been translated in so many different ways, but the most appropriate meaning according to the Muḥaddathīn is : If Ibrāhīm could harbour any doubt, I have a better claim to entertain doubt. But as you see I do not have any doubt in faith, therefore it is quite logical to conceive that Ibrāhīm could not have any doubt in the matter of faith (*Fatḥ-ul-Mulḥim*, Vol. I, pp. 292, 293).

280. The background of this āyat (ii. 160) has been given by Nawawī : When this verse was recited to the people, their minds were especially perturbed on these words "Believeth thou not ?" and they misconstrued them to be an indication of doubt on the part of Ibrāhīm (may peace be upon him). It is at this juncture that the Holy Prophet explained the fact that the Prophet Ibrāhīm did not beg his Lord to show him the signs as he harboured any doubt about the Unseen Realities in which he was required to affirm his faith. He had implicit belief in the Power of Allah. There was no question of doubt about it. He simply wanted to intensify his belief still further by witnessing the Resurrection with his physical eyes so that he might be able to catch a glimpse of the Unseen Truth and thus achieve the position of *'Ain-ul-Yaqīn*, as it had been the privilege of all the Prophets. There was nothing unusual with this innocent demand for the favour of Allah.

Ibn Jarīr, on the authority of authentic chains of transmission, Sa'īd b. Jubair and Mujāhid and others, has explained the words ليطمئن قلبى as يزداد يقينى, i.e. "faith may be intensified" (*Fatḥ-ul-Bāri*, Vol. I, p. 53).

Some of the eminent commentators are of the view that the words of the Qur'ān show that it was not about the belief in the Hereafter (one of the fundamentals of faith) that Ḥaḍrat Ibrāhīm (may peace be upon him) was asking any visible and tangible proof, but it was about the nature of transformation that he wanted to know. And this is not included in the belief in the Hereafter (*Fatḥ-ul-Mulḥim*, Vol. I, p. 293).

This verse of the Qur'ān succinctly defines the attitude of Islam towards the senses and the world of senses. There have been thinkers who look down upon the physical world as a mere illusion. Islam repudiates this and believes that the physical perceptions of man and physical phenomena of Nature are not delusions but, aided by faith, they can prove as vehicles of truth and the means to intensify our belief. These may in a certain figurative, pictorial, suggestive manner embody and enable us to perceive the spiritual realities.

281. This refers to the incident that occurred in the life of Ḥaḍrat Lūṭ (may peace be upon him). His house was visited by angels who came in the form of handsome young boys. The people of the town who were used to sodomy raided his house and attempted to take "these boys" in their

have responded to him who invited me.[282]

(281) 'Abdullah b. Muḥammad narrated the same ḥadīth on the authority of Abū Huraira and in the transmission by Mālik the words are that he (the Holy Prophet) recited the verse: "but that my heart may rest at ease" and completed it.

(282) This ḥadīth has also been narrated by 'Abd b. Ḥumaid Ya'qūb, i.e. son of Ibrāhīm b. Sa'd, Abū Uwais, Zuhrī, like the one narrated by Mālik with the same chain of transmission and said: He recited this verse till he completed it.

Chapter LXXI

THE NECESSITY OF AFFIRMING THE PROPHETHOOD OF OUR APOSTLE MUḤAMMAD (MAY PEACE BE UPON HIM) WHO IS THE APOSTLE SENT TO THE WHOLE OF HUMANITY, AND THE ABROGATION OF OTHER RELIGIONS WITH HIS RELIGION

(283) It is narrated on the authority of Abū Huraira that the Messenger of Allah (may peace be upon him) observed: There has never been a Prophet amongst the prophets who was not bestowed with a sign[283] amongst the signs which were bestowed (on the

custody. Ḥaḍrat Lūṭ (may peace be upon him) reprimanded them and asked them not to disgrace him by laying their hands on his guests. It was at this juncture that he expressed his helplessness saying: Would that I had the power to repel you—rather I shall have a recourse to a strong support (xi. 80).

This verse emphasises the fact that, although Ḥaḍrat Lūṭ was the Apostle of Allah, and had full confidence in the Power of his Lord, yet he was so much agitated at that moment that he wished he had a strong clan at his back to protect his honour and that of his guests.

The Holy Prophet has significantly used the words: "May Allah have mercy on him," implying that Ḥaḍrat Lūṭ was so much obsessed by untoward circumstances and the mischief and high-handedness of the people of his town that he felt helpless and wished for a strong support.

282. It refers to the following verse:

> And the King said: Bring him to me. So when the messenger came to him, he said: Go back to thy Lord and ask him what is the case of the women who cut their hands. Surely, my Lord knows their device (xii. 50).

What Yūsuf stressed was that his innocence was well established before God, but he would not get out of jail unless his honour was vindicated in public.

The Holy Prophet was appreciating Ḥaḍrat Yūsuf's remarkable power of endurance against the hardships of prison life and his longing to vindicate his honour in public.

Before we conclude we should say that there is a meaningful relationship in the different parts of the ḥadīth and that is to emphasise the human aspects of man's life even though he is an apostle. Ibrāhīm had implicit belief in Allah but he wanted to intensify this belief by seeing with the sense of sight the phenomenon of Resurrection. Ḥaḍrat Lūṭ (may peace be upon him) had perfect trust and confidence in Allah but he also felt the need of his men's support in the most trying circumstances as his guests were assailed by the mischief-mongers. Similarly, the innocence of Yūsuf (may peace be upon him) was above all doubt and he knew for certain that the All-Knowing Lord was fully aware of the plot hatched against him, but he wanted to vindicate his honour in public also. This goes to prove that in our physical life of this world, we stand in need of visible proofs, the support of our kith and kin and our nation and human beings at large, and we want to move about in society with honour and respect.

283. No evidence of a Revelation is conceivable which does not partake of the character of a miracle, since nothing but a display of power over the existing system of things can attest the immediate Presence of Him, by Whom it was originally established. Miracles thus hold a prominent

earlier prophets). Human beings believed in it and verily I have been conferred upon revelation (the Holy Qur'ān) which Allah revealed to me.[284] I hope that I will have the greatest following on the Day of Resurrection.[285]

(284) It is narrated on the authority of Abū Huraira that the Messenger of Allah (may peace be upon him) observed: By Him in Whose hand is the life of Muḥammad, he who amongst the community of Jews or Christians hears about me, but does not affirm his belief in that with which I have been sent and dies in this state (of disbelief), he shall be but one of the denizens of Hell-Fire.[286]

(285) It is narrated on the authority of Sha'bī that one among the citizens of Khurāsān asked him: O Abū 'Amr! some of the people amongst us who belong to Khurāsān say that a person who freed his bondswoman and then married her is like one who rode over a sacrificial animal. Sha'bī said: Abū Burda b. Abī Mūsā narrated it to me on the authority of his father that verily the Messenger of Allah (may peace be upon him) said: There are three (classes of persons) who would be given a double reward. One who is amongst the People of the Book and believed in his apostle and (lived) to see the time of Apostle Muḥammad (may peace be upon him) and affirmed his

place as the attestation of all Revelations. They are the most striking and conclusive evidence; because the laws of matter being better understood than those to which mind is conformed, their violation is more easily recognised. This is why every prophet was conferred upon miraculous signs in proof of his being a true messenger of God. These miracles are not perversions of the real order of the world, but Divine acts to restore the sinful world to its proper order. They are amazing occurrences in the sense that they awaken in human beings the consciousness of the Lord which is overlaid by so many aberrations. Signs and Scriptures thus always go together. The general procedure with old prophets was that the minds of the people were first stirred by miracles and it was only when they were prepared to receive the message of Allah that it was vouchsafed to them.

284. There has been a change in the set order of preaching with the advent of Muḥammad (may peace be upon him). In his case, the revelation (the Qur'ān) was presented as the greatest miracle and the people were asked to reflect over it. Miracles there were in the life of Muḥammad, but these were not originally meant to bring conviction of an Almighty Creator. They proffered a testimony what the Holy Qur'ān had instilled in the minds of people. It was the Qur'ān which was made to serve as an effective means to rouse the conscience of the people, to awaken them to a sense of responsibility, to remind them of their duty that they owed to Allah and humanity.

Now the question arises: In what sense the Qur'ān is a miracle? The answer is that it is a miracle both in meaning and diction. There is no book in the world which contains, like the Qur'ān, Unity, Praise and Glorification of the Most High Lord, belief in His apostles and messengers, incitement to good and prohibition of evil, exhortation to Paradise and a dissuasion from Hell. Where in the world can be found a book which covers such a wide range of topics and then discusses them with such sweetness and charm that no sensible mind can remain unaffected, while the man who presents it to the world is unlettered?

285. Muḥammad (may peace be upon him) will have the largest number of sincere followers behind him on the Day of Resurrection.

286. The Holy Prophet has been sent as the final dispenser of the Will of Allah and the Qur'ān is the last scripture from the Lord which embodies the teachings of all the earlier prophets and even those principles and values of life which humanity would stand in need of till the Day of Resurrection.

"Today I have perfected for you your religion and fulfilled My favour unto you" (v. 3).

It implies that the laws of the Qur'ān are the timeless expressions of God's will. These are universal and not hemmed in by space or time. All the previous Sharī'ahs now stand abrogated, for Islam is the culmination of the Divine Code of human life. Thus without believing in it and sincerely adhering to it, no man would be able to attain salvation.

faith in him and followed him and attested his truth, for him is the double reward; and the slave of the master who discharges all those obligations that he owes to Allah and discharges his duties that he owes to his master, for him there is a double reward. And a man who had a bondswoman and fed her and fed her well, then taught her good manners, and did that well and later on granted her freedom and married her, for him is the double reward. Then Sha'bī said: Accept this ḥadīth without (giving) anything. Formerly a man was (obliged) to travel to Medina even for a smaller ḥadīth than this.[287]

(286) This ḥadīth has been narrated by another chain of transmitters like Abū Bakr b. Abī Shaiba, 'Abda b. Sulaimān, Ibn Abī 'Umar Sufyān, 'Ubaidullah b. Mu'ādh, Shu'ba; all of them heard it from Ṣāliḥ b. Ṣāliḥ.

Chapter LXXII

THE DESCENT OF JESUS SON OF MARY, AND HE WILL JUDGE ACCORDING TO THE SHARĪ'AH OF OUR APOSTLE, MUḤAMMAD (MAY PEACE BE UPON HIM)

(287) Abū Huraira reported that the Messenger of Allah (may peace be upon him) said: By Him in Whose hand is my life, the son of Mary (may peace be upon him) will soon descend among you as a just judge.[288] He will break crosses,[289] kill swine[290] and abolish Jizya,[291] and the wealth will pour forth to such an extent that no one will accept it.

(288) The same ḥadīth is transmitted from Zuhrī with the same chain of transmission. But in the tradition narrated by Ibn 'Uyaina the words are: "impartial leader and just judge" and in the tradition narrated by Yūnus: the "judge judging with justice" and "impartial leader" are not mentioned. And in the ḥadīth narrated by Ṣāliḥ like the one transmitted by Laith the words are: "impartial judge". And in the ḥadīth transmitted by Ziyād the words are: "Till one sajda[292] is better than the world," and what it contains. Then Abū Huraira used to say, "recite" if you like: Not one of the People

287. Here Sha'bī was stressing upon the hardships of his ancestors which they underwent for the collection of the Aḥadīth.

288. Since the Sharī'ah of all the earlier prophets stands abrogated with the advent of Muḥammad's apostlehood, Jesus will, therefore, judge according to the law of Islam.

289. Cross is a symbol of Christianity. Jesus will break this symbol after the advent of Muḥammad. Islam is the *dīn* of Allah and no other religion is acceptable to Him. Ḥāfiẓ Ibn Ḥajar 'Asqalānī includes in cross all those instruments which become the means to undermine God-consciousness (*Fatḥ-ul-Bāri*, Vol. VII, p. 302).

290. The flesh of the swine is a favourite dish of the Christians. Jesus would sweep out of existence this dirty and loathsome animal.

291. The whole of the human race would accept Islam and there would be no dhimmī, and thus Jizya would be automatically abolished.

292. Human race would be so much devoted to Allah that it would look upon one act of prostration more valuable than the material wealth of the whole world (*Fatḥ-ul-Bāri*, Vol. VII, p. 303).

of the Book will fail to believe in him[293] before his death.

(289) It is narrated on the authority of Abū Huraira that the Messenger of Allah (may peace be upon him) observed: I swear by Allah that the son of Mary will certainly descend[294] as a just judge and he would definitely break the cross, and kill swine and abolish Jizya and would leave the young she-camel[295] and no one would endeavour[296] to (collect Zakāt on it). Spite, mutual hatred and jealousy against one another will certainly disappear and when he summons people to accept wealth, not even one would do so.[297]

(290) It is narrated on the authority of Abū Huraira that the Messenger of Allah (may peace be upon him) observed: What will be your state when the son of Mary descends amongst you and there will be an Imām[298] amongst you?

(291) It is narrated on the authority of Abū Huraira that he heard the Messenger of Allah (may peace be upon him) as saying: What would you do when the son of Mary would descend and lead you?

(292) It is narrated on the authority of Abū Huraira that the Messenger of Allah

293. This āyat (iv. 159) has been interpreted in so many ways. The two interpretations are authentic. The pronoun "him" is a point of difference between the different commentators of the Holy Qur'ān. Both the Jews and the Christians necessarily believe in the death of Jesus on the cross, while according to the Holy Qur'ān it was not so. The Jews reject his claim to Messiahship on the basis of Deut. 21 : 23 : He that is hanged is accursed of God. According to their belief, since Jesus died on the cross, he was, therefore, accursed of God. Christians, on the other hand, believe that Jesus died on the cross and thus redeemed mankind from the curse of the law. They look upon him as the son of God who died for the atonement of the sins of the human race. The Holy Qur'ān repudiates both the claims. Jesus is not accursed as the Jews think, for he was not crucified. He is an eminent apostle of Allah. But at the same time he is not the son of the Lord, as the Christians believe him to be, but he is His messenger and his bondsman. Thus what the āyat signifies is that, before the actual death of the Christ, the Jews and the Christians would both recognise him as the true prophet of Allah and His bondsman. All mistaken notions about him would be winnowed out before his death in this mortal world. This interpretation is given by Ibn Jarīr and other eminent commentators.

There is also a second interpretation, according to which the pronoun "him" stands for Muḥammad (may peace be upon him). And the āyat would thus mean: That none among the People of the Book, but shall surely believe in him (Muhammad) before his death (*Fatḥ-ul-Bārī*, Vol. VII, p. 303).

294. This ḥadīth, according to a famous commentator of the Ḥadīth, testifies to the descent of Christ near the Day of Resurrection, for if he is believed to have died on the cross, how would he descend to the earth again? (*Fatḥ-ul-Mulḥim*, Vol. I, p. 301).

295. The word is قلاص (qilāṣ). It is one of the finest breeds of camels in Arabia, and this is used simply to stress its value.

296. Qāḍī 'Iyāḍ has explained it: No one would demand Zakāt on it.

297. When love for the material wealth would give way to love for Allah and His Prophet, the hearts would be purified of all such evils which breed sins like spite, mutual hatred and jealousy (*Fatḥ-ul-Mulḥim*, Vol. I, p. 303).

298. According to some commentators of the Ḥadīth, here the word "Imām" stands for *Imām Mahdi* who would, before the descent of Christ, guide people to the path of righteousness. What this ḥadīth (What will you do with your Imām when Christ comes?) implies is: How would you behave with your Imām (Mahdī) after the descent of Christ? The answer is simple that the Imām would then be second in command because the apostle of Allah occupies a higher position than the Imām.

The second and preferable meaning is that Christ would be one amongst the Muslims and would judge according to the Sharī'ah of Islam (*Fatḥ-ul-Bārī*, Vol. VII, pp. 304, 305).

(may peace be upon him) observed: What would you do when the son of Mary would descend amongst you and would lead you as one amongst you? Ibn Abī Dhi'b on the authority of Abū Huraira narrated: Your leader amongst you. Ibn Abi Dhi'b said: Do you know what the words: "He would lead as one amongst you" mean? I said: Explain these to me. He said: He would lead you according to the Book of your Lord (hallowed be He and most exalted) and the Sunnah of your Apostle (may peace be upon him).

(293) Jābir b. 'Abdullah reported: I heard the Messenger of Allah (may peace be upon him) say: A section of my people will not cease fighting[299] for the Truth and will prevail till the Day of Resurrection. He said: Jesus son of Mary would then descend and their (Muslims') commander would invite him to come and lead them in prayer, but he would say: No,[300] some amongst you are commanders over some (amongst you). This is the honour from Allah for this Ummah.

Chapter LXXIII

DESCRIPTION OF THE PERIOD IN WHICH ĪMĀN WOULD NOT BE ACCEPTABLE TO ALLAH

(294) It is narrated on the authority of Abū Huraira that the Messenger of Allah (may peace be upon him) said: The (Last) Hour shall not come till the sun rises from the place of its setting. And on the day when it rises from the place of its setting even if all the people together affirmed their faith, it would not be of any avail to one who did not believe previously and derived no good out of his belief.[301]

(295) This ḥadīth has been narrated by another chain of transmitters, Abū Bakr b. Abī Shaiba, Ibn Numair, Abū Kuraib, Ibn Fuḍail.

(296) It is narrated on the authority of Abū Huraira that the Messenger of Allah (may peace be upon him) observed: When three things appear faith will not benefit one who has not previously believed or has derived no good from his faith: the rising

299. The word "fighting" has been used here in a wider sense. It implies an all-round struggle for the supremacy of Truth. Thus all those noble souls who participate in this struggle are included in this blessed group.

300. Christ would decline the offer and say his prayer behind Imām Mahdī only to show that it was now the Sharī'ah of Islam which was valid. To be led in prayer is not the sign of inferiority in rank. Once 'Abdur-Raḥmān b. 'Auf led the prayer and the Apostle of Allah (may peace be upon him), with all his eminence and dignity, followed him.

301. The real basis of faith is that man believes in the Unseen Realities on the authority of the Apostles of Allah. But when the Lord manifests such startling and visible signs which herald the approach of the Last Hour and by which the veil of the Unseen is rent asunder, then the belief becomes meaningless. The rising of the sun in the west would be a great disturbance in the course of Nature and would shake the mind of every man and awaken him to see for himself the Great Power of the Lord. At this stage the belief in the Unseen would lose its import.

of the sun in its place of setting, the Dajjāl,[302] and the beast [303] of the earth.

(297) It is narrated on the authority of Abū Dharr that the Messenger of Allah (may peace be upon him) one day said: Do you know where the sun goes? They replied: Allah and His Apostle know best. He (the Holy Prophet) observed: Verily it (the sun) glides till it reaches its resting place under the Throne. Then it falls prostrate and remains there until it is asked: Rise up and go to the place whence you came, and it goes back and continues emerging out from its rising place and then glides till it reaches its place of rest under the Throne and falls prostrate and remains in that state until it is asked: Rise up and return to the place whence you came, and it returns and emerges out from its rising place and then it glides (in such a normal way) that the people do not discern anything (unusual in it) till it reaches its resting place under the Throne. Then it would be said to it: Rise up and emerge out from the place of your setting, and it will rise from the place of its setting. The Messenger of Allah (may peace be upon him) said: Do you know when it would happen? It would happen at the time when faith will not benefit one who has not previously believed or has derived no good from the faith.[304]

(298) It is narrated on the authority of Abū Dharr that the Apostle of Allah (may peace be upon him) one day said: Do you know where the sun goes? The remaining part of the ḥadīth is the same.

(299) Abū Dharr reported: I entered the mosque and the Messenger of Allah (may peace be upon him) was sitting there. When the sun disappeared (from the sight) he said: O Abū Dharr! do you know where it goes? He (the narrator) said: Allah and His Apostle know best. He (the Holy Prophet) said: Verily it goes and begs permission

302 Dajjāl, whose equivalent in English is Antichrist, means one who conceals the truth with falsehood, a falsifier, one who deceives, deludes, beguiles, circumvents, is very deceitful or a great deceiver. The verb دجل also means "he smeared the whole body of camel with tar". Thus, according to this, Dajjāl would mean a great falsifier who would cover the whole earth with conceit and delusion and infidelity or with his beguiled adherents as tar covers the body. According to another version, he would be called Dajjāl because he will traverse most of the regions of the earth. There is a good deal of difference of opinion about the personality of Dajjāl and this has raised much academic discussion about it. This thing is, however, certain that at the fag end of the world, a great falsifier would rise and he would, by his vicious tricks and devices, lead people astray from the path of righteousness. Ḥāfiẓ Ibn Ḥajar 'Asqalānī has mentioned the opinion of Qāḍī 'Iyāḍ: Whatever we find in the aḥādīth proves beyond any shadow of doubt that al-Dajjāl is a particular person; he would definitely appear on the plane of the world and through his magic devices mislead people.

303. *Dā'bbat al-arḍ* is one of the signs of the approach of the hour. The Holy Qur'ān also speaks of this:

> And when the word shall come to be fulfilled concerning them, We shall bring forth a beast of the earth speaking unto them, that the people have not been convinced of Our signs (xxvii. 82).

'Allāma Ālūsī, the author of the famous commentary of the Qur'ān, *Rūḥ-ul-Ma'āni*, says that there is a good deal of difference of opinion with regard to the nature of that beast. This much is, however, sure that a strange creature would emerge into being and would be a source of destruction to the people.

304. This ḥadīth is symbolic of the system of orderliness in Nature which exhibits that the whole system of the universe including the sun and the moon runs its course according to the Planning Will of the Creator. The sun emerges out from its rising place so long as it is commanded to do so, and it will change its routine with the Order of the Lord. Prostration before the Throne implies its complete submission and surrender before the Power of the Almighty Creator.

for prostration (to Allah) and the permission is granted to it. Once it would be said: Return to the place whence you came, and then it would rise from its setting place. Then he, after the recitation of 'Abdullah recited it: And that is its appointed term.[305]

(300) Abū Dharr reported: I asked the Messenger of Allah (may peace be upon him) the (implication of the) words of Allah, the Exalted: The sun glides to its appointed resting place. He replied: Its appointed resting place is under the Throne.[306]

Chapter LXXIV

THE BEGINNING OF REVELATION TO THE MESSENGER OF ALLAH (MAY PEACE BE UPON HIM)

(301) 'Ā'isha, the wife of the Apostle of Allah (may peace be upon him), reported: The first (form) with which was started the revelation[307] to the Messenger of Allah was the true vision in sleep.[308] And he did not see any vision but it came like the bright

305. The complete verse is like this: And the sun glides to its appointed term; that is the disposition of the Mighty, the Knowing (xxxvi. 38). This verse explains the meaning of the ḥadīth: God in His perfect wisdom and knowledge has determined a fixed course of action for the heavenly bodies and these cannot deviate even for the fraction of a second from the path set for them.

306. The Throne of Allah represents His Infinite Power and His undisputed Command over everything. What it implies is that it is according to the dictation of the Lord that the sun runs its course.

307. The dictionary meaning of the word *waḥi* is: to suggest, to write the message, to instil in the mind, to speak secretly. According to Ḥāfiẓ Ibn Ḥajar 'Asqalānī, the real purport of waḥī is quick understanding. Imām Rāghib gives its meaning as an instantaneous suggestion thrown in the mind of man. In the religious sense, as used in Islam, a waḥī denotes the means of communication between God and man, either directly or indirectly, through the intermediacy of the angels: "It is not for man that God should speak with him but by revelation, or from behind a veil, or He sendeth a messenger to reveal His permission what He will" (xlii. 50). Waḥī is not something which can be acquired by man's personal endeavour. It is a special favour and gift of the Lord.

308. The first type in which Allah communicated His will to the Messenger and that is *rūyā' ṣādiqa*, Thus the beginning of revelation consisted of dreams anticipating real events. It should, however, be borne in mind that the dreams of the prophets are not like the dreams of common human beings because the level of consciousness of a prophet is quite different from that of an ordinary man. The Holy Prophet (may peace be upon him) said: Their (prophets') eyes are asleep but their hearts do not sleep. Moreover, rūyā' is not a dream in the ordinary sense of the term. It is a vision which gives an indication of some unseen event. The dream is called in Arabic *ḥulm* (حلم). In "Kitāb-ul-Rūyā'" of Bukhārī, there is a ḥadīth which attests it: Rūyā' is from Allah and ḥulm is from the Satan. Then in the dreams there is even a third type which is known as *aḍghath-ul-aḥlām* (confused dreams). All these words have been used in these different senses in Sūra Yūsuf of the Holy Qur'ān:

> O ye chiefs! give me an answer in regard to my vision if a vision you are wont to expound.
>
> They said: Medlays of dreams and in the interpretation of dreams we are not skilled (xii. 43).

According to Maulānā Anwar Shāh Kāshmīrī, it is wrong to interpret rūyā' as a dream. It is a vision which one has in between a state of waking consciousness and sleep (*Faiḍ-ul-Bārī*, Vol. I, pp. 21, 22).

Ḥāfiẓ Ibn Ḥajar 'Asqalānī is of the opinion that the true vision preceded the revelation with a view to attuning the Holy Prophet to receive the message from the Unseen. It was in fact a training period for him in which he was mentally and spiritually prepared to receive Divine Command from the Lord through the angel Gabriel.

gleam of dawn.[309] Thenceforth solitude became dear to him and he used to seclude himself in the cave of Ḥirā', where he would engage in *taḥannuth*[310] (and that is a worship for a number of nights) before returning to his family and getting provisions again for this purpose. He would then return to Khadīja and take provisions for a like period, till Truth came upon him while he was in the cave of Ḥirā'. There came to him the angel and said: Recite, to which he replied: I am not lettered.[311] He took hold of me [the Apostle said] and pressed me, till I was hard pressed;[312] thereafter he let me off and said: Recite. I said: I am not lettered. He then again took hold of me and pressed[313] me for the second time till I was hard pressed and then let me off and said: Recite, to which I replied: I am not lettered.[314] He took hold of me and pressed me for the third time, till I was hard pressed and then let me go and said: Recite in the name of your Lord Who created, created man from a clot of blood. Recite. And your most bountiful Lord is He Who taught the use of pen, taught man what he knew not (al-Qur'ān, xcvi. 1-4).[315] Then the Prophet returned therewith, his heart was trembling, and he went to Khadīja and said: Wrap me up, wrap me up! So they wrapped him till the fear had left him. He then said to Khadīja: O Khadīja! what has happened to me?—and he informed her of the happening, saying: I fear for myself.[316] She replied: It can't be. Be happy. I swear by Allah that He shall never humiliate you.[317] By Allah, you join ties of relationship, you speak the truth, you bear people's burden, you help the destitute, you entertain guests, and you help against the vicissitudes which affect people.[318]

309. There was nothing hazy about it. Whatever the Holy Prophet saw was as bright as daylight.

310. According to Ibn Ḥajar, the original word is يتحنف (*yataḥannaf*) which means: he follows the mode of worship of Ḥanīfiyah, i.e. of Prophet Ibrāhīm (peace be upon him).

311. "I cannot read as I am unlettered and have received no schooling." This also shows that the prophets receive knowledge directly from God.

312. The angel pressed the Holy Prophet in order to make him fully alert and awaken him to the realisation of the fact that what he was seeing before him in the form of an angel was not a vision but an objective reality, and he was going to receive a message from his Lord with which would start his prophetic career.

313. This process was repeated three times with a view to making him fully conscious of the heavy responsibility which was about to be placed on his shoulders.

314. The very first revelation of the Holy Prophet repudiates the charge of all those critics of Islam who claim that Muḥammad's revelations are the outpourings of his own mind. Had it been so, the first revelation would have been the forceful expression concerning either wrong belief or the evils rampant in the then existing society. But we find no reference to them. The first streak of revelation consists of a calm and solemn statement in which the Prophet was exhorted to recite.

315. Ibn Ḥajar has explained its meaning in the following words: Admitted, you cannot recite by your own efforts and by your own knowledge, but read by God's help. He would teach you in the same way as He created you (*Fatḥ-ul-Bāri*, Vol. I, p. 26).

316. This does not mean what some of the critics say that the Holy Prophet feared that he was possessed by an evil spirit. He was afraid of the great burden of prophethood that had fallen on him and the heavy responsibilities which it entailed. Even if we take it to be the fear of the first experience of revelation, it proves his sincerity. If Muḥammad (may peace be upon him) had been comtemplating such a religious enterprise as some of the critics argue, then he must have never felt any fear at the sight of the angel. A man develops a sort of spiritual affinity with the hallucinations which he intentionally tries to conjure before his mind.

317. These words of Khadīja are a source of great comfort to him and reflect her implicit trust in the eminence, piety and virtuous life of her noble husband.

318. These are all social responsibilities which all God-loving persons must undertake.

Khadīja then took him to Waraqa b. Naufal b. Asad b. 'Abd al-'Uzzā, and he was the son of Khadīja's uncle, i.e. the brother of her father. And he was the man who had embraced Christianity in the Days of Ignorance (i.e. before Islam) and he used to write books in Arabic and, therefore, wrote Injīl in Arabic as God willed that he should write. He was very old and had become blind. Khadīja said to him: O uncle! listen to the son of your brother. Waraqa b. Naufal said: O my nephew! what did you see? The Messenger of Allah (may peace be upon him), then, informed him what he had seen, and Waraqa said to him: It is *nāmūs*[319] that God sent down to Mūsā. Would that I were then (during your prophetic career) a young man. Would that I might be alive when your people would expel you! The Messenger of Allah (may peace be upon him) said: Will they drive me out? Waraqa said: Yes. Never came a man with a like of what you have brought but met hostilities. If I see your day I shall help you wholeheartedly.

(302) This ḥadīth has been narrated on the authority of 'Ā'isha with another chain of narrators like one transmitted by Yūnus, i.e. the first thing with which the revelation was initiated with the Messenger of Allah (may peace be upon him) except the words: By Allah, Allah would never humiliate you, and Khadīja said: O son of my uncle! listen to the son of your brother.

(303) This ḥadīth has been reported from 'Ā'isha by another chain of transmitters and the words are: He (the Holy Prophet) came to Khadīja and his heart was trembling. The rest of the ḥadīth has been narrated like one transmitted by Yūnus and Ma'mar, but the first part is not mentioned, i.e. the first thing with which was started the revelation to the Holy Prophet was the true vision. And these words like those transmitted by Yūnus are mentioned thus: By Allah, Allah would never humiliate you. And there is also a mention of the words of Khadīja: O son of my uncle! listen to the son of your brother.

(304) Jābir b. 'Abdullah al-Anṣārī who was one of the Companions of the Messenger of Allah (may peace be upon him) reported: The Messenger of Allah (may peace be upon him) told about the intermission[320] of revelation and narrated: While I was walking

319. *Nāmūs* means the angel who is entrusted with Divine Secrets.

320. After the first experience of the revelation of the Holy Qur'ān, there was a break for some time. It was a sort of respite given to the Holy Prophet so that he should assimilate his first prophetic experience and mentally prepare himself to receive messages from the Lord and try to develop a sort of spiritual affinity with the angel Gabriel whose subsequent appearance was going to become a regular feature of his life.

This period of intermission also proves that the Holy Qur'ān is the word of Allah. During this period the Holy Prophet was pestered by the pagans of Mecca in hundred and one ways. Some jeered at him by saying that he had fallen in the eye of the Lord. Some claimed that his guide Jinn had foresaken him. In short, they said all sorts of things. Had the Holy Qur'ān been the creation of the Prophet's mind, he would have definitely brought forth some verses and made his opponents silent. But he suffered their shafts of taunts during this period of intermission and said nothing and presented the above-mentioned verses (lxxiv. 1-4) only when these were revealed to him.

It is significant to note that there is a very meaningful relation between the first verse revealed to him and the second one. In the first one he was asked to seek the knowledge of Allah and His Attributes or, in other words, deep God-consciousness and devotion to Him. In this verse he has been told that this devotion to God should not lead him to a life of seclusion and withdrawal from the activities of human existence. He is exhorted to warn his fellow beings. Dr Iqbal has told us that the consciousness of the Prophet has an active and social quality which is lacking in that of a

I heard a voice from the sky, and raising my head I saw the angel who had come to me in Ḥirā', sitting on a Throne between heaven and earth. I was terror-stricken on that account and came back (to my family) and said: Wrap me up, wrap me up! So they wrapped me up, and the Blessed and Most Exalted Allah sent down: "You who are shrouded, arise and deliver warning, your Lord magnify, your clothes cleanse, and defilement shun," and "defilement" means idols; and then the revelation was followed continuously.

(305) It is narrated on the authority of Jābir b. 'Abdullah that he heard the Messenger of Allah (may peace be upon him) say: The waḥī was intermitted for me for a small span of time and while I was walking, and then the ḥadīth like the one narrated by Yūnus was transmitted but with the exception of these words: I was terror-stricken till I fell on the ground.[321] Abū Salama said: Defilement means idols. After this the revelation was speeded up and followed rapidly.

(306) This ḥadīth, the like of one narrated by Yūnus, has also been transmitted by Ma'mar on the authority of al-Zuhrī who narrated: Allah the Most Glorious and Exalted revealed this: "You who are shrouded, arise and deliver warning, your Lord magnify, your clothes cleanse and defilement shun," before making the prayer obligatory. I felt terror-stricken as narrated by 'Uqail.

(307) Yaḥyā reported: I asked Abū Salama what was revealed first from the Qur'ān. He said: "O, the shrouded one." I said: Or "Recite." Jābir said: I am narrating to you what was narrated to us by the Messenger of Allah[322] (may peace be upon him).

mystic. "The mystic does not wish," says he, "to return from the repose of 'unitary experience'; and even when he does return, as he must, his return does not mean much for mankind at large. The prophet's return is creative. He returns to insert himself into the sweep of time with a view to control the forces of history, and thereby to create a fresh world of ideals. For the mystic the repose of 'unitary experience' is something final; for the prophet it is the awakening within him, of world-shaking psychological forces, calculated to completely transform the human world. The desire to see his religious experience transformed into a living world-force is supreme in the prophet" (*Reconstruction of Religious Thought in Islam*, p. 124).

321. Some misdirected critics have represented this experience as a fit of epilepsy. This is a sheer fabrication. We do not find any trace of this malady in the life of the Holy Prophet. In an age when soundness of physique was thought to be the chief merit of eminence, this ailment could have never remained unnoticed to the scanning eyes of his bitter enemies who were always looking forward for an opportunity to sling mud at him. In the whole of the literature of early Islam we find all sorts of criticism levelled against Muḥammad (may peace be upon him), but no one ever mentioned or made a direct or indirect reference to this malady.

Moreover, one should see whether it is conceivable that an epileptic could, when the fit comes on, utter those grand religious truths embodied in the Holy Qur'ān or indeed make any coherent statement at all. History does not show a single example of an epileptic whose message created such a noble and balanced civilisation as Islam did, and who presented to the world a marvellous book like the Holy Qur'ān.

322. Apparently there seems to be a contradiction between the two aḥādīth. One in which it was said that the first verse revealed was (xcvi. 1-4): "Recite in the name of your Lord . . ." but here the ḥadīth indicates that opening verses of Sūra al-Muddaththir (lxxiv.) were revealed first of all. A little bit of penetration would easily resolve this contradiction. This ḥadīth has been narrated in the context of intermission. It is, therefore, quite obvious that it is related to the post-intermission period. After intermission the first revelation indeed consisted of the opening verses of Sūra al-Muddaththir. The internal evidence in the ḥadīth also strengthens this and establishes the fact that this ḥadīth speaks of another situation and is related to another context. Here the Holy Prophet did

He said: I stayed in Ḥirā' for one month and when my stay was completed, I came down and went into the heart of the valley. Somebody called me aloud. I looked in front of me, behind me, on the right of my side and on my left, but I did not see anybody. I was again called and I looked about but saw nothing. I was called again and raised my head, and there on the Throne in the open atmosphere he, i.e. Gabriel (peace be upon him) was sitting. I began to tremble on account of fear. I came to Khadīja and said: Wrap me up. They wrapped me up and threw water[323] on me and Allah, the Exalted and Glorious, sent down this: "O you who are shrouded! arise and deliver warning, your Lord magnify, your clothes cleanse."[324]

(308) Yaḥyā b. Abī Kathīr has reported this ḥadīth with the same chain of transmitters and narrated: And there he was sitting on the Throne between the heaven and the earth.

Chapter LXXV

NIGHT JOURNEY[325] OF THE MESSENGER OF ALLAH (MAY PEACE BE UPON HIM) TO HEAVEN, AND THE PRAYER MADE OBLIGATORY

(309) It is narrated on the authority of Anas b. Mālik that the Messenger of Allah

not see a vision in the cave of Ḥirā' but after he had come out of it at the expiry of one month's constant devotion to Allah. And as he was coming down in the valley Gabriel appeared before him. The way how the Prophet of Allah recognised him gives a clear indication that he was not an unfamiliar figure for him, but he had seen him before. These words: "There he was on the Throne in the opening atmosphere" make it clear that it was not the first appearance of the angel before the Holy Prophet (may peace be upon him).

323. Even to this day there is a practice with the physicians to moisten the forehead of a man running temperature.

324. This ḥadīth gives us a clear account of the working of Prophet Muḥammad's mind (may peace be upon him). This shows that he was endowed with this favour by Allah without the least expectation on his part. He was absolutely unaware of what was going to happen. Had his mind been struggling for such a conjure he would have never felt any fear.

325. According to most of the authorities, this miraculous event occurred about one year before the Hijra. The Prophet found himself transported at night to the place of Solomon's Temple in Jerusalem, and was subsequently borne to heaven. The first part of this journey is called the Night Journey (*Isrā'*) and the second, Ascension (*Mi'rāj*). The overwhelming majority of the Companions and of the commentators believes that both the Night Journey and the Ascension were bodily occurrences, although some of them admit of the possibility that the Prophet might have experienced several such night journeys and ascensions, some of which might have been purely spiritual. This journey is described in the Holy Qur'ān in the following words:

> Glory be to Him, Who carried His servant by night from the Sacred Mosque to the distant Mosque—the precincts of which We have blessed—in order that We might show him some of Our signs (xvii. 1).

This event has been described as extraordinary and belies the conclusion that it was a dream experience. Chapter xvii. begins with the glorification of the Lord which is a characteristic style of the Holy Qur'ān adopted on occasions when some extraordinary event is going to be described. Moreover, the expression *'abd* denotes a living human being composed of body and soul.

It is also recorded that as the news of M'irāj spread, the unbelievers scoffed at it. Had it been only a dream, there would have been no occasion for such a reaction about it. Visions like this can flit across the imagination of any man at any time.

(may peace be upon him) said : I was brought al-Burāq[326] who is an animal white and long, larger than a donkey but smaller than a mule, who would place his hoof at a distance equal to the range of vision. I mounted it and came to the Temple (Bait-ul-Maqdis in Jerusalem), then tethered it to the ring used by the prophets. I entered the mosque and prayed two rak'ahs in it, and then came out and Gabriel brought me a vessel of wine and a vessel of milk. I chose the milk, and Gabriel said : You have chosen the natural thing.[327] Then he took me to heaven. Gabriel then asked the (gate of the heaven) to be opened and he was asked who he was. He replied : Gabriel. He was again asked : Who is with you ? He (Gabriel) said : Muḥammad. It was said : Has he been sent for ? Gabriel replied : He has indeed been sent for. And (the door of the heaven) was opened for us and lo ! we saw Adam. He welcomed me and prayed for my good. Then we ascended to the second heaven. Gabriel (peace be upon him) (asked the door of the heaven to be opened), and he was asked who he was. He answered : Gabriel ; and he was again asked : Who is with you ? He replied : Muḥammad. It was said : Has he been sent for ? He replied : He has indeed been sent for. The gate was opened, When I entered 'Īsā b. Maryam and Yaḥya b. Zakariya (peace be upon both of them), cousins from the maternal side, welcomed me and prayed for my good. Then I was taken to the third heaven and Gabriel asked for the opening (of the door). He was asked : Who are you ? He replied : Gabriel. He was (again) asked : Who is with you? He replied : Muḥammad (may peace be upon him). It was said : Has he been sent for ? He replied : He has indeed been sent for. (The gate) was opened for us and I saw Yūsuf (peace of Allah be upon him) who had been given half of (world) beauty. He welcomed me and prayed for my well-being. Then he ascended with us to the fourth heaven. Gabriel (peace be upon him) asked for the (gate) to be opened, and it was said : Who is he ? He replied : Gabriel. It was (again) said : Who is with you ? He said : Muḥammad. It was said : Has he been sent for ? He replied : He has indeed been sent for. The (gate) was opened for us, and lo ! Idrīs was there. He welcomed me and prayed for my well-being. (About him) Allah, the Exalted and the Glorious, has said : "We elevated him (Idrīs) to the exalted position" (Qur'ān xix. 57). Then he ascended with us to the fifth heaven and Gabriel asked for the (gate) to be opened. It was said : Who is he ? He replied : Gabriel. It was (again) said : Who is with thee ? He replied : Muḥammad. It was said : Has he been sent for ? He replied : He has indeed been sent for. (The gate) was opened

> And We made out the vision (of the Prophet's ascent) which We showed thee as an ordeal for mankind (xvii. 60).

This verse testifies to the fact that this unusual event became an ordeal for the people. An ordinary man used to the orderliness in Nature could not imagine that a human being could ascend through the heavens with his body. It, therefore, created a stir amongst the people.

All these arguments go in favour of physical night journey and ascension. The overwhelming majority of the old scholars and mystics believes it to be an experience of both body and soul.

326. The name of the heavenly steed seems to be derived from *barq* (lightning). It alludes to the quickness of its motion.

327. It is a symbolic way of saying that good and evil in the form of milk and wine were brought before the Prophet and he instinctively made a choice for the good. It is very difficult to render the Arabic term *fiṭrah* into English. It denotes the original constitution or disposition, with which a child comes into this world, as contrasted with qualities or inclinations acquired during life ; besides, it refers to the spiritual inclination inherent in man in his unspoilt state (Muhammad Asad, *Ṣaḥiḥ al-Bukhāri*).

for us and then I was with Hārūn (Aaron--peace of Allah be upon him). He welcomed me and prayed for my well-being. Then I was taken to the sixth heaven. Gabriel (peace be upon him) asked for the door to be opened. It was said: Who is he? He replied: Gabriel. It was said: Who is with thee? He replied: Muḥammad. It was said: Has he been sent for? He replied: He has indeed been sent for. (The gate) was opened for us and there I was with Mūsā (Moses—peace be upon him). He welcomed me and prayed for my well-being. Then I was taken up to the seventh heaven. Gabriel asked the (gate) to be opened. It was said: Who is he? He said: Gabriel. It was said: Who is with thee? He replied: Muḥammad (may peace be upon him). It was said: Has he been sent for? He replied: He has indeed been sent for. (The gate) was opened for us and there I found Ibrāhīm (Abraham—peace be upon him) reclining against the Bait-ul-Ma'mūr [328] and there enter into it seventy thousand angels every day, never to visit (this place) again. Then I was taken to Sidrat-ul-Muntahā [329] whose leaves were like elephant ears and its fruit like big earthenware vessels.[330] And when it was covered by the Command of Allah, it underwent such a change that none amongst the creation has the power to praise its beauty. Then Allah revealed to me a revelation and He made obligatory for me fifty prayers every day and night. Then I went down to Moses (peace be upon him) and he said: What has your Lord enjoined upon your Ummah? I said: Fifty prayers. He said: Return to thy Lord and beg for reduction (in the number of prayers), for your community shall not be able to bear this burden, as I have put to test the children of Isrā'īl and tried them (and found them too weak to bear such a heavy burden). He (the Holy Prophet) said: I went back to my Lord and said: My Lord, make things lighter for my Ummah. (The Lord) reduced five prayers for me. I went down to Moses and said: (The Lord) reduced five (prayers) for me. He said: Verily thy Ummah shall not be able to bear this burden; [331] return to thy Lord and ask Him to make things lighter. I then kept going back and forth between my Lord Blessed and Exalted and Moses, till He said: There are five prayers every day and night, O Muḥammad, each being credited as ten, so that makes fifty prayers. He who intends to do a good deed and does not do it will have a good deed recorded for him; and if he does it, it will be recorded for him as ten; whereas he who intends to do an evil deed and does not do, it will not be recorded for him; and if he does it, only one evil deed will be recorded.

328. "The Much-Frequented House" (al-Bait al-Ma'mūr) is mentioned in the Holy Qur'ān (lii. 4). It is a temple which numerous heavenly beings frequently visit for the adoration of their Creator. It is said to have been the spiritual prototype of the Ka'bah in Mecca (Ibn Kathīr, VIII, 76) which is the earthly symbol of the Oneness of God in the same sense as the "Much Frequented House" is its heavenly symbol (Asad, op. cit., p. 192).

329. *Sidrat-ul-Muntahā*: The author of *Mufradāt* suggests, in explanation of this Qur'ānic expression, that the *Sidr* (Arabian lote-tree) is, owing to the abundance of its shade, symbolic of the shade of Paradise. Pursuing this trend of thought we may perhaps assume the expression: Lote-tree of the farthest limit: is indicative of the limit of knowledge allowed to the created beings; though great and wonderful in itself, their knowledge, even in Paradise, can never attain to the limitless perfection of the knowledge which the Creator has reserved for Himself (Asad, op. cit., p. 191).

330. The comparison of the leaves of the lote-tree to elephant ears and of its fruit to earthenware vessels is meant to convey an idea of immeasurably vast heavenly knowledge.

331. Moses had, of all the prophets of old, the greatest experience regarding the guidance of a nation—a fact borne out by the frequent references in the Holy Qur'ān to his history and his heroic endeavours to guide aright the children of Israel.

I then came down and when I came to Moses and informed him, he said: Go back to thy Lord and ask Him to make things lighter. Upon this the Messenger of Allah remarked: I returned to my Lord until I felt ashamed before Him.[332]

(310) It is narrated on the authority of Anas b. Mālik that the Messenger of Allah (may peace be upon him) said: (The angels) came to me and took me to the Zamzam[333] and my heart was opened[334] and washed with the water of Zamzam and then I was left (at my place).

(311) Anas b. Mālik reported that Gabriel came to the Messenger of Allah (may peace be upon him) while he was playing with his playmates. He took hold of him and lay him prostrate on the ground and tore open his breast and took out the heart from it and then extracted a blood-clot out of it and said: That was the part of Satan in thee.[335] And then he washed it with the water of Zamzam in a golden basin and then it was joined together and restored to its place. The boys came running to his mother, i.e. his nurse, and said: Verily Muḥammad has been murdered. They all rushed towards him (and found him all right). His colour was changed. Anas said: I myself saw the marks of needle on his breast.

(312) Anas b. Mālik, while recounting the Night Journey of the Holy Prophet (may peace be upon him), from the mosque of Ka'bah, reported: Three beings (angels) came to him in the mosque of the Ka'bah, while he was sleeping in the sacred mosque before it (the Command of Night Journey and Ascension) was revealed to him. The rest of the ḥadīth is narrated like that of Thābit. However, some portions have occurred before and some of them have occured after; some have been added and some deleted.

(313) Anas b. Mālik reported: Abū Dharr used to relate that the Messenger of Allah (may peace be upon him) said: The roof of my house was cleft when I was in Mecca and Gabriel descended and opened my heart and then washed it with the water of Zamzam. He then brought a gold basin full of wisdom and faith and after emptying it into my breast, he closed it up. Then taking me by the hand, he ascended with me to the heaven, and when we came to the lowest heaven, Gabriel said to the guardian of the lowest heaven: Open. He asked who was there. He replied: It is Gabriel. He again asked whether there was someone with him. He replied: Yes, it is Muḥammad with me. He was asked if he had been sent for. He (Gabriel) said: Yes. Then he opened

332. The beautiful story of the imposition of five daily prayers on Muslims is, of course, not to be taken in the sense that God was ever "undecided" concerning the number of prayers to be imposed on His worshippers. The way this duty was established is merely meant to show that the burden of the Muslims is lighter than that imposed on their predecessors, and that it is well within the individual ability of man (Asad, op. cit., p. 194).

333. It is the sacred well of Mecca, also called the well of Ismā'īl. It is in al-Ḥaram al-Sharīf of the Ka'bah in the corner opposite to the Black Stone. *Zamzam* in Arabic means "abundant water". It is connected with the story af Ibrāhīm. It was opened by the angel Gabriel to save Hājira and her son Ismā'īl who were dying of thirst.

334. The opening of the heart was an experience which the Prophet had had more than once. The best known is that which is said to have happened in his childhood, while he was in the charge of his nurse, Ḥalīma, of the tribe of Sa'd. It was meant to clean and purify the heart of the Holy Prophet of all kinds of alloys.

335. As the Prophet's life was to be made a perfect model of piety and God-consciousness, it was, therefore, essential that his heart should be completely purified of all types of impurities.

(the gate). When we ascended the lowest heaven (I saw) a man seated with parties on his right side and parties on his left side. When he looked up to his right, he laughed and when he looked to his left, he wept. He said: Welcome to the righteous apostle and the righteous son. I asked Gabriel who he was and he replied: He is Adam (peace be upon him) and these parties on his right and on his left are the souls of his descendants. Those of them on his right are the inmates of Paradise and the parties which are on his left side are the inmates of Hell; so when he looked towards his right side, he laughed, and when he looked towards his left side, he wept. Then Gabriel ascended with me to the second heaven. He asked its guardian to open (its gate), and its guardian replied in the same way as the guardian of the lowest heaven had said. He (opened it). Anas b. Mālik said: He (the Holy Prophet) mentioned that he found in the heavens Adam, Idrīs, Jesus, Moses and Abraham (may peace be on all of them), but he did not ascertain as to the nature of their abodes except that he had found Adam in the lowest heaven and Abraham in the sixth heaven. When Gabriel and the Messenger of Allah (may peace be upon him) passed by Idrīs (peace be upon him) he said: Welcome to the righteous apostle and righteous brother. He (the narrator) said: He then proceeded and said: Who is he? Gabriel replied: It is Idrīs. Then I passed by Moses (peace be upon him) and he said: Welcome to the righteous apostle and righteous brother. I said to (Gabriel): Who is he? He replied: It is Moses. Then I passed by Jesus and he said: Welcome to the righteous apostle and righteous brother. I said (to Gabriel): Who is he? He replied: Jesus, son of Mary. He (the Holy Prophet) said: Then I went to Ibrāhīm (peace be upon him). He said: Welcome to the righteous apostle and righteous son.[336] I asked: Who is he? He (Gabriel) replied: It is Abraham. Ibn Shihāb said: Ibn Ḥazm told me that Ibn 'Abbās and Abū Ḥabba al-Anṣārī used to say that the Messenger of Allah (may peace be upon him) said: Thereafter he ascended with me till I was taken to such a height where I heard the scraping of the pens.[337] Ibn Ḥazm and Anas told that the Messenger of Allah (may peace be upon him) said: Allah then made fifty prayers obligatory for my Ummah and I returned with that and passed by Moses. Moses (peace be upon him) said: What has thy Lord enjoined on thy people? I said: Fifty prayers have been made obligatory on them. Moses (peace be upon him) said: Return to thy Lord, for thy Ummah would not be able to bear this burden. Then I came back to my Lord and He remitted a portion out of that. I then again went to Moses (peace be upon him) and informed him about it. He said: Return to thy Lord, for thy Ummah shall not be able to bear this burden. I then went back to my Lord and He said: They are five and at the same time fifty, and what has been said will not be changed. I then returned to Moses and he said: Go back to thy Lord, whereupon I said: I feel ashamed of my Lord. Gabriel then travelled with me till we came to the farthest lote-tree. Many a colour had covered it which I do not know. Then I was admitted to Paradise and saw in it domes of pearls, and its soil of musk.

(314) Anas b. Mālik reported on the authority of Mālik b. Ṣa'ṣa', perhaps a person

336. This shows that all the prophets were joined together by one bond of brotherhood and there was a very close affinity between all of them.

337. The Holy Prophet (may peace be upon him) came so near to Allah that he could hear the scraping of the pens of angels as they were writing the decrees of their Lord. It is a symbolic way of saying that the Holy Prophet (may peace be upon him) was lifted to such heights of spiritual experience where he could distinctly perceive the destiny of human race being decreed.

of his tribe, that the Prophet of Allah (may peace be upon him) said: I was near the House (i.e. Ka'bah) in a state between sleep and wakefulness when I heard someone say: He is the third among the two persons.[338] Then he came to me and took me with him. Then a golden basin containing the water of Zamzam was brought to me and my heart was opened up to such and such (part). Qatāda said: I asked him who was with me (i.e. the narrator) and what he meant by such and such (part). He replied: (It means that it was opened) up to the lower part of his abdomen. (Then the ḥadīth continues): My heart was extracted and it was washed with the water of Zamzam and then it was restored in its original position, after which it was filled with faith and wisdom. I was then brought a white beast which is called al-Burāq, bigger than a donkey and smaller than a mule. Its stride was as long as the eye could reach. I was mounted on it, and then we went forth till we reached the lowest heaven. Gabriel asked for the (gate) to be opened, and it was said: Who is he? He replied: Gabriel. It was again said: Who is with thee? He replied: Muḥammad (may peace be upon him). It was said: Has he been sent for? He (Gabriel) said: Yes. He (the Prophet) said: Then (the gate) was opened for us (and it was said): Welcome unto him! His is a blessed arrival. Then we came to Adam (peace be upon him). And he (the narrator) narrated the whole account of the ḥadīth. (The Holy Prophet) observed that he met Jesus in the second heaven, Yaḥyā (peace be on both of them) in the third heaven, Yūsuf in the third, Idrīs in the fourth, Hārūn in the fifth (peace and blessings of Allah be upon them). Then we travelled on till we reached the sixth heaven and came to Moses (peace be upon him) and I greeted him and he said: Welcome unto righteous brother and righteous prophet. And when I passed (by him) he wept, and a voice was heard saying: What makes thee weep? He said: My Lord, he is a young man whom Thou hast sent after me (as a prophet) and his followers will enter Paradise in greater numbers than my followers. Then we travelled on till we reached the seventh heaven and I came to Ibrāhīm. He (the narrator) narrated in this ḥadīth that the Prophet of Allah (may peace be upon him) told that he saw four rivers which flowed from (the root of the lote-tree of the farthest limits): two manifest rivers and two hidden rivers. I said: O Gabriel! what are these rivers? He replied: The two hidden rivers are the rivers of Paradise, and as regards the two manifest ones, they are the Nile and the Euphrates.[339] Then the Bait-ul-Ma'mūr was

338. Ḥamza and Ja'far were the other two persons (*Fatḥ-ul-Mulhim*, Vol. I, p. 327).

339. Muḥammad Asad (op. cit., p. 192) has explained the significance of these rivers in the following words:

> It appears to me that the two "manifest" rivers, the Nile and the Euphrates, symbolically describe the area—geographical and spiritual—of the religious development which culminated in Islam; for it is in countries between these two rivers that all the prophets mentioned in the Holy Qur'ān as the spiritual precursors of Islam, as well as the Prophet Muḥammad (peace be upon him) himself, lived and preached. The use of the term "manifest" in this connection would imply that the complex religious manifestations which have taken place between the Nile and the Eupharates—that is, the teachings of all the Quranic prophets up to the Holy Prophet of Islam (peace be upon him)—contain all the moral and spiritual truths which God regarded necessary for the life of this world, and which He revealed, or made manifest, to mankind through His Apostles. Besides this, God will reveal to the righteous, in the final illumination of the paradise, hitherto hidden sources of Truth (symbolised by the hidden rivers) and will make them comprehend problems which are beyond the grasp of mortal man.

raised up to me. I said: O Gabriel! what is this? He replied: It is the Bait-ul-Ma'mūr. Seventy thousand angels enter into it daily and, after they come out, they never return again. Two vessels were then brought to me. The first one contained wine and the second one contained milk, and both of them were placed before me. I chose milk. It was said: You did right. Allah will guide rightly through you your Ummah on the natural course. Then fifty prayers daily were made obligatory for me. And then he narrated the rest of the ḥadīth to the end.

(315) It is reported on the authority of Mālik b. Ṣa'ṣa' that the Messenger of Allah (may peace be opon him) narrated the ḥadīth (mentioned above) and added to it: I was brought a gold basin full of wisdom and faith, and then the (part of the body) right from the upper end of the chest to the lower part of the abdomen was opened and it was washed with the water of Zamzam and then filled with wisdom and faith.

(316) Qatāda reported that he heard Abū al-'Āliya saying that the cousin of your Prophet (may peace be upon him), i.e. Ibn 'Abbās, told him: The Messenger of Allah (may peace be upon him), while narrating his night journey observed: Mūsā (peace be upon him) was a man of high stature as if he was of the people of the Shanū'a (tribe), and Jesus was a well-built person having curly hair. He also mentioned Mālik, the guardian of Hell, and Dajjāl.

(317) Abū al-'Āliya reported: Ibn 'Abbās, the son of your Prophet's uncle, told us that the Messenger of Allah (may peace be upon him) had observed: On the night of my night journey I passed by Moses b. 'Imrān (peace be upon him), a man light brown in complexion, tall, well-built as if he was one of the men of the Shanū'a, and saw Jesus son of Mary as a medium-statured man with white and red complexion and crisp hair,[340] and I was shown Mālik the guardian of Fire, and Dajjāl amongst the signs which were shown to me by Allah. He (the narrator) observed: Then do not doubt his (i.e. of the Holy Prophet) meeting with him (Moses). Qatāda elucidated it thus: Verily the Apostle of Allah (may peace be upon him) met Moses (peace be upon him).

(318) Abū al-'Āliya narrated it on the authority of Ibn 'Abbās that the Messenger of Allah (may peace be upon him) passed through the valley of Azraq, and he asked: Which valley is this? They said: This is the valley of Azraq,[341] and he observed: (I perceive) as if I am seeing Moses (peace be upon him) coming down from the mountain track, and he is calling upon Allah loudly (saying: Here I am! at your service![342]). Then he came to the mountain track of Harshā.[343] He (the Holy Prophet) said: Which is this mountain track? They said: It is the mountain track of Harshā. He observed:

340. The word جعد (ja'd) in the previous ḥadīth has been translated as curly and in this ḥadīth it is translated as well-built. Both the meanings are permissible. When it is applied to hair, it means crisp, curly or twisted, but when it is applied to the bodily structure of a man, it means compact in limbs, and strong in make, not flabby nor of slack or incongruous make (Lane, *Arabic-English Lexicon*).

341. It is a valley situated between Mecca and Medina and is named after the name of a person. It is at a distance of one mile from Mecca (*Fatḥ-ul-Mulḥim*, Vol. I, p. 329).

342. In the religious terminology it is known as *talbiya* and the words are: Here I am! O Allah! Here I am! No partner hast Thou. Here I am, ready to obey Thee.

343. It is situated on the way between Syria and Medina near the place al-Juḥfa (*Fatḥ-ul-Mulḥim*, Vol. I, p. 329).

(I feel) as if I am seeing Yūnus (Jonah—peace be upon him) son of Mattā on a well-built red dromedary, with a cloak of wool around him and the rein of his dromedary is made of the fibres of date-palm, and he is calling upon Allah (saying : Here I am! at your service, my Lord!). Ibn Ḥanbal said in the ḥadīth narrated by him : Hushaim said that the meaning of khulba was fibre of date-palm.[344]

(319) Abū al-'Āliya narrated it on the authority of Ibn 'Abbās that he said : We travelled with the Messenger of Allah (may peace be upon him) between Mecca and Medina and we passed by a valley. He (the Holy Prophet) asked : Which valley is this? They said : This is the valley of Azraq. Upon this he (the Holy Prophet) remarked : (I feel) as if I am seeing Moses (peace be upon him), and then he described something about his complexion and hair, which Dāwūd (the narrator) could not remember. He (Moses, as described by the Holy Prophet) was keeping his fingers in his ears and was responding loudly to Allah (saying : I am at Thy service, my Lord) while passing through that valley. We then travelled (further) till we came to the mountain trail. He (the Holy Prophet) said : Which mountain trail is this? They said : It is the Harshā or Lift. He (the Holy Prophet) said : (I perceive) as if I am seeing Yūnus on a red camel, with a cloak of wool around him. The halter of his camel was that of the fibre of date-palm, and he was passing through the valley saying : I am at Thy service! my Lord.[345]

(320) It is narrated on the authority of Mujāhid that he said : We were with Ibn 'Abbās and (the people) talked about al-Dajjāl. (One of them) remarked : There is written between his eyes (the word) *Kāfir* (infidel). The narrator said : Ibn 'Abbās remarked : I did not hear him (the Holy Prophet) say it, but he said : [346] So far as Ibrāhīm is concerned, you may see your companion[347] and so far as Moses is concerned, he is a well-built man with wheat complexion (riding) on a red camel with its halter made of the fibre of date-palm (and I perceive) as if I am seeing towards him as he is going down in the valley saying : I am at Thy service! my Lord.

(321) It is narrated on the authority of Jābir that the Messenger of Allah (may peace be upon him) said : There appeared before me the apostles, and Moses was among

344. Imām Nawawī says on the authority of Qāḍī 'Iyāḍ that this sight may not be connected with the event of Mi'rāj but might be a dream experience. The word "as if" lends support to this point of view (ibid., Vol. I, p. 94).

345. The Holy Prophet (may peace be upon him) could visualise Ḥaḍrat Yūnus and Moses, whereas his companions could not. This unfolds before us the striking difference that exists between a prophet and an ordinary mortal. The prophet is permitted to peep into the mysteries of life and to see the world which is hidden from the view of a common man. The Holy Prophet (may peace be upon him) was, therefore, perceiving which his companions could not perceive. The faith in the Unseen implies that there are so many realities of life which we cannot see or perceive with our senses. But these are there and belief in their existence is important for our right attitude and correct approach to the problems of our life. For the prophets so many aspects of the unseen world are converted into the seen world.

346. The question may be asked what meaningful relation there is between this part of the ḥadīth and the subsequent one. The answer is given by Maulānā Shabbīr Aḥmad and he says : It was perhaps a discussion about the miraculous events connected with the life of the Holy Prophet (may peace be upon him).

347. That is, "Ḥaḍrat Ibrāhīm has a striking resemblance with me and one can see his image in my personality," i.e. personality of Muḥammad (may peace be upon him).

men[348] as if he was one of the people of Shanū'a, and I saw Jesus son of Mary (peace be upon him) and I saw nearest in resemblance with him was 'Urwa b. Mas'ūd, and I saw Ibrāhīm (blessings of Allah be upon him) and I see your companions much in resemblance with him, i.e. his personality, and I saw Gabriel (peace be upon him) and I saw Diḥya[349] nearest in resemblance to him; but in the narration of Ibn Rumḥ, it is Diḥya b. Khalīfa.

(322) It is narrated on the authority of Abū Huraira that the Apostle of Allah (may peace be upon him) said: When I was taken for the night journey I met Moses (peace be upon him). The Apostle of Allah (may peace be upon him) gave his description thus: He was a man, I suppose—and he (the narrator) was somewhat doubtful (that the Holy Prophet observed): (Moses) was a man erect in stature with straight hair on his head as if he was one of the men of the Shanū'a; and I met Jesus and the Apostle of Allah (may peace be upon him) described him as one having a medium stature and a red complexion as if he had (just) come out of the bath.[350] He observed: I saw Ibrāhīm (peace be upon him) and amongst his children I have the greatest resemblance with him. He said: There were brought to me two vessels. In one of them was milk and in the other one there was wine. And it was said to me: Select any one you like. So I selected the vessel containing milk and drank it. He (the angel) said: You have been guided on *al-fiṭra* or you have attained *al-fiṭra*. Had you selected wine, your Ummah would have been misled.

Chapter LXXVI

PERTAINING TO JESUS SON OF MARY AND AL-MASĪḤ AL-DAJJĀL

(323) It is narrated on the authority of 'Abdullah b. 'Umar that the Messenger of Allah (may peace be upon him) said: I found myself one night near the Ka'bah, and I saw a man with wheat complexion[351] amongst the fair-complexioned men that you ever saw. He had a lock of hair the most beautiful of the locks that you ever saw. He had combed it. Water was trickling out of them. He was leaning on two men, or on the shoulders of two men, and he was circumscribing the Ka'bah. I asked: What is he? It

348. ضرب (ḍarab) is interpreted in two different ways. It may mean a person who neither wears too much flesh nor is too much lean. But according to Nawawī and Mulla 'Alī Qārī ضرب من الرجال means a type of men (*Fatḥ-ul-Mulhim*, Vol. I, p. 331).

349. It is read both Diḥya or Daḥya, an eminent Companion of the Holy Prophet (may peace be upon him), and was strikingly handsome (ibid.).

350. The word ديماس (dīmās) is derived from *damasa* which means to hide or conceal in a dungeon or vault or a bath. What it implies is that Jesus Christ appeared fresh as he had just come out from the bath. There was neither any dust on his face nor his countenance showed any sign of weariness. This meaning also resolves the contradiction that we find in this ḥadīth and the previous one in which Jesus had been described as a prophet having a fair complexion. What we understand from the study of these two is that Jesus had a wheat complexion but in this particular case he appeared to be reddish because there was a freshness on his face.

351. آدم. This term applies to camel-colour tinged either with whiteness or with streaks of blackness. It also means a clear white or intensely white complexion (Lane's *Lexicon*).

was said: He is al-Masīḥ son of Mary. Then I saw another person, stout and having too much curly hair, and blind in his right eye as if it was a full swollen grape. I asked: Who is he? It was said: He is al-Masīḥ al-Dajjāl.

(324) It is narrated on the authority of 'Abdullah b. 'Umar that one day the Messenger of Allah (may peace be upon him) mentioned in the presence of people about al-Masīḥ al-Dajjāl. He said: Verily Allah (hallowed be He and High) is not blind of one eye. Behold, but the Masīḥ al-Dajjāl is blind of right eye as if his eye is like a swollen grape, and the Messenger of Allah (may peace be upon him) said: I was shown in a dream in the night that near the Ka'bah there was a man fair-complexioned, fine amongst the white-complexioned men that you ever saw, his locks of hair were falling on his shoulders. He was a man whose hair were neither too curly nor too straight, and water trickled down from his head. He was placing his hands on the shoulders of two persons and amidst them was making a circuit around the Ka'bah. I said: Who is he? They replied: Al-Masīḥ son of Mary. And I saw behind him a man with intensely curly hair, blind of right eye. Amongst the persons I have ever seen Ibn Qaṭan[352] has the greatest resemblance with him. He was making a circuit around the Ka'bah by placing both his hands on the shoulders of two persons. I said: Who is he? They said: It is al-Masīḥ al-Dajjāl.

(325) It is narrated on the authority of Ibn 'Umar that the Messenger of Allah (may peace be upon him) said: I saw near the Ka'bah a man of fair complexion with straight hair, placing his hands on two persons. Water was flowing from his head or it was trickling from his head. I asked: Who is he? They said: He is Jesus son of Mary or al-Masīḥ son of Mary. (The narrator) says: I do not remember which word it was. He (the Holy Prophet) said: And I saw behind him a man with red complexion and thick curly hair, blind in the right eye. I saw in him the greatest resemblance with Ibn Qaṭan. I asked: Who is he? They replied: It is al-Masīḥ al-Dajjāl.

(326) It is narrated on the authority of Jābir b. 'Abdullah that the Messenger of Allah (may peace be upon him) said: When the Quraish belied me, I was staying in Ḥaṭīm[353] and Allah lifted before me Bait-ul-Maqdis and I began to narrate to them (the Quraish of Mecca) its signs while I was in fact looking at it.

(327) 'Abdullah reported on the authority of his father 'Umar b. Khaṭṭāb that he heard from the Messenger of Allah (may peace be upon him) say: I was sleeping when I saw myself making circuit around the Ka'bah, and I saw there a man of fair complexion with straight hair between two men. Water was flowing from his head or water was falling from his head. I said: Who is he? They answered: He is the son of Mary. Then I moved forward and cast a glance and there was a bulky man of red complexion with thick locks of hair on his head, blind of one eye as if his eye was a swollen grape.

352. His name was 'Abdul-'Uzzā after the name of a goddess. He belonged to the tribe of Khuzā'a.

353. The Holy Prophet (may peace be upon him) was staying in Ḥaṭīm when he was commanded to undertake the night journey. The Quraish scoffed and put all sorts of questions. It was at this time that the Holy Prophet (may peace be upon him) was made to see Bait-ul-Maqdis with his own eyes so that he might be able to give correct answers to their inquiries concerning it. It should also be made clear that the word *Ḥijr* in the ḥadith stands for the wall situated on the west side of the Ka'bah; it is a part of Ḥaṭīm.

I asked: Who is he? They said: He is Dajjāl. He had close resemblance with Ibn Qaṭan amongst men.

(328) It is narrated on the authority of Abū Huraira that the Messenger of Allah (may peace be upon him) said: I found myself in Ḥijr and the Quraish were asking me about my night journey. I was asked about things pertaining to Bait-ul-Maqdis which I could not preserve (in my mind). I was very much vexed, so vexed as I had never been before. Then Allah raised it (Bait-ul-Maqdis) before my eyes. I looked towards it, and I gave them the information about whatever they questioned me. I also saw myself among the group of apostles. I saw Moses saying prayer and found him to be a well-built man as if he was a man of the tribe of Shanū'a. I saw Jesus son of Mary (peace be upon him) offering prayer, of all of men he had the closest resemblance with 'Urwa b. Mas'ūd al-Thaqafī. I saw Ibrāhīm (peace be upon him) offering prayer; he had the closest resemblance with your companion (the Prophet himself) amongst people. When the time of prayer came I led them. When I completed the prayer, someone said: Here is Mālik, the keeper of the Hell; pay him salutations. I turned to him, but he preceded me in salutation.[354]

Chapter LXXVII

CONCERNING SIDRAT-UL-MUNTAHĀ [355] (REMOTEST LOTE-TREE)

(329) It is narrated on the authority of 'Abdullah (b. 'Umar) that when the Messenger of Allah (may peace be upon him) was taken for the Night Journey, he was taken to Sidrat-ul-Muntahā, which is situated on the sixth heaven, where terminates everything that ascends from the earth and is held there, and where terminates everything that descends from above it and is held there. (It is with reference to this that) Allah said: "When that which covers covered the lote-tree" (al-Qur'ān, liii. 16). He (the narrator) said: (It was) gold moths. He (the narrator further) said: The Messenger of Allah (may peace be upon him) was given three (things): he was given five prayers, he was given the concluding verses of Sūra al-Baqara, and remission of serious sins[356] for those among his Ummah who associate not anything with Allah.

(330) Al-Shaibānī reported to us: I asked Zirr b. Ḥubaish about the words of Allah (the Mighty and Great): "So he was (at a distance) of two bows or nearer" (al-Qur'ān, liii. 8). He said: Ibn Mas'ūd informed me that, verily, the Apostle of Allah (may peace be upon him) saw Gabriel and he had six hundred wings.

354. It should be remembered that events narrated in this ḥadīth and some of the previous ones are concerned with the spiritual experience in a state of dream. These are separate from the experiences of ascension (Mi'rāj). It is by ignoring this fact that some persons are confused and wrongly infer that the Mi'rāj of the Holy Prophet (may peace be upon him) was just a dream-experience.

355. *Sidrat-ul-Muntahā* has been explained in the previous chapter. One point needs elucidation. There it was said that it is situated in the seventh heaven and in this ḥadīth it is stated to be in the sixth heaven. The answer is that it is a tree which sprouts forth from the sixth heaven and its branches overarch the seventh heaven. This is to give an idea of its immeasurable and countless blessings.

356. It does not mean that he would not suffer at all for his misdeeds in the next world. It simply implies that a person who affirms the oneness of the Lord from the depth of his soul and who does not ascribe divinity to anyone else, would not be eternally doomed to the Fire of Hell (Nawawī).

(331) Al-Shaibānī narrated on the authority of Zirr who narrated it on the authority of 'Abdullah that the (words of Allah): "The heart belied not what he saw" (al-Qur'ān, liii. 11) imply that he saw Gabriel (peace be upon him) and he had six hundred wings.

(332) Zirr b. Ḥubaish narrated it on the authority of 'Abdullah (that the words of Allah): "Certainly he saw of the greatest signs of Allah" (al-Qur'ān, liii. 18) imply that he saw Gabriel in his (original) form [357] and he had six hundred wings.

(333) It is narrated on the authority of Abū Huraira that the (words of Allah): "And certainly he saw him in another descent" (al-Qur'ān, liii. 13) imply that he saw Gabriel.

Chapter LXXVIII

THE MEANING OF THE WORDS OF ALLAH : "HE SAW HIM IN ANOTHER DESCENT" (AL-QUR'ĀN, LIII. 13). DID THE APOSTLE (MAY PEACE BE UPON HIM) SEE HIS LORD ON THE NIGHT OF HIS JOURNEY (TO HEAVEN)?

(334) It is narrated on the authority of Ibn 'Abbās that he (the Holy Prophet) saw (Allah) with his heart.

(335) It is narrated on the authority of Ibn 'Abbās that the words: "The heart belied not what he saw" (al-Qur'ān, liii. 11) and "Certainly he saw Him in another descent" (al-Qur'ān, liii. 13) imply that he saw him twice with his heart.

(336) Abū Bakr b. Abī Shaiba narrated it on the same authorities.

(337) It is narrated on the authority of Masrūq that he said: I was resting at (the house of) 'Ā'isha that she said: O Abū 'Ā'isha (kunya of Masrūq), there are three things, and he who affirmed even one of them fabricated the greatest lie against Allah. I asked what they were. She said: He who presumed that Muḥammad (may peace be upon him) saw his Lord (with his ocular vision) fabricated the greatest lie against Allah. I was reclining but then sat up and said: Mother of the Faithful, wait a bit and do not be in a haste. Has not Allah (Mighty and Majestic) said: "And truly he saw him on the clear horizon" (al-Qur'ān, lxxxi. 23) and "he saw Him in another descent" (al-Qur'ān, liii. 13)? She said: I am the first of this Ummah who asked the Messenger of Allah (may peace be upon him) about it, and he said: Verily he is Gabriel. I have never seen him in his original form in which he was created except on those two occasions (to which these verses refer); I saw him descending from the heaven and filling (the space) from the sky to the earth with the greatness of his bodily structure. She said: Have you not heard Allah saying: "Eyes comprehend Him not, but He comprehends (all) vision, and He is Subtle, and All-Aware" (al-Qur'ān, v. 104)? (She, i.e. 'Ā'isha, further said): Have you not heard that, verily, Allah says: "And it is not vouchsafed to a

357. It was for a number of times that the Holy Prophet had seen Gabriel. He, however, saw him in his original shape on two memorable occasions. One is positively during his ascent to heaven. There is a difference of opinion about the second one. According to the tradition of 'Ā'isha (Allah be pleased with her) it was at Ajyād that the Holy Prophet saw Gabriel in his original form on the second occasion, but the majority of the commentators of the Ḥadīth is of the view that it was in the cave of Ḥirā' and at the time of the first revelation that the Holy Prophet saw Gabriel in his true form.

human being that Allah should speak unto him otherwise than by revelation, or from behind a veil, or that He sendeth a messenger (angel), so that he revealeth whatsoever He wills. Verily He is Exalted, Wise" (al-Qur'ān, xlii. 51). She said: He who presumes that the Messenger of Allah (may peace be upon him) concealed anything from the Book of Allah fabricates the greatest lie against Allah. Allah says: "O Messenger! deliver that which has been revealed to thee from thy Lord, and if thou do (it) not, thou hast not delivered His message" (al-Qur'ān, v. 67). She said: He who presumes that he would inform about what was going to happen tomorrow fabricates the greatest lie against Allah. And Allah says: "Say thou (Muḥammad): None in the heavens and the earth knoweth the unseen save Allah" (al-Qur'ān, xxvii. 65).

(338) Dawūd reported on the same authorities the ḥadīth as narrated above by Ibn 'Uliyya and added: She ('Ā'isha) said: If Muḥammad were to conceal anything which was sent to him, he would have certainly concealed this verse: "And when thou saidst to him on whom Allah had conferred favour and thou too had conferred favour: Keep thy wife to thyself and fear Allah, and thou wast concealing in thy heart that which Allah was going to disclose, and thou wast fearing men while Allah has a better right that thou shouldst fear Him." [358]

(339) Masrūq reported: I asked 'Ā'isha if Muhammad (may peace be upon him) had seen his Lord. She replied: Hallowed be Allah, my hair stood on end when you said this, and he (Masrūq) narrated the ḥadīth as narrated above. The ḥadīth reported by Dāwūd is more complete and longer.

(340) Masrūq reported: I said to 'Ā'isha: What about the words of Allah: "Then he drew nigh and came down, so he was at a distance of two bows or closer still; so He revealed to His servant what He revealed" (al-Qur'ān, liii. 8-10)? She said: It implies Gabriel. He used to come to him (the Holy Prophet) in the shape of men; but he came at this time in his true form and blocked up the horizon of the sky.

358. This is verse 37 of Sūra *al-Ahzāb*, and here the reference is to the marriage of Zainab (Allah be pleased with her) with the Holy Prophet. Zaid (Allah be pleased with him), who was a freed slave and was one of the earliest converts to Islam, was known as the adopted son of Muḥammad (may peace be upon him). He married him to Zainab, the daughter of his aunt, with a view to removing the distinction of birth. Unfortunately, the marriage did not prove to be a happy one, and both the husband and the wife decided to part with each other. It was tragic for both of them, but Zainab was the worst sufferer as she had to carry the stigma of "the divorced spouse of a slave" The marriage had taken place at the suggestion of the Holy Prophet (may peace be upon him). He, therefore, wanted to restore her lost prestige by marrying her himself. But he felt reluctant to do so as it would create an uproar amongst the enemies of Islam who would find an opportunity of slinging mud at him by saying that the Holy Prophet had married his "daughter-in-law". Allah, however, wanted to compensate Zainab and at the same time to give a death-blow to the pre-Islamic custom of treating the adopted sons as real sons.

In the above-mentioned verses the Holy Prophet has been exhorted not to be afraid of public opinion, but to fear Allah only. The verses give a clear indication to the fact that God was not approving the Prophet's attitude of fear from the public. This was the fit case for concealing a fact as it reflected the disapproval of the Lord for his reluctant behaviour. What 'Ā'isha wants to stress is that when Muḥammad (may peace be upon him) did not conceal this fact which savoured of Allah's disapproval, how could he conceal such an illuminating experience of seeing Allah with the ocular vision which could earn him honour even amongst his enemies as one who had seen the Lord with the sight of sense.

Chapter LXXIX

PERTAINING TO HIS (PROPHET'S) WORDS : HE IS A LIGHT ; HOW COULD I SEE HIM ?—AND HIS WORDS : I SAW THE LIGHT

(341) It is narrated on the authority of Abū Dharr : I asked the Messenger of Allah (may peace be upon him) : Did you see thy Lord ? He said : He is a Light ; how could I see Him ?

(342) 'Abdullah b. Shaqīq reported : I said to Abū Dharr : Had I seen the Messenger of Allah, I would have asked him. He (Abū Dharr) said : What is that thing that you wanted to inquire of him ? He said : I wanted to ask him whether he had seen his Lord. Abū Dharr said : I, in fact, inquired of him, and he replied : I saw Light.[359]

(343) Abū Mūsā reported : The Messenger of Allah (may peace be upon him) was standing amongst us and he told us five things. He said : Verily the Exalted and Mighty God does not sleep, and it does not befit Him to sleep. He lowers the scale and lifts it.[360] The deeds in the night are taken up to Him before the deeds of the day, and the deeds of the day before the deeds of the night. His veil is the light. In the ḥadīth narrated by Abū Bakr (instead of the word "light") it is fire. If he withdraws it (the veil), the splendour of His countenance would consume His creation so far as His sight reaches.[361]

359. There is apparently some contradiction between this ḥadīth and the one mentioned above. We have been told in ḥadīth 341 that the Holy Prophet (may peace be upon him) could not see the Lord as He is Light, but in ḥadīth 342 we are told that the Holy Prophet (may peace be upon him) saw the Light. A little bit of penetration would resolve this contradiction. In ḥadīth 341, the word used for Light is نور which implies that the Prophet saw the Light of the Lord as reflected in phenomenal experience of the heaven and the earth and not the Glorious, Illimitable Light of God Himself. Ibn Qayyim has explained the meaning of the words نور انى اراه (*vide* ḥadīth 341). There was intervening between me and His Appearance the veil of Light, as it has been made clear in the ḥadīth that the Veil of Allah is itself a Light (*Zād al-Ma'ād*, Vol. II, p. 126).

All the above-mentioned aḥādīth make it clear that the Holy Prophet (may peace be upon him) did not see his Lord with his carnal eyes, but perceived Him with heart and mind (i.e. eye of the heart, as described in the ḥadīth). There are, however., some aḥādīth, especially reported by Ibn 'Abbās, which lead one to conclude that the Holy Prophet (may peace be upon him) had seen his Lord with his eyes. In Nasā'ī there is a ḥadīth : Do you feel surprised at the friendship of Ibrāhīm with Allah, His talking with Mūsā and His being seen by Muḥammad. Ḥākim too has recorded this ḥadīth and has declared it to be genuine. When we study this ḥadīth and some others like it in the light of the Holy Qur'ān and the Sunnah we come to the conclusion that the Holy Prophet (may peace be upon him) did not see the Lord with his eyes of sense but he did see Him with the eye of the heart. Ibn 'Abbās is not consistent in his words. At some places he calls this experience a sense-perception and at other places he narrates it as an experience of the soul. The ḥadīth reported by 'Ā'isha and Ibn Mas'ūd seems to be more weighty and reliable on this issue.

Some of the commentators are of the opinion that in both the aḥādīth the word "light" stands for the veil of light and the tradition would be like this. In ḥadīth 341 : There is a veil of Light (around Him) ; how could I, therefore, see Him, and in ḥadīth 342 : I saw only the veil of Light.

360. Allah lowers and raises the scales with a view to weighing the deeds of His bondsmen (*Fatḥ-ul-Mulhim*, Vol. I, p. 341).

361. In *Mishkāt* ("Bāb-ul-Masājid") there is a ḥadīth : Between me and Him are seventy thousand veils of Light. Imām Ghazālī has explained this ḥadīth in context with the verse of the Holy Qur'ān (xxiv. 35). The ultimate Light is God, the final fountainhead, Who is Light in and by

(344) A'mash has narrated this ḥadīth on the same authority and said: The Messenger of Allah (may peace be upon him) was standing amongst us and he told us four things. He then narrated the ḥadīth like the one reported by Abū Mu'āwiya, but did not mention the words "His creation" and said: His veil is the light.

(345) Abū Mūsā reported: The Messenger of Allah (may peace be upon him) was standing amongst us and (he said) four (things): Verily Allah does not sleep and it does not befit Him to sleep. He raises the scale and lowers it. The deeds of the day are presented to Him in the night and the deeds of the night in the day.

Chapter LXXX

IN PROOF OF THE FACT THAT THE BELIEVERS WOULD SEE THEIR LORD (HALLOWED BE HE AND EXALTED) ON THE LAST DAY

(346) 'Abdullah b. Qais transmitted on the authority of his father (Abū Mūsā Ash'arī) that the Apostle (may peace be upon him) said: There would be two gardens (in Paradise) the vessels and contents of which would be of silver, and two gardens whose vessels and contents would be of gold. The only thing intervening to hinder the people from looking at their Lord will be the mantle of Grandeur[362] over His face in the Garden of Eden.

(347) Ṣuhaib reported the Apostle (may peace be upon him) saying: When those deserving of Paradise would enter Paradise, the Blessed and the Exalted would ask: Do you wish Me to give you anything more? They would say: Hast Thou not brightened our faces? Hast Thou not made us enter Paradise and saved us from Fire? He (the narrator) said: He (God) would lift the veil, and of things given to them nothing would be dearer to them than the sight of their Lord, the Mighty and the Glorious.

(348) Ḥammād b. Salama narrated it on the same authority and added: He then recited the verse: "Those who do good will have the best reward and even more" (x. 26).[363]

Himself, not a light kindled by other lights. We cannot, however, see this perfect colourless Light of the Lord. We can catch a glimpse of it as it is reflected in colour and is apprehended with the sense of sight. If God were to withdraw this veil, we would not be able to stand His splendour. So, vision cannot perceive Him on account of His very brightness. Human beings have, therefore, been advised to see the signs of the Ultimate Reality and not to make any attempt to see the Reality, as such an effort would result only in their annihilation. How can a finite being comprehend a Being Who is Infinite? Those who make such attempts lose the consciousness of their existence. They are completely blotted out in the sense that with their selves they have no longer anything to do.

Such an attitude defeats the very purpose of human existence. We have a consciousness of the existence of God only when we are conscious of our own being and our own existence, and this is possible when we are aware of the phenomenal world in which we live and in which we should attempt to see the signs of that Great Reality that controls the universe.

It may also be pointed out in this connection that this ḥadīth which elucidates the fact that the veil of Allah is light implies that it is through knowledge, and not through ignorance, that we can understand the Ultimate Reality.

362. The believers will be provided an opportunity to see their Lord in the Paradise. The Unseen Reality would appear in His original shape. The ocular vision would be bestowed such an unusual power with which it would be able to bear His Splendour.

363. The verse, according to Imām Rāghib, indicates that the sight of Allah is the highest achievement of a Muslim which he can possibly conceive. It is a special favour of God.

Chapter LXXXI

THE WAY IN WHICH THE BELIEVERS WOULD SEE THE LORD

(349) Abū Huraira reported: The people said to the Messenger[364] of Allah (may peace be upon him): Messenger of Allah, shall we see our Lord on the Day of Resurrection? The Messenger of Allah (may peace be upon him) said: Do you feel any trouble in seeing the moon on the night when it is full? They said: Messenger of Allah, no. He (the Messenger) further said: Do you feel any trouble in seeing the sun, when there is no cloud over it? They said: Messenger of Allah, no. He (the Holy Prophet) said: Verily you would see Him like this (as you see the sun and the moon). God will gather people on the Day of Resurrection and say: Let every people follow what they worshipped. Those who worshipped the sun would follow the sun, and those who worshipped the moon would follow the moon, and those who worshipped the devils would follow the devils.[365] This Ummah (of Islam) alone would be left behind and there would be hypocrites too amongst it. Allah would then come to them in a form other than His own Form, recognisable to them, and would say: I am your Lord. They would say: We take refuge with Allah from thee. We will stay here till our Lord comes to us, and when our Lord would come we would recognise Him. Subsequently Allah would come to them in His own Form, recognisable to them, and say: I am your Lord. They would say: Thou art our Lord. And they would follow Him, and a bridge would be set over the Hell; and I (the Holy Prophet) and my Ummah would be the first to pass over it; and none but the messengers would speak on that day, and the prayer of the messengers on that day would be: O Allah! grant safety, grant safety. In Hell, there would be long spits like the thorns of Sa'dān. He (the Holy Prophet) said: Have you seen Sa'dān? They replied: Yes, Messenger of Allah. He said: Verily those (hooks) would be like the thorns of Sa'dān, but no one knows their size except Allah. These would seize people for their misdeeds. Some of them would escape for their (good) deeds, and some would be rewarded for their deeds till they get salvation. When Allah would finish judging His bondsmen and because of His mercy

364. Imām Ibn Taimīyya has drawn a distinction between *nabi* (apostle) and *rasūl* (messenger). So long as one is the recipient of the revelation from the Lord he is called *nabi* (apostle), but when he is entrusted with the responsibility of preaching this revelation to the unbelievers he becomes a *rasūl* (messenger). Every messenger is thus an apostle, but every apostle may not necessarily be a messenger, because there have been apostles to whom the revelation was sent, but they were not required to preach it to the hostile groups. They themselves put into practice the commands of Allah and exhorted the class of believers around them to do so. They had not to carry their message to the unbelievers. Thus right from Adam up to Noah it was a class of apostles that preached the teachings of Allah. But with the advent of Noah to Muḥammad (may peace be upon them) the apostles were also made messengers since they not only received revelation from the Lord, but were also assigned the task of preaching that revelation to the groups of unbelievers (*vide* Maulānā Muḥammad Badr-i-'Ālam's *Tarjumān al-Sunnah*, Vol. III, p. 443).

Some of the commentators have given some other marks of distinction between a *nabi* and a *rasūl*, but they all agree on this point that the messenger occupies a higher position than the *nabi*.

365. Originally, *Ṭāghūt* (طاغوت) means one that is exorbitant in pride of corruption or disbelief. In the religious sense it stands for whatever is worshipped, instead of or besides God.

decide to take out of Hell such people as He pleases, He would command the angels to bring out those who had not associated anything with Allah; to whom Allah decided to show mercy, those who would say: There is no god but Allah. They (the angels) would recognise them in the Fire by the marks of prostration, for Hell-fire will devour everything (limb) of the sons of Adam except the marks of prostration. Allah has forbidden the fire to consume the marks of prostration. They will be taken out of the Fire having been burnt, and the water of life would be poured over them, and they will sprout as seed does in the silt carried by flood. Then Allah would finish judging amongst His bondsmen; but a man who will be the last to enter Paradise will remain facing Hell and will say: O my Lord! turn my face away from Hell, for its air has poisoned me and its blaze has burnt me. He will then call to Allah as long as Allah would wish that he should call to Him. Then Allah, Blessed and Exalted, would say: If I did that, perhaps you would ask for more than that. He would say: I would not ask You more than this, and he would give his Lord covenants and agreements as Allah wished, and so He would turn his face away from the Fire. When he turns towards the Paradise and sees it, he will remain silent as long as Allah wishes him to remain so. He will then say: O my Lord! bring me forward to the gate of the Paradise. Allah would say to him: Did you not give covenants and agreements that you would not ask for anything besides what I had given you. Woe to thee! O son of Adam, how treacherous you are! He would say: O my Lord!—and would continue calling to Allah till He would say to him: If I grant you that, perhaps you will ask for more. He will reply: No, by Thy greatness, and he will give His Lord promises and covenants as Allah had wished. He would then bring him to the gate of the Paradise, and when he would stand at the gate of the Paradise, it would lay open before him, and he would see the bounty and the joy that there is in it. He would remain quiet as long as Allah would desire him to remain silent. He would then say: O my Lord, admit me to Paradise. Allah, Blessed and Exalted, would say: Did you not give covenants and agreements that you would not ask for anything more than what I had granted you? Woe to you! son of Adam, how treacherous you are! And he would say: O my Lord, I do not wish to be the most miserable of Thy creatures. He would continue calling upon Allah till Allah, Blessed and Exalted, would laugh. When Allah would laugh at him, He would say: Enter the Paradise. When he would enter, Allah would say: State your wish. He would express his wishes till Allah would remind him (the desire of) such and such (things). When his desires would be exhausted Allah would say: That is for thee and, besides it, the like of it also. 'Aṭā' b. Yazīd said: Abū Sa'īd al-Khudrī was with Abū Huraira and he did not reject anything from the ḥadīth narrated by him, but when Abū Huraira narrated: "Allah said to that man; and its like along with it," Abū Sa'īd said: "Ten like it along with it," O Abū Huraira. Abū Huraira said: I do not remember except the words: "That is for you and a similar one along with it." Abū Sa'īd said: I bear witness to the fact that I remembered from the Messenger of Allah (may peace be upon him) his words: "That is for thee and ten like it." Abū Huraira said: That man was the last of those deserving of Paradise to enter Paradise.

(350) Abū Huraira reported: The people said to the Apostle of Allah (may peace be upon him): Messenger of Allah! shall we see our Lord on the Day of Resurrection?

The rest of the ḥadīth was narrated according to the narration of Ibrāhīm b. Sa'd.

(351) Hammām b. Munabbih said: This is what Abū Huraira transmitted to us from the Messenger of Allah (may peace be upon him),—and he narrated many of them;—one of them was: The Messenger of Allah (may peace be upon him) said: The lowest in rank among you in Paradise would be asked: Desire (whatever you like). And he would express his desire and again and again express a desire. He would be asked: Have you expressed your desire? He would say: Yes. Then He (Allah) would say: For thee is (granted) what thou desirest, and the like of it along with it.

(352) Abū Sa'īd al-Khudrī reported: Some people during the lifetime of the Messenger of Allah (may peace be upon him) said: Messenger of Allah! shall we see our Lord on the Day of Resurrection? The Messenger of Allah (may peace be upon him) said: Yes,[366] and added: Do you feel any trouble in seeing the sun at noon with no cloud over it, and do you feel trouble in seeing the moon (open) in the full moonlit night with no cloud over it? They said: No, Messenger of Allah! He (the Holy Prophet) said: You will not feel any trouble in seeing Allah on the Day of Resurrection any more than you do in seeing any one of them. When the Day of Resurrection comes a Mu'adhdhin (a proclaimer) would proclaim: Let every people follow what they used to worship. Then all who worshipped idols and stones besides Allah would fall into the Fire, till only the righteous and the vicious and some of the people of the Book who worshipped Allah are left. Then the Jews would be summoned, and it would be said to them: What did you worship? They will say: We worshipped 'Uzair, son of Allah. It would be said to them: You tell a lie; Allah had never had a spouse or a son. What do you want now? They would say: We feel thirsty, O our Lord! Quench our thirst. They would be directed (to a certain direction) and asked: Why don't you go there to drink water? Then they would be pushed towards the Fire (and they would find to their great dismay that) it was but a mirage (and the raging flames of fire) would be consuming one another, and they would fall into the Fire. Then the Christians would be summoned and it would be said to them: What did you worship? They would say: We worshipped Jesus, son of Allah. It would be said to them: You tell a lie; Allah did not take for Himself either a spouse or a son. Then it would be said to them: What do you want? They would say: Thirsty we are, O our Lord! Quench our thirst. They would be directed (to a certain direction) and asked: Why don't you go there to get water? But they would be pushed and gathered together towards the Hell, which was like a mirage to them, and the flames would consume one another. They would fall into the Fire, till no one is left except he who worshipped Allah, be he pious or sinful. The Lord of the Universe, Glorified and Exalted, would come to them in a form recognisable to them and say[367]: What are you looking for? Every people follow that which they worshipped. They would say: Our Lord, we kept ourselves separate from the people in

366. The Qur'ān states: "(Some) faces that day will be bright looking to their Lord" (lxxv. 237). The sight of the Lord has been declared as the highest bliss for a man. It should be remembered that the sight of Allah does not imply that the Lord will appear in bodily form; it is either with the heavenly strength added to the ocular vision of the physical world that the believers would see their Lord, or with the spiritual eye.

367. This substantiates the fact that Allah has no bodily form. He is a Light and one can see His Illumination in the Paradise in so many forms.

the world, though we felt great need of them; we, however, did not associate ourselves with them. He would say: I am your Lord. They would say: We take refuge with Allah from thee and do not associate anything with Allah. They would repeat it twice or thrice, till some of them would be about to return. It would be said: Is there any sign between you and Him by which you will recognise Him? They would say: Yes, and the things would be laid bare.[368] Those who used to prostrate themselves before God of their own accord would be permitted by God to prostrate themselves. But there would remain none who used to prostrate out of fear (of people) and ostentation but Allah would make his back as one piece, and whenever he would attempt to prostrate he would fall on his back.[369] Then they would raise their heads and He would assume the Form in which they had seen Him the first time and would say: I am your Lord. They would say: Thou art our Lord. Then the bridge would be set up over the Hell and intercession would be allowed and they will say: O God, keep safe, keep safe. It was asked: Messenger of Allah, what is this bridge? He said: The void in which one is likely to slip. There would be hooks, tongs, spits like the thorn that is found in Najd and is known as Sa'dān. The believers would then pass over within the twinkling of an eye, like lightning, like wind, like a bird, like the finest horses and camels. Some will escape and be safe, some will be lacerated and let go, and some will be pushed into the fire of Hell till the believers will find rescue from the Fire. By One in Whose hand is my life, there will be none among you more eager to claim a right than the believers on the Day of Resurrection for (saving their) brethren in the Fire who would say: O our Lord, they were fasting along with us, and praying and performing pilgrimage. It will be said to them: Take out those whom you recognise. Then their persons would be forbidden to the Fire; and they would take out a large number of people who had been overtaken by Fire up to the middle of the shank or up to the knees. They would then say: O our Lord! not one of those about whom Thou didst give us command remains in it. He will then say: Go back and bring out those in whose hearts you find good of the weight of a dīnār. Then they will take out a large number of people. Then they would say: O our Lord! we have not left anyone about whom You commanded us. He will then say: Go back and bring out those in whose hearts you find as much as half a dīnār of good. Then they will take out a large number of people, and would say: O our Lord! not one of those about whom Thou commanded us we have left in it. Then He would say: Go back and in whose heart you find good to the weight of a particle bring him out. They would bring out a large number of people, and would then say: O our Lord, now we have not left anyone in it (Hell) having any good in him.

Abū Sa'īd Khudrī said: If you don't testify me in this ḥadīth, then recite if you like: "Surely Allah wrongs not the weight of an atom; and if it is a good deed, He multiplies it and gives from Himself a great reward" (al-Qur'ān, iv. 40). Then Allah,

368. يكشف عن ساق is an idiom which means either the disclosing of distress or difficulty or laying bare the truth of the matter. The origin of it is in the fright and the flight and the tucking up of the garments (by women) from their shanks and disclosing of their shanks while fleeing.

369. That refers to the verse of the Holy Qur'ān: "On the day when there is a severe affliction and they are called upon to prostrate themselves, but they are not able" (lxviii. 42).

Exalted and Great, would say: The angels have interceded, the apostles have interceded and the believers have interceded, and no one remains (to grant pardon) but the Most Merciful of the mercifuls. He will then take a handful from Fire and bring out from it people who never did any good and who had been turned into charcoal, and will cast them into a river called the river of life, on the outskirts of Paradise. They will come out as a seed comes out from the silt carried by flood. You see it near the stone or near the tree. That which is exposed to the sun is yellowish or greenish and which is under the shade is white. They said: Messenger of Allah! it seems as if you had been tending a flock in the jungle. He (the Holy Prophet) said: They will come forth like pearls with seals on their necks.[370] The inhabitants of Paradise would recognise them (and say): Those are who have been set free by the Compassionate One, Who has admitted them into Paradise without any (good) deed that they did or any good that they sent in advance. Then He would say: Enter the Paradise; whatevar you see in it is yours. They would say: O Lord, Thou hast bestowed upon us (favours) which Thou didst not bestow upon anyone else in the world. He would say: There is with Me (a favour) for you better than this. They would say: O our Lord! which thing is better than this? He would say: It is My pleasure. I will never be angry with you after this.[371]

(353) It is narrated on the authority of Abū Sa'īd al-Khudrī: We said: Messenger of Allah, shall we see our Lord? The Messenger of Allah (may peace be upon him) said: Do you feel any trouble in seeing the sun on a cloudless day? We said: No. And the remaining part of the ḥadīth has been narrated to the end like the ḥadīth transmitted by Ḥafṣ b. Maisara with the addition of these words: Without the deed that they did or any good that they had sent before. It would be said to them: For you is whatever you see (in it) and with it the like of it. Abū Sa'īd said: I have come to know that the bridge would be thinner even than the hair and sharper than the sword; and in the ḥadīth narrated by Laith these words are not found: They would say, O our Lord! Thou hast bestowed upon us (favours) which Thou didst not bestow on anyone else in the world.

(354) Abū Bakr b. Abī Shaiba, Ja'far b. 'Aun, Hishām b. Sa'd, Zaid b. Aslam narrated the ḥadīth as transmitted by Ḥafṣ b. Maisara, with certain additions and omissions.

Chapter LXXXII

AFFIRMATION OF INTERCESSION AND RESCUE FROM FIRE OF THE BELIEVERS IN ONENESS OF ALLAH

(355) Abū Sa'īd al-Khudrī reported: Verily the Messenger of Allah (may peace be upon him) said: Allah will admit into Paradise those deserving of Paradise, and He will admit whom He wishes out of His Mercy, and admit those condemned to Hell into the Fire (of Hell). He would then say: See, he whom you find having as much faith

370. It may mean seals by which they would be distinguished from others who would attain salvation for their good deeds (*Fatḥ-ul-Mulḥim*, Vol. I, p. 335).

371. This ḥadīth is never meant to underrate the importance of good deeds, but to bring before the mind of man infinite Mercy and Compassion of Allah.

in his heart as a grain of mustard, bring him out. They will then be brought out, burned and turned to charcoal, and would be cast into the river of life, and they would sprout as does a seed in the silt carried away by flood. Have you not seen that it comes out yellow (fresh) and intertwined?

(356) This ḥadīth is transmitted by 'Amr b. Yaḥyā with the same chain of transmitters who narrated: They would be cast into the river which is called (the river of) life, and (both the narrators) did not doubt the ḥadīth. The text transmitted by Khālid is: Just as seeds sprout beside the flood water; and in the ḥadīth of Wuhaib it is: Just as the seed sprouts in the silt or deposit left by flood.

(357) It is reported by Abū Sa'īd that the Messenger of Allah (may peace be upon him) said: The (permanent) inhabitants of the Fire are those who are doomed to it, and verily they would neither die nor live in it (al-Qur'ān, xx. 74; lxxxvii. 13).[372] But the people whom the Fire would afflict (temporarily) on account of their sins, or so said (the narrator) "on account of their misdeeds," He would cause them to die till they would be turned into charcoal. Then they would be granted intercession[373] and would be brought in groups and would be spread on the rivers of Paradise and then it would be said: O inhabitants of Paradise, pour water over them; then they would sprout forth like the sprouting of seed in the silt carried by flood. A man among the people said: (It appears) as if the Messenger of Allah lived in the steppe.

(358) Abū Naḍra narrated it from Abū Saīd al-Khudrī who reported it from the Apostle (may peace be upon him) a similar (ḥadīth) up to the words: "in the mud of the flood," and he did not mention (the words narrated) after it.

(359) 'Abdullah b. Mas'ūd reported that the Messenger of Allah (may peace be upon him) said: I know the last of the inhabitants of Fire to be taken out therefrom, and the last of the inhabitants of Paradise to enter it. A man will come out of the Fire crawling. Then Allah, the Blessed and Exalted, will say to him: Go and enter Paradise. So he would come to it and it would appear to him as if it were full. He would go back and say: O my Lord! I found it full. Allah, the Blessed and Exalted, would say to him: Go and enter Paradise. He would come and perceive as if it were full. He would return and say: O my Lord! I found it full. Allah would say to him:

372. There would be no life in the Hell worth the name, for real life is only for the righteous; neither is there death, because life in the Hereafter is eternal.

373. Of the numerous ways in which Divine Mercy is manifested the one is Shafā'a or intercession. It should, however, be borne in mind that in Islam intercession does not mean a permanent prerogative given to an angel or a prophet or any other saintly person to admit people to the Paradise at his own sweet will. The Holy Qur'ān says that intercession is possible with Allah's permission: "Who is he that can intercede with Him but by permission" (ii. 55). This makes it clear that intercession is not the same as the doctrine of Atonement.

The Holy Qur'ān also tells us that the angels, prophets and pious people will be granted permission to intercede. "And how many an angel is there in the heavens whose intercession is of no use except after Allah has given permission to whom He pleases and chooses" (liii. 26). Speaking of the prophets the Holy Qur'ān says: "He knows what is before them and what is behind them, and they (prophets) do not intercede except for one whom He is pleased with" (xxi. 28). Muḥammad's Shafā'a is recognised by Ijmā'; it is based on this verse of the Holy Qur'ān: "And during a part of the night, keep awake by it, beyond what is incumbent on thee, maybe thy Lord would raise thee to a position of great glory" (xvii. 79). (*Vide* al-Rāzī's commentary.)

Go and enter Paradise, for there is for you the like of the world and ten times like it, or for you is ten times the like of this world. He (the narrator) said: He (that man) would say: Art Thou making a fun of me? or Art Thou laughing at me, though Thou art the King? He (the narrator) said: I saw the Messenger of Allah laugh till his front teeth were visible. And it was said: That would be the lowest rank among the inhabitants of Paradise.

(360) It is narrated on the authority of ʻAbdullah b. Masʻūd that the Messenger of Allah (may peace be upon him) said: I recognise the last of the inhabitants of Fire to be taken out thereof. A man will come out of it crawling. It will be said to him: Go and enter Paradise. He (the Holy Prophet) said: He would go there to enter Paradise, but would find persons who have already occupied all its apartments. It would be said to him: Do you recall the time when you were in it (in the Hell)?[374] He would say: Yes. It would be said to him: Express any desire.[375] And he would express the desire. It would be said to him: For thee is that which thou desireth and ten times the world (worldly resources). He (the Holy Prophet) said: He would say: Art Thou making a fun of me, though Thou art the King?[376] I saw the Messenger of Allah laugh till his front teeth were visible.

(361) Ibn Masʻūd reported: Verily the Messenger of Allah said: The last to enter Paradise would be a man who would walk once and stumble once and be burnt by the Fire once. Then when he gets beyond it, he will turn to it and say: Blessed is He Who has saved me from thee. Allah has given me something He has not given to any one of those in earlier or later times. Then a tree would be raised up for him and he will say: O my Lord! bring me near this tree so that I may take shelter in its shade and drink of its water. Allah, the Exalted and Great, would say: O son of Adam, if I grant you this, you will ask Me for something else. He would say: No, my Lord. And he would promise Him that he would not ask for anything else. His Lord would excuse him because He sees what he cannot help desiring; so He would bring him near it, and he would take shelter in its shade and drink of its water. Afterwards a tree more beautiful than the first would be raised up before him and he would say: O my Lord! bring me near this tree in order that I may drink of its water and take shelter in its shade and I shall not ask Thee for anything else. He (Allah) would say: O son of Adam, if I bring you near it you may ask me for something else. He would promise Him that he would not ask for anything else. His Lord will excuse him because He would see something he cannot help desiring. So He would bring him near it

374. Hell is strait and its atmosphere is stifling. It is, therefore, conceivable that when a person would come out of it, he would, in the first instance, perceive lack of space in the Paradise.

375. It seems that even by this time his mind would be still hemmed in by the narrow bounds of material life, and by no stretch of imagination his desires would be beyond the material comforts and resources.

376. When the infinitely vast resources of Paradise with their boundless blessings would be unfolded before this man and his mind would become familiar with the immensely rich life of heavenly bliss, the comforts of the worldly life would appear ridiculously insignificant in his eyes. All his conceivable desires drawn from his worldly imagination along with the resources of the material world would look to be trifling as compared with the vast and varied bounties of Heaven. The ḥadīth is meant to give us an idea of the insignificance of the material world and its limited resources as compared with the inconceivable vastness and richness of Paradise.

and he would enjoy its shade and drink its water. Then a tree would be raised up for him at the gate of the Paradise, more beautiful than the first two. He would say: O my Lord! bring me near this (tree) so that I may enjoy its shade and drink from its water. I shall not ask Thee for anything else. He (Allah) would say: O son of Adam! did you not promise Me that you would not ask Me anything else? He would say: Yes, my Lord, but I shall not ask Thee for anything else. His Lord would excuse him for He sees something the temptation of which he could not resist. He (Allah) would bring him near to it, and when He would bring him near it he would hear the voices of the inhabitants of the Paradise. He would say: O my Lord! admit me to it. He (Allah) would say: O son of Adam, what will bring an end to your requests to Me? Will it please you if I give you the whole world and a like one along with it? He will say: O my Lord! art Thou mocking at me, though Thou art the Lord of the worlds? Ibn Mas'ūd laughed and asked (the hearers): Why don't you ask me what I am laughing at. They (then) said: Why do you laugh? He said: It is in this way that the Messenger of Allah (may peace be upon him) laughed. They (the companions of the Holy Prophet) asked: Why do you laugh, Messenger of Allah? He said: On account of the laugh of the Lord of the universe, when he (desirer of Paradise) said: Art Thou mocking at me though Thou art the Lord of the worlds? He would say: I am not mocking at you, but I have power to do whatever I will.[377]

Chapter LXXXIII

THE LOWEST OF THE RANKS IN PARADISE

(362) It is transmitted from Abū Sa'īd al-Khudrī that, verily, the Messenger of Allah (may peace be upon him) said: Amongst the inhabitants of Paradise the lowest in rank will be the person whose face Allah would turn away from the Fire towards the Paradise, and make a shady tree appear before him. He would say: O my Lord! direct my steps to this tree so that I (should enjoy) its shade; and the rest of the ḥadīth is like that narrated by Ibn Mas'ūd, but he did not mention: "He (Allah) would say: O son of Adam! what will bring an end to your making requests to Me" to the end of the tradition. In it, he added: Allah will remind him: Ask such and such, and when his expectations would be realised, Allah would say: That is for you, and ten times as much. He said that he would then enter his house and his two wives with large and dark eyes would enter after him. They will say: Praise be to Allah, Who has created you for us and us for you. He will say: No one has been given the like of what I have been given.

(363) It is reported on the authority of al-Mughīra b. Shu'ba that the Messenger of Allah (may peace be upon him) said: Moses asked his Lord: Who amongst the

377. This ḥadīth is indicative of the fact that the new entrant to Paradise would be introduced to this heavenly abode step by step so that he may become familiar with his new spiritual surroundings. The time and its vast mysteries are unfolded to him; the material world, with all its resources, would pale into insignificance and the offer of such worlds from the Lord when he is standing at the threshold of Paradise would seem to him as a joke.

inhabitants of Paradise is the lowest in rank ? He (Allah) said : The person who would be admitted into Paradise last of all among those deserving of Paradise who are admitted to it. It would be said to him : Enter Paradise. He would say : O my Lord ! how (should I enter) while the people have settled in their apartments and taken their shares (portions) ? It would be said to him : Would you be pleased if there be for you like the kingdom of a king amongst the kings of the world ? He would say : I am pleased, my Lord. He (Allah) would say : For you is that, and like that, and like that, and like that, and like that. He would say at the fifth (point) : I am well pleased, my Lord. He (Allah) would say : It is for you and ten times like it, and for you is what your self desires and your eye enjoys. He would say : I am well pleased, my Lord. He (Moses) said : (Which is) the highest of their (inhabitants of Paradise) ranks ? He (Allah) said : They are those whom I choose. I establish their honour with My own hand and then set a seal over it (and they would be blessed with Bounties) which no eye has seen, no ear has heard and no human mind has perceived ;[378] and this is substantiated by the Book of Allah, Exalted and Great : "So no soul knows what delight of the eye is hidden for them ; a reward for what they did" (xxxii. 17).

(364) Sha'bī reported he had heard al Mughīra b. Shu'ba say on the pulpit that Moses (peace be upon him) had asked Allah, Exalted and Great, about the reward of the lowest of the inhabitants of Paradise, and the remaining part of ḥadīth is the same (as narrated) above.

(365) Abū Dharr reported that Allah's Messenger (may peace be upon him) said : I know the last of the inhabitants of Paradise to enter it and the last of the inhabitants of Hell to come out of it. He is a man who would be brought on the Day of Resurrection and it will be said : Present his minor sins to him, and withhold from him his serious sins.[379] Then the minor sins would be placed before him, and it would be said : On such and such a day you did so and so and on such and such a day you did so and so. He would say : Yes. It will not be possible for him to deny, while he would be afraid lest serious sins should be presented before him. It would be said to him : In place of every evil deed you will have good deed.[380] He will say : My Lord ! I have done things I do not see here. I indeed saw the Messenger of Allah laugh till his front teeth were exposed.

(366) This ḥadīth is also narrated by another chain of narrators, i.e. Ibn Numair, Abū Mu'āwiya, Wakī', Abū Bakr b. Abī Shaiba, Abū Kuraib, A'mash.

(367) It is reported on the authority of Abū Zubair that he heard from Jābir b. 'Abdullah, who was asked about the arrival (of people on the Day of Resurrection).

378. This ḥadīth gives us an idea of the various grades in Paradise. It would not be absolutely a strange world for the people, for it will have immeasurably vast bounties of the worldly life too. What the Holy Prophet wanted to stress was that even in the lowest grades of Paradise its dwellers will find life infinitely better than the life of this world. But the higher ranks which provide the comforts of spiritual life can neither be conceived by human mind nor adequately expressed in human words.

379. This is how Allah will reveal to him His kindness and Mercy. Even his minor sins would be so great that he will feel ashamed of them and will not be able to lay any claim for Paradise. It is at this juncture that his attention will turn to the major sins.

380. Allah in His infinite Grace and Mercy pardons his sins for his submissive attitude.

He said: We would come on the Day of Resurrection like this, like[381] this, and see,[382] carefully, that which concerns "elevated people". He (the narrator) said: Then the people would be summoned along with their idols whom they worshipped, one after another. Then our Lord would come to us and say: Whom are you waiting for? They would say: We are waiting for our Lord. He would say: I am your Lord. They would say: (We are not sure) till we gaze at Thee, and He would manifest Himself to them smilingly, and would go along with them and they would follow Him; and every person, whether a hypocrite or a believer, would be endowed with a light, and there would be spikes and hooks on the bridge of the Hell, which would catch hold of those whom Allah willed. Then the light of the hypocrites would be extinguished, and the believers would secure salvation, and the first group to achieve it would comprise seventy thousand men who would have the brightness of full moon on their faces, and they would not be called to account. Then the people immediately following them would have their faces as the brightest stars in the heaven. This is how (the groups would follow one after another). Then the stage of intercession would come, and they (who are permitted to intercede) would intercede, till he who had declared: "There is no god but Allah" and had in his heart virtue of the weight of a barley grain would come out of the Fire. They would be then brought in the courtyard of Paradise and the inhabitants of Paradise would begin to sprinkle water over them till they would sprout like the sprouting of a thing in flood water, and their burns would disappear. They would ask their Lord till they would be granted (the bounties) of the world and with it ten more[383] besides it.

(368) Jābir reported that he had heard with his ears the Apostle (may peace be upon him) saying: Allah will bring out people from the Fire and admit them into Paradise.

(369) Ḥammād b. Zaid reported: I said to 'Amr b. Dīnār: Did you hear Jābir b. 'Abdullah narrating from the Messenger of Allah (may peace be upon him) that Allah would bring out people from the Fire through intercession. He said: Yes.

(370) Jābir b. 'Abdullah reported: The Messenger of Allah (may peace be upon him) said: Verily people would be brought out from the Fire, and they would be burnt except the exterior (surfaces, fronts) of their faces[384]; and they would enter Paradise.

(371) Yāzid al-Faqīr said: This view of the Khwārij (i.e. those who commit major sins and would be eternally doomed to Hell) had obsessed me, and we set out in a large group intending to perform the Ḥajj and then going to the people (for the propaga-

381. The commentators of the ḥadīth are of the opinion that instead of the words كذا كذا the original words are: على كوم (upon the hill).

382. The word أنظر (unẓur) is not a part of the ḥadīth but a word added by a narrator in order to draw the attention of the readers to the fact that there is some discrepancy in the words used here and they should, therefore, read this part with caution.

383. This ḥadīth is *Mauqūf*, i.e. its chain of transmitters does not reach the Holy Prophet. Imām Muslim has in fact avoided the inclusion of such aḥādīth in his compilation. He has, however, made an exception to it because the ḥadīth which relates the events of the Hereafter (matters of the Unseen) cannot but emanate from the Holy Prophet and, therefore, it is as reliable as *Marfū'*.

384. This may be due to the fact that, while prostrating before the Lord, the face touches the ground.

tion of the views of the Khwārij). He (the narrator) said : We happened to pass by Medina and found there Jābir b. 'Abdullah sitting near a column narrating to the people (the aḥādīth of) the Holy Prophet (may peace be upon him). When he mentioned the inhabitants of Hell, I said : O companion of the Messenger of Allah, what is this that thou narrateth, whereas Allah sayeth : "Verily whomsoever Thou shalt commit to the Fire, Thou indeed humiliateth him" (al-Qur'ān, iii. 192) ; and "All those who endeavoured to get out of that would be thrown back into it" (al-Qur'ān, xxxii. 20)?[385] So what is it that you say? He said : Have you read the Qur'ān ? I said : Yes. He said : Have you heard about the (exalted) position of Muḥammad (may peace be upon him), i.e. to which Allah would raise him ? I said : Yes. He said : Verily the position of Muḥammad (may peace be upon him) is that of great glory[386] and that is by which Allah would bring out whomsoever He would wish to bring out. He then described the Path (the Bridge) and the passing of the people over it, and said : I am afraid I may not have remembered (other things) but this much is still in my memory that people would come out of the Hell after having gone into it, and he said : They would come out of it as if they were the wood of the ebony tree.[387] He (the narrator) said : They would enter a river, one of the rivers of Paradise, and would bathe in it, and then come out as if they were (white like) paper. We then turned back and said : Woe be upon you ! How can this old man tell a lie against the Messenger of Allah (may peace be upon him) ? We turned back (from the views of the Khwārij), and by God every one of us abandoned this (band of Khwārij) except one man. A similar statement has been made by Abū Nu'aim.

(372). It is narrated on the authority of Anas b. Mālik that the Messenger of Allah (may peace be upon him) said : Four persons would be brought out from the Fire and would be presented to Allah. One of them would turn (towards the Hell) and say : O my Lord, when Thou hast brought me out from it, do not throw me back into it, and Allah would rescue him from it.

(373) Anas b. Mālik reported : The Messenger of Allah (may peace be upon him) said : Allah would gather people on the Day of Resurrection and they would be concerned about it, and Ibn 'Ubaid said : They would get a Divine inspiration about it, and would say : If we could seek intercession with our Lord, we may be relieved from this predicament of ours. He (the Holy Prophet) said : They would come to Adam and say : Thou art Adam, the father of mankind, Allah created thee with His own hand[388] and breathed unto thee of His spirit[389] and commanded the angels and they prostrated before thee, so intercede for us with thy Lord so that He may relieve us from this position of ours. He would say : I am not in a position to do this, and would recall

385. These verses refer to the unbelievers who are eternally doomed to Hell.

386. This refers to the verse of the Holy Qur'ān : "Maybe thy Lord will raise thee to a position of great glory" (xvii. 79).

387. i.e. they would be turned black like the ebony tree after being burnt in the fire of Hell.

388. Hand is here used not in the literal sense, but in a metaphorical sense.

389. Or "A spirit from Him" and not "His spirit" is the correct rendering of روحه in the context. The reference of Rūḥ towards God is only to indicate its glory as it has been pointed out in the *Tafsir* of Imām Rāzī. Some of the commentators are of the opinion that its reference towards God implies that it is created by Him.

his error,[390] and would fight shy of his Lord on account of that ; go to Noah the first messenger (after me) sent by Allah. He (the Holy Prophet) said : So they would come to Noah (peace be upon him). He would say : I am not in a position to do that for you, and recall his fault which he had committed, and would fight shy of his Lord on account of that, (and would say) : You better go to Ibrāhīm (peace be upon him) whom Allah took for a friend. They would come to Ibrāhīm (peace be upon him) and he would say : I am not in a position to do that for you, and would recall his fault that he had committed and would, therefore, fight shy of his Lord on that account (and would say) : You better go to Moses (peace be upon him) with whom Allah conversed and conferred Torah upon him. He (the Holy Prophet) said : So they would come to Moses (peace be upon him). He would say : I am not in a position to do that for you, and would recall his fault that he had committed and would fight shy of his Lord on account of that (and would say) : You better go to Jesus, the Spirit of Allah and His word.[391] He would say : I am not in a position to do that for you ; you better go to Muḥammad (may peace be upon him), a servant whose former and later sins have been forgiven. He (the narrator) said : The Messenger of Allah (may peace be upon him) observed : So they would come to me and I would ask the permission of my Lord and it would be granted to me, and when I would see Him, I would fall down in prostration, and He (Allah) would leave me thus as long as He would wish, and then it would be said : O Muḥammad, raise your head, say and you would be heard ; ask and it would be granted ; intercede and intercession would be accepted. Then I would raise my head and extol my Lord with the praise which my Lord would teach me. I shall then intercede, but a limit would be set for me. I would bring them out from the Fire and make them enter Paradise (according to the limit). I shall return then and fall down in prostration and Allah would leave me (in that position) as long as He would wish to leave me. It would be said : Rise, O Muḥammad, say and you would be heard ; ask and it would be conferred; intercede and intercession would be granted. I would raise my head and extol my Lord with praise that He would teach me. I would then intercede and a limit would be set for me. I would bring them out of the Fire (of Hell) and make them enter Paradise. He (the narrator) said : I do not remember whether he (the Holy Prophet) said at the third time or at the fourth time : O my Lord, none has been left in the Fire, but those restrained by the Holy Qur'ān, i.e. those who were eternally doomed.[392] Ibn 'Ubaid said in a narration : Qatāda observed : "whose everlasting stay was imperative".

(374) Anas reported : The Messenger of Allah (may peace be upon him) said : The believers would gather on the Day of Resurrection, and they would be concerned about it, or would be made mindful of it (i.e. the trouble for it), (and the remaining part of the ḥadīth would be narrated) like the one transmitted by Abū 'Uwāna, and he said in the ḥadīth : Then I would come for the fourth time, or I would return the fourth time, and would say : O my Lord, no one has been left but he whom the Holy Qur'ān

390. It should be remembered that the prophets are immune from all sins. It is in the sense of minor omissions that the word "error" is used. This point will be discussed in ḥadīth 378.

391. This alludes to the fact that the soul of Jesus was directly infused into the womb of his virgin mother by Divine Command.

392. This refers to disbelievers.

has restrained.

(375) Anas b. Mālik reported: The Prophet of Allah (may peace be upon him) said: Allah will gather the believers on the Day of Resurrection and they would be made mindful of it; and the rest (of the ḥadīth) is like the one narrated above; and then he mentioned the fourth time: And I (the Holy Prophet) would say: O my Lord, no one is left in the Fire except he whom the Qur'ān has restrained, i.e. eternally doomed.

(376) Anas b. Mālik reported: Verily the Apostle (may peace be upon him) said: He who professed: There is no god but Allah, would be brought out of the Fire even though he has in his heart virtue equal to the weight of a barley grain. Then he who professed: There is no god but Allah, would come out of the Fire, even though he has in his heart virtue equal to the weight of a wheat grain. He would then bring out from the Fire he who professed: There is no god but Allah, even though he has in his heart virtue equal to the weight of an atom. Ibn Minhāl has made an addition (of these words) in his narration: Yazīd said: I met Shu'ba and narrated to him this ḥadīth. Shu'ba said: Qatāda transmitted to us this ḥadīth from Anas b. Mālik who heard it from the Apostle of Allah (may peace be upon him) with this alteration that he substituted the word *Zurra* (grain) in place of *Zarra* (atom). Yazīd said: Abū Bisṭām has made a change in it.

(377). Ma'bad b. Hilāl al-'Anazī reported: We went to Anas b. Mālik through Thābit and reached there (his house) while he was offering the forenoon prayer. Thābit sought permission for us and we entered, and he seated Thābit with him on his bedstead. He (Thābit) said to him (Anas b. Mālik): O Abū Ḥamza (kunya of Anas b. Mālik), your brothers from among the inhabitants of Baṣra ask you to narrate to them the ḥadīth of intercession. He said: Muḥammad (may peace be upon him) narrated to us: When it would be the Day of Resurrection, some of the people would rush to one another in bewilderment. They would come to Adam and say: Intercede (with your Lord) for your progeny. He would say: I am not fit to do this, but go to Ibrāhīm (peace be upon him), for he is the Friend of Allah. They would come to Ibrāhīm, but he would say: I am not fit to do this, but go to Moses, for he is Allah's Interlocutor. They would come to Moses, but he would say: I am not fit to do this, but you should go to Jesus, for he is the Spirit[393] of Allah and His word.[394] They would come to Jesus, and he would say: I am not fit to do this; you better go to Muḥammad (may peace be upon him). They would come to me, and I would say: I am in a position to do that. I would go and ask the permission of my Lord and it would be granted to me. I would then stand before

393. "Spirit of Allah" does not mean the incarnation of the Lord, but it simply means the Spirit created directly by Him. This Spirit is the manifestation of God's Glory. The Christians mistook the Spirit created by Allah for His own Spirit and asserted that the Holy Ghost has incarnated Himself in the person of Jesus Christ. It is, however, interesting to note that even the Bible in its present form substantiates the view presented by Islam. "But while he thought on these things, behold, the angel of the Lord appeared unto him in a dream, saying, Joseph, thou son of David, fear not to take unto thee Mary thy wife: for that which is conceived in her is of the Holy Ghost" (Matthew, 1 : 20).

394. "His word" means the Order of God, i.e. it is by His Order that Christ was miraculously born without father. Christians, under the influence of Greeks, however, interpreted it as *Lógos* and then concluded that the very word of Allah was transmuted into flesh and bone in the personality of Jesus Christ.

Him and would extol Him with praises which I am not able to do now, but with which Allah would inspire me, then I would fall in prostration and it would be said to me: O Muḥammad, raise thy head, and say and it would be listened to; ask and it would be granted; intercede and it would be accepted. I shall say: My Lord, my people, my people.[395] It would be said: Go, and bring forth from it (Hell) him who has in his heart faith equal to the weight of a wheat grain or a barley seed. I would go and do that; then I would return to my Lord and extol Him with those praises (taught to me by Allah), then I would fall in prostration. It would be said to me: O Muḥammad, raise your head, and say and it would be heard; ask and it would be granted; intercede and intercession would be accepted. So I would say: My people, my people. It would be said to me: Go and take out from it (Hell) him who has in his heart faith equal to the weight of a mustard seed. I would go and do that. I would again return to my Lord and extol Him with those praises. I would then fall in prostration. It would be said to me: O Muḥammad, raise your head: say, and you would be listened to; ask and it would be granted; intercede and intercession would be accepted. I would say: My Lord, my people, my people. It would be said to me: Go, and bring out of the Fire him who has in his heart as much faith as the smallest, smallest, smallest grain of mustard seed. I would go and do that.

This is the ḥadīth which Anas narrated to us. We went out of his (house) and when we reached the upper part of Jabbān[396] (graveyard) we said: Would that we meet Ḥasan and salute him and he was hiding in the house of Abū Khalīfa.[397] He (Ma'bad b. Hilāl, the narrator) said: We went to him and greeted him and we said: O Abū Sa'īd, we come from your brother Abū Ḥamza (kunya of Anas), and we have never heard a ḥadīth like this relating to intercession, which he has narrated to us. He said: Narrate it. We narrated the ḥadīth. He said: Narrate it (still further). We said: He did not (narrate it) before us more than this. He said: He (Anas) had narrated it to us twenty years back, when he was strong and healthy. He has in fact missed something. I cannot make out whether the old man has forgotten or he has (intentionally) avoided to narrate it to you lest you should rely (absolutely) upon it (and abandon doing good deeds). We said to him: Relate that to us, and he laughed and said: There is haste in the nature of man. I did not make mention of it to you but for the fact that I wanted to narrate that to you (and added that the Holy Prophet said): I would then return to my Lord for the fourth time and extol Him with these praises. I would then fall in prostration. It would be said to me: O Muḥammad, raise your head: say and it will be listened to; ask and it will be granted; intercede and intercession would be accepted. I would say: O my Lord, permit me regarding him who professed: There is no god but Allah. He (the Lord) would say: That is not for thee or that is not what lies with

395. As the Prophet Muḥammad (may peace be upon him) is the leader of all the prophets, therefore all the believers, irrespective of time and place, are his Ummah and he would intercede for all of them.

396. Jabbān is a common place of prayer in a desert tract. This is sometimes called *Jabbānah* because the place of prayer is generally in the burial ground.

397. He was hiding in the house of Abū Khalīfa out of the fear of Ḥajjāj b. Yūsuf.

thee,[398] but by My Honour, Glory, Greatness and Might, I would certainly take him out who professed it: There is no god but Allah. He (the narrator, Ma'bad) said: I bear testimony to the fact that the ḥadīth transmitted to us by Ḥasan was heard by him from Anas b. Mālik and I can see that he reported it twenty years back, when he was hale and hearty.

(378) Abū Huraira reported: Meat was one day brought to the Messenger of Allah (may peace be upon him) and a foreleg was offered to him, a part which he liked. He sliced with his teeth a piece out of it and said: I shall be the leader of mankind on the Day of Resurrection. Do you know why? Allah would gather in one plain the earlier and the later (of the human race) on the Day of Resurrection. Then the voice of the proclaimer would be heard by all of them and the eyesight would penetrate through all of them and the sun would come near. People would then experience a degree of anguish, anxiety and agony which they shall not be able to bear and they shall not be able to stand. Some people would say to the others: Don't you see in which trouble you are? Don't you see what (misfortune) has overtaken you? Why don't you find one who should intercede for you with your Lord? Some would say to the others: Go to Adam. And they would go to Adam and say: O Adam, thou art the father of mankind. Allah created thee by His own Hand and breathed in thee of His spirit and ordered the angels to prostrate before thee. Intercede for us with thy Lord. Don't you see in what (trouble) we are? Don't you see what (misfortune) has overtaken us? Adam would say: Verily, my Lord is angry to an extent to which He had never been angry before nor would He be angry afterward.[399] Verily, He forbade me (to go near) that tree and I disobeyed Him.[400] I am concerned with my own self. Go to someone else; go to Noah. They would come to Noah and would say: O Noah, thou art the first of the Messengers (sent) on the earth (after Adam), and Allah named thee as a "Grateful Servant," intercede for us with thy Lord. Don't you see in what (trouble) we are? Don't you see what (misfortune) has overtaken us? He would say: Verily, my Lord is angry today as

398. The Holy Prophet would, through intercession, bring forth all those believers who believe in the Oneness of the Lord and do some good acts in order to prove their faith in Allah, but those who only make a verbal profession of the Oneness of the Lord and their actions bear not even the slightest imprint of their belief, their case would be decided by Allah because He alone knows what lies hidden in the heart of man.

399. On the Day of Resurrection Allah will take the wrongdoers to task and be wrathful with them.

400. Before we proceed it is essential that we should see the nature of failings on the part of the prophets. All the apostles of Allah are innocent in the sense that they never commit any serious offence and even in minor omissions Allah at once warns them and they rectify themselves immediately. It is in fact very minor acts of omission and commission which they inadvertently do and then immediately beg pardon from the Lord which is readily granted to them. They go before their Lord completely absolved of all their omissions. It should also be noted that in case of prophets even those minor omissions are not actuated by personal motives but by their love for the faith.

But as they are very sensitive in their God-consciousness, they would, therefore, be reluctant to take the initiative before the Lord for the intercession of their people, and shift this responsibility on Muḥammad (may peace be upon him) who, as their leader, would work as their representative and spokesman and by the Will and Permission of Allah would be the first to intercede, and then the apostles, the angels of Allah and the pious believers would come forward and beg intercession for the people.

He had never been angry before, and would never be angry afterwards. There had emanated a curse from me with which I cursed my people.[401] I am concerned with only myself, I am concerned only with myself ; you better go to Ibrāhīm (peace be upon him). They would go to Ibrāhīm and say: Thou art the apostle of Allah and His Friend amongst the inhabitants of the earth ; intercede for us with thy Lord. Don't you see in which (trouble) we are? Don't you see what (misfortune) has overtaken us? Ibrāhīm would say to them: Verily, my Lord is today angry as He had never been angry before and would never be angry afterwards, and (Ibrāhīm) would mention his lies[402] (and then say): I am concerned only with myself, I am concerned only with myself. You better go to someone else: go to Moses. They would come to Moses (peace be upon him) and say: O Moses, thou art Allah's messenger, Allah blessed thee with His messengership and His conversation amongst people. Intercede for us with thy Lord. Don't you see in what (trouble)

401. This is in reference to the mission of Noah and the obstinate attitude of his people:

Lo! We sent Noah unto his people (saying): Warn thy people ere the painful doom come upon them.

He said: O my people! lo! I am a plain warner unto you (bidding you): Serve Allah and keep your duty unto Him and obey me (lxxi. 1-2).

He said: My Lord! lo! I have called upon my people day and night. But my calling only added to their repugnance (lxxi. 5)

Noah said: My Lord! lo! they have disobeyed me (lxxi. 21)

And Noah said: My Lord! leave not any one of the disbelievers in the land (lxxi. 26).

This gives the indication that it was out of disgust that Noah cursed the people.

402. These were not the type of lies which are counted as serious sins in religion. These may be called *tauriya* or *double-entendre* which means using a word, an expression or a phrase, which has an obvious meaning and intending thereby another meaning to which it applies, but which is contrary to the obvious one. Now all the three acts fall under the category of *double-entendre* and cannot be categorised as lies. It was due to intense God-consciousness of Ibrāhīm that he felt them seriously. Now we take all these acts one by one. The first one is that he called the star as his Lord. This matter is referred to in the Holy Qur'ān in the following words:

(*i*) So when the night overshadowed him, he saw a star. He exclaimed: This is my Lord. But when it went down he said: I love not the setting ones (vi. 77).

The words هذا ربي (*hādhā rabbi*), literally "this is my Lord," do not contain Ibrāhīm's conviction. As shown in the previous verse, he was a believer in the Oneness of Allah. These words are uttered as a query (referring to his people's belief who worshipped celestial bodies—stars, moon and sun) in order to awaken them to the realisation of the great reality as to how a transitory being can be an object of worship.

(*ii*) They said: Hast thou done this to our gods, O Ibrāhīm? He said: Surely the chief of them has done it. So ask them, if they can speak (xxi. 62-63).

Apparently it is a prevarication. Ibrāhīm had broken the idols, whereas he made the bigger one responsible for it. It is not, however, a lie but Ibrāhīm's biting irony that cut them to the quick. There is a pause after the words بل فعله and the statement كبيرهم هذا is an independent statement. فعله thus means "some doer has done it". What Ibrāhīm wanted to impress upon them is that they worshipped these lifeless idols, so they had better ask them.

(*iii*) What is then your idea about the Lord of the world? Then he glanced a glance at the stars and said: Surely I am sick (xxxvii. 87-89).

This is the third incident which hung so heavily on the extremely fine and delicate moral consciousness of the Prophet Ibrāhīm (peace be upon him) that he felt it like the burden of a lie. He was not using the word *saqim* in the sense of physical ailment but in the sense of mental aversion. Lane in his *Arabic-English Lexicon* gives the following as one of the explanations of the word *saqim* on the authority of *Tāj al-'Arūs*: "I am sick of your worshipping what is not God."

we are? Don't you see what (misfortune) has overtaken us? Moses (peace be upon him) would say to them: Verily, my Lord is angry as He had never been angry before and would never be angry afterwards. I, in fact, killed a person whom I had not been ordered to kill.[403] I am concerned with myself, I am concerned with myself. You better go to Jesus (peace be upon him). They would come to Jesus and would say: O Jesus, thou art the messenger of Allah and thou conversed with people in the cradle,[404] (thou art) His Word which He sent down upon Mary, and (thou art) the Spirit from Him; so intercede for us with thy Lord. Don't you see (the trouble) in which we are? Don't you see (the misfortune) that has overtaken us? Jesus (peace be upon him) would say: Verily, my Lord is angry today as He had never been angry before or would ever be angry afterwards. He mentioned no sin of his. (He simply said:) I am concerned with myself, I am concerned with myself; you go to someone else: better go to Muḥammad (may peace be upon him). They would come to me and say: O Muḥammad, thou art the messenger of Allah and the last of the apostles. Allah has pardoned thee all thy previous and later sins. Intercede for us with thy Lord; don't you see in which (trouble) we are? Don't you see what (misfortune) has overtaken us? I shall then set off and come below the Throne and fall down prostrate before my Lord; then Allah would reveal to me and inspire me with some of His Praises and Glorifications which He had not revealed to anyone before me. He would then say: Muḥammad, raise thy head; ask and it would be granted; intercede and intercession would be accepted. I would then raise my head and say: O my Lord, my people, my people.[405] It would be said: O

403. The reference is to verse 15 of sūra xxviii.:

> And he entered the city at a time when its people were not vigilant and he found therein two men fighting, one being of his own party and the other of his enemies. And he who was of his party called him for help against him who was of his enemies. So Moses struck him with his fist and killed him. He said: This is the work of Satan. Verily he is an enemy, openly leading astray.

The Israelite (of his own religion), for whose release Moses struck the Egyptian, was one of the down-trodden, oppressed people suffering for years and years the bitterest and the most cruel persecution. The actual situation in which this murder was unintentionally committed may be seen in the following statement:

> The oppressor (an idolatrous Egyptian) turned a deaf ear to remonstrances, persisted in his ill-usage of an unfortunate Hebrew, despite all that Moses could say (Rawlinson, *Moses, His Life and Time*, p. 57).

When Moses found no way of release for the Israelite from the clutches of the Egyptian, he struck him out of sympathy for the helpless, but he did it in a fit of rage and, therefore, the smite being forceful proved to be fatal. Moses never intended to kill him; he just wanted to release the Israelite, but his act produced a result that he had not anticipated.

Such an unintentional act is not a serious offence, but the extremely sensitive soul of the prophet felt it to be a great burden on his conscience and, therefore, he did not pluck courage to intercede with the Lord for his people.

404. Reference is to the following verse of the Holy Qur'ān:

> But she pointed to him. They said: How should we speak to one who is a child in the cradle? He said: I am indeed a servant of Allah. He has given me the Book and made me a prophet (xxviii. 28-30).

405. It has an implied reference to the nature of Muḥammad's prophethood. All the apostles of Allah are sent by Him to call humanity to the path of righteousness and piety. Before the advent of Muḥammad (may peace be upon him) it was the individual aspect of piety that was mainly stressed. But when the last of the prophets came the scope of religion became wide enough to comprehend

Muḥammad, bring in by the right gate of Paradise those of your people who would have no account to render. They would share with the people some other door besides this door. The Holy Prophet then said: By Him in Whose Hand is the life of Muḥammad, verily the distance between two door leaves of the Paradise is as great as between Mecca and Hajar,[406] or as between Mecca and Buṣrā.

(379) It is reported on the authority of Abū Huraira that there was placed before the Messenger of Allah a cup of soft bread, soup and meat. He took part of the foreleg which he liked most. He sliced (with his teeth) a slice (out of that) and said: I would be the leader of mankind on the Day of Resurrection. He then sliced (that meat) for the second time and said: I am the leader of mankind on the Day of Resurrection. When he saw that his companions did not ask him (about this assertion) he said: Why don't you say: How would that be? They said: How would be it, Messenger of Allah? He said: People would stand before the Lord of the worlds. And the rest of the ḥadīth was narrated like the one transmitted by Abū Ḥayyān, on the authority of Abū Zur'a, and in the story of Ibrāhīm, this addition was made. He said and made mention of his words with regard to the star: This is my Lord.[407] And his words with regard to their gods:[408] But the big among them has done that. And his words: I am ailing.[409] He (the Holy Prophet) said: By Him in Whose Hand is the life of Muḥammad, the distance between two leaves of the door from their supporting frames is as the distance between Mecca and Hajar or Hajar and Mecca. I do not remember how he said it (whether Mecca and Hajar or Hajar and Mecca).

(380) It is narrated on the authority of Abū Huraira and Ḥudhaifa that the Messenger of Allah (may peace be upon him) said: Allah, the Blessed and Exalted, would gather people. The believers would stand till the Paradise would be brought near them. They would come to Adam and say: O our father, open for us the Paradise. He would say: What turned ye out from the Paradise was the sin of your father Adam. I am not in a position to do that; better go to my son Ibrāhīm, the Friend of Allah. He (the Holy Prophet) said: He (Ibrāhīm) would say: I am not in a position to do that. Verily I had been the Friend (of Allah) from beyond, beyond;[410] you better approach Moses (peace be upon him) with whom Allah conversed. They would come to Moses (peace be upon him), but he would say: I am not in a position to do that; you better go to Jesus, the Word of Allah and His Spirit. Jesus (peace be upon him) would say: I am not in a position to do that. So they would come to Muḥammad (may peace be upon him). He would then be permitted (to open the door of Paradise). Trustworthiness and kinship[411] would be despatched, and these would stand on the

social responsibility along with individual righteousness. The religious man was henceforth required to attain God-consciousness not only in his individual sphere of life but also in his duties towards other human beings. In other words, a new type of piety was introduced, the basis of which was no doubt individual righteousness but which could be developed only by undertaking social responsibilities with God-consciousness. The words امتی امتی indicate this aspect of Islam.

406. A town in Baḥrain.

407-409. See footnote 400 above.

410. It means: "I am a Friend of Allah no doubt, but like Moses I am not Allah's interlocutor."

411. What it implies is that trustworthiness and responsibility of kinship would be the Guide-posts on the Path of Righteousness. He who is trustworthy and he who undertakes his responsibilities with regard to his kith and kin would find his path to Paradise quite easy. It should be noted that

right and left of the Path and the first of you would pass with (the swiftness) of lightning. He (the narrator) said: I said, O thou who art far dearer to me than my father and my mother! which thing is like the passing of lightning? He said: Have you not seen lightning, how it passes and then comes back within the twinkling of an eye? Then (they would pass) like the passing of the wind, then like the passing of a bird, and the hastening of persons would be according to their deeds, and your Apostle would be standing on the Path saying: Save, O my Lord, save. (The people would go on passing) till the deeds of the servants would be failing in strength, till a man would come who would find it hard to go along (that Path) but crawlingly. He (the narrator) said: And on the sides of the Path hooks would be suspended ready to catch anyone whom these would be required (to catch). There would be those who would somehow or other succeed in trasversing that Path and some would be piled up in Hell. By Him in Whose Hand is the life of Abū Huraira it would take one seventy years to fathom the depth of Hell.

Chapter LXXXIV

PERTAINING TO THE WORDS OF THE APOSTLE OF ALLAH (MAY PEACE BE UPON HIM): "I WOULD BE THE FIRST AMONG PEOPLE TO INTERCEDE IN THE PARADISE AND AMONG THE APOSTLES I WOULD HAVE THE LARGEST FOLLOWING"

(381) Anas b. Mālik reported: The Messenger of Allah (may peace be upon him) said: I would be the first among people to intercede in the Paradise and amongst the apostles I would have the largest following (on the Day of Resurrection).

(382) Anas b. Mālik reported: The Messenger of Allah (may peace be upon him) said: Amongst the apostles I would have the largest following on the Day of Resurrec-

these two qualities are closely linked up with the belief in the Omnipresent Lord and their existence in man proves that he really believes in God. Integrity is something which concerns the heart of man and is commonly hidden from the public gaze. A truly honest man is he who is honest in all affairs of his life. A major part of one's life is not exposed to the public. A man who shows integrity in those hidden aspects of life proves his belief in the existence of the Almighty Lord, and he shows by his deeds that he really loves Him and is afraid of His wrath.

Similarly, responsibility of kinship is such which is also a private affair of a man and the people outside the family cannot peep into this secluded sector of a man's life. It cannot earn one public fame. Thus a person who keeps a regard for the tie of blood and endeavours to discharge his duties towards his kith and kin is one who does good not for public applause but purely for the pleasure of the Lord.

Maulānā 'Abdul Ḥaqq Muḥaddith Dihlavī has given a pointed reference to one more aspect of this blood-relationship. He says that the persons who are not tied to us by the relationship of blood have a feeling of deep obligation when any favour is shown to them since they cannot expect it as a matter of right. But the relatives do expect such "favours" and "sacrifices" as a matter of right and neither express praise nor feel any obligation for them. On the other hand, they often criticise those relatives who show any slackness in their duties towards their kith and kin. It is, therefore, a matter of great piety and love of God that one should carefully perform this "thankless task" only in the hope to get reward from the Lord.

tion, and I would be the first to knock at the door of Paradise.

(383) Anas b. Mālik said: The Apostle of Allah (may peace be upon him) said: I would be the first intercessor in the Paradise and no apostle amongst the apostles has been testified (by such a large number of people) as I have been testified. And verily there would be an apostle among the apostles who would be testified to by only one man from his people.

(384) Anas b. Mālik reported: The Messenger of Allah (may peace be upon him) said: I will come to the gate of Paradise on the Day of Resurrection, and would seek its opening, and the keeper would say: Who art thou? I would say: Muḥammad. He would then say: It is for thee that I have been ordered, and not to open it for anyone before thee.

(385) Abū Huraira reported: Verily the Messenger of Allah (may peace be upon him) said: There is for every apostle a (special) prayer [412] with which he would pray. I wish I could reserve my prayer for intercession of my Ummah on the Day of Resurrection.

(386) Abū Huraira reported: The Messenger of Allah (may peace be upon him) said: There is for every apostle a prayer, and I intend (if Allah so willed) that I would reserve my prayer for the intercession of my Ummah on the Day of Resurrection.

(387) 'Amr b. Abū Sufyān transmitted a ḥadīth like this from Abū Huraira who narrated it from the Messenger of Allah (may peace be upon him).

(388) 'Amr b. Abū Sufyān reported: Abū Huraira said to Ka'b al-Aḥbār that the Apostle of Allah (may peace be upon him) had said: For every apostle there is a (special) prayer by which he would pray (to his Lord). I, however, intend (if Allah so willed) that I would reserve my prayer for the intercession of my Ummah on the Day of Resurrection. Ka'b said to Abū Huraira: Did you hear this from the Messenger of Allah (may peace be upon him)? Abū Huraira said: Yes.

(389) Abū Huraira said: The Prophet of Allah (may peace be upon him) said: There is for every apostle a prayer which is granted, but every prophet showed haste in his prayer. I have, however, reserved my prayer for the intercession of my Ummah on the Day of Resurrection, and it would be granted, if Allah so willed, in case of everyone amongst my Ummah provided he dies without associating anything with Allah.

(390) Abū Huraira said: The Messenger of Allah (may peace be upon him) said: Every Messenger is endowed with a prayer which is granted and by which he would (pray to his Lord) and it would be granted for him. I have, however, reserved my prayer for the intercession of my Ummah on the Day of Resurrection.

(391) Abū Huraira reported: The Messenger of Allah (may peace be upon him) said: There was for every apostle a prayer with which he prayed for his Ummah and it was granted to him; but I wish, if Allah so wills, to defer my prayer for the intercession of my Ummah on the Day of Resurrection.

412. The apostles are dear to Allah and their prayers are very often granted. But with every apostle there is one request which may be called decisive with regard to his Ummah, and with it is decided their fate; for example, Noah in a state of distress uttered: "My Lord! leave not any one of the disbelievers in the land" (al-Qur'ān, lxxi. 26). Muḥammad (may peace be upon him) reserved his prayer for the Day of Resurrection and he would use it for the salvation of the believers (*Fath-ul-Mulhim*, Vol. I, pp. 370-1).

(392) Anas b. Mālik reported: Verily the Apostle of Allah (may peace be upon him) said: There is for every apostle a prayer with which he prays (to Allah) for his Ummah. I have reserved my prayer for the intercession of my Ummah on the Day of Resurrection.

(393) This ḥadīth is narrated with the same chain of narrators by Qatāda.

(394) Mis'ar transmitted it with the same chain of narrators from Qatāda except that in the ḥadīth narrated by Wakī' (the Prophet) said: "He was endowed," and in the ḥadīth reported by Abū Usāma (the words are): "It is reported from the Apostle of Allah (may peace be upon him)."

(395) Muḥammad b. 'Abd al-A'lā reported it to me: Mu'tamir narrated to us on the authority of his father who transmitted it from Anas that verily the Apostle of Allah (may peace be upon him) said, and then narrated the ḥadīth like the one transmitted by Qatāda on the authority of Anas.

(396) Abū Zubair heard Jābir b. 'Abdullah reporting it from the Apostle of Allah (may peace be upon him): For every apostle was a prayer with which he prayed (to his Lord) for his Ummah, but I have reserved my prayer for the intercession of my Ummah on the Day of Resurrection.

Chapter LXXXV

PRAYER OF THE APOSTLE (MAY PEACE BE UPON HIM) FOR HIS UMMAH AND HIS BEING MOVED TO TEARS ON ACCOUNT OF HIS AFFECTION FOR THEM

(397) 'Abdullah b. 'Amr b. al-'Āṣ reported: Verily the Apostle of Allah (may peace be upon him) recited the words of Allah, the Great and Glorious, that Ibrāhīm uttered: My Lord! lo! they have led many of mankind astray: "But whoso followeth me, he verily is of me" (al-Qur'ān, xiv. 35) and Jesus (peace be upon him) said: "If Thou punisheth them, lo! they are Thy slaves, and if Thou forgiveth them—verily Thou art the Mighty, the Wise" (al-Qur'ān, v. 117). Then he raised his hands and said: O Lord, my Ummah, my Ummah, and wept; so Allah the High and the Exalted said: O Gabriel, go to Muḥammad (though your Lord knows it fully well) and ask him: What makes thee weep?[413] So Gabriel (peace be upon him) came to him and asked him, and the Messenger of Allah (may peace be upon him) informed him what he had said (though Allah knew it fully well). Upon this Allah said: O Gabriel, go to Muḥammad and say: Verily We will please[414] thee with regard to your Ummah and would not displease thee.

413. Allah is the Knower of everything. Gabriel was sent to Muḥammad (may peace be upon him) with a view to honouring him.

414. Cf. al-Qur'ān: "And verily thy Lord will give unto thee, so thou wilt be pleased" (xciii. 5).

Chapter LXXXVI

HE WHO DIED WITH UNBELIEF WOULD BE (THROWN) INTO THE FIRE, INTERCESSION WOULD BE OF NO AVAIL TO HIM AND THE RELATIONSHIP OF HIS FAVOURITES WOULD NOT BENEFIT HIM

(398) Anas reported: Verily, a person said: Messenger of Allah, where is my father? He said: (He) is in the Fire. When he turned away, he (the Holy Prophet) called him and said: Verily my father and your father are in the Fire.[415]

Chapter LXXXVII

REGARDING THE WORDS OF ALLAH: "AND WARN THY NEAREST KINDRED"

(399) Abū Huraira reported: When this verse was revealed: "And warn thy nearest kindred" (al-Qur'ān, xxvi. 214), the Messenger of Allah (may peace be upon

415. This ḥadith does not furnish conclusive proof of the fact that the father of the Holy Prophet is doomed to Hell. Here the point which the Apostle wanted to stress was that so far as the reward or the punishment in the Hereafter is concerned it depends only on the right beliefs and good conduct of a man and mere blood-relationship with the pious and dear ones of the Lord is of no avail. Moreover, the Holy Prophet wanted to console him by telling him that his own father and the father of that person would be treated alike by Allah on the Day of Resurrection if they shared common belief in this life; and his father, being the father of the most eminent of the Prophets, would not influence the judgment of God. The fact that the Holy Prophet did not claim any special privilege for himself and his family provided the most convincing proof to his people that he was the true Messenger of Allah and he had no axe of his own to grind and no vested interest to secure and safeguard.

The question may be asked: What would be the position of Prophet's parents in the Hereafter? Different views have been expressed about it. Ibn Ḥajar 'Asqalānī has quoted some of the authorities to support that Allah would grant the requests of the Holy Prophet and would revive his parents to life again and afford them an opportunity to embrace Islam. But most of the Muḥaddithīn have called such assertions as unreliable. After a thorough analysis of such views the only valid conclusion to which the commentators of Ḥadīth have arrived is that nothing can be said with certainty about their status in the Hereafter. The Muslims should talk about them with respect and honour. The fact is that those who die in the intermission period (a period when the teachings of the previous prophets are almost forgotten and no new prophet is raised) would be treated on the belief and action which according to reason are correct and true to the moral conscience of a man.

There is another school of thought which believes that before the advent of Muḥammad, it was the faith of Prophet Ibrāhīm that was the prevailing faith of the time, and, therefore, it is quite reasonable to expect that the parents of the Holy Prophet had been the true believers of that faith.

There is, however, one point which needs a little bit of analysis. A careful study of the above-mentioned ḥadīth in the context of other aḥādīth narrated in this connection gives one some sound reason to believe that the word *Abī* (my father) recorded in the ḥadīth may not refer to his real father but one of those uncles who had died in *Kufr*. The exhortations of the Holy Prophet for the members of his family that we find in the subsequent aḥādīth, and some remission to Abū Ṭālib gives strength to this idea.

After going into the details of all these views, the one commonly held by scholars is that mentioned in the first paragraph. This seems sound. God alone knows best.

him) called the Quraish; so they gathered and he gave them a general warning. Then he made a particular (reference to certain tribes) and said: O sons of Ka'b b. Luwayy, rescue yourselves from the Fire; O sons of Murra b. Ka'b, rescue yourselves from the Fire; O sons of 'Abd Shams, rescue yourselves from the Fire; O sons of 'Abd Manāf, rescue yourselves from the Fire; O sons of Hāshim, rescue yourselves from the Fire; O sons of 'Abd al-Muṭṭalib, rescue yourselves from Fire; O Fāṭimah, rescue thyself from the Fire, for I have no power (to protect you) from Allah in anything except this that I would sustain relationship with you.

(400) The same ḥadīth is narrated by 'Ubaidallah b. 'Umar al-Qawārīrī from Abū 'Uwāna, who transmitted it to 'Abd al-Malik b. 'Umair on the same chain of transmitter, and the ḥadīth of Jarīr is more perfect and comprehensive.

(401) It is narrated on the authority of 'Ā'isha that when this verse was revealed: "And warn thy nearest kindred," the Messenger of Allah (may peace be upon him) stood up on Ṣafā' and said: O Fāṭima, daughter of Muḥammad, O Ṣafiya, daughter of 'Abd al-Muṭṭalib, O sons of 'Abd al-Muṭṭalib, I have nothing which can avail you against Allah; you may ask me what you want of my worldly belongings.

(402) Abū Huraira reported: When (this verse) was revealed to him: "Warn your nearest kinsmen," the Messenger of Allah (may peace be upon him) said: O people of Quraish, buy yourselves from Allah,[416] I cannot avail you at all against Allah; O sons of 'Abd al-Muṭṭalib, I cannot avail you at all against Allah; O 'Abbās b. 'Abd al-Muṭṭalib, I cannot avail you at all against Allah; O Ṣafiya (aunt of the Messenger of Allah), I cannot avail you at all againgst Allah; O Fāṭima, daughter of Muḥammad, ask me whatever you like, but I cannot avail you at all against Allah.[417]

(403) This ḥadīth is narrated fro n the Apostle (may peace be upon him) by another

416. "Secure deliverance from Allah by doing good deeds."

417. We have been studying before aḥādīth with regard to the intercession of Muḥammad (may peace be upon him) with his Lord for his people. It was the Mercy of Allah that was stressed in those aḥādīth, but here it has been made clear that intercession should not be taken in the sense of atonement. "No bearer of burdens shall be made to bear another's burden" (vi. 164). This statement which is also found in xvii. 15, xxxv. 18, xxxix. 17, liii. 38, constitutes a categorical rejection of the Christian doctrine of Atonement. The intercession would be permitted explicitly at the Will of Allah, and mere relationship with the Holy Prophet would not absolve anyone of his sins. Allah is generous no doubt, but He is also just and fair and, therefore, no one can vicariously atone for the sins of others. It is indeed a great revolution in religious thought that the doctrine of Atonement was rejected and mankind was tutored into this belief that mere kinship with the Apostle can secure no special privileges for them on the Day of Resurrection. Even the nearest of the Prophet's kins would be treated by Allah on the same level as other people, and they would be held accountable for their deeds like the rest of humanity.

These aḥādīth have been often criticised by hostile critics of the Ḥadīth and the main line of their criticism is that this event relates to the earlier days of Muḥammad's prophetic career, and these are narrated by Abū Huraira and 'Ā'isha (may Allah be pleased with them) whose presence in that meeting is a remote possibility. This betrays their utter ignorance about the knowledge of Ḥadīth. They should know that these aḥādīth are *Mursal* (traditions in which one of the narrators at the end, the companion who actually narrated it, is unknown). Now these aḥādīth have been transmitted by so many different chains of narrators that these cannot be treated as fabricated ones. Moreover, there is every likelihood, and it is substantiated by a ḥadīth narrated by Abū 'Uwāna contained in Ṭabarānī, that the Holy Prophet gathered his kith and kin in Medina too and he gave them a similar type of warning which he gave standing on the hillock of Ṣafā'.

chain of narrators, 'Amr al-Nāqid, Mu'āwiya b. 'Amr, 'Abdullah b. Dhakwān, A'raj on the authority of Abū Huraira.

(404) Qabīṣa b. al-Mukhāriq and Zuhair b. 'Amr reported: When this verse was revealed: "And warn thy nearest kindred," the Apostle of Allah (may peace be upon him) set off towards a rock of the hill and ascended the highest of the rocks and then called: O sons of 'Abd Manāf! I am a warner; my similitude and your similitude is like a man who saw the enemy and went to guard his people, but, being afraid they might get there before him, he shouted: Be on your guard!

(405) This ḥadīth is narrated from the Apostle of Allah (may peace be upon him) by another chain of narrators, Muḥammad b. 'Abd al-A'lā, Mu'tamir, Abū 'Uthmān, Zuhair b. 'Amr, Qabīṣa b. Mukhāriq.

(406) It is reported on the authority of Ibn 'Abbās that when this verse was revealed: "And warn thy nearest kindred" (and thy group of selected people among them) the Messenger of Allah (may peace be upon him) set off till he climbed Ṣafā' and called loudly: Be on your guard! They said: Who is it calling aloud? They said: Muḥammad. They gathered round him, and he said: O sons of so and so, O sons of so and so, O sons of 'Abd Manāf, O sons of 'Abd al-Muṭṭalib, and they gathered around him. He (the Apostle) said: If I were to inform you that there were horsemen emerging out of the foot of this mountain, would you believe me? They said: We have not experienced any lie from you. He said: Well, I am a warner to you before a severe torment. He (the narrator) said that Abū Lahab then said: Destruction to you! Is it for this you have gathered us? He (the Holy Prophet) then stood up, and this verse was revealed: "Perish the hands of Abū Lahab, and he indeed perished" (cxi. 1). A'mash recited this to the end of the Sūra.

(407) This ḥadīth was narrated by A'mash on the authority of the same chain of narrators and he said: One day the Messenger of Allah (may peace be upon him) climbed the hill of Ṣafā' and said: Be on your guard, and the rest of the ḥadīth was narrated like the ḥadīth transmitted by Usāma; he made no mention of the revelation of the verse: "Warn thy nearest kindred."

Chapter LXXXVIII

INTERCESSON OF THE MESSENGER OF ALLAH (MAY PEACE BE UPON HIM) FOR ABŪ ṬĀLIB AND SOME REMISSION FOR HIM ON THIS ACCOUNT

(408) It is reported on the authority of 'Abbās b. 'Abd al-Muṭṭalib that he said: Messenger of Allah, have you benefited Abū Ṭālib in any way for he defended[418] you and was fervent in your defence? The Messenger of Allah (may peace be upon him) said: Yes; he would be in the most shallow part of the Fire: and but for me he would have been in the lowest part of Hell.[419]

418. *Ghaḍiba* means to become angry, but when it is used with ل it, along with other meanings, gives the meaning "to defend".

419. It proves that even the unbelievers would receive concessions for the good that they did to the Holy Prophet.

(409) 'Abdullah b. al-Ḥārith reported: I heard 'Abbās say: I said: Messenger of Allah, verily Abū Ṭālib defended you and helped you; would it be beneficial for him? He (the Holy Prophet) said: Yes; I found him in the lowest part of the Fire and I brought him to the shallow part.

(410) This ḥadīth is narrated from the Apostle (may peace be upon him) like one narrated by Abū 'Uwāna on the authority of the chain of transmitters like Muḥammad b. Ḥātim, Yaḥyā b. Sa'īd, Abū Sufyān, 'Abbās b. 'Abd al-Muṭṭalib and others.

(411) Abū Sa'īd al-Khudrī reported: A mention was made of his uncle Abū Ṭālib before the Messenger of Allah (may peace be upon him). He said: My intercession may benefit him on the Day of Resurrection, and he may be placed in the shallow part of the Fire which would reach his ankles and his brain would be boiling.

(412) Abū Sa'īd al-Khudrī reported: Verily, the Messenger of Allah (may peace be upon him) said: The least tormented of the inhabitants of the Fire would be he who would wear two shoes of Fire and his brain would boil on account of the heat of the shoes.

(413) Ibn 'Abbās reported: The Prophet (may peace be upon him) said: Among the inhabitants of the Fire Abū Ṭālib would have the least suffering, and he would be wearing two shoes (of Fire) which would boil his brain.

(414) Nu'mān b. Bashīr was delivering an address and saying: I heard the Messenger of Allah (may peace be upon him) say: The least suffering for the inhabitants of Hell on the Day of Resurrection would be for the man under whose soles would be placed two embers and his brain would boil on account of them.

(415) Nu'mān b. Bashīr reported: The Messenger of Allah (may peace be upon him) said: Verily the least suffering for the inhabitants of Fire would be for him who would have two shoes and two laces of Fire (on his feet), and with these would boil his brain as boils the cooking vessel, and he would think that he would not see anyone in a more grievous torment than him, whereas he would be in the least torment.

Chapter LXXXIX

PROOF IN SUPPORT OF THE FACT THAT HE WHO DIED IN UNBELIEF, HIS DEED WOULD NOT BE OF ANY AVAIL TO HIM[420]

(416) 'Ā'isha reported: I said: Messenger of Allah, the son of Jud'ān[421] established

420. Like Paradise, Hell has also numerous grades and ranks. None who does not affirm faith in the Oneness of Allah, Day of Judgment and Apostles is entitled to enter Paradise. The man who denies these fundamental truths of life will have Hell as his permanent abode. Just as the degree of soundness in belief and piety determines one's status in the Paradise, in the same way the nature of unbelief and one's behaviour in life determine one's rank in the Hell. The man who does not believe in God but performs good deeds would be granted some relief in his afflictions there. The question may be asked: Why is it that belief in the Oneness of Allah, in His Apostles and in the Day of Judgment is given basic importance as compared with the deeds and actions of man? The answer is simple. A person who denies this belief is a rebel in the sense that he flouts the fundamental truths which are the fountainhead of goodness and piety. The man who does not believe in them shall have some other considerations before him for doing good deeds. All these considerations would be actuated from material and sensory motives and make the vision of man narrow and cramped.

421. His name was 'Abdullah. He was one of the leaders of the Quraish and was related to 'Ā'isha (may Allah be pleased with her).

ties of relationship, fed the poor. Would that be of any avail to him? He said: It would be of no avail to him as he did not ever say: O my Lord, pardon my sins on the Day of Resurrection.

Chapter XC

FRIENDSHIP WITH BELIEVERS AND DISSOCIATION WITH NON-BELIEVERS AND SEVERANCE FROM THEM

(417) 'Amr b. 'Aṣ reported: I heard it from the Messenger of Allah (may peace be upon him) quite audibly and not secretly: Behold! the posterity of my fathers, that is, so and so, are not my friends. Verily Allah and the pious believers[422] are my friends.

Chapter XCI

THE ADMITTANCE INTO PARADISE OF A GROUP OF MUSLIMS WITHOUT RENDERING ANY ACCOUNT AND SUFFERING PUNISHMENT (TORMENT)

(418) It is narrated on the authority of Abū Huraira that the Apostle of Allah (may peace be upon him) said: Seventy thousand (persons) of my Ummah would enter Paradise without rendering an account. Upon this a person said: Messenger of Allah, pray to Allah that He make me one of them. He (the Holy Prophet) said: O Allah! make him one of them. Then another stood up and said: Messenger of Allah, pray to Allah that He make me one of them. He (the Holy Prophet) said: 'Ukkāsha has preceded you in this matter.[423]

(419) Muḥammad b. Ziyād reported: I heard Abū Huraira narrate this: I heard it from the Messenger of Allah (may peace be upon him) saying a ḥadīth like one narrated by al-Rabī'.

(420) Abū Huraira reported: I heard it from the Messenger of Allah (may peace be upon him) saying: A group of my Ummah consisting of seventy thousand persons would enter Paradise; their faces would be as bright as the brightness of the full moon. Abū Huraira said: 'Ukkāsha b. Miḥṣan al-Asadī then stood up wrapping the blanket around him and said: Messenger of Allah, supplicate (before) Allah that He

422. This ḥadīth comes in the context of those aḥādīth which throw light on the different aspects of the Day of Resurrection. We have been told that the ties of kinship would be of no avail on the Day of Resurrection and everyone would be judged by Allah on the merits of his belief and good deeds. When the ties of blood carry no weight in the Hereafter, it is but natural that the same standard of belief and good conduct should primarily govern and decide human relations in this world too.

This fact also makes it clear that Islam has made belief the rallying force amongst human beings and the basis of Islaicm brotherhood.

423. It could not be determined who the second man was. The scholars of Ḥadīth are of the opinion that he would be either a hypocrite or one whom the Holy Prophet did not deem fit for this favour.

should make me one among them. Upon this the Messenger of Allah (may peace be upon him) said: O Allah, make him among them. Then stood up a man from the Anṣār and said: Messenger of Allah, pray to Allah that He should make me one among them. The Messenger of Allah (may peace be upon him) said: 'Ukkāsha[424] has preceded you in this matter.

(421) Abū Huraira reported: The Messenger of Allah (may peace be upon him) said: Seventy thousand (persons) would enter Paradise as one group and among them (there would be people) whose faces would be bright like the moon.

(422) It is reported on the authority of 'Imrān that the Apostle of Allah (may peace be upon him) said: Seventy thousand people of my Ummah would be admitted into Paradise without rendering any account. They (the companions) said: Who would be those (fortunate persons)? He (the Holy Prophet) said: Those who do not cauterise and practise charm, but repose trust in their Lord. 'Ukkāsha then stood up and said: Supplicate (before) Allah that He should make me one among them. He (the Holy Prophet) said: Thou art one among them. He (the narrator) said: A man stood up and said: Apostle of Allah, supplicate (before) Allah that He should make me one among them. He (the Holy Prophet) said: 'Ukkāsha has preceded you (in this matter).

(423) 'Imran b. Ḥuṣain reported: Verily the Messenger of Allah (may peace be upon him) said: Seventy thousand men of my Ummah would enter Paradise without rendering account. They (the companions of the Holy Prophet) said: Who would be those, Messenger of Allah? He (the Holy Prophet) said: They would be those who neither practise charm, nor take omens, nor do they cauterise, but they repose their trust in their Lord.

(424) Abū Ḥāzim narrated it on the authority of Ibn Sa'd that the Messenger of Allah (may peace be upon him) said: Seventy thousand persons or seven hundred thousand persons (Abū Ḥāzim does not remember the exact number) would enter Paradise holding and supporting one another, and the first among them would not enter till the last among them would enter (therein); (they would enter simultaneously) and their faces would be bright like the full moon.

(425) Ḥuṣain b. 'Abd al-Raḥmān reported: I was with Sa'īd b. Jubair when he said: Who amongst you saw a star shooting last night? I said: It was I; then I said: I was in fact not (busy) in prayer, but was stung by a scorpion (and that is the reason why I was awake and had a glimpse of the shooting star). He said: Then what did you do? I said: I practised charm. He said. What urged you to do this? I said: (I did this according to the implied suggestion) of the ḥadith which al-Shu'ba narrated. He said: What did al-Shu'ba narrate to you? I said: Buraida b. Ḥuṣaib al-Aslamī narrated to us: The charm is of no avail except in case of the (evil influence) of an eye or the sting of a scorpion. He said: He who acted according to what he had heard (from the Holy Prophet) acted rightly, but Ibn 'Abbās narrated to us from the Apostle of Allah (may peace be upon him) that he said: There were brought before me the peoples and I saw an apostle and a small group (of his followers) along with him, another (apostle) and

424. 'Ukkāsha belonged to the tribe of Asad b. Khuzaima and was the ally of Banū Umayya. He was one among the early converts to Islam. He participated in the battle of Badr and fought bravely and manfully, and his sincerity, zeal and devotion to Islam were greatly appreciated by the Holy Prophet (may peace be upon him).

one or two persons (along with him) and (still another) apostle having no one with him. When a very large group was brought to me I conceived as if it were my Ummah. Then it was said to me : It is Moses and his people. You should look at the horizon, and I saw a very huge group. It was again said to me : See the other side of the horizon, and there was (also) a very huge group. It was said to me : This is your Ummah, and amongst them there were seventy thousand persons who would be made to enter Paradise without rendering any account and without (suffering) any torment. He then stood up and went to his house. Then the people began to talk about the people who would be admitted to Paradise without rendering any account and without (suffering) any torment. Some of them said : They may be those who (have had the good fortune of living) in the company of the Messenger of Allah (may peace be upon him) and some of them said : They be those who were born in Islam and did not associate anything with Allah. Some people mentioned other things. Thereupon came forth the Messenger of Allah (may peace be upon him) before them and he said : What was that which you were talking about ? They informed him. He said : They are those persons who neither practise charm, nor ask others to practise it, nor do they take omens, and repose their trust in their Lord. Upon this 'Ukkāsha b. Miḥṣan stood up and said : Supplicate for me that He should make me one among them. Upon this he (Messenger of Allah) said : Thou art one among them. Then another man stood up and said: Supplicate before Allah that He should make me one among them. Upon this he said : 'Ukkāsha has preceded you.[425]

(426) Ibn 'Abbās reported : The Messenger of Allah (may peace be upon him) said : Peoples would be presented to me (on the Day of Resurrection), and then the remaining part of the ḥadīth was narrated like the one transmitted by Hushaim, but he made no mention of the first portion.

Chapter XCII

THIS UMMAH (UMMAH OF ISLAM) WOULD CONSTITUTE HALF OF THE INHABITANTS OF PARADISE

(427) 'Abdullah b. Mas'ūd reported : The Messenger of Allah (may peace be upon him) addressing us said : Aren't you pleased that you should constitute one-fourth of the inhabitants of Paradise ? He (the narrator) said : We glorified (our Lord, i.e. we called

425. This ḥadīth clearly explains the place of charm, spell and enchantment in Islam. There is no denying the fact that some persons can, by practice, develop a mysterious power to influence other people either with the help of enchanting words or penetrating sight. Not to speak of the past, even today patients are treated and cured through this method. The Holy Prophet recognised its efficacy. He, however, purified it from all its evil and devilish practices and taught his followers to invoke Allah and recite the words of the Qur'ān or those of aḥādīth for curing a disease or breaking the spell of an evil eye. But in this connection we have been clearly told that as Muslims we should not take it for granted that these words would certainly be effective, since their efficacy depends on the will of Allah. We should, therefore, repose our trust in God alone. The Holy Prophet has strongly condemned all those practices of enchantment, spell, incantation and sorcery which have an element of idolatry, polytheism and moral depravity in them and which undermine one's faith and trust in God.

aloud Allah-o-Akbar, Allah is the Greatest). He, then, again said : Aren't you pleased that you should constitute one-third of the inhabitants of Paradise ? He (the narrator) said: We glorified (our Lord) and he (the Holy Prophet) then again said : I hope that you would constitute half of the inhabitants of Paradise and I shall explain to you its (reason). The believers among the unbelievers would not be more than a white hair on (the body of a) black ox or a black hair on (the body of a) white ox.[426]

(428) 'Abdullah (b. Mas'ūd) reported : We, about forty men, were with the Messenger of Allah (may peace be upon him) in a camp when he said : Aren't you pleased that you should constitute one-fourth of the inhabitants of Paradise ? He (the narrator) said : Yes. He (the Holy Prophet) again said : Aren't you pleased that you should constitute one-third of the inhabitants of Paradise ? They said : Yes. Upon this he again said : By Him in Whose Hand is my life, I hope that you would constitute one-half of the inhabitants of Paradise and the reason is that no one would be admitted into Paradise but a believer and you are no more among the polytheists than as a white hair on the skin of a black ox or a black hair on the skin of a red ox.

(429) 'Abdullah b. Mas'ūd reported : The Messenger of Allah (may peace be upon him) addressed us and then supported his back (by reclining) against a leather tent and said : Behold, no one but a believing person would enter Paradise. O Allah, (see) have I conveyed (it not) ? O Allah, be witness (to it that I have conveyed it). (Then addressing his companions) he said : Don't you like that you should constitute one-fourth of the inhabitants of Paradise ? We said : Yes, Messenger of Allah. He again said : Don't you like that you should constitute one-third of the inhabitants of Paradise ? They said : Yes, Messenger of Allah. He said : I hope that you would constitute one-half of the inhabitants of Paradise and you would be among the peoples of the world, like a black hair on (the body of) a white ox or like a white hair on the body of a black ox.

(430) Abū Sa'īd reported : The Messenger of Allah (may peace be upon him) said : Allah, the High and Glorious, would say : O Adam ! and he would say : At Thy service, at thy beck and call, O Lord, and the good is in Thy Hand. Allah would say : Bring forth the group of (the denizens of) Fire. He (Adam) would say : Who are the denizens of Hell ? It would be said : They are out of every thousand nine hundred and ninety-nine. He (the Holy Prophet) said : It is at this juncture that every child would become white-haired and every pregnant woman would abort[427] and you would see people in a state of intoxication, and they would not be in fact intoxicated but grievous will be the torment of Allah. He (the narrator) said : This had a very depressing effect upon them (upon the companions of the Holy Prophet) and they said : Messenger of Allah, who amongst us would be (that unfortunate) person (who would be doomed to Hell) ? He said : Good tidings for you, *Yājūj Mājūj*[428] would be those thousands (who would

426. This simile explains so many points. Firstly, the number of true believers would be far less as compared with the number of unbelievers. Secondly, the believers would present a striking contrast to the non-believers and would be fully distinguished among them for their beliefs, honesty of their thought, their integrity, piety, good conduct and commendable behaviour.

427. The children would turn white-haired and pregnant women would abort on account of the dread of that moment.

428. Yājūj Mājūj (Gog and Magog) are the two peoples which figure prominently in Biblical and Muslim eschatology. The Bible as well as Muslim resources connect these peoples with the north-east of the ancient world who have been making inroads on the settled kingdoms and empires at various stages of world's history.

be the denizens of Hell) and a person (selected for Paradise) would be amongst you. He (the narrator) further reported that he (the Messenger of Allah) again said : By Him in Whose Hand is my life, I hope that you would constitute one-fourth of the inhabitants of Paradise. We extolled Allah and we glorified (Him). He (the Holy Prophet) again said : By Him in Whose Hand is my life, I wish you would constitute one-third of the inhabitants of Paradise. We extolled Allah and Glorified (Him). He (the Holy Prophet) again said : By Him in Whose Hand is my life, I hope that you would constitute half of the inhabitants of Paradise. Your likeness among the people is the likeness of a white hair on the skin of a black ox or a strip on the foreleg of an ass.

(431) The same ḥadīth has been narrated from A'mash on the authority of the same chain of transmitters with the exception of these words : You would be no more among men (on the Day of Resurrection) but like a white hair on (the body of) a black ox, or like a black hair on (the body of) a white ox, and he made no mention of : a strip on the foreleg of an ass.[429]

EPILOGUE

Before we close the "Kitāb-ul-Īmān," it seems necessary to bring a few facts before our readers. This book deals with the beliefs, i.e. those unseen realities which we have a strong yearning to comprehend, but which elude the grasp of our senses.

Every person, who is endowed with consciousness, is instinctively impelled to know whence he came and where he would return. What would become of him after crossing the bar of life ? Is the short span of this worldly life the culmination of all his hopes and desires and nothing remains after it ? These are the questions which agitate the mind of every man, whether he is a believer or a non-believer, whether he is a monotheist or a polytheist or an atheist. We cannot silence the echoes of our souls by simply saying that nothing can be said with certainty about them. The mind yearns for definite and satisfactory answers to all of them. That is what is embedded in our very nature and so long as we are human beings we cannot afford to ignore them. We approach scientists for the solution of these spiritual problems of ours which have a direct bearing on our social life, but scientists have no definite answers to give since they are concerned only with observable facts, that is to say, the optically present source of sensation, which forms only a fraction of man's life and the vast sea of "unseen world" lies hidden before them. That is the reason why even a scientist has to fall back upon chance—a very important admission as to the limits of the so-called scientific knowledge and the possibility of another knowledge unknown to science and altogether different from that with the help of which we observe physical phenomena and their laws.

Moreover, the scientific method cannot help us solve the problem of "whence" and "whither". There is always an urge in our hearts to peep across this life hemmed in by space and time and find out our ultimate destiny. Since science deals with "actual," with what is here and now, particularly what can be comprehended with the help

429. In aḥādīth different ratios have been given with regard to the number of the Muslims in Paradise. This difference is due to the fact that a good number of believers in islam would be admitted into Paradise after undergoing a purgatory process in the Hell. Thus the number of the inhabitants of Paradise would increase with the passage of time.

of senses, there is inherent in science a natural tendency to assure that man, too, like inanimate matter, is a bubble that bursts and a vision that fades. If we take this view of man, which is the inevitable conclusion of the so-called "scientific inquiry," the whole of human life in which man plays such a prominent role becomes a meaningless riddle, for he is denied the existence of spiritual yearning in him which is nothing but a sort of cruel joke with man. "Life," says Dr Muhammad Iqbal (*Reconstruction of Religious Thought in Islam*, pp. 50-1), "with its intense feeling of spontaneity constitutes a centre of indetermination, and thus falls outside the domain of necessity. . . . The biologist who seeks a mechanical explanation of life is led to do so because he confines his study to the lower forms of life whose behaviour discloses resemblances to mechanical action. If he studies life as manifested in himself, *i.e.*, his own mind freely choosing, rejecting, reflecting, surveying the past and the present, and dynamically imagining the future, he is sure to be convinced of the inadequacy of his mechanical concepts."

The observable facts or, in other words, the physical entities form only a part of the Reality. On how to know and comprehend the other parts which concern us more intimately than the physical entities, science has nothing definite to say except a meaningful silence which betrays its natural limitation in solving these vital problems of life.

Psychology, too, is inherently incompetent to comprehend the unseen Realities of the universe. Life, as we all know, is a great mystery even in its biological aspects; how mysterious it is in its spiritual and moral aspects, we cannot imagine. Psychology has been able to grope in the darkness of unconscious and sub-conscious chambers and has not been able to bring into light the secrets of the human soul. "Psychology," says Walter Leibrecht (*Religion and Culture*, p. 33), "can show us what man is not. It cannot tell us what man, each one of us, is. The legitimate aim of psychology is the negative, the removal of distortions and illusions, but not the positive, the full and complete knowledge of human being." The fact is that human knowledge and intellect, in spite of their boastful claims, are by nature so much handicapped that they, unaided by revelation, cannot in any way comprehend the unseen Realities. What the intellect at the most can do is to transform the sense-data into conceptual forms, but it has to depend ultimately upon experience and is, therefore, subjected to the same limitations to which the knowledge of physical sciences is subjected. "The intellect," say Ibn Khaldūn, "is a correct scale. Its indications are completely certain and in no way wrong. However, the intellect should not be used to weigh such matters as the oneness of God, the Hereafter, the truth of prophecy, the real character of Divine Attributes, or anything else that lies beyond the level of the intellect. That would mean to aspire for the impossible. One might compare it with a man who sees a scale in which gold is being weighed, and wants to weigh mountains in it. This (the fact that it is impossible) does not prove that the indications of the scale are not true (when it is used for its proper purpose). However, there is a limit at which intellect must stop. It cannot go beyond its own level" (*The Muqaddimah*, translated by Franz Rosenthal, Vol. III, p. 38). What a man in the cold regions of an arid intellectualism can, at his best, infer is only the existence of a Prime Cause, but so far as His Attributes, His will, His behaviour with humanity and His Creation, and our relation with Him are concerned, intellect has nothing positive to say. It is at this stage that man instinctively feels the need of an agency which should provide him authentic information about unseen realities of life. This agency is known as Prophethood. The Great Lord, Who has provided man with material resources for the satisfaction of his material needs, has also made suitable arrangements to acquaint us fully with the Unseen Realities which our souls yearn to know. This knowledge of the Unseen is vouchsafed to us through His trusted Messengers (prophets). This is an immense favour from our Lord, immeasurably more valuable than the material resources for, without it, human souls would have suffered the pangs of privation and would have ultimately died. The Qur'ān says:

> All praise is due to Allah, Who guided us to this. And we would not have found the way if Allah had not guided us. Certainly the Messengers of our Lord brought the Truth (vii. 43).

Just as the information of the Holy Prophet pertaining to our worldly life is perfectly correct judged by any standard, in the same way his revelations concerning the Unseen, e.g. the Day of Resurrection, Paradise and Hell, will also be perfectly true, because he is Amīn, the Truthful. We should, however, bear in mind that since we are living in a world of senses it is, therefore, through sensory experiences that we comprehend it. A man's mind is so much hemmed in by space and time and his vision is so much limited by the material aspects of his life that it is only through material concepts that his mind is led to the knowledge of the Unseen. That is the reason why one can easily find frequent use of metaphors and similes in the language of the Holy Prophet as he explained the Unseen Realities of existence. These are not myths but the Great undeniable Truths which our souls yearn to know, affirm and believe, but which our own intelligence fails to comprehend.

KITAB AL-TAHARAH

THE BOOK OF PURIFICATION

INTRODUCTION

We have read in the first Book that the love of Allah is the highest aim of a true believer. It is for the achievement of this single end that he affirms his faith in Him by renouncing all other types of godhood.

The love of God is not something inert or lifeless ; it is dynamic in the sense that it calls for a complete change in the life of man : change in his thoughts and ideas and change in his conduct and behaviour. One who claims to be a believer in Allah has to make a good deal of effort with a view to pleasing his Lord. He has to purify his soul from all evil thoughts and fancies so that the love of God should reside in it. Unless the soul is purged of all impurities one cannot achieve salvation. This is known as *Ṭahārah* in Islam, and it is the foundation-stone of Īmān. This high objective of the purification of the soul requires intentional and deliberate efforts and a good deal of sacrifice on the part of man, and the most elementary stage in this sacred path is the cleanliness of body.

By enjoining cleanliness of body upon man Islam awakens him to the realisation of the fact that when impurities on the body of a man produce such unhealthy effects on his physical being and corrode his mental health, how miserable his life would be when his soul is polluted with impurities. The process of the purification of the soul should, therefore, start with the physical efforts of purifying the body.

Chapter XCIII

MERIT OF WUḌŪ'

(432) Abū Mālik al-Ash'arī reported : The Messenger of Allah (may peace be upon him) said : Cleanliness is half of *faith*[430] and *al-Ḥamdu Lillāh* (Praise be to Allah) fills the scale,[431] and *Subḥān Allah* (Glory be to Allah) and *al-Ḥamdu Lillāh* (Praise be to Allah)

430. Faith covers two aspects : (*a*) purification of one's soul of all evil thoughts and ideas and banishing from it the love of all false deities ; (*b*) entertaining in one's heart the love of Allah alone. Cleanliness is said to be half of faith because, unless the work of purification of heart is not complete, one cannot have full devotion to Allah. Thus half of faith is purification of the soul and half is devotion to Allah to the exclusion of devotion to any other godhood.

If we take *al-Ṭahūr* in the sense of cleanliness of body, then the word "faith" would imply prayer, because prayer is the first visible expression of faith. We find in the Holy Qur'ān : و ما كان الله ليضيع ايمانكم [Nor was Allah going to make your prayers go waste (ii. 143)]. Here the word "Īmān" stands for prayer.

431. Adoration of Allah is the sum and substance of faith and the real basis of piety and God-consciousness ; it is, therefore, weighty enough to fill the scale of his destiny with virtuous deeds and secure salvation for him.

fill up what is between the heavens and the earth,[432] and prayer is a light,[433] and charity is proof[434] (of one's faith) and endurance is a brightness[435] and the Holy Qur'ān is a proof on your behalf or against you.[436] All men go out early in the morning and sell themselves, thereby setting themselves free or destroying themselves.[437]

Chapter XCIV

PURIFICATION IS ESSENTIAL FOR PRAYER

(433) Mus'ab b. Sa'd reported: 'Abdullah son of 'Umar came to Ibn 'Āmir in order to inquire after his health as he was ailing. He said: O Ibn 'Umar, why don't you pray

432. The whole universe, as it is created with an amazingly artistic skill, provides a living testimony to the Glory of the Lord. Right from the insignificant ant to the huge and massive animals, and from the tiny atom to the mighty constellations gliding in the heavens—all represent but a very small aspect of His Infinite Might and Glory and they all sing His Praises. No sensible man can shut his eye to this Grand Truth. The recognition of His Glory must find expression in His Praise, Adoration and Worship. Thus the Glorification of Allah and His Praise in right earnest are such significant acts of God-consciousness and religious piety that they can fill the whole universe with their bulk.

433. Prayer is called Light. In Sūra Yūnus the Holy Qur'ān says: هو الذى جعل الشمس ضياءً و القمر نوراً [He it is Who appointed the sun a brightness and the moon a light (x. 6)]. Here the brightness of the moon is called light and it can, therefore, be inferred that prayer has the same blessings for us as the light of the moon. It guides erring people to the right path. The Holy Qur'ān says: "Verily prayer prohibits (people) from abomination and detestable (acts)" (xxix. 45). The light of the moon is very soothing and comfortable, so is the case with prayer. It provides great comfort to the soul by bringing it into the presence of the Merciful Lord. The Holy Prophet (may peace be upon him) has said: جعلت قرة عينى فى الصلٰوة (Coolness of my eyes lies in the prayer).

434. Charity, i.e. parting with one's wealth for the sake of Allah, is a proof of the fact that one is sincerely devoted to Him and one is prepared to make sacrifice for His sake.

435. Endurance is compared to brightness mainly for two reasons: (*a*) It is by endurance that the life of man glistens with faith and provides an undeniable proof of his belief in Allah. So long as man does not feel the Presence of the Lord in his heart as the brightness of the sun, he cannot suffer hardships for His sake. His suffering for His sake bears out the fact that his faith in Allah is beyond doubt and he believes in Him as a Great Reality far more bright than the brightness of the sun. (*b*) Endurance is compared to the brightness of the sun which signifies that its splendour is greater than that of the prayer which is compared to the gleam of the moon. Prayer represents the positive aspect of one's devotion to Allah. It implies that a believer holds the love of Allah uppermost in his heart and all other attachments are subservient to it. Ṣadaqa represents the negative aspect, i.e. love for wealth is insignificant in his eye as compared to the love of God and he is always ready to sacrifice material riches for the love of God. Endurance covers both the aspects: love for Allah and preparedness to undergo hardships cheerfully for His sake.

436. "The Holy Qur'ān is a proof on your behalf or against you" means that your destiny would be determined by your attitude towards the Holy Qur'ān. If you act according to the teachings embodied in the Holy Qur'ān with sincerity and devotion, you would gain salvation, but if you contravene them, you will suffer disgrace and humiliation at the hand of Allah.

437. Life is a sort of trade in the sense that we barter our physical strength, our inborn and acquired qualities for certain desires and ends. If these desires and ends are moral and are inspired by a spirit of piety and God-consciousness, then we are doing a profitable business which would ensure salvation in the Hereafter. But if we are mortgaging ourselves for vain desires and fancies we are ruining ourselves.

to Allah for me? He said: I heard the Messenger of Allah (may peace be upon him) say: Neither the prayer is accepted without purification[438] nor is charity[439] accepted out of the ill-gotten (wealth), and thou wert the (governor) of Basra.[440]

(434) A ḥadīth like this is narrated from the Apostle (may peace be upon him) with the same chain of transmitters by Muḥammad b. Muthannā, Ibn Bashshār, Muḥammad b. Ja'far, Shu'ba.

(435) Hammām b. Munabbih, who is the brother of Wahb b. Munabbih, said: This is what has been transmitted to us by Abū Huraira from Muḥammad, the Messenger of Allah (may peace be upon him), and then narrated aḥādīth out of them and observed that the Messenger of Allah (may peace be upon him) said: The prayer of none amongst you would be accepted in a state of impurity till he performs ablution.[441]

Chapter XCV

HOW TO PERFORM ABLUTION

(436) Ḥumrān, the freed slave of 'Uthmān, said: 'Uthmān b. 'Affān called for ablution water and this is how he performed the ablution. He washed his hands thrice. He then rinsed his mouth and cleaned his nose with water (three times), He then washed his face three times; then washed his right arm up to the elbow three times, then washed his left arm like that, then wiped his head; then washed his right foot up to the ankle three times, then washed his left foot like that, and then said: I saw the Messenger of Allah (may peace be upon him) performing ablution like this ablution of mine. Then the Messenger of Allah (may peace be upon him) said: He who performs ablution like this ablution of mine and then stood up (for prayer) and offered two rak'ahs of prayer without allowing his thoughts to be distracted, all his previous sins are expiated. Ibn Shihāb said: Our scholars remarked: This is the most complete of the ablutions performed for prayer.

(437) Ḥumrān, the freed slave of 'Uthmān, said: I saw 'Uthmān calling for a vessel (of water) and poured water over his hands three times and then washed them. Then he put his right hand in the vessel and rinsed his mouth and cleaned his nose. Then he

438. Just as the purification of the body is essential for the performance of formal prayer, in the same way purification of the soul is necessary for the earnest and sincere supplication to the Lord.

439. Charity is the symbol of real devotion and love for Allah and spirit of sacrifice for His sake. This expression of religious piety is meaningful if one is prepared to part with the wealth earned by moral and legitimate means. The spending of ill-gotten wealth cannot purify one's soul which is the main function of charity.

> (O Prophet!) Accept that (part) of their possession which is (to be) offered as charity for the sake of Allah (ix. 103).
>
> O you who believe! spend out of the good things which you may have acquired, and that which We bring forth for you from the earth; and choose not for your spending the bad things which you (yourselves) would not accept without averting your eyes (ii. 267).

440. "You must recall to your mind that you had been the governor of Basra and during the tenure of your office, you laid your hands upon the rights of the people and polluted your soul; how can then the supplication in your case be effective? You should better repent at this hour of trouble."

441. This ḥadīth makes it clear that Wuḍū' (ablution) is obligatory for prayer.

washed his face three times and his hands up to the elbow three times; then wiped his head, then washed his feet three times. Then he said that the Messenger of Allah (may peace be upon him) had said: He who performed ablution like this ablution of mine and offered two rak'ahs of prayer without allowing his thoughts to be distracted, all his previous sins would be expiated.

Chapter XCVI

THE MERIT OF WUḌŪ' AND THAT OF PRAYER AFTER IT

(438) Ḥumrān, the freed slave of 'Uthmān, said: I heard from 'Uthmān b. 'Affān and he was in the courtyard of the mosque, when the Mu'adhdhin (announcer of the hour of prayer) came to him at the time of afternoon prayer. So he ('Uthmān) called for the ablution water and performed ablution and then said: By Allah, I am narrating to you a ḥadīth. If there were not a verse[442] in the Book of Allah, I would have never narrated it to you. I heard the Messenger of Allah (may peace be upon him) say: If a Muslim performs ablution and does it well and offers prayer, all his (sins)[443] during the period from one prayer to another would be pardoned by Allah.

(439) This ḥadīth is also narrated on the authority with the same chain of transmitters, and in the ḥadīth of Abū Usāma the words are: "He who performed the ablution well and then offered the obligatory prayer."

(440) Ḥumrān reported when 'Uthmān performed ablution he said: By Allah, I am narrating to you a ḥadīth. Had there not been this verse in the Book of Allah, I would not have narrated it to you. Verily I heard the Messenger of Allah (may peace be upon him) say: Not a person is there who performed ablution, and did it well, then offered prayer, but his sins (which he committed) were not pardoned between the prayer that he offered and the next one. 'Urwa said: The verse is this: "Those who suppress the clear proofs and the guidance which We have sent down" . . . to His words: "the Cursers" (ii. 15).

(441) 'Amr b. Sa'īd b. al-'Āṣ reported: I was with 'Uthmān that he called for ablution water and said: I heard the Messenger of Allah (may peace be upon him) say: When the time for a prescribed prayer comes, if any Muslim performs ablution well and offers (his prayer) with humility and bowing, it will be an expiation for his past sins, so long as he has not committed a major sin; and that means for all times.

(442) Ḥumrān, the freed slave of 'Uthmān, reported: I brought for 'Uthmān b. 'Affān the ablution water. He performed ablution and then said: Verily the people narrate from the Messenger of Allah (may peace be upon him) aḥādīth. I do not know what these are, but (I know this fact) that I saw the Messenger of Allah (may peace be

442 It has reference to the following verse:

> Those who suppress the clear proofs and the guidance which We have sent down (and this) after We have made it clear unto mankind in the Book, these it is whom Allah curses, and curse them also the Cursers (ii. 159).

What it implies is that "I am not narrating to you this ḥadith in order to display my knowledge of ḥadīth but simply as a matter of religious obligation" as we have been instructed to convey to others all that we have received from the Apostle of Allah (may peace be upon him).

443. Here the sins stand for minor sins.

upon him) performing ablution like this ablution of mine and then he said: He who performed ablution like this, all his previous sins would be expiated and his prayer and going towards the mosque would have an extra reward. In the tradition narrated by Ibn 'Abda (the words are): "I came to 'Uthmān and he performed ablution."

(443) Abū Anas[444] reported that 'Uthmān performed ablution at Maqā'id[445] and said: Should I not show you the ablution performed by the Messenger of Allah (may peace be upon him)? And he then washed (the different parts of the body) three times.[446] Qutaiba has added in his narration the words: "There were with him (with Uthmān) Companions of the Messenger of Allah (may peace be upon him)."

(444) Ḥumrān b. Abān reported: I used to fetch water for 'Uthmān for his purification. Never was there a day that he did not take bath with a small quantity of water. And 'Uthmān said: The Messenger of Allah (may peace be upon him) at the time of our returning from our prayer told us (certain things pertaining to purification). Mis'ar said: I find that it was afternoon prayer. He said: I do not know whether I should tell you a thing or keep quiet. We said: Messenger of Allah, tell us if it is good and if it is otherwise, Allah and His Apostle know better. Upon this he said: A Muslim who purifies (himself) and completes purification as enjoined upon him by Allah and then offers the five prayers, that will be expiatious (of his sins that he committed) between these (prayers).

(445) Jāmi' b. Shaddād reported: I heard Ḥumrān b. Abān narrating to Abū Burda in this very mosque during the governorship of Bishr that 'Uthmān b. 'Affān said: The Messenger of Allah (may peace be upon him) observed: He who completed ablution as Allah, the Exalted, enjoined upon him, his obligatory prayers would be expiatious (for his minor sins that he would commit) during (the interval) between them. This ḥadīth is transmitted by Ibn Mu'ādh, and in the ḥadīth narrated by Ghundar, the words "during the governorship of Bishr" are omitted and there is no mention of the obligatory prayers.

(446) Ḥumrān, the freed slave of 'Uthmān, reported: One day 'Uthmān b. 'Affān performed the ablution well, and then said: I saw the Messenger of Allah (may peace be upon him) performing ablution, the best ablution, and then observed: He who performed ablution like this and then went towards the mosque and nothing (but the love of) prayer urged him (to do so), all his previous (minor) sins would be expiated.

(447) Ḥumrān, the freed slave of 'Uthmān b. 'Affān, reported on the authority of 'Uthmān b. 'Affān that he heard the Messenger of Allah (may peace be upon him) say: He who performed ablution for prayer, and performed it properly, and then went (to observe) obligatory prayer and offered it along with people or with the congregation or in the mosque, Allah would pardon his sins.

(448) Abū Huraira reported: The Messenger of Allah (may peace be upon him) said: Five prayers and from one Friday prayer to (the next) Friday prayer is an expiation

444. His name was Mālik b. Abū 'Āmir. He was the grandfather of Imām Mālik. He died in 94 H.

445. Different meanings have been given to this word. Some of the scholars are of the view that it stands for the shops which 'Uthmān (Allah be pleased with him) had built in front of his house. Some take it to be a raised platform where the pious Caliph used to sit along with his friends.

446. This ḥadīth gives a clear indication of the fact that it is essential to wash each part of the body thrice.

(of the sins committed in between their intervals) if major sins are not committed.

(449) Abū Huraira reported that the Messenger of Allah (may peace be upon him) said: Five prayers and one Friday prayer to (the next) Friday prayer are expiatious (for the sins committed in the intervals) between them.

(450) Abū Huraira reported: Verily the Messenger of Allah (may peace be upon him) said: Five (daily) prayers and from one Friday prayer to the (next) Friday prayer, and from Ramaḍān to Ramaḍān are expiatious for the (sins) committed in between (their intervals) provided one shuns the major sins.[447]

(451) 'Uqba b. 'Āmir reported: We were entrusted with the task of tending the camels. On my turn when I came back in the evening after grazing them in the pastures, I found the Messenger of Allah (may peace be upon him) standing and addressing the people. I heard these words of his: If any Muslim performs ablution well, then stands and prays two rak'ahs setting about them with his heart as well as his face, Paradise would be guaranteed to him. I said: What a fine thing is this! And a narrator who was before me said: The first was better than even this. When I cast a glance, I saw that it was 'Umar who said: I see that you have just come and observed: If anyone amongst you performs the ablution, and then completes the ablution well and then says: I testify that there is no god but Allah and that Muḥammad is the servant of Allah and His Messenger, the eight gates of Paradise would be opened for him and he may enter by whichever of them he wishes.[448]

(452) 'Uqba b. 'Āmir al-Juhanī reported: Verily the Messenger of Allah (may peace be upon him) said, and then narrated (the ḥadīth) like one (mentioned above) except (this) that he said: He who performed ablution and said: I testify that there is no god but Allah, the One, there is no associate with Him and I testify that Muḥammad is His servant and His Messenger.

(453) 'Abdullah b. Zaid b. 'Āṣim al-Anṣārī, who was a Companion (of the Holy Prophet), reported: It was said to him (by people): Perform for us the ablution (as it was performed) by the Messenger of Allah (may peace be upon him). He ('Abdullah b. Zaid) called for a vessel (of water), and poured water from it on his hands and washed them three times. Then he inserted his hand (in the vessel) and brought it (water) out, rinsed his mouth and snuffed up water from the palm of one hand, doing that three times. He again inserted his hand and brought it out and washed his face three times, then inserted his hand and brought it out and washed each arm up to the elbow twice, then inserted his hand and brought it out and wiped his head both front and back with his hands. He then washed his feet up to the ankles, and then said: This is how God's Messenger (peace be upon him) performed ablution.

(454) This ḥadīth is narrated by 'Amr b. Yaḥyā with the same chain of transmitters, but there is no mention of ankles.[449]

(455) Mālik b. Anas narrated it from 'Amr b. Yaḥyā with the same chain of trans-

447. This point has been stressed in the Qur'ān: "If ye shun the major sins from which you are prohibited, We shall expiate from you your misdeeds and make you enter a noble entrance" (iv. 31).

448. It is recorded in Tirmidhī that it is a matter of great virtue to recite the following supplication after Wuḍū' اللهم اجعلني من التوابين و اجعلني من المتطهرين.

[O Allah! make me of the penitents, and make me of those who seek purification.]

449. The ankle is a part of the foot and, therefore, it was not mentioned.

mitters and mentioned the rinsing (of mouth) and snuffing (of water into the nostrils) three times, but he did not mention "from one palm," and made this addition: He moved them (his hands) for wiping to the front of his head and then the nape of his neck, then bringing them back till he reached the place from which he had begun, after which he washed his feet.

(456) Bahz reported: This ḥadīth has been narrated by Wuhaib on the authority of 'Amr b. Yaḥyā with the same chain of transmitters and it has been mentioned therein: He rinsed his mouth, snuffed up water in nostrils and cleaned the nose with three handfuls and wiped his head moving (his hand) in front and then back once. Bahz said: Wuhaib narrated this ḥadith to me and Wuhaib said: 'Amr b. Yaḥyā narrated to me this ḥadīth twice.

(457) 'Abdullah b. Zaid b. 'Āṣim al-Māzinī reported: He saw the Messenger of Allah (may peace be upon him) performing the ablution. He rinsed his mouth, then cleaned his nose, then washed his face three times, then washed his right hand thrice and then the other one, thrice. He then took fresh water and wiped his head and then washed his feet till he cleaned them.

Chapter XCVII

WHILE CLEANING THE NOSE AND USING OF PEBBLES IN TOILET, THE ODD NUMBER IS PREFERABLE

(458) Abū Huraira reported Allah's Apostle (may peace be upon him) as saying: When anyone wipes himself with pebbles (after answering the call of nature) he must make use of an odd number and when any one of you performs ablution, he must snuff in his nose water and then clean it.

(459) Hammām b. Munabbih reported: This is what Abū Huraira transmitted to us from Muḥammad, the Messenger of Allah (may peace be upon him), and he mentioned a number of aḥādīth, of which this is one: that the Messenger of Allah (may peace be upon him) said: When anyone amongst you (performs ablution) he must snuff his nostrils with water and then clean them.

(460) Abū Huraira reported: The Messenger of Allah (may peace be upon him) said: When anyone performs ablution he must clean his nose, and when anyone wipes himself with pebbles (after answering the call of nature) he must do that odd number of times.

(461) It has been transmitted by Abū Huraira and Abū Sa'īd al-Khudrī (both of them the reputed Companions of the Holy Prophet) that the Messenger of Allah (may peace be upon him) said like that.

(462) Abū Huraira reported: The Apostle of Allah (may peace be upon him) said: When any one of you awakes from sleep and performs ablution, he must clean his nose three times, for the devil spends the night in the interior of his nose.[450]

450. The presence of impurities in the nostrils has a very unhealthy effect on the mind of a man and he sees nightmares in sleep (Shāh Walīullāh's *Ḥujjatullāh al-Bāligha*, Vol. I, p. 145).

(463) Jābir b. 'Abdullah reported that he heard the Messenger of Allah (may peace be upon him) say: When anyone wipes himself with pebbles (after answering the call of nature) he should do this odd number of times.[451]

Chapter XCVIII

THE WASHING OF FEET PROPERLY IS INDISPENSABLE IN WUḌŪ'

(464) Sālim, the freed slave of Shaddād, said: I came to 'Ā'isha, the wife of the Holy Prophet (may peace be upon him), on the day when Sa'd b. Abī Waqqāṣ died. 'Abd al-Raḥmān b. Abū Bakr also came there and he performed ablution in her presence. She (Ḥaḍrat 'Ā'isha) said: O 'Abd al-Raḥmān, complete the ablution as I have heard the Messenger of Allah (may peace be upon him) say: Woe to the heels because of hell-fire.[452]

(465) 'Abdullah, the freed slave of Shaddād, came to 'Ā'isha and transmitted from her a ḥadīth like this (which she narrated) from the Holy Prophet (may peace be upon him).

(466) Sālim, the freed slave of Mahrī, reported: I and 'Abd al-Raḥmān b. Abū Bakr went out (in order to join) the funeral procession of Sa'd b. Abī Waqqāṣ and passed by the door of the residence of 'Ā'isha, and then he transmitted a ḥadīth like this from her who (narrated it) from the Holy Prophet (may peace be upon him).

(467) Sālim, the freed slave of Shaddād b. al-Hād said: I was in the presence of 'Ā'isha, and then narrated on her authority a ḥadīth like this from the Holy Prophet (may peace be upon him).

(468) 'Abdullah b. 'Amr reported: We returned from Mecca to Medina with the Messenger of Allah (may peace be upon him), and when we came to some water on the way, some of the people were in a hurry at the time of the afternoon prayer and performed ablution hurriedly; and when we reached them, their heels were dry, no water had touched them. The Prophet (may peace be upon him) said: Woe to (dry) heels, because of hell-fire. Make your ablution thorough.

(469) In the ḥadīth transmitted by Shu'ba these words are not there: "Complete the Wuḍū'," and there is the name of Abū Yaḥyā al-A'raj (a narrator).

(470) 'Abdullah b. 'Amr reported: The Messenger of Allah (may peace be upon him) lagged behind us on a journey. We travelled (back) and betook him; and then came the time of the afternoon prayer, and as we were going to wipe our feet he (the Holy Prophet) called out: Woe to the heels because of hell-fire.

451 There are so many aḥādīth which tell us that the number used for it should be at least three, since it can ensure proper wiping and then the private part of the body should be carefully washed. If pebbles are not available, other things, e.g. a clod or a piece of rough cloth, can also be used.

452. When ablution is performed carelessly, some parts of the body are not properly washed, and it betrays the fact that the man is not performing his religious duty with the seriousness that it rightly deserves. In this state of carelessness it is generally the heels which are not thoroughly washed. In order to make believers fully conscious of the importance of Wuḍū' for prayer it has been stressed that it should be performed well and every part of the body that has to be washed in a Wuḍū' should be carefully cleaned.

(471) Abū Huraira reported : The Apostle of Allah (may peace be upon him) saw a man who did not wash his heel and he remarked : Woe to the heels because of hell-fire.

(472) Abū Huraira reported : He saw people performing ablution with the help of a water jar and he said : Complete the Wuḍū' for I have heard Abū al-Qāsim (may peace be upon him) say : Woe to the hamstrings because of hell-fire.

(473) Abū Huraira reported : The Messenger of Allah (may peace be upon him) said : Woe to the heels because of hell-fire.

Chapter XCIX

IT IS OBLIGATORY TO WASH ALL PARTS OF THE BODY NECESSARY FOR PURIFICATION

(474) Jābir reported : 'Umar b. Khaṭṭāb said that a person performed ablution and left a small part equal to the space of a nail (unwashed). The Apostle of Allah (may peace be upon him) saw that and said : Go back and perform ablution well. He then went back (performed ablution well) and offered the prayer.

Chapter C

PURGING OF SINS WITH ABLUTION WATER

(475) Abū Huraira reported : The Messenger of Allah (may peace be upon him) said : When a bondsman—a Muslim or a believer—washes his face (in course of ablution), every sin he contemplated with his eyes will be washed away from his face along with water, or with the last drop of water ; when he washes his hands, every sin they wrought will be effaced from his hands with the water, or with the last drop of water ; and when he washes his feet, every sin towards which his feet have walked will be washed away with the water, or with the last drop of water, with the result that he comes out pure from all sins.

(476) 'Uthmān b. 'Affān reported : The Messenger of Allah (may peace be upon him) said : He who performed ablution well, his sins would come out from his body, even coming out from under his nails.[453]

453. One single meaning of these two aḥādīth is that God would pardon all sins when one performs ablution as it is the preliminary step to prayer. The person who makes himself ready for prayer by performing ablution gives a clear proof of his devotion to Allah and, therefore, one can rightly expect from the Generous Lord that his sins would be pardoned. It should also be remembered that here sin stands for a minor offence, and not a major one.

Shāh Walīullāh is of the opinion that the impurities settled on the body produce very unhealthy effects on the mind of a man, and when a person purifies his body, his mind is purified of all evil thoughts and this helps him in expiation of his sins (*Ḥujjatullāh al-Bāligha*, Vol. I, p. 174).

Moreover, we find in the Qur'ān that the doing of good deeds wipes out the sins of man : "Surely good deeds take away evil deeds" (xi. 115).

Chapter CI

IT IS COMMENDABLE TO INCLUDE FOREHEAD IN WASHING THE FACE AND ELBOW AND ANKLE IN WASHING THE HANDS AND FEET, WHILE PERFORMING ABLUTION

(477) Nu'aim b. 'Abdullah al-Mujmir reported: I saw Abū Huraira performing ablution. He washed his face and washed it well. He then washed his right hand including a portion of his arm. He then washed his left hand including a portion of his arm. He then wiped his head. He then washed his right foot including his shank, and then washed his left foot including shank, and then said: This is how I saw the Messenger of Allah (may peace be upon him) perform his ablution. And (Abū Huraira) added that the Messenger of Allah (may peace be upon him) had observed: You shall have your faces, hands and feet bright on the Day of Resurrection on account of your perfect ablution. He who can afford among you, let him increase the brightness of his forehead and that of hands and legs.[454]

(478) Nu'aim b. 'Abdullah reported: He saw Abū Huraira performing ablution. He washed his face and washed his hands up to the arms. He then wased his feet and reached up to the shanks, and then said: I heard the Messenger of Allah (may peace be upon him) say: My people would come with bright faces, and bright hands and feet on account of the marks of ablution, so he who can increase the lustre of his forehead (and that of his hands and legs) should do so.

(479) Abū Huraira reported: Verily the Messenger of Allah (may peace be upon him) said: My Cistern[455] has its dimensions wider than the distance between Aila[456] and Aden,[457] and its water is whiter than ice and sweeter than the honey diluted with milk, and its cups are more numerous than the numbers of the stars. Verily I shall prevent the (faithless) people therefrom just as a man prevents the camels of the people from his fountain. They said: Messenger of Allah, will you recognise us on that day? He said: Yes, you will have distinctive marks which nobody among the peoples (except you) will have; you would come to me with blazing forehead and bright hands and feet on account of the traces of ablution.

(480) Abū Huraira reported: The Messenger of Allah (may peace be upon him) said: My people would come to me on the Cistern and I would drive away persons (from it) just as a person drives away other people's camels from his camels. They (the hearers) said: Apostle of Allah, would you recognise us? He replied: Yes, you would have a mark which other people will not have. You would come to me with a white blaze on

454. Performing of Wuḍū' well is an indication of one's devotion to Allah, and he will have its distinctive marks on his body on the Day of Resurrection.

455. Every prophet will have a fountain for his followers to drink from. The fountain given to Muḥammad (may peace be upon him) is known as Kauthar. [To thee have We given the fount of abundance (cviii. 1)]. This heavenly Fountain of unbounded grace and knowledge, mercy and goodness, truth and wisdom, spiritual power and insight, would quench the highest spiritual thirst of man who had been quenching it in a degree with the help of prayers in this mortal world. The ablution is the first step to prayer and it shows that one has prepared oneself both spiritually and morally to bow before the Lord and develop an intimate spiritual contact with that Great Power.

456. Situated at the farthest end of the Syrian seashore.

457. Situated at the farthest end of Yemen.

your foreheads and white marks on your feet because of the traces of ablution. A group among you would be prevented from coming to me, and they would not meet me, and I would say: O my Lord, they are my companions. Upon this an angel would reply to me saying: Do you know what these people did after you?[458]

(481) Ḥudhaifa reported: The Messenger of Allah (may peace be upon him) said: My Cistern is bigger than the space between Aila and Aden. By Him in Whose Hand is my life, I will drive away persons (from it) just as a person drives away unknown camels from his cistern. They (the companions) said: Messenger of Allah, would you recognise us? He said: Yes, you would come to me with white faces, and white hands and feet on account of the traces of ablution. None but you would have (this mark).

(482) Abū Huraira reported: The Messenger of Allah (may peace be upon him) came to the graveyard and said: Peace be upon you! the abode of the believing people and we, if God so wills, are about to join you. I love to see my brothers. They (the hearers) said: Arn't we your brothers, Messenger of Allah? He said: You are my companions, and our brothers are those who have, so far, not come into the world.[459] They said: Messenger of Allah, how would you recognise those persons of your Ummah who have not yet been born? He said: Supposing a man had horses with white blazes on foreheads and legs among horses which were all black, tell me, would he not recognise his own horses? They said: Certainly, Messenger of Allah. He said: They would come with white faces and arms and legs owing to ablution, and I would arrive at the Cistern before them. Some people would be driven away from my Cistern as the stray camel is driven away. I would call out: Come, come. Then it would be said (to me): These people changed themselves after you, and I would say: Be off, be off.

(4 3) Abū Huraira reported: The Messenger of Allah (may peace be upon him) went out to the graveyard and said: Peace be upon you, the abode of the believing people, and if Allah so wills we shall join you, . . . (and so on and so forth) like the ḥadīth narrated by Ismā'īl b. Ja'far except the words of Mālik: Then some persons would be driven away from my Cistern.

(484) Abū Ḥāzim reported: I was (standing) behind Abū Huraira and he was performing the ablution for prayer. He extended the (washing) of his hand that it went up to his armpit.[460] I said to him: O Abū Huraira, what is this ablution? He said: O of the tribe of Farrukh,[461] you are here; if I knew that you were here, I would have never performed ablution like this; I have heard my Friend (may peace be upon him) say: In a believer adornment would reach the places where ablution reaches.

(485) Abū Huraira reported: The Messenger of Allah (may peace be upon him) said: Should I not suggest to you that by which Allah obliterates the sins and elevates the

458. Here the reference is made to those tribes who had abandoned the faith of Islam during the caliphate of Abū Bakr Ṣiddīq (Allah be pleased with him) after the death of the Holy Prophet.

459. This ḥadīth gives us a clear indication that the Companions of the Holy Prophet hold the most eminent position in Islamic Brotherhood, because they are both brothers and friends of the Holy Prophet (may peace be upon him). But it has a special message of happiness for those who would be believers after him.

460. Abū Huraira was over-zealous in washing the different parts of his body while performing the ablution. It was his personal zeal in observing cleanliness.

461. Farrukh is the name of a son of Ibrāhīm and his progeny settled in Persia. Abū Ḥāzim belonged to this non-Arab tribe.

ranks (of a man). They (the hearers) said: Yes, Messenger of Allah. He said: Performing the ablution thoroughly despite odds, tranversing of more paces towards the mosque, and waiting for the next prayer after observing a prayer,[462] and that is mindfulness.[463]

(486) This ḥadīth has been narrated on the authority of 'Alā' b. 'Abd al-Raḥmān with the same chain of transmitters and there is no mention of the word of *al-Ribāṭ* in the ḥadīth transmitted by Shu'ba and in the ḥadīth narrated by Mālik "Ribāṭ" has been mentioned twice. This is the "Ribāṭ" for you, this is the "Ribāṭ" for you.

Chapter CII

PERTAINING TO TOOTH-STICK[464]

(487) Abū Huraira reported: The Apostle (may peace be upon him) said: Were it not that I might over-burden the believers—and in the ḥadīth transmitted by Zuhair "people"—I would have ordered them to use tooth-stick at every time of prayer.

(488) Miqdām b. Shuraiḥ narrated it from his father who said: I asked 'Ā'isha what Allah's Apostle (may peace be upon him) did first when he entered his house, and she replied: He used tooth-stick (first of all).

(489) 'Ā'isha reported: Whenever the Apostle of Allah (may peace be upon him) entered his house, he used tooth-stick first of all.

(490) Abū Mūsā reported: I went to the Apostle (may peace be upon him) and found one end of the tooth stick upon his tongue (i.e. he was rinsing his mouth).

(491) Ḥudhaifa reported: Whenever the Messenger of Allah (may peace be upon him) got up for Tahajjud[465] prayer, he cleansed his mouth with the tooth-stick.

(492) This ḥadīth is reported from Ḥudhaifa by another chain of transmitters. Whenever he (the Holy Prophet) got up in the night, they (the transmitters) have not mentioned the words: for offering Tahajjud prayer.

(493) Ḥudhaifa reported: Whenever he (the Holy Prophet) got up for prayer during the night, he cleansed his mouth with the tooth-stick.

(494) Ibn 'Abbās reported that he spent a night at the house of the Apostle of Allah (may peace be upoh him). The Apostle of Allah (may peace be upon him) got up for prayer in the latter part of the night. He went out and looked towards the sky and then recited this verse (190th) of Āl-i-'Imrān: "Verily in the creation of the heavens and the earth and the alternation of night and day," up to the (words) "save us from the torment of Hell." He then returned to his house, used the tooth-stick, performed the ablution, and then got up and offered the prayer. He then lay down on the bed,

462. All these acts show that the person is devoted to his Lord and he lives in this world with his heart set on the Hereafter.

463. The original meaning of this word is "keeping to the post," or "remaining alert and watchful on the frontier against the attack of the enemy". These acts of piety mentioned above have been called *ribāṭ* besause these provide safeguard to the person against the attack of the devil.

464. سواک or مسواک (Siwāk or Miswāk): a piece of small stick with which the teeth are rubbed and cleaned, the end being made like a brush by beating or chewing it so as to separate the fibres.

465. It is offered at the latter part of the night before the morning prayer.

and again got up and went out and looked towards the sky and recited this verse (mentioned above), then returned, used the tooth-stick, performed ablution and again offered the prayer.

Chapter CIII

CHARACTERISTICS OF FIṬRA

(495) Abū Huraira reported: Five are the acts quite close to the Fiṭra, or five are the acts of Fiṭra:[466] circumcision,[467] shaving the pubes, cutting the nails, plucking the hair under the armpits[468] and clipping the moustache.

(496) Abū Huraira reported: Five are the acts of fitra: circumcision, shaving the pubes, clipping the moustache, cutting the nails, plucking the hair under the armpits.

(497) Anas reported: A time limit has been prescribed for us for clipping the moustache, cutting the nails, plucking hair under the armpits, shaving the pubes, that it should not be neglected far more than forty nights.[469]

(498) Ibn 'Umar said: The Apostle of Allah (may peace be upon him) said: Trim closely the moustache, and let the beard grow.

(499) Ibn 'Umar said: The Apostle of Allah (may peace be upon him) ordered[470] us to trim the moustache closely and spare the beard.

(500) Ibn 'Umar said: The Messenger of Allah (may peace be upon him) said: Act

466. The word *fiṭra* has been explained in "Kitāb al-Īmān". A few words may be said here. Here *fiṭra* (lit. nature) stands for the Sunnah of the Apostles of Allah, because in a ḥadīth transmitted by Abū 'Awāna, there is the word *Sunnah* instead of fiṭra. The conduct of the Apostle is quite close to nature. Some of the commentators have explained this word by the religion of Islam, because it is given to man by the same Lord Who has created nature and thus there is a very close affinity between the two. Some of the scholars are of the view that fiṭra here implies the inner sense of cleanliness in a man which is a proof of his moral and mental health.

467. It is an old form of minor operation in which the foreskin of the male sexual organ is cut away. "The hygienic value of circumcision has today been generally conceded, and some physicians recommended the operation as a routine measure for all male infants. It is part of the routine of bathing an uncircumcised boy to draw back the foreskin and sponge the head of the penis, for general cleanliness and also to remove pasty white secretion called smegma, which accumulates under the foreskin and may lead to local irritation unless it is regularly cleansed. Whenever a new-born is found to have a foreskin so long or so tight that it will be difficult to draw it back for washing or it will interfere with urination, the physician recommends circumcision" (Jerome and Julia Rainer, *Sexual Pleasure in Marriage*, pp. 185-6).

468. Plucking the hair under the armpits does not mean that these should necessarily be uprooted. Their shaving can also serve the purpose since the aim is to make the body clean and remove impurities from it.

469. This is the uppermost limit. The keen sense of cleanliness in man can urge him to do these things even after short intervals. It is cleanliness that is desired in Islam, and the higher its standard is achieved, the better it is.

470. It is on the basis of this word that wearing of a beard by a Muslim has been declared *wājib*, since it is of the nature of a command.

against the polytheists, trim closely the moustache and grow beard.[471]

(501) Abū Huraira reported : The Messenger of Allah (may peace be upon him) said : Trim closely the moustache, and grow beard, and thus act against the fire-worshippers.

(502) 'Ā'isha reported : The Messenger of Allah (may peace be upon him) said : Ten are the acts according to fitra : clipping the moustache, letting the beard grow, using the tooth-stick, snuffing up water in the nose, cutting the nails, washing the finger joints, plucking the hair under the armpits, shaving the pubes, and cleaning one's private parts with water. The narrator said : I have forgotten the tenth, but it may have been rinsing the mouth.

(503) This ḥadīth has been narrated by Mus'ab b. Shaiba with the same chain of transmitters except for these words : "His father said : I forgot the tenth one."

Chapter CIV

HOW TO CLEANSE ONESELF AFTER RELIEVING ONESELF

(504) Salmān reported that it was said to him : Your Apostle (may peace be upon him) teaches you about everything,[472] even about excrement. He replied : Yes, he has forbidden us to face the Qibla[473] at the time of excretion or urination, or cleansing with right hand[474] or with less than three pebbles, or with dung or bone.

(505) Salmān said that (one among) the polytheists remarked : I see that your friend even teaches you about the excrement. He replied : Yes. He has in fact forbidden us that anyone amongst us should cleanse himself with his right hand, or face the Qibla. He has forbidden the use of dung or bone for it, and he has also instructed us not to use less than three pebbles (for this purpose).

(506) Jābir reported : The Messenger of Allah (my peace be upon him) forbade the use of bone or the droppings of camels for wiping (after excretion).

(507) Abū Ayyūb reported : The Apostle of Allah (may peace be upon him) said : Whenever you go to the desert, neither turn your face nor turn your back towards the Qibla while answering the call of nature, but face towards the east or the west. Abū Ayyūb said : When we came to Syria we found that the latrines already built there

471. This ḥadīth explains the importance and significance of the beard in a Muslim society. Islam created a new brotherhood on the basis of belief and good conduct. It exhorted its followers to develop a keen sense of moral consciousness as a hallmark of its new community. For the identification of faces, the Muslims have been ordered to trim the moustache and wear the beard, so that they may be distinguished from the non-Muslims who grow moustache and shave beards.

472. The Holy Prophet has to purify both our bodies and souls. He has, therefore, guided us in all details of life. For leading a pious life it is essential that, along with the purity of the soul, our bodies should also be neat and clean. It is for this reason that the Holy Prophet has given us instructions how we should properly answer the call of nature.

473. We turn our faces towards the Qibla for offering prayers ; it is, therefore, quite desirable that we should not turn our faces towards it while answering the call of nature.

474. We eat food, write and do so many other good things with our right hands, and the sense of decency and cleanliness, therefore, demands that we should avoid its use for cleansing the private parts of our body.

were facing towards the Qibla. We turned our faces away from them and begged forgiveness of the Lord. He said : Yes.

(508) Abū Huraira said : When anyone amongst you squats for answering the call of nature, he should neither turn his face towards the Qibla nor turn his back towards it.

(509) Wāsi' b. Ḥabbān reported : I was offering my prayer in the mosque and 'Abdullah b. 'Umar was sitting there reclining with his back towards the Qibla. After completing my prayer, I went to him from one side. 'Abdullah said : People say when you go to the latrine, you should neither turn your face towards the Qibla nor towards Bait-ul-Maqdis. 'Abdullah said (further) : I went up to the roof of the house and saw the Messenger of Allah (may peace be upon him) squatting on two bricks for relieving himself with his face towards Bait-al-Maqdis.

(510) 'Abdullah b. 'Umar said : I went up to the roof of the house of my sister Ḥafṣa and saw the Messenger of Allah (may peace be upon him) relieving himself facing Syria, with his back to the Qibla.[475]

(511) Abū Qatāda reported it from his father : The Messenger of Allah (may peace be upon him) said : None of you should hold penis with his right hand while urinating, or wipe himself with his right hand in privy, and should not breathe into the vessel (from which he drinks).

(512) Abū Qatāda reported it from his father that the Messenger of Allah (may peace be upon him) said : When anyone amongst you enters the privy, he must not touch his penis with his right hand.

(513) Abū Qatāda reported : The Messenger of Allah (may peace be upon him) forbade (us) to breathe into the vessel, to touch the penis with the right hand and to wipe after relieving with right hand.

Chapter CV

STARTING FROM THE RIGHT-HAND SIDE FOR ABLUTION, ETC.

(514) 'Ā'isha reported : The Messenger of Allah (may peace be upon him) loved to start from the right-hand side for performing ablution,[476] for combing (the hair) and wearing the shoes.

(515) 'Ā'isha reported : The Messenger of Allah (may peace be upon him) loved to start from the right-hand side in his every act, i.e. in wearing shoes, in combing (his hair) and in performing ablution.

475. The scholars of Hadīth have resolved the apparent contradiction between the above-mentioned aḥādīth. It is forbidden to face Qibla or to turn one's back towards it, when we go out for toilet in the wilderness or desert, where we can easily avoid it, but in a built-up area or enclosure, we are permitted to do so.

476. It is narrated in the aḥādīth that the Holy Prophet preferred to use his right hand and to start from the right-hand side for performing all desirable acts. There is a ḥadīth in Abū Dāwūd which explains the conduct of the Holy Prophet : "God's Messenger used his right hand for getting water for ablution and taking food, and his left hand for his evacuations and anything repugnant. If there is imperative necessity to act against it, it is pardonable, otherwise it is makrūh (undesirable)."

Chapter CVI

EASING IS FORBIDDEN IN THE STREETS AND UNDER THE SHADE

(516) Abū Huraira reported : The Messenger of Allah (may peace be upon him) said : Be on your guard against two things which provoke cursing. They (the hearers) said : Messenger of Allah, what are those things which provoke cursing ? He said : Easing on the thoroughfares (where people walk) or under the shades (where they take shelter and rest).[477]

(517) Anas b. Mālik reported : The Messenger of Allah (may peace be upon him) entered an enclosure while a servant was following him with a jar of water and he was the youngest amongst us and he placed it by the side of a lote-tree. When the Messenger of Allah (may peace be upon him) relieved himself, he came out and had cleansed himself with water.

(518) Anas b. Mālik reported : When the Messenger of Allah (may peace be upon him) entered the privy, a servant and I used to carry a skin of water, and a pointed staff, and he would cleanse himself with water.

(519) Anas b. Mālik reported : The Messenger of Allah (may peace be upon him) went to a far-off place in the desert (hidden from the sight of human beings)[478] for relieving himself. Then I brought water for him and he cleansed himself.

Chapter CVII

WIPING OVER THE SOCKS

(520) Hammām reported : Jarīr urinated, then performed ablution and wiped[479] over the socks. It was said to him : Do you do like this ? He said : Yes, I saw that the Messenger of Allah (may peace be upon him) urinated, then performed ablution and then wiped over his shoes. A'mash said : Ibrāhīm had observed that this ḥadīth had a surprise for them (the people) because Jarīr had embraced Islam after the revelation of

477. In the *Sunan* of Abū Dāwūd, along with these two places, i.e. thoroughfares and shades, the third place is also mentioned, i.e. watering places. The ḥadīth is reported like this on the authority of Mu'ādh : The Messenger of Allah (may peace be upon him) said : Guard against the three things which provoke cursing : relieving oneself in watering places, on the thoroughfares and in the shade.

478. The Holy Prophet had an exceedingly keen sense of modesty and was thus very much particular in concealing the private parts of his body. That is the reason why he either relieved himself in privy or went far away into the desert where he was absolutely hidden from the sight of human beings. It is narrated on the authority of Jābir that whenever the Apostle of Allah (may peace be upon him) felt the need of relieving himself he went far away so that no one could see him (Abū Dāwūd).

479. Islam does not inflict rigorous rules in anything. In Wuḍū' or ablution, the concession of wiping over the socks has been granted in order to provide relief to the people. With the exception of the Khwārij and Shī'a, there is a consensus of opinion amongst the Muslims that it is permissible to wipe the socks while performing ablution without doing it any harm. Difference, if there is any, is about the nature of the socks. Imām Mālik is of the view that wiping is permitted only on leather socks. Imām Shāfi'ī deems it desirable only when a man is wearing shoes along with socks. Imām Abū Yūsuf and Imām Muḥammad consider it permissible in case of thick socks.

Sūrat al-Mā'ida.[480]

(521) This ḥadīth is narrated on the same authority from A'mash by another chain of transmitters like one transmitted by Abū Mu'āwyia. The ḥadīth reported by 'Īsā and Sufyān has these words also : "This ḥadīth surprised the friends of 'Abdullah," for Jarīr had embraced Islam after the revelation of al-Mā'ida.

(522) Ḥudhaifa reported : I was with the Apostle of Allah (may peace be upon him) when he came to the dumping ground of filth belonging to a particular tribe. He urinated while standing,[481] and I went aside. He (the Holy Prophet) asked me to come near him[482] and I went so near to him that I stood behind his heels. He then performed ablution and wiped over his socks.

(523) Abū Wā'il reported : Abū Mūsā inflicted extreme rigour upon himself in the matter of urination and urinated in a bottle and said : When the skin of anyone amongst the Israelites was besmeared with urine, he cut that portion with a cutter. Ḥudhaifa said : I wish that your friend should not inflict such an extreme rigour. I and the Messenger of Allah (may peace be upon him) were going together till we reached the dumping ground of filth behind an enclosure. He stood up as one among you would stand up, and he urinated. I tried to turn away from him, but he beckoned to me, so I went to him and I stood behind him, till he had relieved himself.[483]

(524) The son of Mughīra b. Shu'ba reported : The Messenger of Allah (may peace be upon him) went out for relieving himself. Mughīra went with him carrying a jug full of water. When he (the Holy Prophet) came back after relieving himself, he poured water over him and he performed ablution and wiped over his socks ; and in the narration of Ibn Rumḥ there is "till" instead of "when".

(525) This ḥadīth has been transmitted with the same chain of transmitters by Yaḥyā b. Sa'īd with the addition of these words : "He washed his face and hands, and wiped his head and then wiped his socks."

(526) Mughīra b. Shu'ba reported : I was with the Messenger of Allah (may peace be upon him) one night. He came down (from the ride) and relieved himself. He then

480. This part of the ḥadīth explains the importance of the teachings of the Holy Prophet in Islam. Had Sūrat al-Mā'ida been revealed after this act of the Holy Prophet, it was then quite logical to argue that it had been abrogated by the verse of the Qur'ān (v. 7) in which washing of feet to the ankles had been made compulsory. But as Jarīr had embraced Islam after the revelation of this verse, it implies that wiping over the socks is permitted, as the act and the word of the Holy Prophet explain the true significance of the teachings of the Qur'ān. His interpretation is divinely inspired and is, therefore, to be accepted as final in all matters of Islam.

481. The common practice with the Holy Prophet was that he urinated in a sitting posture. He made an exception to it because he was feeling pain in his back and he could not sit or, according to some of the scholars of Ḥādīth, he did not find there a proper place to sit.

482. He was asked to stand behind the Holy Prophet with his back turned towards him with a view to providing him with a sort of privacy.

483. This ḥadīth makes it clear that it is no virtue and piety to impose unnecessary burden and inflict rigours upon oneself. The purpose of religion is to make life well regulated and not to make it intolerably hard.

The Qur'ān after describing the general rules of cleanliness and purification of the body says :

> God does not want to impose any hardship on you, but wants to make you pure, and to bestow upon you the full measure of His blessings, so that you might have cause to be grateful (v. 6).

came back and I poured water upon him from the jar that I carried with me. He performed ablution and wiped over his socks.

(527) Mughīra b. Shu'ba reported: I was in the company of the Messenger of Allah (may peace be upon him) on a journey when he said: Mughīra, take hold of this jar (of water). I took hold of it and I went out with him. (I stopped but) the Messenger of Allah (may peace be upon him) proceeded on till he was out of my sight. He relieved himself and then came back and he was wearing a tight-sleeved Syrian gown. He tried to get his forearms out, but the sleeve of the gown was very narrow, so he brought his hands out from under the gown. I poured water over (his hands) and he performed ablution for prayer, then wiped over his socks and prayed.

(528) Mughīra b. Shu'ba reported: The Messenger of Allah (may peace be upon him) went out for relieving himself. When he came back I brought for him a jar (of water) and poured water upon his hands and He washed his face. He tried to wash his forearms, but as the (sleeves of the) gown were tight, he, therefore, brought them out from under the gown. He then washed them, wiped his head, and wiped his socks and then prayed.

(529) 'Urwa b. Mughīra reported his father having said: I was one night with the Apostle of Allah (may peace be upon him) on a journey. He said to me: Have you any water with you? I said: Yes. He (the Holy Prophet) came down from his ride and went on till he disappeared in the darkness of night. He then came back and I poured water for him from the jar. He washed his face. He had a woollen gown on him and he could not bring out his forearms from it (i.e. from its sleeves) and consequently he brought them out from under his gown. He washed his forearms, wiped over his head. I then bent down to take off his socks. But he said: Leave them, for my feet were clean when I put them in, and he only wiped over them.[484]

(530) 'Urwa b. al-Mughīra reported it from his father: He (Mughīra) helped the Apostle (may peace be upon him) in performing the ablution, and he performed it and wiped over his shoes. He (Mughīra) said to him (about the washing of the feet after putting them off), but he (the Holy Prophet) said: I put them (feet) in when these were clean.

Chapter CVIII

WIPING (OVER) THE FORELOCK AND TURBAN

(531) 'Urwa b. al-Mughīra b. Shu'ba reported it on the authority of his father that he said: The Messenger of Allah (may peace be upon him) lagged behind (in a journey) and I also lagged behind along with him. After having relieved himself he said: Have you any water with you? I brought to him a jar of water; he washed his palms, and face, and when he tried to get his forearms out (he could not) for the sleeve of the gown was tight. He, therefore, brought them out from under the gown and, throwing it over his shoulders, he washed his forearm. He then wiped his forelock and his turban and his socks. He then mounted and I also mounted (the ride) and came to the people.

484. Ablution is complete by merely wiping over the socks only when these are worn after ablution.

They had begun the prayer with 'Abd ar-Raḥmān b. 'Auf leading them and had completed a *rak'a*. When he perceived the presence of the Apostle of Allah (may peace be upon him) he began to retire. He (the Holy Prophet) signed to him to continue and offered prayer along with them. Then when he had pronounced the salutation, the Apostle (may peace be upon him) got up and I also got up with him, and we offered the rak'a which had been finished before we came.

(532) Ibn Mughīra narrated it from his father: The Apostle of Allah (may peace be upon him) wiped over his socks and over his forehead and over his turban.

(533) This ḥadīth has been transmitted by Ibn Mughīra on the authority of his father by another chain of transmitters.

(534) Bakr reported that he had heard from the son of Mughīra that verily the Apostle of Allah (may peace be upon him) performed ablution and wiped over his forehead and wiped over his turban and over his socks.

(535) It is narrated from Bilāl that the Messenger of Allah (may peace be upon him) wiped over the socks and turban, and in the ḥadīth transmitted by 'Īsā b. Yūnus the words are: "Bilāl narrated it to me."

(536) This tradition is transmitted by A'mash with this addition: "I saw the Messenger of Allah (may peace be upon him)."

Chapter CIX

TIME LIMIT FOR WIPING OVER THE SHOES

(537) Shuraiḥ b. Hānī said: I came to 'Ā'isha to ask her about wiping over the socks. She said: You better ask ('Alī) son of Abū Ṭālib for he used to travel with the Messenger of Allah (may peace be upon him). We asked him and he said: The Messenger of Allah (may peace be upon him) stipulated (the upper limit) of three days and three nights for a traveller and one day and one night for the resident.

(538) This ḥadīth is narrated by 'Ubaidullah b. 'Amr and Zaid b. Abī Unaisa with the same chain of transmitters.

(539) Shuraiḥ b. Hānī reported: I asked 'Ā'isha about wiping over the shoes. She said: You better go to 'Alī, for he knows more about this than I.[485] I, therefore, came to 'Alī and he narrated from the Apostle (may peace be upon him) like this.

(540) Sulaimān b. Buraida narrated it from his father that the Apostle of Allah

485. This ḥadīth throws a good deal of light on the humility, sincerity, mutual respect and trust and straightforwardness of the Companions of the Holy Prophet. Whenever any one of them was consulted for opinion on any matter, he was directed to go to a more proper person who was considered to be an authority on that matter. Ḥaḍrat 'Alī had a special insight in Fiqh. Moreover, he accompanied the Holy Prophet (may peace be upon him) on journeys. Ḥaḍrat 'Ā'isha (Allah be pleased with her), therefore, directed the man to go to 'Alī (Allah be pleased with him), for the most reliable and correct information, as he was in a position to tell about the Prophet's conduct outside the four walls of his house. This ḥadīth also categorically falsifies the stories about the mistrust between 'Alī and 'Ā'isha (Allah be pleased with them) and establishes the fact beyond any shadow of doubt that 'Ā'isha had full trust in 'Alī, because of his devotion to the Holy Prophet, his sincerity and correct and right understanding of the teachings of Islam.

(may peace be upon him) offered prayers with one ablution on the day of the Conquest (of Mecca) and wiped over the socks. Umar said to him: You have today done something that you have not been accustomed to before. He (the Holy Prophet) said: O 'Umar, I have done that on purpose.

Chapter CX

IT IS UNDESIRABLE TO PUT ONE'S HAND IN THE UTENSIL BEFORE WASHING IT

(541) Abū Huraira said: When anyone amongst you wakes up from sleep, he must not put his hand in the utensil till he has washed it three times, for he does not know where his hand was during the night.

(542) This ḥadīth is transmitted from Abū Huraira by another chain of transmitters.

(543) Zuhrī and Ibn Musayyab have both transmitted a ḥadīth like this from Abū Huraira who narrated it from the Apostle (may peace be upon him).

(544) Abū Huraira reported: The Apostle of Allah (may peace be upon him) said: When anyone amongst you wakes up from sleep, he should wash his hands three times before putting it in the utensil, for he does not know where his hand was during the night.

(545) This ḥadīth has been transmitted through many other chains of transmitters on the authority of Abū Huraira in which it is reported that the Apostle of Allah (may peace be upon him) made a mention of washing the hand, and did not instruct to wash it three times. But the aḥādīth narrated from Jābir and Ibn Musayyab, Abū Salama, and 'Abdullah b. Shaqīq, Abū Ṣāliḥ, Abū Razīn, there is a mention of "three times".

Chapter CXI

INSTRUCTIONS PERTAINING TO THE LICKING OF A DOG [486]

(546) Abū Huraira reported the Messenger of Allah (may peace be upon him) to have said: When a dog licks a utensil belonging to any one of you, (the thing contained in it) should be thrown away and then (the utensil) should be washed seven times.

486. The dog is one of the unclean beasts according to Islam and eating of its flesh is forbidden and its keeping in the house as a pet is also prohibited for the Muslims. They have, however, been permitted to keep dogs for hunting, herding and watching. The food or water or the vessel which the dog licks are rendered impure. Thus such food and water should be thrown away and the vessel should be cleaned several times in order to purify it. Islam has declared the dog to be an unclean beast because its sliva has the germs of rabies in it. The writer of the article on "Dog" in the *Encyclopaedia Britannica* says: "It [rabies] is more common in dogs than in any other animal" (Vol. VII, p. 497). The dog is also responsible for the spread of "Canine Plague". The virus causing this disease is airborne and affects the other dogs very quickly.

(547) This ḥadīth has been transmitted by another chain of transmitters in which there is no mention of "throwing away".

(548) Abū Huraira reported: The Messenger of Allah (may peace be upon him) said: When a dog drinks out of a vessel belonging to any one of you, he must wash it seven times.

(549) Abū Huraira reported: The Messenger of Allah (may peace be upon him) said: The purification of the utensil belonging to any one of you, after it is licked by a dog, lies in washing it seven times, using sand for the first time.

(550) Hammām b. Munabbih reported: Of the aḥādīth narrated by Abū Huraira from Muḥammad, the Messenger of Allah (may peace be upon him), one is this: The Messenger of Allah (may peace be upon him) said: The purification of the utensil belonging to one amongst you, after it is licked by a dog, lies in washing it seven times.

(551) Ibn Mughaffal reported: The Messenger of Allah (may peace be upon him) ordered killing of the dogs,[487] and then said: What about them, i.e. about other dogs?—and then granted concession (to keep) the dog for hunting and the dog for (the security) of the herd, and said: When the dog licks the utensil, wash it seven times, and rub it with earth the eighth time.

(552) A ḥadīth like this has been narrated from Shu'ba with the same chain of transmitters except for the fact that in the ḥadīth transmitted by Yaḥyā those words are: "He (the Holy Prophet) gave concession in the case of the dog for looking after the herd, for hunting and for watching the cultivated land," and there is no mention of this addition (i.e. concession in case of watching the cultivated lands) except in the ḥadīth transmitted by Yaḥyā.

Chapter CXII

IT IS FORBIDDEN TO URINATE IN STAGNANT WATER

(553) Jābir reported: The Messenger of Allah (may peace be upon him) forbade to urinate in stagnant water.

(554) Abū Huraira reported: The Messenger of Allah (may peace be upon him) said: None amongst you should urinate in standing water, and then wash in it.

(555) Hammām b. Munabbih said: Of the aḥādīth narrated to us by Abū Huraira from Muḥammad the Messenger of Allah (may peace be upon him) one is this: The Messenger of Allah (may peace be upon him) said: You should not urinate in standing water, that is not flowing, then wash in it.[488]

487. The word used in the ḥadīth is *al-kilāb* which means particular dogs and not all dogs. What the Holy Prophet, therefore, ordered was not the indiscriminate killing of dogs as a species, but the killing of stray dogs and those which were infected by rabies and other dangerous diseases.

488. Water is used for ablution, washing and drinking purposes; it is, therefore, essential that it should be kept clean from all kinds of impurities. Special care must be taken in case of standing and stagnant water, because any impurity added to it would not be washed away. The Holy Prophet has, therefore, forbidden to urinate in standing water and has prohibited the Muslims to wash themselves in such water in which the people are accustomed to urinate. It may also be added that

Chapter CXIII

IT IS FORBIDDEN TO WASH ONESELF IN STANDING WATER

(556) Abū Huraira reported the Messenger of Allah (may peace be upon him) saying: None of you must wash in standing water[489] when he is in a state of Junub.[490] And Abū Huraira was asked how it was to be done; he said: It was to be taken out in handfuls.

Chapter CXIV

IT IS OBLIGATORY TO CLEANSE THE MOSQUE WHEN THERE ARE IMPURITIES IN IT AND THE EARTH BECOMES CLEAN OF IMPURITIES WITH THE HELP OF WATER WITHOUT SCRAPING (THE PART OF IT)

(557) Anas reported: A Bedouin urinated in the mosque. Some of the persons stood up (to reprimand him or to check him from doing so), but the Messenger of Allah (may peace be upon him) said: Leave him alone; [491] don't interrupt him. He (the narrator) said: And when he had finished, he called for a bucket of water and poured it over.

(558) Anas b. Mālik narrated that a desert Arab (Bedouin) stood in a corner of the mosque and urinated there. The people (the Companions of the Holy Prophet who were present there) shouted, but the Messenger of Allah (may peace be upon him) said: Leave him alone. When he had finished, the Messenger of Allah (may peace be upon him) ordered that a bucket (of water) should be brought and poured over it.

(559) Anas b. Mālik reported: While we were in the mosque with Allah's Messenger

urination even in flowing water is not desirable and this evil practice must be avoided.

The second point to be noted is that if standing water is like a big lake or a pond, one can wash oneself in it even if it has impurities, but on condition that those impurities have neither changed its colour, nor odour, nor taste. But if the water containing such impurities is small in quantity (less than 6½ maunds) it is unfit for washing or performing ablution, even if its colour, odour or taste are unchanged.

489. The scholars of Ḥadīth are of the opinion that it is not totally forbidden, but it is to be discouraged especially when the water is not in the lake, pond or the ocean, but in the well or any other small tank or tub.

490. It must be made clear that the word *Junub* does not mean sexual defilement as is commonly translated by the European writers. There is no idea of defilement or pollution in relation to sex in Islam. The sexual act is a spiritual act if it is performed according to the commands of God. The word *Junub* means side or remote. What it signifies is that one who has sexual intercourse is on the side of or remote from prayer (Imām Rāghib), unless he takes a bath. The word *Junub* may also convey the sense of lying on the side of one's wife and thus it is a metaphorical expression for sexual act. The necessity of bathing arises in case of emission of seminal fluid due to sexual intercourse, or *pollutio nocturna*.

491. These words are sufficient to give us an idea of the tenderly human feelings of the Holy Prophet. The desert Arab was doing something noxious and had justifiably provoked the anger of the Companions of the Holy Prophet, but he calmed their ruffled feelings and exhorted them to treat him kindly as he was ignorant of the etiquette of the mosque.

(may peace be upon him), a desert Arab came and stood up and began to urinate in the mosque. The Companions of Allah's Messenger (may peace be upon him) said: Stop, stop; but the Messenger of Allah (may peace be upon him) said: Don't interrupt him; leave him alone. They left him alone, and when he finished urinating, Allah's Messenger (may peace be upon him) called him and said to him: These mosques are not the places meant for urine and filth, but are only for the remembrance of Allah, prayer and the recitation of the Qur'ān,[492] or Allah's Messenger said something like that. He (the narrator) said that he (the Holy Prophet) then gave orders to one of the people who brought a bucket of water and poured it over.

Chapter CXV

PERTAINING TO THE URINE OF THE SUCKLING BABE, AND HOW IT IS TO BE WASHED AWAY

(560) 'Ā'isha, the wife of the Apostle (may peace be upon him) said: Babies were brought to the Messenger of Allah (may peace be upon him) and he blessed them, and after having chewed (something, e.g. dates or any other sweet thing) he rubbed therewith their soft palates. A baby was brought to him and he passed water over him (over his garment), so he asked water to be brought and sprinkled it, but he did not wash it.

(561) 'Ā'isha reported: A suckling babe was brought to the Messenger of Allah (may peace be upon him) and he urinated in his lap. He (the Holy Prophet) sent for water and poured it over.

(562) Hishām narrated the ḥadīth like one transmitted by Ibn Numair (the above-mentioned one) with the same chain of transmitters.

(563) Umm Qais daughter of Miḥṣan reported that she came to the Messenger of Allah (may peace be upon him) with her child, who was not yet weaned, and she placed him in his lap; and he urinated in his (Holy Prophet's) lap. He (the Holy Prophet) did nothing more than spraying water over it.

(564) This ḥadīth has also been narrated from al-Zuhrī with the same chain of narrators, (but for the words): "He (the Holy Prophet) sent for water and sprinkled it over."

(565) 'Ubaidullah b. 'Abdullah b. 'Utba b. Mas'ūd said: Umm Qais, daughter of Miḥṣan, was among the earliest female emigrants who took the oath of allegiance to the Messenger of Allah (may peace be upon him), and she was the sister of 'Ukkasha b. Miḥṣan, one amongst the sons of Asad b. Khuzaima. He (the narrator) said: She (Umm Qais) told me that she came to the Messenger of Allah (may peace be upon him) with her son and he had not attained the age of eating food. He (the narrator, 'Ubaidullah), said: She told me that her son passed urine in the lap of the Messenger of Allah (may peace be upon him). The Messenger of Allah (may peace be upon him) sent for water

492. Herein is explained the true purpose of the mosque. It implies that the mosque should be protected from impure things, and one must refrain from talking loudly, or transacting business or wrangling in them. One should enter them with single-minded devotion to Allah and with full consciousness of His Great Majesty and Power.

and sprayed it over his garment (over that part which was contaminated with the urine of the child) and he did not wash it thoroughly.[493]

Chapter CXVI

WASHING AWAY OF THE SEMEN FROM THE GARMENT AND ITS SCRAPING

(566) 'Alqama and Aswad reported: A person stayed in the house of 'Ā'isha and in the morning began to wash his garment. 'Ā'isha said: In case you saw it (i.e. drop of semen), it would have served the purpose (of purifying the garment) if you had simply washed that spot; and in case you did not see it, it would have been enough to sprinkle water around it, for when I saw that on the garment of the Messenger of Allah (may peace be upon him), I simply scraped it off and he offered prayer, while putting that on.

(567) Al-Aswad and Hammām reported 'Ā'isha as saying: I used to scrape off the (drop of) semen from the garment of the Messenger of Allah (may peace be upon him).

(568) Qutaiba b. Sa'īd, Isḥāq b. Ibrāhīm, Ibn Abī 'Arūba, Abū Ma'shar, Abū Bakr b. Abū Shaiba, Manṣūr and Mughīra have all transmitted from Ibrāhīm, who transmitted it on the authority of 'Ā'isha's narration pertaining to the scraping off of the (drop) of semen from the garment of the Messenger of Allah (may peace be upon him) like the ḥadīth of Khālid on the authority of Abū Ma'shar.

(569) Hammām narrated the ḥadīth from 'Ā'isha like the (above-mentioned) traditions.

(570) 'Amr b. Maimūn said: I asked Sulaimān b. Yasār whether the semen that gets on to the garment of a person should be washed or not. He replied: 'Ā'isha told me: The Messenger of Allah (may peace be upon him) washed the semen, and then went out for prayer in that very garment and I saw the mark of washing on it.

(571) Abū Kuraib, Ibn al-Mubārak, Ibn Abū Zā'ida all of them narrated from 'Amr b. Maimūn with the same chain of transmitters. Ibn Abū Zā'ida narrated as was transmitted from Ibn Bishr that the Messenger of Allah (may peace be upon him) washed semen, and in the ḥadīth transmitted on the authority of Ibn Mubārak and 'Abdul Wāḥid the words are: "She ('Ā'isha) reported: I used to wash it from the garment of the Messenger of Allah (may peace be upon him)."

(572) 'Abdullah b. Shihāb al-Khaulānī reported: I stayed in the house of 'Ā'isha and had a wet dream (and perceived its effect on my garment), so (in the morning) I dipped both (the clothes) in water. This (act of mine) was watched by a maid-servant of 'Ā'isha and she informed her. She (Ḥaḍrat 'Ā'isha) sent me a message: What prompted you to act like this with your clothes? He (the narrator) said: I told that I saw

493. This law relates to the urine of the suckling babe (male) and not to the weaned child. Moreover, it does not apply to the urine of a female baby. In her case, the impurity is to be cleaned by washing. According to the Ḥanafite school of Fiqh, washing is essential in case of passing urine, whether it is of the female or the male child. This difference of opinion is based upon the verb نضح (naḍaḥa) which implies both sprinkling and washing. So far as the clause لم يغسل is concerned, according to Imām Abū Ḥanīfa, it simply tells that one should not lay too much stress on washing it.

in a dream what a sleeper sees. She said: Did you find (any mark of the fluid) on your clothes? I said: No. She said: Had you found anything you should have washed it. In case I found that (semen) on the garment of the Messenger of Allah (may peace be upon him) dried up, I scraped it off with my nails.[494]

Chapter CXVII

THE IMPURITY OF THE BLOOD OF MENSES AND ITS WASHING

(573) Asmā' (daughter of Abū Bakr) reported: A woman came to the Apostle of Allah (may peace be upon him) and said: What should one do if the blood of menses smears the garment of one amongst us? He (the Holy Prophet) replied: She should scrape it, then rub it with water, then pour water over it and then offer prayer in it.

(574) This tradition is narrated by Abū Kuraib, Ibn Numair, Abū Ṭāhir, Ibn Wahb, Yaḥyā b. 'Abdullah b. Sālim, Mālik b. Anas, 'Amr b. Ḥārith on the authority of Hishām b. 'Urwa, with the same chain of transmitters like one transmitted by Yaḥyā b. Sa'id like the above-mentioned.

Chapter CXVIII

PROOF OF THE IMPURITY OF URINE AND THAT IT IS OBLIGATORY TO SAFEGUARD ONESELF FROM IT

(575) Ibn 'Abbās reported: The Messenger of Allah (may peace be upon him) happened to pass by two graves and said: They (their occupants) are being tormented, but they are not tormented for a grievous sin. One of them carried tales and the other did not keep himself safe from being defiled by urine.[495] He then called for a fresh

494. There is a difference of opinion amongst the jurists whether the semen is impure or clean. Imām Sufyān Thaurī, Aḥmad, Isḥāq, and Shāfi'ī take it to be clean, whereas Imām Abū Ḥanīfa, Imām Mālik, and Shāh Walīullāh consider it to be unclean. The opinion of the first group of the jurists rests on the ground that had it been clean, its mere scraping off from the garment would not have made it clean. The second group derives its argument from the fact that its washing away or scraping from the garment is a clear proof of the fact that it is unclean. Had it not been so, there would have been no need at all for removing it from the garment.

It should also be remembered that in case of dry marks of semen, scraping can make the garment clean and fit for prayer, but it is preferable to wash it.

This tradition also sheds a good deal of light how the mothers of the faithful guided their spiritual posterity in all matters pertaining to religion. They, like affectionate mothers, taught their sons even the elementary rules of personal cleanliness and purity.

495. These two sins are such that a man commits them unconsciously. They are indicative of the carelessness on the part of a man: the first one is carelessness in speech and the second one shows the carelessness of action. The ḥadīth stresses that one should be very careful about the words that one utters and should realise that their expression leads to hardship of this world and torments in the grave,

twig and split it into two parts, and planted them on each grave[496] and then said: Perhaps, their punishment may be mitigated as long as these twigs remain fresh.

(576) This ḥadīth is transmitted from A'mash by Aḥmad b. Yūsuf al-Azdī, Mu'allā b. Asad, 'Abd al-Wāḥid, Sulaimān with the same chain of transmitters but for the words: "The other did not keep himself safe from being defiled by urine."[497]

496. This act of the Holy Prophet reveals that a man who is dead retains in some respect relations with those who survive him. They can be a source of service and benefit to him, if they ask forgiveness for him from the Lord and do acts of piety. It has been inferred from this tradition that the reciting of the Holy Qur'ān, giving of alms and charity and supplication for the soul of the dead can be beneficial to him and can alleviate his sufferings in the grave, in case he dies as a Muslim.

497. In one case the phrase is عن البول ('ani'l-baul) and in the second case it is من البول (min al-baul), but there is no change in the meaning, as both عن and من are translated with the word "from" in English. One can see the utmost care which has been so zealously observed in transmitting the traditions.

KITAB AL-HAID[498] (Menstruation)

Chapter CXIX

LYING WITH ONE IN MENSTRUATION ABOVE THE WAIST-WRAPPER

(577) 'Ā'isha reported : When anyone amongst us (amongst the wives of the Holy Prophet) menstruated, the Messenger of Allah (may peace be upon him) asked her to tie a waist-wrapper over her (body) and then embraced her.[499]

(578) 'Ā'isha reported : When anyone amongst us was menstruating the Messenger of Allah (may peace be upon him) asked her to tie waist-wrapper during the time when the menstrual blood profusely flowed and then embraced her ; and she ('Ā'isha) observed: And who amongst you can have control over his desires as the Messenger of Allah (may peace be upon him) had over his desires.[500]

(579) Maimūna (the wife of the Holy Prophet) reported : The Messenger of Allah (may peace be upon him) contacted and embraced his wives over the waist-wrapper when they were menstruating.

(580) Kuraib, the freed slave of Ibn 'Abbās, reported : I heard it from Maimūna, the wife of the Apostle of Allah (may peace be upon him) : The Messenger of Allah (may peace be upon him) used to lie with me when I menstruated, and there was a cloth between me and him.

(581) Umm Salama reported : While I was lying with the Messenger of Allah (may peace be upon him) in a bed cover I menstruated, so I slipped away and I took up the clothes (which I wore) in menses. Upon this the Messenger of Allah (may peace be upon him) said : Have you menstruated? I said : Yes. He called me and I lay down

498. The menstrual discharge is looked upon as pollution in many religions and, among the Hindus and the Jews, the woman who has her courses on is segregated. Islam does not subscribe to their views. It looks upon menses as an impurity which does not make the whole body of the woman polluted. Sexual intercourse is made unlawful during these days, but lying with one's wife, kissing and embracing her, eating and drinking with her are permitted. There is no idea of segregation on this account in Islam.

499. This tradition has been the target of worst criticism by the hostile critics of the Ḥadīth. They assert that it contravenes the teaching of the Qur'ān (ii. 222), in which it has been commanded to keep aloof from women during menstrual period. But these critics little realise that it is the sexual intercourse with the menstruating women which is prohibited. The ḥadīth gives no indication that the Holy Prophet acted against this injunction of the Qur'ān. The very wording that he ordered to tie a waist-wrapper on the lower part of her body gives a clear indication that the Holy Prophet did not have sexual intercourse with his wives during this period of menstrual discharge ; he simply embraced them. The verb يباشره (yubāshira) does not necessarily mean sexual intercourse. It denotes to have a contact, to touch (Lane's *Arabic-English Lexicon*).

500. This observation of Ḥaḍrat 'Ā'isha leads to the conclusion that a young man who cannot exercise proper restraint on his sexual lust should refrain from doing such an act.

with him in the bed cover. (And she further) said that she and the Messenger of Allah used to take bath from the same vessel after sexual intercourse.[501]

Chapter CXX

THE MENSTRUATING WOMAN IS PERMITTED TO WASH THE HEAD OF HER HUSBAND, COMB HIS HAIR, AND HER LEFT-OVER IS CLEAN, AND ONE IS PERMITTED TO RECLINE IN HER LAP AND RECITE THE QUR'ĀN

(582) It is reported from 'Ā'isha that she observed : When the Messenger of Allah (may peace be upon him) was in I'tikāf,[502] he inclined his head towards me and I combed[503] his hair, and he did not enter the house but for the natural calls (for relieving himself).

(583) 'Amra daughter of 'Abd al-Raḥmān reported : 'Ā'isha, wife of the Apostle of Allah (may peace be upon him) observed : When I was (in I'tikāf), I entered the house for the call of nature, and while passing I inquired after the health of the sick (in the family), and when the Messenger of Allah (may peace be upon him) was (in I'tikāf), he put out his head towards me, while he himself was in the mosque, and I combed his hair ; and he did not enter the house except for the call of nature so long as he was in I'tikāf ; and Ibn Rumḥ stated : As long as they (the Prophet and his wives) were among the observers of I'tikāf.

(584) 'Ā'isha, the wife of the Apostle (may peace be upon him), reported : The Messenger of Allah (may peace be upon him) put out from the mosque[504] his head for me as he was in I'tikāf, and I washed it in the state that I was menstruating.

(585) 'Urwa reported it from 'Ā'isha that she observed : The Messenger of Allah (may peace be upon him) inclined his head towards me (from the mosque) while I was in my apartment and I combed it in a state of menstruation.

(586) Al-Aswad narrated it from 'Ā'isha that she observed : I used to wash the head of the Messenger of Allah (may peace be upon him), while I was in a state of menstruation.

501. What it implies is that sexual intercourse does not physically defile a man. The original word is *Junub* from *Janb* meaning a side. To call this a state of pollution or defilement is not correct. In Islam there is no idea of pollution around sex as found in Christianity and other religions. In a technical sense it means one who is under the obligation to take a full bath. The connection with the root meaning is that such a man remains away from prayer and recitation of the Holy Qur'ān.

502. This word is derived from *'akafa 'alaihi,* meaning he kept, or clave to it constantly, or perseveringly, and I'tikāf means literally to stay in a place ; technically, it is staying in a mosque for a certain number of days, especially the last ten days of the month of Ramaḍān.

503. The menstruating woman is not allowed to enter the mosque, but she is not to be segregated from the family. She is permitted to have contacts with the members of the household and participate in all the household activities.

504. The dwelling place of the Holy Prophet was adjacent to the mosque, and he could easily put out his head and get it combed and washed by his wives.

(587) 'Ā'isha reported : The Messenger of Allah (may peace be upon him) said to me : Get me the mat from the mosque. I said : I am menstruating. Upon this he remarked : Your menstruation is not in your hand.[505]

(588) 'Ā'isha reported : The Messenger of Allah (may peace be upon him) ordered me that I should get him the mat from the mosque. I said : I am menstruating. He (the Holy Prophet) said : Do get me that, for menstruation is not in your hand.

(589) Abū Huraira reported : While the Messenger of Allah (may peace be upon him) was in the mosque, he said : O 'Ā'isha, get me that garment. She said : I am menstruating. Upon this he remarked : Your menstruation is not in your hand, and she, therefore, got him that.

(590) 'Ā'isha reported : I would drink when I was menstruating, then I would hand it (the vessel) to the Apostle (may peace be upon him) and he would put his mouth where mine had been, and drink, and I would eat flesh from a bone when I was menstruating, then hand it over to the Apostle (may peace be upon him) and he would put his mouth where mine had been. Zuhair made no mention of (the Holy Prophet's) drinking.

(591) 'Ā'isha reported : The Messenger of Allah (may peace be upon him) would recline in my lap when I was menstruating, and recite the Qur'ān.

(592) Thābit narrated it from Anas : Among the Jews, when a woman menstruated, they did not dine with her, nor did they live with them in their houses ; so the Companions of the Apostle (may peace be upon him) asked the Apostle (may peace be upon him), and Allah, the Exalted revealed : "And they ask you about menstruation ; say it is a pollution, so keep away from woman during menstruation" to the end (Qur'ān, ii. 222). The Messenger of Allah (may peace be upon him) said : Do everything[506] except intercourse.[507] The Jews heard of that and said : This man does not

505. *Mahiḍ* (محيض), menstruation which has been described in the Qur'ān as اذىً (pollution), is a noun of place (*momina loci*). It is, therefore, the female organ which secretes the blood of menstruation that is polluted and not the whole of woman's body. If women are not permitted to enter the mosque during this period, it is not because they are defiled or polluted but due to the reason that the drops of blood may fall in the sacred place.

506. Compare the attitude of Islam towards the menstruating woman with that of Biblical regulations : " . . . she shall be put apart seven days : and whosoever toucheth her shall be unclean until the even. And every thing that she lieth upon in her separation shall be unclean : every thing also that she sitteth upon shall be unclean. And whosoever toucheth her shall wash his clothes, and bath himself in water, and be unclean until the even. . . . And if any man lie with her at all, and her flowers be upon him, he shall be unclean seven days ; and all the bed whereon he lieth shall be unclean" (Leviticus 15, 19-24).

More onerous still are the laws prescribed by the Jewish doctors. "According to them woman must reckon seven days after the termination of the period. If, then, this lasts seven days, she cannot become pure until the fifteenth day. Purification, furthermore, can be gained only by a ritual bath : and until the woman has taken this, she remains unclean. In addition to all this, a woman who does not menstruate regularly is unclean for a certain time before she becomes aware that the period has begun and objects which she touches are defiled" (*The Jewish Encyclopaedia*, IX, p. 301).

507. The prohibition of sexual intercourse with a menstruating woman is justified on medical and hygienic grounds. According to a well-known authority, severe menorrhagia, perimetritic [illegible] tion, and parametritic inflammations have been observed to follow such indiscretion ([illegible] (Kisch, *Sexual Life of Women*, p. 173).

want to leave anything we do without opposing us in it. Usaid b. Ḥuḍair and 'Abbād b. Bishr came and said: Messenger of Allah, the Jews say such and such thing. We should not have, therefore, any contact[508] with them (as the Jews do). The face of the Messenger of Allah (may peace be upon him) underwent such a change that we thought he was angry with them, but when they went out, they happened to receive a gift of milk which was sent to the Apostle of Allah (may peace be upon him). He (the Holy Prophet) called for them and gave them drink, whereby they knew that he was not angry with them.

Chapter CXXI

ON AL-MADHĪ[509]

(593) 'Alī reported: I was one whose prostatic fluid flowed readily and I was ashamed to ask the Apostle (may peace be upon him) about it, because of the position of his daughter.[510] I, therefore, asked Miqdād b. al-Asad and he inquired of him (the Holy Prophet). He (the Holy Prophet) said: He should wash his male organ and perform ablution.

(594) 'Alī reported: I felt shy of asking about prostatic fluid from the Apostle (may peace be upon him) because of Fāṭimah. I, therefore, asked al-Miqdād (to ask on my behalf) and he asked. He (the Holy Prophet) said: Ablution is obligatory in such a case.

(595) Ibn 'Abbās reported it from 'Alī: We sent al-Miqdād b. al-Aswad to the Messenger of Allah (may peace be upon him) to ask him what must be done about prostatic fluid which flows from (the private part of) a person. The Messenger of Allah (may peace be upon him) said: Perform ablution and wash your sexual organ.

508. In one version it is: فلا تجامعهن, i.e. you should not have contact with them (as the Jews desire). The colour of the Holy Prophet underwent a change because these two noble Companions seemed to be influenced by the taunts of the Jews and showed an inclination to act according to their wishes so that their clamour might be pacified. But in most of the texts the words are افلا نجامعهن: "then why may we not have sexual intercourse with them, so that we should oppose Jews in all details?" The colour of the Holy Prophet changed because these words of theirs showed that they had not fully appreciated the true nature and significance of Islam. The teachings of Islam are divinely inspired and the Lord in His Infinite Wisdom has vouchsafed them to humanity to lead a righteous and pious life. These are far above the customs and practices of people and the man-made laws. They are meant neither to oppose nor to contradict any individual or community, nor are they meant to support and substantiate the views of any group. They are poised, based on Divine Knowledge and Mercy and can, therefore, under no circumstances, be changed or altered by the pressure of worldly considerations or public opinion. Here the point which the Holy Prophet wanted to make them realise was that when sexual intercourse with a menstruating woman had been prohibited in the Qur'ān (ii. 222), how these believers could dare suggest otherwise at the sarcastic remarks and taunts of the Jews. This attitude of the Holy Prophet clearly shows that the teachings of the Qur'ān and the Sunnah are derived from no human agency and these are all inspired by God and, therefore, transcend all material or worldly considerations.

509. There is a difference between the Arabic words *Madhi* (prostatic fluid) and *Mani* (semen). The former comes out in watery form before copulation and the latter comes out after copulation in thick form. In case of the former, ablution is necessary and in case of the latter bath is obligatory.

510. 'Alī (may Allah be pleased with him) was the son-in-law of the Holy Prophet, and he, therefore, felt shy of asking anything pertaining to sexual problems directly from his father-in-law.

Chapter CXXII

WASHING OF FACE AND HANDS AFTER WAKING UP FROM SLEEP

(596) Ibn 'Abbās reported: The Apostle (may peace be upon him) woke up at night, relieved himself, and then washed his face and hands and then again slept.

Chapter CXXIII

IT IS PERMISSIBLE FOR A PERSON TO SLEEP AFTER SEXUAL INTERCOURSE (WITHOUT A BATH) AND THE DESIRABILITY OF ABLUTION FOR HIM, AND WASHING OF THE SEXUAL ORGAN AS HE INTENDS TO EAT, DRINK, OR SLEEP OR COHABIT

(597) 'Ā'isha reported: Whenever the Messenger of Allah (may peace be upon him) intended to sleep after having sexual intercourse, he performed ablution as for the prayer before going to sleep.[511]

(598) 'Ā'isha reported: Whenever the Messenger of Allah (may peace be upon him) had sexual intercourse and intended to eat or sleep, he performed the ablution of prayer.

(599) This ḥadīth has been transmitted by Shu'ba with the same chain of transmitters. Ibn al-Muthannā said in his narration: Al-Ḥakam narrated to us who heard from Ibrāhīm narrating that.

(600) Ibn 'Umar reported: 'Umar said: Is one amongst us permitted to sleep in a state of impurity (i.e. after having sexual intercourse)? He (the Holy Prophet) said: Yes, after performing ablution.

(601) Ibn 'Umar said: 'Umar asked the verdict of the Sharī'ah from the Apostle (may peace be upon him) thus: Is it permissible for any one of us to sleep in a state of impurity? He (the Holy Prophet) said: Yes, he must perform ablution and then sleep and take a bath when he desires.

(602) Ibn 'Umar reported: 'Umar b. al-Khaṭṭāb said to the Messenger of Allah (may peace be upon him) that he became Junbi during the night. The Messenger of Allah (may peace be upon him) said to him: Perform ablution, wash your sexual organ and then go to sleep.

(603) 'Abdullah b. Abu'l-Qais reported: I asked 'Ā'isha about the Witr (prayer) of the Messenger of Allah (may peace be upon him) and made mention of a ḥadīth, then I said: What did he do after having sexual intercourse? Did he take a bath before sleeping or did he sleep before taking a bath? She said: He did all these. Sometimes he took a bath and then slept, and sometimes he performed ablution only and went to sleep. I (the narrator) said: Praise be to Allah Who has made things easy (for human beings).

511. This was done so that the soul of man may be transported from the urges of the flesh to its original spiritual domain.

(604) This ḥadīth has been transmitted with the same chain of transmitters from Mu'āwyia b. Ṣāliḥ by Zuhair b. Ḥarb, 'Abd al-Raḥmān b. Mahdī, Hārūn b. Sa'īd al-'Ailī and Ibn Wahb.

(605) Abū Sa'īd al-Khudrī reported: The Messenger of Allah (may peace be upon him) said: When anyone amongst you has sexual intercourse with his wife and then he intends to repeat it, he should perform ablution.[512] In the ḥadīth transmitted by Abū Bakr (the words are): "Between the two (acts) there should be an ablution," or he (the narrator) said: "Then he intended that it should be repeated."[513]

(606) Anas reported: The Messenger of Allah (may peace be upon him) used to have sexual intercourse with his wives with a single bath.[514]

Chapter CXXIV

BATHING IS OBLIGATORY FOR A WOMAN AFTER EXPERIENCING ORGASM IN DREAM

(607) Anas b. Mālik reported: Umm Sulaim who was the grandmother of Isḥāq came to the Messenger of Allah (may peace be upon him) in the presence of 'Ā'isha and said to him: Messenger of Allah, in case a woman sees what a man sees in dream and she experiences in dream what a man experiences (i.e. experiences orgasm)? Upon this 'Ā'isha remarked: O Umm Sulaim, you brought humiliation to women;[515] may your right hand be covered with dust.[516] He (the Holy Prophet) said to 'Ā'isha: Let your hand be covered with dust,[517] and (addressing Umm Sulaim) said: Well, O Umm Sulaim, she should take a bath if she sees that (i.e. she experiences orgasm in dream).

512. It is one of the greatest contributions of Islam to human morality that it has illuminated the carnal desire of man with the glow of spirituality and religious piety. The idea behind ablution is that even sexual intercourse (a sensual act) should be performed with the decency of a spiritual life and not like beasts and animals.

513. Mark how meticulously have the words of the Holy Prophet been preserved by the Muḥaddithīn. The verbs. يعود (ya'ūd) and يعادو (yu'ādū) belong to the same root. The first one belongs to the category of فعل (fa'ala) which denotes an act that immediately affects an object, while the second one falls under فاعل (fā'ala) which expresses the effort or attempt to perform that act upon the object, in which case the idea of reciprocity is added when the effort is necessarily or accidentally a mutual one.

514. The Holy Prophet (may peace be upon him) did not take a bath after every intercourse; he simply performed ablution and took a bath at the end.

515. Sexual dream, i.e. experiencing of orgasm, is not so common with woman and, therefore, 'Ā'isha did not approve of its expression before the Apostle of Allah. What actually happens with women is that, because of vaginal secretions from bartholins' glands or due to "sweating reaction" occurring on the walls of vagina their clothes are soiled (Ruth and Edward Brecher, ed., *An Analysis of Human Sexual Response*, p. 24).

516. This is not a kind of curse but a common expression of disapproval in Arabic.

517. The Holy Prophet did not approve of the attitude of 'Ā'isha in discouraging Umm Sulaim from asking him a matter pertaining to cleanliness. This was one of the problems that confronted women and guidance was genuinely needed at every step. It was, therefore, their duty to seek guidance from the Apostle of Allah (may peace be upon him), because if his guidance were not sought there was none else to explain to them these matters with the help of Divine Knowledge.

(608) Anas b. Mālik reported that Umm Sulaim narrated it that she asked the Apostle of Allah (may peace be upon him) about a woman who sees in a dream what a man sees (sexual dream). The Messenger of Allah (may peace be upon him) said: In case a woman sees that, she must take a bath Umm Sulaim said: I was bashful on account of that and said: Does it happen? Upon this the Apostle of Allah (may peace be upon him) said: Yes (it does happen), otherwise how can (a child) resemble her? Man's discharge (i.e. sperm) is thick and white and the discharge of woman is thin and yellow; so the resemblance comes from the one whose genes prevail or dominate.[518]

(609) Anas b. Mālik reported: A woman asked the Messenger of Allah (may peace be upon him) about a woman who sees in her dream what a man sees in his dream (sexual dream). He (the Holy Prophet) said: If she experiences what a man experiences, she should take a bath.

(610) Umm Salama reported: Umm Sulaim went to the Apostle of Allah (may peace be upon him) and said: Apostle of Allah, Allah is not ashamed of the truth.[519] Is bathing necessary for a woman when she has a sexual dream? Upon this the Messenger of Allah (may peace be upon him) said: Yes, when she sees the liquid (vaginal secretion).[520] Umm Salama said: Messenger of Allah, does a woman have

518. Various explanations of this statement have been given by writers, old and new. We quote two. One given by Mr Asad: "The Prophet's answer raises the very complex problem of heredity. Modern science is not yet decided as to the exact connection between the details of a sexual act and characteristics of the offspring resulting therefrom. . . . It has certainly an indirect import on the conception, for it is a physiological expression of the degree or quality of the woman's emotion during the act; and it goes without saying that in a highly developed organism like the human body emotional conditions must, to a great extent, influence the reproductive processes. Moreover, it is quite possible that the popular expression *ma ar-rajul* and *ma al-mar'ah* do not refer, in this context, merely to the ejaculation of the sperm on the part of the man and the vaginal secretion of the woman, but to the gemetic processes in entirety. This brings us considerably nearer to an understanding of the problem. . . . The above utterance of the Holy Prophet would thus imply that the sex of the offspring is determined by the greater vigour of either of the parents at the time of mating. This idea is supported by one of the most influential modern theories in this domain, namely, that propounded by the biologist Girou, who connects the sex of the offspring with that of the more vigorous parent" (*Ṣaḥiḥ al-Bukhārī's* translation, Vol. V, 4th instalment, p. 242).

The recent researches in Genetics are embodied in the following words: "Experiments with plants and animals, and particularly Goldschmidt's experiment, on the gypsy moth Lymantria, have shown that the sex of an individual is not the result of either pure male or pure female tendencies. Rather, in the development of either sex, both male and female determiners are at work; stronger male to the female ones in the origin of males and reverse in the origin of females. We may assume that some 'balance theory' of sex holds for man. Perhaps human male has genes for maleness not only in the y-chromosome but also in the x-chromosome, or the autosomes, or in both of these; and, in addition, genes for femaleness in x-chromosome, or autosomes, or in both. He is the male because male determiners 'outweigh' the female ones. Conversely, although a human female presumably has genes for both maleness and femaleness, in the absence of strong male-determining factor carried by the y-chromosome, the female determiners outweigh the male ones" (Curt Stern, *Principles of Human Genetics*, p. 401).

519. Cleanliness is a part of faith and, therefore, Allah teaches all those things which we need in matters of cleanliness. A man or a woman should not feel shy in asking questions pertaining to sex, and Allah is not bashful in giving their replies, since sexual urge is a part of human nature for the perpetuation of the race.

520. Woman feels the sexual urge like her male counterpart and it is a result of this urge that there is mating between them. It should also be remembered that in case of orgasm of woman, the

sexual dream? He (the Holy Prophet) said: Let your hand be covered with dust, in what way does her child resemble her?

(611) This ḥadīth with the same sense (as narrated above) has been transmitted from Hishām b. 'Urwa with the same chain of narrators but with this addition that she (Umm Salama) said: "You humiliated the women."

(612) 'Ā'isha the wife of the Apostle (may peace be upon him) narrated: Umm Sulaim, the mother of Banī Abū Ṭalḥa, came to the Messenger of Allah (may peace be upon him), and a ḥadīth (like that) narrated by Hishām was narrated but for these words: " 'Ā'isha said: I expressed disapproval to her, saying! Does a woman see a sexual dream?"

(613) It is reported on the authority of 'Ā'isha that a woman came to the Messenger of Allah (may peace be upon him) and inquired: Should a woman wash herself when she sees a sexual dream and sees (the marks) of liquid? He (the Holy Prophet) said: Yes. 'Ā'isha said to her: May your hand be covered with dust and injured. She narrated: The Messenger of Allah (may peace be upon him) said: Leave her alone. In what way does the child resemble her but for the fact that when the genes contributed by woman prevail upon those of man, the child resembles the maternal family, and when the genes of man prevail upon those of woman the child resembles the paternal family.[521]

fluid may not necessarily flow out of her private part.

Kinsey and others write: "Because the male may find tangible evidence that he has ejaculated during sleep, his record may be somewhat more accurate than the females; but vaginal secretions often bear similar testimony to the female's arousal and/or orgasm during sleep. As with the male, the female is often awakened by the muscular spasms or convulsions which follow her orgasms. Consequently, the record seems as trustworthy as her memory can make it" (*Sexual Behaviour in the Human Female*, p. 192).

521. The words of the Holy Prophet have become more clear from the study of modern genetics. A.M. Winchester writes: "When meiosis occurs in children and grand children are born, we find that each grand-child will be expected to receive about one-fourth of its genes from each of the four grand-parents. Here, however, the number is subject to considerable flexibility. While a child receives exactly half of its chromosomes from each parent there is an independent assortment during the meiosis in the child; consequently, the number of chromosomes from the father (paternal) and the number from the mother (maternal) that go into any one gamete will vary according to chance arrangement of the chromosomes in meiosis. Thus a particular child could inherit considerably more from the paternal grandfather than from the maternal grandmother" (*Heredity, An Introduction to Genetics*, p. 38).

The main purpose of the Holy Prophet in talking of the sexual urge in woman and her contribution to the production of the child was to dispel the wrong notion from the minds of the people that woman makes no contribution in this process, and she acts merely as a ' receiver". This false notion had taken such a firm hold on the minds of people that it was long after the invention of microscope that this could be removed. The Holy Prophet (may peace be upon him) emphasised that the procreating substance is contributed not only by male but by female also. As a proof of this he said that the child sometimes resembles the father and sometimes the mother. So he dispelled this misconception that woman is just a "necessary site". In this way the Holy Prophet (may peace be upon him) enhanced the status of woman as a co-sharer in the production of a child.

Another misconception under which the people, especially the Westerners, had been labouring up to the Victorian times was that they conceived woman to be completely devoid of sexual desires. Kenneth Walker says: "A century ago it was thought that women have no sexual needs" (*The Physiology of Sex*, p. 74).

Chapter CXXV

THE CHARACTERISTIC OF THE MALE REPRODUCTIVE SUBSTANCE (SPERM) AND FEMALE REPRODUCTIVE SUBSTANCE (OVUM), AND THAT THE OFFSPRING IS PRODUCED BY THE CONTRIBUTION OF BOTH

(614) Thaubān, the freed slave of the Messenger of Allah (may peace be upon him), said: While I was standing beside the Messenger of Allah (may peace be upon him) one of the rabbis of the Jews came and said: Peace be upon you, O Muḥammad. I pushed him back[522] with a push that he was going to fall. Upon this he said: Why do you push me? I said: Why don't you say: O Messenger of Allah? The Jew said: We call him by the name by which he was named by his family. The Messenger of Allah (may peace be upon him) said: My name is Muḥammad with which I was named by my family. The Jew said: I have come to ask you (something). The Messenger of Allah (may peace be upon him) said: Should that thing be of any benefit to you, if I tell you that?[523] He (the Jew) said: I will lend my ears to it. The Messenger of Allah (may peace be upon him) drew a line[524] with the help of the stick that he had with him and then said: Ask (whatever you like). Thereupon the Jew said: Where would the human beings be on the Day[525] when the earth would change into another earth and the heavens too (would change into other heavens)? The Messenger of Allah (may peace be upon him) said: They would be in darkness beside the Bridge.[526] He (the Jew) again said: Who amongst people would be the first to cross (this bridge)? He said: They would be the poor[527] amongst the refugees. The Jew said: What would constitute their breakfast when they would enter Paradise? He (the Holy Prophet) replied: A

The Holy Prophet repudiated it and made it clear that women like their male counterparts have also the sexual urge and it is the duty of the husband to satisfy it with a sense of responsibility like all other duties of married life. Woman can legitimately claim this right and if a husband is negligent or wilfully avoids it, it can be referred to the court. It is one of the contributions of Islam that it has provided Divine Guidance even in matters pertaining to sex, a sphere which has been woefully neglected by other religions, and this negligence on their part has led to so many sexual and moral evils. Kenneth Walker rightly laments: "Unfortunately the great spiritual leaders of mankind, Christ and Buddha, spoke little about sex, and what they said is often difficult to interpret" (ibid., p. 93).

522. The Jews were in the habit of using the words of ambiguous import for the Holy Prophet, and the Muslims were, therefore, anxious that the Holy Prophet must be addressed as the Messenger of Allah. It was for evil intention of the Jews that the Companion pushed him, but the Holy Prophet came to his rescue and permitted him to address him by his name.

523. The Holy Prophet (may peace be upon him) did not approve of useless discussions. He was always ready to explain things which seemed to be useful and beneficial for man.

524. It is one of those acts which people do for the concentration of their minds. It is a sort of mental preparation.

525. Doomsday.

526. Bridge where the entrants of Paradise would cross into that heavenly abode.

527. Poor in the sense that they had sacrificed all material possessions for the sake of Allah and proved by their deed that the love of Allah and that of His Apostle (may peace be upon him) is dearer to them than worldly riches.

caul of the fish-liver.[528] He (the Jew) said: What would be their food after this? He (the Holy Prophet) said: A bullock[529] which was fed in the different quarters of Paradise would be slaughtered for them. He (the Jew) said: What would be their drink? He (the Holy Prophet) said: They would be given drink from the fountain which is named *Salsabīl*. He (the Jew) said: I have come to ask you about a thing which no one amongst the people on the earth knows except an apostle or one or two men besides him. He (the Holy Prophet) said: Would it benefit you if I tell you that? He (the Jew) said: I would lend ears to that. He then said: I have come to ask you about the child. He (the Holy Prophet) said: The reproductive substance of man is white and that of woman (i.e. ovum central portion) yellow,[530] and when they have sexual intercourse and the male's substance (chromosomes and genes) prevails upon the female's substance (chromosomes and genes), it is the male child that is created by Allah's Decree, and when the substance of the female prevails upon the substance contributed by the male, a female child is formed by the Decree of Allah. The Jew said: What you have said is true; verily you are an Apostle. He then returned and went away. The Messenger of Allah (may peace be upon him) said: He asked me about such and such things of which I have had no knowledge till Allah gave me that.

(615) This tradition has been narrated by Mu'āwyia b. Salām with the same chain of transmitters except for the words: "I was sitting beside the Messenger of Allah" and some other minor alterations.

Chapter CXXVI

BATHING AFTER SEXUAL INTERCOURSE OR SEMINAL EMISSION

(616) 'Ā'isha reported: When Allah's Messenger (may peace be upon him) bathed because of sexual intercourse, he first washed his hands; he then poured water with his right hand on his left hand and washed his private parts. He then performed ablution

528. Liver is the most tasty and nutritive part of the animal's body. "Many commentators have been perplexed by this strange description of 'the food of Paradise' by the Prophet. In reality, however, the above picturesque expression is not difficult to understand. We see here one more instance of the Prophet's genius for conveying, by means of easily comprehensible metaphors and parables, abstract ideas to the people of widely divergent intellectual levels or of habits of thinking different from that of the speaker. The Jews of Medina appear to have had a particular predilection for fish, and fish-liver was regarded by them as the rarest of the delicacies If we remember in addition, that 'the caul of the liver' (not particularly fish-liver, to be sure) is amongst those parts of the meat of sacrificial animals, which, according to the elaborate instructions given in the Bible, were to be used for a 'burnt offering,' a sweet savour before the Lord (cf. Exodus XXIX, 22-25), and we can easily imagine that for a Jew of that period there could have been hardly a more appropriate symbol of the sublime enjoyment provided by the food of the Paradise, than that contained in the Prophet's answer to 'Abd Allah Ibn Salam" (Asad, op. cit., pp. 241-2).

529. Exactly is the case of the bullock as that of the caul of fish-liver. For the Jews it is one of the finest sacrificial animals whose sacrifice would please the Lord (Exdous, xxix, 10-13).

530. The central part of the ovum which plays its part in conception is yellow in colour. According to *Tāj-ul-'Urūs*, *mani* is so called because it has the capacity to produce a new life. So the yellow central part of ovum can be called *mani* according to this definition.

as is done for prayer. He then took some water and put his fingers and moved them through the roots of his hair. And when he found that these had been properly moistened, then poured three handfuls on his head and then poured water over his body and subsequently washed his feet.

(617) This ḥadīth is narrated by Abū Kuraib, Ibn Numair and others, all on the authority of Hishām with the same chain of transmitters, but in their narration these words are not there : "washed his feet."

(618) Hishām narrated it from his father, who narrated it on the authority of 'Ā'isha that when the Apostle (may peace be upon him) took a bath because of sexual intercourse, he first washed the palms of his hands three times, and then the whole ḥadīth was transmitted like that based on the authority of Abū Mu'āwyia, but no mention is made of the washing of feet.

(619) 'Urwa has narrated it on the authority of 'Ā'isha that when Allah's Messenger (may peace be upon him) took a bath because of sexual intercourse, he first washed his hands before dipping one of them into the basin, and then performed ablution as is done for prayer.

(620) Ibn 'Abbās reported it on the authority of Maimūna, his mother's sister, that she said : I placed water near the Messenger of Allah (may peace be upon him) to take a bath because of sexual intercourse. He washed the palms of his hands twice or thrice and then put his hand in the basin and poured water over his private parts and washed them with his left hand. He then struck his hand against the earth and rubbed it with force and then performed ablution for the prayer and then poured three handfuls of water on his head and then washed his whole body after which he moved aside from that place and washed his feet, and then I brought a towel (so that he may wipe his body), but he returned it.[531]

(621) This ḥadīth is narrated by A'mash with the same chain of transmitters, but in the ḥadīth narrated by Yaḥyā b. Yaḥyā and Abū Kuraib there is no mention of : "pouring of three handfuls of water on the head," and in the ḥadīth narrated by Wakī' all the features of ablution have been recorded : rinsing (of mouth), snuffing of water (in the nostrils) ; and in the ḥadīth transmitted by Abū Mu'āwyia, there is no mention of a towel.

(622) Ibn 'Abbās narrated it on the authority of Maimuna that the Apostle of Allah (may peace be upon him) was given a towel, but he did not rub (his body) with it, but he did like this with water, i.e. he shook it off.

(623) 'Ā'isha reported : When the Messenger of Allah (may peace be upon him) took a bath because of sexual intercourse, he called for a vessel and took a handful of water from it and first (washed) the right side of his head, then left, and then took a handful (of water) and poured it on his head.[532]

531. This returning of the towel does not imply complete forbiddance of its use but an indication that it is not a part of bath. One is permitted to wipe water from one's body with the help of one's hands, or with the help of a towel, and if in the hot weather one is inclined to keep one's body wet, one is allowed to do so. The Holy Prophet has, by his personal example, approved all these acts.

532. These traditions give an integrated view how the Holy Prophet took a bath because of sexual intercourse. The various steps are : He first washed his hand twice or thrice and then dipped his right hand in water and then washed the other one very well. He poured water over the left hand with the right hand and cleansed the private parts of the body. Afterwards he rubbed his left hand

Chapter CXXVII

THE QUANTITY OF WATER THAT IS DESIRABLE FOR A BATH BECAUSE OF SEXUAL INTERCOURSE, BATHING OF THE MALE AND FEMALE WITH ONE VESSEL IN THE SAME CONDITION AND WASHING OF ONE OF THEM WITH THE LEFT-OVER OF THE OTHER

(624) 'Ā'isha reported: The Messenger of Allah (may peace be upon him) washed himself with water from a vessel (measuring seven to eight seers) because of sexual intercourse.

(625) 'Ā'isha reported: The Messenger of Allah (may peace be upon him) took a bath from the vessel (which contained seven to eight seers, i.e. fifteen to sixteen pounds) of water. And I and he (the Holy Prophet) took bath from the same vessel.[533] And in the ḥadīth narrated by Sufyān the words are: "from one vessel". Qutaiba said: Al-Faraq is three Ṣā' (a cubic measuring of varying magnitude).

(626) Abū Salama[534] b. 'Abd al-Raḥmān reported: I along with the foster brother of 'Ā'isha went to her and he asked about the bath of the Apostle (may peace be upon him) because of sexual intercourse. She called for a vessel equal to a Ṣā' and she took a bath, and there was a curtain between us and her. She poured water on her head thrice and he (Abū Salama) said: The wives of the Apostle (may peace be upon him) collected [535] hair on their heads and these lopped up to ears[536] (and did not go beyond that).

against the earth and washed it properly so tha; no trace of impurity was left on it. He then performed ablution and paid special attention to the rinsing of the mouth and snuffing of water into his nostrils. He then moved his wet fingers in his beard and washed his hair so thoroughly that water reached their roots. He then poured water on the right side of his head and then on its left side and then washed his body properly. Lastly, he moved aside from the spot where he took the bath and washed his feet.

533. What the ḥadīth makes clear is that the left-over of the water is not impure and can make the body clean. If a male or a female uses water from a vessel and some part of it is left over, there is no harm in utilising it for the purification of the body povided the person taking bath does not sit in the tub.

534. Abū Salama was the foster son of Ḥaḍrat 'Ā'isha's sister Umm Kulthūm daughter of Abū Bakr (may Allah be pleased with all of them). 'Abdullah b. Yazīd was himself 'Ā'isha's foster brother. They were thus both *Maḥram* of Ḥaḍrat 'Ā'isha and she could uncover her face and head in their presence. There was a curtain hanging between her and his brother and nephew and they could see only the head of Ḥaḍrat 'Ā'isha.

535. Long hair were worn by the women of Arabia for the sake of grace. Qāḍī 'Iyāḍ is of the opinion that after the death of the Holy Prophet, his noble wives (may Allah be pleased with them) collected hair on the head and did not hang them down, since they did not feel any urge for adornment. Maulānā Shabbīr Aḥmad 'Uthmānī has explained this ḥadīth in the following words: In my opinion the ḥadīth explains that the wives of the Apostle (may peace be upon him) used to curtail their hanging hair and bind them on the backs of their heads or on the heads without making ringlets or tresses, with the result that their hair did not hang beyond their ears as is commonly done by old ladies of our time or by women while taking bath especially after washing the head. If the long hair is not twisted and is allowed to hang down, the water trickles down over the body (*Fatḥ-ul-Mulhim*, Vol. I, p. 472).

536. وفره (*wafra*) has different meanings. It may be hair collected together upon the head, or

(627) Salama b. 'Abd al-Raḥmān narrated it on the authority of 'Ā'isha that when the Messenger of Allah (may peace be upon him) took a bath, he started from the right hand and poured water over it and washed it, and then poured water on the impurity with the right hand and washed it away with the help of the left hand, and after having removed it, he poured water on his head. 'Ā'isha said: I and the Messenger of Allah (may peace be upon him) took a bath from the same vessel, after sexual intercourse.

(628) Ḥafṣa, daughter of 'Abd al-Raḥmān b. Abū Bakr, reported that 'Ā'isha narrated to her that she and the Apostle of Allah (may peace be upon him) took a bath from the same vessel which contained water equal to three Mudds[537] or thereabout.

(629) 'Ā'isha reported: I and the Messenger (may peace be upon him) took a bath from the same vessel and our hands alternated into it in the state that we had had sexual intercourse.[538]

(630) 'Ā'isha reported: I and the Messenger of Allah (may peace be upon him) took bath from one vessel which was placed between me and him and he would get ahead of me, so that I would say: Spare (some water for) me, spare (some water for) me; and she said that they had had sexual intercourse.

(631) Ibn 'Abbās said: Maimūna (the wife of the Holy Prophet) reported to me that she and the Apostle of Allah (may peace be upon him) took a bath from one vessel.

hair hanging down upon the ears, or hair extending to the lobes of the ears, or hair extending to the lobes of the ears (Lane's *Arabic-English Lexicon*).

537. *Mudd* (مد) is a standard of measurement which varies according to the place and circumstances. But it is generally equal to one bushel.

538. This ḥadīth and others like it have been the target of criticism by the hostile critics of the Ḥadīth, though there is nothing noxious in it. It is a simple act of purification. These critics deliberately conjure up before the minds of people the modern system of tub bath in the glaring light of bulbs and tubes, and then try to create an opinion that it is unworthy of the modesty and high sense of chastity of the Holy Prophet that such things should be attributed to him, and then jump to the conclusion that all the collections of aḥādīth are mere fabrications having no truth in them. The whole argument and the case on which it rests is fallacious and wrong. There are so many authentic aḥādīth which show that the Holy Prophet had a very keen sense of modesty.

Secondly, although the Holy Prophet and his wives, on occasions, took bath from one vessel, it had never been a tub bath wherein the couple sat together and washed themselves. What they did was that they took out water from one vessel and bathed separately.

Thirdly, the bathroom of the Holy Prophet was not illuminated with light so that his body and that of his pious wife could be visible to each other. He and his wives took bath before Tahajjud prayer, i.e. much before the dawn in pitch darkness, and, therefore, there was no question of their seeing the body of each other. The very words of the ḥadīth تختلف ايدينا فيه clearly indicate that their hands touched each other since they could not see them.

These critics ignore the conditions under which the Holy Prophet (may peace be upon him) and his pious wives (may Allah be pleased with them) lived, and resort to indiscriminate criticism. The fact is that there was no practice of taking bath, because of sexual intercourse, in broad daylight. Every Muslim got up for Tahajjud prayer and especially in the house of the Holy Prophet prayer, meditation and dhikr were the most common feature, and the whole family spent the latter part of the night in the remembrance of the Lord. The pious members of this sacred house, therefore, bathed themselves long before daybreak.

The point of importance here is that the left-over of the water is not defiled, even if it is used by a person who has had a sexual intercourse.

(632) Ibn 'Abbas reported that the Messenger of Allah (may peace be upon him) took a bath with the water left over by Maimūna.

(633) Zainab bint Umm Salama (the wife of the Holy Prophet) reported that Umm Salama and the Messenger of Allah (may peace be upon him) took bath from the same vessel.

(634) Anas reported that the Messenger of Allah (may peace be upon him) took a bath with five Makkuks[539] of water and performed ablution with one Makkuk. Ibn Muthannā has used the words five Makakiyya, and Ibn Mu'ādh narrated it from 'Abdullah b. 'Abdullah and he made no mention of Ibn Jabr.

(635) Anas said: The Apostle of Allah (may peace be upon him) performed ablution with one Mudd and took bath with a Ṣā' up to five Mudds.

(636) Safīna reported: The Messenger of Allah (may peace be upon him) took a bath with one Ṣā' of water because of sexual intercourse and performed ablution with one Mudd.

(637) Safīna reported that Abū Bakr, the Companion of the Messenger of Allah (may peace be upon him), observed: The Messenger of Allah (may peace be upon him) took a bath with one Ṣā' of water and performed ablution with one Mudd (of water); and in the ḥadīth narrated by Ibn Ḥujr the words are: One Mudd sufficed for his (Holy Prophet's) ablution. And Ibn Ḥujr said that (his Shaikh) Ismā'īl was much advanced in age, and it was because of this that he could not fully rely on him for this tradition.

Chapter CXXVIII

THE DESIRABILITY OF POURING WATER THRICE ON THE HEAD AND OTHER PARTS (OF THE BODY)

(638) Jubair b. Muṭ'im reported: The people contended amongst themselves in the presence of the Messenger of Allah (may peace be upon him) with regard to bathing. Some of them said: We wash our heads like this and this. Upon this the Messenger (may peace be upon him) said: As for me I pour three handfuls of water upon my head.

(639) Jubair b. Muṭ'im reported it from the Apostle of Allah (may peace be upon him) that a mention was made before him about bathing because of sexual intercourse and he said: I pour water over my head thrice.

(640) Jābir b. 'Abdullah reported: A delegation of the Thaqīf said to the Apostle of Allah (may peace be upon him): Our land is cold; what about our bathing then? He (the Holy Prophet) said: I pour water thrice over my head.[540]

(641) Ibn Sālim in his narration reported: "The delegation of the Thaqīf said: Messenger of Allah."[541]

(642) Jābir b. 'Abdullah reported: When the Messenger of Allah (may peace be upon him) took a bath because of sexual intercourse, he poured three handfuls of water

539. It is a plural of Makkuk and is equal to Mudd.

540. Pouring of water thrice would serve the purpose, and there is no need of using unnecessary water for bathing.

541. Mark how even the minutest details have been recorded by the Muḥaddithīn.

upon his head. Ḥasan b. Muḥammad said to him (the narrator): My hair is thick. Upon this Jābir observed. I said to him: O son of my brother, the hair of the Messenger of Allah (may peace be upon him) was thicker than your hair and these were more fine (than yours).

Chapter CXXIX

LAW OF SHARĪ'AH PERTAINING TO THE PLAITED HAIR OF THE WOMAN WHO TAKES A BATH

(643) Umm Salama reported: I said: Messenger of Allah, I am a woman who has closely plaited hair on my head; should I undo it for taking a bath, because of sexual intercourse? He (the Holy Prophet) said: No, it is enough for you to throw three handfuls of water on your head and then pour water over yourself, and you shall be purified.

(644) This ḥadīth has been narrated by 'Amr al-Nāqid, Yazīd b. Hārūn, 'Abd b. Ḥumaid, 'Abd al-Razzāq, Thaurī, Ayyūb b. Mūsā, with the same chain of transmitters. In ḥadīth narrated by 'Abd al-Razzāq there is a mention of the menstruation and of the sexual intercourse. The rest of the ḥadīth has been transmitted like that of Ibn 'Uyaina.

(645) This ḥadīth is narrated by the same chain of transmitters by Aḥmad al-Dārimī, Zakariyā b. 'Adī, Yazīd, i.e. Ibn Zurai', Rauḥ b. al-Qāsim, Ayyūb b. Mūsā with the same chain of transmitters, and there is a mention of these words: "Should I undo the plait and wash it, because of sexual intercourse?" and there is no mention of menstruation.

(646) 'Ubaid b. 'Umair reported: It was conveyed to 'Ā'isha that 'Abdullah b. 'Amr ordered the women to undo the (plaits) of hair on their heads. She said: How strange it is for Ibn 'Amr that he orders the women to undo the plaits of their head while taking a bath; why does he not order them to shave their heads? I and the Messenger of Allah (may peace be upon him) took bath from one vessel. I did no more than this that I poured three handfuls of water over my head.[542]

Chapter CXXX

THE DESIRABILITY OF USING MUSK AT THE SPOT OF BLOOD WHILE BATHING AFTER MENSTRUATION

(647) 'Ā'isha reported: A woman asked the Apostle of Allah (may peace be upon him) how to wash herself after menstruation. She mentioned that he taught her how to take bath and then told her to take a piece of cotton with musk and purify herself. She said: How should I purify myself with that? He (the Holy Prophet) said: Praise be to

542. According to Imām Nawawī, the order of 'Abdullah b. 'Amr was conditional in so far as the water did not reach the roots of the hair; if water could penetrate there, there was no need to undo the plaits, and there is also the possibility that 'Abdullah had not heard the aḥādīth of Umm Salama and 'Ā'isha (Allah be pleased with them) to this effect, or it would have been the result of his exceedingly high sense of purification.

Allah, purify yourself with it, and covered his face. Sufyān b. ʿUyaina gave a demonstration by covering his face (as the Holy Prophet had done). ʿĀ'isha reported: I dragged her to my side for I had understood what the Apostle of Allah (may peace be upon him) intended and, therefore, said: Apply this cotton with musk to the trace of blood. Ibn ʿUmar in his ḥadīth (has mentioned the words of ʿĀ'isha thus): Apply it to the marks of blood.

(648) ʿĀ'isha reported: A woman asked the Apostle of Allah (may peace be upon him) how she should wash herself after the menstrual period. He (the Holy Prophet) said: Take a cotton with musk and purify yourself, and the rest of the ḥadīth was narrated like that of Sufyān.

(649) ʿĀ'isha reported: Asmā' (daughter of Shakal) asked the Apostle of Allah (may peace be upon him) about washing after menstruation. He said: Everyone amongst you should use water (mixed with the leaves of) the lote-tree and cleanse herself well, and then pour water on her head and rub it vigorously till it reaches the roots of the hair. Then she should pour water on it. Afterwards she should take a piece of cotton smeared with musk and cleanse herself with it. Asmā' said: How should she cleanse herself with the help of that? Upon this he (the Apostle of Allah) observed: Praise be to Allah, she should cleanse herself. ʿĀ'isha said in a subdued tone that she should apply it to the trace of blood. She (Asmā') then further asked about bathing after sexual intercourse. He (the Holy Prophet) said: She should take water and cleanse herself well or complete the ablution and then (pour water) on her head and rub it till it reaches the roots of the hair (of her) head and then pour water on her. ʿĀ'isha said: How good are the women of Anṣār (helpers) that their shyness does not prevent them from learning religion.

(650) This ḥadīth is narrated by ʿUbaidullah b. Muʿādh with the same chain of transmitters (but for the words) that he (the Holy Prophet) said: Cleanse yourself with it, and he covered (his face on account of shyness).

(651) ʿĀ'isha reported: Asmā' b. Shakal came to the Messenger of Allah (may peace be upon him) and said: Messenger of Allah, how one amongst us should take a bath after the menstruation, and the rest of the ḥadīth is the same and there is no mention of bathing because of sexual intercourse.

Chapter CXXXI

THE WOMAN WHO HAS A PROLONGED FLOW OF BLOOD,[543] HER BATHING AND PRAYER

(652) ʿĀ'isha reported: Fāṭimah b. Abū Ḥubaish came to the Apostle (may peace be upon him) and said: I am a woman whose blood keeps flowing (even after the menstruation period). I am never purified; should I, therefore, abandon prayer? He

543. The woman who bleeds not on account of menses or after childbirth is known as *Mustaḥāḍa*. Prayer and fasting are binding on her like other women and sexual intercourse is permitted with her. There is, however, one condition for prayer which has been pointed out in the forthcoming aḥādīth.

(the Holy Prophet) said: Not at all, for that is only a vein,[544] and is not menstruation, so when menstruation comes, abandon prayer, and when it ends, wash the blood from yourself and then pray.

(653) The ḥadīth narrated by Wakī' and with its chain of narrators has been transmitted on the authority of Hishām b. 'Urwa, but in the ḥadīth narrated by Qutaiba on the authority of Jarīr, the words are: "There came Fāṭimah b. Abū Ḥubaish, b. 'Abd al-Muṭṭalib, b. Asad, and she was a woman amongst us," and in the ḥadīth of Ḥammād b. Zaid there is an addition of these words: "We abandoned mentioning him."

(654) 'Ā'isha reported: Umm Ḥabība b. Jahsh thus asked for a verdict from the Messenger of Allah (may peace be upon him): I am a woman whose blood keeps flowing (after the menstrual period). He (the Holy Prophet) said: That is only a vein, so take a bath and offer prayer; and she took a bath at the time of every prayer. Laith b. Sa'd said: Ibn Shihāb made no mention that the Messenger of Allah (may peace be upon him) had ordered her to take a bath at the time of every prayer, but she did it of her own accord.[545] And in the tradition transmitted by Ibn Rumḥ there is no mention of Umm Ḥabība (and there is mention of the daughter of Jahsh only.)

(655) 'Ā'isha, the wife of the Messenger of Allah (may peace be upon him), reported: Umm Ḥabība b. Jahsh who was the sister-in-law of the Messenger of Allah (may peace be upon him) and the wife of 'Abd al-Raḥmān b. 'Auf, remained mustaḥāḍa for seven years, and she, therefore, asked for the verdict of Sharī'ah from the Messenger of Allah (may peace be upon him) about it. The Messenger of Allah (may peace be upon him) said: This is not menstruation, but (blood from) a vein: so bathe yourself and offer prayer. 'Ā'isha said: She took a bath in the wash-tub placed in the apartment of her sister Zainab. b. Jahsh, till the redness of the blood came over the water. Ibn Shihāb said: I narrated it to Abū Bakr b. 'Abd al-Raḥmān b. al-Ḥārith b. Hishām about it who observed: May Allah have mercy on Hinda! would that she listened to this verdict. By Lord, she wept for not offering prayer.[546]

(656) This ḥadīth has been thus reported by another chain of transmitters: Umm Ḥabība b Jahsh came to the Messenger of Allah (may peace be upon him) and she had been a mustaḥāḍa for seven years, and the rest of the ḥadīth was narrated like that of 'Amr b. al-Ḥārith up to the words: "There came the redness of the blood over

544. The blood during menstrual period oozes out from endometrium of uterus along with secretions of ovary (with the drops of semen). This period extends normally from five to ten days at the most. But due to some abnormalities in the normal process of menstruation blood continues to flow beyond the menses period. It may be due to haemorrhage in the vein or any other harmonic trouble. This blood is free from female sex cells and comes from the ovary.

545. It was due to the highly keen sense of purification of Umm Ḥabība that she took bath before every prayer. What the Shar'īah has made obligatory for mustaḥiḍa is only ablution at the time of every prayer. Some of the Muḥaddithīn are of the opinion that bath for every prayer is not obligatory but a mustaḥāḍa should wash herself every day. In Abū Dāwūd there is a tradition which points towards it (Shaukānī, *Nail-ul-Autār*, Vol. I, p. 242).

546. This verdict of the Sharī'ah had not reached the ears of Hinda and she, therefore, conceived this prolonged flow of blood in the sense of menstrual flow and abandoned prayer. Had she listened to it, she would have offered the prayers. What intense devotion early Muslims, both men and women, had for prayer and other religious duties!

water," and nothing was narrated beyond it.

(657) This ḥadīth has been narrated by 'Ā'isha through another chain of transmitters (in these words) : "The daughter of Jahsh had been mustaḥāḍa for seven years," and the rest of the ḥadīth is the same (as mentioned above).

(658) On the authority of 'Ā'isha : Umm Ḥabība asked the Messenger of Allah (may peace be upon him) about the blood (which flows beyond the period of menstruation). 'Ā'isha said : I saw her wash-tub full of blood. The Messenger of Allah (may peace be upon him) said : Remain away (from prayer) equal (to the length of time) that your menses prevented you. After this (after the period of usual courses) bathe yourself and offer prayer.

(659) 'Ā'isha, the wife of the Apostle (may peace be upon him), said : Umm Ḥabība b. Jahsh who was the spouse of 'Abd al-Raḥmān b. 'Auf made a complaint[547] to the Messenger of Allah (may peace be upon him) about blood (which flows beyond the menstrual period). He said to her : Remain away (from prayer) equal (to the length of time) that your menstruation holds you back. After this bathe yourself.[548] And she washed herself before every prayer.

Chapter CXXXII

IT IS OBLIGATORY FOR A MENSTRUATING WOMAN TO COMPLETE THE ABANDONED FASTS, BUT NOT THE ABANDONED PRAYERS

(660) Mu'ādha reported : A woman asked 'Ā'isha : Should one amongst us complete prayers abandoned during the period of menses ? 'Ā'isha said : Are you a Ḥarūriya ?[549] When any one of us during the time of the Messenger of Allah (may peace be upon him) was in her menses (and abandoned prayer) she was not required to complete them.

(661) It is reported from Mu'ādha[550] that she asked 'Ā'isha : Should a menstruating woman complete the prayer (abandoned during the menstrual period) ? 'Ā'isha said : Are you a Ḥarūriya ? The wives of the Messenger of Allah (may peace be upon him) have had their monthly courses, (but) did he order them to make compensation (for the abandoned prayers) ? Muḥammad b. Ja'far said : (Compensation) denotes their completion.

547. See how every man and woman sought guidance from the Holy Prophet in every matter in a spirit with which one approaches one's kind and loving father.

548. The Holy Prophet had told her to take a bath after the usual period of menstruation and then offer regular prayers, but she washed at the time of every prayer for her intensely keen sense of purification. It was not the order from the Messenger of Allah (may peace be upon him) but her self-imposed discipline.

549. This name is given after the name of a village Ḥarūra at a distance of two miles from Kūfa. The Khawārij first of all settled at this place. They were of the opinion that the abandoned prayers during the menstrual period must be completed as the abandoned fasts of Ramaḍān. This view is the fabrication of their own minds and runs counter to the principles of Sharī'ah.

550. She was the daughter of 'Abdullah 'Aladwiya, and she was one among the women jurists belonging to a class of successors.

(662) Mu'ādha said: I asked 'Ā'isha: What is the reason that a menstruating woman completes the fasts (that she abandons during her monthly course), but she does not complete the prayers? She (Ḥaḍrat 'Ā'isha) said: Are you a Ḥarūriya? I said: I am not a Ḥarūriya, but I simply want to inquire. She said: We passed through this (period of menstruation), and we were ordered to complete the fasts, but were not ordered to complete the prayers.[551]

Chapter CXXXIII

ONE SHOULD DRAW AROUND A CURTAIN WHILE TAKING A BATH

(663) Umm Hānī b. Abū Ṭālib reported: I went to the Messenger of Allah (may peace be upon him) on the day of the conquest (of Mecca) and found him taking a bath, while his daughter Fāṭimah was holding a curtain around him.

(664) Umm Hānī b. Abū Ṭālib reported: It was the day of the conquest (of Mecca) that she went to the Messenger of Allah (may peace be upon him) and he was staying at a higher part (of that city). The Messenger of Allah (may peace be upon him) got up for his bath. Fāṭimah held a curtain around him (in order to provide him privacy).[552] He then put on his garments and wrapped himself with that and then offered eight rak'ahs of the forenoon prayer.

(665) This ḥadīth is narrated by Sa'īd b. Abū Hind with the same chain of transmitters and said: His (the Holy Prophet's) daughter Fāṭimah provided him privacy with the help of his cloth, and when he had taken a bath he took it up and wrapped it around him and then stood and offered eight rak'ahs of the forenoon prayer.

(666) Maimūna reported: I placed water for the Apostle (may peace be upon him) and provided privacy for him, and he took a bath.

551. Allah does not impose unbearable burden upon people. The fasts of Ramaḍān are observed once during the year, and it is quite easy to compensate the abandoned fasts (from five to ten) during the whole year. But the completion of abandoned prayers which must range between twenty-two and fifty every month, is quite difficult. Islam has not put this burden upon women and has granted them this concession. It should also be borne in mind that it was one of the characteristics of the Khawārij that they put themselves to unnecessary hardships in matters of religion and imposed upon themselves such duties as Islam never ordained. Psychological studies have made it clear that such an attitude towards religion is born out of self-conceitedness and pride in one's piety. True religion teaches humility and modesty.

552. Islam has strictly enjoined upon its followers to cover private parts of their bodies and not to expose them before anybody except under great necessity, for example, before one s wife at the time of sexual intercourse or before a physician or surgeon for medical treatment. The Holy Prophet has ordered to observe strict privacy while taking bath and if no other arrangement could be possible the sheets of cloth were used as curtains for this purpose. It is narrated in Abū Dāwūd and al-Nisā'ī on the authority of Ya'lā that the Messenger of Allah once saw a man bathing in a public place. He mounted the pulpit, and after he had praised and extolled Allah, he said: Allah is characterised by modesty and concealment and loves modesty and concealment, so when any one of you takes a bath, he should conceal himself.

Chapter CXXXIV

IT IS FORBIDDEN TO SEE THE PRIVATE PARTS OF SOMEONE ELSE

(667) 'Abd al-Raḥmān, the son of Abū Sa'īd al-Khudrī, reported from his father: The Messenger of Allah (may peace be upon him) said: A man should not see the private parts of another man, and a woman should not see the private parts of another woman,[553] and a man should not lie with another man under one covering, and a woman should not lie with another woman under one covering.[554]

(668) This ḥadīth has been narrated by Ibn Abū Fudaik and Daḥḥāk b. 'Uthmān with the same chain of transmitters and they observed: Private parts of man are the nakedness (which is concealed).

Chapter CXXXV

IT IS PERMISSIBLE TO TAKE A BATH NAKED IN COMPLETE PRIVACY[555]

(669) Amongst the traditions narrated from Muḥammad, the Messenger of Allah (may peace be upon him) on the authority of Abū Huraira, the one is that Banū Isrā'īl used to take a bath naked, and they looked at the private parts of one another.[556] Moses (peace be upon him), however, took a bath alone[557] (in privacy); and they said (tauntingly): By Allah, nothing prohibits Moses to take a bath along with us, but sacrotal hernia.[558] He (Moses) once went for a bath and placed his

553. It is also forbidden both for man and woman to see private parts of the opposite sex. The husband can expose his private parts before his wife and *vice versa* at the time of sexual intercourse, but it is not desirable to see them. It is, however, permitted in case of dire necessity, for example medical examination and treatment.

554. This is forbidden especially when one or both of them are naked, because the contact of the two bodies may cause sexual excitement. Islam has not only recommended the most severe punishment for fornication, but has taken full care to adopt those measures which control the sexual urge of the people and has blocked all those paths and channels which can possibly excite it and lead a person astray.

555. What Islam commends in bath is that one should cover one's private parts and then wash oneself. It is not desirable to expose the private parts of oneself even before one's own self. In case of necessity, however, or due to lack of proper arrangement for it, one is permitted to take bath nakedly.

556. They had lost every sense of modesty and had been reduced to such a low level of moral depravity that they freely exposed their private parts before one another. It is a sign of moral bankruptcy and runs counter to the delicate sense of religious piety.

557. Moses as a true Messenger of Allah was extremely chaste and modest and did not follow the common practice of bathing naked in an open place along with other men. He observed complete seclusion and privacy while washing himself.

558. There had been so much moral deterioration among Banū Isrā'īl, that they, instead of feeling ashamed at their immodest and shameful act, taunted Moses for his modesty and insulted him by saying that he was suffering from sacrotal hernia, and, therefore, refrained from exposing his private parts to the public.

clothes on a stone and the stone moved on[559] with his clothes. Moses ran after it saying: O stone, my clothes, O stone, my clothes, and Banū Isrā'īl had the chance to see the private parts of Moses, and said: By Allah, Moses does not suffer from any ailment. The stone then stopped, till Moses had been seen by them, and he then took hold of his clothes and struck the stone. Abū Huraira said: By Allah, there are the marks of six or seven strokes made by Moses on the stone.

Chapter CXXXVI

UTMOST CARE FOR KEEPING PRIVATE PARTS OF BODY CONCEALED

(670) Jābir b. 'Abdullah reported: When the Ka'ba[560] was constructed the Apostle of Allah (may peace be upon him) and 'Abbās went and lifted stones. 'Abbās said to the Messenger of Allah (may peace be upon him): Place your lower garment on your shoulder (so that you may protect yourself from the roughness and hardness of stones). He (the Holy Prophet) did this, but fell down upon the ground in a state of unconsciousness and his eyes were turned towards the sky. He then stood up and said: My lower garment, my lower garment; and this wrapper was tied around him.[561] In the ḥadīth transmitted by Ibn Rāfi', there is the word: "On his neck" and he did not say: "Upon his shoulder."

(671) Jābir b. 'Abdullah reported: The Messenger of Allah (may peace be upon him) was carrying along with them (his people) stones for the Ka'ba and there was a waist-

It should be remembered that a prophet is free from physical defects. He is perfect in all respects, both in body and soul. So it was something very insulting for Moses and he was very much aggrieved at such slander and calumny. It was quite necessary to bring the real fact before the people with the help of clear evidence that Moses had no such defect and it could be possible only when his private parts were exposed before the people so that they could see with their own eyes the blatant falsehood.

559. Banū Isrā'īl were the people who were accustomed to see the signs of the Lord in the unusual phenomena of the Universe. The miracles were, therefore, quite frequent during those days and Allah shook people out of their heedlessness by this unusual phenomenon of Nature.

560. It was not for the first time that the Ka'ba was being reconstructed. According to Suhaylī, it was first built by Shīth son of Adam during his lifetime. Later on it was reconstructed by Ḥaḍrat Ibrāhīm (peace be upon him). The Quraish before the birth of Muḥammad also rebuilt it, and in the early life of Prophet Muḥammad (may peace be upon him) it was constructed once again.

561. This ḥadīth brings into prominence some facts about prophethood. The Prophet is born as a prophet and his mind and thought, his character and behaviour are moulded and directed by Allah right from his very birth. He is no doubt made conscious of his exalted position when he attains maturity, and then the responsibilities of prophethood are put on his shoulders, but he is fully trained for this high office from the very day that he comes into this mortal world. Allah guards him against all pitfalls and all acts of omission and commission, and he is made to grow as a perfectly pious and God-loving man so that he should be mentally and morally well prepared to undertake full responsibilities of prophethood.

Modesty is one of the qualities of religious piety and, therefore, even in childhood when some slackness was shown by the Holy Prophet with regard to concealing of the lower part of his body under the influence of his dear uncle, Allah in His infinite Mercy gave him a mild warning in order to make him realise that this act was not approved by the Lord.

wrapper around him. His uncle, 'Abbās, said to him: O son of my brother! if you take off the lower garment and place it on the shoulders underneath the stones, it would be better. He (the Holy Prophet) took it off and placed it on his shoulder and fell down unconscious. He (the narrator) said: Never was he seen naked after that day.

(672) Al-Miswar b. Makhrama reported: I was carrying a heavy stone and my lower garment was loose, and it, therefore, slipped off (so soon) that I could not place the stone (on the ground) and carry to its proper place. Upon this the Messenger of Allah (may peace be upon him) said: Return to your cloth (lower garment), take it (and tie it around your waist) and do not walk naked.

Chapter CXXXVII

CONCEALING ONE'S PRIVATE PARTS WHILE RELIEVING ONESELF

(673) 'Abdullah b. Ja'far reported: The Messenger of Allah (may peace be upon him) one day made me mount behind him and he confided to me something secret[562] which I would not disclose to anybody; and the Messenger of Allah (may peace be upon him) liked the concealment provided by a lofty place or cluster of dates (while answering the call of nature). Ibn Asmā' said in his narration: It implied an enclosure of the date-trees.

Chapter CXXXVIII

EMISSION OF SEMEN MAKES BATH OBLIGATORY

(674) Sa'id al-Khudrī narrated it from his father: I went to Qubā' with the Messenger of Allah (may peace be upon him) on Monday till we reached (the habitation) of Banū Sālim. The Messenger of Allah (may peace be upon him) stood at the door of 'Itbān and called him loudly. So he came out dragging his lower garment. Upon this the Messenger of Allah (may peace be upon him) said: We have made this man to make haste. 'Itbān said: Messenger of Allah, if a man parts with his wife suddenly without seminal emission, what is he required to do (with regard to bath)? The Messenger of Allah (may peace be upon him) said: It is with the seminal emission that bath becomes obligatory.[563]

562. It must be something which had a concern with 'Abdullah b. Ja'far alone and none else. He, therefore, kept it to himself and did not disclose it to others.

There is a meaningful relationship between the two parts of the ḥadīth. What this implies is that just as the matter was kept secret, in the same way private parts should be carefully concealed and these should not be exposed before others.

563. According to Nawawī, there is consensus of opinion amongst the jurists that sexual intercourse necessitates a bath, whether there is seminal emission or not. This ḥadīth is abrogated by the later commands of the Apostle of Allah. It must be remembered that the later verdicts of the Holy Prophet abrogate the earlier ones if they directly conflict with one another and no reconciliation is possible between them. According to Ibn 'Abbās, this ḥadīth is not abrogated, because it refers not to the actual sexual intercourse, but only to the sexual dream, in which there is no seminal emission.

(675) Abū al-'Alā' b. al-Shikhkhīr said: The Messenger of Allah (may peace be upon him) abrogated some of his commands by others, just as the Qur'ān abrogates[564] some part with the other.

(676) Abū Sa'īd al-Khudrī reported: The Messenger of Allah (may peace be upon him) happened to pass by (the house) of a man amongst the Anṣār, and he sent for him. He came out and water was trickling down from his head. Upon this he (the Holy Prophet) said: Perhaps we put you to haste. He said: Yes, Messenger of Allah. He (the Holy Prophet) said: When you made haste or semen is not emitted, bathing is not obligatory for you, but ablution is binding. Ibn Bashshār has narrated it with a minor alteration.

(677) Ubayy ibn Ka'b reported: I asked the Messenger of Allah (may peace be upon him) about a man who has sexual intercourse with his wife, but leaves her before orgasm.[565] Upon this he (the Holy Prophet) said: He should wash the secretion of his wife, and then perform ablution and offer prayer.

(678) Ubayy ibn Ka'b narrated it from the Messenger of Allah (may peace be upon him) that he said: If a person has sexual intercourse with his wife, but does not experience orgasm, he should wash his organ and perform an ablution.

(679) Abū Sa'īd al-Khudrī reported: The Apostle of Allah (may peace be upon him) observed: Bathing is obligatory in case of seminal emission.

(680) Zaid b. Khālid al-Juhanī reported that he asked 'Uthmān b. 'Affān: What is your opinion about the man who has sexual intercourse with his wife, but does not experience orgasm? 'Uthmān said: He should perform ablution as he does for prayer, and wash his organ. 'Uthmān also said: I have heard it from the Messenger of Allah (may peace be upon him).

(681) Abū Ayyūb reported that he had heard like this from the Messenger of Allah (may peace be upon him).

Chapter CXXXIX

ABROGATION OF (THE COMMAND THAT) BATH IS OBLIGATORY (ONLY) BECAUSE OF SEMINAL EMISSION AND INSTEAD CONTACT OF THE CIRCUMCISED PARTS MAKES BATH OBLIGATORY

(682) Abū Huraira reported: The Apostle of Allah (may peace be upon him) said:

564. Abrogation in the technical sense does not mean total elimination or complete cancellation of the previous commands, but some alteration in their practical implications. This change is not in fundamentals of the Sharī'ah but only in details. The whole misconception about *Naskh* starts from its English rendering, abrogation, whereas what it implies is limiting the import of a command to a certain aspect, or to widen the implication of a command to other spheres (*Tafsir Madārik al-Tanzil*). For a detailed discussion, see *Itqān* of Jalāl-ud-Dīn Suyūṭī.

565. See with what zeal and earnestness the Companions of the Holy Prophet sought his guidance and neither concealed nor kept back anything from him. We do not find any trace of pretension or mental reservation or mental inhibition in them.

When a man has sexual intercourse,[566] bathing becomes obligatory (both for the male and the female). In the ḥadīth of Maṭar the words are: Even if there is no orgasm. Zuhair has narrated it with a minor alteration of words.

(683) This ḥadīth is narrated by Qatāda with the same chain of transmitters, but with minor alterations. Here instead of the word جهد (*Jahada*), اجتهد (*Ijtahada*) has been used, and the words: "Even if there is no orgasm" have been omitted.

(684) Abū Mūsā reported: There cropped up a difference of opinion between a group of Muhājirs (Emigrants) and a group of Anṣār (Helpers) (and the point of dispute was) that the Anṣār said: The bath (because of sexual intercourse) becomes obligatory only when the semen spurts out or ejaculates. But the Muhājirs said: When a man has sexual intercourse (with the woman), a bath becomes obligatory (no matter whether or not there is seminal emission or ejaculation). Abū Mūsā said: Well, I satisfy you on this (issue). He (Abū Mūsā, the narrator) said: I got up (and went) to 'Ā'isha and sought her permission and it was granted, and I said to her: O Mother, or Mother of the Faithful, I want to ask you about a matter on which I feel shy. She said: Don't feel shy of asking me about a thing which you can ask your mother, who gave you birth, for I am your mother too.[567] Upon this I said: What makes a bath obligatory for a person? She replied: You have come across one well informed![568] The Messenger of Allah (may peace be upon him) said: When anyone sits amidst four parts (of the woman) and the circumcised parts touch each other a bath becomes obligatory.

(685) 'Ā'isha the wife of the Apostle of Allah (may peace be upon him) reported: A person asked the Messenger of Allah (may peace be upon him) about one who has sexual intercourse with his wife and parts away (without orgasm) whether bathing is obligatory for him. 'Ā'isha was sitting by him. The Messenger of Allah (may peace be upon him) said: I and she (the Mother of the Faithful) do it and then take a bath.

Chapter CXL

ABLUTION IS ESSENTIAL WHEN ONE TAKES SOMETHING COOKED WITH THE HELP OF FIRE

(686) Zaid b. Thābit reported: I heard the Messenger of Allah (may peace be upon

566. The actual words of the ḥadīth are: "When anyone sits between the four parts of her body and then makes effort." What it implies is that a male sits within the thighs of the female and then cohabits. The Holy Prophet was an eloquent speaker and his expressions are very exquisite. He uses similes and metaphors for conveying the true sense of the meaning. This act of sexual intercourse could not rightly be expressed with the English word "mating". He, therefore, used a metaphor to explain the real nature of the act.

This ḥadīth abrogates the previous one and makes it clear that the sexual intercourse makes a bath obligatory both for the man and the woman.

567. Mark the intense love of the Mother of the Believers for her children in faith.

568. Ḥaḍrat 'Ā'isha was the most competent authority who could deliver final verdict on this matter on the basis of her personal experience. It is indeed one of the greatest sacrifices on the part of the Holy Prophet and his noble wives that they disclosed even the most private and personal affairs of their lives, and it is due to this sacrifice on their part that we have been able to learn these matters pertaining to purity and religious piety in the sphere of our private and personal life.

him) say this: Ablution is obligatory (for one who takes anything) touched by fire.[569]

(687) 'Abdullah b. Ibrāhīm b. Qāriẓ reported that he found Abū Huraira performing ablution in the mosque, who said: I am performing ablution because of having eaten pieces of cheese, for I heard the Messenger of Allah (may peace be upon him) say: Perform ablution (after eating anything) touched by fire.

(688) 'Urwa reported on the authority of 'Ā'isha, the wife of the Messenger of Allah (may peace be upon him), saying this: The Messenger of Allah (may peace be upon him) said: Perform ablution (after eating anything) touched by fire.

Chapter CXLI

ABROGATION OF THE ḤADĪTH THAT ABLUTION IS OBLIGATORY FOR HIM WHO TAKES SOMETHING COOKED WITH THE HELP OF FIRE

(689) Ibn 'Abbās reported: The Messenger of Allah (may peace be upon him) took (meat of) goat's shoulder and offered prayer and did not perform ablution.

(690) Ibn 'Abbās reported: The Messenger of Allah (may peace be upon him) took flesh from the bone or meat, and then offered prayer and did not perform ablution, and (in fact) he did not touch water.

(691) Ja'far b. 'Amr b. Umayya al-Ḍamarī reported on the authority of his father who said: I saw the Messenger of Allah (may peace be upon him) taking slices from goat's shoulder, and then eating them. And then offered prayer but did not perform ablution.

(692) Ja'far b. 'Amr b. Umayya al-Ḍamarī reported on the authority of his father who said: I saw the Messenger of Allah (may peace be upon him) taking slices from goat's shoulder and then eating them. He was called for prayer and he got up, leaving aside the knife, and offered prayer but did not perform ablution.

(693) Ibn 'Abbās reported it on the authority of Maimūna, the wife of the Apostle of Allah (may peace be upon him), that the Apostle of Allah (may peace be upon him) took (a piece of goat's) shoulder at her place, and then offered prayer but did not perform ablution.

(694) This ḥadīth has been narrated by Ibn 'Abbās on the authority of Maimūna, the wife of the Apostle (may peace be upon him), by another chain of transmitters.

(695) Abū Rāfi' reported: I testify that I used to roast the liver of the goat for the Messenger of Allah (may peace be upon him) and then he offered prayer but did not perform ablution.

(696) Ibn 'Abbās reported: The Apostle (may peace be upon him) took milk and then called for water and rinsed[570] (his mouth) and said: It contains greasiness.

(697) This ḥadīth has been narrated by another chain of transmitters.

569. Anything cooked with the help of fire. This ḥadīth stands abrogated by other aḥādīth of the later period.

570. From this act of the Holy Prophet it can be safely inferred that it is desirable to rinse the mouth after taking anything (Nawawī).

(698) Ibn 'Abbās reported: The Messenger of Allah (may peace be upon him) dressed himself, and then went out for prayer, when he was presented with bread and meat. He took three morsels out of that, and then offered prayer along with other people and did not touch water.

(699) This ḥadīth is narrated by Muḥammad b. 'Amr b. 'Aṭā' with these words: I was with Ibn 'Abbās, and Ibn 'Abbās saw the Apostle of Allah (may peace be upon him) doing like this, and it is also said that the words are: He (the Holy Prophet) offered prayer; and the word "people" is not mentioned.

Chapter CXLII

THE QUESTION OF ABLUTION AFTER EATING THE FLESH OF THE CAMEL

(700) Jābir b. Samura reported: A man asked the Messenger of Allah (may peace be upon him) whether he should perform ablution after (eating) mutton. He (the Messenger of Allah) said: Perform ablution if you so desire, and if you do not wish, do not perform it. He (again) asked: Should I perform ablution (after eating) camel's flesh? He said: Yes, perform ablution (after eating) camel's flesh [571] He (again) said: May I say prayer in the sheepfolds? He (the Messenger of Allah) said: Yes. He (the narrator) again said: May I say prayer where camels lie down? He (the Holy Prophet) said: No.[572]

(701) This ḥadīth is also narrated by another chain of transmitters.

571. There is a difference of opinion amongst the jurists about this matter. Some of the scholars of Ḥadīth are of the opinion that the eating of camel's flesh does not break the ablution, but, according to others, e.g. Aḥmad b. Ḥanbal, Isḥāq b. Rahwai, and Yaḥyā and Ibn Munḍar, it does break. The question naturally arises why such an exception is made for the flesh of the camel. Various reasons have been put forward for this. Maulānā Shabbīr Aḥmad deems its offensive smell to be the main cause of it. Shāh Walīullāh of Delhi has given a different view His argument is that the eating of camel's flesh had been forbidden in the Torah and all the apostles of Banū Isrā'īl agreed on it, but it was made permissible for the followers of Muḥammad (may peace be upon him) and ablution was enjoined upon them as an expression of thankfulness to the Lord for this favour. Similarly, other scholars have given other arguments, but to my mind the most convincing reason is given by Maulānā Shabbīr Aḥmad 'Uthmānī, that this order of ablution after eating the flesh of camel is one of the main phases through which new converts had to pass for learning the laws of purification. Firstly, ablution was made obligatory for everyone who ate food touched by fire. This was done in order to accustom people to this habit of purification. Later on concession was granted in this matter but it was ordained to continue this practice of ablution in case of camel's flesh and subsequently the full concession was given. (For detailed study see *Fatul-Mulhim*, Vol. I, p. 490, and Shāh Walīullāh's *Ḥujjat Allāh al-Bāligha*, Vol. I, p. 177.)

572. Different are the conditions in the folds of sheep and camels. The sheep and goats are small and meek animals and one feels no danger from them and, therefore, one has no cause to fear them. But this is not the case of camels; they at times become violent and one has to exercise great care in living by their side. Prayer in their folds may cause distraction of mind.

Chapter CXLIII

A MAN WHO IS SURE OF HIS PURIFICATION, BUT ENTERTAINS DOUBT OF ANYTHING BREAKING IT, CAN SAFELY OFFER PRAYER WITHOUT PERFORMING A NEW ABLUTION

(702) ʻAbbād b. Tamīm reported from his uncle that a person made a complaint to the Apostle (may peace be upon him) that he entertained (doubt) as if something had happened to him breaking his ablution. He (the Holy Prophet) said: He should not return (from prayer) unless he hears a sound or perceives a smell (of passing wind). Abū Bakr and Zuhair b. Ḥarb have pointed out in their narrations that it was ʻAbdullah b. Zaid.

(703) Abū Huraira reported: The Messenger of Allah (may peace be upon him) said: If any one of you has pain in his abdomen, but is doubtful whether or not anything has issued from him, he should not leave the mosque unless he hears a sound or perceives a smell.[573]

Chapter CXLIV

PURIFICATION OF THE SKINS OF THE DEAD ANIMALS BY TANNING THEM

(704) The freed slave-girl of Maimūna was given a goat in charity but it died. The Messenger of Allah (may peace be upon him) happened to pass by that (carcass). Upon this he said: Why did you not take off its skin? You could put it to use, after tanning it. They (the Companions) said: It was dead. Upon this he (the Messenger of Allah) said: Only its eating is prohibited. Abū Bakr and Ibn ʻUmar in their narrations said: It is narrated from Maimūna (may Allah be pleased with her).

(705) Ibn ʻAbbās said: The Messenger of Allah (may peace be upon him) saw a dead goat, which had been given in charity to the freed slave-girl of Maimūna. The Messenger of Allah (may peace be upon him) said: Why don't you make use of its skin? They (the Companions around the Holy Prophet) said: It is dead. Upon this he said: It is the eating (of the dead animal) which is prohibited.

(706) This ḥadīth is narrated by Ibn Shihāb with the same chain of transmitters as transmitted by Yūnus.

(707) Ibn ʻAbbās reported: The Messenger of Allah (may peace be upon him) happened to pass by a goat thrown (away) which had been in fact given to the freed slave-girl of Maimūna as charity. Upon this the Messenger of Allah (may peace be upon him) said: Why did they not get its skin? They had better tan it and make use of it.

(708) Ibn ʻAbbās reported on the authority of Maimūna that someone amongst the

573. According to Nawawī it is one of those aḥādīth which lay down the basic principles of Islamic Sharīʻah. Here we have been told not to go after doubts, but to hold things valid unless there is some concrete evidence against it. Islam does not make a man whimsical but makes him a man of trust and confidence.

wives of the Messenger of Allah (may peace be upon him) had a domestic animal[574] and it died. Upon this the Messenger of Allah (may peace be upon him) said: Why did you not take off its skin and make use of that?

(709) Ibn 'Abbās reported: The Apostle of Allah (may peace be upon him) happened to pass by (the dead body) of the goat which belonged to the freed slave-girl of Maimūna and said: Why did you not make use of its skin?

(710) 'Abdullah b. 'Abbās said: I heard the Apostle of Allah (may peace be upon him) say: When the skin is tanned it becomes purified.[575]

(711) This ḥadīth has been transmitted on the authority of Ibn 'Abbās by another chain of transmitters.

(712) Abū al-Khair reported: I saw Ibn Wa'la al-Sabā'ī wearing a fur. I touched it. He said: Why do yot touch it?[576] I asked Ibn 'Abbās saying: We are the inhabitants of the western regions, and there (live) with us Berbers and Magians. They bring with them rams and slaughter them, but we do not eat (the meat of the animals) slaughtered by them, and they come with skins full of fat. Upon this Ibn 'Abbās said: We asked the Messenger of Allah (may peace be upon him) about this and he said: Its tanning makes it pure.[577]

(713) Ibn Wa'la al-Sabā'ī reported: I asked 'Abdullah b. 'Abbās saying: We are the inhabitants of the western regions.[578] The Magians come to us with skins full of water and fat. He said: Drink. I said to him: Is it your own opinion? Ibn 'Abbās said: I heard the Messenger of Allah (may peace be upon him) say: Tanning purifies it (the skin).

Chapter CXLV

TAYAMMUM[579]

(714) 'Ā'isha reported: We went with the Apostle of Allah (may peace be upon

574. According to Maulānā Shabbīr Aḥmad 'Uthmānī, داجن may be a bird or a goat or any other animal or bird which is kept in the house, but here it implies goat only (*Fatḥ-ul-Mulhim*, Vol. I, p. 492).

575. There is a good deal of difference of opinion amongst the jurists whether tanning purifies the skin of all animals. But after taking into consideration the different arguments of the various scholars, one can easily reach the conclusion that tanning purifies the skin of ḥalāl animals only, and we are permitted to use their skins. But so far as ḥarām (forbidden) animals are concerned, especially the dog and the swine, their skins can neither be purified nor is a Muslim permitted to use them.

576. He touched it in a manner which indicated that he did not consider it something proper for him.

577. It implies that tanning makes the skin pure, even if it is tanned by non-Muslims.

578. The region which is known as the Far East now-a-days, e.g. Tunis, Algeria.

579. The word "tayammum" is derived from "amma": "he repaired to a thing," and "tayammum," therefore, means, originally, betaking oneself to a thing, and since the word is used here in connection with betaking oneself to pure earth, tayammum has come technically to mean this particular practice of touching the earth and then wiping over the face and hands.

Tayammum is a practice of special significance in Islam. We have said in previous pages that the main purpose behind ablution and bath is religious one and the hygienic one is a matter of secondary importance. These practices have been enjoined upon us as religious duties in order to prepare ourselves physically and mentally for the performance of the main duty (prayer).

him) on one of his journeys[580] and when we reached the place Baidā' or Dhāt al-Jaish,[581] my necklace was broken (and fell somewhere). The Messenger of Allah (may peace be upon him) along with other people stayed there for searching it. There was neither any water at that place nor was there any water with them (the Companions of the Holy Prophet). Some persons came to my father Abū Bakr and said: Do you see what 'Ā'isha has done? She has detained the Messenger of Allah (may peace be upon him) and persons accompanying him, and there is neither any water here or with them. So Abū Bakr came there and the Messenger of Allah (may peace be upon him) was sleeping with his head on my thigh. He (Abū Bakr) said: You have detained the Messenger of Allah (may peace be upon him) and other persons and there is neither water here nor with them. She ('Ā'isha) said: Abū Bakr scolded me and uttered what Allah wanted him to utter and nudged my hips with his hand. And there was nothing to prevent me from stirring but for the fact that the Messenger of Allah (may peace be upon him) was lying upon my thigh. The Messenger of Allah (may peace be upon him) slept till it was dawn at a waterless place. So Allah revealed the verses pertaining to tayammum[582] and they (the Holy Prophet and his Companions) performed tayammum. Usaid b. al-Ḥuḍair who was one of thel eaders[583] said: This is not the first of your blessings, O Family of Abū Bakr.[584] 'Ā'isha said: We made the camel stand which was my mount and found the necklace under it.

(715) 'Ā'isha reported she had borrowed from Asmā' (her sister) a necklace and it was lost. The Messenger of Allah (may peace be upon him) sent men to search for it. As it was the time for prayer, they offered prayer without ablution (as water was not available there). When they came to the Messenger of Allah (may peace be upon

Allah has directed us to perform tayammum in case water is not available or we are handicapped to make use of that. This practice is meant to retain the spiritual value of ablution as a means of distracting us from the mundane activities of life and directing us to the presence of Lord.

The Qur'ān says: "And if you are sick or on a journey or one of you come from the privy, or you have touched the women, and you cannot find water, then betake yourself to clean earth and wipe your faces and hands therewith" (v. 6).

The question may be asked why earth has been recommended for purification. The answer is that after water the next most easily available thing in the world is earth. Secondly, its use reminds a man of his birth and his abode in the grave. Moreover, its wiping over the face and hands strikes at the very root of man's vanity and pride and inculcates in him a spirit of humility (Shāh Walīullāh, *Ḥujjat Allāh al-Bāligha*, p. 180).

580. It was an expedition to dhāt al-Raqā'.

581. The two places between Medina and Khaybar.

582. It refers to the verses of Sūrat al-Nisā' rather than those of Mā'ida: "And if you be ailing or on a journey or one of you comes from the privy, or you have touched women, and you find no water, then betake yourselves to clean earth and wipe your faces and your hands therewith. Verily Allah is ever Pardoning, Forgiving" (iv. 43).

Ḥāfiz Ibn Ḥajar 'Asqalānī is of the opinion that the expression فتيمموا (then, betake yourselves) clearly shows that Niyyah (intention) is essential in tayammum and almost all the jurists subscribe to this view.

583. Usaid b. al-Ḥuḍair was one of those twelve eminent personalities of the Anṣār who pledged allegiance to the Holy Prophet on the night of second pledge of 'Aqaba and the Holy Prophet entrusted him with the sacred task of teaching Islam to the Muslims of Medina.

584. These words clearly show the eminence of Abū Bakr and his family in the millah of Islam and the love of God and that of the Holy Prophet for these noble souls.

him), they made a complaint about it, and the verses pertaining to tayammum were revealed. Upon this Usaid b. Ḥuḍair said (to 'Ā'isha): May Allah grant you a good reward! Never has been there an occasion when you were beset with difficulty and Allah did not make you come out of that and made it an occasion of blessing for the Muslims.

(716) Shaqīq reported: I was sitting in the company of 'Abdullah and Abū Mūsā, when Abū Mūsā said: O 'Abd al-Raḥmān (kunya of 'Abdullah b. Mas'ūd), what would you like a man to do about the prayer if he experiences a seminal emission or has sexual intercourse but does not find water for a month? 'Abdullah said. He should not perform tayammum even if he does not find water for a month.[585] 'Abdullah said: Then what about the verse in Sūra Mā'ida: "If you do not find water, betake yourself to clean dust"? 'Abdullah said: If they were granted concession on the basis of this verse, there is a possibility that they would perform tayammum with dust on finding water very cold for themselves. Abū Mūsā said to 'Abdullah: You have not heard the words of 'Ammār: The Messenger of Allah (may peace be upon him) sent me on an errand and I had a seminal emission, but could find no water, and rolled myself in dust just as a beast rolls itself. I came to the Messenger of Allah (may peace be upon him) then and made a mention of that to him and he (the Holy Prophet) said: It would have been enough for you to do thus. Then he struck the ground with his hands once and wiped his right hand with the help of his left hand and the exterior of his palms and his face.[586] 'Abdullah said: Didn't you see that 'Umar was not fully satisfied with the words of 'Ammār only?[587]

(717) This ḥadīth is narrated by Shaqīq with the same chain of transmitters but with the alteration of these words: He (the Holy Prophet) struck hands upon the earth, and then shook them and then wiped his face and palm.

(718) 'Abd al-Raḥmān b. Abzā narrated it on the authority of his father that a man came to 'Umar and said: I am (at times) affected by seminal defilement but find no water. He ('Umar) told him not to say prayer. 'Ammār then said: Do you remember, O Commander of the Faithful, when I and you were in a military detachment and we had had a seminal emission and did not find water (for taking bath) and you did not say prayer, but as for myself I rolled in dust and said prayer, and (when it was mentioned before) the Apostle (may peace be upon him) said: It was enough for you to strike the ground with your hands and then blow (the dust) and then wipe your face and palms. 'Umar said: 'Ammār, fear Allah. He said: If you so like, I would not

585. 'Abdullah b. Mas'ūd and Ḥaḍrat 'Umar (may Allah be pleased with them) were both of the opinion that tayammum does not purify a man who is sexually defiled. But the overwhelming majority of the Companions of the Holy Prophet and their successors do not subscribe to this view and they believe that with tayammum the same objectives can be achieved as with ablution or bathing, provided water is not available or there is any other handicap in its use. Both 'Abdullah b. Mas'ūd and 'Umar (Allah be pleased with them) changed their views and accepted the view held by the majority.

586. The Holy Prophet explained to him practically that tayammum purifies the man whether he needs ablution or bathing.

587. It does not imply that Ḥaḍrat 'Umar had no faith in 'Ammār (Allah be pleased with them). What it means is that Ḥaḍrat 'Umar made inquiries from some other Companions too and then shifted his stand.

narrate it.

A ḥadīth like this has been transmitted with the same chain of transmitters but for the words: " 'Umar said: We hold you responsible for what you claim."

(719) 'Abd al-Raḥmān b. Abzā narrated it on the authority of his father that a man came to 'Umar and said: I have had a seminal emission but I found no water, and the rest of the ḥadīth is the same but with this addition: 'Ammār said: O Commander of the Faithful, because of the right given to you by Allah over me, if you desire, I would not narrate this ḥadīth to anyone.

(720) 'Umair, the freed slave of Ibn 'Abbās, reported: I and 'Abd al-Raḥmān b. Yasār, the freed slave of Maimūna, the wife of the Apostle (may peace be upon him), came to the house of Abu'l-Jahm b. al-Ḥārith al-Ṣimma Anṣārī and he said: The Messenger of Allah (may peace be upon him) came from the direction of Bi'r Jamal and a man met him; he saluted him but the Messenger of Allah (may peace be upon him) made no response, till he (the Holy Prophet) came to the wall, wiped his face and hands and then returned his salutations.

(721) Ibn 'Umar reported: A person happened to pass by the Messenger of Allah (may peace be upon him) when he was making water, and saluted him, but he did not respond to his salutation.

Chapter CXLVI

A MUSLIM IS NOT DEFILED

(722) Abū Huraira reported that he met the Apostle of Allah (may peace be upon him) on one of the paths leading to Medina in a state of (sexual) defilement and he slipped away and took a bath. The Apostle of Allah (may peace be upon him) searched for him and when he came, he said to him: O Abū Huraira, where were you? He said: Messenger of Allah, you met me when I was (sexually) defiled and I did not like to sit in your company before taking a bath. Upon this the Messenger of Allah (may peace be upon him) said: Hallowed be Allah, verily a believer is never defiled.

(723) Ḥudhaifa reported: The Messenger of Allah (may peace be upon him) happened to meet him and he was (sexually) defiled, and he slipped away and took a bath and then came and said: I was (sexually) defiled. Upon this he (the Holy Prophet) remarked: A Muslim is never defiled.[588]

588. The soul of man is purified by belief in Allah and His Prophets and other articles of faith and taking to the path of righteousness and religious piety. The seminal emission does not pollute him. He is, even in this state, pure, because his soul is purified by his belief in Islam. He is barred from prayer and recitation of the Holy Qur'ān and entering into the mosque simply to make him conscious of the immeasurably high spiritual value of these acts of devotion to Allah.

So far as man as a human being is concerned no person is defiled, not even a non-believer, because the Lord has created man in the best make (xcv. 4), and then he lowered himself by his own misdeeds. Man as such is the recipient of the special favours of the Lord. The Holy Qur'ān says:

> And surely We have honoured the children of Adam, and we carry them in the land and the sea, and We provide them with good things, and We have made them to excel highly most of them whom We have created (xvii. 70).

This verse of the Holy Qur'ān makes it clear that man has received the greatest honour from the Lord and he is created pure and is not defiled and polluted. It is his wrong beliefs and vicious acts

Chapter CXLVII

REMEMBRANCE OF ALLAH EVEN IN A STATE OF SEXUAL DEFILEMENT

(724) 'Ā'isha said: The Apostle of Allah (may peace be upon him) used to remember Allah at all moments.[589]

Chapter CXLVIII

IT IS PERMISSIBLE TO EAT WITHOUT ABLUTION AND THERE IS NO ABHORRENCE IN IT AND PERFORMING OF ABLUTION IMMEDIATELY (AFTER THAT) IS NOT ESSENTIAL

(725) Ibn 'Abbās reported: The Apostle of Allah (may peace be upon him) came out of the privy, and he was presented with some food, and the people reminded him about ablution, but he said: Am I to say prayer that I should perform ablution?[590]

(726) Ibn 'Abbās reported: We were with the Apostle of Allah (may peace be upon him) and he had come out of the privy. Food was presented to him. It was said to him (by the Companions around him): Wouldn't you perform ablution? Upon this he said: Why, am I to say prayer that I should perform ablution?

(727) Ibn 'Abbās reported: The Messenger of Allah (may peace be upon him) went to the privy and when he came back, he was presented with food. It was said to him: Messenger of Allah, wouldn't you perform ablution? He said: Why, am I to say prayer?

(728) Ibn 'Abbās reported: The Apostle of Allah (may peace be upon him) came out of the privy after relieving himself, and food was brought to him and he took it, and did not touch water. In another narration transmitted by Sa'īd b. al-Ḥuwairith it is like this: It was said to the Apostle of Allah (may peace be upon him): You have not performed ablution. He said: I do not intend to say prayer that I should perform ablution.

that make him unclean. The verse of the Holy Qur'ān (ix. 28) in which the polytheists have been declared as unclean points to their evil beliefs and practices. The jurists of Islam have elaborated this point and have drawn the conclusion that no man as a man is impure or defiled. It is because of his idolatrous beliefs and evil deeds that he becomes defiled. Imām Shaukānī has given sound arguments in support of his answer: "The Muslims have been permitted to marry the women of the People of the Book; they have been allowed to use their utensils provided they do not contain impurities of the forbidden things; they can accept their gifts, etc. All these facts go to prove that the Holy Prophet never treated them as inherently defiled and polluted persons, for if he had thought them so, he would have never come into contact with them. He called them unclean for their wrong beliefs and acts" (*Nail-ul-Autār*, Vol. I, pp. 20, 21).

589. This means that one is always permitted to glorify the Lord, remember Him and extol Him. There is, however, a difference of opinion whether one can recite the Holy Qur'ān in a state of Janāba or in case of menses of a woman. The general view is that it is not permitted. It is also forbidden to remember Allah while one is in the privy or is busy in sexual intercourse (*Fatḥ-ul-Mulhim* Vol. I, p. 498).

590. Mere washing of hand is enough; there is no need of ablution before taking food.

Chapter CXLIX

WHAT SHOULD BE UTTERED WHILE ENTERING THE PRIVY?

(729) Anas reported: When the Messenger of Allah (may peace be upon him) entered the privy, and in the ḥadīth transmitted by Hushaim (the words are): When the Messenger of Allah (may peace be upon him) entered the lavatory, he used to say: O Allah, I seek refuge in Thee from wicked and noxious things.

(730) This ḥadīth is also transmitted by 'Abd al-'Azīz with the same chain of transmitters, and the words are: I seek refuge with Allah from the wicked and noxious things.[591]

Chapter CL

ABLUTION DOES NOT BREAK BY DOZING IN A SITTING POSTURE

(731) Anas reported: (The people) stood up for prayer and the Messenger of Allah (may peace be upon him) was whispering to a man, and in the narration of 'Abd al-Wārith (the words are): The Apostle of Allah (may peace be upon him) was having a private conversation with a man, and did not start the prayer till the people dozed off.

(732) Anas b. Mālik reported: (The people) stood up for prayer and the Apostle of Allah (may peace be upon him) was talking in whispers with a man, and he did not discontinue the conversation till his Companions dozed off; he then came and led the prayer.

(733) Qatāda reported: I heard Anas saying that the Companions of the Messenger of Allah (may peace be upon him) dozed off and then offered prayer and did not perform ablution. He (the narrator) said: I asked him if he had actually heard it from Anas. He said: By Allah, yes.

(734) Anas reported: (The people) stood up for the night prayer when a man spoke forth: I need to say something. The Apostle of Allah (may peace be upon him) entered into secret conversation[592] with him, till the people dozed off[593] or some of the people (dozed off), and then they said the prayer.

591. أعوذ بالله من الخبث و الخبائث. See how even the slightest difference in words has been recorded in the aḥādīth. In ḥadīth 729, the words are: "O Allah, I seek refuge in Thee..." and in the next one the expression is: "I seek refuge with Allah." Where one can find such a meticulous care as is shown in the transmission of ḥadīth.

592. It must have been something very important that the Messenger of Allah postponed the prayer. This generous act of the Holy Prophet gives us an idea of what great regard he had for the sentiments of the people and how dearly he loved them. Prayer is the most effective means for the purification of the soul and it, therefore, inculcates in man a spirit of humility, love, selflessness and fellow feeling and readiness to alleviate the sorrows of other human beings.

593. I have translated the word نوم with dozing because it is in dozing and half sleeping only that the ablution does not break. There is a ḥadīth recorded in Tirmidhī and Abū Dāwūd which makes this point very clear. It is reported by Ibn 'Abbās that the Messenger of Allah (may peace be upon him) said: Ablution is necessary for one who sleeps in a state of lying down, for when he lies down his joints are relaxed.

From the above aḥādīth it can be easily concluded that the aḥādīth recorded above refer not to sleep but to dozing only when neither the leather strap of anus is loosened nor joints relax. It is not in sound sleep but in a state between waking and sleep that one can remain conscious of one's ablution.

KITAB AL-SALAT[594]

INTRODUCTION

Prayer is the soul of religion. Where there is no prayer, there can be no purification of the soul. The non-praying man is rightly considered to be a soulless man. Take prayer out of the world, and it is all over with religion because it is with prayer that man has the consciousness of God and selfless love for humanity and inner sense of piety. Prayer is, therefore, the first, the highest, and the most solemn phenomenon and manifestation of religion.

The way in which prayer is offered and the words which are recited in it explain the true nature of religion of which it is the expression of man's contact with the Lord.

Prayer in Islam gives in a nutshell the teachings of Islam. The very first thing which comes into prominence in Islamic prayer is that it is accompanied by bodily movements. It implies that Islam lifts not only the soul to the spiritual height, but also illuminates the body of man with the light of God-consciousness. It aims at purifying both body and soul, for it finds no cleavage between them. Islam does not regard body and soul as two different entities opposed to each other, or body as the prison of the soul from which it yearns to secure freedom in order to soar to heavenly heights. "The soul is an organ of the body which exploits it for physiological purposes, or body is an instrument of the soul" (Iqbal, *Reconstruction of Religious Thought in Islam*, p. 105), and thus both need spiritual enlightenment.

Secondly, Islamic prayer does not aim at such a spiritual contact with God in which the world and self are absolutely denied, in which human personality is dissolved, disappears and is absorbed in the Infinite Lord. Islam does not favour such a meditation and absorption in which man ceases to be conscious of his own self and feels himself to be perfectly identified with the Infinite, and claims in a mood of ecstasy: My "I" has become God, or rather he is God. Islam wants to inculcate the consciousness of the indwelling of the light of God in body and soul but does allow him to transport himself in the realm of Infinity. It impresses upon his mind that he is the humble servant of the Great and Glorious Lord and his spiritual development and

594. Some of the lexicographers are of the opinion that the word *al-Ṣalāt* means to pray, supplicate, to make petition or to perform the divinely appointed act. This meaning becomes clear in one of the famous traditions of the Holy Prophet (may peace be upon him) :

من دعى الى وليمة فليجب و الا فليصل

Whosoever is invited to a banquet, or a marriage feast, let him comply, or, if not, let him pray for the inviter.

It also means to give blessings as it is found in the Holy Qur'ān :

ان الله و ملا ئكة يصلون على النبى

Verily God and His angels bless the Apostle (xxxiii. 56).

Ṣalāt in the technical sense means that particular mode of prayer which is enjoined upon the Muslims as a foremost religious duty. Prayers are of various kinds : five obligatory prayers daily, Friday prayer, funeral prayer, 'Īd prayers, etc., etc.

religious piety lies in sincere and willing obedience to Allah. The very first step towards the achievement of this objective is that man should have a clear consciousness of his own finiteness and Infiniteness of the Lord, and clearly visualise and feel that he is created as a human being by the Creator and Master of the universe, and he cannot, therefore, become demi-god or god. His success lies in proving himself by his outlook and behaviour that he is the true and loyal servant of his Great Master. Islamic prayer is, therefore, the symbol of humble reverence before the Majesty of the Glorious Lord.

Chapter CLI

THE BEGINNING OF ADHĀN

(735) Ibn 'Umar reported : When the Muslims came to Medina, they gathered and sought to know the time of prayer but no one summoned them. One day they discussed the matter, and some of them said : Use something like the bell of the Christians and some of them said : Use horn like that of the Jews. 'Umar said : Why may not a man be appointed who should call (people) to prayer ? The Messenger of Allah (may peace be upon him) said : O Bilāl, get up and summon (the people) to prayer.[595]

(736) Anas reported : Bilāl was commanded (by the Apostle of Allah) to repeat (the phrases of) Adhān twice and once in Iqāma.[596] The narrator said : I made a mention of it before Ayyūb who said : Except for saying : Qāmat-iṣ-Ṣalāt [the time for prayer has come].

(737) Anas b. Mālik reported : They (the Companions) discussed that they should know the timings of prayer by means of something recognised by all. Some of them said that fire should be lighted or a bell should be rung. But Bilāl was ordered to repeat the phrases twice in Adhān, and once in Iqāma.

(738) This ḥadīth is transmitted by Khālid Ḥadhdhā' with the same chain of transmitters (and the words are) : When the majority of the people discussed they should know, like the ḥadīth narrated by al-Thaqafī (mentioned above) except for the words : "They (the people) should kindle fire."

595. The full account of Adhān, as it was introduced in Islam, is given in so many traditions. The proposals mentioned above were brought before the Holy Prophet, but he did not feel drawn at all towards these customs and practices of calling people to prayer, as he considered them inappropriate for such a sacred purpose. He felt that human voice could better communicate the inspiration and emotion which should be dedicated to the solemnity of the occasion. It is narrated that when this problem was being discussed, one day 'Abdullah b. Zayd came to the Holy Prophet and told him : I saw last night a visitant in a dream who had a clapper in his hand and I asked him to sell that to me. When he questioned what I wanted to do with that, I replied that it was to summon people for prayer, whereupon he said : Should I not show you a better way than this ? I replied in the affirmative. Upon this he informed me about the words of Adhān. The Holy Prophet said : Your vision, by the Grace of God, is true. Go to Bilāl and communicate it to him so that he should call people to prayer accordingly. When 'Umar heard this in his house he came there dragging his waist-wrapper on the ground and said : By Him Who has sent you with truth, I have seen precisely the same vision as has been shown to 'Abdullah b. Zayd. The Prophet said : God be praised for that (Abū Dāwūd, "Kitāb al-Ṣalāt," Bāb Badā' al-Adhān).

596 Iqāma is a sort of Adhān which is uttered in a comparatively lower tone than Adhān just at the time of beginning the actual prayer.

(739) Anas reported: Bilāl was commanded (by the Holy Prophet) to repeat the phrases twice[597] in Adhān, and once in Iqāma.

Chapter CLII

HOW ADHĀN IS TO BE PRONOUNCED

(740) Abū Maḥdhūra said that the Apostle of Allah (may peace be upon him) taught him Adhān like this: Allah is the Greatest, Allah is the Greatest[598]; I testify that there is no god but Allah, I testify that there is no god but Allah; I testify that Muḥammad is the Messenger of Allah, I testify that Muḥammad is the Messenger of Allah, and it should be again repeated[599]: I testify that there is no god but Allah, I testify that there is no god but Allah; I testify that Muḥammad is the Messenger of Allah, I testify that Muḥammad is the Messenger of Allah. Come to the prayer (twice). Come to the prayer (twice). Isḥāq added: Allah is the Greatest, Allah is the Greatest; there is no god but Allah.

Chapter CLIII

THERE CAN BE TWO PRONOUNCERS OF ADHĀN FOR ONE MOSQUE

(741) Ibn 'Umar reported: The Messenger of Allah (may peace be upon him) had

597. The original word شفع (Shaf') signifies one of a pair or couple, and sometimes a pair or couple altogether (Lane). Since *Allah-o-Akbar* in Adhān is uttered twice in one breath, it is, therefore, one utterance and when it is repeated again then it becomes a pair. In this ḥadīth we have been told to utter the phrases once in Iqāma, i.e. twice *Allah-o-Akbar* at the beginning and at the end, and twice *Qad Qāmat-iṣ-Ṣalāt*. Imām Shāfi'ī and Imām Aḥmad b. Ḥanbal are of this opinion, but according to Imām Mālik the phrase *Qad Qāmat-iṣ-Ṣalāt* should also be pronounced only once in Iqāma.

Imām Abū Ḥanīfa, Imām Sufyān Thaurī, Ibn Mubārak and other jurists of Kūfa are of the opinion that Iqāma should be pronounced as Adhān with the addition of the phrase (*Qad Qāmat-iṣ-Ṣalāt*) twice. They hold this opinion on the basis of a ḥadīth mentioned in Abū Dāwūd, Nisā'ī, Ibn Māja, which is narrated on the authority of Maḥdhura. The fact is that both the styles are correct.

598. So many other authentic traditions speak of the fact that *Allah-o-Akbar* is to be repeated four times and then twice at the end and the testifications, e.g. I testify that there is not god but Allah and I testify that Muḥammad is the Messenger of Allah, should be repeated twice. This ḥadīth gives the various phrases uttered in the Adhān but not an integrated form of that which we find in the aḥādīth.

599. This process is known as ترجيع (*Tarji'*) which means that in the first instance the opening phrases should be uttered in a lower voice and then repeated in a louder voice. If we keep in view the circumstances under which Abū Maḥdhūra was asked to say Adhān, it becomes quite clear that it was a special case with him.

After the conquest of Mecca when the Holy Prophet was moving towards Ḥunain, he had with him quite a good number of persons who had been granted pardon. Abū Maḥdhūra was one of them. He had a loud, ringing voice. The Prophet, therefore, asked him to pronounce Adhān. As it embodies the sum and substance of the teachings of Islam, the Holy Prophet asked him to repeat them for a number of times. He was exhorted to repeat especially the phrases: I testify that there is no god but Allah and I testify that Muḥammad is the Messenger of Allah, in order to imprint on his mind the two important fundamentals of Islam. Abū Maḥdhūra got the blessing of Islam through these phrases and he, therefore, repeated them in this very style in the subsequent period of his life. Otherwise the most accepted form of Adhān is one which has been transmitted to us through 'Abdullah b. Zaid.

two Mu'adhdhins, Bilāl and 'Abdullah b. Umm Maktūm, who (latter) was blind.

(742) This ḥadīth has been narrated on the authority of 'Ā'isha by another chain of transmitters.

(743) 'Ā'isha reported: Ibn Umm Maktūm used to pronounce Adhān at the behest of the Messenger of Allah (may peace be upon him) (despite the fact) that he was blind.

(744) A ḥadīth like this has been transmitted by Hishām.

Chapter CLIV

THE HOLY PROPHET REFRAINED FROM ATTACKING PEOPLE LIVING IN DĀR AL-KUFR ON HEARING ADHĀN FROM THEM

(745) Anas b. Mālik reported: The Messenger of Allah (may peace be upon him) used to attack the enemy when it was dawn.[600] He would listen to the Adhān; so if he heard an Adhān, he stopped,[601] otherwise made an attack. Once on hearing a man say: Allah is the Greatest, Allah is the Greatest, the Messenger of Allah (may peace be upon him) remarked: He is following al-Fiṭra (al-Islam). Then hearing him say: I testify that there is no god but Allah, there is no god but Allah, the Messenger of Allah (may peace be upon him) said: You have come out of the Fire (of Hell). They looked at him and found that he was a goatherd.

Chapter CLV

HE WHO HEARS THE ADHĀN SHOULD RESPOND LIKE IT, INVOKE BLESSINGS UPON THE APOSTLE (MAY PEACE BE UPON HIM) AND THEN BEG FOR HIM THE WAṢĪLA

(746) Abū Sa'īd al-Khudrī reported: When you hear the call (to prayer), repeat what the Mu'adhdhin pronounces.

(747) 'Abdullah b. 'Amr b. al 'Āṣ reported Allah's Messenger (may peace be upon him) as saying: When you hear the Mu'adhdhin, repeat what he says, then invoke a blessing on me, for everyone who invokes a blessing on me will receive ten blessings from Allah; then beg from Allah al-Waṣīla for me, which is a rank in Paradise fitting for only one of Allah's servants, and I hope that I may be that one. If anyone who asks that I be given the Waṣīla, he will be assured of my intercession.

600. The greatest contribution made by the Holy Prophet in the sphere of warfare is that he elevated it from the surface of reckless murder and slaughter to the level of humanised struggle for the uprooting of evil in society. The Holy Prophet, therefore, did not allow his Companions to take the enemy unawares under the cover of darkness of night.

601. The hearing of Adhān in an overwhelming population of unbelievers gives an indication that the non-Muslim society is not rotten to the core and there is at least this much decency that it allows the Muslims to live within it and practise their religion freely.

(748) 'Umar b. al-Khaṭṭāb reported: The Messenger of Allah (may peace be upon him) said: When the Mu'adhdhin says: Allah is the Greatest, Allah is the Greatest, and one of you should make this response: Allah is the Greatest, Allah is the Greatest; (and when the Mu'adhdhin) says: I testify that there is no god but Allah, one should respond: I testify that there is no god but Allah, and when he says: I testify that Muḥammad is the Messenger of Allah, one should make a response: I testify that Muḥammad is Allah's Messenger. When he (the Mu'adhdhin) says: Come to prayer, one should make a response: There is no might and no power except with Allah. When he (the Mu'adhdhin) says: Come to salvation, one should respond: There is no might and no power except with Allah, and when he (the Mu'adhdhin) says: Allah is the Greatest, Allah is the Greatest, then make a response: Allah is the Greatest, Allah is the Greatest. When he (the Mu'adhdhin) says: There is no god but Allah, and he who makes a response from the heart: There is no god but Allah, he will enter Paradise.

(749) Sa'd b. Abū Waqqāṣ reported: The Messenger of Allah (may peace be upon him) said: If anyone says on hearing the Mu'adhdhin: I testify that there is no god but Allah alone, Who has no partner, and that Muḥammad is His servant and His Messenger, (and that) I am satisfied with Allah as my Lord, with Muḥammad as Messenger, and with Islam as dīn (code of life), his sins would be forgiven. In the narration transmitted by Ibn Rumḥ the words are: "He who said on hearing the Mu'adhdhin 'and verily I testify.'" Qutaiba has not mentioned his words: "And I."

Chapter CLVI

THE EXCELLENCE OF ADHĀN[602] AND RUNNING AWAY[603] OF THE SATAN ON HEARING IT

(750) Yaḥyā narrated it on the authority of his uncle that he had been sitting in the company of Mu'āwiya b. Abū Sufyān when the Mu'adhdhin called (Muslims) to

602. The Adhān beautifully sums up the teachings of Islam. If we study the Holy Qur'ān and the Sunnah we will find that there are four fundamentals on which the entire superstructure of Islam rests: (*a*) Belief in the oneness of Allah and in the fact that there is no Power greater than Him; (*b*) He alone is the Creator and the Master of the universe and none other can claim share in His God-hood or sovereignty; (*c*) Muḥammad is the final dispenser of the Will of Allah and it is in his words and deeds that His will finds expression; (*c*) it is not the material utility that determines the value of things or acts in Islam but their spiritual significance—thus salvation in Islam lies in the purification of the soul which can be achieved only by willing and conscious obedience to the Commands of Allah, and prayer is the most important of that obedience; (*d*) the highest aim of the life of a Muslim is to live a life of eternal bliss.

Looking into the character of the contents of Adhān, it becomes apparent that the teachings of the Qur'ān and the Sunnah have been beautifully summed up in Adhān. If a person were to read and listen to nothing but Adhān and grasp its meaning, he could understand all essentials of the Faith. The main purpose behind the loud pronouncement of Adhān five times a day in every mosque is to make available to everyone an easily intelligible brief version of Islam. It is intended to bring to the mind of every believer or non-believer the substance of Islamic beliefs, or its spiritual ideology, as well as his goal in life and programme of righteous living.

603. Where there is Islam, there is naturally no scope of Satan to penetrate and exercise its influence. It must fly from that place.

prayer. Mu'āwiya said: I heard the Messenger of Allah (may peace be upon him) saying: The Mu'adhdhins will have the longest necks on the Day of Resurrection.[604]

(751) Abū Sufyān reported it on the authority of Jābir that he had heard the Apostle of Allah (may peace be upon him) say: When Satan hears the call to prayer, he runs away to a distance like that of Rauḥā'. Sulaimān said: I asked him about Rauḥā'. He replied: It is at a distance of thirty-six miles from Medina.

(752) Abū Mu'āwiya narrated it on the authority of A'mash with the same chain of transmitters.

(753) Abū Huraira reported the Messenger of Allah (may peace be upon him) saying: When Satan hears the call to prayer, he turns back and breaks the wind so as not to hear the call being made, but when the call is finished he turns round and distracts (the minds of those who pray), and when he hears the Iqāma he again runs away so as not to hear its voice, and when it subsides, he comes back and distracts (the minds of those who stand for prayer).[605]

(754) Abū Huraira reported: The Messenger of Allah (may peace be upon him) said: When the Mu'adhdhin calls to prayer, Satan runs back vehemently.

(755) Suhail reported that his father sent him to Banū Ḥāritha along with a boy or a man. Someone called him by his name from an enclosure. He (the narrator) said: The person with me looked towards the enclosure, but saw nothing. I made a mention of that to my father. He said: If I knew that you would meet such a situation I would have never sent you (there), but (bear in mind) whenever you hear such a call (from the evil spirits) pronounce the Adhān, for I have heard Abū Huraira say that the Messenger of Allah (may peace be upon him) said: Whenever Adhān is proclaimed, Satan runs back vehemently.[606]

(756) Abū Huraira reported: The Apostle (may peace be upon him) said: When the call to prayer is made, Satan runs back and breaks wind so as not to hear the call being made, and when the call is finished, he turns round. When Iqāma is proclaimed he turns his back, and when it is finished he turns round to distract a man, saying: Remember such and such; remember such and such, referring to something the man did not have in his mind, with the result that he does not know how much he has prayed.

604. They would figure prominently on the Day of Resurrection.

605. This ḥadīth explains how evil forces work against the forces of piety. Whenever the forces of piety and righteousness become active, the forces of evil turn back because they cannot stand against the moral forces. The breaking of wind indicates that evil forces try to resist the forces of good by foul means and evil persons even in their own selves avoid the healthy influence of the forces of righteousness by deliberately harbouring evil thoughts and ideas in their minds so that the good may not penetrate into them. When the forces of good become inert or inactive, the forces of evil become active and march against them. But they seldom make a direct advance; they try to distract the minds of the religious people from goodness and piety by stuffing them with worldly temptations and planting various kinds of doubts and suspicions in them.

This ḥadīth also explains the fact that while reciting Adhān and Iqāma the minds of the people are free from evil promptings but as soon as the actual prayer begins these begin to haunt them. It is a common experience of our lives.

606. حصاص (Ḥuṣāṣ). This word has so many meanings. One is mange or scab which implies that vehement running makes the hair fall off. It also means the quick running of an ass while straightening and erecting its ears, and moving about or wagging the tail and running. It also means an emission of wind from the anus with a sound.

(757) A ḥadīth like it has been narrated by Abū Huraira but for these words: "He (the man saying the prayer) does not know how much he has prayed."

Chapter CLVII

THE DESIRABILITY OF RAISING THE HANDS APPOSITE THE SHOULDERS AT THE TIME OF BEGINNING THE PRAYER AND AT THE TIME OF BOWING AND AT THE TIME OF RETURNING TO THE ERECT POSITION AFTER BOWING 607

(758) Sālim narrated it on the authority of his father who reported: I saw the Messenger of Allah (may peace be upon him) raising his hands apposite the shoulders at the time of beginning the prayer and before bowing down and after coming back to the erect position after bowing, but he did not raise them between two prostrations.608

(759) Ibn 'Umar reported that the Messenger of Allah (may peace be upon him),

607. We have discussed at the beginning of "Kitāb al-Ṣalāt" the spiritual significance of the bodily movements in prayer and stated that these are meant to awaken the consciousness of man's being present before the Lord. Raising of hands at different stages of prayer is meant to serve the same purpose. It was, therefore, stressed in earlier years when the present form of prayer was made obligatory so that the minds of people should remain active and they should fully realise what a sacred duty they were performing, and how humbly they were standing before the Gracious Master and supplicating before Him as His loyal and obedient servants. Later on when the Muslims were accustomed to it and movements of bowing and prostration alone could keep their minds alert relaxation was granted in it. According to some Ṣūfīs, the spiritual implication of raising of hands is that the man devoting himself to prayer shows by his gestures that he is going to take off his hand from all the material pursuits of life for the sake of Allah.

608. Raising of hands is a matter of great significance and importance in prayer, and opinions differ at what stages in prayer it is essential. There is consensus of opinion amongst the jurists that it is essential at the time of beginning of the prayer along with the recitation of the takbīr. It is in the subsequent stages of prayer, i.e. at the time of bowing and prostration, that there is a difference of opinion with regard to the raising of hands. Imām Shāfi'ī and Imām Aḥmad consider this act to be desirable while bowing, coming back to the erect position and prostrating. They base their assertion on the aḥādīth narrated by 'Abdullah b. 'Umar, Wā'il b. Ḥujr, Abū Ḥumaid as-Sā'idī (may Allah be pleased with all of them).

Imām Abū Ḥanīfa asserts that raising of hands is essential only at the time of beginning of prayer, and it is needless at the subsequent stages. He bases his argument on the traditions narrated by 'Abdullah b. Mas'ūd and Barā' b. 'Āzib. The fact is that both the practices are correct and have been narrated to us by authentic traditionists. It is, therefore, a gross ignorance to dispute with one another on this point. The difference of opinion amongst the jurists is on which practice is preferable to the other. The life of the Holy Prophet was neither stereotyped nor mechanical. The fundamental form of prayer is the same. So far as details are concerned, he acted differently on different occasions and, therefore, all these acts are valid. The Holy Prophet did this so that the devotional life of the Muslims may not become absolutely rigid. He wanted to retain the natural flexibility of religious life.

Moreover, the Holy Prophet wanted to inculcate a spirit of tolerance for minor issues and train the minds of his followers to differentiate between the fundamentals and details of religious acts and show respect for an honest difference of opinion. In fact, he aimed at broadening the outlook of the Muslims.

when he stood up for prayer, used to raise his hands apposite the shoulders and then recited takbīr (Allah-o-Akbar), and when he was about to bow he again did like it and when he raised himself from the rukū' (bowing posture) he again did like it, but he did not do it at the time of raising his head from prostration.

(760) This ḥadīth has been transmitted with the same chain of transmitters by al-Zuhrī as narrated by Ibn Juraij (who) said: When the Messenger of Allah (may peace be upon him) stood up for prayer, he raised hands (to the height) apposite the shoulders and then recited takbīr.

(761) Abū Qilāba reported that he saw Mālik b. Ḥuwairith raising his hands at the beginning of prayer and raising his hands before kneeling down, and raising his hands after lifting his head from the state of kneeling, and he narrated that the Messenger of Allah (may peace be upon him) used to do like this.

(762) Mālik b. Ḥuwairith reported: The Messenger of Allah (may peace be upon him) raised his hands apposite his ears at the time of reciting the takbīr (i.e. at the time of beginning the prayer) and then again raised his hands apposite the ears at the time of bowing and when he lifted his head after bowing he said: Allah listened to him who praised Him, and did like it (raised his hands up to the ears).

(763) This ḥadīth has been transmitted by Qatāda with the same chain of transmitters that he saw the Apostle of Allah (may peace be upon him) doing like this (i.e. raising his hands) till they were apposite the lobes of ears.

Chapter CLVIII

THE RECITING OF TAKBĪR AT THE TIME OF BOWING AND RISING IN PRAYER EXCEPT RISING AFTER RUKŪ' WHEN IT IS SAID: ALLAH LISTENED TO HIM WHO PRAISED HIM

(764) Abū Salama reported: Abu Huraira led prayer for them and recited takbīr when he bent and raised himself[609] (in rukū' and sujūd) and after completing (the prayer) he said: By Allah I say prayer which has the best resemblance with the prayer of the Holy Prophet (may peace be upon him) amongst you.

(765) Abū Huraira reported: When the Messenger of Allah (may peace be upon him) got up for prayer, he would say the takbīr (Allah-o-Akbar) when standing, then say the takbīr when bowing, then say: "Allah listened to him who praised him," when coming to the erect position after bowing, then say while standing: "To Thee, our Lord, be the praise," then recite the takbīr when getting down for prostration, then

609. While going back to the standing position after rukū', it is not the takbīr that is pronounced but these words are uttered: Sami' Allāhu li-man ḥamidah," meaning: "Allah listened to him who praised Him." And with this, the words of Divine Praise are uttered: Rabba-nā wa lak-al ḥamd, that is, "Our Lord ! all praise is due to Thee."

The second exception to the utterance of takbīr on a change of posture is at the completion of prayer when it is concluded with salutation (as-Salāmu-'alaikum wa raḥmat Allah=peace be upon you and mercy of Allah).

say the takbīr on raising his head, then say the takbīr on prostrating himself, then say the takbīr on raising his head. He would do that throughout the whole prayer till he would complete it, and he would say the takbīr[610] when he would get up at the end of two rak'as after adopting the sitting posture. Abū Huraira said: My prayer has the best resemblance amongst you with the prayer of the Messenger of Allah (may peace be upon him).

(766) Ibn al-Ḥārith reported: He had heard Abū Huraira say: The Messenger of Allah (may peace be upon him) recited takbīr on standing for prayer, and the rest of the ḥadīth is like that transmitted by Ibn Juraij (recorded above), but he did not mention Abū Huraira saying: "My prayer has the best resemblance amongst you with the prayer of the Messenger of Allah (may peace be upon him)."

(767) Abū Salama b. 'Abd al-Raḥmān reported: When Marwān appointed Abū Huraira as his deputy in Medina, he recited takbīr whenever he got up for obligatory prayer, and the rest of the ḥadīth is the same as transmitted by Ibn Juraij (but with the addition of these words): On completing the prayer with salutation,[611] and he turned to the people in the mosque and said. . . .

(768) Abū Salama reported that Abū Huraira recited takbīr in prayer on all occasions of rising and bending. We said: O Abū Huraira, what is this takbīr? He said: Verily it is the prayer of the Messenger of Allah (may peace be upon him).

(769) Suhail reported on the authority of his father that Abū Huraira used to recite takbīr on all occasions of rising and bending (in prayer) and narrated that the Messenger of Allah (may peace be upon him) used to do like that.

(770) Muṭarrif reported: I and 'Imrān b. Ḥuṣain said prayer behind 'Alī b. Abū Ṭālib. He recited takbīr when he prostrated, and he recited takbīr when he raised his head and he recited takbīr while rising up (from the sitting position at the end of two rak'ahs). When we had finished our prayer, 'Imrān caught hold of my hand and said: He (Ḥaḍrat 'Alī) has led prayer like Muḥammad (may peace be upon him) or he said: He in fact recalled to my mind the prayer of Muḥammad (may peace be upon him.)

Chapter CLIX

THE RECITING OF AL-FĀTIḤA IN EVERY RAK'AH OF PRAYER IS OBLIGATORY

(771) 'Ubāda b. aṣ-Ṣāmit reported from the Apostle of Allah (may peace be upon him): He who does not recite Fātiḥat al-Kitāb is not credited with having observed the prayer.[612]

610. Reciting of takbīr at the time of changing the postures in prayer is quite significant. It implies that in prayer one should have full consciousness of the fact that Allah is the Greatest and He alone is to be adored, and man is His humble servant.

611. The prayer is concluded with السلام عليكم و رحمة الله.

612. The recitation of Sūra Fātiḥa or the opening Sūra of the Holy Qur'ān in every rak'ah of prayer has been made essential for it brings before the mind of man the sum and substance of the Qur'ān. If we reflect over the teachings of the Qur'ān we find that these converge on four points: (*a*) attributes of Allah in proper perspective; (*b*) man's relation with Allah; (*c*) exhortation

(772) 'Ubāda b. aṣ-Ṣāmit reported: The Messenger of Allah (may peace be upon him) said: He who does not recite Umm al-Qur'ān is not credited with having observed the prayer.

(773) Maḥmūd b. al-Rabī', on whose face the Messenger of Allah (may peace be upon him) squirted water from the well, reported on the authority of 'Ubāda b. aṣ-Ṣāmit that the Messenger of Allah (may peace be upon him) said: He who does not recite Umm al-Qur'ān[613] is not credited with having observed prayer.

(774) This ḥadīth has also been transmitted by Ma'mar from al-Zuhrī with the same chain of transmitters with the addition of these words: "and something more".[614]

(775) Abū Huraira reported: The Apostle of Allah (may peace be upon him) said: If anyone observes prayer in which he does not recite Umm al-Qur'ān, it is deficient [he said this three times] and not complete. It was said to Abū Huraira: At times we are behind the Imām. He said: Recite it inwardly, for he had heard the Messenger of Allah (may peace be upon him) declare that Allah the Exalted had said: I have divided the prayer into two halves between Me and My servant, and My servant will

to do good deeds and avoid evil ones; (*d*) accountability of one's deeds before Allah. The whole Qur'ān is an elucidation and elaboration of these points and all these points have been beautifully summed up in Sūrat al-Fātiḥa. Herein we have been told that Allah alone is the Creator, Nourisher and Master of the universe. He is infinitely Kind, Compassionate and Merciful and looks to the well-being of His creation at every step. He is the Powerful Lord, and comprehends the whole universe in His All-Pervading Power and Authority. He is a Just and Kind Ruler and rules over the universe with unbounded Benevolence and Perfect Wisdom. Man is not sent in this world as a free lancer, but with moral responsibility, and thus he is made answerable to his Master for all his deeds. The Lord in His infinite Mercy would judge man's actions on the Day of Resurrection and will reward or punish him according to his conduct and behaviour in the worldly life.

So far as man's relation with Allah is concerned, it should be that of complete devotion and absolute submission to Him.

Lastly, it has been laid down in the Sūra that the right path in the eye of Allah, i.e. the path of true virtue and piety as outlined by Him, is one on which have gone those who have received favours from Him, and the wrong path is one which has been trodden by those who have earned His wrath. A Muslim should cherish an earnest desire and then make effort to go on the path of righteousness and avoid the pitfalls of evil.

In every rak'ah of prayer this substance of the teachings of the Qur'ān is recited by every Muslim so that he should be constantly aware of the aims and objects of his life, the virtues which he should practise, the evils which he must avoid with a deep sense of moral responsibility and God-consciousness. That is why the recitation of Sūrat al-Fātiḥa in every rak'ah of the prayer has been made obligatory.

613. This Sūra has many names: e.g. Sūrat al-Fātiḥa, Sab' al-Mathānī (the oft-repeated seven), Umm al-Qur'ān (the essence of the Qur'ān), al-Kāfī (the sufficient), al-Kanz (the treasure), Asās al-Qur'ān (the basis of the Qur'ān).

614. After Sūrat al-Fātiḥa, some verses of the Qur'ān should also be recited.

Sūra I (al-Fātiḥa) forms a good preface to the Qur'ān. The Qur'ān begins with not only a hymn and prayer but it sums up in the tersest manner the main attributes of Allah—beneficence, mercy, Creator and Perfector of the worlds, and the Lord of the Day of Judgment when the attributes of مُلك (sovereignty) and مِلك (ownership) will belong only to Him (cf. الملك يومئذ لله : xxii. 56 and يوم لا تملك نفس لنفس شيئاً (lxxvii. 19). Then it establishes, so to say, a real workable relationship between man and God (without which mere belief in the existence of God is meaningless), of Master

receive what he asks. When the servant says: Praise be to Allah, the Lord of the universe, Allah the Most High says: My servant has praised Me. And when he (the servant) says: The Most Compassionate, the Merciful, Allah the Most High says: My servant has lauded Me. And when he (the servant) says: Master of the Day of Judgment, He remarks: My servant has glorified Me, and sometimes He would say: My servant entrusted (his affairs) to Me. And when he (the worshipper) says: Thee do we worship and of Thee do we ask help, He (Allah) says: This is between Me and My servant, and My servant will receive what he asks for. Then, when he (the worshipper) says: Guide us to the straight path, the path of those to whom Thou hast been Gracious--not of those who have incurred Thy displeasure, nor of those who have gone astray, He (Allah) says: This is for My servant, and My servant will receive what he asks for. Sufyān said: 'Alā b. 'Abd al-Raḥmān b. Ya'qūb narrated it to me when I went to him and he was confined to his home on account of illness, and I asked him about it.

(776) It is narrated on the authority of Abū Huraira that he had heard the Messenger of Allah (may peace be upon him) say: He who observed prayer but he did not recite the Umm al-Qur'ān in it, and the rest of the ḥadīth is the same as transmitted by Sufyān, and in this ḥadīth the words are: "Allah, the Most High said: The prayer is divided into two halves between Me and My servant. The half of it is for Me and the half of it for My servant."[615]

and servant, Lord and slave, who should carry out his Master's injunctions. To such a Being we must give our unstinted obedience and from Him seek help. What help? To guide us on the right path. Which path? The path of those upon whom He bestowed His favours and not of those, etc. This brief Sūra contains not only the basis of the Qur'ān but of any religion:

(*a*) Belief in a Supreme Being—Creator and Perfector, Beneficent and Merciful, Who is supreme here and in the next world, from Whom we can expect every good and perfection;

(*b*) Reward and Punishment in this world and the next;

(*c*) The Last Judgment Day; and indirectly

(*d*) Revelation and Prophethood.

As you open the Qur'ān you at once know where you stand with relation to your Creator; what you have to do in this world to merit reward and avoid punishment: the path you have to follow. Your mind is prepared for what follows.

You asked for guidance; you wanted to learn to differentiate between the good people and those who had gone astray and those who had incurred the wrath of God—so that you may follow the "Straight Path". Your prayer is heard, so to say, in the very next Sūra:

ذلک الکتاب لا ریب فیه هدی للمتقین۔

Of course "guidance" must come to you through a book which is free from all sorts of doubts, otherwise you will find yourself on a very shaky ground; and the prerequisite to that guidance is faith or belief in Allah and ultimate truths (Dr 'Ābid Aḥmad 'Alī, *Language for Prayer*).

615. In half of the verses of Sūrat al-Fātiḥa there is the praise and glorification of Allah and in the other half we find supplication on the part of the worshipper for favours from the Great Lord.

The way how a man glorifies and begs mercy from his Lord and how He responds to the worshipper produces the consciousness of abiding communion of man with God and an intense feeling of his being in the Divine Presence. Whenever a worshipper raises up his voice in prayer he is responded to by Allah with a comforting message. A prayer is thus a spiritual echo. Philosophy is apt to regard prayer as merely a petition for moral good and resignation or an expression of one's failings, but this is not correct. Prayer is as deep, vast and rich as the human soul. The entire range of

(777) Abū Huraira reported : The Messenger of Allah (may peace be upon him) said : He who said his prayer, but did not recite the opening chapter of al-Kitāb, his prayer is incomplete. He repeated it thrice.[616]

(778) Abū Huraira reported : The Messenger of Allah (may peace be upon him) said : One is not credited with having observed the prayer without the recitation (of al-Fātiḥa). So said Abū Huraira : (The prayer in which) the Messenger of Allah (may peace be upon him) recited in a loud voice,[617] we also recited that loudly for you (and the prayer[618] in which) he recited inwardly we also recited inwardly for you (to give you a practical example of the prayer of the Holy Prophet).

(779) 'Aṭā' narrated on the authority of Abū Huraira who said that one should recite (al-Fātiḥa) in every (rak'ah of) prayer. What we heard (i.e. recitation) from the Messenger of Allah (may peace be upon him), we made you listen to that. And that

noble feelings and moods, religious emotions and judgments of moral values appear in it. The prayer in Islam is not, therefore, a bargain between man and God, but a feeling of the indwelling of the Lord in the heart and soul of man.

616. This ḥadīth and the foregoing ones in this chapter prove beyond doubt that the recitation of Sūrat al-Fātiḥa in every rak'ah of the prayer is essential, and if it is not recited one is not credited with having oberved one's prayer. There is perfect agreement amongst the jurists on this basic point. The difference, however, is on the nature of recitation. Imām S..āfi'ī and some other Fuqahā' are of the view that the recitation of Sūra Fātiḥa by each individual is essential in all rak'ahs and in both types of prayer (*jahri*, in which the Imām recites loudly and in *sirri* in which the Imām recites inwardly).

Imām Mālik and Imām Aḥmad b. Ḥanbal are of the opinion that in *jahri* prayers when the recitation of the Imām is audible to his followers, one should only listen to him attentively as the recitation of the Imām would absolve the followers of the responsibility of its recitation.

According to Imām Abū Ḥanīfa even in *sirri* prayers, the followers need not recite Sūrat al-Fātiḥa as the recitation of the Imām (even though it is done inwardly) is sufficient for the followers. Imām Abū Ḥanīfa draws his argument from a ḥadīth recorded in Abū Dāwūd, Nasā'ī, Ibn Māja, in which the Messenger of Allah said : The Imām is conferred upon (this privilege) that his followers should follow him. So when the Imām recites the takbīr, you must also recite it, and when he recites (the Qur'ān) you should listen to him. This ḥadīth is an elucidation of the following verse of the Qur'ān : "And when the Qur'ān is recited, listen to it and remain silent, that mercy may be shown to you" (vii. 204).

One can easily find in these arguments the true nature of the difference amongst the opinions of the jurists. They all draw their argument from the Qur'ān and the Sunnah, so their difference is only a difference of interpretation and understanding. It is, in fact, a difference of preference rather than that of kufr and Islam. In the above-mentioned case all the opinions are valid since their base is one and the same. Difference is on the issue as to which view should be held preferable to the other. In the opinion of the translator, the view of Imām Mālik and Imām Aḥmad b. Ḥanbal seems to be the most valid. So far as the *jahrī* prayers are concerned the Muqtadī (follower in prayer) should only listen to the recitation of the Imām, and in *sirri* prayer, the Muqtadī should recite Sūrat al-Fātiḥa inwardly. The verse : "When the Qur ān is recited, listen to it and remain silent" (vii. 204) lends support to this opinion. This verse gives a clear indication that it relates to loud recitation of the Qur'ān, for one can listen to it only when it is read loudly. Thus one should silently listen to the recitation of Sūrat al-Fātiḥa and some other portion of the Qur'ān in *jahri* prayers, and in *sirri* prayers, when the recitation of the Imām is not audible to his followers, one should recite Sūrat al-Fātiḥa oneself.

617. The morning prayer, evening prayer and the night prayer (Fajr, Maghrib and 'Ishā) are the *jahrī* prayers. In these prayers the recitation is done loudly.

618. Ẓuhr and 'Aṣr (noon and afternoon prayers) are *sirri* prayers as the recitation is done inwardly.

which he (recited) inwardly, we (recited) inwardly for you. A person said to him : If I add nothing to the (recitation) of the Umm al-Qur'ān (Sūrat al-Fātiḥa), would it make the prayer incomplete? He (Abū Huraira) said : If you add to that (if you recite some of verses of the Qur'ān along with Sūrat al-Fātiḥa), that is better for you. But if you are contented with it (Sūrat al-Fātiḥa) only, it is sufficient for you.[619]

(780) 'Aṭā' reported it on the authority of Abū Huraira who said : Recitation (of Sūrat al-Fātiḥa) in every (rak'ah) of prayer is essential. (The recitation) that we listened to from the Apostle of Allah (may peace be upon him) we made you listen to it. And that which he recited inwardly to us, we recited it inwardly for you. And he who recites Umm al-Qur'ān, it is enough for him (to complete the prayer), and he who adds to it (recites some other verses of the Holy Qur'ān along with Sūrat al-Fātiḥa), it is preferable for him.

(781) Abū Huraira reported : The Messenger of Allah (may peace be upon him) entered the mosque and a person also entered therein and offered prayer, and then came and paid salutation to the Messenger of Allah (may peace be upon him). The Messenger of Allah (may peace be upon him) returned his salutation and said : Go back and pray, for you have not offered the prayer. He again prayed as he had prayed before, and came to the Apostle of Allah (may peace be upon him) and saluted him. The Messenger of Allah (may peace be upon him) returned the salutation and said : Go back and say prayer, for you have not offered the prayer. This (act of repeating the prayer) was done three times. Upon this the person said : By Him Who hast sent you with Truth, whatever better I can do than this, please teach me. He (the Holy Prophet) said : When you get up to pray, recite takbīr, and then recite whatever you conveniently can from the Qur'ān, then bow down and remain quietly in that position, then raise yourself and stand erect ; then prostrate yourself and remain quietly in that attitude ; then raise yourself and sit quietly ; and do that throughout all your prayers.[620]

(782) Abū Huraira reported : A person entered the mosque and said prayer while the Messenger of Allah (may peace be upon him) was sitting in a nook (of the mosque), and the rest of the ḥadīth is the same as mentioned above, but with this addition : "When you get up to pray, perform the ablution completely, and then turn towards the Qibla and recite takbīr (Allah o Akbar=Allah is the Most Great)."

Chapter CLX

THE ONE LED IN PRAYER IS FORBIDDEN TO RECITE LOUDLY BEHIND THE IMĀM

(783) 'Imrān b. Ḥuṣain reported : The Messenger of Allah (may peace be upon him) led us in Ẓuhr or 'Aṣr prayer (noon or the afternoon prayer). (On concluding it) he said : Who recited behind me (the verses) : *Ṣabbiḥ Isma Rabbik al-a'lā* (Glorify the

619. What this implies is that recitation of Sūrat al-Fātiḥa in prayer is the bare minimum by which it is observed. Recitation of other verses along with it is creditable.

620. Prayer is the highest act of devotion to Allah. It should, therefore, be performed not in haste but with perfect tranquillity of mind.

name of thy Lord, the Most High) ?[621] Thereupon a person said : It was I, but I intended nothing but goodness. I felt that some one of you was disputing with me in it (or he was taking out from my tongue what I was reciting), said the Holy Prophet (may peace be upon him).

(784) 'Imrān b. Ḥuṣain reported : The Messenger of Allah (may peace be upon him) observed the Ẓuhr prayer and a person recited *Sabbiḥ Isma Rabbik al-a'lā* (Glorify the name of thy Lord, the Most High) behind him. When he (the Holy Prophet) concluded the prayer he said : Who amongst you recited (the above-mentioned verse) or who amongst you was the reciter ? A person said : It was I. Upon this he (the Holy Prophet) observed : I thought as if someone amongst you was disputing with me (in what I was reciting).

(785) This ḥadīth has been narrated by Qatāda with the same chain of transmitters that the Messenger of Allah (may peace be upon him) observed Ẓuhr prayer and said : I felt that someone amongst you was disputing with me (in what I was reciting).

Chapter CLXI

ARGUMENT OF THOSE WHO SAY THAT HE (THE HOLY PROPHET) DID NOT RECITE BISMILLĀH (IN THE NAME OF ALLAH) LOUDLY

(786) Anas reported : I observed prayer along with the Messenger of Allah (may peace be upon him) and with Abū Bakr, 'Umar and 'Uthmān (may Allah be pleased with all of them), but I never heard any one of them reciting *Bismillāh-ir-Raḥmān-ir-Raḥīm* loudly.

(787) Shu'ba reported it with the same chain of transmitters, with the addition of these words : "I said to Qatāda : Did you hear it from Anas ? He replied in the affirmative and added : We had inquired of him about it."

(788) 'Abda reported : 'Umar b. al-Khaṭṭāb used to recite loudly these words : *Subḥānak Allahumma wa bi ḥamdika wa tabārakasmuka wa ta'āla jadduka wa lā ilāha ghairuka* [Glory to Thee, O Allah, and Thine is the Praise, and Blessed is Thy Name, and Exalted is Thy Majesty, and there is no other object of worship besides Thee]. Qatāda informed in writing that Anas b. Mālik had narrated to him : I observed prayer behind the Apostle of Allah (may peace be upon him) and Abū Bakr and 'Umar and 'Uthmān. They started (loud recitation) with : *Al-ḥamdu lillāhi Rabb al-'Ālamīn* [All Praise is due to Allah, the Lord of the worlds] and did not recite *Bismillāh ir-Raḥmān-ir-Raḥīm* (loudly) at the beginning of the recitation or at the end of it.

(789) It is reported on the authority of Abū Ṭalḥa that he had heard Anas b. Mālik narrating this.

621. Al-Qur'ān, lxxxvii. 1.

Chapter CLXII

ARGUMENT OF THOSE WHO ASSERT THAT BISMILLĀH IS A PART OF EVERY SŪRA EXCEPT SŪRA TAUBA

(790) Anas reported : One day the Messenger of Allah (may peace be upon him) was sitting amongst us that he dozed off. He then raised his head smilingly. We said : What makes you smile, Messenger of Allah ? He said : A Sūra has just been revealed to me, and then recited : In the name of Allah, the Compassionate, the Merciful. Verily We have given thee Kauthar (fount of abundance). Therefore turn to thy Lord for prayer and offer sacrifice, and surely thy enemy is cut off (from the good).[622] Then he (the Holy Prophet) said : Do you know what Kauthar is ? We said : Allah and His Messenger know best. The Holy Prophet (may peace be upon him) said : It (Kauthar) is a canal which my Lord, the Exalted and Glorious, has promised me, and there is an abundance of good in it. It is a cistern and my people would come to it on the Day of Resurrection, and tumblers there would be equal to the number of stars. A servant would be turned away from (among the people gathered there). Upon this I would say : My Lord, he is one of my people, and He (the Lord) would say : You do not know that he innovated new things (in Islam) after you. Ibn Ḥujr made this addition in the ḥadīth : "He (the Holy Prophet) was sitting amongst us in the mosque, and He (Allah) said : (You don't know) what he innovated after you."

(791) Mukhtār b. Fulful reported that he had heard Anas b. Mālik say that the Messenger of Allah (may peace be upon him) dozed off, and the rest of the ḥadīth is the same as transmitted by Mus-hir except for the words that he (the Holy Prophet) said: It (Kauthar) is a canal which my Lord the Exalted aud the Glorious has promised me in Paradise. There is a tank over it, but he made no mention of the tumblers like the number of the stars.

Chapter CLXIII

THE PLACING OF THE RIGHT HAND OVER THE LEFT HAND AFTER THE FIRST TAKBĪR IN PRAYER (TAKBĪR-I-TAḤRĪMA) BELOW THE CHEST AND ABOVE THE NAVEL AND THEN PLACING THEM APPOSITE THE SHOULDERS IN PROSTRATION

(792) Wā'il b. Ḥujr reported: He saw the Apostle of Allah (may peace be upon him) raising his hands at the time of beginning the prayer and reciting takbīr, and according to Hammām (the narrator), the hands were lifted opposite to ears. He (the Holy Prophet) then wrapped his hands in his cloth and placed his right hand over his left hand. And when he was about to bow down, he brought out his hands from the cloth, and then lifted them, and then recited takbīr and bowed down, and when (he came back to the erect position) he recited: "Allah listened to him who praised Him." And when prostrated, he prostrated between the two palms.

622. A full discussion of al-Kauthar can be seen in "Kitāb al-Īmān."

Chapter CLXIV

THE TASHAHHUD[623] IN PRAYER

(793) 'Abdullah (b. Mas'ūd) said: While observing prayer behind the Messenger of Allah (may peace be upon him) we used to recite: Peace be upon Allah, peace be upon so and so. One day the Messenger of Allah (may peace be upon him) said to us: Verily Allah is Himself Peace. When any one of you sits during the prayer, he should say: All services rendered by words, by acts of worship, and all good things are due to Allah. Peace be upon you, O Prophet, and Allah's mercy and blessings. Peace be upon us and upon Allah's upright servants, for when he says this it reaches every upright servant in heaven and earth (and say further): I testify that there is no god but Allah and I testify that Muḥammad is His servant and Messenger. Then he may choose any supplication which pleases him and offer it.

(794) Shu'ba has narrated this on the authority of Manṣūr with the same chain of transmitters, but he made no mention of this: "Then he may choose any supplication which pleases him."

(795) This ḥadīth has been narrated on the authority of Manṣūr with the same chain of transmitters and he made a mention of this: "Then he may choose any supplication which pleases him or which he likes."

(796) 'Abdullah b. Mas'ūd reported: We were sitting with the Apostle (may peace be upon him) in prayer, and the rest ofthe ḥadīth is the same as narrated by Manṣūr. He (also said): After (reciting tashahhud) he may choose any prayer.

(797) Ibn Mas'ūd is reported to have said: The Messenger of Allah (may peace be upon him) taught me tashahhud taking my hand within his palms, in the same way as he taught me a Sūra of the Qur'ān, and he narrated it as narrated above.

(798) Ibn 'Abbās reported: The Messenger of Allah (may peace be upon him) used to teach us tashahhud just as he used to teach us a Sūra of the Qur'ān, and he would say: All services rendered by words, acts of worship, and all good things are due to Allah. Peace be upon you, O Prophet, and Allah's mercy and blessings. Peace be upon us and upon Allah's upright servants. I testify that there is no god but Allah, and I testify that Muḥammad is the Messenger of Allah. In the narration of Ibn Rumḥ (the words are): "As he would teach us the Qur'ān."

(799) Ṭāwūs narrated it on the authority of Ibn 'Abbās that he said: The Messenger of Allah (may peace be upon him) used to teach us tashahhud as he would teach us a Sūra of the Qur'ān.

(800) Ḥaṭṭān b. 'Abdullah al-Raqāshī reported: I observed prayer with Abū Mūsā al-Ash'arī and when he was in the qa'dah, one among the people said: The prayer has been made obligatory along with piety and Zakāt. He (the narrator) said: When Abū Mūsā had finished the prayer after salutation he turned (towards the people) and said: Who amongst you said such and such a thing? A hush fell on the people. He again said: Who amongst you has said such and such a thing? A hush fell on the people. He (Abū Musā) said: Ḥaṭṭān, it is perhaps you that have uttered it. He (Ḥaṭṭān) said:

623. Tashahhud means to say the words in prayer beginning with *at-tahiyāt lillāhi*. These words are recited while sitting after two rak'ahs or at the final sitting before salutations in prayer.

No, I have not uttered it. I was afraid that you might be annoyed with me on account of this. A person amongst the people said: It was I who said it, and in this I intended nothing but good. Abū Mūsā said: Don't you know what you have to recite in your prayers? Verily the Messenger of Allah (may peace be upon him) addressed us and explained to us all its aspects and taught us how to observe prayer (properly). He (the Holy Prophet) said: When you pray make your rows straight and let anyone amongst you act as your Imām. Recite the takbīr when he recites it and when he recites: Not of those with whom Thou art angry, nor of those who go astray, say: Āmīn. Allah would respond you. And when he (the Imām) recites the ṭakbīr, you may also recite the takbīr, for the Imām bows before you and raises himself before you. Then the Messenger of Allah (may peace be upon him) said: The one is equivalent to the other. And when he says: Allah listens to him who praises Him, you should say: O Allah, our Lord, to Thee be the praise, for Allah, the Exalted and Glorious, has vouchsafed (us) through the tongue of His Apostle (may peace be upon him) that Allah listens to him who praises Him. And when he (the Imām) recites the takbīr and prostrates, you should also recite the takbīr and prostrate, for the Imām prostrates before you and raises himself before you. The Messenger of Allah (may peace be upon him) said: The one is equivalent to the other. And when he (the Imām) sits for Qa'da (for tashahhud) the first words of every one amongst you should be: All services rendered by words, acts of worship and all good things are due to Allah. Peace be upon you, O Apostle, and Allah's mercy and blessings. Peace be upon us and upon the upright servants of Allah. I testify that there is no god but Allah, and I testify that Muḥammad is His servant and His Messenger.

(801) Qatāda bas narrated a ḥadīth like this with another chain of transmitters. In the ḥadīth transmitted by Jarīr on the authority of Sulaimān, Qatāda's further words are: When (the Qur'ān) is recited (in prayer), you should observe silence, and (the following words are) not found in the ḥadīth narrated by anyone except by Abū Kāmil who heard it from Abū 'Awāna (and the words are): Verily Allah vouchsafed through the tongue of the Apostle of Allah (may peace be upon him) this: Allah listens to him who praises Him. Abū Isḥāq (a student of Imām Muslim) said: Abū Bakr the son of Abū Naḍr's sister has (critically) discussed this ḥadīth. Imām Muslim said: Whom can you find a more authentic transmitter of ḥadīth than Sulaimān? Abū Bakr said to him (Imām Muslim): What about the ḥadīth narrated by Abū Huraira, i.e. the ḥadīth that when the Qur'ān is recited (in prayer) observe silence? He (Abū Bakr again) said: Then, why have you not included it (in your compilation)? He (Imām Muslim) said: I have not included in this every ḥadīth which I deem authentic; I have recorded only such aḥādīth on which there is an agreement (amongst the Muḥaddithīn apart from their being authentic).

(802) This ḥadīth has been transmitted by Qatāda with the same chain of transmitters (and the words are): "Allah, the Exalted and the Glorious, commanded it through the tongue of His Apostle (may peace be upon him): Allah listens to him who praises Him.[624]

624. These aḥādīth categorically reject the views of those who assert that nothing has been revealed to the Holy Prophet by Allah besides the Holy Qur'ān. It also makes it clear that the mode of prayer and the words recited in it have been revealed to Muḥammad (may peace be upon him).

Chapter CLXV

BLESSINGS ON THE PROPHET (MAY PEACE BE UPON HIM) AFTER TASHAHHUD

(803) 'Abdullah b. Zaid—he who was shown the call (for prayer in a dream)—narrated it on the authority of Mas'ūd al-Anṣārī who said: We were sitting in the company of Sa'd b. 'Ubāda when the Messenger of Allah (may peace be upon him) came to us. Bashīr b. Sa'd said: Allah has commanded us to bless you,[625] Messenger of Allah! But how should we bless you? He (the narrator) said: The Messenger of Allah (may peace be upon him) kept quiet (and we were so much perturbed over his silence) that we wished we had not asked him. The Messenger of Allah (may peace be upon him) then said: (For blessing me) say: "O Allah, bless Muḥammad and the members[626] of his household as Thou didst bless the members of Ibrāhīm's[627] household. Grant favours

625. This refers to the verse of the Qur'ān: "Surely Allah and His angels bless the Prophet. O you who believe, call for blessings on him and salute him with a (becoming) salutation" (xxxiii. 56). The blessings of Allah upon the Holy Prophet are too numerous to be counted. He has been elevated to the highest position amongst the Prophets. He has been sent as a Mercy for the worlds and has been made as the final dispenser of the Will of Allah. The angels too bless the Holy Prophet, for he has been able to show by his words and deeds that the human beings, in spite of the freedom of will, can lead a life of perfect submission to the Almighty and this helps in creating an atmosphere of spiritual piety in the world, an atmosphere which is congenial to the angels. The Muslims have been commanded to bless the Holy Prophet as a token of love and gratitude for that august personality who showed them the right path, the path of God-consciousness, virtue, and religious piety.

The word *Ṣalāt*, when it is appended with the preposition *'alā*, conveys three meanings: to incline towards one with love and affection, to magnify one, or to supplicate for one. When this word is used for Allah, it would be used in the first two meanings and when it is used for angels and human beings it would cover the three shades of meanings.

The reciting of *Darūd* has been made essential in the prayer for various reasons. The two obvious reasons are: The prayer has been called the highest ascent (*mi'rāj*) of a believer and this has been made known to the Muslims by Muḥammad (may peace be upon him). It has, therefore, been made obligatory for the believers to bless the Holy Prophet in the best state of communion with Allah as an acknowledgment of their gratitude to him. Secondly, it strikes at the very root of shirk.

The Prophet Muḥammad is the most eminent personality amongst those noble beings who have been directly deputed by Allah to guide people to the path of righteousness and who received revelations from Him. The exhortation to bless him implies that with all unusual eminence and greatness of Muḥammad and his nearness to Allah, he needs blessings of the Master; therefore, he cannot, in spite of his most eminent position amongst the apostles, be attributed with godhood.

626. آل (*āl*). This word has been translated as members of the household, but in Arabic, especially in the context of the Qur'ān and the Sunnah, it gives a wide range of meanings. It means all the devoted members of the household and all those persons who are related to another person not by ties of blood but by ties of love and companionship Thus all the sincere followers are included in the *āl* of Muḥammad (may peace be upon him).

In the present context of *darūd*, *āl* implies the pious and noble family of Muḥammad, i.e. his wives, his daughters, and other members of his household who believed in him as a prophet and shared the hardships of life along with him, and all of his Companions and followers who sincerely obeyed his command and tried to live by the ideals prescribed by him.

627. Different interpretations have been offered as to why the Muslims have been exhorted to supplicate for blessings on Muḥammad (may peace be upon him) like those with which Ḥaḍrat Ibrāhīm (peace be upon him) was blessed by Allah. The most valid explanation is that Ḥaḍrat

to Muḥammad and the members of his household as Thou didst grant favours to the members of the household of Ibrāhīm in the world. Thou art indeed Praiseworthy and Glorious" ; and salutation as you know.

(804) Ibn Abī Lailā reported : Ka'b b. 'Ujra met me and said : Should I not offer you a present (and added) : The Messenger of Allah (may peace be upon him) came to us and we said : We have learnt how to invoke peace upon you ; (kindly tell us) how we should bless you. He (the Holy Prophet) said : Say : "O Allah : bless Muḥammad and his family as Thou didst bless the family of Ibrāhīm. Verily Thou art Praiseworthy and Glorious, O Allah."

(805) A ḥadīth like this has been narrated by Mis'ar on the authority of al-Ḥakam, but in the ḥadīth transmitted by Mis'ar these words are not found : "Should I not offer you a present ?"

(806) A ḥadīth like this has been narrated by al-Ḥakam except that he said : "Bless Muḥammad (may peace be upon him)" and he did not say : "O Allah !"

(807) Abū Ḥumaid as-Sā'idī reported : They (the Companions of the Holy Prophet) said : Apostle of Allah, how should we bless you ? He (the Holy Prophet) observed : Say : "O Allah ! bless Muḥammad, his wives and his offspring as Thou didst bless Ibrāhīm, and grant favours to Muḥammad, and his wives and his offspring as Thou didst grant favours to the family of Ibrāhīm ; Thou art Praiseworthy and Glorious."

(808) Abū Huraira reported : The Messenger of Allah (may peace be upon him) said : He who blesses me once, Allah would bless him ten times.[628]

Ibrāhīm had some special points of eminence which the other apostles besides Muḥammad did not have. Prophet Muḥammad (may peace be upon him) was the direct descendant of Ibrāhīm for the birth of whom the supplication was made by him. Haḍrat Ibrāhīm and his illustratious son Haḍrat Ismā'īl (peace be upon them), while raising the foundations of Ka'ba, supplicated before the Lord:

> Our Lord ! make us both submissive to Thee, and raise from our offspring a nation submissive to Thee, and show us our ways of devotion and turn to us (mercifully). Surely Thou art the oft-returning (to mercy), the Merciful, our Lord, and raise up in them a Messenger from among them (al-Qur-ān, ii. 128-129).

Secondly, Ibrāhīm was made a leader of mankind (ii. 124). This was indeed a special favour of Allah upon him that he was the head of an international religious movement. All those peoples who believe in Allah, revelation and apostlehood even up to this day rever and respect him as their head. The Muslims have been commanded to beg for the same favour for the Holy Prophet Muḥammad. And this favour has actually been conferred upon him that he has been made the final dispenser of a universal message and a "Mercy for the worlds".

628. Our blessing on the Holy Prophet is a token of our love and devotion, of our great debt of gratitude that we owe to him for guiding us to the path of Allah, and saving the human race from moral ruin and destruction. What can be a better favour upon humanity than this that the mysteries of the universe are unfolded before mankind and the human beings have been taught to live according to the moral ideals rather than the material ends. The Holy Prophet raised human beings from the low level of animality to the pinnacle of moral glory and eminence. It is indeed an utmost favour of Allah upon us that by just acknowledging the favours of Muḥammad (may peace be upon him), which is a bare statement of fact, we have been entitled to ten favours from our Lord.

Chapter CLXVI

THE RECITING OF TASMĪʿ (ALLAH LISTENS TO HIM WHO PRAISES HIM), TAḤMĪD (O, OUR LORD, FOR THEE IS THE PRAISE), AND TĀMĪN (ĀMĪN)

(809) Abū Huraira reported: The Messenger of Allah (may peace be upon him) said: When the Imām says: "Allah listens to him who praises Him," you should say: "O Allah, our Lord, for Thee is the praise," for if what anyone says synchronises with what the angels say, his past sins will be forgiven.

(810) A ḥadīth like this is narrated by Abū Huraira by another chain of transmitters.

(811) Abū Huraira reported: The Messenger of Allah (may peace be upon him) said: Say Āmīn[629] when the Imām says Āmīn, for if anyone's utterance of Āmīn synchronises with that of the angels,[630] he will be forgiven his past sins.

(812) Abū Huraira said: I heard from the Messenger of Allah (may peace be upon him) the ḥadīth like one transmitted by Mālik, but he made no mention of the words of Shihāb.

(813) Abū Huraira reported: The Messenger of Allah (may peace be upon him) said: When anyone amongst you utters Āmīn in prayer and the angels in the sky also utter Āmīn, and this (utterance of the one) synchronises with (that of) the other, all his previous sins are pardoned.

(814) Abū Huraira reported: The Messenger of Allah (may peace be upon him) said: When anyone amongst you utters Āmīn and the angels in the sky also utter Āmīn and (the Āmīn) of the one synchronises with (that of) the other, all his previous sins are pardoned.

(815) A ḥadīth like this is transmitted by Maʿmar from Hammām b. Munabbih on the authority of Abū Huraira who reported it from the Apostle of Allah (may peace be upon him).

(816) Abū Huraira reported: The Messenger of Allah (may peace be upon him) said: When the reciter (Imām) utters: "Not of those on whom (is Thine) wrath and not the erring," and (the person) behind him utters Āmīn and his utterance synchronises with that of the dwellers of heavens, all his previous sins would be pardoned.[631]

629. The reciting of Āmīn at the end of Sūrat al-Fātiḥa is known as *Tāmīn*. (It means: O Allah, grant our prayer.) This is in fact a sort of very humble appeal before the Lord for granting our prayer. The concluding sentences of Sūrat al-Fātiḥa (Guide us in the straight path, the path of those to whom Thou art generous, not of those with whom Thou art angry, nor of those who go astray) is a fervent supplication before the Lord for leading us to the path of righteousness. At the end of the supplication we have been commanded to make a humble appeal to our Master to grant it out of His Grace and Mercy, and not as a matter of right.

630. Various explanations have been given for this, but the most simple and straightforward explanation is that the synchronising of one's Āmīn with that of the angels implies that it should be uttered along with the Imām.

631. The utterance of Āmīn by both the Imām and his followers at the end of Sūrat al-Fātiḥa is essential and there is no difference of opinion on this issue. The difference, however, is on the point

Chapter CLXVII

THE MUQTADĪ (FOLLOWER) SHOULD STRICTLY FOLLOW THE IMĀM IN PRAYER

(817) Anas b. Mālik reported: The Apostle of Allah (may peace be upon him) fell down from a horse and his right side was grazed. We went to him to inquire after his health when the time of prayer came. He led us in prayer in a sitting posture and we said prayer behind him sitting, and when he finished the prayer he said: The Imām is appointed only to be followed; so when he recites takbīr, you should also recite that; when he prostrates, you should also prostrate; when he rises up, you should also rise up, and when he says: "God listens to him who praises Him," you should say: "Our Lord, to Thee be the praise," and when he prays sitting, all of you should pray sitting.[632]

(818) Anas bin Mālik reported: The Messenger of Allah (may peace be upon him) fell down from a horse and he was grazed and he led the prayer for us sitting, and the rest of the ḥadīth is the same.

(819) Anas b. Mālik reported: The Messenger of Allah (may peace be upon him) fell down from a horse and his right side was grazed, and the rest of the ḥadīth is the same with the addition of these words: "When he (the Imām) says prayer standing, you should also do so."

(820) Anas reported: The Messenger of Allah (may peace be upon him) rode a horse and fell down from it and his right side was grazed, and the rest of the ḥadīth is the same, and (these words) are found in it: "When he (the Imām) says prayer in an erect posture, you should also say it in an erect posture."

(821) Anas b. Mālik reported: The Messenger of Allah (may peace be upon him) fell down from his horse and his right side was grazed, and the rest of the ḥadīth is the same. In this ḥadīth there are no additions (of words) as transmitted by Yūnus and Mālik.

(822) 'Ā'isha reported: The Messenger of Allah (may peace be upon him) fell ill and some of his Companions came to inquire after his health. The Messenger of Allah (may

whether it should be uttered in a loud voice or in a subdued tone. So far as the *sirri* prayers (noon and afternoon prayers) are concerned, there is unanimity of opinions amongst the jurists that it should be uttered inwardly. According to Shāfi'ites, Ḥanbalites and Ahl al-Ḥadīth, Āmīn should be uttered loudly in *jahri* prayers both by the Imām and his followers. Imām Mālik is of the opinion that in such prayers the Imām should utter it in a subdued tone, whereas the followers should recite it loudly. The Ḥanafites and some other jurists of Kūfah deem it preferable to utter Āmīn in a subdued tone both in *sirri* and *jahri* prayers. They base their argument primarily on a ḥadīth recorded in Tirmidhī that the Holy Prophet uttered Āmīn and kept his tone low.

The fact is that both the modes of utterance are correct since the Holy Prophet uttered Āmīn both loudly and in subdued tone at different occasions.

632. According to Imām Auzā'ī and Imām Mālik, this mode is essential in offering prayer. Imām Shāfi'ī and Imām Abū Ḥanīfa are of the opinion that it is not advisable to say prayer sitting behind an Imām who has been obliged to say prayer in a sitting posture due to illness or some other reason. They base their argument on the fact that the Holy Prophet led the prayer before his death in a sitting posture while the followers observed it in a standing position, and assert that when there is valid reason to offer prayer in a sitting position, one should not do so, even if his Imām is doing that.

peace be upon him) said prayer sitting, while (his Companions) said it (behind him) standing. He (the Holy Prophet) directed them by his gesture to sit down, and they sat down (in prayer). After finishing the (prayer) he (the Holy Prophet) said: The Imām is appointed so that he should be followed, so bow down when he bows down, and rise up when he rises up and say (prayer) sitting when he (the Imām) says (it) sitting.

(823) This ḥadīth is transmitted with the same chain of transmitters by Hishām b. 'Urwa.

(824) Jābir reported: The Messenger of Allah (may peace be upon him) was ill and we said prayer behind him and he was sitting. And Abū Bakr was making audible to the people his takbīr. As he paid his attention towards us he saw us standing and (directed us to sit down) with a gesture. So we sat down and said our prayer with his prayer in a sitting posture. After uttering salutation he said: You were at this time about to do an act like that of the Persians and the Romans. They stand before their kings while they sit, so don't do that; follow your Imāms. If they say prayer standing, you should also do so, and if they say prayer sitting, you should also say prayer sitting.[633]

(825) Jābir said: The Messenger of Allah (may peace be upon him) led the prayer and Abū Bakr was behind him. When the Messenger of Allah (may peace be upon him) recited the takbīr, Abū Bakr also recited (it) in order to make it audible to us. And the rest of the ḥadīth is like one transmitted by Laith.

(826) Abū Huraira reported: The Messenger of Allah (may peace be upon him) said: The Imām is appointed so that he should be followed, so don't be at variance with him. Recite takbīr when he recites it; bow down, when he bows down and when he says: "Allah listens to him who praises Him," say: "O Allah, our Lord, to Thee be the Praise." And when he (the Imām) prostrates, you should also prostrate, and when he says prayer sitting, you should all observe prayer sitting.

(827) A ḥadīth like this has been transmitted by Hammām b. Munabbih from the Apostle of Allah (may peace be upon him) on the authority of Abū Huraira.

(828) Abū Huraira reported: The Messenger of Allah (may peace be upon him), while teaching us (the principles of faith), said: Do not try to go ahead of the Imām, recite takbīr when he recites it, and when he says, "Nor of those who err," you should say Āmīn, bow down when he bows down, and when he says: "Allah listens to him who praises Him," say: "O Allah, our Lord, to Thee be the praise."

(829) Abū Huraira reported from the Apostle of Allah (may peace be upon him)

633. According to Shāh Walīullāh of Dehli, this command is concerned with the earlier period when the present mode of prayer was made obligatory. The Holy Prophet stressed this point with a view to effacing out of the minds of his people the undue respect and reverence which the neighbouring people of Persia and Rome showed to their kings. They kept standing before them in all humility and dared not sit down before them. The Holy Prophet did not approve of this type of respect which is against the dignity of man He, therefore, in contravention of the practices amongst the Romans and the Greeks, ordered them to sit down when the Imām was sitting and not to observe this type of ceremonious respect. But when the sense of human dignity and equality took hold of the minds of the Muslims, then this practice was abrogated and the Muslims were permitted to say their prayer standing behind a sitting Imām, when there is no valid reason for it, as standing in prayer is a part of prayer and it should not be abandoned in normal circumstances (*Ḥujjatullāh-il-Bāligha*, Vol. II, p. 27).

(a ḥadīth) like it, except the words: "Nor of those who err, say Āmīn" and added: "And don't rise up ahead of him."

(830) Abū Huraira reported: The Messenger of Allah (may peace be upon him) said: Verily the Imām is a shield,[634] say prayer sitting when he says prayer sitting. And when he says: "Allah listens to him who praises Him," say: "O Allah, our Lord, to Thee be the praise," and when the utterance of the people of the earth synchronises with that of the beings of heaven (angels), all the previous sins would be pardoned.

(831) Abū Huraira reported Allah's Messenger (may peace be upon him) saying: The Imām[635] is appointed to be followed. So recite takbīr when he recites it, and bow down when he bows down and when he utters: "Allah listens to him who praises Him," say: "O Allah, our Lord for Thee be the praise." And when he prays standing, you should pray standing. And when he prays sitting, all of you should pray sitting.

Chapter CLXVIII

THE IMĀM IS AUTHORISED TO APPOINT ONE AS HIS DEPUTY WHEN THERE IS A VALID REASON FOR IT (FOR EXAMPLE, ILLNESS OR JOURNEY OR ANY OTHER), AND IF AN IMĀM LEADS THE PRAYER SITTING AS HE CANNOT DO SO STANDING, HIS FOLLOWERS SHOULD SAY PRAYER STANDING PROVIDED THEY ARE ABLE TO DO IT AND THERE IS AN ABROGATION OF SAYING PRAYER SITTING BEHIND A SITTING IMĀM

(832) 'Ubaidullah b. 'Abdullah reported: I visited 'Ā'isha and asked her to tell about the illness of the Messenger of Allah (may peace be upon him). She agreed and said: The Apostle (may peace be upon him) was seriously ill and he asked whether the people had prayed.[636] We said: No, they are waiting for you, Messenger of Allah. He (the Holy Prophet) said: Put some water in the tub for me. We did accordingly and he (the Holy Prophet) took a bath and, when he was about to move with difficulty, he fainted.[637] When he came round, he again said: Have the people said prayer? We said: No ,they are waiting for you, Messenger of Allah. He (the Holy Prophet) again said: Put some water for me in the tub. We did accordingly and he took a bath,

634. The Imām serves as a safeguard against the omissions and commissions of his followers in prayer.

635. Islam teaches discipline—spiritual, moral, social and political. This purpose can be achieved through obedience in prayer, the most important act of devotion in any religious system.

636. This incident refers to the last illness of the Holy Prophet. He ran alarmingly high temperature but even in this precarious condition his mind was set on prayer, because prayer is the heart and soul of religion and God-consciousness. This gives an idea of the intense love which the Holy Prophet had for the Lord. Nothing was so dear to his heart as prayer.

637. Due to high temperature the Holy Prophet fainted but soon recovered and talked about prayer only.

but when he was about to move with difficulty, he fainted. When he came round, he asked whether the people had prayed. We said: No, they are waiting for you, Messenger of Allah. He said: Put some water for me in the tub. We did accordingly and he took a bath and he was about to move with difficulty when he fainted. When he came round, he said: Have the people said prayer? We said: No, they are waiting for you, Messenger of Allah. She ('Ā'isha) said: The people were staying in the mosque and waiting for the Messenger of Allah (may peace be upon him) to lead the last (night) prayer. She ('Ā'isha) said: The Messenger of Allah (may peace be upon him) sent (instructions) to Abū Bakr[638] to lead the people in prayer. When the messenger came, he told him (Abū Bakr): The Messenger of Allah (may peace be upon him) has ordered you to lead the people in prayer. Abū Bakr who was a man of very tenderly feelings asked 'Umar to lead the prayer. 'Umar said: You are more entitled to that. Abū Bakr led the prayers during those days. Afterwards the Messenger of Allah (may peace be upon him) felt some relief and he went out supported by two men, one of them was al-Abbās, to the noon prayer. Abū Bakr was leading the people in prayer. When Abū Bakr saw him, he began to withdraw, but the Apostle of Allah (may peace be upon him) told him not to withdraw. He told his two (companions) to seat him down beside him (Abū Bakr). They seated him by the side of Abū Bakr. Abū Bakr said the prayer standing while following the prayer of the Apostle (may peace be upon him) and the people said prayer (standing) while following the prayer of Abū Bakr. The Apostle (may peace be upon him) was seated. 'Ubaidullah said: I visited 'Abdullah b. 'Abbās and said: Should I submit to you what 'Ā'isha had told about the illness of the Apostle (may peace be upon him)? He said: Go ahead. I submitted to him what had been transmitted by her ('Ā'isha). He objected to none of it, only asking whether she had named to him the man who accompanied al-'Abbās. I said: No. He said: It was 'Alī.[639]

(833) 'Ā'isha reported: It was in the house of Maimūna that the Messenger of Allah (may peace be upon him) first fell ill. He asked permission from his wives to stay in her ('Ā'isha's) house during his illness.[640] They granted him permission. She ('Ā'isha) narrated: He (the Holy Prophet) went out (for prayer) with his hand over

638. This is a convincing proof of Abū Bakr's most eminent position amongst the Companions of the Holy Prophet. That Abū Bakr was deputed by Muḥammad (may peace be upon him) to lead the prayer is a clear indication that he was the most competent person to head the commonwealth of Islam. Islam draws no line of demarcation between religious and secular, and the Imām of prayer is also the Imām of the State. This was what the Muslims acknowledged at the time of the election of the first Caliph. They said: We are pleased with him with regard to our worldly affairs with whom the Holy Prophet was pleased with regard to our *dīn*. In Islamic polity religion reigns supreme and the worldly aspects of life are subservient to it.

639. Ḥaḍrat 'Ā'isha (Allah be pleased with her) did not intentionally ignore the name of Ḥaḍrat 'Alī (Allah be pleased with him) as some of the people allege. The fact is that Ḥaḍrat 'Abbās supported the Holy Prophet on one side, whereas on the other side there was not one person to support but three persons, e.g. Usāma b. Zaid, Faḍl b. 'Abbās and Ḥaḍrat 'Alī (Allah be pleased with all of them). And it was for this reason that Ḥaḍrat 'Ā'isha made no mention of them. The story of ill-will against Ḥaḍrat 'Alī is a mere myth (*Fatḥ-al-Mulhim*, Vol. II, p. 58).

640. One can find in it a high sense of justice which the Holy Prophet observed in his ideal treatment towards his wives. He was seriously ill and was unable to move out of his bed, but even in this condition he was highly sensitive to the feelings of his wives. He, therefore, asked their permission to let him stay in the house of 'Ā'isha.

al-Faḍl b. 'Abbās and on the other hand there was another person and (due to weakness) his feet dragged on the earth. 'Ubaidullah said: I narrated this ḥadīth to the son of 'Abbās ('Abdullah b. 'Abbās) and he said: Do you know who the man was whose name 'Ā'isha did not mention? It was 'Alī.

(834) 'Ā'isha, the wife of the Apostle (may peace be upon him), said: When the Messenger of Allah (may peace be upon him) fell ill and his illness became serious, he asked permission from his wives to stay in my house during his illness. They gave him permission to do so. He stepped out (of 'Ā'isha's apartment for prayer) supported by two persons. (He was so much weak) that his feet dragged on the ground and he was being supported by 'Abbās b. 'Abd al-Muṭṭalib and another person. 'Ubaidullah said: I informed 'Abdullah (b. 'Abbās) about that which 'Ā'isha had said. 'Abdullah b. 'Abbās said: Do you know the man whose name 'Ā'isha did not mention? He said: No. Ibn 'Abbās said: It was 'Alī.

(835) 'Ā'isha, the wife of the Apostle of Allah (may peace be upon him), said: I tried to dissuade the Messenger of Allah (may peace be upon him) from it[641] (i.e. from appointing Abū Bakr as the Imām) and my insistence upon it was not due to the fact that I entertained any apprehension in my mind[642] that the people would not love the man who would occupy his (Prophet's) place (i.e. who would be appointed as his caliph) and I feared that the people would be superstitious[643] about one who would occupy his place. I, therefore, desired that the Messenger of Allah (may peace be upon him) should leave Abū Bakr aside in this matter.

(836) 'Ā'isha reported: When the Messenger of Allah (may peace be upon him) came to my house, he said: Ask Abū Bakr to lead people in prayer. 'Ā'isha narrated: I said, Messenger of Allah, Abū Bakr is a man of tenderly feelings; as he recites the Qur'ān, he cannot help shedding tears: so better command anyone else to lead the prayer. By Allah, there is nothing disturbing in it for me but the idea that the people may not take evil omen with regard to one who is the first to occupy the place of the Messenger of Allah (may peace be upon him). I tried to dissuade him (the Holy Prophet) twice or thrice (from appointing my father as an Imām in prayer), but he ordered Abū

641. Ḥaḍrat 'Ā'isha could easily visualise that the Imāmah of prayer would burden her kind-hearted father with the heavy responsibilities as the head of the State. It was out of sheer love for her father that she requested the Holy Prophet not to appoint Abū Bakr as the Imām. One can easily find in this ḥadīth the grave and heavy responsibilities which fall on the shoulders of the head of an Islamic State. As Ḥaḍrat 'Ā'isha was fully conscious of the difficulty of the task which lay ahead for her father, she persuaded the Holy Prophet to spare him as he was a man of very tenderly feelings and she thought that he would not be able to run the administration well which at times needs stern actions.

The coming events proved that Abū Bakr was the best choice and he, in spite of his kind and generous heart, was fully competent to run the affairs of the State with perfect efficiency and brilliance and was strong enough to cope with any situation, however alarming it might be.

642. This can be translated like this also: "It was not due to anything else except that I did not think that the people would love the man. . . ."

643. The Prophet's health was fast deteriorating and one could easily perceive that he was about to leave for his heavenly abode. Ḥaḍrat 'Ā'isha thought that the appointment of Ḥaḍrat Abū Bakr as an Imām at this critical juncture would be taken as a bad omen by the people since his installation to this high office would mark the final departure of the Holy Prophet from this mortal world.

Bakr to lead the people in prayer and said: You women are like those (who had) surrounded Yūsuf.[644]

(837) 'Ā'isha reported: When the Messenger of Allah (may peace be upon him) was confined to bed, Bilāl came to him to summon him to prayer. He (the Holy Prophet) said: Ask Abū Bakr to lead the people in prayer. She ('Ā'isha) reported: I said: Messenger of Allah, Abū Bakr is a tender-hearted man,[645] so when he would stand at your place (he would be so overwhelmed by feelings) that he would not be able to make the people hear anything (his recitation would not be audible to the followers in prayer). You should better order 'Umar (to lead the prayer). He (the Holy Prophet) said: Ask Abū Bakr to lead people in prayer. She ('Ā'isha) said: I asked Ḥafṣa to (convey) my impression to him (the Holy Prophet) that Abū Bakr was a tender-hearted man, so when he would stand at his place, he would not be able to make the people hear anything. He better order 'Umar. Ḥafṣa conveyed this (message of Ḥaḍrat 'Ā'isha) to him (the Holy Prophet). The Messenger of Allah (may peace be upon him) said: (You are behaving) as if you are the famales who had gathered around Yūsuf. Order Abū Bakr to lead the people in prayer. She ('Ā'isha) reported: So Abū Bakr was ordered to lead the people in prayer. As the prayer began, the Messenger of Allah (may peace be upon him) felt some relief; he got up and moved supported by two persons and his feet dragged on earth (due to excessive weakness). 'Ā'isha reported: As he (the Holy Prophet) entered the mosque, Abū Bakr perceived his (arrival). He was about to withdraw, but the Messenger of Allah (may peace by upon him) by the gesture (of his hand) told him to keep standing at his place. The Messenger of Allah (may peace be upon him) came and seated himself on the left side of Abū Bakr. She ('Ā'isha) reported: The Messenger of Allah (may peace be upon him) was leading people in prayer sitting. Abū Bakr was following the prayer of the Apostle (may peace be upon him) in a standing posture and the people were following the prayer of Abū Bakr.[646]

(838) A'mash reported: When the Messenger of Allah (may peace be upon him) suffered from illness of which he died, and in the ḥadīth transmitted by Ibn Mus-hir the words are: The Messenger of Allah (may peace be upon him) was brought till he was seated by his (Abū Bakr's) side and the Apostle (may peace be upon him) led

644. Two reasons have been given by commentators for similarity between the act of Ḥaḍrat 'Ā'isha and that of the women around Ḥaḍrat Yūsuf (peace be upon him). In case of Ḥaḍrat Yūsuf the wife of 'Azīz tried to prevail upon him, but he remained firm and unmoved. In the present case Ḥaḍrat 'Ā'isha tried to prevail upon the Holy Prophet, but he did not yield to her, since it was a matter of principle, and sentimentalism could not be allowed to influence his decision.

The second reason is that the wife of 'Azīz invited some of the ladies of the town apparently for honouring them with a royal feast, but inwardly she wanted to exhibit before them the rare beauty of Yūsuf. 'Ā'isha was requesting the Holy Prophet to spare her father from the responsibility of Imāmah on the ostensible plea that he was very sensitive and would weep while reciting the Qur'ān in prayer. This reason was no doubt there. But inwardly the more important idea behind that was the fear that the people might regard her father's appointment as a bad omen, in case of the death of the Holy Prophet (*Fath-ul-Mulhim*, Vol. II, p. 59).

645. رجل آسيف : means a grieving person, or one who is quickly affected by grief. It also implies a tender-hearted man (Lane's *Lexicon*).

646. This ḥadīth abrogates those recorded in the previous chapter, wherein a follower in prayer was commanded to say prayer sitting when the Imām was sitting. Here the Messenger of Allah was leading the prayer in a sitting posture but Abū Bakr said it in a standing posture behind him.

the people in prayer and Abū Bakr was making takbīr audible to them, and in the ḥadīth transmitted by 'Īsā the (words are): "The Messenger of Allah (may peace be upon him) sat and led the people in prayer and Abū Bakr was by his side and he was making (takbīr) audible to the people."

(839) 'Ā'isha reported: The Messenger of Allah (may peace be upon him) ordered Abū Bakr that he should lead people in prayer during his illness, and he led them in prayer. 'Urwa said: The Messenger of Allah (may peace be upon him) felt relief and went (to the mosque) and Abū Bakr was leading the people in prayer. When Abū Bakr saw him he began to withdraw, but the Messenger of Allah (may peace be upon him) signed him to remain where he was. The Messenger of Allah (may peace be upon him) sat opposite to Abū Bakr by his side. Abū Bakr said prayer following the prayer of the Messenger of Allah (may peace be upon him), and the people said prayer following the prayer of Abū Bakr.

(840) Anas b. Mālik reported: Abū Bakr led them in prayer due to the illness of the Messenger of Allah (may peace be upon him) of which he died. It was a Monday and they stood in rows for prayer. The Messenger of Allah (may peace be upon him) drew aside the curtain of ('Ā'isha's) apartment and looked at us while he was standing, and his (Prophet's) face was (as bright) as the paper of the Holy Book.[647] The Messenger of Allah (may peace be upon him) felt happy and smiled. And we were confounded with joy while in prayer due to the arrival (among our midst) of the Messenger of Allah (may peace be upon him). Abū Bakr stepped back upon his heels to say prayer in a row perceiving that the Messenger of Allah (may peace be upon him) had come out for prayer. The Messenger of Allah (may peace be upon him) with the help of his hand signed to them to complete their prayer. The Messenger of Allah (may peace be upon him) went back (to his apartment) and drew the curtain. He (the narrator) said: The Messenger of Allah (may peace be upon him) breathed his last on that very day.

(841) Anas reported: The last glance that I have had of the Messenger of Allah (may peace be upon him) (before his death) was that when he on Monday drew the curtain aside. The ḥadīth transmitted by Ṣāliḥ is perfect and complete.

(842) This ḥadīth is narrated on the authority of Anas b. Mālik by another chain of transmitters.

(843) Anas reported: The Apostle of Allah (may peace be upon him) did not come to us for three days. When the prayer was about to start, Abū Bakr stepped forward (to lead the prayer), and the Apostle of Allah (may peace be upon him) lifted the curtain. When the face of the Apostle of Allah (may peace be upon him) became visible to us, we (found) that no sight was more endearing to us than the face of the Apostle of Allah (may peace be upon him) as it appeared to us. The Apostle of Allah (may peace be upon him) with the gesture of his hand directed Abū Bakr to step forward

647. 'Allāma Sindhī has explained why the Holy Prophet's face has been compared to the leaf of the Holy Book. He says that the Prophet's pious face was bright, gleaming with religious piety and it, therefore, commanded deep love and profound reverence from the Muslims just as the Holy Books command (*Fatḥ-ul-Mulhim*, Vol. II, p. 60).

There is another explanation of comparing the Prophet's sacred face to the Holy Book. In the old days the Holy Books were written on *qirṭās*, the colour of which turned pale with the passage of time. As the Holy Prophet's face had become somewhat pale on account of illness, the narrator might have, therefore, compared him to a leaf of the Holy Book. Allah knows best.

(and lead the prayer). The Apostle of Allah (may peace be upon him) then drew the curtain, and we could not see him till he died.

(844) Abū Mūsā reported: When the Messenger of Allah (may peace be upon him) became ill and illness became serious he ordered Abū Bakr to lead the people in prayer. Upon this 'Ā'isha said: Messenger of Allah, Abū Bakr is a man of tenderly feelings; when he would stand in your place (he would be so much overwhelmed by grief that) he would not be able to lead the people in prayer. He (the Holy Prophet) said: You order Abū Bakr to lead the people in prayer, and added: You are like the female companions of Yūsuf. So Abū Bakr led the prayer (during this period of illness) in the life of the Messenger of Allah (may peace be upon him).

Chapter CLXIX

IF THE IMĀM ARRIVES LATE AND THERE IS NO DANGER OF AN UNPLEASANT HAPPENING, ANOTHER IMĀM CAN BE APPOINTED TO LEAD THE PRAYER

(845) Sahl b. Sa'd al-Sā'idī reported: The Messenger of Allah (may peace be upon him) went to the tribe of Banī 'Amr b. 'Auf in order to bring reconciliation amongst (its members), and it was a time of prayer. The Mu'adhdhin came to Abū Bakr and said: Would you lead the prayer in case I recite takbīr (taḥrīma, with which the prayer begins)? He (Abū Bakr) said: Yes. He (the narrator) said: He (Abū Bakr) started (leading) the prayer. The people were saying the prayer when the Messenger of Allah (may peace be upon nim) happened to come there and made his way (through the people) till he stood in a row. The people began to clap (their hands), but Abū Bakr paid no heed (to it) in prayer. When the people clapped more vigorously, he (Abū Bakr) then paid heed and saw the Messenger of Allah (may peace be upon him) there. (He was about to withdraw when) the Messenger of Allah (may peace be upon him) signed to him to keep standing at his place. Abū Bakr lifted his hands and praised Allah for what the Messenger of Allah (may peace be upon him) had commanded him and then Abū Bakr withdrew himself till he stood in the midst of the row and the Messenger of Allah (may peace be upon him) stepped forward and led the prayer. When (the prayer) was over, he (the Holy Prophet) said: O Abū Bakr, what prevented you from standing (at that place) as I ordered you to do? Abū Bakr said: It does not become the son of Abū Quḥāfa to lead prayer before the Messenger of Allah (may peace be upon him). The Messenger of Allah (may peace be upon him) said (to the people) around him: What is it that I saw you clapping so vigorously? (Bear in mind) when anything happens in prayer, say: *Subḥān Allah*, for when you would utter it, it would attract the attention, while clapping of hands is meant for women.[648]

648. This ḥadīth sheds light on so many aspects.

(*a*) It is one of the main duties of the man in power to look into various aspects of social and individual life and try to cure all the ills which find their way into it. Whenever there is bitterness in any section of society, it should be removed and every attempt should be made to create an atmosphere of harmony and cordial relations amongst its members.

(*b*) It establishes the priority of Abū Bakr as the righteous Caliph of the Holy Prophet.

(*c*) It teaches us an object lesson for Imāmah. Only a right person should be asked to lead the

(846) This ḥadīth is transmitted by Sahl b. Sa'd in the same way as narrated by Mālik, with the exception of these words: "Abū Bakr lifted his hands and praised Allah and retraced his (steps) till he stood in a row."

(847) Sahl b. Sa'd al-Sā'idī reported: The Apostle of Allah (may peace be upon him) went to Banī 'Amr b. 'Auf in order to bring about reconciliation amongst them. The rest of the ḥadīth is the same but with (the addition of these words): "The Messenger of Allah (may peace be upon him) came and made his way through the rows till he came to the first row and Abū Bakr retraced his steps."[649]

(848) Mughīra b. Shu'ba reported that he participated in the expedition of Tabūk along with the Messenger of Allah (may peace be upon him). The Messenger of Allah (may peace be upon him) went out to answer the call of nature before the morning prayer, and I carried along with him a jar (full of water). When the Messenger of Allah (may peace be upon him) came back to me (after relieving himself), I began to pour water upon his hands out of the jar and he washed his hands three times, then washed his face three times. He then tried to tuck up the sleeves of his cloak upon his forearms, but since the sleeves were tight he inserted his hands in the cloak and then brought out his forearms up to the elbow, below the cloak and then wiped over his shoes and then moved on. Mughīra said: I also moved along with him till he came to the people and (he found) that they had been saying their prayer under the Imāmah of 'Abd al-Raḥmān b. 'Auf. The Messenger of Allah (may peace be upon him) could get one rak'ah out of two and said (this) last rak'ah along with the people. When 'Abd al-Raḥmān b. 'Auf pronounced the salutation, the Messenger of Allah (may peace be upon him) got up to complete the prayer. This made the Muslims terrified and most of them began to recite the glory of the Lord. When the Apostle of Allah (may peace be upon him) finished his prayer, he turned towards them and then said: You did well, or said with a sense of joy: You did the right thing that you said prayer at the appointed hour.

(849) This ḥadīth is transmitted by Ḥamza b. Mughīra by another chain of transmitters (but with the addition of these words): "I made up my mind to hold 'Abd al-Raḥmān b. 'Auf back, but the Messenger of Allah (may peace be upon him) said: Leave him."

Chapter CLXX

IF SOMETHING HAPPENS IN PRAYER, MEN SHOULD GLORIFY ALLAH AND WOMEN SHOULD CLAP HANDS

(850) Abū Huraira reported: The Messenger of Allah (may peace be upon him)

prayer and that too with the verbal or implied consent of the permanent Imām.

(*d*) Every care should be taken to avoid dissension as far as possible and one should accept this office only if the general opinion is in one's favour. One must not thrust oneself as Imām of the people contrary to their will.

(*e*) In case one has to point out any omission or commission in prayer one should do this with a sense of dignity keeping in view the sublimity of the occasion.

(*f*) The womenfolk should clap their hands but men should say *Subḥān Allah* (Hallowed be Allah) when they want to rectify their Imām. This shows that females should not unnecessarily raise their voice before males thus inviting their attention.

649. While retracing one's steps in prayer one should not turn one's back towards the Qibla.

said : Glorification of Allah is for men and clapping of hands is meant for women (if something happens in prayer). Ḥarmala added in his narration that Ibn Shibāb told him: I saw some of the scholars glorifying Allah and making a gesture.[650]

(851) This ḥadīth is narrated on the authority of Abū Huraira by another chain of transmitters.

(852) This ḥadīth is transmitted by Muḥammad b. Rāfi', Abu'l-Razzāq, Ma'mar, Hammām on the authority of Abū Huraira with the addition of (the word) "prayer".

Chapter CLXXI

COMMAND TO OBSERVE PRAYER WELL, PERFECTING IT, AND DEVOTION IN IT

(853) Abū Huraira reported : One day the Messenger of Allah (may peace be upon him) led the prayer. Then turning (towards his Companions) he said : O you, the man, why don't you say your prayer well?[651] Does the performer of prayer not see how he is performing the prayer for he performs it for himself ?[652] By Allah, I see behind me as I see in front of me.[653]

(854) Abū Huraira reported : The Messenger of Allah (may peace be upon him) said: Do you find me seeing towards the Qibla only? By Allah, your bowing and your prostrating are not hidden from my view. Verily I see them behind my back.

(855) Anas b. Mālik reported : The Messenger of Allah (may peace be upon him) said : Perform bowing and prostration well. By Allah, I see you even if you are behind me, or he said : (I see you) behind my back when you bow or prostrate.

(856) Anas reported : The Apostle of Allah (may peace be upon him) said: Complete the bowing and prostration well. By Allah, I see you behind my back as to how you bow and prostrate or when you bow and prostrate.

Chapter CLXXII

IT IS FORBIDDEN TO BOW AND PROSTRATE AHEAD OF THE IMĀM

(857) Anas reported : The Messenger of Allah (may peace be upon him) one day led

650. According to one school of thought, gesture is permissible in case of necessity, but according to Imām Ṭaḥāvī, it has been abrogated by an explicit injunction of the Holy Prophet (may peace be upon him) to observe perfect calmness and tranquillity in prayer.

651. Prayer is the most important act of religious devotion ; it should, therefore, be observed with dignity and tranquillity of mind.

652. He is observing the prayer for the purification and elevation of his own soul.

653. This part of the ḥadīth has been interpreted in different ways. In one of the interpretations it has been asserted that the Holy Prophet's keen power of perception could acquaint him with the behaviour of his followers in prayer. The second view is that the Holy Prophet had been endowed with a special sight which could enable him to see behind him, but this faculty could work only in prayer. It was in fact a miraculous power (*Fatḥ-ul-Mulhim*, Vol. II, p. 63).

us in the prayer, and when he completed the prayer he turned his face towards us and said: O people, I am your Imām, so do not precede me in bowing and prostration and in standing and turning (faces, i.e. in pronouncing salutation), for I see you in front of me and behind me, and then said: By Him in Whose hand is the life of Muḥammad, if you could see what I see, you would have laughed little and wept much more. They said: What did you see, Messenger of Allah? He replied: (I saw) Paradise and Hell.

(858) This ḥadīth is transmitted by Anas with another chain of transmitters, and in the ḥadīth transmitted by Jarīr there is no mention of "turning (faces)".

(859) Abū Huraira reported: The Messenger of Allah (may peace be upon him) said: Does the man who lifts his head ahead of the Imām (from prostration) not fear that Allah may change his head into the head of an ass?[654]

(860) Abū Huraira reported: The Messenger of Allah (may peace be upon him) said: Does the man who lifts his head before the Imām not fear that Allah may change his face into that of an ass?

(861) This ḥadīth has been narrated by Abū Huraira by another chain of transmitters except for the words narrated by Rabī' b. Muslim: "Allah may make his face like the face of an ass."

Chapter CLXXIII

IT IS FORBIDDEN TO LIFT ONE'S EYES TOWARDS THE SKY IN PRAYFR

(862) Jābir b. Samura reported: The Messenger of Allah (may peace be upon him) said: The people who lift their eyes towards the sky in prayer should avoid it or they would lose their eyesight.[655]

(863) Abū Huraira reported: People should avoid lifting their eyes towards the sky while supplicating in prayer, otherwise their eyes would be snatched away.[656]

654. These words are uttered by the Holy Prophet as a warning that one should be vigilant in prayer and should consciously follow the Imām and should not behave in an irresponsible way.

655. We have told before that the object of prayer is to inculcate God-consciousness and make man realise that he is the loyal servant of the Lord. This object can be achieved if one is in commune with Allah and is at the same time aware of one's surroundings and of one's own self. This is possible if the mind is set on Allah and the eyes are transferred towards the Qibla, and one is conscious of where he stands and what he is doing. Lifting of one's eyes towards the sky may help in the elevation of the soul, but at the same time it severes man's relation with the material world and dissolves the consciousness of his own being.

Moreover, transfixing one's eyes in the sky is something which does not seem appropriate to the dignity which a man must observe in prayer.

656. There is consensus of opinion amongst the scholars of the Ḥadīth that it is not permissible to lift one's eyes during the ṣalāt, but there is difference of opinion with regard to supplication (du'ā'). Qāḍī Shuraiḥ is of the opinion that even in du'ā' it is not desirable to lift one's eyes towards heaven, but the other scholars deem it permissible as the heaven has been called the Qibla of du'ā'.

Chapter CLXXIV

THE COMMAND TO OBSERVE PRAYER WITH TRANQUILLITY AND CALMNESS AND FORBIDDANCE OF MAKING GESTURES WITH HANDS AND LIFTING THEM WHILE PRONOUNCING SALUTATION, AND THE COMPLETING OF FIRST ROWS AND JOINING TOGETHER WELL IN THEM

(864) Jābir b. Samura reported: The Messenger of Allah (may peace be upon him) came to us and said: How is it that I see you lifting your hands like the tails of headstrong horses?[657] Be calm in prayer. He (the narrator) said: He then again came to us and saw us (sitting) in circles; he said: How is it that I see you in separate groups? He (the narrator) said: He again came to us and said: Why don't you draw yourselves up in rows as angels do in the presence of their Lord? We said: Messenger of Allah, how do the angels draw themselves up in rows in the presence of their Lord? He (the Holy Prophet) said: They make the first rows complete and keep close together in the row.

(865) This ḥadīth has been transmitted by A'mash with the same chain of transmitters.

(866) Jābir b. Samura reported: When we said prayer with the Messenger of Allah (may peace be upon him) we pronounced: Peace be upon you and Mercy of Allah, peace be upon you and Mercy of Allah, and made gesture with the hand on both the sides. Upon this the Messenger of Allah (may peace be upon him) said: What do you point out with your hands as if they are the tails of headstrong horses? This is enough for you that one should place one's hand on one's thigh and then pronounce salutation upon one's brother on the right side and then on the left.

(867) Jābir b. Samura reported: We said our prayer with the Messenger of Allah (may peace be upon him) and, while pronouncing salutations, we made gestures with our hands (indicating) "Peace be upon you, peace be upon you." The Messenger of Allah (may peace be upon him) looked towards us and said: Why is it that you make gestures with your hands like the tails of headstrong horses? When any one of you pronounces salutation (in prayer) he should only turn his face towards his companion and should not make a gesture with his hand.

657. It implies that one should observe prayer with dignity and should not unnecessarily move one's hands. Some of the scholars of Ḥadīth are of the opinion that with this command of the Holy Prophet was forbidden the practice of lifting one's hands while pronouncing salutations.

Chapter CLXXV

STRAIGHTENING OF ROWS AND THE EXCELLENCE OF THE FIRST ROW AND THEN OF THE SUBSEQUENT ROWS AND COMPETING AND VYING WITH ONE ANOTHER FOR THE FIRST ROW AND PRIORITY OF THE MEN OF VIRTUES AND THEIR NEARNESS TO THE IMĀM

(868) Abū Mas'ūd reported: The Messenger of Allah (may peace be upon him) used to touch our shoulders in prayer and say: Keep straight, don't be irregular, for there would be dissension in your hearts.[658] Let those of you who are sedate and prudent[659] be near me, then those who are next to them, then those who are next to them. Abū Mas'ūd said: Now-a-days there is much dissension amongst you.

(869) This ḥadīth is transmitted by Ibn 'Uyaina with the same chain of transmitters.

(870) 'Abdullah b. Mas'ūd reported: The Messenger of Allah (may peace be upon him) said: Let those who are sedate and prudent be near me, then those who are next to them (saying it three times), and beware of the tumult of the markets.[660]

(871) Anas b. Mālik reported: The Messenger of Allah (may peace be upon him) said: Straighten your rows, for the straightening of a row is a part of the perfection of prayer.

(872) Anas b. Mālik reported: The Messenger of Allah (may peace be upon him) said: Complete the rows, for I can see you behind my back.

(873) Hammām b. Munabbih reported: This is what was transmitted to us by Abū Huraira from the Messenger of Allah (may peace be upon him) and, while making a mention of few aḥādīth, said: (The Messenger of Allah directed us thus:) Establish rows in prayer, for the making of a row (straight) is one of the merits of prayer.

(874) Nu'mān b. Bashīr reported: I heard the Messenger of Allah (may peace be upon him) say: Straighten your rows or Allah would create dissension amongst you.[661]

(875) Nu'mān b. Bashīr reported: The Messenger of Allah (may peace be upon him) used to straighten our rows as if he were straightening an arrow with their help until he saw that we had learnt it from him. One day he came out, stood up (for prayer) and was about to say: Allah is the Greatest, when he saw a man, whose chest was bulging out from the row, so he said: Servants of Allah, you must straighten your rows

658. Irregular rows in prayer give a clear indication that the Muslims are slackening in self-discipline which would surely lead them to dissension and mutual distrust. The disciplined behaviour is a blessing and the Holy Prophet not only stressed its importance in words, but also saw it observed in religious acts, for example in prayer and pilgrimage.

659. It implies that it is not the worldly status of man which is given importance in Islam, but his religious piety, his integrity and wisdom; and the social position of a man is not determined by his material possessions but by his God-consciousness.

660. It means that the gathering in the mosque should assume the dignity of a religious assembly, and it should not present the picture of a tumult in the busy markets.

661. That is, your discordant behaviour in prayer would create disunity in your ranks. It is psychological—outward behaviour creates a corresponding mental attitude.

or Allah would create dissension amongst you.

(876) Abū 'Awāna transmitted this ḥadīth with the same chain of transmitters.

(877) Abū Huraira reported: The Messenger of Allah (may peace be upon him) said: If the people were to know what excellence is there in the *Adhān* and in the first row, and they could not (get these opportunities) except by drawing lots, they would have definitely done that. And if they were to know what excellence lies in joining the prayer in the first takbīr (prayer), they would have vied with one another. And if they were to know what excellence lies in night prayer and morning prayer, they would have definitely come even if crawling (on their knees).

(878) Abū Sa'īd al-Khudrī reported: The Messenger of Allah (may peace be upon him) saw (a tendency[662]) among his Companions to go to the back, so he said to them: Come forward and follow my lead, and let those who come after you follow your lead. People will continue to keep back till Allah will put them at the back.[663]

(879) Abū Sa'īd al-Khudrī reported: The Messenger of Allah (may peace be upon him) saw people at the end of the mosque, and then the (above-mentioned ḥadīth) was narrated.

(880) Abū Huraira reported: The Messenger of Allah (may peace be upon him) said: If you were to know, or if they were to know, what (excellence) lies in the front rows, there would have been drawing of lots (for filling them); and Ibn Ḥarb said: For (occupying) the first row there would have been drawing of lots.

(881) Abū Huraira said: The best rows for men are the first rows, and the worst ones the last ones, and the best rows for women are the last ones and the worst ones for them are the first ones.[664]

(882) This ḥadīth is transmitted by Suhail with the same chain of transmitters.

Chapter CLXXVI

THE PRAYING WOMEN HAVE BEEN COMMANDED NOT TO PRECEDE MEN IN LIFTING THEIR HEADS FROM PROSTRATION

(883) Sahl b. Sa'd reported: I saw men having tied (the ends) of their lower garments around their necks, like children, due to shortage of cloth and offering their prayers, behind the Apostle of Allah (may peace be upon him). One of the proclaimers said: O womenfolk, do not lift your heads till men raise (them).[665]

662. This tendency shows that the people lack interest in acts of devotion and they are becoming slack in the performance of their religious duties.

663. This indifference on their part would deprive them of the favours and bounties of Allah.

664. This injunction about women is true only when they join with men in prayer.

665. This ḥadīth relates to the early period of Islam when most of the Companions of the Holy Prophet were so poor that they could not find enough cloth to hide even the private parts of their bodies well. Their lower garments were small and they were, therefore, obliged to tie their ends around their necks as the children usually do so that their private parts might not be exposed. There was, however, a possibility left that during their movements in prayer some part of their *satr* might have been exposed. It was for this reason that women were instructed not to precede men in lifting their heads so that men might adjust their clothing before the women lifted their heads.

Chapter CLXXVII

WOMEN COMING OUT (FROM THEIR HOUSES) FOR GOING TO THE MOSQUE WHEN THERE IS NO APPREHENSION OF WICKEDNESS, BUT THEY SHOULD NOT COME OUT SCENTED

(884) Sālim narrated it from his father ('Abdullah b. 'Umar) that the Messenger of Allah (may peace be upon him) said: When women ask permission for going to the mosque, do not prevent them.

(885) 'Abdullah b. 'Umar reported: I heard the Messenger of Allah (may peace be upon him) say: Don't prevent your women from going to the mosque when they seek your permission. Bilāl[666] b. 'Abdullah said: By Allah, we shall certainly prevent them. On this 'Abdullah b. 'Umar turned towards him and reprimanded him so harshly as I had never heard him do before. He ('Abdullah b. 'Umar said): I am narrating to you that which comes from the Messenger of Allah (may peace be upon him) and you (dare) say: By Allah we shall certainly prevent them.

(886) Ibn 'Umar reported: The Messenger of Allah (may peace be upon him) said: Do not prevent the maid-servants of Allah from going to the mosque.

(887) Ibn 'Umar reported: I heard the Messenger of Allah (may peace be upon him) say: When your women seek your permission for going to the mosque, you grant them (permission).

(888) Ibn 'Umar reported: The Messenger of Allah (may peace be upon him) said: Do not prevent women from going to the mosque at night. A boy said to 'Abdullah b. 'Umar: We would never let them go out, that they may not be caught in evil. He (the narrator) said: Ibn 'Umar reprimanded him and said: I am saying that the Messenger of Allah (may peace be upon him) said this, but you say: We would not allow![667]

(889) A ḥadīth like this has been transmitted by A'mash with the same chain of transmitters.

(890) Ibn 'Umar reported: Grant permission to women for going to the mosque in the night. His son who was called Wāqid said: Then they would make mischief. He (the narrator) said: He thumped his (son's) chest and said: I am narrating to you the ḥadīth of the Messenger of Allah (may peace be upon him), and you say: No!

(891) Ibn 'Umar reported: The Messenger of Allah (may peace be upon him) said: Do not deprive women of their share of the mosques, when they seek permission from

666. Bilāl was not doing something in contravention of the command of the Holy Prophet but he had in his mind the injunction of the Messenger of Allah in which women were instructed to pray preferably in their houses rather than go to the mosques (Abū Dāwūd). Moreover, Bilāl felt that the conditions had undergone a change and it was a period of unrest; so it was not advisible for women to observe prayers in the mosque.

'Abdullah b. 'Umar was also justified in scolding him, because, according to his view, the social atmosphere of the Muslim society was not so uncongenial that women should not be permitted to go to the mosques. He was annoyed, as Shāh Walīullāh rightly maintains, on the apprehension that the Muslims were not permitting their women to join with others in prayer on account of tribal pride and vanity which, according to him, had still some traces left in their minds.

667. This ḥadīth gives a clear idea how enviably the words of the Holy Prophet were respected.

you. Bilāl said : By Allah, we would certainly prevent them. 'Abdullah said : I say that the Messenger of Allah (may peace be upon him) said it and you say: We would certainly prevent them !

(892) Zainab Thaqafiya reported: The Messenger of Allah (may peace be upon him) said : When any one of you (women) participates in the 'Ishā' prayer, she should not perfume herself that night.

(893) Zainab, the wife of 'Abdullah (b. 'Umar), reported : The Messenger of Allah (may peace be upon him) said to us: When any one of you comes to the mosque, she should not apply perfume.

(894) Abū Huraira said : The Messenger of Allah (may peace be upon him) said: Whoever (woman) fumigates herself with perfume should not join us in the 'Ishā' prayer.

(895) 'Amra, daughter of 'Abd al-Raḥmān, reported : I heard 'Ā'isha, the wife of the Apostle of Allah (may peace be upon him), say: If the Messenger of Allah (may peace be upon him) had seen what new things the women have introduced (in their way of life) he would have definitely prevented them from going to the mosque, as the women of Banī Isrā'īl were prevented.[668]

668. Before we close this chapter, it seems advisable that we should explain the standpoint of the Islamic Sharī'a with regard to women joining men in prayer in the mosque. The fact is that the Holy Prophet deemed it preferable for women to say their prayers within the four walls of their houses or in the nearest mosque. Umm Ḥumaid once said to the Holy Prophet: Messenger of Allah, I long to pray with you. Upon this the Messenger of Allah (may peace be upon him) observed: I know it that you love to say prayer with me but the prayer you offer in your chamber is more excellent than that you offer in your apartment, and the prayer that you say in your apartment is more excellent than that you offer in your courtyard, and the prayer which you say in your courtyard is better than that you observe in the mosque of your tribe (which is near to your house) and your prayer in the mosque of your tribe is better than that which you say in my mosque (narrated by Aḥmad, *Kanz al-'Ummāl*).

This ḥadīth is strengthened and supported by a ḥadīth recorded in Abū Dāwūd and transmitted by Ibn Mas'ūd in which the Messenger of Allah is reported to have said : It is more excellent to pray in her house than in her courtyard and more excellent for her to pray in her private chamber than in her house.

These aḥādīth clearly indicate that it is better for women to pray in their own houses. But on the other hand there are a number of aḥādīth some of which have been recorded in this chapter which exhort men to grant permission to Muslim women for praying in the mosque.

Apparently there seems to be some contradiction between these groups of aḥādīth, but the exposition given by the scholars of Ḥadīth, especially by Shāh Walī Ullāh of Delhi, resolves it altogether. The actual fact is that the women who had the good fortune to live during the lifetime of Muḥammad (may peace be upon him) had a deep longing to say their prayer under his Imāmah as it was an enviable privilege for them. They, therefore, sought permission to join prayers in the mosque. Moreover, the moral atmosphere of that blessed period was quite congenial to the coming out of women from their houses and there was not even the slightest chance of indecency towards them. Under such conditions the Holy Prophet did not like to put any curb on their desire to join prayer in the mosque before daybreak and during night. The Holy Prophet could well visualise that moral conditions would change ; therefore women were advised to say their prayers in their houses when there would be deterioration in the moral standards of the people in general.

It should also be kept in mind that even if women are permitted to go to the mosque they should observe purdah and should not perfume themselves or do anything which can attract the attention of the people.

(896) This ḥadīth has been transmitted by Yaḥya b. Sa'īd with the same chain of transmitters.

Chapter CLXXVIII

MODERATION BETWEEN LOUD AND LOW RECITATION IN JAHRĪ PRAYER, WHEN THERE IS A FEAR OF TURMOIL IN RECITING LOUDLY

(897) Ibn 'Abbās reported: The word of (Allah) Great and Glorious: "And utter not thy prayer loudly, nor be low in it" (xvii. 110) was revealed as the Messenger of Allah (may peace be upon him) was hiding himself in Mecca. When he led his Companions in prayer he raised his voice (while reciting the) Qur'ān. And when the polytheists heard that, they reviled the Qur'ān and Him Who revealed it and him who brought it. Upon this Allah, the Exalted, said to His Apostle (may peace be upon him): Utter not thy prayer so loudly that the polytheists may hear thy recitation and (recite it) not so low that it may be inaudible to your Companions. Make them hear the Qur'ān, but do not recite it loudly and seek a (middle) way between these. Recite between loud and low tone.[669]

(898) 'Ā'isha reported that so far as these words of (Allah) Glorious and High are concerned: "And utter not thy prayer loudly nor be low in it" (xvii. 110) relate to supplication (du'ā').

(899) A ḥadīth like this has been narrated by Hishām with the same chain of transmitters.

Chapter CLXXIX

LISTENING TO THE RECITATION OF THE QUR'ĀN

(900) Ibn 'Abbās reported with regard to the words of Allah, Great and Glorious: "Move not thy tongue therewith" (lxxv. 16) that when Gabriel brought revelation to him (the Holy Prophet) he moved his tongue and lips (with a view to committing it to memory instantly). This was something hard for him and it was visible (from his face). Then Allah, the Exalted, revealed this: "Move not thy tongue therewith to make haste (in memorising it). Surely on Us rests the collecting of it and the reciting of it" (lxxv. 16), i.e. Verily it rests with Us that We would preserve it in your heart and (enable you) to recite it. You would recite it when We would recite it and so follow its recitation, and He (Allah) said: "We revealed it, so listen to it attentively. Verily its exposition rests with Us, i.e. We would make it deliver by your tongue." So when Gabriel

669. The Holy Prophet was instructed to recite the Qur'ān in a low voice so that the hostile element might not be provoked, but he was at the same time asked not to recite so low that it might become inaudible to the congregation. This instruction concerned special circumstances when the Muslims were obliged to say their prayers privately, hidden from the view of the polytheists.

But it should be remembered that even if such circumstances do not prevail, prayer should be pronounced with earnestness and humility and the Holy Qur'ān should be recited in a tone neither too loud nor too low.

came to him (to the Holy Prophet), he kept silent, and when he went away he recited as Allah had promised him.[670]

(901) Ibn 'Abbās reported with regard to the words: "Do not move thy tongue therewith to make haste," that the Apostle of Allah (may peace be upon him) felt it hard and he moved his lips. Ibn 'Abbās said to me (Sa'īd b. Jubair): I move them just as the Messenger of Allah (may peace be upon him) moved them. Then said Sa'īd: I move them just as Ibn 'Abbās moved them, and he moved his lips. Allah, the Exalted, revealed this: "Do not move your tongue therewith to make haste. It is with Us that its collection rests and its recital" (al-Qur'ān, lxxv. 16). He said: Its preservation in your heart and then your recital. So when We recite it, follow its recital. He said: Listen to it, and be silent and then it rests with Us that you recite it. So when Gabriel came to the Messenger of Allah (may peace be upon him), he listened to him attentively and when Gabriel went away, the Apostle of Allah (may peace be upon him) recited as he (Gabriel) had recited it.

Chapter CLXXX

RECITATION OF THE QUR'ĀN LOUDLY IN THE DAWN PRAYER

(902) Ibn 'Abbās reported: The Messenger of Allah (may peace be upon him) neither recited the Qur'ān to the Jinn nor did he see them.[671] The Messenger of Allah (may peace be upon him) went out with some of his Companions with the intention of going to the bazaar of 'Ukāẓ.[672] And there had been (at that time) obstructions between satans and the news from the Heaven, and there were flung flames upon them.[673] So satans went back to their people and they said: What has happened to you? They said: There have been created obstructions between us and the news from the Heaven. And there have been flung upon us flames.[674] They said: It cannot happen but for some (important) event. So traverse the eastern parts of the earth and the western parts and find out why is it that there have been created obstructions between us and the news from the Heaven. So they went forth and traversed the easts of the

670. This ḥadīth conclusively proves that the Qur'ān is the word of Allah and not the outpouring of Muḥammad's mind. Every word of it was revealed by God. Had it not been so, there was no need for Muḥammad to repeat the words uttered by the angel in haste. It shows that the words of the Qur'ān were not his own words and these were being conveyed to him from someone else.

671. This incident relates to the early period of apostlehood. The next ḥadīth gives a clear proof that the Holy Prophet had recited the Qur'ān to the Jinn and had seen them.

672. It was a fair which was held in the valley between Mecca and Ṭā'if and was known as the Sūq of 'Ukāz.

673. Before the advent of the Holy Prophet the astrologers and soothsayers had a thriving trade. They tried to have an access to divination with the help of Jinn and other mysterious beings, but with the revelation of the Qur'ān all those practices were abandoned as it was told in clear terms that henceforth no one could have a knowledge of the unseen but through the Holy Prophet. All ancient oracles found themselves gradually and automatically becoming dumb.

674. Shooting stars are sometimes hurled at the devils when they endeavour stealthily to listen to the heavenly secrets which they impart to men on earth who by means of talisman or certain invocations make them serve the purposes of magical performances.

earth and its wests. Some of them proceeded towards Tihāma and that is a nakhl towards the bazaar of 'Ukāẓ and he (the Holy Prophet) was leading his Companions in the morning prayer. So when they heard the Qur'ān, they listened to it attentively and said: It is this which has caused obstruction between us and news from the Heaven. They went back to their people and said: O our people, we have heard a strange Qur'ān which directs us to the right path; so we affirm our faith in it and we would never associate anyone with our Lord. And Allah, the Exalted and Glorious, revealed to His Apostle Muḥammad (may peace be upon him): "It has been revealed to me that a party of Jinn listened to it" (Qur'ān, lxxii. 1).

(903) Dāwūd reported from 'Āmir who said: I asked 'Alqama if Ibn Mas'ūd was present with the Messenger of Allah (may peace be upon him) on the night of the Jinn (the night when the Holy Prophet met them). He (Ibn Mas'ūd) said: No, but we were in the company of the Messenger of Allah (may peace be upon him) one night and we missed him. We searched for him in the valleys and the hills and said: He has either been taken away (by Jinn) or has been secretly killed. He (the narrator) said: We spent the worst night which people could ever spend. When it was dawn we saw him coming from the side of Ḥirā'. He (the narrator) reported: We said: Messenger of Allah, we missed you and searched for you, but we could not find you and we spent the worst night which people could ever spend. He (the Holy Prophet) said: There came to me an inviter on behalf of the Jinn and I went along with him and recited to them the Qur'ān. He (the narrator) said: He then went along with us and showed us their traces and traces of their embers. They (the Jinn) asked him (the Holy Prophet) about their provision and he said: Every bone on which the name of Allah is recited is your provision. The time it will fall in your hand it would be covered with flesh, and the dung of (the camels) is fodder for your animals. The Messenger of Allah (may peace be upon him) said: Don't perform *istinjā* with these (things) for these are the food of your brothers (Jinn).

(904) This ḥadīth has been transmitted by Dāwūd with the same chain of transmitters up to the word(s): "The traces of their embers." Sha'bī said: They (the Jinn) asked about their provision, and they were the Jinn of al-Jazīra, up to the end of the ḥadīth, and the words of Sha'bī have been directly transmitted from the ḥadīth of 'Abdullah.

(905) This ḥadīth has been narrated on the authority of 'Abdullah from the Apostle (may peace be upon him) up to the words: "The traces of the embers," but he made no mention of what followed afterward.

(906) 'Abdullah (b. Mas'ūd) said: I was not with the Messenger of Allah (may peace be upon him) but I wish I were with him.

(907) Ma'n reported: I heard it from my father who said: I asked Masrūq who informed the Messenger of Allah (may peace be upon him) about the night when they heard the Qur'ān. He said: Your father, Ibn Mas'ūd, narrated it to me that a tree[675] informed him about that.

675. It was a miracle and there can be no doubt that one who believes in the prophetic doctrine of Allah, the Creator and the Sustainer of the universe, can find no *a priori* difficulty about testifying to the miracles of the prophets. These are not unworthy of God, nor are they arbitrary acts. These are in fact occasional expressions of God's special purpose in the universe, designed to serve as an eye-opener to the people and give an idea of His Great Might.

Chapter CLXXXI

RECITATION IN NOON AND AFTERNOON PRAYERS

(908) Abū Qatāda reported : The Messenger of Allah (may peace be upon him) led us in prayer and recited in the first two rak'ahs of noon and afternoon prayers Sūrat al-Fātiḥa and two (other) sūras. And he would sometimes recite loud enough for us the verses. He would prolong the first rak'ah more than the second. And he acted similarly in the morning prayer.

(909) Abū Qatāda reported it on the authority of his father : The Messenger of Allah (may peace be upon him) would recite in the first two rak'ahs of noon and afternoon prayers the opening chapter of the Book and another sūra. He would sometimes recite loud enough to make audible to us the verse[676] and would recite in the last two rak'ahs Sūrat al-Fātiḥa (only).

(910) Abū Sa'īd al-Khudrī reported : We used to estimate how long Allah's Messenger (may peace be upon him) stood in noon and afternoon prayers, and we estimated that he stood in the first two rak'ahs of noon prayer as long as it takes to recite *Alif Lām Mīm, Tanzīl*, i.e. as-Sajda.[677] We estimated that he stood half that time in the last two rak'ahs ; that he stood in the first two of the afternoon as long as he did in the last two at noon ; and in the last two of the afternoon prayer about half that time.

Abū Bakr in his narration has made no mention of *Alif Lām Mīm, Tanzīl*, but said : As long as it takes to recite thirty verses.

(911) Abū Sa'īd al-Khudrī reported : The Apostle of Allah (my peace be upon him) used to recite in every rak'ah of the first two rak'ahs of noon prayer about thirty verses and in the last two about fifteen verses or half (of the first rak'ah) and in every rak'ah of the 'Aṣr prayer of the first two rak'ahs about fifteen verses and in the last two verses half (of the first ones).

(912) Jābir b. Samura reported : The people of Kūfa complained to 'Umar b. Khaṭṭāb about Sa'īd and they made a mention of his prayer. 'Umar sent for him. He came to him. He ('Umar) told him that the people had found fault with his prayer. He said : I lead them in prayer in accordance with the prayer of the Messenger of Allah (may peace be upon him). I make no decrease in it. I make them stand for a longer time in the first two (rak'ahs) and shorten it in the last two.[678] Upon this 'Umar remarked : This is what I deemed of thee, O Abū Isḥāq.[679]

(913) This ḥadīth has been transmitted by 'Abd al-Malik with the same chain of transmitters.

676. In *sirri* prayers, i.e. noon and afternoon, the recitation is done in a low voice. The Holy Prophet, however, made an exception to this rule, because it was through him that we could learn what to recite in *sirri* prayers.

677. Al-Qur'ān, sūra xxxii. This sūra has thirty verses.

678. This ḥadīth shows what great importance was given to prayer in the early period of Islam. It was one of the fundamental duties of the head of the State to see that it was observed properly by all Muslims.

679. This is the kunyah of Sa'd.

(914) Jābir b. Samura reported: 'Umar said to Sa'd: They complain against you in every matter, even in prayer. He (Sa'd) said: I prolong (standing) in the first two (rak'ahs) and shorten it in the last two, and I make no negligence in following the prayer of the Messenger of Allah (may peace be upon him). He ('Umar) remarked: This is what is expected of you, or, that is what I deemed of you.

(915) This ḥadīth is narrated by Jābir b. Samura but with the addition of these words: "(Sa'd said): These bedouins presume to teach me prayer."[680]

(916) Abū Sa'īd al-Khudrī reported: The noon prayer would start and one would go to al-Baqī' and after having relieved himself he would perform ablution and then come, while the Messenger of Allah (may peace be upon him) would be in the first rak'ah because he would prolong it so much.

(917) Qaz'a reported: I came to Abū Sa'īd al-Khudrī and he was surrounded by people. When the people departed from him I said: I am not going to ask you what these people have been asking you. I want to ask you about the prayer of the Messenger of Allah (may peace be upon him). He (Abū Sa'īd) said: There is no good for you in this.[681] He (Qaz'a), however, repeated (his demand). He then said: The noon prayer would start and one of us would go to Baqī' and, having relieved himself, would come to his home, then perform ablution and go to the mosque, and (he would find) the Messenger of Allah (may peace be upon him) in the first rak'ah.

Chapter CLXXXII

RECITATION IN THE MORNING PRAYER

(918) 'Abdullah b. Sā'ib reported: The Apostle of Allah (may peace be upon him) led us in morning prayer in Mecca and began Sūrat al-Mū'minūn (xxiii.) but when he came to the mention of Moses and Aaron (verse 45) or to the mention of Jesus (verse 50), a cough got the better of him, and he bowed. 'Abdullah b. Sā'ib was present there, and in the ḥadīth narrated by 'Abd al-Razzāq (the words are): He cut short (the recitation) and bowed.

(919) 'Amr b. Ḥuwairith reported: I heard the Apostle of Allah (may peace be upon him) reciting in the morning prayer "*Wa'l-lail-i-idhā 'As'asa*" (lxxxi. 17).

(920) Quṭba b. Mālik reported: I said prayer and the Messenger of Allah (may peace be upon him) led it and he recited "Qāf. (l.): By the Glorious Qur'ān," till he recited "and the tall palm trees" (l. 10). I wanted to repeat it but I could not follow its significance.

(921) Quṭba b. Mālik reported that he had heard the Messenger of Allah (may peace be upon him) reciting in the morning prayer this: "And the tall palm trees having flower spikes piled one above another" (l. 10).

680. Maulānā Shabbīr Aḥmad states: "These words indicate that those who had complained against Sa'd were not scholars and they thought that the rak'ahs should be of equal length" (*Fatḥ-ul-Mulhim*, Vol. II, p. 28).

681. "It is of no avail to know how long the Holy Prophet stood in prayer, because you cannot show so much patience and devotion as he did."

(922) Ziyād b. 'Ilāqa reported it on the authority of his uncle that he said the morning prayer with the Apostle of Allah (may peace be upon him) and he recited in the first rak'ah : "And the tall palm trees having flower spikes piled one above another (l. 10) or perhaps Sūra Qāf.

(923) Jābir b. Samura reported : The Apostle of Allah (may peace be upon him) used to recite in the morning prayer "Qāf. By the Glorious Quran," and his prayer afterward shortened.

(924) Simāk asked Jābir b. Samura about the prayer of the Apostle (may peace be upon him). He said : He (the Holy Prophet) shortened the prayer and he did not pray like these people then, and he informed me that the Messenger of Allah (may peace be upon him) used to recite "Qāf.[682] By the (Glorious) Qur'ān," and a passage of similar length.

(925) Jābir b. Samura reported : The Apostle of Allah (may peace be upon him) used to recite in noon prayer : "By the night when it envelopes" (xcii.), and in the afternoon like this, but he prolonged the morning prayer as compared to that (noon and afternoon prayers).

(926) Jābir b. Samura reported : The Apostle of Allah (may peace be upon him) used to recite in the noon prayer : "Glorify the name of thy Most High Lord in the morning prayer longer than this" (lxxxvii.).

(927) Abū Barza reported : The Messenger of Allah (may peace be upon him) used to recite in the morning prayer from sixty to one hundred verses.

(928) Abū Barza Aslamī[683] reported : The Messenger of Allah (may peace be upon him) used to recite from sixty to one hundred verses in the morning prayer.

(929) Ibn 'Abbās reported : Umm al-Faḍl daughter of al-Ḥārith heard him reciting : "By those sent forth to spread goodness" (lxxvii.). (Upon this) she remarked : O my son, you reminded me by the recitation of this sūra (the fact) that it was the last sūra that I heard from the Messenger of Allah (may peace be upon him) and he recited it in the evening prayer.

(930) This ḥadīth has been transmitted by Zuhrī with the same chain of transmitters but with this addition : "And he did not lead the prayer after this till his death."[684]

(931) Jubair b. Muṭ'im reported : I heard the Messenger of Allah (may peace be upon him) reciting Sūrat al-Ṭūr (Mountain) (lii.) in the evening prayer.[685]

682. In the earlier period the Holy Prophet recited long verses but in the later period when the congregation in prayer consisted of a large number of men and women having different bodily strength and belonging to different age groups, the Holy Prophet shortened the recitation.

683. He was one of the earlier converts to Islam and it was he who killed 'Abdullah b. Khaṭṭal. He participated in almost all the battles along with the Apostle of Allah (may peace be upon him). He later on settled in Baṣra and joined battle in Khurāsān and died in 60 H.

684. Apparently this ḥadīth seems to conflict with the ḥadīth transmitted by 'Ā'isha in which we have been told that the last prayer which the Holy Prophet led was noon prayer, but here it is said it was evening. The fact is that the ḥadīth narrated by 'Ā'isha relates to the prayer in the mosque and this ḥadīth relates to the last prayer which he led in his house (*Fatḥ-ul-Mulhim*, Vol. II, p. 81).

685. The Holy Prophet usually recited a few number of verses and short sūras in the evening prayer. Here he made a departure from his usual practice with a view to showing that it was permissible to recite long sūras if one so desires.

(932) This ḥadīth has been transmitted by Zuhrī with the same chain of transmitters.

Chapter CLXXXIII

RECITATION IN THE NIGHT PRAYER

(933) 'Adī reported: I heard al-Barā' narrating it from the Apostle of Allah (may peace be upon him) that while in a journey he said night prayer and recited in one of the two rak'ahs: "By the Fig and the Olive" (Sūra xcv.).

(934) Al-Barā' b. 'Āzib reported that he said prayer with the Messenger of Allah (may peace be upon him) and he recited: "By the Fig and the Olive."

(935) Al-Barā' b. 'Āzib reported: I heard the Apostle of Allah (may peace be upon him) reciting in the night prayer: "By the Fig and the Olive," and I have never heard anyone with a sweeter voice than he.

(936) Jābir reported that Mu'ādh b. Jabal used to pray with the Apostle (may peace be upon him), then came and led his people in prayer. One night he said the night prayer with the Apostle of Allah (may peace be upon him). He then came to his people and led them in prayer beginning with Sūrat al-Baqara. A man turned aside, pronounced the *taslīm* (salutation for concluding the prayer), then prayed alone and departed. The people said to him: Have you become a hypocrite, so and so? He said: I swear by Allah that I have not, but I will certainly go to Allah's Messenger (may peace be upon him) and will inform (him) about this. He then came to the Messenger of Allah (may peace be upon him) and said: Messenger of Allah, we look after camels used for watering and work by day. Mu'ādh said night prayer with you. He then came and began with Sūrat al-Baqara. Allah's Messenger (may peace be upon him) then turned to Mu'ādh and said: Are you there to (put the people) to trial? Recite such and recite such (and such a sūra). It is transmitted on the authority of Jābir, as told by Sufyān, that he (the Holy Prophet) had said: "By the Sun and its morning brightness" (Sūra xci.). "By brightness" (Sūra xciii.), "By the night when it spreads" (Sūra xcii.), and "Glorify the name of thy most high Lord" (Sūra lxxxii.).[686]

(937) Jābir reported: Mu'ādh b. Jabal al-Anṣārī led his companions in night prayer and prolonged it for them. A person amongst us said prayer (after having separated himself from the congregation). Mu'ādh was informed of this, and he remarked that he was a hypocrite. When it (the remark) was conveyed to the man, he went to the Messenger of Allah (may peace be upon him) and informed him of what Mu'ādh had said. Upon this the Apostle of Allah (may peace be upon him) said to him: Mu'ādh, do you want to become a person putting (people) to trial? When you lead people in prayer, recite: "By the Sun and its morning brightness (Sūra xci), "Glorify the name of thy most high Lord" (Sūra lxxxvi.), and "Read in the name of Lord" (Sūra xcvi.), and "By the

686. This ḥadīth tells us that one must show moderation even in prayer and devotion, and especially one who has to lead the prayer should see that no one is put to trouble in the congregation behind him.

night when it spreads" (Sūra xcii.).

(938) Jābir b. 'Abdullah reported: Mu'ādh b. Jabal said night prayer with the Messenger of Allah (may peace be upon him) and then returned to his people and then led them in this prayer.[687]

(939) Jābir b. 'Abdullah reported: Mu'ādh said night prayer with the Messenger of Allah (may peace be upon him). He then came to the mosque of his people and led them in prayer.

Chapter CLXXXIV

THE DUTY OF THE IMĀM IS TO BE BRIEF AND PERFECT IN PRAYER

(940) Abū Mas'ūd al-Anṣārī reported: A person came to the Messenger of Allah (may peace be upon him) and said: I keep away from the morning prayer on account of such and such (a man), because he keeps us so long. I never saw God's Messenger (may peace be upon him) more angry when giving an exhortation than he was that day. He said: O people, some of you are scaring people away, so whoever of you leads the people in prayer he must be brief, for behind him are the weak, the aged, and the people who have (urgent) business to attend.

(941) This ḥadīth like one narrated by Hushaim has been transmitted from Ismā'īl with the same chain of transmitters.

(942) Abū Huraira reported: The Apostle of Allah (may peace be upon him) said: When any one of you leads the people in prayer, he should be brief, for among them are the young and the aged, the weak and the sick. But when one of you prays by himself, he may (prolong) as he likes.

(943) Hammām b. Munabbih reported: This is what Abū Huraira transmitted to us from Muḥammad the Messenger of Allah (may peace be upon him), and he narrated (some) aḥādīth out of (these narrations and one of them is this): The Messenger of Allah (may peace be upon him) said: When any one of you stands to lead people in prayer, he should shorten it, for amongst them are the aged, and amongst them are the weak, but when he prays by himself, he may prolong his prayer as he likes.

(944) Abū Huraira reported: The Messenger of Allah (may peace be upon him) said: When any one of you leads people in prayer, he must shorten it for among them are the weak, the infirm and those who have business to attend.

(945) Abū Bakr b. 'Abd al-Raḥmān reported that he had heard Abū Huraira say that the Messenger of Allah (may peace be upon him) said like it, but he substituted "the aged" for "the infirm".

687. This ḥadīth has been discussed at length by the scholars of Ḥadīth. The point of difference is whether Mu'ādh said Farḍ prayer with the Holy Prophet or Nafl (supererogatory prayer). If it was Farḍ, then the second prayer in which he led his people becomes Nafl prayer; and is it advisable for a person offering Nafl prayer to lead people in Farḍ prayer? There have been long discussions over these issues. After reading them the general conclusion that can be drawn is that it was as a Nafl prayer that Mu'ādh said with the Messenger of Allah and then led his people in Farḍ prayer.

(946) 'Uthmān b. Abu'l-'Āṣ[688] al-Thaqafī reported: The Apostle of Allah (may peace be upon him) said to him: Lead your people in prayer. I said: Messenger of Allah, I perceive something (disturbing) in my soul. He (the Holy Prophet) asked me to draw near him and making me sit down in front of him he placed his hand on my breast between my nipples, and then, telling me to turn round, he placed it on my back between my shoulders. He then said: Act as an Imām for your people. He who acts as Imām of the people, he must be brief, for among them are the aged, among them are the sick, among them are the weak, and among them are the people who have business to attend. But when any of you prays alone, he may pray as he likes.

(947) 'Uthmān b. Abu'l-'Āṣ reported: The last thing which the Messenger of Allah (may peace be upon him) instructed me was: When you lead the people in prayer, be brief.

(948) Anas reported: The Apostle of Allah (may peace be upon him) used to be brief and perfect in prayer.

(949) Anas reported: The Messenger of Allah (may peace be upon him) was among those whose prayer was brief and perfect.

(950) Anas reported: I never prayed behind an Imām who was more brief and more perfect in prayer than the Messenger of Allah (may peace be upon him).

(951) Anas reported: The Messenger of Allah (may peace be upon him) would listen to the crying of a lad in the company of his mother, in prayer, and he would recite a short sūra or a small sūra.

(952) Anas b. Mālik reported the Messenger of Allah (may peace be upon him) having said: When I begin the prayer I intend to make it long, but I hear a boy crying; I then shorten it because of his mother's feelings.

Chapter CLXXXV

MODERATION IN THE ARTICLES OF PRAYER AND THEIR SHORTENING AND PERFECTION

(953) Al-Barā' b. 'Āzib reported: I noticed the prayer of Muḥammad (may peace be upon him) and saw his Qiyām (standing), his bowing, and then going back to the standing posture after bowing, his prostration, his sitting between the two prostrations,[689] and his prostration and sitting between salutation and going away,[690] all these were

688. 'Uthmān b. Abu'l-'Āṣ—he is one of the Companions of the Holy Prophet who appointed him as the Governor of Ṭā'īf. He held this post during the caliphate of Abū Bakr and also in the first two years of 'Umar's. Later on he was appointed the Governor of 'Ammān and Baḥrain. He was twenty-nine when he came to the Holy Prophet in the delegation of Banū Thaqīf. He died in 51 H. in Baṣra.

689. This is known in Arabic as *Jalsa Istrāḥat*.

690. The scholars of Ḥadīth are of the opinion that it was not a common practice with the Holy Prophet, but at times he said his prayers like this in order to show that this was also permissible. The other interpretation is that equality does not imply that Qiyām, Sujūd, Rukū' and Jalsa should be of equal duration but it means that there should be a sense of proportion in the different postures of prayer. If the Qiyām is longer, the Rukū' should be correspondingly longer, and so should be the Sajda (*Fatḥ al-Mulhim*, Vol. II, p. 87).

nearly equal to one another.

(954) Ḥakam reported: There dominated in Kūfa a man whose name was mentioned as Zaman b. al-Ash'ath,[691] who ordered Abū 'Ubaidah b. 'Abdullah to lead people in prayer and he accordingly used to lead them. Whenever he raised his head after bowing, he stood up equal to the time that I can recite (this supplication): O Allah! our Lord! unto Thee be the praise which would fill the heavens and the earth, and that which will please Thee besides them! Worthy art Thou of all praise and glory. None can prevent that which Thou bestowest, and none can bestow that which Thou preventest. And the greatness of the great will not avail him against Thee. Ḥakam (the narrator) said: I made a mention of that to 'Abd al-Raḥmān ibn Abī Lailā who reported: I heard al-Barā' b. 'Āzib say that the prayer of the Messenger of Allah (may peace be upon him) and his bowing, and when he lifted his head from bowing, and his prostration, and between the two prostrations (all these acts) were nearly proportionate. I made a mention of that to 'Amr b. Murrah and he said: I saw Ibn Abī Lailā (saying the prayer), but his prayer was not like this.

(955) Ḥakam reported: When Maṭar b. Nājiya dominated Kūfa he ordered Abū 'Ubaid to lead people in prayer, and the rest of the ḥadīth is the same.

(956) Thābit reported it on the authority of Anas: While leading you in prayer I do not shorten anything in the prayer. I pray as I saw the Messenger of Allah (may peace be upon him) leading us. He (Thābit) said: Anas used to do that which I do not see you doing; when he lifted his head from bowing he stood up (so long) that one would say: He has forgotten (to bow down in prostration). And when he lifted his head from prostration, he stayed in that position, till someone would say: He has forgotten (to bow dow in prostration for the second sajda).

(957) Thābit reported it on the authority of Anas: I have never said such a light and perfect prayer as I said behind the Messenger of Allah (may peace be upon him). The prayer of the Messenger of Allah (may peace be upon him) was well balanced. And so too was the prayer of Abū Bakr well balanced. When it was the time of 'Umar b. al-Khaṭṭāb he prolonged the morning prayer. When the Messenger of Allah (may peace be upon him) said: Allah listened to him who praised Him, he stood erect till we said: He has forgotten. He then prostrated and sat between two prostrations till we said: He has forgotten.[692]

Chapter CLXXXVI

FOLLOWING THE IMĀM AND ACTING AFTER HIM

(958) Al-Barā' (b. 'Āzib), and he was no liar (but a truthful Companion of the Holy Prophet), reported: They used to say prayer behind the Messenger of Allah (may peace be upon him). I never saw anyone bending his back at the time when he (the

691. He was Muḥammad b. al-Ash'ath, who beleaguered Muslim b. 'Aqīl (Allah be pleased with him) and took him to 'Ubaidullah b. Ziyād (*Fatḥ al-Mulhim*, Vol. II, p. 87).

692. This ḥadīth gives a clear indication that there is no iron formula for the duration of Qiyām, Rukū' and Sajda in prayer. The Holy Prophet at times observed equal duration in them and he would sometimes lengthen any one of them. All these practices had been followed by the Holy Prophet and so these are all permissible.

Holy Prophet) raised his head, till the Messenger of Allah (may peace be upon him) placed his forehead on the ground. They then fell in prostration after him.[693]

(959) Al-Barā' reported, and he was no liar: When the Messenger of Allah (may peace be upon him) said: Allah listened to him who praised Him, none of us bent his back till he (the Holy Prophet) prostrated; we then, afterwards, went down in prostration.

(960) Al-Barā' reported: They (the Companions) said prayer with the Messenger of Allah (may peace be upon him), and they bowed when he (the Holy Prophet) bowed, and when he raised his head after bowing, he pronounced: "Allah listened to him who praised Him," and we kept standing till we saw him placing his face on the ground and then we followed him.

(961) Al-Barā' reported: When we were (in prayer) with the Messenger of Allah (may peace be upon him) none of us bent his back till we saw he prostrated. Zuhair and others reported: "till we saw him prostrating."

(962) 'Amr b. Ḥuraith reported: I said dawn prayer behind the Apostle of Allah (may peace be upon him) and heard him reciting: "Nay, I call to witness the stars, running their courses and setting" (al-Qur'ān, lxxxi. 15-16) and none of us bent his back till he completed prostration.

(963) ('Abdullah b.) Ibn Abī Aufā[694] reported: When the Messenger of Allah (may peace be upon him) raised his back from the rukū' he pronounced: Allah listened to him who praised Him. O Allah! our Lord! unto Thee be praise that would fill the heavens and the earth and fill that which will please Thee besides them.

(964) 'Abdullah b. Aufā reported: The Messenger of Allah (may peace be upon him) used to recite this supplication: O Allah! our Lord, unto Thee be praise that would fill the heavens and the earth and fill that which will please Thee besides them.

(965) 'Abdullah b. Abū Aufa reported from the Apostle of Allah (may peace be upon him) used to recite (this supplication): O Allah! our Lord, unto Thee be praise that would fill the heavens and the earth and fill that which will please Thee besides (them). O Allah! purify me with snow, (water of) hail and with cold water;[695] O Allah, cleanse me from the sins and errors just as a white garment is cleansed from dirt.[696]

693. This implies that the followers must not precede the Imām in acts of prayer. When an Imām completes an act, then the followers should start it. In other words, the prayer should be performed in a manner as to show that the "followers" do actually *follow* the Imām.

694. He was a famous Companion of the Holy Prophet. His father's name was 'Alqama b. Qais al-Aslamī and kunyah was Abū Aufā. 'Abdullah participated in Ḥudaybiya and Khaybar and joined all the subsequent battles fought by the Muslims. He stayed in Medina till the death of the Holy Prophet and then shifted to Kūfa. He was the last amongst the Companions of the Messenger of Allah. He died in Kūfa in 87 H.

695. There has been a good deal of discussion in the commentaries of Ḥadīth as to why snow and hail have been used along with cold water. The one answer is that it is meant to emphasise the process of purification. The answer given by Ṭībī seems to be more appropriate. The idea of sin is always accompanied with the idea of Hell-fire. Hail, snow and cold water would not only purify the sins of man but also effectively extinguish the fire of Hell.

696. This supplication of the Holy Prophet is meant to teach the Muslims how to pray, and it should in no way be taken to mean that the Holy Prophet committed sins. The Messenger of Allah was pure from sins. The very minor omissions on his part, which were also corrected by Allah there and then, can in no way be counted as sins.

(966) This ḥadīth with the same chain of transmitters has been narrated by Shu'ba, and in the narration of Mu'ādh the words are: "just as the white garment is cleansed from filth," and in the narration of Yazīd: "from dirt".

(967) Abū Sa'īd al-Khudrī reported: When the Messenger of Allah (may peace be upon him) raised his head after bowing, he said: O Allah! our Lord, to Thee be the praise that would fill all the heavens and the earth, and all that it pleases Thee besides (them).[697] O, Thou art worthy of praise and glory, most worthy of what a servant says, and we all are Thy servants, no one can withhold what Thou givest or givẹ what Thou withholdest, and riches cannot avail a wealthy person against Thee.

(968) Ibn 'Abbās reported: When the Apostle of Allah (may peace be upon him) raised his head after bowing, he said: O Allah! our Lord, to Thee be the praise that would fill the heavens and the earth and that which is between them, and that which will please Thee besides (them). Worthy art Thou of all praise and glory. No one can withhold what Thou givest, or give what Thou withholdest. And the greatness[698] of the great availeth not against Thee.

(969) Ibn 'Abbās reported from the Apostle of Allah (may peace be upon him) the words: "And that would fill that which will please Thee besides (them)!" and he did not mention the subsequent (portion of supplication).

(970) Ibn 'Abbās reported: The Messenger of Allah (may peace be upon him) drew aside the curtain (of his apartment) and (he saw) people in rows (saying prayer) behind Abū Bakr. And he said: Nothing remains of the glad tidings of apostlehood, except good visions,[699] which a Muslim sees or someone is made to see for him. And see that I have been forbidden to recite the Qur'ān in the state of bowing and prostration. So far as Rukū' is concernrd, extol in it the Great and Glorious Lord, and while prostrating yourselves be earnest in supplication, for it is fitting that your supplications should be answered.

(971) 'Abdullah b. 'Abbās reported: The Messenger of Allah (may peace be upon him) drew aside the curtain and his head was bandaged on accaunt of illness in which he died, he said: O Allah, have I not delivered (Thy Message)? (He repeated it) three times. Nothing has been left out of the glad tidings of apostlehood, but good vision,

697. "Besides them" implies that there are other worlds which "are beyond my comprehension. Your Mercy knows no bound and it covers far more wider spheres which a human mind can possibly conceive of."

698. The word *al-jadd* (الجد), according to Imām Nawawī, means a portion out of the material world. It may be out of worldly riches, children, or worldly prestige or domination.

699. This incident relates to the last day of Muḥammad's life in this transcient world. He was thus emphasising the most important points of his mission and one of those was that prophethood has been finalised in him and no new prophet is to be raised after him. The manifestation of Divine Will in belief and law has been finally accomplished in the Holy Qur'ān and the Sunnah and there would be no more revelation from the Lord. Out of the *Mubashshirat Nubuwwa*, it is true visions which still exist.

It should be noted in this connection that it is not a fraction of *Nubuwwa* that is left, but a portion of its *Mubashshira* only. *Mubashshira* is not a part of *Nubuwwa*, but a prelude to that. Just as the streaks of light announce the dawn, in the same way the good visions foretell *Mubashshira*. Moreover, these visions have not been declared as the *Mubashshira* of *Risāla*, but those of *Nubuwwa*. This is highly meaningful and indicates that the good visions would only sometimes forecast some of the events shrouded in the mist of future. But those have nothing to do with the high office of the messengership of Allah.

which a pious servant (of Allah) sees or someone else is made to see for him. He then narrated like the ḥadīth transmitted by Sufyān.

(972) ʻAlī b. Abī Ṭālib reported: The Messenger of Allah (may peace be upon him) forbade me to recite (the Qur'ān) in a state of bowing and prostration.[700]

(973) ʻAlī b. Abī Ṭālib reported: The Messenger of Allah (may peace be upon him) forbade to recite the Qur'ān, while I am in the state of bowing and prostration.

(974) ʻAlī b. Abī Ṭālib reported: The Messenger of Allah (may peace be upon him) forbade me from the recitation (of the Qur'ān) in bowing and prostration and I do not say that he forbade you.

(975) ʻAlī reported: My loved one (the Holy Prophet) forbade me that I should recite (the Qur'ān) in a state of bowing and prostration.

(976) This ḥadīth has been narrated by some other narrators, Ibn ʻAbbās and others, and they all reported that ʻAlī said: The Apostle of Allah (may peace be upon him) forbade me to recite the Qur'ān while I am in a state of bowing and prostration, and in their narration (there is a mention of) forbiddance from that (recital) in the state of prostration as it has been transmitted by Zuhrī, Zaid b. Aslam, al-Waḥīd b. Kathīr, and Dawūd b. Qais.

(977) This ḥadīth is transmitted on the authority of ʻAlī, but he made no mention of "while in prostration".

(978) Ibn ʻAbbās reported: I was forbidden to recite (the Qur'ān) while I was bowing, and there is no mention of ʻAlī in the chain of transmitters.

Chapter CLXXXVII

WHAT IS TO BE RECITED IN BOWING AND PROSTRATION

(979) Abū Huraira reported: The Messenger of Allah (may peace be upon him) said: The nearest a servant comes to his Lord is when he is prostrating[701] himself, so make supplication (in this state).

(980) Abū Huraira reported: The Messenger of Allah (may peace be upon him) used to say when prostrating himself: O Lord, forgive me all my sins, small and great, first and last, open and secret.

(981) ʻĀ'isha reported: The Messenger of Allah (may peace be upon him) often said while bowing and prostrating himself: "Glory be to Thee, O Allah, our Lord, and praise be to Thee, O Allah, forgive me," thus complying with the (command in) the

700. These are the two states in prayer when a man expresses his humility before his Lord. It is, therefore, obvious that in these states Allah should be praised and glorified. The words of the Qur'ān should be recited in a state of Qiyām before the Almighty Lord.

701. The state of prostration is the highest state of humility and submission before the Lord. It is a state when a man by his act of devotion throws himself upon the Lord's mercy, and states that He alone is Great and Mighty and he himself is an insignificant humble servant before Him, begging for His Mercy. It is in this state that one rightly demonstrates how a man is related to his Master. Moreover, this state is the best expression of man's consciousness of God and consciousness of his whole humble being. This is the reason why this state has been declared as the most befitting state for supplication.

Qur'ān. 702

(982) 'Ā'isha reported that the Messenger of Allah (may peace be upon him) before his death recited often: Hallowed be Thou, and with Thy praise, I seek foregiveness from Thee and return to Thee. She reported: I said: Messenger of Allah, what are these words that I find you reciting? He said: There has been made a sign for me in my Ummah; when I saw that, I uttered them (these words of glorification for Allah), and the sign is: "When Allah's help and victory . . ." to the end of the Sūrah. 703

(983) 'Ā'isha reported: Never did I see the Apostle of Allah (may peace be upon him) after the revelation (of these verses): "When Allah's help and victory came," observing his prayer without making (this supplication) or he said in it (supplication): Hallowed be Thee, my Lord, and with Thy praise, O Allah, forgive me.

(984) 'Ā'isha reported: The Messenger of Allah (may peace be upon him) recited often these words: Hallowed be Allah and with His praise, I seek the forgiveness of Allah and return to Him. She said: I asked: Messenger of Allah, I see that you often repeat the saying سبحان الله بحمده استغفر الله واتوب اليه, whereupon he said: My Lord informed me that I would soon see a sign in my Ummah, so when I see it I often recite (these) words: Hallowed be Allah and with His Praise, I seek forgiveness of Allah and return to Him. Indeed I saw it (when this verse) was revealed: "When Allah's help and victory came, it marked the victory of Mecca, and you see people entering into Allah's religion in troops, celebrate the praise of Thy Lord and ask His forgiveness. Surely He is ever returning to Mercy."

(985) Ibn Juraij reported: I asked 'Aṭā': What do you recite when you are in a state of bowing (in prayer)? He said: "Hallowed be Thou, and with Thy praise, there is no god, but Thou." Son of Abū Mulaika narrated to me on the authority of 'Ā'isha (who reported): I missed one night the Apostle of Allah (may peace be upon him) (from his bed). I thought that he might have gone to one of his other wives. I searched for him and then came back and (found him) in a state of bowing, or prostration, saying: Hallowed be Thou and with Thy praise; there is no god but Thou. I said: With my father mayest thou be ransomed and with my mother. I was thinking of (another) affair, whereas you are (occupied) in another one. 704

(986) 'Ā'isha reported: One night I missed Allah's Messenger (may peace be upon him) from the bed, and when I sought him my hand touched the soles of his feet while he was in the state of prostration; they (feet) were raised and he was saying: "O Allah, I seek refuge in Thy pleasure from Thy anger, and in Thy forgiveness from Thy

702. What it means is that the Holy Prophet praised and glorified Allah complying with the command in the Qur'ān found in Sūrat al-Naṣr: "When Allah's help and victory came, and thou seest men entering the religion of Allah in companies, celebrate the praise of thy Lord and ask His protection. Surely, He is ever-returning (to Mercy)."

703. This Sūra (No. cx.), in which the Holy Prophet had been exhorted to glorify Allah, was revealed after the conquest of Mecca, when the people had begun to enter into the fold of Islam in large numbers. It marked the final victory of Islam over the forces of Jāhilīyya The Prophet was, therefore, instructed to glorify the Lord Who had granted him success. This sūra also gave an implied indication of the fact that the Holy Prophet was soon going to depart from this mortal world.

704. "I thought that you would be in the company of some of your wives, whereas I find you occupied in glorifying Allah."

punishment, and I seek refuge in Thee from Thee (Thy anger). I cannot reckon Thy praise. Thou art as Thou hast lauded Thyself."

(987) 'Ā'isha reported that the Messenger of Allah (may peace be upon him) used to pronounce while bowing and prostrating himself: All Glorious, All Holy, Lord of the Angels and the Spirit.[705]

(988) This ḥadīth has been narrated on the authority of 'Ā'isha by another chain of transmitters.

Chapter CLXXXVIII

THE EXCELLENCE OF PROSTRATION AND EXHORTATION TO OBSERVE IT

(989) Ma'dān b. Ṭalḥa reported: I met Thaubān, the freed slave of Allah's Messenger (may peace be upon him), and asked him to tell me about an act for which, if I do it, Allah will admit me to Paradise, or I asked about the act which was loved most by Allah. He gave no reply. I again asked and he gave no reply. I asked him for the third time, and he said: I asked Allah's Messenger (may peace be upon him) about that and he said: Make frequent prostrations before Allah, for you will not make one prostration without raising you a degree because of it, and removing a sin from you, because of it. Ma'dān said that then he met Abū al-Dardā' and when he asked him, he received a reply similar to that given by Thaubān.

(990) Rābi'a b. Ka'b[706] said: I was with Allah's Messenger (may peace be upon him) one night, and I brought him water and what he required. He said to me: Ask (anything you like). I said: I ask your company in Paradise. He (the Holy Prophet) said: or anything else besides it. I said: That is all (what I require). He said: Then help me to achieve this for you by devoting yourself often to prostration.

Chapter CLXXXIX

HOW THE LIMBS SHOULD WORK IN PROSTRATION AND FORBIDDANCE TO FOLD CLOTHING AND HAIR AND PLAITING OF HAIR IN THE PRAYER

(991) Ibn 'Abbās reported: The Apostle of Allah (may peace be upon him) had been commanded that he should prostrate on the seven (bones) and he was forbidden to fold back the hair and clothing. And in the narration transmitted by Abū Rabī' (the words are): "on the seven bones and I was forbidden to fold back the hair and clothing." According to Abu'l-Rabī' (the seven bones are): The hands, the knees, and the (extremities) of the feet and the forehead.

705. The reference is to the Qur'ān, cx. 3.

706. He was the son of Ka'b. His kunyah was Abū Faras Aslamī. He was one of the eminent Companions of the Holy Prophet who spent most of his time among the people of Ṣuffa. He tried to remain in the company of the Messenger of Allah as it was practically possible. He died in 63 H.

(992) Ibn 'Abbās reported from the Apostle of Allah (may peace be upon him): I was commanded to prostrate myself on seven bones and not to fold back clothing or hair.

(993) Ibn 'Abbās reported: The Messenger of Allah (may peace be upon him) had been commanded to prostrate on seven (bones) and forbidden to fold back hair and clothing.

(994) Ibn 'Abbās reported that the Messenger of Allah (may peace be upon him) said: I have been commanded to prostrate myself on seven bones: "forehead," and then pointed with his hand towards his nose, hands, feet, and the extremities of the feet; and we were forbidden to fold back clothing and hair.

(995) Ibn 'Abbās reported: The Messenger of Allah (may peace be upon him) said: I was commanded to prostrate myself on the seven (bones) and forbidden to fold back hair and clothing. (The seven bones are): forehead, nose, hands, knees and feet.

(996) 'Abdullah b. 'Abbās reported that he saw 'Abdullah b. al-Ḥārith observing the prayer and (his hair) was plaited behind his head. He ('Abdullah b. 'Abbās) stood up and unfolded them. While going back (from the prayer) he met Ibn 'Abbās and said to him: Why is it that you touched my head? He (Ibn 'Abbās) replied: (The man who observes prayer with plaited hair) is like one who prays with his hands tied behind.

Chapter CXC

MODERATION IN PROSTRATION, PLACING THE PALMS ON THE EARTH (GROUND) AND KEEPING AWAY ELBOWS FROM THE SIDES AND THE BELLY FROM THE THIGHS WHILE PROSTRATING

(997) Anas reported: The Messenger of Allah (may peace be upon him) said: Observe moderation in prostration, and let none of you stretch out his forearms (on the ground) like a dog.

(998) This ḥadith has been narrated by Shu'ba with the same chain of transmitters. And in the ḥadīth transmitted by Ibn Ja'far (the words are): "None of you should stretch out his forearms like the stretching out of a dog."

(999) Al-Barā' (b. 'Āzib) reported: The Messenger of Allah (may peace be upon him) said: When you prostrate yourself, place the palms of your hands on the ground and raise your elbows.

(1000) 'Abdullah b. Mālik ibn Bujainah[707] reported: When the Prophet (may peace be upon him) prostrated, he spread out his arms so that the whiteness of his armpits was visible.

(1001) This ḥadīth has been transmitted by Ja'far b. Rabī' with the same chain of transmitters. And in the narration transmitted by 'Amr b. al-Ḥārith (the words are): "When the Messenger of Allah (may peace be upon him) prostrated, he spread out his arms so that the whiteness of his armpits was visible." And in the narration transmitted by al-Laith (the words are): "When the Messenger of Allah (may peace be upon him)

707. His full name is 'Abdullah b. Mālik b. al Qishāb al-Azdī. His mother's name was Bujaina who was the daughter of Ḥārith b. 'Abd al-Muṭṭalib. He died in 58 H., during the reign of Mu'āwiya.

prostrated, he spread his hands from the armpits so that I saw their whiteness."

(1002) Maimūna reported: When the Apostle of Allah (may peace be upon him) prostrated himself, if a lamb wanted to pass between his arms, it could pass.

(1003) Maimūna, the wife of the Apostle of Allah (may peace be upon him), reported: When the Messenger of Allah (may peace be upon him) prostrated himself, he spread his arms, i.e. he separated them so much that the whiteness of his armpits became visible from behind and when he sat (for Jalsa) he rested on his left thigh.

(1004) Maimūna daughter of Ḥārith reported: When the Messenger of Allah (may peace be upon him) prostrated, he kept his hands so much apart from each other that when it was seen from behind the armpits became visible. Wakī' said: That is their whiteness.

Chapter CXCI

THE EXCELLENCE OF THE PRAYER AND THE WAY IT IS BEGUN AND THE EXCELLENCE OF RUKU' AND MODERATION IN IT, AND PROSTRATION AND MODERATION IN IT, ETC.

(1005) 'Ā'isha reported: The Messenger of Allah (may peace be upon him) used to begin prayer with takbīr (saying Allāh-o-Akbar) and the recitation: "Praise be to Allah, the Lord of the Universe." When he bowed he neither kept his head up nor bent it down, but kept it between these extremes; when he raised his head after bowing he did not prostrate himself till he had stood erect; when he raised his head after prostration he did not prostrate himself again till he sat up. At the end of every two rak'ahs he recited the *taḥiyya*; and he used to place his left foot flat (on the ground) and raise up the right; he prohibited the devil's way of sitting on the heels, and he forbade people to spread out their arms like a wild beast. And he used to finish the prayer with the taslīm.

Chapter CXCII

SUTRA[708] FOR PRAYER

(1006) Mūsā b. Ṭalḥa[709] reported it on the authority of his father: The Messenger of Allah (may peace be upon him) said: When one of you places in front of him something such as the back of a saddle, he should pray without caring who passes on the other side of it.

(1007) Mūsā b. Ṭalḥā reported on the authority of his father: We used to say prayer and the animals moved in front of us. We mentioned it to the Messenger of Allah (may peace be upon him) and he said: If anything equal to the back of a saddle is in front of you, then what walks in front, no harm would come to him. Ibn Numair

708. *Sutra* means a covering or screen. In religious terms of Islam it means an object a worshipper places in front of him when engaged in prayer so that there should be a sort of screen between him and other passersby in front of him.

709. His kunya was Abū 'Īsā Tamīmī Qarshī. He transmitted aḥādīth from a large number of Companions. He died in 104 H.

said: No harm would come whosoever walks in front.

(1008) 'Ā'isha reported: The Messenger of Allah (may peace be upon him) was asked about sutra of a worshipper; he said: Equal to the back of the saddle.

(1009) 'Ā'isha reported: The Messenger of Allah (may peace be upon him) was asked in the expedition of Tabūk about the sutra of the worshipper; he said: Like the back of the saddle.

(1010) Ibn 'Umar reported: When the Messenger of Allah (may peace be upon him) went out on the 'Īd day, he ordered to carry a spear and it was fixed in front of him, and he said prayer towards its (direction), and the people were behind him. And he did it in the journey, and that is the reason why the Amīrs carried it.

(1011) Ibn 'Umar reported: The Apostle of Allah (may peace be upon him) set up (sutra), and Abū Bakr said: He implanted iron-tipped spear and said prayer towards its direction. Ibn Abū Shaiba made this addition to it: " 'Ubaidullah said that it was a spear."

(1012) Ibn 'Umar said: The Apostle of Allah (may peace be upon him) used to place his camel (towards the Ka'ba) and said prayer in its direction.

(1013) Ibn 'Umar reported: The Apostle of Allah (may peace be upon him) used to say prayer towards his camel. Ibn Numair said: The Apostle of Allah (may peace be upon him) said prayer towards the camel.[710]

(1014) Abū Juḥaifa[711] reported it on the authority of his father: I came to the Apostle of Allah (may peace be upon him) in Mecca and he was (at that time) at al-Abṭaḥ in a red leather tent. And Bilāl stepped out with ablution water for him. (And what was left out of that water) some of them got it (whereas others could not get it) and (those who got it) rubbed themselves with it. Then the Apostle of Allah (may peace be upon him) stepped out with a red mantle on him and I was catching a glimpse of the whiteness of his shanks. The narrator said: He (the Holy Prophet) performed the ablution, and Bilāl pronounced Adhān and I followed his mouth (as he turned) this side and that as he said on the right and the left: "Come to prayer, come to success." A spear was then fixed for him (on the ground). He stepped forward and said two rak'ahs of Ẓuhr, while there passed in front of him a donkey and a dog, and these were not checked. He then said two rak'ahs of 'Aṣr prayer, and he then continued saying two rak'ahs till he came back to Medina.

(1015) Abū Juḥaifa reported on the authority of his father: I saw the Messenger of Allah (may peace be upon him) (in Mecca at al-Abṭaḥ) in a red leather tent, and I saw Bilāl take the ablution water (left by Allah's Messenger), and I saw the people racing with one another to get that ablution water. If anyone got some of it, he rubbed himself with it, and anyone who did not get any got some of the moisture from his companion's hand. I then saw Bilāl take a staff and fix it in the ground, after which the Messenger of Allah (may peace be upon him) came out quickly in a red mantle and

710. What it means is that the Holy Prophet during his journey set his riding animal towards the Qibla as sutra and then said prayer.

711. His name was Wahb b. 'Abdullah al-'Āmirī. He belonged to Kūfa and was counted among the younger generations of the Companions who had not attained maturity at the time of the death of the Holy Prophet. He died in Kūfa in 74 H. A good number of transmitters belonging to the group of successors (Tābi'īn) have transmitted the aḥādīth on his authority.

led the people in two rak'ahs facing the staff, and I saw people and animals passing in front of the staff.

(1016) 'Aun b. Abū Juḥaifa narrated from the Apostle of Allah (may peace be upon him) on the authority of his father a ḥadīth like that of Sufyān, and 'Umar b. Abū Zā'ida made this addition: Some of them tried to excel the others (in obtaining water), and in the ḥadīth transmitted by Mālik b. Mighwal (the words are): When it was noon, Bilāl came out and summoned (people) to (noon) prayer.

(1017) Abū Juḥaifa reported: The Messenger of Allah (may peace be upon him) went at noon towards al-Baṭḥā', he performed ablution, and said two rak'aḥs of Ẓuhr prayer and two of 'Aṣr prayer, and there was a spear in front of him. Shu'ba said and 'Aun made this addition to it on the authority of his father Abū Juḥaifa: And the woman and the donkey passed behind it.

(1018) Shu'ba narrated the same on the basis of two authorities and in the ḥadīth transmitted by Ḥakam (the words are): The people began to get water that was left out of his (the Prophet's) ablution.

(1019) Ibn 'Abbās reported: I came riding on a she-ass, and I was on the threshold of maturity, and the Messenger of Allah (may peace be upon him) was leading people in prayer at Minā. I passed in front of the row and got down, and sent the she-ass for grazing and joined the row, and nobody made any objection to it.

(1020) 'Abdullah b. 'Abbās reported that he came riding on a donkey, and the Messenger of Allah (may peace be upon him) was leading the people in prayer at Minā on the occasion of the Farewell Pilgrimage and (the narrator) reported: The donkey passed in front of the row and then he got down from it and joined the row along with the people.

(1021) This ḥadīth has been transmitted by Ibn 'Uyaina on the authority of al-Zuhrī with the same chain of transmitters and he reported: The Apostle of Allah (may peace be upon him) was leading prayer at 'Arafa.

(1022) This ḥadīth has been transmitted by Ma'mar on the authority of al-Zuhrī with the same chain of transmitters, but here no mention has been made of Minā or 'Arafa, and he said: It was in the Farewell Pilgrimage or on the Day of Victory.

(1023) Abū Sa'īd al-Khudrī reported that the Messenger of Allah (may peace be upon him) said: When any one of you prays he should not let anyone pass in front of him (if there is no sutra), and should try to turn him away as far as possible, but if he refuses to go, he should turn him away forcibly[712] for he is a devil.[713]

(1024) Abū Ṣāliḥ al-Sammān reported: I narrate to you what I heard and saw from Abū Sa'īd al-Khudrī: One day I was with Abū Sa'īd and he was saying prayer on Friday turning to a thing which concealed him from the people when a young man from Banū Mu'aiṭ came there and he tried to pass in front of him; he turned him back by striking his chest. He looked about but finding no other way to pass except in front of Abū Sa'īd, made a second attempt. He (Abū Sa'īd) turned him away by striking his chest more vigorously than the first stroke. He stood up and had a scuffle with Abū

712. The original word is فليقاتله which means "then he should fight him". But here it does not actually mean fighting but resisting him to do this act (*Fatḥ-ul-Mulhim*, Vol. II, p. 105).

713. This is a satanic act that one does not observe the sanctity of prayer.

Sa'īd. Then the people gathered there. He came out and went to Marwān and complained to him what had happened to him. Abū Sa'īd too came to Marwān. Marwān said to him: What has happened to you and the son of your brother that he came to complain against you? Abū Sa'īd said: I heard from the Messenger of Allah (may peace be upon him) saying: When any one of you prays facing something which conceals him from people and anyone tries to pass in front of him, he should be turned away, but if he refuses, he should be forcibly restrained from it, for he is a devil.

(1025) 'Abdullah b. 'Umar reported that the Messenger of Allah (may peace be upon him) said: When any one of you prays, he should not allow anyone to pass before him, and if he refuses, he should be then forcibly resisted, for there is a devil with him.

(1026) This ḥadīth has been transmitted by Ibn 'Umar by another chain of trasmitters.

(1027) Busr b. Sa'īd reported that Zaid b. Khālid al-Juhanī sent him to Abū Juhaim in order to ask him what he had heard from the Messenger of Allah (may peace be upon him) with regard to the passer in front of the worshipper. Abū Juhaim reported that the Messenger of Allah (may peace be upon him) said: If anyone who passes in front of a man who is praying knew the responsibility he incurs, he would stand still forty (years) rather than to pass in front of him. Abū Naḍr said: I do not know whether he said forty days or months or years.

(1028) This ḥadīth has been transmitted from Abū Juhaim Anṣārī by another chain of transmitters.

(1029) Sahl b. Sa'd al-Sā'idī reported: Between the place of worship where the Messenger of Allah (may peace be upon him) prayed and the wall, there was a gap through which a goat could pass.

(1030) Salama b. Akwa' reported: He sought the place (in the mosque) where the copies of the Qur'ān were kept and glorified Allah there, and the narrator made a mention that the Messenger of Allah (may peace be upon him) sought that place and that was between the pulpit and the qibla—a place where a goat could pass.

(1031) Yazīd reported: Salama sought to say prayer near the pillar which was by that place where copies of the Qur'ān were kept. I said to him: Abū Muslim, I see you striving to offer your prayer by this pillar. He said: I saw the Messenger of Allah (may peace be upon him) seeking to pray by its side.

(1032) Abū Dharr reported: The Messenger of Allah (may peace be upon him) said: When any one of you stands for prayer and there is a thing before him equal to the back of the saddle that covers him and in case there is not before him (a thing) equal to the back of the saddle, his prayer would be cut off[714] by (passing of an) ass, woman, and black dog. I said: O Abū Dharr, what feature is there in a black dog which distinguishes it from the red dog and the yellow dog? He said: O, son of my brother, I

714. Here cutting off does not mean that it would become absolutely invalid and one would be required to repeat the prayer. What it implies is that by the passing of a woman, a black dog and an ass the deep communion that a worshipper holds with his Lord while praying would be temporarily disturbed. Now the question may be asked why an ass, a dog and a woman have been especially mentioned. The answer is that these three things are strikingly significant for bad voice, ugliness and charm, respectively, and these can, therefore, distract the attention of the worshipper (*Fatḥ-ul-Mulhim*, Vol. II, p. 110).

asked the Messenger of Allah (may peace be upon him) as you are asking me, and he said : The black dog is a devil.

(1033) This ḥadīth has been transmitted by Ḥumaid b. Hilāl on the authority of Yūnus.

(1034) Abū Huraira reported : The Messenger of Allah (may peace be upon him) said : A woman, an ass and a dog disrupt the prayer, but something like the back of a saddle guards against that.

(1035) 'Ā'isha reported : The Prophet (may peace be upon him) used to pray at night while I lay interposed between him and the Qibla like a corpse on the bier.[715]

(1036) 'Ā'isha reported : The Apostle of Allah (may peace be upon him) said his whole prayer (Tahajjud prayer) during the night while I lay between him and the Qibla. When he intended to say witr[716] (prayer) he awakened me and I too said witr (prayer).

(1037) 'Urwa b. Zubair reported : 'Ā'isha asked : What disrupts the prayer ? We said : The woman and the ass. Upon this she remarked : Is the woman an ugly animal? I lay in front of the Messenger of Allah (may peace be upon him) like the bier of a corpse and he said prayer.[717]

(1038) Masrūq reported : It was mentioned before 'Ā'isha that prayer is invalidated (in case of passing) of a dog, an ass and a woman (before the worshipper, when he is not screened). Upon this 'Ā'isha said : You likened us to the asses and the dogs. By Allah! I saw the Messenger of Allah (may peace be upon him) saying prayer while I lay on the bedstead interposing between him and the Qibla. When I felt the need, I did not like to sit in front (of the Holy Prophet) and perturb the Messenger of Allah (may peace be upon him) and quietly moved out from under its (i.e. of the bedstead) legs.

(1039) Al-Aswad reported that 'Ā'isha said : You have made us equal to the dogs and the asses, whereas I lay on the bedstead and the Messenger of Allah (may peace be upon him) came there and stood in the middle of the bedstead and said prayer. I did not like to take off the quilt from me (in that state) so I moved away quietly from the front legs of the bedstead and thus came out of the quilt.

(1040) 'Ā'isha reported : I was sleeping in front of the Messenger of Allah (may peace be upon him) with my legs between him and the Qibla. When he prostrated himself, he pinched me and I drew up my legs, and when he stood up, I stretched them out. She said : At that time there were no lamps in the houses.

(1041) Maimūna, the wife of the Apostle (may peace be upon him), reported : The Messenger of Allah (may peace be upon him) said prayer and I (lay) opposite to him while I was in menses. Sometimes his clothe touched me when he prostrated.

(1042) 'Ā'isha reported : The Apostle of Allah (may peace be upon him) said prayer at night and I was by his side in a state of menses and I had a sheet pulled over me a portion of which was on his side.

715. This ḥadīth lends support to the view that the prayer does not become invalid if a woman passes in front of the worshipper.

716. Witr may consist of three rak'ahs or only one.

717. See in what high esteem a woman is held in Islam.

Chapter CXCIII

PRAYER IN A SINGLE GARMENT

(1043) Abū Huraira reported: An inquirer asked the Messenger of Allah (may peace be upon him) about the prayer in a single garment. He (the Holy Prophet) said: Has every one of you two garments? [718]

(1044) A ḥadīth like this has been narrated by Abū Huraira with another chain or transmitters.

(1045) Abū Huraira reported: A person addressed the Apostle of Allah (may peace be upon him) and said to him: Can any one of us say prayer in one garment. He said: Do all of you possess two garments?

(1046) Abū Huraira reported: The Messenger of Allah (may peace be upon him) said: None of you must pray in a single garment of which no part comes over his shoulders.

(1047) 'Umar b. Abū Salama reported: I saw the Messenger of Allah (may peace be upon him) praying in Umm Salama's house in a single garment, placing its two ends over his shoulders.

(1048) This ḥadīth has been transmitted by Hishām b. 'Urwa with the same chain of transmitters except (with this difference) that the word *mutawashshiḥan* [719] (متوشحا) was used and not the word *mushtamilan* (مشتملا).

(1049) 'Umar b. Abū Salama reported: I saw the Messenger of Allah (may peace be upon him) saying prayer in the house of Umm Salama in a single garment with its extremities crossing each other.

(1050) 'Umar b. Abū Salama reported: I saw the Messenger of Allah (may peace be upon him) praying in a single garment with its ends crossing each other. 'Īsā b. Ḥammad added: "placing on his shoulders"

(1051) Jābir reported: I saw the Messenger of Allah (may peace be upon him) praying in a single garment crossing the two ends.

(1052) This ḥadīth has been transmitted by Sufyān with the same chain of transmitters and in the ḥadīth transmitted by Numair the words are: "I called upon the Messenger of Allah (may peace be upon him)."

(1053) Abū Zubair reported that he saw Jābir b. 'Abdullah praying in a single garment crossing its ends even though he had the garments, [720] and Jābir said: He saw the Messenger of Allah (may peace be upon him) doing like this.

(1054) Abū Sa'īd al-Khudrī reported: I visited the Apostle (may peace be upon him) and saw him praying on a reed mat on which he was prostrating himself. And I saw him praying in a single garment with ends crossed with each other.

718. These words of the Holy Prophet are clearly indicative of the fact that it is better to say prayer in two garments, i.e. loin covering and covering for the upper part of the body, but as these are not available to everyone, it is, therefore, permissible to say prayer in a single garment. Permission of praying in a single dress is thus a matter of expediency rather than a normal routine.

719. توشح, means throwing a portion of one's garment over one's left shoulder and drawing its extremity under one's right arm, and then tying the two extremities together in a knot upon one's bosom.

720. Jābir b. 'Abdullah did it simply to show that it was permissible under the stress of expediency.

(1055) This ḥadīth has been transmitted by A'mash with the same chain of transmitters and in the narration of Abū Kuraib the words are : "Placing its (mantle's) ends on his shoulders" ; and the narration transmitted by Abū Bakr and Suwaid (the words are) : "the ends crossing with each other".

Chapter CXCIV

MOSQUES AND THE PLACE OF WORSHIP

(1056) Abū Dharr reported : I said : Messenger of Allah, which mosque was set up first on the earth ? He said : Al-Masjid al-Ḥarām[721] (the sacred). I (again) said : Then which next ? He said : It was the Masjid Aqṣā.[722] I (again) said : How long the space of time (between their setting up) ? He (the Holy Prophet) said : It was forty years.[723] And whenever the time comes for prayer, pray there, for that is a mosque ; and in the ḥadīth transmitted by Abū Kāmil (the words are) : "Whenever time comes for prayer, pray, for that is a mosque (for you)."

(1057) Ibrāhīm b. Yazīd al-Taymī reported : I used to read the Qur'ān with my father in the vestibule (before the door of the mosque). When I recited the āyāt (verses) concerning prostration, he prostrated himself. I said to him : Father, do you prostrate yourself in the path ? He said : I heard Abū Dharr saying : I asked the Messenger of Allah (may peace be upon him) about the mosque that was first set up on the earth. He said : Masjid Ḥarām. I said : Then which next ? He said : The Masjid al-Aqṣā. I said : How long is the space of time between the two ? He said : Forty years. He (then) further said : The earth is a mosque for you, so wherever you are at the time of prayer, pray there.

(1058) Jābir b. 'Abdullah al-Anṣārī reported : The Prophet (may pe ce be upon him) said : I have been conferred upon five (things) which were not granted to anyone before me (and these are) : Every apostle was sent particularly to his own people, whereas I have

721. This refers to the Ka'ba.

722. The great mosque at Jerusalem.

723. This part of the ḥadīth has often been made a target of criticism by the hostile critics of the Ḥadīth. They contend that Ka'ba was built by Ḥaḍrat Ibrāhīm and the Temple of Jerusalem was built by Ḥaḍrat Sulaimān and there is a span of one thousand years between these two Messengers of Allah, whereas this ḥadīth asserts that there is a difference of only forty years between the setting up of these two Houses of Worship. The fact is that it is wrong to suppose that Ka'ba was built by Ibrāhīm and the Temple of Aqṣā was built by Ḥadart Sulaimān. Both these houses of worship were built by Adam and there was a difference of forty years between the two. Ḥaḍrat Ibrāhīm rebuilt it on the old foundations. The second view is that the Temple of Jerusalem was built not by Sulaimān but by Ya'qūb b. Isḥāq b. Ibrāhīm who laid its foundation forty years after the rebuilding of the Ka'ba by Ḥaḍrat Ibrāhīm (*Fatḥ-ul-Mulhim*, Vol. II, p. 114).

This point has been stressed by Ḥāfiz Ibn Qayyim. He says : This ḥadīth creates doubt in the mind of one who does not know its correct implication. It is said that it was Sulaimān b. Dāwūd who built the Masjid Aqṣā, whereas there yawns a space of time more than one thousand years between the two. The fact is that Sulaimān rebuilt the Aqṣā Mosque and he was not the first to build it for the first time. It was built by Ya'qūb b. Isḥāq (peace be upon him) after the building of the Ka'ba by Ibrāhīm equal to so much space of time (*Zād al-Ma'ād*, Vol. I, p. 11).

been sent to all the red and the black,[724] the spoils of war have been made lawful for me, and these were never made lawful to anyone before me,[725] and the earth has been made sacred and pure and mosque for me,[726] so whenever the time of prayer comes for any one of you he should pray wherever he is, and I have been supported by awe[727] (by which the enemy is overwhelmed) from the distance (which one takes) one month to cover and I have been granted intercession.[728]

(1059) Jābir b. 'Abdullah related that the Messenger of Allah (may peace be upon him) said, and he related like this.

(1060) Ḥudhaifa reported: The Messenger of Allah (may peace be upon him) said: We have been made to excel (other) people in three (things): Our rows have been made like the rows of the angels[729] and the whole earth has been made a mosque for us, and its dust has been made a purifier for us in case water is not available. And he mentioned another characteristic too.[730]

(1061) Ḥudhaifa reported: The Messenger of Allah (may peace be upon him) said like this.

(1062) Abū Huraira reported that the Messenger of Allah (may peace be upon him) said: I have been given superiority over the other prophets in six respects: I have been given words which are concise but comprehensive in meaning; I have been helped

724. "My apostlehood is universal and I have been sent as a messenger to the whole human race." The Qur'ān says: Say (O Muḥammad): O mankind! lo, I am the Messenger of Allah to you, (the Messenger of) Him unto Whom belongeth the sovereignty of the heaven and the earth" (vii. 158); "And We have not sent thee but as a bringer of good tidings and as a warner unto all mankind, but most of mankind know not" (xxxiv. 28).

725. Khaṭṭābī explains it in this way: Either the earlier prophets were not allowed to wage war against their enemies and thus the question of spoils did not arise, or if they were permitted to lift arms, they were not allowed to take any booty. A lightning from the sky came and burnt the whole lot of it.

726. This is a matter of great significance. Before Islam it was thought that the material world is profane and has nothing to do with the spiritual life of man. One who is interested in spirituality should look down upon this world as something impure. But with the advent of the Holy Prophet it was made clear that the material world is neither profane nor impure and it is as sacred as the spiritual and the moral world. The whole earth has been made a fit place of worship for you. This signifies that there is no impurity attached to it and a prayer house is not necessary for prayer.

727. It implies that "at times I would win victory even without confrontation and armed encounter." This is testified by history and many a battle was won even by fear that haunted the minds of the enemies of Islam.

728. The privilege of intercession has been granted to many others. Here it is the mention of a special privilege which the Holy Prophet would use on the Doomsday when there would be general consternation and all the apostles would express their helplessness.

729. Just as angels keep their ranks and do whatever service is assigned to them and do not question God's plan, similarly the Muslims believe in willing submission to the Creator. This ḥadīth has a reference to the following verse of the Holy Qur'ān:

> And we are verily ranged in ranks (for service). And we are verily those who declare God's Glory (xxxvii. 166).

730 This has a reference to the concluding verses of Sūra Baqara which the Holy Prophet received under the Throne, which deal with Īmān, willing submission before the Lord, belief in the earlier prophets, angels and the Books, supplication for forgiveness and burden which is not unbearable, Allah's mercy and triumph of the Muslims.

by terror (in the hearts of enemies); spoils have been made lawful to me; the earth has been made for me clean and a place of worship; I have been sent to all mankind; and the line of prophets is closed with me.

(1063) Abū Huraira reported: The Messenger of Allah (may peace be upon him) said: I have been commissioned with words which are concise but comprehensive in meaning; I have been helped by terror (in the hearts of enemies); and while I was asleep I was brought the keys[731] of the treasures of the earth which were placed in my hand. And Abū Huraira added: The Messenger of Allah (may peace be upon him) has left (for his heavenly home) and you are now busy in getting them.

(1064) Abū Huraira reported: I heard the Messenger of Allah (may peace be upon him) saying a ḥadīth like that of Yūnus.

(1065) This ḥadīth has been transmitted by Abū Huraira by another chain of transmitters.

(1066) Abū Huraira reported: The Messenger of Allah (may peace be upon him) said: I have been helped by terror (in the heart of the enemy); I have been given words which are concise but comprehensive in meaning; and while I was asleep I was brought the keys of the treasures of the earth which were placed in my hand.

(1067) Hammām b. Munabbih reported: That is what Abū Huraira reported to us from the Messenger of Allah (may peace be upon him) and he narrated (some) aḥādīth one of which is that the Messenger of Allah (may peace be upon him) said: I have been helped by terror (in the hearts of enemies) and I have been given words which are concise but comprehensive in meaning.

Chapter CXCV

BUILDING OF THE PROPHET'S MOSQUE IN MEDINA

(1068) Anas b. Mālik reported: The Messenger of Allah (may peace be upon him) came to Medina and stayed in the upper part of Medina for fourteen nights with a tribe called Banū 'Amr b. 'Auf. He then sent for the chiefs of Banū al-Najjār, and they came with swords around their necks. He (the narrator) said: I perceive as if I am seeing the Messenger of Allah (may peace be upon him) on his ride with Abū Bakr behind him and the chiefs of Banū al-Najjār around him till he alighted in the court-yard of Abū Ayyūb. He (the narrator) said: The Messenger of Allah (may peace be upon him) said prayer when the time came for prayer, and he prayed in the fold of goats and sheep. He then ordered mosques to be built and sent for the chiefs of Banū al-Najjār, and they came (to him). He (the Holy Prophet) said to them: O Banū al-Najjār, sell these lands of yours to me. They said: No, by Allah, we would not demand their price, but (reward) from the Lord. Anas said: There (in these lands) were trees and graves of the polytheists, and ruins. The Messenger of Allah (may peace be

731. Keys denote riches, honour and power and victory, and all these things were conferred upon the Holy Prophet. He was given both the worldly and the spiritual wealth, but he chose the latter. He has been given an honour the like of which is not found in history. He was given unrivalled power and he won great triumphs and victories.

upon him) ordered that the trees should be cut, and the graves should be dug out, and the ruins should be levelled. The trees (were thus) placed in rows towards the Qibla and the stones were set on both sides of the door, and (while building the mosque) they (the Companions) sang rajaz verses along with the Messenger of Allah (may peace be upon him):

O Allah! there is no good but the good of the next world,
So help the Anṣār and the Muhājirīn.

(1069) Anas reported: The Messenger of Allah (may peace be upon him) used to pray in the folds of the sheep and goats before the mosque was built.

(1070) Abū al-Tīyyāḥ reported: I heard from Anas a narration like this from the Messenger of Allah (may peace be upon him).

Chapter CXCVI

CHANGE OF QIBLA FROM BAIT-UL-MAQDIS TO KA'BA

(1071) Al-Barā' b. 'Āzib reported: I said prayer with the Apostle (may peace be upon him) turning towards Bait-ul-Maqdis for sixteen months till this verse of Sūra Baqara was revealed: "And wherever you are turn your faces towards it" (ii. 144). This verse was revealed when the Apostle (may peace be upon him) had said prayer. A person amongst his people passed by the people of Anṣār as they were engaged in prayer. He narrated to them (this command of Allah) and they turned their faces towards the Ka'ba.[732]

(1072) Abū Isḥāq reported: I heard al-Barā' saying: We prayed with the Messenger of Allah (may peace be upon him) (with our faces) towards Bait-ul-Maqdis for sixteen months or seventeen months. Then we were made to change (our direction) towards the Ka'ba.

(1073) Ibn 'Umar reported: As the people were praying at Qubā' a man came to them and said: It has been revealed to the Messenger of Allah (may peace be upon him) during the night and he has been directed to turn towards the Ka'ba. So turn towards it. Their faces were towards Syria and they turned round towards Ka'ba.

(1074) Ibn 'Umar reported: As the people were engaged in morning[733] prayer a man came to them. The rest of the ḥadīth is the same.

732. This was a change of far-reaching importance, and it had different reactions in different circles. It strengthened the loyalty of the Muslims to Islam and the Prophet. They expressed their implicit faith in Muḥammad (may peace be upon him) as a recipient of Divine Faith and accepted this change most willingly. The Jews were indignant. The hypocrites labelled it as an inconsistent, rather contradictory, behaviour of the Holy Prophet in matters of religion. The Holy Qur'ān explains the significance of this change in the following words:

> And We appointed not the Qibla which you have had but that We might distinguish him who follows the Apostle from him who turns back upon his heels, and surely this was hard except for those whom Allah has guided aright (xi. 143).

This change of direction, says Arnold, "has a deeper significance than at first sight appears. It was really the beginning of the national life of Islam; it established the Ka'bah at Mecca as a religious centre for all the Muslim people" (*The Preaching of Islam*, p. 27).

733. The only difference between the two is that in ḥadīth 1073 the word صبح has been used for morning prayer and in this ḥadīth it is غداة.

(1075) Anas reported: The Messenger of Allah (may peace be upon him) used to pray towards Bait-ul-Maqdis, that it was revealed (to him): "Indeed We see the turning of the face to heaven, wherefore We shall assuredly cause thee to turn towards Qibla which shall please thee. So turn thy face towards the sacred Mosque (Ka'ba)" (ii. 144). A person from Banū Salama was going; (he found the people) in rukū' (while) praying the dawn prayer and they had said one rak'ah. He said in a loud voice: Listen! the Qibla has been changed and they turned towards (new) Qibla (Ka'ba) in that very state.

Chapter CXCVII

FORBIDDANCE TO BUILD MOSQUES ON THE GRAVES AND DECORATING THEM WITH PICTURES AND FORBIDDANCE TO USE THE GRAVES AS MOSQUES

(1076) 'Ā'isha reported: Umm Ḥabība and Umm Salama made a mention before the Messenger of Allah (may peace be upon him) of a church which they had seen in Abyssinia and which had pictures in it. The Messenger of Allah (may peace be upon him) said: When a pious person amongst them (among the religious groups) dies they build a place of worship on his grave, and then decorate it with such pictures. They would be the worst of creatures on the Day of Judgment in the sight of Allah.[734]

(1077) 'Ā'isha reported: They (some Companions of the Holy Prophet) were conversing with one another in the presence of the Messenger of Allah (may peace be upon him) (during his last) illness. Umm Salama and Umm Ḥabība made a mention of the church, and then (the ḥadīth was) narrated.

(1078) 'Ā'isha reported: The wives of the Apostle of Allah (may peace be upon him) made a mention of the church which they had seen in Abyssinia which was called Marya,[735] and the rest of the ḥadīth is the same.

(1079) 'Ā'isha reported: The Messenger of Allah (may peace be upon him) said during his illness from which he never recovered: Allah cursed the Jews and the Christians that they took the graves of their prophets as mosques. She ('Ā'isha) reported: Had it not been so, his (Prophet's) grave would have been in an open place,[736] but it could not be due to the fear that it may not be taken as a mosque.

(1080) Abū Huraira reported: The Messenger of Allah (may peace be upon him) said: Let Allah destroy the Jews for they have taken the graves of their apostles as places of worship.

734. The Holy Prophet has explained how polytheism gradually develops. It starts from the pious intention, i.e. building of a temple by the grave of a pious man so that there should be association of a religious piety to a place of worship. But steadily the people begin to look upon the religious man as a demigod and then elevate him to a higher status of Godhood. This undermines the belief in the oneness of Allah.

The pictures of the pious men are displayed in the temples in order to keep alive their sacred memories, but with the march of time the people begin to worship them.

735. Perhaps this church was named after Mary, the mother of Jesus.

736. The Holy Prophet was buried in the small room of Ḥaḍrat 'Ā'isha (Allah be pleased with her) where he died. It is a covered place with walls built on all sides of it.

(1081) Abū Huraira reported: The Messenger of Allah (may peace be upon him) said: Let there be curse of Allah upon the Jews and Christians for they have taken the graves of their apostles as places of worship.

(1082) 'Ā'isha and 'Abdullah reported: As the Messenger of Allah (may peace be upon him) was about to breathe his last, he drew his sheet upon his face and when he felt uneasy, he uncovered his face and said in this very state: Let there be curse upon the Jews and the Christians that they have taken the graves of their apostles as places of worship. He in fact warned (his men) against what they (the Jews and the Christians) did.

(1083) Jundub reported: I heard from the Apostle of Allah (may peace be upon him) five days before his death and he said: I stand acquitted before Allah that I took any one of you as friend,[737] for Allah has taken me as His friend, as he took Ibrāhīm as His friend. Had I taken any one of my Ummah as friend, I would have taken Abū Bakr as a friend.[738] Beware of those who preceded you and used to take the graves of their prophets and righteous men as places of worship, but you must not take graves as mosques; I forbid you to do that.

Chapter CXCVIII

THE VIRTUE OF BUILDING THE MOSQUES AND EXHORTATION TO IT

(1084) 'Ubaidullah al-Khaulānī reported: 'Uthmān b. 'Affān listened to the opinion of the people (which was not favourable) when he rebuilt the mosque of the Messenger of Allah (may peace be upon him). Thereupon he said: You have not been fair to me for I have heard from the Messenger of Allah (may peace be upon him) saying: He who built mosque for Allah, the Exalted, Allah would build for him a house in Paradise. Bukair said: I think he (the Holy Prophet) said: While he seeks the pleasure of Allah (by building the mosque). And in the narration of Ibn 'Isā (the words are): "(a house) like that (mosque) in Paradise."

(1085) Maḥmūd b. Labīd reported: When 'Uthmān b. 'Affān intended to build the mosque (of the Prophet) the people did not approve of it. They liked that it should be kept in the same state. Thereupon he said: I heard the Messenger of Allah (may peace be upon him) say: He who built a mosque for Allah, Allah would build a house for him like it in Paradise.

737. Khalīl may be derived from al-Khulla which may mean true or sincere friendship, love and affection Here Khalīl stands for one to whom one turns in moments of need. What the ḥadīth signifies is that "I have looked to my God alone for help and assistance at every step of my life."

738. It implies: "If I ever looked for help and assistance to anyone out of the worldly supporters I would have chosen Abū Bakr for it." This clearly explains the eminence of Abū Bakr in Islam. Abū Bakr was no doubt a sincere friend of the Holy Prophet and he too loved him dearly but he was in no way the ultimate resort of the Holy Prophet. Muḥammad had explicit faith in Allah and he depended on Him alone for guidance and assistance. He alone was his ultimate Resort and a constant source of strength and power.

Chapter CXCIX

CONCERNING THE COMMAND OF PLACING ONE'S HANDS ON THE KNEES WHILE IN RUKŪ' AND ABROGATION OF AL-TAṬBĪQ[739]

(1086) Al-Aswad and 'Alqama reported: We came to the house of 'Abdullah b. Mas'ūd. He said: Have these people[740] said prayer behind you? We said: No. He said: Then stand up and say prayer. He neither ordered us to say Adhān nor Iqāma.[741] We went to stạnd behind him. He caught hold of our hands and made one of us stand on his right hand and the other on his left side.[742] When we bowed, we placed our hands on our knees. He struck our hands and put his hands together, palm to palm, then put them between his thighs. When he completed the prayer he said: There would soon come your Amīrs, who would defer prayers from their appointed time and would make such delay that a little time is left before sunset. So when you see them doing so, say prayer at its appointed time and then say prayer along with them as (Nafl), and when you are three, pray together (standing in one row), and when you are more than three, appoint one amongst you as your Imām. And when any one of you bows he must place his hands upon his thighs and kneel down, and putting his palms together place (them within his thighs). I perceive as if I am seeing the gap between the fingers of the Messenger of Allah (may peace be upon him).

(1087) This ḥadīth is narrated on the authority of 'Alqama and Aswad by another chain of transmitters and in the ḥadīth transmitted by Ibn Mus-hir and Jabīr the words are: "I preceive as if I am seeing the gap between the fingers of the Messenger of Allah (may peace be upon him) as he was bowing."

(1088) 'Alqama and Aswad reported that they went to 'Abdullah. He said: Have (people) behind you said prayer? They said: Yes. He stood between them ('Alqama and Aswad). One was on his right side and the other was on his left. We then bowed and placed our hands on our knees. He struck our hands and then putting his hands together, palm to palm, placed them between his thighs.[743] When he completed the prayer he said: This is how the Messenger of Allah (may peace be upon him) used to do.

(1089) Muṣ'ab b. Sa'd reported: I said prayer by the side of my father and placed my hands between my knees. My father said to me: Place your hands on your knees. I repeated that (the previous act) for the second time, and he struck at my hands and said: We have been forbidden to do so and have been commanded to place our palms on the knees.

(1090) This ḥadīth has been transmitted by Abū Ya'fūr with the same chain of transmitters up to these words: We have been forbidden from it and no mention of

739. It means putting of hands together, palm to palm, and then putting them between one's thighs. This practice is now abrogated in prayer.

740. The rich and the dignitaries.

741. This is permissible when the prayer is said in the house.

742. This is abrogated. The actual position is that when there are only two persons to say prayer, they should stand in one row and when there are more than two, one acts as the Imām and the other two stand behind him.

743. This practice now stands abrogated by a tradition which has been transmitted by Sa'd b. Abī Waqqāṣ as we find it in ḥadīth 1089.

that has been made what follows it.

(1091) Ibn Sa'd reported: I bowed and my hands were in this state, i.e. they were put together, palm to palm, and were placed between his thighs. My father said: We used to do like this but were later on commanded to place them on the knees.

(1092) Mus'ab b. Sa'd b. Abū Waqqāṣ reported: I said prayer by the side of my father. When I bowed I intertwined my fingers and placed them between my knees. He struck my hands. When he completed the prayer he said: We used to do this, but then were commanded to lift (our palms) to the knees.

Chapter CC

SITTING ON THE BUTTOCKS

(1093) Ṭāwūs reported: We asked Ibn 'Abbās about sitting on one's buttocks (in prayer) (على القدمين). He said: It is sunnah. We said to him: We find it a sort of cruelty to the foot. Ibn 'Abbās said: It is the sunnah of your Apostle (may peace be upon him).[744]

Chapter CCI

FORBIDDANCE OF TALKING IN PRAYER AND ABROGATION OF WHAT WAS PERMISSIBLE

(1094) Mu'āwiya b. al-Ḥakam said: While I was praying with the Messenger of Allah (may peace be upon him), a man in the company sneezed. I said: Allah have mercy on you! The people stared at me with disapproving looks, so I said: Woe be upon me, why is it that you stare at me?[745] They began to strike their hands on their thighs, and when I saw them urging me to observe silence (I became angry) but I said nothing. When the Messenger of Allah (may peace be upon him) had said the prayer (and I declare that neither before him nor after him have I seen a leader who gave better instruction than he for whom I would give my father and mother as ransom), I swear that he did not scold, beat or revile me but said:[746] Talking to persons is not fitting during the prayer, for it consists of glorifying Allah, declaring His Greatness, and recitation of the Qur'ān or words to that effect. I said: Messenger of Allah, I was till recently a pagan, but Allah has brought Islam to us; among us there are men who have recourse to Kāhins.[747] He said: Do not have recourse to them. I said: There are men who take omens [748] That is something which they find in their breasts,[749] but let

744. There is a pressure on the feet which has been said as cruelty. Prayer is a training in patience and perseverance and such a minor hardship is desirable. But if a man cannot observe this practice he can change the posture of sitting.

745. The Companions of the Holy Prophet were staring at him angrily because he talked in prayer, an act which is not permissible.

746. It reflects how kindly the Holy Prophet treated his men and with what wisdom and sagacity he instructed the people.

747. Kāhin is a diviner or a soothsayer who claims to unfold the secrets lying in the womb of future. This is forbidden in Islam because it is God alone Who has the perfect knowledge of the unseen.

748. It was a common practice with the Arabs that they took omens from the flight of birds.

749. This is just a prompting of their own soul.

it not turn their way (from freedom of action).[750] I said: Among us there are men who draw lines. He said: There was a prophet who drew lines,[751] so if they do it as they did, that is allowable.[752] I had a maid-servant who tended goats by the side of Uḥud and Jawwāniya.[753] One day I happened to pass that way and found that a wolf had carried a goat from her flock. I am after all a man from the posterity of Adam. I felt sorry as they (human beings) feel sorry. So I slapped her. I came to the Messenger of Allah (may peace be upon him) and felt (this act of mine) as something grievous. I said: Messenger of Allah, should I not grant her freedom? He (the Holy Prophet) said: Bring her to me. So I brought her to him. He said to her: Where is Allah? She said: He is in the heaven.[754] He said: Who am I? She said: Thou art the Messenger of Allah.[755] He said: Grant her freedom, she is a believing woman.[756]

((1095) This ḥadīth has been transmitted by Yaḥā b. Abū Kathīr with the same chain of transmitters.

(1096) 'Abdullah (b. Mas'ūd) reported: We used to greet the Messenger of Allah (may peace be upon him) while he was engaged in prayer and he would respond to our greeting. But when we returned from the Negus we greeted him and he did not respond to us;[757] so we said: Messenger of Allah, we used to greet you when you were engaged in prayer and you would respond to us. He replied: Prayer demands whole attention.

(1097) This ḥadīth has been transmitted by A'mash with the same chain of transmitters.

(1098) Zaid b. Arqam reported: We used to talk while engaged in prayer and a person talked with a companion on his side in prayer till (this verse) was revealed: "And stand before Allah in devout obedience" (ii. 238) and we were commanded to observe

750. This wave of prompting should in no way affect their mind and behaviour. The one meaning is that one should not allow an omen to determine one's course of action and according to Ṭībī it implies that this omen should not deviate one from the straight path (*Fatḥ-ul-Mulhim*, Vol. II, p. 135).

751. In this case the diviner draws many lines and then reveals secrets of the unseen. Here the practice of divination attributed to the Prophets is quite different from geomancy. The Prophets alluded to are Idrīs and Dāniyāl.

752. What it means is that they were the Prophets who divined things by drawing lines and as they were blessed with the prophetic vision so their information was correct, but since prophethood has been finalised in Muḥammad (may peace be opon him) it is, therefore, quite logical to conclude that this practice cannot be held as valid and authentic. Khaṭṭābī is right in asserting that these words imply forbiddance of such practice.

753. This place is situated in the north of Medina (*Fatḥ-ul-Mulhim*, Vol. II, p. 136).

754. She was a simple woman and had no knowledge of the subtleties of the metaphysical life. Her answer did not imply that she confined Allah to heaven only. What it means is that Allah is above all of us and universe, and He is the Greatest of the great.

755. This ḥadīth gives a clear idea that mere belief in Allah does not make a man Muslim. To be a Muslim one has also to affirm belief in the Prophethood of Muḥammad, because it is through him that we know Allah and the mysteries of the moral and spiritual life are unfolded to us.

756. It does not mean that a non-Muslim woman must be kept in the bondage of slavery. What it implies is that being a Muslim she has a better right to secure freedom.

757. In the earlier period of Islam one could in case of dire necessity speak while praying, but when the Prophet had migrated to Medina and those who had sought asylum in Abyssinia had come back to Medina, the conditions had considerably changed. Apart from other changes the one was that the concession of talking in prayer had been withdrawn.

silence (in prayer) and were forbidden to speak.

(1099) A ḥadīth like this has been transmitted by Ismā'īl b. Abū Khālid.

(1100) Jābir reported : The Messenger of Allah (may peace be upon him) sent me on an errand. I (having done the business assigned to me came back and) joined him as he was going (on a ride). Qutaiba said that he was saying prayer while he rode. I greeted him. He gestured to me. When he completed the prayer, he called me and said : You greeted me just now while I was engaged in prayer. (Qutaiba said) : His (Prophet's face) was towards the east,[758] as he was praying.

(1101) Jābir reported : The Messenger of Allah (may peace be upon him) sent me (on an errand) while he was going to Banū Muṣṭaliq. I came to him and he was engaged in prayer on the back of his camel. I talked to him and he gestured to me with his hand, and Zuhair gestured with his hand. I then again talked and he again (gestured to me with his hand). Zuhair pointed with his hand towards the ground. I heard him (the Holy Prophet) reciting the Qur'ān and making a sign with his head.[759] When he completed the prayer he said : What have you done (with regard to that business) for which I sent you ? I could not talk with you but for the fact that I was engaged in prayer. Zuhair told that Abū Zubair was sitting with his face turned towards Qibla (as he transmitted this ḥadīth). Abū Zuhair pointed towards Banū Muṣṭaliq with his hand, and the direction to which he pointed with his hand was not towards the Ka'ba.

(1102) Jābir reported : We were in the company of the Messenger of Allah (may peace be upon him), and he sent me on an errand, and when I came back (I saw him) saying prayer on his ride and his face was not turned towards Qibla. I greeted him but he did not respond to me. As he completed the prayer, he said : Nothing prevented me from responding to your greeting but the fact that I was praying.

(1103) This ḥadīth that the Messenger of Allah (may peace be upon him) sent Jābir on an errand has been transmitted by him through another chain of transmitters.

Chapter CCII

IT IS ALLOWABLE TO CURSE SATAN DURING PRAYER AND SEEK THE PROTECTION (OF THE LORD) AND MINOR ACTS (OF COMMISSION) IN PRAYER

(1104) Abū Huraira reported that he heard the Messenger of Allah (may peace be upon him) saying : A highly wicked one amongst the Jinn escaped yesternight to interrupt my prayer, but Allah gave me power over him, so I seized him and intended to tie him to one of the pillars of the mosque in order that you, all together or all, might look at him, but I remembered the supplication of my brother Sulaimān : "My Lord, forgive me; give me such a kingdom as will not be possible for anyone after me" (Qur'ān xxxvii. 35).

(1105) This ḥadīth has been transmitted by Ibn Abī Shaiba.

(1106) Abū Dardā' reported : Allah's Messenger (may peace be upon him) stood up

758. When a man offers the Nafl prayer on the ride, the keeping of direction towards Qibla is not very essential for it is not practicable.

759. For rukū' and prostration.

(to pray) and we heard him say: "I seek refuge in Allah from thee." Then said: "I curse thee with Allah's curse" three times, then he stretched out his hand as though he was taking hold of something. When he finished the prayer, we said: Messenger of Allah, we heard you say something during the prayer which we have not heard you say before, and we saw you stretch out your hand. He replied: Allah's enemy Iblīs came with a flame of fire to put it in my face, so I said three times: "I Seek refuge in Allah from thee." Then I said three times: "I curse thee with Allah's full curse." But he did not retreat (on any one of these) three occasions. Thereafter I meant to seize him. I swear by Allah that had it not been for the supplication of my brother Sulaimān, he would have been bound, and made an object of sport for the children of Medina.

Chapter CCIII

PERMISSIBILITY OF CARRYING CHILDREN IN PRAYER

(1107) Abū Qatāda reported: I saw the Messenger of Allah (may peace be upon him) saying the prayer while he was carrying Umāma,[760] daughter of Zainab, daughter of the Messenger of Allah (may peace be upon him), and Abu'l-'Āṣ b. al-Rabī'. When he stood up, he took her up and when he prostrated he put her down. Yaḥyā said: Mālik replied in the affirmative.

(1108) Abū Qatāda al-Anṣārī reported: I saw the Apostle (may peace be upon him) leading the people in prayer with Umāma, daughter of Abu'l-'Āṣ and Zainab, daughter of the Apostle of Allah (may peace be upon him), on his shoulder. When he bowed, he put her down, and when he got up after prostration, he lifted her again.

(1109) Abū Qatāda reported: I saw the Messenger of Allah (may peace be upon him) leading the people in prayer with Umāma daughter of Abu'l-'Āṣ on his neck; and when he prostrated he put her down.

(1110) Abū Qatāda reported: As we were sitting in the mosque, the Messenger of Allah (may peace be upon him) came to us, and the rest of the ḥadīth is the same except that he made no mention that he led people in this prayer.

Chapter CCIV

THE PERMISSIBILITY OF MOVING TWO STEPS IN THE PRAYER

(1111) Abū Ḥāzim reported on the authority of his father: Some people came to Sahl b. Sa'd and began to differ about the wood of which the (Prophet's) pulpit was

760. It is the *'aml kathir* (major act) by which the prayer is broken; the *'aml qalil* (the minor act) does not break it. According to Imām Abū Ḥanīfa, *'aml kathir* is that in which both the hands are used, and *'aml qalil* is that in which only one hand is involved So it was the *'aml qalil* which the Holy Prophet did This act of the Holy Prophet has a deep moral significance The Holy Prophet was born in an age and society where female children were looked down upon with deep contempt. They were thought unclean. The Holy Prophet took them up even in prayer, with a view to showing that they are innocent and pure and deserve our love and kindness even in the act of highest devotion to Allah. They do not in any way affect adversely our spiritual life; they are rather means by which our souls are elevated. (For details see *Fatḥ-ul-Mulhim,* Vol. II, pp. 140-1.)

made. He (Sahl b. Sa'd) said: By Allah, I know of which wood it is made and who made it, and the day when I saw the Messenger of Allah (may peace be upon him) seated himself on it on the first day. I said to him: O Abū 'Abbās (kunya of Sahl b. Sa'd), narrate to us (all these facts). He said: The Messenger of Allah (may peace be upon him) sent a person to a woman asking her to allow her slave, a carpenter, to work on woods (to prepare a pulpit) so that I should talk to the people (sitting on it). Abū Ḥāzim said: He (Sahl b. Sa'd) pointed out the name of (that lady) that day. So he (the carpenter) made (a pulpit) with these three steps. Then the Messenger of Allah (may peace be upon him) commanded it to be placed here (where it is lying now). It was fashioned out of the wood[761] of al-Ghāba.[762] And I saw the Messenger of Allah (may peace be upon him) standing upon it and glorifying Allah and the people also glorified Allah after him, while he was on the pulpit. He then raised (his head from prostration) and stepped back (on his heels) till he prostrated himself at the base of pulpit, and then returned (to the former place and this movement of one or two steps continued),[763] till the prayer was complete. He then turned towards the people and said: O people, I have done it so that you should follow me and learn (my mode of) prayer.[764]

(1112) Abū Ḥāzim reported: They (the people) came to Sahl b. Sa'd and they asked him of what thing the pulpit of the Apostle of Allah (may peace be upon him) was made, and the rest of the ḥadīth is the same.

Chapter CCV

IT IS NOT ADVISABLE TO SAY PRAYER WHILE KEEPING ONE'S HAND ON ONE'S WAIST

(1113) Abū Huraira reported from the Apostle of Allah (may peace be upon him) that he forbade keeping one's hand on one's waist while praying, and in the narration of Abū Bakr (the words are): The Messenger of Allah[765] (may peace be upon him) forbade to do so.

Chapter CCVI

IT IS FORBIDDEN TO REMOVE PEBBLES AND SMOOTH THE GROUND WHILE ENGAGED IN PRAYER

(1114) Mu'aiqīb quoted the Apostle of Allah (may peace be upon him) mentioning the removal of pebbles from the ground where he prostrated himself. He (the Prophet)

761. The original word is *ṭarfā'* which is a kind of tree, of which there are four species, one of these being athal. The name is now generally applied to the common, or French, tamarisk (Lane's *Lexicon*).

762. It is a place situated on the height, nine miles away from Medina.

763. Movement of one or two steps in prayer without turning the back is permissible in case of necessity.

764. "I am doing it," i.e. "saying prayer on a higher plane in order to make myself visible to you while praying so that you should learn it properly."

765. The only difference is that in the ḥadīth transmitted by Abū Huraira the words "Apostle of Allah" have been used and in the ḥadīth narrated by Abū Bakr, the words used are: "Messenger of Allah".

said: If you must do so, do it only once.

(1115) Mu'aiqīb said: They asked the Apostle (may peace be upon him) about the removal of (pebbles) in prayer, whereupon he said: If you do it, do it only once.[766]

Chapter CCVII

FORBIDDANCE TO SPIT IN THE MOSQUE WHILE ENGAGED IN PRAYER

(1116) 'Abdullah b. 'Umar reported: The Messenger of Allah (may peace be upon him) saw spittle on the wall towards Qibla, and scratched it away[767] and then turning to the people said: When any one of you prays, he must not spit in front of him, for Allah[768] is in front of him when he is engaged in prayer.

(1117) Ibn 'Umar reported that the Messenger of Allah (may peace be upon him) saw sputum sticking to the Qibla wall of the mosque, the rest of the ḥadīth is the same.

(1118) Abū Sa'īd al-Khudrī reported: The Apostle of Allah (may peace be upon him) saw sputum sticking to the Qibla of the mosque. He scratched it off with a pebble and then forbade spitting on the right side or in front, but (it is permissible) to spit on the left side or under the left foot.

(1119) Abū Huraira and Abū Sa'īd narrated that the Messenger of Allah (may peace be upon him) saw sputum, and the rest of the ḥadīth is the same.

(1120) 'Ā'isha reported: The Apostle of Allah (may peace be upon him) saw spittle, or snot or sputum, sticking to the wall towards Qibla and scratched it off.

(1121) Abū Huraira reported that the Messenger of Allah (may peace be upon him) saw some sputum in the direction of the Qibla of the mosque. He turned towards people and said: How is it that someone amongst you stands before his Lord and then spits out in front of him? Does any one of you like that he should be made to stand in front of someone and then spit at his face? So when any one of you spits, he must spit on his left side under his foot. But if he does not find (space to spit) he should do like this. Qāsim (one of the narrators) spat in his cloth and then folded it and rubbed it.

(1122) Abū Huraira reported: I perceive as if I am looking at the Messenger of Allah (may peace be upon him) folding up a part of his cloth with another one.

(1123) Anas b. Mālik reported: The Messenger of Allah (may peace be upon him) said: When any one of you is engaged in prayer, he is holding intimate conversation with his Lord, so none of you must spit in front of him, or towards his right side, but towards his left side under his foot.

(1124) Anas b. Mālik reported: The Messenger of Allah (may peace be upon him) said: Spitting in a mosque is a sin, and its expiation is that it should be buried.

766. One is permitted to do so only once and not to repeat it.

767. It indicates that it is one of the duties of the Imām to look to the cleanliness and neatness of the mosque (*Fatḥ-ul-Mulhim*, Vol. II, p. 144).

768. The worshipper perceives while praying that he is standing in the presence of the Lord; he should not, therefore, spit in front of him. According to Nawawī, here presence of Allah signifies Qibla.

(1125) Shu'ba reported: I asked Qatāda about spitting in the mosque. He said: I heard Anas b. Mālik say: I heard the Messenger of Allah (may peace be upon him) say: Spitting in the mosque is a sin, and its expiation is that it should be buried.

(1126) Abū Dharr reported: The Apostle of Allah (may peace be upon him) said: The deeds of my people, good and bad, were presented before me, and I found the removal of something objectionable from the road among their good deeds, and the sputum mucus left unburied in the mosque among their evil deeds.

(1127) 'Abdullah b. Shakhkhīr reported on the authority of his father that he said: I said prayer with the Messenger of Allah (may peace be upon him) and saw him spitting and rubbing it off with his shoe.

(1128) 'Abdullah b. Shakhkhīr narrated it on the authority of his father that he said prayer with the Messenger of Allah (may peace be upon him), and he spat and then rubbed it off with his left shoe.

Chapter CCVIII

PERMISSIBILITY OF WEARING SHOES IN PRAYER

(1129) Sa'd b. Yazīd reported: I said to Anas b. Mālik: Did the Messenger of Allah (may peace be upon him) pray while putting on the shoes? He said: Yes.[769]

(1130) Sa'd b. Yazīd Abū Maslama reported: I said to Anas like (that mentioned above).

Chapter CCIX

IT IS NOT ADVISABLE TO PRAY WEARING A CLOTH WHICH HAS DESIGNS OR MARKINGS OVER IT

(1131) 'Ā'isha reported: The Apostle of Allah (may peace be upon him) prayed in a garment which had designs over it, so he (the Holy Prophet) said: Take it to Abū Jahm and bring me a plain blanket from him, because its designs have distracted me.

(1132) 'Ā'isha reported: The Messenger of Allah (may peace be upon him) stood for prayer with a garment which had designs over it. He looked at these designs and after completing the prayer said: Take this garment to Abū Jahm b. Ḥudhaifa and bring me a blanket[770] for it has distracted me just now.

769. It is permissible to say prayer with shoes on one's feet provided these are not soiled with impurities. Before saying prayer it is essential to remove the impurities by rubbing them against dust or on sand.

770. This ḥadīth reveals how sensitive the Holy Prophet was to the feelings of others and what care he took in respecting them. He did not like to return the gift which had been given to him by Abū Jahm straightway perceiving that it might disturb him. He, therefore, asked him to give him another one in its place.

This ḥadīth also sheds a good deal of light on the fact that one must avoid all such things which can be a source of distraction in prayer. Some of the scholars are of the view that the mosques must also be simple and should be free from attractive designs and decorations.

(1133) 'Ā'isha reported: The Apostle of Allah (may peace be upon him) had a garment which had designs upon it and this distracted[771] him in prayer. He gave it to Abū Jahm and took a plain garment in its place which is known *anbijāniya*.

Chapter CCX

WHEN FOOD IS BROUGHT BEFORE A MAN AND HE IS INCLINED TO TAKE IT, HE SHOULD NOT SAY PRAYER BEFORE EATING IT AND UNDESIRABILITY OF PRAYING WHILE FEELING THE CALL OF NATURE

(1134) Anas b. Mālik reported the Apostle of Allah (may peace be upon him) saying: When the supper is brought and the prayer begins, one should first take food.

(1135) Anas b. Mālik reported: The Messenger of Allah (may peace be upon him) said: When the supper is brought before you, and it is also the time to say prayer, first take food before saying evening prayer and do not hasten (to prayer, leaving aside the food).

(1136) This ḥadīth has been narrated on the authority of Anas by another chain of transmitters.

(1137) Ibn 'Umar reported: The Messenger of Allah (may peace be upon him) said: When the supper is served to any one of you and the prayer also begins, (in such a case) first take supper, and do not make haste (for prayer) till you have (taken the food).

(1138) A ḥadīth like this has been narrated from the Apostle of Allah (may peace be upon him) on the authority of Ibn 'Umar with another chain of transmitters.

(1139). Ibn 'Ātiq[772] reported: Al-Qāsim[773] was in the presence of 'Ā'isha (may Allah be pleased with her) that I narrated a ḥadīth and Qāsim was a man who committed errors in (pronouncing words[774]) and his mother was a freed slave-girl.[775] 'Ā'isha said to him: What is the matter with you that you do not narrate as this son of my brother narrated (the aḥādīth)? Well I know from where you picked it up. This

771. This gives us an idea of one of the chief characteristics of prayer in Islam. The prayer in other religions is purely deep meditation and losing of all contact with the external world. But prayer in Islam is devotion and meditation and communion with Allah without losing contact and consciousness of the material world. This contact is essential because Islam desires that what a man gains in prayer in the form of moral and spiritual elevation must not be left off in the sphere of spiritual life; it must be externalised in the material world too so that the material life should be permeated with spiritual and moral blessings.

772. He was 'Abdullah b. Muḥammad b. 'Abd al-Raḥmān b. Abū Bakr.

773. Al-Qāsim son of Muḥammad son of Abū Bakr was the nephew of Ḥaḍrat 'Ā'isha (may Allah be pleased with her).

774. The original words are رجلاً لحانة which mean a person who commits mistakes in speaking. لحن (*laḥn*) also means an ambiguous mode of speech.

775. ام ولد (*Umm Walad*) is that woman who is first a slave, but she becames free due to the birth of a child from the loins of a free man.

is how his mother brought him up and how your mother brought you up.[776] Qāsim felt angry (on this remark of Ḥaḍrat 'Ā'isha) and showed bitterness towards her. When he saw that the table had been spread for 'Ā'isha, he stood up. 'Ā'isha said : Where are you going? He said : (I am going) to say prayer. She said : Sit down (to take the food). He said : I must say prayer. She said : Sit down, O faithless,[777] for I have heard the Messenger of Allah (may peace be upon him) say : No prayer can be (rightly said) when the food is there (before the worshipper), or when he is prompted by the call of nature.

(1140) 'Abdullah b. 'Atīq narrated from the Apostle (may peace be upon him) on the authority of 'Ā'isha, but he made no mention of the account of Qāsim.

Chapter CCXI

FORBIDDANCE TO EAT GARLIC, ONIONS, AND ANYTHING OF OFFENSIVE SMELL WHILE COMING TO THE MOSQUE

(1141) Ibn 'Umar reported : The Messenger of Allah (may peace be upon him) said during the battle of Khaybar : He who ate of this plant, i.e. garlic, he should not come to the mosques. In the narration of Zuhair, there is only a mention of "battle" and not of Khaybar.

(1142) Ibn 'Umar reported : The Messenger of Allah (may peace be upon him) said : He who eats of this (offensive) plant, he must not approach our mosque, till its odour dies : (plant signifies) garlic.

(1143) Ibn Ṣuhaib reported : Anas was asked about the garlic ; he stated that the Messenger of Allah (may peace be upon him) had said : He who eats of this plant (garlic) should not approach us and pray along with us.

(1144) Abū Huraira reported : The Messenger of Allah (may peace be upon him) said : He who eats of this plant (garlic) should not approach our mosque and should not harm us with the odour of garlic.

(1145) Jābir reported : The Messenger of Allah (may peace be upon him) forbade eating of onions and leek. When we were overpowered by a desire (to eat) we ate them. Upon this he (the Holy Prophet) said : He who eats of this offensive plant, he must not approach our mosque, for the angels are harmed by the same things as men.

(1146) Jābir reported : The Messenger of Allah (may peace be upon him) said : He who eats garlic or onion, he should remain away from us or from our mosque and stay in his house. A kettle was brought to him which had (cooked) vegetables in it. He smelt (offensive) odour in it. On asking he was informed of the vegetables (cooked in

776. It is a bare statement of fact. Qāsim was brought up in the lap of a slave-girl and she could not give him proper training, whereas 'Ātīq was the son of a free lady and thus he had better opportunities of receiving training in language. The other possibility is that Qāsim's mother might be non-Arab and, therefore, he could not learn to speak correct and chaste Arabic and thus he committed mistakes in grammar and pronunciation.

777. 'Ā'isha called him faithless for there was no occasion for Qāsim to be angry. She was the Mother of the Faithful and thus she had every right to reprimand him on his mistakes. Moreover, she was the sister of his father Muḥammad and after his father's death brought him up like her real son. So it was her duty to give him proper training. "Faithless" here does not mean a man who has actually proved to be a traitor, but it is a word of disapproval for Qāsim's behaviour.

it). He said: Take it to such and such Companion. When he saw it, he also disliked eating it. (Upon this), he (the Holy Prophet) said: You may eat it, for I converse with one with whom you do not converse.[778]

(1147) Jābir b. 'Abdullah reported the Apostle of Allah (may peace be upon him) saying: He who eats of this (offensive) plant, i.e. garlic, and sometimes he said: He who eats onion and garlic and leek, he should not approach our mosque for the angels are harmed by the same things as the children of Adam.

(1148) Ibn Juraij has narrated it with the same chain of transmitters: He who eats of this plant, i.e. garlic, he should not come to us in our mosque, and he made no mention of onions or leek.[779]

(1149) Abū Sa'īd reported: We made no transgression but Khaybar was conquered. We, the Companions of the Messenger of Allah (may peace be upon him), fell upon this plant, i.e. garlic, because the people were hungry. We ate it to our heart's content and then made our way towards the mosque. The Messenger of Allah (may peace be upon him) sensed its odour and he said: He who takes anything of this offensive plant must not approach us in the mosque. The people said: Its (use) has been forbidden; its (use) has been forbidden. This reached the Apostle of Allah (may peace be upon him) and he said: O people, I cannot forbid (the use of a thing) which Allah has made lawful, but (this garlic) is a plant the odour of which is repugnant to me.[780]

(1150) Abū Sa'īd al-Khudrī reported: The Messenger of Allah (may peace be upon him) along with his Companions happened to pass by a field in which onions were sown. The people stopped there and ate out of that, but some of them did not eat. Then they (Prophet's Companions) went to him. He (first) called those who had not eaten the onions and kept the others (who had taken onion) waiting till its odour vanished.

(1151) Ma'dān b. Ṭalḥa reported: 'Umar b. Khaṭṭāb delivered the Friday sermon and he made a mention of the Apostle of Allah (may peace be upon him) and Abū Bakr. He (further) said: I saw in a dream that a cock pecked me thrice, and I perceive that my death is near. Some people have suggested me to appoint my successor.[781] And Allah would not destroy His religion, His caliphate and that with which

778. "I converse with the angel whereas you do not."

779. It is a certain herb, or leguminous plant, well known for its foul odour and of its disagreeable juice, the common leek (Lane's *Lexicon*).

780. This ḥadīth gives us the actual position with regard to the eating of garlic and onion. These vegetables are not ḥarām (forbidden) and, therefore, their use does not incur the wrath of Allah. The only care which Islam wants us to take in their use is that we should refrain from going to the mosque, or joining prayer, while our mouth emits foul odour. These should be either well cooked so that the odour is lost or we should rinse our mouths or wait till it dies out. This odour is repugnant to the fine and delicate sense of the Prophet and the angels.

This ḥadīth also makes it clear that the Holy Prophet obeys the commands of Allah and is not authorised to give command on his own behalf or make even the slightest alteration in it. The Qur'ān says:

> Say: It is not for me to change it of my own accord. I follow naught but what is revealed to me. Indeed I fear, if I disobey my Lord, the chastisement of a grievous day (x. 15).

781. "I am not going to nominate my successor. This matter would be decided by the mutual consultation of the eminent Muslims."

He sent His Apostle (may peace be upon him).[782] If death approaches me soon, the (issue) of Caliphate (would be decided) by the consent of these six men[783] with whom the Messenger of Allah (may peace be upon him) remained well pleased till his death. And I know fully well that some people would blame me that I killed with these very hands of mine some persons who apparently professed (Islam).[784] And if they do this (blame me) they are the enemies of Allah, and are non-believers and have gone astray. And I leave not after me anything which to my mind seems more important than Kalāla.[785] And I never turned towards the Messenger of Allah (may peace be upon him) (for guidance) more often than this Kalāla, and he (the Holy Prophet) was not annoyed with me on any other (issue) than this. (And he was so perturbed) that he struck his fingers on my chest and said: Does this verse, that is at the end[786] of Sūrat al-Nisā', which was revealed in the hot season not suffice you? And if I live longer I would decide this (problem so clearly) that one who reads the Qur'ān, or one who does not read it, would be able to take (correct) decisions (under its light). He ('Umar) further said: Allah! I call You witness on these governors of lands, that I sent them to (the peoples of these lands) so that they should administer justice amongst them, teach them their religion, and the Sunnah of the Apostle of Allah (may peace be upon him), and distribute amongst them the spoils of war and refer to me that which they find difficult to perform.[787] O people, you eat these two plants and these are onions and garlic, and I find them nothing but repugnant for I saw that when the Messenger of Allah (may peace be upon him) sensed the odour of these two from a person in a mosque, he was made to go to al-Baqī'. So he who eats it should (make its odour) die by cooking it well.

782. Allah would preserve Islam and a society in which one can see the precepts of Islam translated into practice and the teachings of the Holy Qur'ān crystallised into reality. These three things would never be completely swept out of existence. Caliphate here may also signify the vicegerency of the Lord on the earth, meaning thereby that a group of Muslims would always strive to fulfil the designs of the Lord upon this earth.

783. They are 'Uthmān, 'Alī, Ṭalḥa, Zubair, Sa'd b. Abī Waqqāṣ, 'Abd al-Raḥman b. 'Auf (may Allah be pleased with all of them).

784. It refers to those persons who tried to flout the Caliphate and became apostates, though they made profession of Islam.

785. *Al-Kalāla*: any inheritor except father and children is Kalāla. According to Ibn 'Abbās, Kalāla includes every inheritor excepting one's children. It is reported that the Messenger of Allah was once asked about Kalāla and he replied: Every dead person who is not survived by father and children is Kalāla. Kalāla is an infinitive which is used both for an inheritor and for one who leaves an inheritance (***Mufradāt fī Gharā'ib al-Qur'ān*** by Imām Rāghib).

786. Al-Qur'ān, iv. 177.

787. This beautifully sums up the duties of an Islamic State:

(*a*) To observe social, legal justice in society and protect the people from the hands of oppressors and exploiters.

(*b*) To make elaborate arrangement for training people in religion and elevating them morally and spiritually.

(*c*) Proper and fair distribution of wealth in society.

(*d*) The teaching of Sunnah so that the people may have an unceasing contact with the Holy Prophet who is the real focus of a Muslim's loyalty and the messenger of Divine Will. The Sunnah of the Holy Prophet is the only way by which one can understand "Dīn" correctly. Its teaching is, therefore, one of the basic duties of the Islamic State.

(1152) This ḥadīth has been transmitted by Qatāda with the same chain of transmitters.

Chapter CCXII

IT IS FORBIDDEN TO CRY OUT FOR FINDING OUT THE LOST THING IN THE MOSQUE

(1153) Abū Huraira reported: The Messenger of Allah (may peace be upon him) said: If anyone hears a man crying out in the mosque about something he has lost, he should say: May Allah not restore it to you, for the mosques were not built for this.

(1154) Abū Huraira reported Allah's Messenger (may peace be upon him) saying like this.

(1155) Sulaimān b. Buraida narrated it on the authority of his father that a man cried out in the mosque saying: Who had called out for the red camel? Upon this the Apostle of Allah (may peace be upon him) said: May it not be restored to you! The mosques are built for what they are meant.[788]

(1156) Sulaimān b. Buraida reported on the authority of his father that when the Apostle of Allah (may peace be upon him) had said prayer a man stood up and said: Who called for a red camel? (Upon this) the Apostle of Allah (may peace be upon him) said: May it not be restored to you![789] The mosques are built for what they are meant.

(1157) Ibn Buraida narrated it on the authority of his father that a Bedouin came when the Apostle of Allah (may peace be upon him) had completed the morning prayer. He thrust his head in the door of the mosque, and then the ḥadīth (as narrated above) was narrated.

(1158) This ḥadīth has been transmitted by another chain of transmitters.

Chapter CCXIII

FORGETFULNESS IN PRAYER AND PROSTRATION AS COMPENSATION FOR IT

(1159) Abū Huraira reported: The Messenger of Allah (may peace be upon him) said: When any one of you stands up to pray, the devil comes to him and confuses him so that he does not know how much he has prayed. If any one of you has such an experience he should perform two prostrations while sitting down (in qa'da).[790]

788. These are meant for prayer and meditation.

789. The Holy Prophet did not curse him. It is just an expression of disapproval. The mosques are meant for prayer, meditation and remembrance of Allah, and it is, therefore, essential to preserve the serenity and sanctity of their atmosphere.

790. According to the scholars of Ḥadīth, forgetfulness also includes confusion and one is required to perform two prostrations in order to make amends for the loss done to the prayer on this account. There is, however, a difference of opinion on the point as to when these two prostrations should be performed. According to Imām Abū Ḥanīfa, they should be performed after tashahhud and pronouncing taslīm on the right side but, according to Imām Shāfi'ī, it should be done before taslīm.

(1160) This ḥadīth has been narrated by al-Zuhrī with the same chain of transmitters.

(1161) Abū Huraira reported: The Messenger of Allah (may peace be upon him) said: When there is a call to prayer the devil runs back breaking the wind so that he may not hear the call, and when the call is complete he comes back. And when the takbīr is pronounced he again runs back, and when takbīr is over he comes back and distracts a man saying: Remember such and such, remember such and such, referring to something the man did not have in his mind, with the result that he does not know how much he has prayed; so when any one of you is not sure how much he has prayed, he should perform two prostrations while sitting (qa'da).[791]

(1162) Abū Huraira reported: The Messenger of Allah (may peace be upon him) said: The devil takes to his heels breaking wind when the prayer begins, and the rest is the same but with this addition: "He (the devil) makes him think of pleasant things (or things productive of enjoyment) and of the things wished for, and reminds him of such needs which he had forgotten."

(1163) 'Abdullah b. Buḥaina reported: The Messenger of Allah (may peace be upon him) led us two rak'ahs of prayer in one of the (obligatory) prayers and then got up and did not sit, and the people stood up along with him. When he finished the prayer and we expected him to pronounce salutation, he said: "Allah is Most Great" while sitting and made two prostrations before salutation and then pronounced (the final) salutation.[792]

(1164) 'Abdullah b. Buḥaina al-Asadī, the ally of 'Abd al-Muṭṭalib, reported: The Messenger of Allah (may peace be upon him) stood up in noon prayer (though) he had to sit (after the two rak'ahs). When he completed the prayer he performed two prostrations and said, "Allah is the Most Great" in each prostration, while he was sitting before pronouncing salutation, and the people performed prostration along with him That was a compensation for he had forgotten to observe jalsa (after two rak'ahs).

(1165) 'Abdullah b. Mālik ibn Buḥaina al-Asadī reported: The Messenger of Allah (may peace be upon him) stood up (at the end of two rak'ahs) when he had to sit and proceeded on with the prayer. But when he was at the end of prayer, he performed a prostration before the salutation and then pronounced the salutation.

(1166) Abū Sa'īd al-Khudrī reported: The Messenger of Allah (may peace be upon him) said: When any one of you is in doubt about his prayer and he does not know how much he has prayed, thee or four (rak'ahs), he should cast aside his doubt and

791. In a state of confusion when a person cannot decide how many rak'ahs he has prayed, he should take the minimum into account and then complete the prayers, e g. one man is saying the prayer and he is confused whether he has completed three rak'ahs or four. In this case he should take it for granted that he has completed three rak'ahs and then say the fourth one and at the end perform two prostrations.

792. Imām Shāfi'ī derives the strength of his argument for prostrations before salutation from this ḥadīth. Imām Abū Ḥanīfa and Sufyān Thaurī are of the view that prostrations should be performed after salutations.

Imām Mālık says: If it is an act of omission in prayer, then prostrations should be done before salutations and if it is an act of commission it should be done after the prostrations. This difference is only a difference of preference rather than that of right or wrong.

base his prayer on what he is sure of, then perform two prostrations before giving salutations. If he has prayed five rak'ahs, they will make his prayer an even number for him, and if he has prayed exactly four, they will be humiliation for the devil.[793]

(1167) This ḥadīth has been narrated by Zaid b. Aslam with the same chain of transmitters and he said: He should perform two prostrations before the salutation, as it was mentioned by Sulaimān b. Bilāl.

(1168) 'Alqama[794] narrated it on the authority of 'Abdullah (b. Mas'ūd) who said: The Messenger of Allah (may peace be upon him) said the prayer; (the narrator added): He made some act of omission or commission when he pronounced salutation; it was said to him: Messenger of Allah, is there something new about the prayer? He (the Holy Prophet) said: What is it? They said: You said prayer in such and such a way. He (the narrator) said: He (the Holy Prophet) turned his feet and faced the Qibla and performed two prostrations and then pronounced salutations, and then turned his face towards us and said: If there is anything new about prayer (new command from the Lord) I informed you of that. But I am a human being and I forget as you forget, so when I forget, remaind me, and when anyone of you is in doubt about his prayer, he should aim at what is correct, and complete his prayer in that respect and then make two prostrations.

(1169) This ḥadīth has been transmitted by Manṣūr with the same chain of transmitters, with a slight modification of words.

(1170) This ḥadīth is transmitted by Manṣūr with the same chain of transmitters, but with these words: "He should aim at correct (prayer) and it is advisable."

(1171) This ḥadīth has been transmitted by Manṣūr with the same chain of transmitters with the words: "He should aim at what is correct and complete."

(1172) This ḥadīth has been transmitted by Manṣūr with the same chain of transmitters and said: "He should aim at correctness and that is right."

(1173) This ḥadīth has been transmitted by Manṣūr with the same chain of transmitters and he said: "He should aim at what is according to him correct."

(1174) This ḥadīth has been transmitted by Manṣūr and he said: "He should aim at correctness."

(1175) 'Abdullah (b. Mas'ūd) reported: The Apostle of Allah (may peace be upon him) said five rak'ahs of the noon prayer and when he completed the prayer, it was said to him: Has there been (commanded) an addition in prayer? He said: What is it? They said: You have said five rak'ahs, so he performed two prostrations.

(1176) 'Alqama reported: He (the Holy Prophet) had led them five rak'ahs in prayer.

(1177) Ibrāhīm b. Suwaid reported: 'Alqama led us in noon prayer and he offered five rak'ahs; when the prayer was complete, the people said to him: Abu Shibl, you have offered five rak'ahs. He said: No, I have not done that. They said: Yes (you said five rak'ahs). He (the narrator) said: And I was sitting in a corner among people

793. It means that the devil has met failure in confusing the man.

794. He was the son of Waqqāṣ and belonged to the tribe of Laith. He was born during the lifetime of the Holy Prophet, and joined the battle of Khandaq (Ditch). He died in Medina during the reign of 'Abd al-Malik b. Marwān.

and I was just a boy. I (also) said: Yes, you have offered five (rak'ahs). He said to me: O, one-eyed, do you say the same thing? I said: Yes. Upon this he turned (his face) and performed two prostrations and then gave salutations, and then reported 'Abdullah as saying: The Messenger of Allah (may peace be upon him) led us in prayer and offered five rak'ahs. And as he turned away the people began to whisper amongst themselves. He (the Holy Prophet) said: What is the matter with you? They said: Has the prayer been extended? He said: No. They said: You have in fact said five raka'hs. He (the Holy Prophet) then turned his back (and faced the Qibla) and performed two prostrations and then gave salutations and further said: Verily I am a human being like you, I forget just as you forget. Ibn Numair made this addition: "When any one of you forgets, he must perform two prostrations."

(1178) 'Abdullah (b. Mas'ūd) reported: The Messenger of Allah (may peace be upon him) led us five (rak'ahs in prayer). We said: Messenger of Allah, has the prayer been extended? He said: What is the matter? They said: You have said five (rak'ahs). He (the Holy Prophet) said: Verily I am a human being like you. I remember as you remember and I forget just as you forget. He then performed two prostrations as (compensation of) forgetfulness.

(1179) 'Abdullah (b. Mas'ūd) reported: The Messenger of Allah (may peace be upon him) said prayer and he omitted or committed (something). Ibrāhīm (one of the narrators of this ḥadīth) said: It is my doubt, and it was said: Messenger of Allah, has there been any addition to the prayer? He (the Holy Prophet) said: Verily I am a human being like you I forget just as you forget, so when any one of you forgets, he must perform two prostrations, and he (the Holy Prophet) was sitting. and then the Messenger of Allah (may peace be upon him) turned (his face towards the Qibla) and performed two prostrations.

(1180) 'Abdullah b. Mas'ūd reported: The Apostle of Allah (may peace be upon him) performed two prostrations for forgetfulness after salutation and talking.

(1181) 'Abdullah reported: We prayed along with the Messenger of Allah (may peace be upon him) and he committed or omitted (something). Ibrāhīm said: By Allah, this is a misgiving of mine only. We said: Messenger of Allah, is there something new about the prayer? He (the Holy Prophet) said: No. We told him about what he had done. He (the Holy Prophet) said: When a man commits or omits (something in prayer), he should perform two prostrations, and he then himself performed two prostrations.

(1182) Ibn Sīrīn reported Abū Huraira as saying: The Messenger of Allah (may peace be upon him) led us in one of the two evening prayers, Ẓuhr or 'Aṣr,[795] and gave salutations after two rak'ahs and going towards a piece of wood which was placed to the direction of the Qibla in the mosque, leaned on it looking as if he were angry. Abū Bakr and 'Umar were among the people and they were too afraid to speak to him and the people came out in haste (saying): The prayer has been shortened. But among them was a man called Dhu'l-Yadain[796] who said: Messenger of Allah, has the prayer been

795. *'Ashiy* generally means evening or night, but it also means the time between the declining of the sun after the meridian and sunset or morning, so the two prayers here mentioned are the noon (Ẓuhr) prayer and the afternoon ('Aṣr) prayer.

796. His name was Khirbaq Aslamī al-Ḥijāzī or 'Umair; he was so called because of his long arms.

shortened or have you forgotten? The Apostle of Allah (may peace be upon him) looked to the right and left and said: What was Dhu'l-Yadain saying? They said: He is right. You (the Holy Prophet) offered but two rak'ahs. He offered two (more) rak'ahs and gave salutation, then said takbīr and prostrated and lifted (his head) and then said takbīr and prostrated, then said takbīr and lifted (his head). He (the narrator) says: It has been reported to me by 'Imrān b. Ḥuṣain that he said: He (then) gave salutation.

(1183) Abū Huraira reported: The Messenger of Allah (may peace be upon him) led us in one of the evening prayers. And this ḥadīth was narrated like one transmitted by Sufyān.

(1184) Abū Huraira reported: The Messenger of Allah (may peace be upon him) led us in 'Aṣr prayer and gave salutation after two rak'ahs. Dhu'l-Yadain (the possessor of long arms) stood up and said: Messenger of Allah, has the prayer been shortened or have you forgotten? The Messenger of Allah (may peace be upon him) said: Nothing like this has happened (neither the prayer has been shortened nor have I forgotten). He (Dhu'l-Yadain) said: Messenger of Allah, something has definitely happened. The Messenger of Allah (may peace be upon him) turned towards people and said: Is Dhu'l-Yadain true (in his assertion)? They said: Messenger of Allah, he is true. Then the Messenger of Allah (may peace be upon him) completed the rest of the prayer, and then performed two prostrations while he was sitting after salutation.

(1185) Abū Huraira reported: The Messenger of Allah (may peace be upon him) said two rak'ahs of the noon prayer and then gave salutation when a man from Banū Sulaim came to him and said: Messenger of Allah, has the prayer been shortened, or have you forgotten?—and the rest of the ḥadīth is the same.

(1186) Abū Huraira reported: I offered with the Apostle of Allah (may peace be upon him) the noon prayer and the Messenger of Allah (may peace be upon him) gave salutation after two rak'ahs. A person from Banī Sulaim stood up, and the rest of the ḥadīth was narrated as mentioned above.

(1187) 'Imrān b. Ḥuṣain reported: The Messenger of Allah (may peace be upon him) said afternoon prayer and gave the salutation at the end of three rak'ahs and then went into his house. A man called al-Khirbāq, who had long arms, got up and went to him, and addressed him as Messenger of Allah and mentioned to him what he had done. He came out angrily trailing his mantle, and when he came to the people he said: Is this man telling the truth? They said: Yes. He then said one rak'ah and then gave salutation and then performed two prostrations and then gave salutation.

(1188) 'Imrān b. Ḥuṣain reported: The Messenger of Allah (may peace be upon him) said three rak'ahs of the 'Aṣr prayer and then got up and went to his apartment. A man possessing large arms stood up and said: Messenger of Allah, has the prayer been shortened? He came out angrily, and said the rak'ah which he had omitted and then gave salutation, then performed two prostrations of forgetfulness and then gave salutation.[797]

797. According to the Ḥanafites *Sajda Sahv* (prostration of forgetfulness) is valid only if the Imām makes no movement and he does not speak. They believe that all these traditions are abrogated by the ḥadīth of Ibn 'Abbās in which the Holy Prophet forbade to talk in prayer.

Chapter CCXIV

PROSTRATION[798] WHILE RECITING THE QUR'ĀN

(1189) Ibn 'Umar reported: The Messenger of Allah (may peace be upon him) while reciting the Qur'ān recited its sūra containing sajda, and he performed prostration and we also prostrated along with him (but we were so overcrowded) that some of us could not find a place for our forehead (when prostrating ourselves).

(1190) Ibn 'Umar reported: Sometimes the Messenger of Allah (may peace be upon him) recited the Qur'ān, and would pass by (recite) the verse of sajda and performed prostration and he did this along with us, but we were so crowded in his company that none of us could find a place for performing prostration, (and it was done on occasions) other than prayer.

(1191) 'Abdullah (ibn 'Umar) reported: The Apostle of Allah (may peace be upon him) recited (Sūrat) al-Najm[799] and performed prostration during its recital and all those who were along with him also prostrated themselves except one old man who took a handful of pebbles or dust in his palm and lifted it to his forehead and said: This is sufficient for me. 'Abdullah said: I saw that he was later killed in a state of unbelief.

(1192) 'Aṭā' b. Yasār reported that he had asked Zaid b. Thābit about recital along with the Imām, to which he said: There should be no recital along with the Imām in anything,[800] and alleged that he recited: "By the star when it sets" (Sūra Najm) before the Messenger of Allah (may peace be upon him) and he did not prostrate himself.

(1193) Abū Salama b. 'Abd al-Raḥmān reported: Abū Huraira recited before them: "When the heaven burst asunder" (al-Qur'ān, lxxxiv. 1) and performed prostration. After completing (the prayer) he informed them that the Messenger of Allah (may peace be upon him) had prostrated himself at it (this verse).

798. The significance of this prostration is that, while reciting the Qur'án, one makes a humble submission before the Lord on all those occasions where His Greatness has been strikingly emphasised. Prostration is a visible expression of man's humility before the Almighty and it is one of the characteristics of a Muslim which means one who submits himself willingly to his Master. There are in all fifteen occasions in the Qur'ān where the believers are required to perform prostration, and the Prophet's practice was to prostrate himself when reciting such verses whether it was a recital during prayer or an ordinary occasion. These verses are vii. 205, xiii. 15, xvi. 50, xvii. 109, xix. 58, xxii. 18, 77, xxv. 60, xxvii. 26, xxxii. 15, xxxviii. 24, xli. 38, liii. 62, lxxxiv. 21, xcvi. 19.

It should also be remembered that if one is listening to these verses it is desirable for him to perform prostration.

799. Verse 62 of Sūra Najm is the first verse on the recital of which the Holy Prophet prostrated himself. This was in fact the beginning of the prostration of recital. The ḥadīth indicates that this sūra when first revealed was read in a large assembly comprising Muslims and non-Muslims. When the Holy Prophet, in obedience to the command, prostrated himself, not only did the Muslims prostrate themselves, but even the unbelievers and polytheists and the idolaters also fell down in prostration overawed by the sublimity and the grandeur of the atmosphere which the recital of this verse created at that time. Umayya b. Khalf was the only exception. He only raised gravel to his forehead. This man was later killed in a state of unbelief.

800. It is on the basis of this ḥadīth that Imām Abū Ḥanīfa does not consider it proper to recite verses behind the Imām in prayer. Ḥāfiẓ Ibn Ḥajar 'Asqalānī is of the opinion that the Holy Prophet postponed this prostration on account of some reason.

(1194) A ḥadīth like this has been narrated by Abū Salama on the authority of Abū Huraira.

(1195) Abū Huraira reported : We performed prostration along with the Messenger of Allah (may peace be upon him) (as he recited these verses :)"When the heaven burst asunder" and "Read in the name of Thy Lord" (al-Qur'ān, xcvi. 1).

(1196) Abū Huraira reported : The Messenger of Allah (may peace be upon him) prostrated himself (while reciting these verses) : "When the heaven burst asunder"; "Read in the name of Thy Lord."

(1197) A ḥadīth like this has been transmitted by 'Abd al-Raḥmān al-'Araj on the authority of Abū Huraira.

(1198) Abū Rāfi' reported : I said night prayer along with Abū Huraira and as he recited : "When the heaven burst asunder," he performed prostration. I said to him : What prostration is this ? He said : I prostrated myself (on this occasion of recital) behind Abu'l-Qāsim (Muḥammad, may peace be upon him), and I would go on doing this till I meet him (in the next world). Ibn 'Abd al-A'lā said : (Abū Huraira uttered this :) I would not abandon performing prostration.

(1199) This ḥadīth has been transmitted by Tamīmī with the same chain of transmitters except for this that they made no mention of : "Behind Abu'l-Qāsim" (may peace be upon him).

(1200) Abu Rāfi' reported : I saw Abū Huraira performing prostration (while reciting this verse :) "When the heaven burst asunder." I said to him : Do you prostrate yourself (while reciting) it ? He said : Yes, I saw my best Friend (may peace be upon him) prostrating himself on (the recital of this verse) and I shall continue prostrating till I meet him. Shu'ba asked : Do you mean (by Friend) the Apostle of Allah (may peace be upon him) ? He said : Yes.

Chapter CCXV

HOW JALSA IS TO BE OBSERVED

(1201) 'Abdullah b. Zubair narrated on the authority of his father : When the Messenger of Allah (may peace be upon him) sat in prayer, he placed the left foot between his thigh and shank and stretched the right foot and placed his left hand on his left knee[801] and placed his right hand on his right thigh, and raised his finger.

(1202) 'Abdullah b. Zubair narrated on the authority of his father that when the Messenger of Allah (may peace be upon him) sat for supplication, i.e. tashahhud (blessing and supplication), he placed his right hand on his right thigh and his left hand

801. The sitting posture which has been explained above is known as *Tawarruk.* There is, however, one difference here and that is stretching of the right foot. The actual position is that the right foot is to be kept in a standing position, as in the sajda, the tips of the toes touching the ground, while the left foot is stretched with its back in contact with ground and the open hands placed on the knees. Here the stretching of the right foot has been mentioned simply to show that if a man by any difficulty cannot assume this position with ease, he may adopt even this sitting posture.

on his left thigh, and pointed with his forefinger,[802] and placed his thumb on his (middle) finger, and covered his knee with the palm of his left hand.

(1203) Ibn 'Umar reported that when the Messenger of Allah (may peace be upon him) sat for tashahhud he placed his left hand on his left knee, and his right hand on his right knee, and he raised his right finger, which is next to the thumb, making supplication in this way, and he stretched his left hand on his left knee. Another version on the authority of Ibn 'Umar says: When the Messenger of Allah (may peace be upon him) sat for tashahhud, he placed his left hand on his left knee and placed his right hand on his right knee, and he formed a ring like ٥٣ (fifty-three) and pointed with his finger of attestation.

(1204) 'Alī b. 'Abd al-Raḥmān al-Mu'āwī reported: 'Abdullah b. 'Umar saw me playing with pebbles during prayer. After finishing the prayer he forbade me (to do it) and said: Do as the Messenger of Allah (may peace be upon him) used to do. I said: How did Allah's Messenger (may peace be upon him) do? He said that he (the Messenger of Allah) sat at tashahhud, placed his right palm on the right thigh and closed all his fingers and pointed with the help of finger, next to the thumb, and placed his left palm on his right thigh.[803]

(1205) This ḥadīth has been narrated by another chain of transmitters.

Chapter CCXVI

TASLĪM[804] AT THE COMPLETION OF THE PRAYER

(1206) Abū Ma'mar reported: There was an Amīr in Mecca who pronounced taslīm twice. 'Abdullah said: Where did he get this sunnah? Al-Ḥakam said: There is a ḥadīth to the effect that the Messenger of Allah (may peace be upon him) did like it.

(1207) 'Abdullah reported: An Amīr or a person pronounced taslīm twice. 'Abdullah said: Where did he get this sunnah?

(1208) 'Āmir b. Sa'd reported: I saw the Messenger of Allah (may peace be upon him) pronouncing taslīm on his right and on his left till I saw the whiteness of his cheek.

Chapter CCXVII

DHIKR AFTER THE PRAYER

(1209) Ibn 'Abbās said: We used to know that Allah's Messenger (may peace be upon him) had finished his prayer when we heard the takbīr (Allah-o-Akbar).

(1210) Ibn 'Abbās reported: We knew the finishing of the prayer of the Messenger of Allah (may peace be upon him) through takbīr. 'Amr (b. Dīnār) said: I made a

802. While reciting *Attahiyyah*, when the worshipper reads *Ashhadu an la ilāha ill-Allāhu* he raises his forefinger and, along with his verbal affirmation of the Oneness of Allah, he attests it with the movement of his finger.

803. In the ḥadīth at places we find the word "thigh" and at places the word "knee". There is no contradiction in it. The fact is that the hands should be placed at the lower ends of the thighs covering the knees too.

804. The prayer is concluded with *taslīm : As-salāmu 'alaikum wa raḥmatullāh* (peace be upon you and mercy of Allah).

mention of it to Abū Ma'bad, but he rejected it and said: I never narrated it to you. 'Amr said: He did narrate it before this.[805]

(1211) Ibn 'Abbās reported: Dhikr (mentioning the name of Allah) in a loud voice after obligatory prayers was (a common practice) during the lifetime of the Apostle of Allah (may peace be upon him); and when I heard that I came to know that they (the people) had finished the prayer.

Chapter CCXVIII

DESIRABILITY OF SEEKING REFUGE FROM THE TORMENT OF THE GRAVE

(1212) 'Ā'isha reported: The Holy Prophet (may peace be upon him) entered my house when a Jewess was with me and she was saying: Do you know that you would be put to trial in the grave? The Messenger of Allah (may peace be upon him) trembled (on hearing this) and said: It is the Jews only who would be put to trial. 'Ā'isha said: We passed some nights and then the Messenger of Allah (may peace be upon him) said: Do you know that it has been revealed to me: "You would be put to trial in the grave"? 'Ā'isha said: I heard the Messenger of Allah (may peace be upon him) seeking refuge from the torment of the grave after this.[806]

(1213) Abū Huraira reported: I heard the Messenger of Allah (may peace be upon him) seeking refuge from the torment of the grave after this (after the revelation).

(1214) 'Ā'isha reported: There came to me two old women from the old Jewesses of Medina and said: The people of the grave are tormented in their graves. I contradicted them and I did not deem it proper to testify them. They went away and the Messenger of Allah (may peace be upom him) came to me and I said to him: Messenger of Allah! there came to me two old women from the old Jewesses of Medina and asserted that the people of the graves would be tormented therein. He (the Prophet) said: They told the truth; they would be tormented (so much) that the animals would listen to it. She ('Ā'isha) said: Never did I see him (the Holy Prophet) afterwards but seeking refuge from the torment of the grave in prayer.

805. 'Amr b. Dīnār, the transmitter of this ḥadīth, is authentic and, therefore, it must be accepted as valid and there is no reason to reject it. A ḥadīth which is transmitted by a more authentic narrator is valid even though it is rejected by a comparatively less authentic narrator, provided it fits into the general framework of the teachings of Islam and does not conflict with its spirit.

806. This ḥadīth provides a conclusive proof of the fact that the Holy Prophet received revelation from Allah besides the Qur'ān and this revelation is also binding upon the Muslims. It also proves that the Holy Prophet strictly adhered to the revelation. His opinion was different before the revelation, but when the revelation came he told the people frankly what was contrary to his own views. This incident establishes his sincerity. Had the revelation been a prompting of his own mind, and had it been motivated by his desire to establish his supremacy over people, he would have never changed his mind and views, which could undermine his prestige.

This revelation also categorically rejects the views of the Orientalists who either assert that Muḥammad (may peace be upon him) borrowed his teachings from the Jews and Christians or he did nothing but subverted the teachings of these religions. Muḥammad's revelations came from the Lord. He neither borrowed anything from the Jews and Christians, nor did he base his system of teachings on their contradictions and subversions. He preached and practised only what had been revealed to him by his Lord, irrespective of the fact whether it subscribed to the views held by the Christians and Jews or ran contrary to them.

(1215) Masrūq reported this ḥadīth on the authority of 'Ā'isha who said: Never did he (the Holy Prophet) say prayer after this in which I did not hear him seeking refuge from the torment of the grave.

(1216) 'Ā'isha reported: I heard the Messenger of Allah (may peace be upon him) seeking refuge from the trial of Dajjāl (Antichrist) in prayer.

(1217) Abū Huraira reported: The Messenger of Allah (may peace be upon him) said: When any one of you utters tashahhud (in prayer) he must seek refuge with Allah from four (trials) and should thus say: "O Allah! I seek refuge with Thee from the torment of the Hell, from the torment of the grave, from the trial of life and death and from the evil of the trial of Masīḥ al-Dajjāl" (Antichrist).

(1218) 'Ā'isha, the wife of the Apostle of Allah (may peace be opon him), reported: The Apostle of Allah (may peace be upon him) used to supplicate in prayer thus: "O Allah! I seek refuge with Thee from the torment of the grave, and I seek refuge with Thee from the trial of the Masīḥ al-Dajjāl (Antichrist) and I seek refuge with Thee from the trial of life and death. O Allah! I seek refuge with Thee from sin and debt." She ('Ā'isha) reported: Someone said to him (the Holy Prophet): Messenger of Allah! why is it that you so often seek refuge from debt? He said: When a (person) incurs debt, (he is obliged) to tell lies and break promise.

(1219) Abū Huraira reported: The Messenger of Allah (may peace be upon him) said: When any one of you completes the last tashahhud, he should seek refuge with Allah from four (trials), i.e. from the torment of Hell, from the torment of grave, from the trial of life and death, and from the mischief of Masīḥ al-Dajjāl (Antichrist). This ḥadīth has been narrated by al-Auzā'ı with the same chain of transmitters but with these words: "When any one of you completes the tashahhud" and he made no mention of the words "the last".

(1220) Abū Huraira reported: The Apostle of Allah (may peace be upon him) said: O Allah! I seek refuge with Thee from the torment of the grave, and the torment of Hell, and the trial of life and death and the mischief of Masīḥ al-Dajjāl.

(1221) Abū Huraira reported the Messenger of Allah (may peace be upon him) as saying: Seek refuge with Allah from the torment of Hell, seek refuge with Allah from the torment of the grave, and seek refuge with Allah from the trial of Masīḥ al-Dajjāl, and seek refuge with Allah from the trial of life and death.

(1222) A ḥadīth like this has been transmitted by Ibn Ṭāwūs from his father on the authority Abū Huraira.

(1223) A ḥadīth like this has been transmitted by A'raj on the authority of Abū Huraira.

(1224) Abū Huraira reported that the Apostle of Allah (may peace be upon him) used to seek refuge from the torment of the grave, torment of Hell and the trial of Dajjāl.

(1225) Ibn 'Abbās reported that the Messenger of Allah (may peace be upon him) used to teach them this supplication (in the same spirit) with which he used to teach them a sūra of the Qur'ān. He would thus instruct us: "Say, O Allah! we seek refuge with Thee from the torment of Hell, and I seek refuge with Thee from the torment of the grave, and I seek refuge with Thee from the trial of Masīḥ al-Dajjāl, and I seek refuge with Thee from the trial of life and death." Muslim b. Ḥajjāj said: It has reached me that Ṭāwūs said to his son: Did you make this supplication in prayer? He said: No. (Upon this) he (Ṭāwūs) said: Repeat the prayer.[807] Ṭāwūs has narrated this ḥadīth through three or four (transmitters) with words to the same effect.

Chapter CCXIX

EXCELLENCE OF DHIKR AFTER PRAYER AND ITS DESCRIPTION

(1226) Thaubān reported: When the Messenger of Allah (may peace be upon him) finished his prayer, he begged forgiveness [808] three times and said: O Allah! Thou art Peace, and peace comes from Thee Blessed art Thou, O Possessor of Glory and Honour.[809] Walīd reported: I said to Auzā'ī: How is the seeking of forgiveness? He replied: You should say: "I beg forgiveness from Allah, I beg forgiveness from Allah."

(1227) 'Ā'isha reported: When the Messenger of Allah (may peace be upon him) pronounced salutation, he sat no longer than it took him to say: O Allah! Thou art Peace, and peace comes from Thee, blessed art Thou, Possessor of Glory and Honour; and in the narration of Ibn Numair the words are: "O Possessor of Glory and Honour."

(1228) Ibn Numair narrated it with the same chain of transmitters and said: O Possessor of Glory and Honour.

(1229) A ḥadīth like this has been transmitted by 'Abdullah b. Ḥārith on the authority of 'Ā'isha except for the words that he (the Holy Prophet) used to say: "O Possessor of Glory and Honour."

(1230) Mughīra b. Shu'ba [810] wrote to Mu'āwiya: When the Messenger of Allah (may peace be upon him) finished the prayer and pronounced salutation he uttered (this supplication): "There is no god but Allah He is alone, Who has no partner. To Him belongs the sovereignty and to Him praise is due and He is Potent over everything. O Allah! no one can withhold what Thou givest, or give what Thou withholdest, and the riches cannot avail a wealthy person with Thee."

(1231) A ḥadith like this has been narrated by Mughīra b. Shu'ba with another chain of transmitters. Abū Bakr and Abū Kuraib narrated in their narration (that Warrād [811] reported): Mughīra gave me dictation of it and I wrote it to Mu'āwiya.

(1232) Warrād, the freed slave of Mughīra b. Shu'ba, reported: Mughīra b. Shu'ba wrote to Mu'āwiya (it was Warrād who wrote this letter for him, i.e. Mughīra): I heard the Messenger of Allah (may peace be upon him) saying: "When the salutation is pronounced," and the rest of the ḥadīth is the same except this that he made no mention of: "He is Potent over everything."

(1233) Warrād, the scribe of Mughīra b. Shu'ba, reported: Mu'āwiya wrote to

807. The utterance of this supplication is not obligatory but as a matter of excellence. Ṭāwūs asked him to repeat the prayer just for emphasising its importance upon him (Nawawī, p. 218).

808. استغفر الله = "I seek forgiveness from Allah."

809. It is often seen that while making this supplication these words are also uttered: اليك يرجع السلام فحينا ربنا بالسلام وادخلنا الجنة دارالسلام along with those mentioned above. These words of the supplication are not authentic.

810. His name is Mughīra b. Shu'ba al-Thaqafī. He embraced Islam in the year of the Battle of the Ditch and settled in Medina. He was appointed Amīr of Kūfa by Mu'āwiya b Abū Sufyān. He died i 50 H at the age of seventy in Kūfa.

811. He was the freed slave of Mughīra b. Shu'ba.

Mughīra (the contents) of the ḥadīth as transmitted by Manṣūr and A'mash.

(1234) Warrād, the scribe of Mughīra b. Shu'ba, reported: Mu'āwiya wrote to Mughīra: Write to me anything which you heard from the Messenger of Allah (may peace be upon him). So he (Mughīra) wrote to him (Mu'āwiya): I heard the Messenger of Allah (may peace be upon him) uttering (these words) at the completion of prayer: "There is no god but Allah. He is alone and there is no partner with Him. Sovereignty belongs to Him and to Him is praise due and He is Potent over everything. O Allah! no one can withhold what Thou givest, or give what Thou withholdest, and riches cannot avail a wealthy person with Thee."

(1235) Abū Zubair reported: Ibn Zubair uttered at the end of every prayer after pronouncing salutation (these words): "There is no god but Allah. He is alone. There is no partner with Him. Sovereignty belongs to Him and He is Potent over everything. There is no might or power except with Allah. There is no god but Allah and we do not worship but Him alone To Him belong all bounties, to Him belongs all Grace, and to Him is worthy praise accorded. There is no god but Allah, to Whom we are sincere in devotion, even though the unbelievers should disapprove it" (The narrator said): He (the Holy Prophet) uttered it at the end of every (obligatory) prayer.

(1236) Abū Zubair reported: 'Abdullah b. Zubair used to say *Lā ilāha il-Allāh* at the end of every prayer like the ḥadīth narrated by Ibn Numair and he reported it in the end, and then reported Ibn Zubair saying: The Messenger of Allah (may peace be upon him) uttered *Lā ilāha il-Allāh* at the end of every prayer.

(1237) Abū Zubair reported: I heard 'Abdullah b. Zubair[812] addressing (people) on the pulpit and saying: When the Messenger of Allah (may peace be upon him) pronounced salutation at the end of the prayer or prayers, and then he made a mention of the ḥadīth as transmitted by Hishām b. 'Urwa.

(1238) Abū Zubair al-Makkī[813] reported that he had heard 'Abdullah b Zubair uttering (the words) like that of the ḥadīth (narrated above) at the end of the prayer after pronouncing salutation. He at the conclusion also said that he was making a mention of that from the Messenger of Allah (may peace be upon him).

(1239) Abū Huraira reported: The poor amongst the emigrants came to the Messenger of Allah (may peace be upon him) and said: The possessors of great wealth have obtained the highest ranks and the lasting bliss. He (the Holy Prophet) said: How is that? They said: They pray as we pray, and they observe fast as we observe fast, and they give charity but we do not give charity, and they set slaves free but we do not set slaves free. Upon this the Messenger of Allah (may peace be upon him) said: Shall I not teach you something by which you will catch up on those who have preceded you, and get ahead of those who come after you, only those who do as you do being more excellent than you? They said: Yes, Messenger of Allah. He (the Holy Prophet) said: Extol Allah, declare His Greatness, and Praise Him thirty-three times after every prayer. Abū Ṣāliḥ said: The poor amongst the emigrants returned to the Messenger of Allah

812. His kunyah was Abū Bakr after the name of his illustrious maternal grandfather Abū Bakr. His mother's name was Asmā'. He was born in 1 H. and was the first child to be born in Medina in the family of the Muhājirīn. He was brought to the Holy Prophet and he blessed him. He was a very pious man. He was executed by Ḥajjāj b. Yūsuf in Mecca on 17 Jumadat al-Thānīya in 64 H.

813. His name was Muḥammad b. Aslam. He was the freed slave of Ḥakim b. Ḥizām. He was one of the successors (*tābi'in*) in Mecca. He died in 125 H.

(may peace be upon him) saying: Our brethren, the possessors of property have heard what we have done and they did the same. So the Messenger of Allah (may peace be upon him) said: This is Allah's Grace[814] which He gives to whom He wishes. Sumayy reported: I made a mention of this ḥadīth to some members of my family (and one of them) said: You have forgotten; he (the Holy Prophet) had said (like this): "Extol Allah thirty-three times, Praise Allah thirty-three times and declare His Greatness thirty-three times. Ibn 'Ajlān said: I made a mention of this ḥadīth to Rajā' b. Ḥaiwata and he narrated to me a ḥadīth like this from Abū Ṣāliḥ from the Messenger of Allah (may peace be upon him) on the authority of Abū Huraira.

(1240) Abū Huraira narrated it from the Messenger of Allah (may peace be upon him) that they (the poor among the emigrants) said: Messenger of Allah, the possessors of great wealth have obtained the highest ranks and lasting bliss, and the rest of the ḥadīth is the same as transmitted by Qutaiba on the authority of Laith except that he inserted the words of Abū Ṣāliḥ in the narration of Abū Huraira that "the poor of the emigrants came back," to the end of the ḥadīth, but this addition was made that Suhail said (that every part of the supplication, i.e. Glorification of Allah, His Praise and declaration of His Greatness) should be uttered eleven times making the total as thirty-three.[815]

(1241) Ka'b b. 'Ujra reported Allah's Messenger (may peace be upon him) as saying: There are certain ejaculations,[816] the repeaters of which or the performers of which after every prescribed prayer will never be caused disappointment: "Glory be to Allah" thirty-three times, "Praise be to Allah" thirty-three times, and "Allah is most Great" thirty-four times.

(1242) Ka'b b. 'Ujra reported Allah's Messenger (may peace be upon him) as saying: There are certain ejaculations, the repeaters of which or the performers of which at the end of every prayer will never be caused disappointment: "Glory be to Allah" thirty-three times, "Praise be to Allah" thirty-three times, and "Allah is most Great" thirty-four times.

(1243) Abū Huraira reported Allah's Messenger (may peace be upon him) as say-

814. Mere possession of wealth is not the grace of Allah. Wealth is a trial for man. If he spends it on good purposes and that too for seeking the pleasure of Allah alone, that is a grace of God; but if he squanders it away on immoral pursuits and does not perform the duties which its possession lays upon him, it is a symbol of the wrath of God Ḥāfiẓ Ibn Ḥajar 'Asqalānī states on the authority of Qurṭubī that Allah's Grace in the above-mentioned ḥadīth does not imply material riches, but merely the favour of Allah. What the Holy Prophet wanted to make clear to them was that they should not entertain this idea in their minds that the rich people are always entitled to better rewards. It is Allah alone Who gives reward and He knows how to apportion it. He showers Graces upon the people as He wishes (*Fatḥ al-Bārī*, Vol. II, p. 475).

815. This does not conflict with those aḥādīth in which it has been stressed to utter each part of supplication thirty-three times. It simply implies that this is also permitted. In some traditions it has been laid down that the total number should be one hundred, thirty-three times "Ṣubḥān Allah," thirty-three times "Alḥamdu lillāh" and thirty-four times "Allah-o-Akbar".

The second thing to be noted in this ḥadīth is the utmost care which was observed in recording and transmitting the words of the Holy Prophet (may peace be upon him). The Muḥaddathīn have very carefully transmitted the ḥadīth and have clearly pointed out any insertion made by the narrator on his behalf.

816. The original word is معقبات (Mu'aqqibāt,) which implies the ejaculation repeated at the end of prayer. These ejaculations are said to be Mu'aqqibāt as these are repeated after the Prayer (*Fatḥ-ul-Mulhim*, Vol. II, p. 179).

ing : If anyone extols Allah after every prayer thirty-three times, and praises Allah thirty-three times, and declares His Greatness thirty-three times, ninety-nine times in all, and says to complete a hundred : "There is no god but Allah, having no partner with Him, to Him belongs sovereignty and to Him is praise due, and He is Potent over everything," his sins will be forgiven even if these are as abundant as the foam of the sea.[817]

(1244) This ḥadīth has been transmitted by Abū Huraira by another chain of transmitters.

Chapter CCXX

WHAT IS TO BE RECITED BETWEEN TAKBĪR TAḤRĪMA AND RECITATION OF THE QUR'ĀN

(1245) Abū Huraira reported that Allah's Messenger (may peace be upon him) used to observe silence for a short while between the takbīr (at the time of opening the prayer) and the recitation of the Qur'ān. I said to him : Messenger of Allah, for whom I would give my father and mother in ransom, what do you recite during your period of silence between the takbīr and the recitation ? He said : I say (these words) : "O Allah, remove my sins from me as Thou hast removed the East from the West. O Allah ! purify me from sins as a white garment is purified from filth. O Allah ! wash away my sins with water, snow and hail."

(1246) Abū Huraira reported that when the Messenger of Allah (may peace be upon him) stood up for the second rak'ah he opened it with the recitation of the praise of Allah, the Lord of universe (al-Fātiḥa), and he did not observe silence (before the recitation of al-Fātiḥa).

(1247) Anas reported : A man came panting and entered the row of worshippers and said : Praise be to Allah, much praised and blessed. When the Messenger of Allah (may peace be upon him) finished the prayer he said : Who amongst you uttered these words ? The people remained silent. He (the Holy Prophet again said) : Who amongst you uttered these words ? He said nothing wrong. Then a man said : I came and had a difficulty in breathing, so I uttered them. He replied : I saw twelve angels racing one another as to who will take them up (to Allah).

(1248) Ibn 'Umar reported : While we said prayer with the Messenger of Allah (may peace be upon him), one among the people said : Allah is truly Great, praise be to Allah in abundance. Glory be to Allah in the morning and the evening. The Messenger of Allah (may peace be upon him) said : Who uttered such and such a word ? A person among the people said : It is I, Messenger of Allah (who have recited these words). He (the Holy Prophet) said : It (its utterance) surprised me, for the doors of heaven were opened for it. Ibn 'Umar said : I have not abandoned them (these words) since I heard the Messenger of Allah (may peace be upon him) saying this.[818]

817. This refers to minor sins (Nawawī).

818. It should be remembered in connection with this chapter that different supplications narrated above in the aḥādīth do not include all of them. In the other compilations of the aḥādīth other supplications are also recorded for this occasion, for example, the common supplication which is often recited in every prayer :

سبحانک اللهم وبحمدك و تبارك اسمک وتعالی جدك ولا اله غيرك

[Glory to Thee, Allah, and Thine is the praise and blessed is Thy name and Exalted is Thy majesty and there is no god besides Thee.]

Chapter CCXXI

DESIRABILITY OF GOING TO PRAYER WITH DIGNITY AND TRANQUILLITY AND FORBIDDANCE OF GOING TO IT IN HOT HASTE

(1249) Abū Huraira reported : I heard the Messenger of Allah (may peace be upon him) saying : When the Iqāma has been pronounced for prayer, do not go running to it, but go walking in tranquillity, and pray what you are in time for and complete what you have missed.[819]

(1250) Abū Huraira reported that the Messenger of Allah (may peace be upon him) said : When the words of Iqāma are pronounced, do not come to (prayer) running, but go with tranquillity, and pray what you are in time for, and complete (what you have missed) for when one of you is preparing for prayer he is in fact engaged in prayer.[820]

(1251) Abū Huraira reported aḥādīth from the Messenger of Allah (may peace be upon him), and one of ṭhem is that the Messenger of Allah (may peace be upon), said : When the call is made for prayer come to it walking with tranquillity, and pray what you are in time for, and complete what you have missed.

(1252) Abū Huraira reported : The Messenger of Allah (may peace be upon him) said : When the words of Iqāma are pronounced, none of you should run to it (to join the prayer) but walk with tranquillity and dignity, and pray what you are in time for and complete what has gone[821] before (what the Imām has completed).

This ḥadīth is transmitted on the authority of 'Ā'isha (Allah be pleased with her) and is recorded in Tirmidhī and Abū Dāwūd. Then there is another supplication transmitted by Ḥadrat 'Alī (Allah be pleased with him) which we find in the books of aḥādīth :

انی وجهت وجهی للذی فطر السموت والارض حنیفاً وما انا من المشرکین ان صلوتی ونسکی ومحیای ومماتی
لله رب العالمین لا شریک له و بذالک امرت و انا من المسلمین -

[I have turned my face as *hanif* towards Him Who created the heavens and the earth, and I am not an associator with Allah. My prayer and my devotion, my life and my death belong to Allah, the Lord of the universe, Who has no partner. That is what I have been commanded, and I am a Muslim.]

Imām Nawawī makes it clear that one can make any supplication out of these. These are all transmitted from the Holy Prophet (may peace be upon him).

819. The act of running to join the prayer is an indication of immature mind and carelessness. Worship is the most sacred act of devotion and it should be performed well in time and with perfect calmness and tranquillity (*Mazhar-i-Ḥaqq* by Maulānā Quṭub-ud-Dīn, Vol. I, p. 243).

820. Some people find this ḥadīth contradicting a verse of the Holy Qur'ān in which it has been said : "When the call is made for prayer on Friday, hasten to the remembrance of Allah and leave off business" (lxii. 9). It is asserted by the critics that in both places the word سعی (sa'ī) is used. The famous commentator of Ḥadīth, Ṭībī says that in the Qur'ānic verse سعی (sa'ī) stands for قصد (*qaṣd*) : to intend. Imām Ḥasan Baṣrī is of the opinion that سعی (sa'ī) does not merely imply the hastening of footsteps ; it also signifies the quickness of intention ('Alī b. Sulṭān b. al-Qārī, *Mirqāt al-Mafātiḥ*, Vol. II, p. 179).

821. It is on the basis of this word that the Ḥanafites believe that the late-comer in prayer should complete that part of the prayer which he has missed. The Shāfi'ites and others are of the view that the part of the prayer offered by the worshipper along with the Imām would form the earlier part and the remaining part would be completed accordingly. Let us take an example to make this point clear. A worshipper joins two rak'ahs in prayer in which four rak'ahs are to be offered. It means

(1253) **'Abdullah b. Abū Qatāda reported on the authority of his father : While we said our prayer with the Messenger of Allah (may peace be upon him) he heard tumult. (At the end of the prayer) he (the Holy Prophet) said : What is the matter with you ? They said : We hastened to prayer. He (the Holy Prophet) said : Don't do that ; when you come for prayer, there should be tranquillity upon you. Pray (along with the Imām) what you can find and complete what preceded you.**

(1254) This ḥadīth has been narrated by Shaibān with the same chain of transmitters.

Chapter CCXXII

WHEN SHOULD THE PEOPLE STAND UP FOR PRAYER

(1255) Abū Qatāda reported : The Messenger of Allah (may peace be upon him) said : When the Iqāma is pronounced, do not get up till you see me. Ibn Ḥātim was in doubt whether it was said : "When the Iqāma is pronounced" or "When call is made".

(1256) Abū Salama son of 'Abd al-Raḥmān b. 'Auf reported Abū Huraira as saying : Iqāma was pronounced and we stood up and made rows straight till he (the Holy Prophet) stood at his place of worship (the place ahead of the rows where he stood to lead the prayer) before takbīr taḥrīma. He reminded to (himself something [822]) and went back saying that we should stand at our places and not leave them. We waited, till he came back to us and he had taken a bath and water trickled out of his head and then led us in prayer.

(1257) Abū Salama[823] reported Abū Huraira as saying : Iqāma was pronounced, and the people had formed themselves into rows. The Messenger of Allah (may peace be upon him) came out and stood at his place, and then pointed out with his hand that we should stand at our places. He then went away and took a bath and water trickled from his head and then led them in prayer.

(1258) Abū Salama reported on the authority of Abū Huraira that when Iqāma was pronounced for the Messenger of Allah (may peace be upon him), the people occupied their places in the rows before the Apostle of Allah (may peace be upon him) stood up at his place.

that he has missed the first two rak'ahs. According to the Ḥanafites, he would complete the first two, i.e. he would start from the Glorification of Allah, and then recite Fātiḥa and verses from the Qur'ān as is done in the opening rak ah. Similarly, he would perform the second rak'ah as is commonly done. In other words, he would complete the first two rak'ahs in the same way as it is ordinarily done. The Shāfi'ites complete the missed part in a different way. They take the third and the fourth rak'ahs offered along with the Imām as the first and the second rak'ahs and complete the third and fourth in the same way as these are generally performed.

822. This proves the humanness of the Prophets. The Prophets are the best of the human lot and they are safeguarded by Allah against committing any fault but, in order to teach the human race the true implication of the Divine Command, their human characteristics are brought into prominence. Forgetfulness is one of the features of human beings. Probably the Holy Prophet forgot that he needed an obligatory bath, so he hastened to perform it as soon as be remembered this.

823. He was not the son of 'Abd al-Raḥmān b 'Auf (Allah be pleased with him) but his real nephew. He was one of the seven jurists of Medina and was counted amongst the eminent Successors. He died in 94 H. at the age of seventy-two.

(1259) Jābir b. Samura reported: Bilāl summoned to prayer as the sun declined but did not pronounce Iqāma till the Apostle of Allah (may peace be upon him) came out and the Iqāma was pronounced on seeing him.

Chapter CCXXIII

HE WHO CAME UP WITH THE RAK'AH, HE IN FACT CAME UP WITH THE PRAYER (LED IN CONGREGATION WITH THE IMĀM)

(1260) Abū Huraira reported the Apostle of Allah (may peace be upon him) as saying: He who finds a rak'ah of the prayer, he in fact finds the prayer.

(1261) Abū Huraira reported the Messenger of Allah (may peace be upon him) as saying: He who finds one rak'ah of the prayer with the Imām, he in fact finds the prayer.

(1262) This ḥadīth has been narrated on the authority of Mālik and there is no mention of "along with the Imām" and in the ḥadīth transmitted by 'Abdullah the words are: "he in fact finds the entire prayer".

(1263) Abū Huraira reported: The Messenger of Allah (may peace be upon him) said: He who finds one rak'ah at dawn before the rising of the sun, he in fact finds the dawn prayer, and he who finds one rak'ah of the afternoon prayer before sunset, he in fact finds the afternoon prayer.

(1264) 'Ā'isha reported: The Messenger of Allah (may peace be upon him) said: He who finds a prostration before sunset or at dawn (prayer) before the rising (of the sun) he in fact finds that (prayer), and prostration implies a rak'ah.

(1265) This ḥadīth is narrated by Abū Huraira with another chain of transmitters.

(1266) Abū Huraira reported: The Messenger of Allah (may peace be upon him) said: He who finds (gets) a rak'ah of the afternoon (prayer) before the setting of the sun, he in fact gets (the full prayer), and he who gets a rak'ah of the morning (prayer) before the rising of the sun he in fact gets (the full prayer).[824]

(1267) This ḥadīth has been transmitted by Ma'mar with another chain of transmitters.

Chapter CCXXIV

TIMES OF PRAYER

(1268) Ibn Shihāb reported: 'Umar b. 'Abd al-'Azīz deferred the afternoon prayer somewhat and 'Urwa said to him: Gabriel came down and he led the Messenger of Allah (may peace be upon him) in prayer. 'Umar said to him: O 'Urwa, are you aware of what you are saying? Upon this he (Urwa) said: I heard Bashīr b. Abū Mas'ūd say that he heard Abū Mas'ūd say that he heard the Messenger of Allah (may peace be upon him) say: Gabriel came down and acted as my Imām, then I prayed with him, then I prayed with him, then I prayed with him, then I prayed with him, then I prayed with him, reckoning with his fingers five times of prayer.

824. These aḥādīth imply that the man who came up with a rak'ah in prayer gets the reward of saying prayer in congregation.

(1269) Ibn Shihāb reported: 'Umar b. 'Abd al-'Azīz one day deferred the prayer. 'Urwa b. Zubair came to him and informed him that one day as Mughīra b. Shu'ba was in Kūfa (as its governor), he deferred the prayer, Abū Mas'ūd al-Anṣārī came to him and said: What is this, O Mughīra? Did you know that it was Gabriel who came and said prayer and (then) the Messenger of Allah (may peace be upon him) said the prayer (along with him), then (Gabriel) prayed and the Messenger of Allah (may peace be upon him) also prayed, then (Gabriel) prayed and the Messenger of Allah (may peace be upon him) also prayed, then (Gabriel) prayed and the Messenger of Allah (may peace be upon him) prayed (along with him), then Gabriel prayed and the Messenger of Allah (may peace be upon him) also prayed (along with him) and then said: This is how I have been ordered to do.[825] 'Umar (b. 'Abd al-'Azīz) said: O 'Urwa! be mindful of what you are saying that Gabriel (peace be upon him) taught the Messenger of Allah (may peace be upon him) the times of prayer. Upon this 'Urwa said: This is how Bashīr b. Abū Mas'ūd narrated on the authority of his father and (also said): 'Ā'isha, the wife of the Apostle (may peace be upon him), narrated it to me that the Messenger of Allah (may peace be upon him) used to say the afternoon prayer, when the light of the sun was there in her apartment before it went out (of it).

(1270) 'Ā'isha reported: The Apostle of Allah (may peace be upon him) said afternoon prayer as the sun shone in my apartment, and the afternoon shadow did not extend further. Abū Bakr said: The afternoon shadow did not appear to extend further.

(1271) 'Ā'isha, the wife of the Apostle (may peace be upon him), said that the Messenger of Allah (may peace be upon him) said the afternoon prayer (at the time) when the sun shone in her apartment and its shadow did not extend beyond her apartment.

(1272) 'Ā'isha reported: The Messenger of Allah (may peace be upon him) said afternoon prayer (at time) when the (light) of the sun was there in my apartment.

(1273) 'Abdullah b. 'Amr reported the Apostle (may peace be upon him) saying: The time of the noon prayer (lasts) as long as it is not afternoon, and the time of the afternoon prayer (lasts) as long as the sun does not turn pale, and the time of the evening prayer (lasts) as long as the spreading appearance of the redness above the horizon after sunset does not sink down, and the time of the night prayer (lasts) by midnight and the time of the morning prayer (lasts) as long as the sun does not rise.

(1274) Abū Bakr b. Abū Shaiba and Yaḥyā b. Abū Bukair both of them transmitted this ḥadīth with the same chain of transmitters.

(1275) 'Abdullah b. 'Amr reported: The Messenger of Allah (may peace be upon him) said: The time of the noon prayer is when the sun passes the meridian and a man's shadow is the same (length) as his height, (and it lasts) as long as the time for the afternoon prayer has not come; the time for the afternoon prayer is as long as the sun has not become pale; the time of the evening prayer is as long as the twilight has not ended; the time of the night prayer is up to the middle of the average night,[826] and the time of the morning prayer is from the appearance of dawn, as long as the sun has not risen; but when the sun rises, refrain from prayer, for it rises

825. It means that the timings of prayers have been scheduled by Allah.

826. The word *al-ausaṭ* (اوسط) qualifies the night, i.e. the night which is neither long nor short. However, there can be another translation for it if al-Ausaṭ is made the quality, i.e. *niṣf* (half), then it would be exact midnight (*Mirqāt*, Vol. II, p. 121).

between the horns of the devil.[827]

(1276) 'Abdullah b. 'Amr b. al-'Āṣ reported: The Messenger of Allah (may peace be upon him) was asked about the time of prayers. He said: The time for the morning prayer (lasts) as long as the first visible part of the rising sun does not appear, and the time of the noon prayer is when the sun declines from the zenith and there is not a time for the afternoon prayer and the time for the afternoon prayer is so long as the sun does not become pale and its first visible part does not set, and the time for the evening prayer is that when the sun disappears and (it lasts) till the twilight[828] is no more and the time for the night prayer is up to the midnight.

(1277) 'Abdullah narrated it on the authority of his father Yaḥyā: Knowledge cannot be acquired with sloth.[829]

(1278) Sulaimān b. Buraida narrated it on the authority of his father that a person asked the Apostle of Allah (may peace be upon him) about the time of prayer. Upon this he said: Pray with us these two, meaning two days. When the sun passed the meridian, he gave command to Bilāl who uttered the call to prayer, then he commanded him and pronounced Iqāma for noon prayer. (Then at the time of the afternoon prayer) he again commanded and Iqāma for the afternoon prayer was pronounced, when the sun was high, white and clear. He then commanded and Iqāma for the evening prayer was pronounced, when the sun had set. He then commanded him and the Iqāma for the night prayer was pronounced when the twilight had disappeared. He then commanded him and the Iqāma for the morning prayer was pronounced, when the dawn had appeared. When it was the next day, he commanded him to delay the noon prayer till the extreme heat had passed and he did so, and he allowed it to be delayed till the extreme heat had passed. He observed the afternoon prayer when the sun was high, delaying it beyond the time he had previously observed it. He observed the evening prayer before the twilight had vanished; he observed the night prayer when a third of the night had passed; and he observed the dawn prayer when there was clear daylight. He (the Holy Prophet) then said: Where is the man who inquired about the time of prayer? He (the inquirer) said: Messenger of Allah! here I am. He (the Holy Prophet) said: The time for your prayer is within the limits of what you have seen.[830]

(1279) Buraida narrated on the authority of his father that a man came to the Prophet (may peace be upon him) and asked about the times of prayer. He said: You observe with us the prayer. He commanded Bilāl, and he uttered the call to prayer in

827. This has already been explained in "Kitāb al-Īmān".

828. There is a difference of opinion among the jurists about twilight. Most of them believe that twilight is that redness which appears after sunset. Imām Abū Ḥanīfa is of the same view. But there is another opinion of Imām Abū Ḥanīfa and other scholars according to which twilight includes both redness and whiteness which appear after the sinking of the sun (*Mirqāt*, Vol. II, p. 120.)

829. Apparently there seems to be no occasion of the narration of this ḥadīth under this chapter. Here the times of prayers are being specified and this ḥadīth has no concern with it. According to Imām Nawawī, its narration has a special significance in this context. We have been seeing with what care the aḥādīth concerning the times of prayers are being narrated by 'Abdullah b. 'Amr. He must have done a good deal of labour in collecting them and then transmitting them, and this ḥadīth refers to it.

830. The Holy Prophet clearly demarcated the extreme limits for the times of five prayers and showed them by saying prayers on these two limits.

the darkness of night preceding daybreak and he said the morning prayer till dawn had appeared. He then commanded him (Bilāl) to call for the noon prayer when the sun had declined from the zenith. He then commanded him (Bilāl) to call for the afternoon prayer when the sun was high. He then commanded him for the evening prayer when the sun had set. He then commanded him for the night prayer when the twilight had disappeared. Then on the next day he commanded him (to call for prayer) when there was light in the morning. He then commanded him (to call) for the noon prayer when the extreme heat was no more. He then commanded him for the afternoon prayer when the sun was bright and clear and yellowness did not blend with it. He then commanded him to observe the sunset prayer. He then commanded him for the night prayer when a third part of the night had passed or a bit less than that. Ḥaramī (the narrator of this ḥadīth) was in doubt about that part of the mentioned ḥadīth which concerned the portion of the night. When it was dawn, he (the Holy Prophet) said : Where is the inquirer (who inquired about the times of prayers and added) : Between (these two extremes) is the time for prayer.

(1280) Abū Mūsā narrated on the authority of his father that a person came to the Messenger of Allah (may peace be upon him) for inquiring about the times of prayer. He (the Holy Prophet) gave him no reply (because he wanted to explain to him the times by practically observing these prayers). He then said the morning prayer when it was daybreak, but the people could hardly recognise one another. He then commanded and the Iqāma for the noon prayer was pronounced when the sun had passed the meridian and one would say that it was midday but he (the Holy Prophet) knew batter than them. He then again commanded and the Iqāma for the afternoon prayer was pronounced when the sun was high. He then commanded and Iqāma for the evening prayer was pronounced when the sun had sunk. He then commanded and Iqāma for the night prayer was pronounced when the twilight had disappeared. He then delayed the morning prayer on the next day (so much so) that after returning from it one would say that the sun had risen or it was about to rise. He then delayed the noon prayer till it was near the time of afternoon prayer (as it was observed yesterday). He then delayed the afternoon prayer till one after returning from it would say that the sun had become red. He then delayed the evening prayer till the twilight was about to disappear. He then delayed the night prayer till it was one-third of the night. He then called the inquirer in the morning and said : The time for prayers is between these two (extremes).

(1281) Abū Mūsā reported on the authority of his father that an inquirer came to the Prophet (may peace be upon him) and asked him about the times of prayer, and the rest of the ḥadīth is the same (as narrated above) but for these words : "On the second day he (the Holy Prophet) observed the evening prayer before the disappearance of the twilight."

Chapter CCXXV

DESIRABILITY OF SAYING THE NOON PRAYER WHEN THE EXTREME HEAT IS OVER

(1282) Abū Huraira reported that the Messenger of Allah (may peace be upon him) said : When it is very hot, say (noon prayer) when the extreme heat passes away, for intensity of heat is from the exhalation of Hell.[831]

(1283) Another ḥadīth like this has been transmitted by Abū Huraira.

(1284) Abū Huraira reported: The Messenger of Allah (may peace be upon him) said: When it is a hot day, (delay) the prayer till extreme heat passes away, for the intensity of heat is from the exhalation of Hell.

(1285) Abū Huraira reported: Refrain from saying (noon prayer) till the extreme heat passes away, for the intensity of heat is from the exhalation of Hell.

(1286) Abū Huraira narrated this ḥadīth from the Messenger of Allah (may peace be upon him) by another chain of transmitters.

(1287) Abū Huraira reported that the Messenger of Allah (may peace be upon him) said: This heat is from the exhalation of Hell-fire, so delay the prayer till it is cool.

(1288) Hammām b. Munabbih reported: This is what Abū Huraira narrated to us from the Holy Prophet and he transmitted some aḥādīth—one of them was that the Messenger of Allah (may peace be upon him) said: Let the heat become less severe before prayer, for the intesity of heat is from the exhalation of Hell.

(1289) Abū Dharr reported: The Mu'adhdhin (the announcer of the hour of prayer) of the Messenger of Allah (may peace be upon him) called for the noon prayer. Upon this the Apostle of Allah (may peace be upon him) said: Let it cool down, let it cool down, or he said: Wait, wait, for the intensity of heat is from the exhalation of Hell. When the heat is intense, delay the prayer till it becomes cooler. Abū Dharr said: (We waited) till we saw the shadow of the mounds.[832]

(1290) Abū Huraira reported: The Messenger of Allah (may peace be upon him) said: The Fire made a complaint before the Lord saying: "O Lord, some parts of mine have consumed the others."[833] So it was allowed to take two exhalations, one exhalation in winter and the other exhalation in summer. That is why you find extreme heat (in summer) and extreme cold (in winter).[834]

(1291) Abū Huraira reported: The Messenger of Allah (may peace be upon him) said: When it is hot, make delay (in the noon prayer) till it cools down, for the intensity of heat is from the exhalation of Hell; and he also mentioned that the Hell-fire complained to the Lord (about the congested atmosphere) and so it was permitted to take two exhalations during the whole year, one exhalation during the winter and one exhalation during the summer.

(1292) Abū Huraira reported that the Messenger of Allah (may peace be upon him) said: The Fire said to the Lord: O Lord! some parts of mine have consumed the others, so allow me to exhale (in order to find some relief from this congestion). It was granted permission to take two exhalations, one exhalation during the winter and the other exhalation during the summer. So whatever you perceive in the form of intense cold or hurting cold is from the exhalation of Hell. And whatever you perceive in the form of extreme heat or intense heat is from the exhalation of Hell.

831. This has been said to give us an idea of the dreadful heat in the Hell-fire.

832. The shadow of the mounds does not immediately appear on the earth after the passing of the sun over the meridian. It is after some time that it casts its shadow on the earth.

833 It refers to overcrowding in the Hell.

834. It is a metaphorical way of saying that extreme cold in winter and extreme hot in summer are the characteristic features of Hell. Exhalation is the very sign of life. The life-breath of Hell is, therefore, its highly uncogenial atmosphere either too much cold or too much hot. This state of torment can be visualised from the extreme heat and cold on this earth.

Chapter CCXXVI

DESIRABILITY OF OBSERVING THE NOON PRAYER AT THE EARLIER HOUR (OF TIMES PRESCRIBED FOR IT) WHEN THERE IS NO INTENSE HEAT

(1293) Jābir b. Samura reported : The Apostle of Allah (may peace be upon him) used to offer the noon prayer when the sun declined.

(1294) Khabbāb reported : We complained to the Messenger of Allah (may peace be upon him) (the difficulty of) saying prayer on the intensely heated (ground or sand)[835] but he paid no heed to our complaint.[836]

(1295) Khabbāb reported : We came to the Messenger of Allah (may peace be upon him) and we complained to the Messenger of Allah (may peace be upon him) about (saying prayer) on the extremely heated ground (or sand), but he paid no head to us. Zuhair said : I asked Abū Isḥāq whether it was about the noon prayer. He said : Yes. I again said whether it concerned the (offering) of noon (prayer) in earlier hours. He said : Yes. I said : Did it concern expediting[837] it ? He said : Yes.

(1296) Anas b. Mālik reported : We used to say (noon prayer) with the Messenger of Allah (may peace be upon him) in the intense heat, but when someone amongst us found it hard to place his forehead on the ground, he spread his cloth and prostrated on it.

Chapter CCXXVII

PREFERENCE FOR SAYING THE 'AṢR PRAYER AT THE COMMENCEMENT OF THE PRESCRIBED TIME

(1297) Anas b. Mālik reported that the Messenger of Allah (may peace be upon him) used to pray the afternoon prayer when the sun was high and bright, then one would go off to al-'Awālī[838] and get there while the sun was still high. Ibn Qutaiba made no mention of "one would go off to al-'Awālī".

(1298) This ḥadīth that the Messenger of Allah (may peace be upon him) used to offer the afternoon prayer like the one narrated above has been transmitted by Anas b. Mālik by another chain of transmitters.

(1299) Anas b. Mālik reported : We used to offer the 'Aṣr prayer, then one would go to Qubā'[839] and reach there and the sun would be still high.

835. *Ramḍā'* means ground, land or stones, or sand intensely hot, or intensely heated by the sun.

836. This ḥadīth apparently conflicts with those mentioned in the previous chapter. The scholars of Ḥadīth have given very satisfactory reply to remove this contradiction. In the hot season the ground and sand remain extremely hot even in the afternoon. Ḥaḍrat Khabbāb demanded a concession to an extent which could not be granted by the Holy Prophet (Ibn Ḥajar 'Asqalānī, *Fatḥ al-Bārī* Vol. II, p 156).

837. It means that unnecessary delay should in no way be caused in offering the noon prayer even in hot season. If one waits for the coolness to prevail in the atmosphere during summer, one shall have to delay the noon prayer for such long hours that the prescribed time would be over. This ḥadīth also determines the meaning of the phrase ابردوا بالصلوة used in the earlier aḥādīth (1282, 1284). It indicates that the word ابردوا should not be taken in the sense of coldness here, but in the sense that when the intolerably extreme heat is over and one can stand the hot rays of the declining sun.

838. Villages on high ground around Medina.

839. Qubā' is situated at a distance of three miles from Medina.

(1300) Anas b. Mālik reported : We used to offer the afternoon prayer (at such a time) that a person would go to Banū 'Amr b. 'Auf[840] and he would find them busy offering the afternoon prayer.

(1301) 'Alā' b. 'Abd al-Raḥmān reported that they came to the house of 'Anas b. Mālik in Baṣra after saying the noon prayer. His (Anas's) house was situated by the side of the mosque. As we visited him he (Anas) said : Have you said the afternoon prayer ? We said to him : It is just a few minutes before that we finished the noon prayer. He said : Offer the afternoon prayer. So we stood up and said our prayer. And when we completed it, he said : I have heard the Messenger of Allah (may peace be upon him) saying : This is how the hypocrite prays : he sits watching the sun, and when it is between the horns of devil, he rises and strikes the ground four times (in haste) mentioning Allah a little during it.[841]

(1302) Abu Umāma b. Sahl reported : We offered the noon prayer with 'Umar b. 'Abd al-'Azīz. We then set out till we came to Anas b. Mālik and found him busy in saying the afternoon prayer. I said to him : O uncle![842] which is this prayer that you are offering ? He said : It is the afternoon prayer, and this is the prayer of the Messenger of Allah (may peace be upon him) that we offered along with him.

(1303) Anas b. Mālik reported : The Messenger of Allah (may peace be upon him) led us in the afternoon prayer. When he completed it, a person from Banū Salama came to him and said : Messenger of Allah, we intend to slaughter our camel and we are desirous that you should also be present there (on this occasion). He (the Holy Prophet) said : Yes. He (the person) went and we also went along with him and we found that the camel had not been slaughtered yet. Then it was slaughtered, and it was cut into pieces and then some of those were cooked, and then we ate (them) before the setting of the sun. This ḥadīth has also been transmitted by another chain of transmitters.[843]

(1304) Rāfi' b. Khadīj reported : We used to say the afternoon prayer with the Messenger of Allah (may peace be upon him), and then the camel was slaughtered and ten parts of it were distributed, then it was cooked and then we ate this cooked meat before the sinking of the sun.

(1305) This ḥadīth has been transmitted by 'Auzā'ī with the same chain of transmitters : We used to slaughter the camel during the lifetime of the Messenger of Allah (may peace be upon him) after the 'Aṣr prayer, but he made no mention of : "We used to pray along with him."

840. This is situated at a distance of two miles from Medina (*Fatḥ-ul-Mulhim*, Vol. II, p. 201.)

841. This ḥadīth is clearly indicative of the fact that it is not desirable to say the 'Aṣr prayer when the sun wears yellow hue. The man who does it intentionally is a sort of hypocrite. The Holy Prophet (may peace be upon him) has exhorted his followers to be prompt in offering this prayer, because the time prescribed for it is short and one is very busy in one's transactions during these hours. Now if a person offers this prayer at the last hour he would do so in haste, and would not be able to offer prayer in full devotion.

842. He addressed him in this way simply out of respect.

843. According to Imām Nawawī, this has been mentioned to emphasise the importance of observing the 'Aṣr prayer at the commencement of its time and not to delay it. Moreover, it also indicates the fact that invitation to a feast should be accepted, whether it is before noon or in the afternoon.

Chapter CCXXVIII

THE SEVERITY (OF PUNISHMENT) IN MISSING THE 'AṢR PRAYER

(1306) Ibn 'Umar reported that the Messenger of Allah (may peace be upon him) said: He who misses[844] the afternoon prayer, it is as though he has been deprived of his family and his property.[845]

(1307) This ḥadīth has been narrated as *Marfū'* by another chain of transmitters.

(1308) 'Abdullah relates on the authority of his father: He who missed his afternoon prayer, it is as though he was deprived of his family and property.

(1309) 'Alī reported: When it was the day (of the Battle) of Aḥzāb, the Messenger of Allah (may peace be upon him) said: May Allah fill their graves and houses with fire, as they detained us and diverted us from the middle[846] prayer, till the sun set.

(1310) This ḥadīth has been transmitted by Hishām with the same chain of transmitters.

(1311) 'Alī reported: The Messenger of Allah (may peace be upon him) said: On the day (of the Battle) of Aḥzāb we were diverted from the middle prayer, till the sun set. May Allah fill their graves or their houses, or their stomachs, with fire. The narrator is in doubt about "houses" and "stomachs".

(1312) This ḥadīth has been narrated by Qatāda with the same chain of transmitters. And he said: Their houses and their graves (be filled with fire), and did not express doubt over the words, "houses" and "graves".

(1313) Yaḥyā heard 'Alī saying that the Messenger of Allah (may peace be upon him) said on the day (of the Battle) of Aḥzāb, while sitting in one of the openings of the ditch: They (the enemies) have diverted us from the middle prayer, till the sun set. May Allah fill their graves and their houses with fire, or their graves and stomachs with fire.

(1314) 'Alī reported: The Messenger of Allah (may peace be upon him) said on the day (of the Battle) of Aḥzāb: They diverted us from saying the middle prayer, i.e. the 'Aṣr prayer. May Allah fill their houses and graves with fire; he then observed this

844 The word *faut*, according to Sayyid Anwar Shāh Kāshmīrī, has different connotations in the Ḥadīth. It may mean the missing of congregation, or missing of the preferable time for offering the prayer, or the missing of its due time altogether (*Faiḍ al-Bīri* Vol. II, p. 115).

845. According to Shāh Walīullāh, cutting off from one's family and property here implies to be deprived of one's good deeds (*Muṣaffā*, Vol. I, p. 76).

This ḥadīth can be translated in various other ways. By whomsoever the prayer of the afternoon passeth unobserved, he has, as though, had his family slain and his property taken away; or as though he had his family and his property taken away; or as though he were deprived of his family and property and remaind alone. The loss of the family and property is thus likened to the loss of the recompense.

What the ḥadīth in simple words means is that the missing of the afternoon prayer is a great privation for a Muslim.

846. *Wasaṭ*, of which *wusṭa* is the comparative form, means both middle and excellent, for *wasaṭ* refers sometimes to place and sometimes to degree (Imām Rāghib). There is a good deal of difference of opinion as to which is the middle prayer, but an overwhelming majority is of the view that it implies the 'Aṣr prayer.

prayer between the evening prayer and the night prayer.

(1315) 'Abdullah (b. Mas'ūd) reported that the polytheists detained the Messenger of Allah (may peace be upon him) from observing the afternoon prayer till the sun became red or it became yellow. Upon this the Messenger of Allah (may peace be upon him) said: They have diverted us from (offering) the middle prayer, i.e. the 'Aṣr prayer. May Allah fill their bellies and their graves with fire, or he said: May Allah stuff their bellies and their graves with fire.

(1316) Abū Yūnus, the freed slave of 'Ā'isha said: 'Ā'isha ordered me to transcribe a copy of the Qur'ān for her and said: When you reach this verse: "Guard the prayers and the middle prayer" (ii. 238), inform me; so when I reached it, I informed her and she gave me dictation (like this): Guard the prayers and the middle prayer,[847] and the afternoon prayer, and stand up truly obedient to Allah. 'Ā'isha said: This is how I have heard from the Messenger of Allah (may peace be upon him).

(1317) Al-Barā' b. 'Āzib reported: This verse was revealed (in this way): "Guard the prayers and the 'Aṣr prayer." We recited it (in this very way) so long as Allah desired. Allah, then, abrogated it and it was revealed: "Guard the prayers, and the middle prayer." A person who was sitting with Shaqīq (one of the narrators in the chain of transmitters) said: Now it implies the 'Aṣr prayer. Upon this al-Barā' said: I have already informed you how this (verse) was revealed and how Allah abrogated it, and Allah knows best. Imām Muslim said: Ashja'ī narrated it from Sufyān al-Thaurī, who narrated it from al-Aswad b. Qais, who narrated it from 'Uqba, who narrated it from al-Barā' b. 'Āzib who said: We recited with the Prophet (may peace be upon him) (the above-mentioned verse like this, i.e. instead of *Ṣalāt al-Wuṣṭā*, *Ṣalāt al-'Aṣr*) for a certain period, as it has been mentioned (in the above-quoted ḥadīth).

(1318) Jābir b. 'Abdullah reported that 'Umar b. al-Khaṭṭāb had been cursing the pagans of the Quraish on the day (of the Battle) of Khandaq (Ditch). (He came to the Holy Prophet) and said: Messenger of Allah, by God, I could not say the 'Aṣr prayer till the sun set. Upon this the Messenger (may peace be upon him) said: By Allah I, too, have not observed it. So we went to a valley.[848] The Messenger of Allah (may peace be upon him) performed ablution and we too performed ablution, and then the Messenger of Allah (may peace be upon him) said the 'Aṣr prayer after the sun had set, and then said the evening prayer after it.

(1319) This ḥadīth has been transmitted by Yaḥyā b. Abū Kathīr with the same chain of transmitters.

Chapter CCXXIX

MERIT OF THE MORNING AND AFTERNOON PRAYERS AND EXHORTATION TO GUARD THEM

(1320) Abū Huraira reported: The Messenger of Allah (may peace be upon him) said: Angels take turns among you by night and by day, and they all assemble at the

847 Ḥaḍrat 'Ā'isha had by that time not come to know that this part (and the middle prayer) had, so far as words were concerned, been abrogated (*Fatḥ al-Mulhim*, Vol. II, p. 205).

848. It is a valley by the side of Medina (*Fatḥ al-Mulhim*, Vol. II, p. 205).

dawn and afternoon prayers Those (of the angels) who spend the night among you, then ascend, and their Lord asks them, though He is the best informed about them: How did you leave My servants ?[849]—they say: We left them while they were praying and we came to them while they were praying.

(1321) Abū Huraira reported Allah's Messenger (may peace be upon him) as saying: Angels take turns among you by night and by day, and the rest of the ḥadīth is the same.

(1322) Jarīr b. 'Abdullah is reported to have said: We were sitting with the Messenger of Allah (may peace be upon him) that he looked at the full moon and observed: You shall see your Lord as you are seeing this moon, and you will not be harmed[850] by seeing Him. So if you can, do not let yourselves be overpowered in case of prayer observed before the rising of the sun and its setting, i.e. the 'Aṣr prayer and the morning prayer. Jarīr then recited it: "Celebrate the praise of Thy Lord before the rising of the sun and before its setting" (xx. 130).

(1323) Wakī' reported (this ḥadīth) with the same chain of transmitters (that the Holy Prophet) said: You will be soon presented before your Lord, and you will see Him as you are seeing this moon, and then recited (the above-mentioned verse). But (in this ḥadīth) no mention is made of Jarīr.

(1324) 'Umāra b. Ruwaiba is reported to have said on the authority of his father: I heard the Messenger of Allah (may peace be upon him) saying: He who observed prayer before the rising of the sun and its setting, i.e. the dawn prayer and the afternoon prayer, would not enter the (Hell) fire. A person belonging to Baṣra said to him: Did you yourself hear it from the Messenger of Allah (may peace be upon him) ? He said: Yes. The person (from Baṣra) said: I bear witness that I heard it from the Messenger of Allah (may peace be upon him) ; my ears heard it and my heart retained it.

(1325) 'Umāra b. Ruwaiba reported on the authority of his father that the Messenger of Allah (may peace be upon him) said: He who said prayer before the rising of the sun and its setting would not enter the fire (of Hell), and there was a man from Baṣra (sitting) beside him who said: Did you hear it from the Apostle of Allah (may peace be upon him) ? He said: Yes, I bear witness to it. The man from Baṣra

849. The main purpose behind asking the angels was not to seek information through them, but simply to show them the preference of man over angels and herein is an implied answer to the question which was asked by the angels on the day when man was going to be created and entrusted with vicegerency of the Lord on the earth: "Wilt Thou place in it such as make mischief in it and shed blood" (ii. 30).

Allah wanted to show them that their misgivings were unfounded They were now themselves the witnesses of the religious devotion of man (*Mirqāt*, Vol. II. p. 143).

This ḥadīth emphasises the utmost importance of the dawn and afternoon prayers.

850. *Ḍāmma* (ضام) means "he wronged," "he harmed and inflicted damage," or "he treated unjustly". All these meanings fit here. According to Maulānā Shabbīr Aḥmad 'Uthmānī, it denotes the absence of overcrowding. What it actually means is that there would be no hustle and bustle and everyone would gaze at Allah with perfect peace of mind and that too in a free atmosphere (*Fath al-Mulhim*, Vol. II, p. 207).

It also implies that everyone would be given opportunity to gaze at his Lord and no one would be treated unjustly in getting this privilege.

This ḥadīth also shows that the unbelievers would be deprived of this great blessing of the sight of Allah.

said: I bear witness that I did hear from the Apostle of Allah (may peace be upon him) saying it from the place that you heard from him.

(1326) Abū Bakr reported on the authority of his father that the Messenger of Allah (may peace be upon him) said: He who observed two prayers at two cool (hours)[851] would enter Paradise.

(1327) This ḥadīth has been narrated by the same chain of transmitters by Hammām, and said about Abū Bakr that he was Ibn Abū Mūsā.

Chapter CCXXX

COMMENCEMENT OF THE TIME FOR THE EVENING PRAYER IS IMMEDIATELY AFTER SUNSET

(1328) Salama b. al-Akwa'[852] reported that the Messenger of Allah (may peace be upon him) used to say the evening prayer when the sun had set and disappeared (behind the horizon).

(1329) Rāfi' b. Khadīj[853] reported: We used to observe the evening prayer with the Messenger of Allah (may peace be upon him) and then one of us would go away and he could see the (distant) place where his arrow would fall.[854]

(1330) A ḥadīth like this, i.e. "We used to observe evening prayer..." so on and so forth, has been narrated by Rāfi' b. Khadīj by another chain of transmitters.

Chapter CCXXXI

TIME FOR THE NIGHT PRAYER AND ITS DELAY

(1331) 'Ā'isha, the wife of the Apostle of Allah (may peace be upon him), reported: The Messenger of Allah (may peace be upon him) deferred one night the 'Ishā' prayer. And this is called *'Atama*. And the Messenger of Allah (may peace be upon him) did not come out till 'Umar b. Khaṭṭāb told (him) that the women and children had gone to sleep. So the Messenger of Allah (may peace be upon him) came out towards them and said to the people of the mosque:[855] None except you from the people of the earth waits[856] for it (for the night prayer at this late hour), and it was before Islam had

851. This refers to the morning and afternoon prayers.

852. His kunyah was Abū Muslim Aslamī He belonged to Medina, and was one of those who gave an oath of allegiance in the famous Bay'ah taken under the Tree. He was a brave warrior and participated in most of the battles. He died in 74 H. in Medina at the age of eighty.

853. Rāfi' b. Khadīj. His kunyah is Abū 'Abdullah. He belonged to the tribe of Ḥārith and is one of the Anṣār of Medina. He was wounded by an arrow in the Battle of Uḥud and the Holy Prophet remarked: "I shall stand as witness on the Day of Judgment for you because of this wound. He died in 73 H in Medina at the age of eighty-six.

854. As the prescribed limit for the evening prayer is short, it should, therefore, be observed immediately after the commencement of its time.

855. This means the people who had assembled in the mosque for prayer. The Holy Prophet's wording has an implied reference to their devotion, the mosque and prayer.

856. No other Ummah of the world is so much devoted to prayer, especially at such odd hours, as the Ummah of Islam, and this is a testimony of their better God-consciousness as compared with other nations.

spread amongst people. And in the narration transmitted by Ibn Shihāb the Messenger of Allah (may peace be upon him) is reported to have said: It is not meant that you should compel the Messenger of Allah (may peace be upon him) for prayer.[857] And (this he said) when 'Umar b. Khaṭṭāb called (the Holy Prophet) in a loud voice.

(1332) A ḥadīth like this has been narrated by Ibn Shihāb with the same chain of transmitters, but therein no mention has been made of the words of al-Zuhri: It was narrated to me, and that which followed.

(1333) 'Ā'isha reported: The Apostle of Allah (may peace be upon him) one night delayed (observing the 'Ishā' prayer) till a great part of the night was over, and the people in the mosque had gone to sleep. He (the Holy Prophet) then came out and observed prayer and said: This is the proper time for it; were it not that I would impose a burden on my people (I would normally pray at this time). In the ḥadīth transmitted by 'Abd al-Razzāq (the words are): "Were it not that it would impose burden on my people."

(1334) 'Abdullah b 'Umar reported: We waited one night in expectation of the Messenger of Allah (may peace be upon him) for the last prayer of the night, and he came out to us when a third of the night had passed even after that. We do not know whether he had been occupied with family business or something else. When he came out he said: You are waiting for prayer, for which the followers of no other religion wait, except you. Were it not a burden for my Ummah, I would have led them (in the 'Ishā' prayer) at this hour. He then ordered the Mu'adhdhin (to call for prayer) and then stood up for prayer and observed prayer.

(1335) 'Abdullah b. 'Umar reported that the Messenger of Allah (may peace be upon him) was one night occupied (in some work) and he delayed it ('Ishā' prayer) till we went to sleep in the mosque. We then woke up and again went to sleep and again woke up. The Messenger of Allah (may peace be upon him) then came to us and said: None among the people of the earth except you waits for prayer in the night.

(1336) Thābit reported: They (the believers) asked Anas about the ring of the Messenger of Allah (may peace be upon him) and he said: One night the Messenger of Allah (may peace be upon him) delayed (observing) the 'Ishā' prayer up to the midnight or midnight was about to be over. He then came and said: (Other) people have offered prayers and slept, but you are constantly in prayer as long as you wait for prayer. Anas said: I perceive as if I am seeing the lustre of his silver ring, and lifted his small left finger (in order to show how the Holy Prophet had lifted it).

(1337) Anas b. Mālik reported: We waited for the Messenger of Allah (may peace be upon him) one night, till it was about midnight. He (the Holy Prophet) came and observed prayer and then turned his face towards us, as if I was seeing the lustre of the silver ring on his finger.

(1338) This ḥadīth has been narrated by Qurra with the same chain of transmitters, but therein he did not mention: "He turned his face towards us."

(1339) Abū Mūsā reported: I and my companions who had sailed along with me in

857. What it implies is that as the Messenger is guided by Allah, therefore none has a right to advise him on religious matters. The Holy Prophet in fact wanted to show the last limit of the night prayer. Delay on his part had a purpose behind it which others could not see.

the boat landed with me in the valley of Buṭḥān[858] while the Messenger of Allah (may peace be upon him) was staying in Medina. A party of people amongst them went to the Messenger of Allah (may peace be upon him) every night at the time of the 'Ishā' prayer turn by turn. Abū Mūsā said: (One night) we (I and my companions) went to the Messenger of Allah (may peace be upon him) and he was occupied in some matter till there was a delay in prayer so much so that it was the middle of the night. The Messenger of Allah (may peace be upon him) then came out and led them (Mūsā's companions) in prayer. And when he had observed his prayer he said to the audience present: Take it easy, I am going to give you information and glad tidings that it is the blessing of Allah upon you for there is none among the people, except you, who prays at this hour (of the night), or he said: None except you observed prayer at this (late) hour. He (i e. the narrator) said: I am not sure which of these two sentences he actually uttered. Abū Mūsā said: We came back happy for what we heard from the Messenger of Allah (may peace be upon him).

(1340) Ibn Juraij reported: I said to 'Aṭā': Which time do you deem fit for me to say the 'Ishā' prayer,—as an Imām or alone,—that time which is called by people 'Atama? He said: I heard Ibn 'Abbās saying: The Apostle of Allah (may peace be upon him) one night delayed the 'Ishā' prayer till the people went to sleep. They woke up and again went to sleep and again woke up. Then 'Umar b. Khaṭṭāb stood up and said (loudly) "Prayer." 'Aṭā' further reported that Ibn 'Abbās said: The Apostle of Allah (may peace be upon him) came out, and as if I am still seeing him with water trickling from his head, and with his hand placed on one side of the head, and he said: Were it not hard for my Ummah, I would have ordered them to observe this prayer like this (i.e. at late hours).[859] I inquired from 'Aṭā' how the Apostle of Allah (may peace be upon him) placed his hand upon his head as Ibn Abbās had informed.[860] So 'Aṭā' spread his fingers a little and then placed the ends of his fingers on the side of his head. He then moved them like this over his head till the thumb touched that part of the ear which is near the face and then it (went) to the earlock and the part of the beard. It (the hand) neither held nor caught anything but this is how[861] (it moved on). I said to 'Aṭā': Was it mentioned to you (by Ibn 'Abbās) how long did the Apostle (may peace be upon him) delay it (the prayer) during that night? He said: I do not know (I cannot give you the exact time). 'Aṭā' said: I love that I should say prayer, whether as an Imām or alone at delayed hours as the Apostle of Allah (may peace be

858. Abū Mūsā started from Yemen to owe allegiance to the Holy Prophet But the wind drifted him to Abyssinia and he stayed there for seven years and then came to Medina along with those emigrants who had taken refuge there. They all came before the Battle of Khaibar (*Fatḥ al-Mulhim*, Vol. II, p. 209).

859. Observing the night prayer at late hours is good because it shows that one is prepared to undergo hardship for one's devotion to Allah. But herein we have been told one important principle of Divine faith that it does not impose such hardship upon its followers as may be unbearable for them. Islam preaches easiness in religion and not intolerable rigours. The Fuqahā' have kept this principle before them for enunciating their Fiqhī deductions.

860. This was meant to find out how clearly 'Aṭā' could recapitulate the situation before his mind and so how accurately he could narrate the words of the Holy Prophet as transmitted by Ibn 'Abbās. The Arabs as a nation have very clear concepts and vivid memories and are distinguished for preserving in their minds both words and conceptual images.

861. The Holy Prophet was moving his hand in order to remove water from his head.

upon him) said that night, but if it is hard upon you in your individual capacity or upon people in the congregation and you are their Imām, then say prayer ('Ishā') at the middle hours, neither too early nor too late.

(1341) Jābir b. Samura reported that the Messenger of Allah (may peace be upon him) postponed the last 'Ishā' prayer.

(1342) Jābir b. Samura reported: The Messenger of Allah (may peace be upon him) used to observe prayers like your prayers, but he would delay the prayer after nightfall to a little after the time you observed it, and he would shorten the prayer.

(1343) 'Abdullah b. 'Umar reported: I heard the Messenger of Allah (may peace be upon him) as saying: Let the bedouin not gain upper hand over you in regard to the name of your prayer. See! (The night prayer should be called) 'Ishā' (and the bedouins call it 'Atama (because) they milk their camels late.

(1344) Ibn 'Umar said: The Messenger of Allah (may peace be upon him) said: Let the bedouin not gain upper hand over you in regard to the name of your prayer, i.e. night prayer, for it is mentioned 'Ishā' in the Book of Allah (i.e. the Qur'ān). (The bedouin call it 'Atama because) they make delay in milking their she-camels.[862]

Chapter CCXXXII

DESIRABILITY OF OBSERVING THE MORNING PRAYER AT EARLIER HOUR AND THAT IS THE TIME WHEN THERE IS DARKNESS BEFORE DAWN AND THE EXPOSITION ABOUT THE LENGTH OF RECITATION IN IT

(1345) 'Ā'isha reported: The believing women used to pray the morning prayer with the Messenger of Allah and then return wrapped in their mantles.[863] No one could recognise them.

(1346) 'Ā'isha, the wife of the Apostle of Allah (may peace be upon him), reported: The believing women observed the morning prayer with the Messenger of Allah (may peace be upon him) wrapped in their mantles. They then went back to their houses and were unrecognisable, because of the Messenger of Allah's (may peace be upon him) praying in the darkness before dawn.

(1347) 'Ā'isha reported: The Messenger of Allah (may peace be upon him) used to observe the morning prayer, and the women would go back wrapped in their mantles being unrecognisable because of the darkness before dawn. (Isḥāq b. Mūsā) al-Anṣārī (one of the narrators in this chain of narration) narrated "wrapped" (only) in his narration. (No mention was made of mantles.)

862. Herein we have been given special instructions about the use of the terms and language in expressing the teachings of Islam. The Qur'ān has Divine language having special shades of meaning. The terms used in the Holy Book have implication of their own. No human language can provide substitutes for them. 'Ishā' is a term for night prayer used by the Qur'ān and it should not, therefore, be substituted by any other word which is used by the people of Jāhilīyya. Ṣalāt-ul-'Ishā' occurs in Sūra Nūr, verse 58, in the Qur'ān.

863. *Mirṭ* (مرط) the plural of which is *Murūṭ* (مروط) was a mantle which the women in those days threw over their heads and also wrapped themselves in. It also means a garment which is not sewed.

(1348) Muḥammad b. 'Amr b. al-Ḥasan b. 'Alī reported : When Ḥajjāj came to Medina we asked Jābir b. 'Abdullah (about the timings of prayer as observed by the Holy Prophet). He said : The Messenger of Allah (may peace be upon him) used to pray the noon prayer in the midday heat ; the afternoon prayer when the sun was bright ; the evening prayer when the sun had completely set ; and as for the night prayer, he sometimes delayed and sometimes (observed it) at earlier hours. When he found them (his Companions) assembled (at earlier hours) he (prayed) early, and when he saw them coming late, he delayed the (prayer), and the morning prayer the Apostle of Allah (may peace be upon him) observed in the darkness before dawn.

(1349) Muḥammad b. 'Amr al-Ḥasan b. 'Alī reported : Ḥajjāj used to delay the prayers, and so we asked Jābir b. 'Abdullah, and the rest of the ḥadīth is the same [864]

(1350) Sayyār b. Salāma reported : I heard my father asking Abū Barza (al-Aslamī) about the prayer of Allah's Messenger (may peace be upon him). I (Shu'ba, one of the narrators) said : Did you hear it (from Abū Barza). He said : I feel as if I am hearing you at this very time. He said : I heard my father asking about the prayer of the Messenger of Allah (may peace be upon him) and he (Abū Barza) making this reply : He (the Holy Prophet) did not mind delaying some (prayer), i.e 'Ishā' prayer, even up to the midnight and did not like sleeping before observing it, and talking after[865] it. Shu'ba said : I met him subsequently and asked him (about the prayers of the Holy Prophet) and he said : He observed the noon prayer when the sun was past the meridian, he would pray the afternoon prayer, after which a person would go to the outskirts of Medina and the sun was still bright ; (I forgot what he said about the evening prayer) ; I then met him on a subsequent occasion and asked him (about prayers of the Holy Prophet) and he said : He would observe the morning prayer (at such a time) so that a man would go back and would recognise his neighbour by casting a glance at his face, and he would recite from sixty to one hundred verses in it.

(1351) Sayyār b. Salāma reported : I heard Abū Barza saying that the Messenger of Allah (may peace be upon him) did not mind some delay in the 'Ishā' prayer even up to the midnight and he did not like sleeping before (observing it) and talking after it. Shu'ba said : I again met him (Sayyār b. Salāma) for the second time and he said : Even up to the third (part) of the night.

(1352) Abū Barza b. Aslamī is reported to have said : The Messenger of Allah (may peace be upon him) delayed the night prayer till a third of the night had passed and he did not approve of sleeping before it, and talking after it, and he used to recite in the morning prayer from one hundred to sixty verses (and completed the prayer at such hours) when we recognised the faces of one another.[866]

864. This ḥadīth shows how careful the early Muslims were about prayers and their observance at the prescribed times. Ḥajjāj b. Yūsuf used to delay the prayers and that caused consternation among the people They saw in it lack of religious devotion on the part of the Muslim rulers.

865. Both sleeping before 'Ishā' prayer and talking after it are permissible if there is any necessity for it, but ordinarily these practices should be avoided. One is liable to miss the prescribed time for the 'Ishā' prayer when one is overpowered by sleep and one is liable to find it troublesome to get up early in the morning for the dawn prayer, if one occupies oneself in conversation late in the night.

866. Both the limits have been explained : the earliest one and the latest one. The earliest one is that when faces cannot be recognised due to the darkness of dawn and the latest one is that when the faces can be easily recognised.

Chapter CXXXIII

DISAPPROVAL OF DELAYING THE PRAYER FROM ITS PRESCRIBED TIME ; WHAT ONE WHO IS LED IN PRAYER SHOULD DO WHEN THE IMĀM DELAYS IT ?

(1353) Abū Dharr reported : The Messenger of Allah (may peace be upon him) said to me : How would you act when you are under the rulers who would delay the prayer beyond its prescribed time, or they would make prayer a dead thing [867] as far as its proper time is concerned ? I said, what do you command ? He (the Holy Prophet) said : Observe the prayer at its proper time, and if you can say it along with them do so, for it would be a supererogatory prayer for you. Khalaf (one of the narrators in the above ḥadīth) has not mentioned "beyond their (prescribed) time".

(1354) Abū Dharr reported : The Messenger of Allah (may peace be upon him) said to me : O Abū Dharr, you would soon find after me rulers who would make their prayers dead. You should say prayer at its prescribed time. If you say prayer at its prescribed time that would be a supererogatory prayer for you, otherwise you saved your prayer.

(1355) Abū Dharr reported : My friend (the Holy Prophet) bade me to hear and obey (the ruler) even if he is a slave having his feet and arms cut off, and observe prayer at its prescribed time. (And further said) : If you find people having observed the prayer, you in fact saved your prayer, otherwise (if you join with them) that would be a Nafl prayer for you.

(1356) Abū Dharr reported : The Messenger of Allah (may peace be upon him) struck my thigh (and said) : How would you act if you survive among the people who would delay prayers beyond their (prescribed) time ? He (Abū Dharr) said : What do you command (under this situation) ? He (the Holy Prophet) said : Observe prayer at its prescribed time, then go (to meet) your needs and if the Iqāma is pronounced, and you are present in the mosque, then observe prayer (along with the Jamā'at).

(1357) Abu'l-'Āliyat al-Barā' reported : Ibn Ziyād delayed the prayer. 'Abdullah b. Ṣāmit came to me and I placed a chair for him and he sat in it and I made a mention of what Ibn Ziyād had done. He bit his lips (as a sign of extreme anger and annoyance) and struck at my thigh and said : I asked Abū Dharr as you have asked me, and he struck my thigh just as I have struck your thigh, and said : I asked the Messenger of Allah (may peace be upon him) as you have asked me and he struck my

867. It has the same meaning as delaying the prayer. In this ḥadīth the Holy Prophet has told how to act when the rulers delay in prayer. Prayers should be observed at their prescribed times. But when the rulers cause delay, one should join the congregation in order to avoid dissension and rift in the Muslim society. But that would be counted as Nafl (supererogatory) prayer. It should be borne in mind that it is possible only in case of Ẓuhr and 'Ishā' prayers, for it is not permissible to observe the Nafl prayer after the morning (before the sunrise) and afternoon prayers (before sunset). The evening prayer consists of three rak'ahs and one is not allowed to observe Nafl in three rak'ahs.

This ḥadīth does not imply that one should silently co-operate and willingly submit before the rulers whatever they do. The Muslims must object to everything that is wrong and should try to set their rulers on the right path. They should persuade them to conform their behaviour to the Qur'ān and the Sunnah and should try to dissuade them from going astray, but at the same time they should avoid creating any dissension in the Muslim society.

thigh just as I have struck your thigh, and he (the Holy Prophet) said : Observe prayer at its prescribed time, and if you can say prayer along with them, do so, and do not say : "I have observed prayer and so I shall not pray." 868

(1358) Abū Dharr reported : (The Messenger of Allah) said : How would you, or how would thou, act if you survive to live among people who delay prayer beyond the (prescribed) time ? (The narrator said : Allah and His Messenger know best), whereupon he said : Observe prayer at its prescribed time, but if the Iqāma is pronounced for (congregational) prayer, then observe prayer along with them, for herein is an excess of virtue.

(1359) Abu'l-'Āliyat al Barrā' reported : I said to 'Abdullah b. Ṣāmit : We say our Jumu'a prayer behind those rulers who delay the prayer. He ('Abdullah b. Ṣāmit) struck my thigh that I felt pain and said : I asked Abū Dharr about it, he struck my thigh and said : I asked the Messenger of Allah (may peace be upon him) about it. Upon this he said : Observe prayer at its prescribed time, and treat prayer along with them (along with those Imāms who delay prayer) as Nafl. 'Abdullah said : It was narrated to me that the Messenger of Allah (may peace be upon him) struck the thigh of Abū Dharr.

Chapter CCXXXIV

EXCELLENCE OF PRAYERS IN CONGREGATION AND GRIM WARNING FOR REMAINING AWAY FROM IT 869

(1360) Abū Huraira reported Allah's Messenger (may peace be upon him) as saying : Prayer said in a congregation is twenty-five degrees more excellent than prayer said by a single person.

(1361) Abū Huraira reported Allah's Apostle (may peace be upon him) as saying : Prayer said in a congregation is twenty-five degrees more excellent than prayer said by a single person. He (Abū Huraira further) said : The angels of the night and the angels of the day meet together. Abū Huraira said : Recite if you like : "Surely the recital of the Qur'ān at dawn is witnessed" (al-Qur'ān, xvii. 78).870

868 Do not show a defiant attitude towards the Imām. When there is time for prayer join the congregation and treat that prayer observed earlier as Nafl and in this way you would not be committing an offence of telling a lie.

869. The aim of religion, as we have said before, is to develop a spirit of piety and God-consciousness in man. Islam heightens this aim by saying that this God-consciousness must be externalised in a social order permeated by religious sanctity and goodness. It is for this reason that prayer in Islam has been divided into two parts, one individual devotion to Allah in which a person as a single entity is trained to develop love for God ; it is a Nafl prayer. The second part is collective prayer which trains a person how religious piety is to be transfused into society. The five obligatory prayers are all congregational prayers in which every Muslim, who has no valid reason to remain aloof, has been enjoined to participate. It is in fact social training in God-consciousness which Islam exhorts its followers to develop and which distinguishes this faith from other religions. Moreover, meeting together five times a day in the mosque and showing submission to the Lord bind the Muslims together in tender chords of spiritual affinity. The prayer in congregation is meant to lift the individual to a higher stage of devotion. Narrow self-seeking wishes are silenced in the presence of congregation. The little and the weak who join the congregational prayer with low and earthly thoughts are carried to the heights of spiritual devotion in the company of more pious and God-fearing persons.

870. The guardian angels bear special testimony to the observer of the morning prayer.

(1362) A ḥadīth like this has been transmitted by Abū Huraira with another chain of transmitters with a very slight change of words.[871]

(1363) Abū Huraira reported Allah's Messenger (may peace be upon him) as saying: Prayer said in a congregation is equivalent to twenty-five (prayers) as compared with the prayer said by a single person.

(1364) Abū Huraira reported: The Messenger of Allah (may peace be upon him) said: Prayer along with the Imām is twenty-five times more excellent than prayer said by a single person.

(1365) Ibn 'Umar reported Allah's Messenger (may peace be upon him) as saying: Prayer said in a congregation is twenty-seven [872] degrees more excellent than prayer said by a single person.

(1366) Ibn 'Umar reported Allah's Apostle (may peace be upon him) as saying: The prayer of a person in congregation is twenty-seven times in excess to the prayer said alone.

(1367) Ibn Numair reported it on the authority of his father (a preference of) more than twenty (degrees) and Abū Bakr in his narration (has narrated it) twenty-seven degrees.

(1368) Ibn 'Umar reported from the Apostle of Allah (may peace be upon him) as some and twenty (degrees).

(1369) Abū Huraira reported: The Messenger of Allah (may peace be upon him) found some people absenting from certain prayers and he said: I intend that I order (a) person to lead people in prayer, and then go to the persons who do not join the (congregational prayer) and then order their houses to be burnt by the bundles of fuel. If one amongst them were to know that he would find a fat fleshy bone he would attend the night prayer.[873]

871. There is no change of meaning but a slight difference in the expression. In the earlier ḥadīth it is خمساً و عشرين درجه and in this ḥadīth it is بخمس و عشرين جزءاً.

872. There is no contradiction between twenty-five degrees as narrated in the previous ḥadīth and twenty-seven degrees as recorded in this ḥadīth. It is meant to exhort Muslims to join congregation and stress the importance of Jamā'at and the great reward which is in store for people participating in it. It is not a degree of exact measurement, but a measure of preference for congregational over the prayer said alone. According to Ḥāfiẓ Ibn Ḥajar 'Asqalānī, twenty-seven degrees of excellence refer to Jahrī prayers (morning, evening, and night) and twenty-five for Sirrī prayers (noon and afternoon) (*Fatḥ al-Bāri*, Vol. II, p. 274).

873. This is one among those aḥādīth in which the importance of congregation in prayer has been fully stressed. Some jurists (Imām Aḥmad b. Ḥanbal is one of them) on the basis of this ḥadīth assert that praying in congregation is as obligatory as prayer itself. But this is not correct deduction. According to Shāh Walīullāh, the Messenger of Allah only made an intention of burning the houses of those who miss congregations without any valid reason or justification, but he never did it. That shows that he wanted to stress its importance. Moreover, in those days only hypocrites remained absent from the congregation. The Holy Prophet wanted to show that these people join Islam and participate in religious practices in order to gain worldly ends. They have no sincere devotion for Islam (as is clear from the words of the Holy Prophet): If one amongst them were to find...). Ḥāfiẓ Ibn Ḥajar also subscribes to the same view that it is not Farḍ. Mullā 'Alī Qārī has, on the authority of this ḥadīth, refuted the claim of those who treat congregational prayer as Farḍ-i-Kifāya (meaning that obligatory act which, if the few perform, absolves all others of its responsibility). Thus collective prayer is neither obligatory, nor optional, but Wājib (positive act) or Sunnat-i-Muwakkad.

(1370) Abū Huraira reported Allah's Messenger (may peace be upon him) as saying: The most burdensome prayers for the hypocrites are the night prayer and the morning prayer.[874] If they were to know the blessings they have in store, they would have come to them, even though crawling, and I thought that I should order the prayer to be commenced and command a person to lead people in prayer, and I should then go along with some persons having a fagot of fuel with them to the people who have not attended the prayer (in congregation) and would burn their houses with fire.

(1371) Hammām b. Munabbih reported: This is what Abū Huraira reported to us from the Messenger of Allah (may peace be upon him) and (in this connection) he narrated some aḥādīth, one of them is: The Messenger of Allah (may peace be upon him) said: I intend that I should command my young men to gather bundles of fuel for me, and then order a person to lead people in prayer, and then burn the houses with their inmates (who have not joined the congregation).

(1372) A ḥadīth like this has been narrated by Abū Huraira.

(1373) 'Abdullah reported Allah's Messenger (may peace be upon him) as saying about people who are absent from Jumu'a prayer: I intend that I should command a person to lead people in prayer, and then burn those persons who absent themselves from Jumu'a prayer in their houses.

Chapter CCXXXV

HE WHO HEARS THE CALL FOR PRAYER IT IS ESSENTIAL FOR HIM TO COME TO THE MOSQUE

(1374) Abū Huraira reported: There came to the Apostle of Allah (may peace be upon him) a blind man and said: Messenger of Allah, I have no one to guide me to the mosque. He, therefore, asked Allah's Messenger (may peace be upon him) permission to say prayer in his house. He (the Holy Prophet) granted him permission. Then when the man turned away he called him and said: Do you hear the call to prayer? He said: Yes. He (the Holy Prophet then) said: Respond to it.[875]

874. Prayer, especially morning and evening, are burdensome for those who are not deeply attached to Allah Prayer is a symbol of man's intimate contact with his Creator and devotion to His religion. The person who does not develop God-consciousness cannot willingly submit before His Command and he always looks forward for an opportunity to evade any burden that religion might put on him. The 'Ishā' prayer and the morning prayer demand from a person that he should sacrifice the sweetness of sleep for the sake of Allah. The people who are given to worldly pleasures find it hard to meet this demand.

875. Ordinarily one is permitted to say prayer at home if there is a valid reason for it. That is why permission has been granted to the blind, the infirm and the sick. It was according to this rule that Ibn Umm Maktūm, the seeker of this concession, was granted this permission. The Holy Prophet made an exception to this rule in his case simply because he was one of his eminent Companions and he had a special regard for him because it was due to indifference towards him that the Holy Qur'ān revealed this verse: "He frowned and turned away, because the blind man came to him" (lxxx. 1-2). The Holy Prophet, therefore, desired his being present in the mosque. Moreover, he was appointed many a time Imām in place of the Messenger of Allah (may peace be upon him) when he was out of Medina, and for occupying this high office it was essential that he should receive training in Imāmah.

(1375) 'Abdullah (b. Mas'ūd) reported: I have seen the time when no one stayed away from prayer except a hypocrite, whose hypocrisy was well known, or a sick man, but if a sick man could walk between two persons (i.e. with the help of two persons with one on each side) he would come to prayer. And (further) said: The Messenger of Allah (may peace be upon him) taught us the paths of right guidance, among which is prayer in the mosque in which the Adhān is called.

(1376) 'Abdullah (b. Mas'ūd) reported: He who likes to meet Allah tomorrow as Muslim, he should persevere in observing these prayers, when a call is announced for them, for Allah has laid down for your Prophet the paths of right guidance, and these (prayers) are among the paths of right guidance If you were to pray in your houses, as this man who stays away (from the mosque) prays in his house, you would abandon the practice of your Prophet, and if you were to abandon the practice of your Prophet, you would go astray. No man purifies himself, doing it well, then makes for one of those mosques, without Allah recording a blessing for him for every step he takes raising him a degree for it, and effacing a sin from him for it. I have seen the time when no one stayed away from it, except a hypocrite, who was well known for his hypocrisy, whereas a man would be brought swaying (due to weakness) between two men till he was set up in a row.

Chapter CCXXXVI

FORBIDDANCE TO GO OUT OF THE MOSQUE AFTER THE ADHĀN[876] HAS BEEN ANNOUNCED BY THE MU'ADHDHIN

(1377) Abū Sha'thā' reported: While we were sitting with Abū Huraira in a mosque a man went out of the mosque after the call to prayer had been announced. (A man stood up in the mosque and set off.) Abū Huraira's eyes followed him till he went out of the mosque. Upon this Abū Huraira said: This man has disobeyed Abu'l-Qāsim (Muḥammad) (may peace be upon him).

(1378) Abū Sha'thā' al-Muḥāribī reported on the authority of his father, who said: I heard it from Abū Huraira that he saw a person getting out of the mosque after the call to prayer had been announced. Upon this he remarked: This (man) disobeyed Abu'l-Qāsim (may peace be upon him).

Chapter CCXXXVII

EXCELLENCE OF PRAYING THE 'ISHĀ' AND MORNING PRAYERS IN CONGREGATION

(1379) 'Abd al-Raḥmān b. Abū 'Amra reported: 'Uthmān b. 'Affān entered the mosque after evening prayer and sat alone. I also sat along with him, so he said: O, son of my brother, I heard the Messenger of Allah (may peace be upon him) say:

876. It is not permissible to go out of the mosque after Adhān but when it is imperative to do so, one is permitted (Nawawī).

He who observed the 'Ishā' prayer in congregation, it was as if he prayed up to the mid-night, and he who prayed the morning prayer in congregation, it was as if he prayed the whole night.[877]

(1380) This ḥadīth has been narrated by the chain of transmitters by Abū Sahl 'Uthmān b. Ḥakīm.

(1381) Jundab b. 'Abdullah reported Allah's Messenger (may peace be upon him) as saying : He who prayed the morning prayer (in congregation) he is in fact under the protection of Allah. And it can never happen that Allah should demand anything from you in connection with the protection (that He guarantees) and one should not get it. He would then throw him in the fire of Hell

(1382) Anas b. Sīrīn reported : I heard Jundab b. Qasrī saying that the Messenger of Allah (may peace be upon him) said : He who observed the morning prayer (in congre-gation), he is in fact under the protection of Allah and it never happens that Allah should make a demand in connection with the protection (that He guarantees and should not get it) for when he asks for anything in relation to His protection, he definitely secures it. He then throws him flatly in the Hell-fire.[878]

(1383) This ḥadīth has been narrated by Jundab b. Sufyān from the Apostle of Allah (may peace be upon him) with the same chain of transmitters, but this has not been mentioned : "He would throw him in fire."

Chapter CCXXXVIII

PERMISSION TO REMAIN AWAY FROM THE CONGREGATIONAL PRAYER FOR ANY VALID REASON

(1384) Maḥmūd b. al-Rabī' reported that 'Itbān b. Mālik, who was one of the Companions of the Apostle of Allah (may peace be upon him) and who participated in the (Battle of) Badr[879] and was among the Anṣār (of Medina), told that he came to the

877. The man who observes the night prayer in congregation spends a good deal of his time at night and deprives himself of the rest for the love of God ; he is, therefore, given reward of praying up till midnight. But the man who gets out of the bed early in the morning and gives up the sweetness of the morning sleep for the sake of Allah is like one who spends the whole night in God-consciousness waiting for the dawn, when he can stand before his Lord and beg His Mercy ; he is, therefore, given the reward of praying for the whole night. Getting up early in the morning is more burdensome than awaking late in the night. It is easy for a man to remain awake for some time, but it is difficult for him to get up from sleep in the morning Only a very keen sense of responsibility can exhort him to do so.

878. Apparently there seems to be some gap between the first portion and the last one. But this is not the case. There is a meaningful relation between the two. What the Prophet means to say is that the man who observes morning prayer in congregation is guaranteed protection by Allah Now if any other person annoys him or usurps his right or tortures him, he in fact tries to wrong that person who is under the protection of Allah. Allah would, therefore, punish this tyrant.

879. Those who joined the Battle of Badr are held in high esteem in Islam, because they were the first to offer their lives and properties for the sake of Divine faith. They came forward to fight on the side of the Messenger of Allah (may peace be upon him) when the Muslims were weak and lacked material resources. Only a deep and intense devotion to Islam and the Holy Prophet could exhort them to such a tremendous sacrifice.

Messenger of Allah (may peace be upon him) and said : Messenger of Allah, I have lost my eyesight and I lead my people in prayer. When there is a downpour there is then a current (of water) in the valley that stands between me and them and I find it impossible to go to their mosque and lead them in prayer.[880] Messenger of Allah, I earnestly beg of you that you should come and observe prayer at a place of worship (in my house) so that I should then use it as a place of worship [881] The Messenger of Allah (may peace be upon him) said : Well, if God so wills, I would soon do so.[882] 'Itbān said : On the following day, when the day dawned, the Messenger of Allah (may peace be upon him) came along with Abū Bakr al-Ṣiddīq, and the Messenger of Allah (may peace be upon him) asked permission (to get into the house). I gave him the permission, and he did not sit after entering the house, when he said : At what place in your house you desire me to say prayer? I ('Itbān b. Mālik) said : I pointed to a corner in the house. The Messenger of Allah (may peace be upon him) stood (at that place for prayer) and pronounced *Allah-o-Akbar* (Allah is the Greatest) (as an expression for the commencement of prayer). We too stood behind him, and he said two rak'ahs and then pronounced salutation (marking the end of the prayer). We detained him (the Holy Prophet) for the meat curry we had prepared for him. The people of the neighbouring houses came and thus there was a good gathering in (our house). One of them said : Where is Mālik b. Dukhshun? Upon this one of them remarked : He is a hypocrite ; he does not love Allah and His Messenger. Thereupon the Messenger of Allah (may peace be upon him) said : Do not say so about him. Don't you see that he utters *Lā ilāha Ill-Allah* (There is no god but Allah) and seeks the pleasure of Allah through it.[883] They said : Allah and His Messenger know best. One (among the audience) said : We see his inclination and well-wishing for hypocrites only.[884] Upon this the Messenger of Allah (may peace be upon him) again said : Verily Allah has forbidden the Fire for one who says : There is no god but Allah, thereby seeking Allah's pleasure. Ibn Shihāb said : I asked Ḥusain b. Muḥammad al-Anṣārī (he was one of the leaders of Banū Sālim) about the ḥadīth transmitted by Maḥmūd b. Rabī' and he testified it.[885]

(1385) 'Itbān b. Mālik reported : I came to the Messenger of Allah (may peace be upon him), and the rest of the ḥadīth is the same as narrated (above) except this that

880. This shows that one is permitted to stay away from congregational prayer if there is any sound reason or justification for it.

881. The presence of the pious people at places and performance of the virtuous deeds there can sanctify them and one is allowed to secure such blessings in Islam.

882. The Holy Prophet had a very great regard for the feelings of his Companions, especially his weak Companions, and he readily responded to their invitations and paid visits to their houses.

883. The Messenger of Allah did not like backbiting and so he silenced them by saying that Mālik b. Dukhshun was a Muslim and would be saved from the Hell-fire. The words : "Seek the pleasure of Allah through Kalima" show that the Holy Prophet had been divinely informed of the sincerity of this man.

884. He was a true Muslim as the Holy Prophet made an attestation. His mixing with the hypocrites might be due to some dire necessity and he was, therefore, to be excused for that as we find in case of Ḥātib b. Abū Balta'a, who was one of the participants of Badr (*Fatḥ al-Mulhim* Vol. II, p. 225).

885. Imām Nawawī makes a deduction on the basis of this ḥadīth that it is permissible to pray in congregation even in case of Nafl prayers.

a man said: Where is Mālik b. Dukhshun or Dukhaishin, and also made this addition that Maḥmūd said: I narrated this very ḥadīth to many people and among them was Abū Ayyūb al-Anṣārī who said: I cannot think that the Messenger of Allah (may peace be upon him) could have said so as you say.[886] He (the narrator) said: I took an oath that if I ever go to 'Itbān, I would ask him about it. So I went to him and found him to be a very aged man, having lost his eyesight, but he was the Imām of the people. I sat by his side and asked about this ḥadīth and he narrated it in the same way as he had narrated it for the first time. Then so many other obligatory acts and commands were revealed which we see having been completed[887] So he who wants that he should not be deceived would not be deceived.[888]

(1386) Maḥmūd b. Rabī' reported: I well remember the disgorge of the Messenger of Allah (may peace be upon him) that he did (with water) from a bucket of our house.[889] Maḥmūd said: 'Itbān b. Mālik narrated it to me that he had said: Messenger of Allah, I have lost my eyesight, and the rest of the ḥadīth is the same up to these words: "He led us in two rak'ahs of prayer and we detained the Messenger of Allah (may peace be upon him) for serving him the pudding[890] that we had prepared for him," and no mention has been made of what follows next from the addition[891] made by Yūnus and Ma'mar.

Chapter CCXXXIX

PERMISSIBILITY OF OBSERVING NAFL (SUPEREROGATORY) PRAYER IN CONGREGATION AND THAT TOO ON THE MAT OR THE COVERING CLOTH OR ANY OTHER THING WHICH IS FREE FROM FILTH AND RUBBISH

(1387) Anas b. Mālik reported that his grandmother, Mulaika, invited the Messenger of Allah (may peace be upon him) to a dinner which she had prepared.[892] He (the Holy Prophet) ate out of that and then said: Stand up so that I should observe prayer (in

886. Ḥaḍrat Ayyūb al-Anṣārī could not think how a mere profession of Kalima could safeguard a person from the Hell-fire. He had in his mind so many verses of the Qur'ān and aḥādīth of the Holy Prophet in which it has been made clear that Īmān is to be accompanied by good deeds. It had perhaps slipped out of his mind that this safeguard against fire had been guaranteed against one's everlasting stay in Fire and it was not a guarantee for a temporary chastisement which would be given to the evil-doers for the purgation of their souls (*Fatḥ al-Mulhim*, Vol. II, p. 225).

887. This shows that this event is related to the earlier period of Islam, when so many commands had not been revealed.

888. The path of Islam is now bright and clear and one can safely tread over it if one so desires. Nothing can lead one astray. Moreover, Allah would through Muḥammad vouchsafe many an act of Do's and Dont's and strict adherence to them would draw a line of distinction between a hypocrite and a true believer.

889. That the Holy Prophet threw water at his face shows how tenderly and affectionately he treated the children. This affection must be shown to the children by light acts of humour.

890. Jashīsh is prepared by cooking the flour along with meat or dates.

891. It does not mean that Yūnus and Ma'mar had made addition from their own mind. What they narrated was from the Messenger of Allah (may peace be upon him). But so far as the above context of the ḥadīth is concerned, it does not contain their words.

892. A woman can also invite a pious man to dinner.

order to bless) you.[893] Anas b. Mālik said: I stood up on a mat (belonging to us) which had turned dark on account of its long use. I sprinkled water over it (in order to soften it), and the Messenger of Allah (may peace be upon him) stood upon it, and I and an orphan [894] formed a row behind him (the Holy Prophet) and the old woman was behind us, and the Messenger of Allah (may peace be upon him) led us in two rak'ahs of prayer and then went back.

(1388) Anas b. Mālik reported that the Messenger of Allah (may peace be upon him) was the best among people in character. On occasions, the time of prayer would come while he was in our house. He would then order to spread the mat lying under him. That was dusted and then water was sprinkled over it The Messenger of Allah (may peace be upon him) then led the prayer and we stood behind him, and that mat was made of the leaves of date-palm.

(1389) Thābit reported on the authority of Anas: The Apostle of Allah (may peace be upon him) came to us and there was none in our house but I, my mother and my aunt Umm Ḥarām. He (the Holy Prophet) said: Stand up so that I may lead you in prayer (and there was no time for prescribed prayer). He led us in prayer. A person said to Thābit: Where stood Anas with him (the Holy Prophet)? He replied: He was on his right side. He then blessed us, the members of the household with every good of this world and of the Hereafter. My mother said: Messenger of Allah (and then, pointing towards Anas, said) here is your little servant, invoke the blessing of Allah upon him too. He then blessed me with [895] every good, and he concluded his blessings for me (with these words): Allah! increase his wealth, and his children and make (them the source of) blessing for him.

(1390) 'Abdullah b. al-Mukhtār heard Mūsā b. Anas narrating on the authority of Anas b. Mālik that the Messenger of Allah (may peace be upon him) led him, his mother or his aunt in prayer. He made me stand on his right side and made the woman stand behind us.

(1391) This ḥadīth has also been transmitted by Shu'ba with this chain of transmitters.

(1392) Maimūna, the wife of the Apostle of Allah (may peace be upon him), reported: The Messenger of Allah (may peace be upon him) said prayer while I was by

893. The Holy Prophet wanted to bless that house and family by saying prayer there. But, apart from it, he would go often to the houses of the people and pray there so that the inmates of the house should see how the Holy Prophet observed prayer. These feasts had a religious purpose behind them and the Holy Prophet got opportunities to teach and instruct the womenfolk as they could not actively participate in public meetings.

894. His name was Ḍamīr the grandfather of Ḥusain b. 'Abdullah b. Ḍamīr (*Fatḥ al-Mulhim*, Vol. II, p. 226).

895. Anas b. Mālik was one of the most dedicated servants of the Holy Prophet, when the Prophet came to Medina The mother of Anas, Umm Sulaim, presented him to the Messenger of Allah and from this time onward up to the Prophet's death he remained with him as a devoted companion. The Prophet was very kind to him and it was Anas who said that during his long stay in the Prophet's house, the Messenger of Allah never, not even once, used any harsh word for him. He died in 91 H. attaining the age of more than one hundred years.

his side, and at times when he prostrated his cloth touched me,[896] and he prayed on a small mat.

(1393) Abū Sa'īd al Khudrī reported that he went to the Messenger of Allah (may peace be upon him) and found him observing prayer on a mat and prostrating on that.

Chapter CCXL

MERIT OF PRAYING IN CONGREGATION AND WAITING FOR PRAYER

(1394) Abū Huraira reported Allah's Messenger (may peace be upon him) as saying: A man's prayer in congregation is more valuable than twenty degrees and some above them as compared with his prayer in his house and his market, for when he performs ablution doing it well, then goes out to the mosque, and he is impelled (to do so) only by (the love of congregational) prayer, he has no other objective before him but prayer. He does not take a step without being raised a degree for it and having a sin remitted for it, till he enters the mosque, and when he is busy in prayer after having entered the mosque, the angels continue to invoke blessing on him as long as he is in his place of worship, saying: O Allah, show him mercy, and pardon him! Accept his repentance (and the angels continue this supplication for him) so long as he does not do any harm in it, or as long as his ablution is not broken.[897]

(1395) A ḥadīth having the same meaning (as mentioned above) has been transmitted by A'mash.

(1396) Abū Huraira reported Allah's Messenger (may peace be upon him) as saying: The angels invoke blessings on everyone among you so long as he is in a place of worship with these words: O Allah! pardon him, O Allah, have mercy upon him, (and they continue to do so) as long as the ablution (of the worshipper) is not broken, and one among you is in prayer and so long as he is detained for the prayer.[898]

(1397) Abū Huraira reported Allah's Messenger (may peace be upon him) as saying: The servant is constantly in prayer so long as he is in a place of worship waiting for the prayer (to be observed in congregation), and the angels invoke (blessings upon him in these words): O Allah! pardon him, O Allah! show mercy to him, (and they continue to do so) till he returns (from the mosque having completed the prayer) or his ablution

896. This part is very significant so far as the status of woman is concerned. In so many other religions of the world woman is thought to be evil and the spirit of Satan. Her very presence is supposed to pollute the sanctity of an occasion, and her participation especially in prayers is thus totally disallowed. Islam categorically rejects all such misconceptions about woman, and asserts that she is as respectable an individual as man. There is nothing profane about her. Her presence in the religious ceremonies and prayers in no way mars the sanctity of these occasions. Even touching of cloth does not in the least harm the solemnity of religious devotion.

897. Imām Bukhārī, on the basis of this ḥadīth, draws the conclusion that the man who is without ablution is not one who is defiled; he is, therefore, permitted to enter the mosque (*Fatḥ al-Bāri*, Vol. II, p. 267).

898 What it means is that the angels begin invoking blessings upon him the time the worshipper enters the mosque after performing ablution and they continue to do so as long as he waits for the congregational prayer, then observes it.

breaks. I said: How is the ablution broken? He said: By breaking of the wind noiselessly or with noise.

(1398) Abū Huraira reported the Messenger of Allah (may peace be upon him) as saying: Everyone among you is constantly in prayer so long as the prayer detains him (for this noble objective) and nothing prevents him to return to his family but the prayer.

(1399) Abū Huraira reported: The Messenger of Allah (may peace be upon him) said: Anyone amongst you who sat in a place of worship waiting for the prayer is in prayer and his ablution is not broken, the angels invoke blessing upon him (in these words): O Allah! pardon him, O Allah! have mercy upon him.

(1400) A ḥadīth like this has been narrated by Hammām b. Munabbih on the authority of Abū Huraira.

Chapter CCXLI

EXCELLENCE OF TAKING MANY STEPS FOR REACHING THE MOSQUE

(1401) Abū Mūsā reported Allah's Messenger (may peace be upon him) as saying: The most eminent among human beings (as a recipient of) reward (is one) who lives farthest away, and who has to walk the farthest distance, and he who waits for the prayer to observe it along with the Imām, his reward is greater than one who prays (alone) and then goes to sleep. In the narration of Abū Kuraib (the words are): "(He waits) till he prays along with the Imām in congregation." 899

(1402) Ubayy b. Ka'b reported: There was a man, and I do not know of any other man, whose house was farther than his from the mosque and he never missed the prayer (in congregation). It was said to him or I said to him: If you were to buy a donkey you could ride upon it in the dark nights and in the burning sand. He said: I do not like my house to be situated by the side of the mosque, for I (eagerly) desire that my steps towards the mosque, and back from it, should be recorded when I return to my family. Upon this the Messenger of Allah (may peace be upon him) said: Allah has gathered all (rewards) for you.

(1403) This ḥadīth has been transmitted by Taimī with the same chain of transmitters.

(1404) Ubayy b. Ka'b reported: There was a person among the Anṣār whose house was situated at the farthest end of Medina, but he never missed any prayer along with the Messenger of Allah (may peace be upon him). We felt pity for him and said to him: O, so and so, had you bought a donkey it would have saved you from the burn-

899. Imām Quṭb-ud-Dīn observes: The man who waits for the Imām deserves better reward than one who prays alone earlier than the Imām. Moreover, the man who waits for a bigger congregation and seeks to observe prayer behind an Imām who is more competent for this job, would get more reward as compared with one who hurriedly absolves himself of this responsibility. It shows a lack of devotion on his part (*Mazhar-i-Ḥaqq*, Vol. I, p. 248).

The man who covers a greater distance for coming to the mosque is entitled to a greater reward, because he puts in more labour and spends more time in the path of Allah and thus shows more devotion to Allah.

ing sand and would have saved you from the reptiles of the earth. He said: Listen! by Allah, I do not like my house to be situated by the side of Muḥammad (may peace be upon him). I took (these words of his)[900] ill and came to the Apostle of Allah (may peace be upon him) and informed him about (these words). He (the Holy Prophet) called him and he said exactly like that (which he had mentioned to Ubbay b. Ka'b), but made a mention of this (also) that he wanted a reward for his steps. Upon this the Apostle of Allah (may peace be upon him) said: In fact for you is the reward which you expect.

(1405) A ḥadīth like this has been transmitted by 'Āṣim with the same chain of transmitters.

(1406) Jābir b. 'Abdullah narrated: Our houses were situated far away from the mosque; we, therefore, decided to sell our houses so that we may be able to come near the mosque. The Messenger of Allah (may peace be upon him) forbade us (to do so) and said: There is for every step (towards the mosque) a degree (of reward) for you.

(1407) Jābir b. 'Abdullah reported: There were some plots vacant around the mosque. Banū Salama decided to shift (to this land) and come near the mosque. This (news) reached the Messenger of Allah (may peace be upon him) and he said to them (Banū Salama): I have received (information) that you intend to shift near the mosque. They said: Yes, Messenger of Allah, we have taken this decision. Upon this he (the Holy Prophet) said: O Banū Salama, live in your houses, for your steps are recorded; live in your houses, for your steps are recorded.

(1408) Jābir b. 'Abdullah reported that Banū Salama decided to shift near the mosque (as there were) some plots vacant. This (news) reached the Apostle of Allah (may peace be upon him), whereupon he said: O people of the Salama tribe, you better stay in your houses (where you are living), for your footsteps are recorded. They said: We could not be more delighted even by shifting (near the mosque) as we were delighted (on hearing these words from the Messenger of Allah [may peace be upon him]).

(1409) Abū Huraira reported: The Messenger of Allah (may peace be upon him) said: He who purified himself in his house, and then he walked to one of the hou es of Allah for the sake of performing a Farḍ (obligatory act) out of the Farā'iḍ (obligatory acts) of Allah, both his steps (would be significant) as one of them would obliterate his sin and the second one would raise his status.

(1410) In the ḥadīth narrated on the authority of Abū Huraira the Messenger of

900 This shows the love of the Prophet's Companions for the Holy Prophet. Such a stand could be least expected from a Muslim; it was, therefore, a matter of great shock for Ubayy b. Ka'b and he went to the Holy Prophet and told him that there was a man who apparently seemed to remain at a distance from him which was, according to him, an indication of the lack of love for the Holy Prophet Such an indifferent attitude towards the Messenger of Allah was then a sign of great moral depravity and the Muslim society could not tolerate it. Ka'b at once went to the Holy Prophet and apprised him of the situation, and the Messenger of Allah followed the same course which Islam has shown He neither felt angry nor passed any verdict against him, but called him and asked him to clarify the point, and was not only perfectly satisfied with the explanation that he offered, but gave him glad tidings that he would get reward according to his expectation. This incident also shows that sometimes more than one interpretation can be put upon the same words and we should not hasten to derive wrong meanings from them.

Allah (may peace be upon him) is reported to have said, while in the ḥadīth narrated by Bıkr (the words are like this): He heard the Messenger of Allah (may peace be upon him) as saying: Just see, can anything of his filthiness remain (on the body of) any one of you if there were a river at his door in which he washed himself five times daily? They said: Nothing of his filthiness will remain (on his body). He said: That is like the five prayers by which Allah obliterates sins.[901]

(1411) Jābir son of 'Abdullah reported that the Messenger of Allah (may peace be upon him) said: The similitude of five prayers is like an overflowing river passing by the gate of one of you in which he washes five times daıly. Ḥasan said: No filthiness can remain on him.

(1412) 'Aṭā' b Yasār[902] reported, on the authority of Abū Huraira, the Apostle of Allah (may peace be upon him) as saying: He who went towards the mosque in the morning or evening, Allah would arrange a feast for him morning or evening in the Paradise.

Chapter CCXLII

EXCELLENCE OF SITTING AT THE PLACE OF WORSHIP AFTER THE DAWN PRAYER AND EXCELLENCE OF THE MOSQUE

(1413) Simāk b. Ḥarb[903] reported: I said to Jābir b. Samura: Did you sit in the company of the Messenger of Allah (may peace be upon him)? He said: Yes, very often. He (the Holy Prophet) used to sit at the place where he observed morning or dawn prayer till the sun rose or when it had risen; he would stand, and they (his Companions) would talk about matters (pertaining to the days) of ignorance, and they would laugh (on these matters) while (the Holy Prophet) only smiled.[904]

(1414) Simāk narrated on the authority if Jābir b Sımura that when the Apostle

901. This is a very appropriate simile Just as water removes filth and dirt from the body and makes it clean, in the same way prayer washes out all types of moral impurities from the heart of man and makes him a pious and virtuous human being. The scholars of Ḥadīth are of the view that prayer obliterates all types of minor sins; the major sins, e.g. murder, committing of adultery, etc, cannot be removed simply by prayer. The man who commits such heinous crimes would be punished by Allah for some time (*Fatḥ al-Mulhim*, Vol. II, p. 229).

902. He was the freed slave of Ḥadrat Maimūna, the wife of the Holy Prophet. His kunyah is Abū Muḥammad. He was counted as one of the eminent *tābi is* (successors) of Medina. He has transmitted so many traditions on the authority of Ibn 'Abbās.

903. Simāk b. Ḥarb. His kunyah is Abū Mughīra. He narrates on the authority of Jābir b. Samura, and Nu'mān b. Bashīr and Shu'ba and Ziyāda transmit from him. About two hundred aḥādīth have been transmitted through him. He was considered to be a very reliable and authentic transmitter of Ḥadīth but his memory afterwards became weak due to old age. That is why he is considered to be a weak transmitter. He died in 123 H.

904 It often happened that the Companions of the Holy Prophet recalled to their minds the foolish rites and rituals which they observed in the name of religion before embracing Islam. Now when they had been brought to light from darkness they discerned striking contrast between the two different phases of their life. Some of their religious practices and social customs were so ridiculous and fantastic and from the moral point of view so depraving that their very idea would make them laugh. The Holy Prophet was happy to see that his Companions (Allah be pleased with them) had become fully conscious of the immeasurably vast distance that yawns between Jahilīyya and Is'am and they had realised the worth of that great wealth which they had received in the form of Islam. The Holy Prophet did not have a boistrous laugh; he only smiled.

of Allah (may peace be upon him) observed the dawn prayer, he sat at the place of worship till the sun had risen enough.

(1415) This ḥadīth has been narrated by Simāk with the same chain of transmitters, but no mention has been made of "enough".

(1416) Abū Huraira reported that the Messenger of Allah (may peace be upon him) said: The parts of land dearest to Allah are its mosques, and the parts most hateful to Allah are markets [905]

Chapter CCXLIII

WHO DESERVES MOST TO ACT AS IMĀM

(1417) Abū Sa'īd al-Khudrī reported Allah's Messenger (may peace be upon him) as saying: When there are three persons, one of them should lead them. The one among them most worthy to act as Imām is one who is best versed in the Qur'ān.[906]

(1418) A ḥadīth like this has been narrated by Qatāda with the same chain of transmitters.

(1419) This ḥadīth has been narrated by Abū Sa'īd al-Khudrī by another chain of transmitters.

(1420) Abū Mas'ūd al-Anṣārī reported Allah's Messenger (may peace be upon him) as saying: The one who is most versed in Allah's Book should act as Imām for the people, but if they are equally versed in reciting it, then the one who has most knowledge regarding Sunnah; if they are equal regarding the Sunnah, then the earliest one to emigrate; if they emigrated at the same time, then the earliest one to embrace Islam.[907] No man must lead another in prayer where (the latter) has authority,[908] or sit in his

905. Mosques are the sacred places where such noble qualities as religious piety, devotion to Allah and God-consciousness are inculcated in man, whereas the bazaars are the places where the evil in man is prompted. He is inclined to selfishness and is impelled to deceive and take undue advantage of the ignorance of others. Moreover, in bazaars the activities of the people are centred around material interests and gains.

906. The original word (اقرأهم) means one who is the greatest reciter (of the Qur'ān) among them. But here recitation does not mean mere reading; it implies one who is well versed in the Qur'ān, who has a deep insight into it, who has the greatest devotion to it and who can recite it well.

907 This ḥadīth sums up the qualities of a Muslim leader. An Imām who has to lead the prayer should be the most versed in the Qur'ān and the Sunnah among all his followers, and should be more willing to undergo hardship for the sake of Islam. Then there is a distinction of his earlier conversion to Islam which implies that his mind is more receptive to good and virtue as compared with those who delayed in accepting the Divine Faith. Moreover, the man who spends longer time in the fold of Islam gets more opportunities of training in the practices of this religion and thus he is more competent to lead people in prayer and in other matters concerning life. The whole life of a Muslim is a kind of prayer, as he has been commanded to show submission to the Lord in all phases of his life. This ḥadīth, though it enumerates the qualities of an Imām in prayer, clearly points out the attributes of the leader of the Muslim nation.

908. Islam teaches sense of responsibility, humility and discipline. If a particular person is entrusted with the responsibility of leading the people in prayer, it means that the people of that locality have after due consideration delegated him the authority of leading the prayer and if another person without the willing consent of worshippers leads the prayer, this may create ill-feeling among them and may disturb the peaceful atmosphere of the mosque. That is why the Messenger of Allah (may peace be upon him) has forbidden persons to lead the people in prayer without the permission of the one who is already acting as an Imām there.

place of honour[909] in his house, without his permission. Ashajj in his narration used the word "age" in place of "Islam".

(1421) A ḥadīth like this has been transmitted by A'mash by the same chain of transmitters.

(1422) Abū Mas'ūd al-Anṣārī reported: The Messenger of Allah (may peace be upon him) said to us: The one who is most versed in Allah's Book and is distinguished among them in recitation should act as Imām for the people, and if they are equally versed in reciting it, then the one who has most knowledge regarding Sunnah; if they are equal regarding the Sunnah, then the earliest one to emigrate; if they emigrated at the same time, then the oldest one in age.[910] No man must lead another in prayer in latter's house or where (the latter) has authority, or sit in his place of honour in his house, except that he gives you permission or with his permission.

(1423) Mālik b. Ḥuwairith reported: We came to the Messenger of Allah (may peace be upon him) and we were all young men of nearly equal age. We stayed with him (the Holy Prophet) for twenty nights,[911] and as the Messenger of Allah (may peace be upon him) was extremely kind and tender of heart, he, therefore, thought[912] that we were eager (to see) our family (we felt home-sickness). So he asked us about the members of the family that we had left behind and when we informed him, he said: Go back to your family, stay with them, and teach them (beliefs and practices of Islam) and exhort them to good,[913] and when the time for prayer comes, one amongst you should announce Adhān, and then the oldest among you should lead the prayer.

(1424) This ḥadīth has been transmitted by Ayyūb with the same chain of transmitters.

(1425) Mālik b. Ḥuwairith Abū Sulaimān reported: I came to the Messenger of Allah (may peace be upon him) along with other persons and we were young men of nearly equal age, and the rest of the ḥadīth was transmitted like the ḥadīth narrated before.

(1426) Mālik b. Ḥuwairith reported: I came to the Apostle of Allah (may peace be upon him) along with a companion of mine, and when we intended to return from him, he said: When there is time for prayer, announce prayer, pronounce Iqāma, and the oldest amongst you should lead the prayer.

(1427) This ḥadīth has been transmitted with the same chain of transmitters, but al-Ḥadhā' made this addition: "They both were equal in recitation."

909. No man should occupy the place in the house of another person which is reserved for him, e.g. his bed, his special carpet, except with his permission.

910. Islam gives importance to age. Other things being equal, a person with more advanced age commands greater respect in Muslim society as compared with a younger person. The aged man is more rich in experience, more balanced in emotion, more catholic in outlook and has wider vision of life; thus he is looked upon with greater honour among people

911. They stayed there for twenty nights and learnt from the Holy Prophet the beliefs and practices of religion. It is inferred from this that we should go to people who are far ahead of us in learning and piety and stay with them to learn the teachings of Islam.

912. That shows what a great regard the Prophet had for the feelings of others He was fully aware of the various problems of human beings and did not subject them to unnecessary hardships and labour. He always looked to their needs.

913. مروهم means to command them to do good and avoid things forbidden in Islam, and then give wide publicity to permissible and forbidden acts.

Chapter CCXLIV

THE EXCELLENCE OF QUNŪT 914 IN ALL THE PRAYERS WHEN ANY CALAMITY BEFALLS THE MUSLIMS

(1428) Abū Salama son of 'Abd al-Raḥmān b. 'Auf heard Abū Huraira say: (When) Allah's Messenger (may peace be upon him) (wished to invoke curse or blessing on someone, he would do so at the end) of the recitation in the dawn prayer, when he had pronounced *Allah-o-Akbar* (for bending) and then lifted his head (saying): "Allah listened to him who praised Him; our Lord! to Thee is all praise"; he would then stand up and say: "Rescue al-Walīd b. Walīd, 915 Salama 916 b. Hishām, and 'Ayyāsh b. Abū Rabī'a,917 and the helpless among the Muslims. O Allah! trample severely Muḍar 918 and cause them a famine (which broke out at the time) of Joseph. O Allah! curse Liḥyān, 919 Ri'l, Dhakwān, 'Uṣayya, 920 for they disobeyed Allah and

914. The word *Qunūt* means being obedient, being humble, or the act of standing, but in the context of prayer it implies a special supplication which is made either in Witr or in other prayers especially when the Muslims are overtaken by a calamity. This supplication is of three types:

(*a*) *Qunūt Nāzila.* This supplication is made at the time of a calamity upon the Muslims. There is no prescribed time for it and it can be offered in any prayer though it is preferably offered in Jahrī prayers (morning, evening and night).

(*b*) *Qunūt Witr.* According to the Ḥanafites, this supplication is made in the third rak'ah of Witr of the 'Ishā' prayer and the Imām and his followers recite it silently.

(*c*) *Qunūt Fajr.* Imām Shāfi'ī is of the opinion that it is essential to offer this supplication in the dawn prayer throughout the year. The Ḥanafites do not subscribe to this view. They deem it permissible only in case of a calamity.

Qunūt Nāzila is offered after the rukū' whereas Qunūt Witr is offered before it. The Shāfi'ites differ with it and offer it after the rukū'. The opinion of the Ḥanafites seems to be more weighty in this respect.

915. Walīd b. Walīd was the brother of Khālid b. Walīd. He fought in the Battle of Badr against the Muslims and was caught as a prisoner. He, however, secured freedom after paying ransom and then went back to Mecca and embraced Islam He was imprisoned by the Meccans and put to unspeakable tortures.

916. Salama b. Hishām was the brother of Abū Jahl and was one of the earliest converts to Islam. He was subjected to horrifying atrocities at the hands of the pagans of Mecca.

917. 'Ayyāsh b. Rabī'a was the step brother of Abū Jahl and was among the earliest converts to Islam. He first migrated to Abyssinia and later to Medina. Abū Jahl succeeded in taking him back to Mecca by narrating false stories of the miserable plight of his mother and then put him under arrest. He managed to escape to Medina and died as a martyr in the Battle of Tabūk.

918. That is the name of a tribe which was a staunch enemy of Islam and which perpetrated atrocities upon the Muslims.

919. That was the notorious tribe which put to death six reciters of the Holy Qur'ān at Rajī' in 4 H. whom the Holy Prophet had sent to instruct them in Islam at their invitation. Banū Liḥyān came there and arrested them. The leader of the Muslim delegation 'Āṣim b. Thābit fought against them and fell as a martyr. Khubaib and Zaid were imprisoned and sold to the Meccans who later put them to death with the most painful tortures.

920. These are the tribes who killed seventy eminent reciters of the Holy Qur'ān at Bi'r Ma'ūna in 4 H. They went to the Holy Prophet and requested him to send some preachers to preach them Islam and give them practical instructions in the teachings of the Divine Faith. But when these preachers reached there, they attacked and killed them.

The Holy Prophet was deeply sad at the treacheries of these tribes and the great loss of the Muslim scholars and the curse inevitably escaped his lips. It was but natural; such heinous acts and horrifying atrocities were sufficient to ruffle his feelings.

His Messenger." (The narrator then adds): Then news reached us that he abandoned (this) when this verse was revealed: "Thou hast no concern in the matter whether He turns to them (mercifully) or chastises them; surely they are wrongdoers" (iii. 127). 921

(1429) This ḥadīth has been transmitted on the authority of Abū Huraira by another chain of transmitters up to the words: "And cause them a famine like that (which broke out at the time) of Joseph," but the subsequent portion was not mentioned.

(1430) Abū Salama reported it on the authority of Abū Huraira that the Apostle of Allah (may peace be upon him) recited Qunūt after rukū' in prayer for one month at the time of reciting (these words): "Allah listened to him who praised Him," and he said in Qunūt: "O Allah! rescue al-Walīd b. al-Walīd; O Allah! rescue Salama b. Hishām; O Allah! rescue 'Ayyāsh b. Abū Rabī'a; O Allah! rescue the helpless amongst the Muslims; O Allah! trample Muḍar severely; O Allah! cause them a famine like that (which was caused at the time) of Joseph." Abū Huraira (further) said: I saw that the Messenger of Allah (may peace be upon him) afterwards abandoned this supplication. I, therefore, said: I see the Messenger of Allah (may peace be upon him) abandoning this blessing upon them. It was said to him (Abū Huraira): Don't you see that (those for whom was blessing invoked by the Holy Prophet) have come (i.e. they have been rescued)?

(1431) Abū Salama narrated that Abū Huraira told him that when the Messenger of Allah (may peace be upon him) pronounced: "Allah listened to him who praised Him," and before prostration, he would recite this in the 'Ishā' prayer: O Allah! rescue 'Ayyāsh b. Abū Rabī'a, and the rest of the ḥadīth is the same as narrated by Auzā'ī to the words: "Like the famine (at the time) of Joseph," but he made no mention of that which follows afterwards.

(1432) Abū Salama b. 'Abd al-Raḥmān is reported to have said that he had heard Abū Huraira saying: I would say prayer along with you which is near to the prayer of the Messenger of Allah (may peace be upon him), and Abū Huraira recited Qunūt in the noon and in the 'Ishā' and in the morning prayer, and invoked blessing (of Allah) upon Muslims and curse upon the unbelievers.

(1433) Anas b. Mālik reported that the Messenger of Allah (may peace be upon him) invoked curse in the morning (prayer) for thirty days upon those who killed the Companions (of the Holy Prophet) at Bi'r Ma'ūna. He cursed (the tribes) of Ri'l, Dhakwān, Liḥyān, and 'Uṣayya, who had disobeyed Allah and His Messenger (may peace be upon him). Anas said: Allah the Exalted and Great, revealed (a verse)

921. This verse does not imply that the invoking of curse upon the enemy has been forbidden altogether. The Holy Prophet was greatly shocked at the heart-rendering news of how his Companions were mercilessly treated and killed by the enemies; he was, therefore, overwhelmed by feelings of resentment against the tyrants and invoked curse upon them It is at this juncture that Allah comforted and consoled him by saying that it is Allah Who knows His plan to bring sinners to repentance and to teach them righteousness or to punish them for their misdeeds, "so O Prophet! you should not be swayed by emotions; as a Mercy to the worlds you should pray for their righteousness and welfare." It has been said keeping in view the eminently high status of the Holy Prophet, otherwise invoking of curse is not completely forbidden in Islam for it is the natural outburst of a victim of tyranny and oppression A ḥadīth in Abū Dāwūd indicates that what is forbidden by this verse is naming of the enemy while invoking curse for no one knows that he may embrace Islam at a later stage (*Maẓhar-i-Ḥaqq*, Vol. I, p. 442).

regarding those who were killed at Bi'r Ma'ūna, and we recited it, till it was abrogated later on (and the verse was like this): "Convey it to our people the tidings that we have met our Lord, and He was pleased with us and we were pleased with Him."[922]

(1434) Muḥammad reported: I asked Anas whether the Messenger of Allah (may peace be upon him) observed Qunūt in the dawn prayer. He said: Yes, (he did so) after the rukū' for a short while.

(1435) Anas b. Mālik reported: The Messenger of Allah (may peace be upon him) observed Qunūt for a month in the dawn prayer after rukū', and invoked curse upon Ri'l, Dhakwān, and said that 'Uṣayya had disobeyed Allah and His Apostle (may peace be upon him).

(1436) Anas b. Mālik reported that the Messenger of Allah (may peace be upon him) observed Qunūt for a month in the dawn prayer after rukū' and invoked curse upon Banū 'Uṣayya.

(1437) 'Āṣim reported: I asked Anas whether Qunūt was observed (by the Holy Prophet) before rukū' or after rukū'. He replied: Before Rukū'. I said: People conceive that the Messenger of Allah (may peace be upon him) observed Qunūt after the rukū'. He said: The Messenger of Allah (may peace be upon him) observed Qunūt (after the rukū' as the people conceive it) for a month invoking curse upon those persons who had killed men among his Companions who were called the reciters[923] (of the Qur'ān).

(1438) 'Āṣim reported: I heard Anas saying: Never did I see the Messenger of Allah (may peace be upon him) so much grieved (at the loss of a) small army as I saw him grieved at those seventy men who were called "reciters" (and were killed) at Bi'r Ma'ūna; and he invoked curse for full one month upon their murderers.

(1439) This ḥadīth has been narrated by Anas with another chain of transmitters and with minor additions.

(1440) Anas b. Mālik reported that the Messenger of Allah (may peace be upon him) observed Qunūt for one month invoking curse upon Ri'l, Dhakwān, 'Uṣayya, those who disobeyed Allah and His Messenger (may peace be upon him).

(1441) A ḥadīth like this has been transmitted by Anas from the Apostle of Allah (may peace be upon him).

(1442) Anas reported that the Messenger of Allah (may peace be upon him) observed Qunūt for one month invoking curse upon some tribes of Arabia (those who were responsible for the murders in Bi'r Ma'ūna and Rajī'), but then abandoned it.

(1443) Al-Barā' b. 'Āzib reported that the Messenger of Allah (may peace be upon him) observed Qunūt in the morning and evening (prayers).

(1444) Al-Barā' reported that the Messenger of Allah (may peace be upon him) observed Qunūt in the dawn and evening (prayers).

(1445) Khufāf b. Īmā' al-Ghifārī reported that the Messenger of Allah (may peace be upon him) said in prayer: O Allah! curse the tribes of Liḥyān, Ri'l, Dhakwān, and

922. This āyah was revealed in a particular context and it was substituted by so many other verses having the same meaning but far wider implications (e.g. v. 122, ix. 101, lviii. 22, xcviii. 9).

923. This ḥadīth lends strong support to the opinion of the Ḥanafites. It clearly testifies to the fact that it is Qunūt Nāzila (humble supplication offered in case of a calamity) only which is to be observed after the rukū', but so far as Qunūt Witr is concerned it is to be observed before bowing.

'Uṣayya for they disobeyed Allah and His Messenger (may peace be upon him). Allah pardoned (the tribe of) Ghifār,[924] and Allah granted protection to (the tribe of) Aslam.

(1446) Khufāf b. Īmā' reported that the Messenger of Allah (may peace be upon him) bowed (in prayer) and then lifted his head and then said: So far as the tribe of Ghifār is concerned, Allah had pardoned it, and Allah had granted protection to the tribe of Aslam, and as for the tribe of 'Uṣayya it had disobeyed Allah and His Messenger, (and further said): O Allah! curse the tribe of Liḥyān, curse Ri'l, and Dhakwān, and then fell in prostration. It is after this that the cursing of the unbelievers got a sanction.[925]

(1447) A ḥadīth like this has been transmitted by Khufāf b. Īmā' except this that he did not mention (these words): "cursing of unbelievers got a sanction".

Chapter CCXLV

COMPENSATION OF THE MISSED PRAYER AND EXCELLENCE OF OBSERVING IT PROMPTLY

(1448) Abū Huraira reported that when the Messenger of Allah (may peace be upon him) returned from the expedition to Khaibar, he travelled one night, and stopped for rest when he became sleepy. He told Bilāl to remain on guard during the night and he (Bilāl) prayed as much as he could, while the Messenger of Allah (may peace be upon him) and his Companions slept. When the time for dawn approached Bilāl leaned against his camel facing the direction from which the dawn would appear but he was overcome by sleep while he was leaning against his camel, and neither the Messenger of Allah (may peace be upon him) nor Bilāl, nor anyone else among his Companions got up,[926] till the sun shone on them. Allah's Messenger (may peace be upon him) was the first of them to awake and, being startled, he called to Bilāl who said: Messenger of Allah! may my father and mother be offered as ransom for thee, the same thing overpowered me which overpowered you. He (the Holy Prophet, then) said: Lead the beasts on; so they led their camels to some distance. The Messenger of Allah

924. Before embracing Islam, the people of the Ghifār tribe were notorious for stealing the articles of the pilgrims (*Fatḥ al-Mulhim*, Vol. II, p. 238).

925. Thus cursing of the enemy got a religious sanction in Islam (*Fatḥ al-Mulhim*, Vol. II, p. 238).

926. Mullā 'Alī Qārī has resolved this apparent contradiction between the fact mentioned in this ḥadīth and the one narrated by Ḥaḍrat 'Ā'isha in which the Messenger of Allah (may peace be upon him) is reported to have said: "My eyes sleep but the heart does not sleep." If the ḥadīth narrated by 'Ā'isha is accepted as valid, then it seems strange that the Holy Prophet was so much overpowered by sleep that he could not wake up for the dawn prayer. There are two valid reasons for it. Firstly, the "heart does not sleep" does not imply that the heart of the Holy Prophet (may peace be upon him) had always been active and retained conscious contact with the world of senses. What it really means is that his heart was always in deep communion with the Divine and was fully aware of the depth of his soul. The second and the most appropriate reply is that it was for Divine guidance in respect of missed prayer that the Holy Prophet (may peace be upon him) was overpowered by sleep for if he did not forget prayer in sleep and did not miss the prescribed time for it, how could his followers learn how to observe the missed prayer (*Mirqāt*, Vol. II, pp. 177-8).

(may peace be upon him) then performed ablution and gave orders to Bilāl who pronounced the Iqāma[927] and then led them in the morning prayer. When he finished the prayer he said: When anyone forgets the prayer, he should observe it when he remembers it,[928] for Allah has said: "And observe the prayer for remembrance of Me" (Qur'ān, xx. 14).[929] Yūnus said: Ibn Shihāb used to recite it like this: "(And observe the prayer) for remembrance."[930]

(1449) Abū Huraira reported: We stopped for rest along with the Apostle of Allah (may peace be upon him) and did not awake till the sun rose. The Apostle of Allah (may peace be upon him) then told us that everybody should take hold of his camel's nosestring (get out of this ground) for it was the place where devil had visited us.[931] We did accordingly. He then called for water and performed ablution and then performed two prostrations.[932] Ya'qūb said: Then he prayed (performed) two prostrations, then takbīr was pronounced for prayer and then he offered the morning prayer (in congregation).

(1450) Abū Qatāda reported: The Messenger of Allah (may peace be upon him) addressed us and said: You would travel in the evening and the night till (God willing) you would come in the morning to a place of water. So the people travelled (self-absorbed) without paying any heed to one another, and the Messenger of Allah (may peace be upon him) also travelled till it was midnight. I was by his side. The Messenger of Allah (may peace be upon him) began to doze and leaned (to one side) of his camel. I came to him and I lent him support without awaking him till he sat poised on his ride. He went on travelling till a major part of the night was over and (he again) leaned (to one side) of his camel. I supported him without awaking him till he sat poised on his ride, and then travelled till it was near dawn. He (again) leaned which was far more inclined than the two earlier leanings and he was about to fall down. So I came to him and supported him and he lifted his head and said: Who is this? I said: It is Abū Qatāda. He (the Holy Prophet again) said: Since how long have you been travelling along with me like this? I said: I have been travelling in this very state since the night. He said: May Allah protect you, as you have protected His Apostle[933] (from falling down) and again said: Do you see that we are hidden from the people?—

927. Not only was Iqāma pronounced, but Adhān was also announced as it has been said in a ḥadīth recorded in Abū Dāwūd. Imām Shāfi'ī is of the opinion that in case of missed prayer there is no need of Adhān (*Mirqāt*, Vol II, p. 178).

928. It should be observed in the times permitted for observing prayer (*Faiḍ al-Bāri*, Vol. II, p. 147).

929. Keeping in view the context of this verse in the ḥadīth mentioned above, it would mean: Observe prayer when you remember it, for the remembrance of prayer is the remembrance of Allah. The use of first person by God in remembrance has been done for the glorification of prayer.

930. This recitation "(observe the prayer) for remembrance" lends support to the meaning explained above in note 928 (*Mirqāṭ*, Vol. II, p 135).

931. It was a place where they had been so much overpowered by sleep that they had missed the prayer. They must, therefore, vacate that place. It is on this ground that it is forbidden to pray in bathrooms where evil thoughts haunt the minds of man (Nawāwī, Vol. I, p. 238).

932. Herein lies the justification of observing the missed Sunnah prayer (Nawāwī, Vol I, p. 238).

933. This shows how kind the Holy Prophet was to his Companions and how he blessed them even on very small acts of help to him.

and again said : Do you see anyone ? I said : Here is a rider. I again said : Here is another rider till we gathered together and we were seven riders. The Messenger of Allah (may peace be upon him) stepped aside of the highway and placed his head (for sleep and said) : Guard for us our prayers. The Messenger of Allah (may peace be upon him) was the first to wake up and the rays of the sun were falling on his back. We got up startled. He (the Holy Prophet) said : Ride on. So we rode on till the sun had (sufficiently) risen. He then came down from his camel and called for a jug of water which I had with me. There was a little water in that. He performed ablution with that which was less[934] thorough as compared with his usual ablutions and some water of that had been left. He (the Holy Prophet) said to Abū Qatāda : Keep a watch over your jug of water ; it would have (a miraculous[935]) condition about it. Then Bilāl summoned (people) to prayer and then the Messenger of Allah (may peace be upon him) observed two rak'ahs and then said the morning prayer as he said every day. The Messenger of Allah (may peace be upon him) (then) rode on and we rode along him and some of us whispered to the others saying : How would there be compensation for omission in our prayers ? Upon this he (the Apostle of Allah) said : Is there not in me (my life) a model for you ? There is no omission in sleeping.[936] The (cognizable) omission is that one should not say prayer (intentionally) till the time of the other prayer comes. So he who did like it (omitted prayer in sleep or due to other unavoidable circumstances) should say prayer when he becomes aware of it and on the next day he should observe it at its prescribed time. He (the Holy Prophet) said : What do you think the people would have done (at this hour) ? They would have in the morning found their Apostle missing from amongst them and then Abū Bakr and 'Umar would have told them that the Messenger of Allah (may peace be upon him) must be behind you, he cannot leave you behind (him)[937] but the people said : The Messenger of Allah (may peace be upon him) is ahead of you. So if you had obeyed Abū Bakr and 'Umar, you would have gone on the right path.[938] So we proceeded on till we came up to the people (from whom we had lagged behind) and the day had considerably risen and everything became hot, and they (the Companions of the Holy Prophet) said : Messenger of Allah, we are dying of thirst. Upon this he (the Holy Prophet) remarked : There is no destruction for you. And again said : Bring that small cup of mine and he then asked for the jug of water to be brought to him. The Messenger of Allah (may peace be upon him) began to pour water (in that small cup) and Abū Qatāda gave them to drink. And when the people saw that there

934. He could not perform ablution well, but did it hurriedly and that too with a little water that the jug contained.

935. This came to be true for the small water in it, with the blessing of the Holy Prophet, satiated numerous people.

936. This omission is not caused by intentional negligence on the part of a man, but simply by sleep over which man has no control.

937. This gives us an idea what deep insight Abū Bakr and 'Umar had in the conduct of the Holy Prophet. They knew it fully well that it was not the habit of the Messenger of Allah to leave behind his Companions. He would either go along with them or go after them to see that everything was all right and no Companion of his had fallen into trouble and thus lagged behind He was a great protector of his fellow men.

938. This shows the eminence of Ḥaḍrat Abū Bakr and 'Umar (Allah be pleased with them). The Holy Prophet gave a clear verdict that their approach was more correct and realistic and their judgment and opinion were more sound than of any other man.

was (a little) water in the jug, they fell upon it. Upon this the Messenger of Allah (may peace be upon him) said : Behave well ; the water (is enough) to satiate all of you. Then they (the Companions) began to receive (their share of) water with calmness (without showing any anxiety) and the Messenger of Allah (may peace be upon him) began to fill (the cup), and I began to serve them till no one was left except me and the Messenger of Allah (may peace be upon him). He then filled (the cup) with water and said to me : Drink it. I said : Messenger of Allah, I would not drink till you drink. Upon this he said : The server of the people is the last among them to drink [939] So I drank and the Messenger of Allah (may peace be upon him) also drank and the people came to the place of water quite happy and satiated. 'Abdullah b. Rabāḥ said : I am going to narrate this ḥadīth in the great mosque, when 'Imrān b. Ḥuṣain said : See, O young man, how will you narrate for I was also one of the riders on that night ? I said : So you must be knowing this ḥadīth well. He said : Who are you ? I said : I am one of the Anṣār. Upon this he said : You narrate, for you know your ḥadīth better. I, therefore, narrated it to the people. 'Imrān said : I was also present that night, but I know not anyone else who learnt it so well as you have learnt.

(1451) 'Imrān b. Ḥuṣain reported : I was with the Apostle of Allah (may peace be upon him) in a journey. We travelled the whole of the night, and when it was about to dawn, we got down for rest, and were overpowered (by sleep) till the sun shone. Abū Bakr was the first to awake amongst us, and we did not awake the Apostle of Allah (may peace be upon him) from his sleep allowing him to wake up (of his own accord).[940] It was 'Umar who then woke up. He stood by the side of the Apostle of Allah (may peace be upon him) and recited takbīr in a loud voice till the Messenger of Allah (may peace be upon him) woke up. When he lifted his head, he saw that the sun had arisen ; he then said : Proceed on. He travelled along with us till the sun shone brightly. He came down (from his camel) and led us in the morning prayer. A person, however, remained away from the people and did not say prayer along with us. After having completed the prayer, the Messenger of Allah (may peace be upon him) said to him : O, so and so, what prevented you from observing prayer with us ? He said : Apostle of Allah ! I was not in a state of purity. The Messenger of Allah (may peace be upon him) ordered him and he performed Tayammum with dust and said prayer. He then urged me to go ahead immediately along with other riders to find out water, for we felt very thirsty. We were travelling when we came across a woman who was sitting (on a camel) with her feet hanging over two leathern water-bags. We said to her : How far is water available ? She said : Far, very far, very far. You cannot get water. We (again) said : How much distance is there between (the residence of) your family and water ? She said : It is a day and night journey. We said to her : You go to the

939. This gives an idea of the responsibility of a leader in a Muslim society. He is the father of the nation and as such it is his foremost duty to look to the welfare of the people and make the maximum sacrifice for their sake and should be last to derive personal benefit out of a thing which is needed by the people. Can history furnish any example of such selflessness and love as we find in the life of the Holy Prophet ?

940. Abū Bakr had a very deep insight into the mind of the Holy Prophet and he did not awake him lest it should disturb the revelation which he might be receiving from his Lord at that time (*Fatḥ al-Mulhim*, Vol. II, p. 244).

Messenger of Allah (may peace be upon him). She said: Who is the Messenger of Allah? We somehow or the other managed to bring her to the Messenger of Allah (may peace be upon him) and he asked about her, and she informed him as she had informed us that she was a widow having orphan children. He ordered that her camel should be made to kneal down and he gargled in the opening (of her leathern water-bag). The camel was then raised up and we forty thirsty men drank water till we were completely satiated, and we filled up all leathern water-bags and water-skins that we had with us and we washed our companions,[941] but we did not make any camel drink, and (the leathern water-bags) were about to burst (on account of excess of water). He then said: Bring whatever you have with you. So we collected the bits (of eatable things) and dates and packed them up in a bundle, and said to her: Take it away. This is meant for your children, and know that we have not in any way done any loss to your water. When she came to her family she said: I have met the greatest magician amongst human beings, or he is an apostle, as he claims to be, and she then narrated what had happened and Allah guided aright those people through that woman. She affirmed her faith in Islam and so did the people embrace Islam.

(1452) 'Imrān b. Ḥuṣain reported: We were with the Messenger of Allah (may peace be upon him) in a journey and we travelled throughout the night till at the end, just before dawn, we lay down (for rest), and nothing is sweeter for a traveller than this and none awakened us but the heat of the sun, and the rest of the ḥadīth is the same (as mentioned above) except this addition: "When 'Umar b. Khaṭṭāb woke up, he saw what had happened to the people. And he was a man having a big belly and strongly built; he recited takbīr in a loud voice till the Messenger of Allah (may peace be upon him) woke up by the loudness of his voice in takbīr. When the Messenger of Allah (may peace be upon him) got up, the people told him what had happened. Upon this the Messenger of Allah (may peace be upon him) said: There is no harm; you better proceed further," and (the rest of the ḥadīth) was narrated.

(1453) Abū Qatāda reported that when the Messenger of Allah (may peace be upon him) was in a journey he got down for rest at night, and he used to lie down on his right side, and when he lay down for rest before the dawn, he used to stretch his forearm and place his head over his palm.

(1454) Qatāda reported from Anas b. Mālik that the Messenger of Allah (may peace be upon him) said: He who forgets the prayer should say it, when he remembers it, there is no expiation for it, except this. Qatada said: (Allah says) "And observe prayer for remembrance of Me."

(1455) This ḥadīth has been narrated by Qatāda, but here no mention has been made of "There is no expiation for it except this."

(1456) Qatāda narrated it on the authority of Anas b. Mālik that the Apostle of Allah (may peace be upon him) said: He who forgets the prayer, or he slept (and it was omitted), its expiation is this only that he should observe it when he remembers it.

(1457) Qatāda reported it on the authority of Anas b. Mālik that the Messenger of Allah (may peace be upon him) said: When any one of you omits the prayer due to sleep or he forgets it, he should observe it when he remembers it, for Allah has said: "Observe prayer for remembrance of Me."

941. We made our campanions take their bath.

Chapter CCXLVI

THE PRAYER OF TRAVELLERS AND ITS SHORTENING

(1458) 'Ā'isha, the wife of the Messenger of Allah (may peace be upon him), reported: The prayer was prescribed as two rak'ahs, two rak'ahs both in journey and at the place of residence. The prayer while travelling remained as it was (originally prescribed), but an addition was made in the prayer (observed) at the place of residence.[942]

(1459) 'Ā'isha, the wife of the Messenger of Allah (may peace be upon him), said: Allah prescribed the prayer as two rak'ahs, then it was completed (to four rak'ahs) at the place of residence, but was retained in the same position in journey as it was first made obligatory.

(1460) 'Ā'isha reported: The prayer was prescribed as consisting of two rak'ahs, the prayer in travelling remained the same, but the prayer at the place of residence was completed.[943] (Zuhrī said he asked 'Urwa why 'Ā'isha said prayer in the complete form during journey, and he replied that she interpreted the matter herself as 'Uthmān did.)

(1461) Ya'la b. Umayya said: I told 'Umar b. al-Khaṭṭāb that Allah had said: "You may shorten the prayer, only if you fear that those who are unbelievers may afflict you" (Qur'ān, iv. 101),[944] whereas the people are now safe. He replied: I wondered about it in the same way as you wonder about it, so I asked the Messenger of Allah (may peace be upon him) about it and he said: It is an act of charity which Allah has done to you, so accept His charity.[945]

(1462) Ya'la b. Umayya reported: I said to 'Umar b. al-Khaṭṭāb, and the rest of the ḥadīth is the same.

(1463) Ibn 'Abbās reported: Allah has prescribed the prayer through the word of your Prophet (may peace be upon him)[946] as four rak'ahs when resident, two when travelling, and one when danger is present.

(1464) Ibn 'Abbās reported: Allah has prescribed the prayer by the tongue of

942. Imām Shāfi'ī and Mālik b. Anas and many other jurists are of the opinion that both short and full prayers are permissible in a journey, whereas others think that, although both are permissible, yet it is better to shorten the prayer in a travel, but Imām Abū Ḥanīfa is of the view that shortening of prayer in a journey is obligatory and it is not permissible to observe complete prayer deliberately. According to Nawawī, the most appropriate view is that it is excellent to shorten the prayer in a journey.

943. It was completed to four rak'ahs in the noon, afternoon and night prayers and three in case of the evening prayer.

944. 'Uthmān said prayer in complete form on the basis of this verse of the Qur'ān: "You may shorten the prayer only if you fear that those who are unbelievers may afflict you." 'Uthmān was of the view that according to this verse shortening of prayer is only permissible, it is not obligatory.

945. It is on the basis of this ḥadīth that Imām Abū Ḥanīfa and some other scholars assert that shortening of prayer is obligatory in a journey and it should not be observed completely.

946. According to some of the scholars, e g. Ḥasan and Ḍuḥāk and Isḥāq b. Rahwai in case of danger only one rak'ah is obligatory, but Imām Shāfi'ī and Imām Mālik believe that Ṣalāt-ul-Khauf (prayer in danger) is equal to the prayer where there is no danger, i.e. two rak'ahs in journey and four when resident. The one rak'ah mentioned in the ḥadīth refers to that single rak'ah which one observes along with the Imām during the time of danger as the method of prayer in danger reveals (*Fatḥ al-Mulhim*, Vol. II, p 250).

your Apostle (may peace be upon him) as two rak'ahs for the traveller, four for the resident, and one in danger.

(1465) Mūsā b. Salama Ḥudhalī said: I asked Ibn 'Abbās: How should I say prayer when I am in Mecca,[947] and when I do not pray along with the Imām? He said: Two rak'ahs (of prayer) is the Sunnah of Abu'l-Qāsim[948] (may peace be upon him).

(1466) A ḥadīth like this has been transmitted by Abū Qatāda with the same chain of transmitters.

(1467) Ḥafṣ b. 'Āṣim said: I accompanied Ibn 'Umar on the road to Mecca and he led us in two rak'ahs at the noon prayer, then he went forward and we too went along with him to a place where he alighted, and he sat and we sat along with him, and he cast a glance to the side where he said prayer and he saw people standing and asked: What are they doing? I said: They are engaged in glorifying Allah offering Sunnah prayer. He said: If I had done so I would have perfected my prayer; O my nephew! I accompanied the Messenger of Allah (may peace be upon him) on a journey, and he made no addition to two rak'ahs, till Allah called him. I accompanied Abū Bakr and he made no addition to two rak'ahs till Allah caused him to die. I accompanied 'Umar and he made no addition to two rak'ahs till Allah caused him to die. I accompanied 'Uthmān and he made no addition to two rak'ahs till Allah caused him to die, and Allah has said: "There is a model pattern for you in the Messenger of Allah" (al-Qur'ān, xxxiii. 21).

(1468) Ḥafṣ b. 'Āṣim reported: I fell ill and Ibn 'Umar came to inquire after my health, and I asked him about the glorification of Allah (i.e. prayer) while travelling. Thereupon he said: I accompanied the Messenger of Allah (may peace be upon him) on a journey but I did not see him glorifying Him, and were I to glorify (Him), I would have completed the prayer.[949] Allah, the Exalted, has said: "Verily there is a model pattern for you in the Messenger of Allah."

(1469) Anas reported: The Messenger of Allah (may peace be upon him) said four rak'ahs in the noon prayer while at Medina, but he offered two rak'ahs in afternoon prayer at Dhu'l-Ḥulaifa.[950]

(1470) Anas b. Mālik is reported to have said: I observed four rak'ahs in the noon prayer with the Messenger of Allah (may peace be upon him) at Medina, and said two rak'ahs in the afternoon prayer at Dhu'l-Ḥulaifa.

(1471) Yaḥyā b. Yazīd al-Hunā'ī reported: I asked Anas b. Mālik about shortening of prayer. He said: When the Messenger of Allah (may peace be upon him) had covered a distance of three miles or three farsakh[951] (Shu'ba, one of the narrators, had

947. When he was on a journey, as his residence was in Medina.

948. Kunyah of the Holy Prophet.

949. It is on the basis of these words of Ibn 'Umar that it is considered permissible not to observe Sunnah while travelling. Imam Shāfi'ī believes that Sunnah prayer in a journey becomes Nafl.

950. Dhu'l-Ḥulaifa which is situated at a distance of six miles from Medina was not the destination of the Holy Prophet. He had undertaken the journey for Ḥajj or 'Umra and Dhu'l-Ḥulaifa was the first habitation where he reached at the time of the afternoon prayer. This habitation is the famous Mīqāt for the people of Medina which implies that it is at this place that they should put on Iḥrām before entering the Ḥaram of the Ka'ba (*Fatḥ al-Bārī*, Vol. IV, p. 579).

951. It is a measure of distance and is equal to three miles.

some doubt about it) he observed two rak'ahs.[952]

(1472) Jubair b. Nufair reported: I went along with Shuraḥbīl b. al-Simṭ to a village which was situated at a distance of seventeen or eighteen miles,[953] and he said only two rak'ahs of prayer. I said to him (about it) and he said: I saw 'Umar observing two rak'ahs at Dhu'l-Ḥulaifa and I (too) said to him (about it) and he said: I am doing the same as I saw the Messenger of Allah (may peace be upon him) doing. (This ḥadīth has been transmitted by Shu'ba with the same chain of transmitters and it is narrated from Simṭ, and the name of Shuraḥbīl has not been mentioned, and he said that he had gone to a place called Dūmīn, situated at a distance of eighteen miles from Ḥims.)

(1473) Anas b. Mālik reported: We went out from Medina to Mecca with the Messenger of Allah (may peace be upon him) and he prayed two rak'ahs at each time of prayer till we returned to Medina. I said: For how long did he stay in Mecca? He said: (For) ten (days).[954]

(1474) A ḥadīth like this has been transmitted by Anas by another chain of transmitters.

(1475) Yaḥyā b. Abū Isḥāq reported: I heard Anas b. Mālik say: We went out for Pilgrimage from Medina. The rest is the same.

(1476) A ḥadīth like this has been transmitted by Anas, but no mention has been made of Pilgrimage.

(1477) Sālim b. 'Abdullah (b. 'Umar) reported on the authority of his father that Allah's Messenger (may peace be upon him) observed the prayer of a traveller, i.e. two rak'ahs, in Minā, and other places; so did Abū Bakr and 'Umar, and 'Uthmān too observed two rak'ahs at the beginning of his caliphate, but he then completed

952. The actual position is not the same what this ḥadīth apparently indicates. The Holy Prophet and his Companions shortened the prayer on a journey the time they had got out of the outskirts of their habitations. Here the Messenger of Allah (may peace be upon him) shortened the prayer after covering a distance of three miles, because it must have been the place where the time for the prayer had actually come.

953. According the Ḥanafites it cannot be inferred from this ḥadīth that the minimum journey for shortening the prayer is eighteen miles. It was not the destination, but one of the stations towards the destination. But this is not correct. Herein no mention has been made of the subsequent journey. The preposition ال indicates that their destination was the same village. The fact is that no hard and fast rule has been laid down for the distance which may be treated as journey in the Sharī'ah.

954. This relates to the Farewell Pilgrimage of the Holy Prophet (may peace be upon him). He reached Mecca on the 4th of Dhu'l-Ḥajj and came back on the 14th to Medina and shortened the prayers during these days. It shows that a person is a traveller for this period. According to Imām Abū Ḥanīfa, the minimum period for a temporary stay which brings a person to the position of a Muqīm is fifteen days having a previous intention to do so, but if there is no previous intention and he is compelled to stay at a place even for a longer period, he should treat himself as a traveller and shorten his prayer. According to Imām Shāfi'ī, the time limit is four days' stay with previous intention and eighteen days without intention.

It is interesting to note that Imām Shāfi'ī has inferred from this ḥadīth as four days' stay on the basis that the Prophet stayed in Mecca only for three days, i e. on the 5th, 6th and 7th of Dhu'l-Ḥajj continuously. So far as the rest of the days are concerned he has been moving in Minā and 'Arafāt for Ḥajj ceremonies.

four.[955]

(1478) A ḥadīth like this has been transmitted by Zuhrī, with the same chain of transmitters, and in it mention was made of Minā only, but not of other places.

(1479) Ibn 'Umar reported: The Messenger of Allah (may peace be upon him) said two rak'ahs at Minā, and Abū Bakr after him, and 'Umar after Abū Bakr, and 'Uthmān at the beginning of his caliphate; then 'Uthmān observed four rak'ahs, and when Ibn 'Umar prayed with the Imām, he said four rak'ahs, but when he observed prayer alone, he said two rak'ahs.[956]

(1480) A ḥadīth like this has been transmitted by the same chain of transmitters.

(1481) Ibn 'Umar reported: The Apostle of Allah (may peace be upon him) said in Minā the prayer of a traveller (short prayer); Abū Bakr and 'Umar did the same, and 'Uthmān did it for eight years or six years. Ḥafṣ (one of the narrators) said: Ibn 'Umar would also say two rak'ahs at Minā and then go to bed. I said to him: O uncle, I wish you could have said two rak'ahs (of Sunnah prayer after shortening the Farḍ prayer). He said: Were I to do that, I would have completed the prayer.

(1482) This ḥadīth has been transmitted by Shu'ba with the same chain of transmitters but no mention has been made of Minā, but they (the narrators) only said: He prayed while travelling.

(1483) Ibrāhīm reported: I heard 'Abd al-Raḥmān as saying; 'Uthmān led us four rak'ahs of prayer at Minā. It was reported to 'Abdullah b. Mas'ūd and he recited: "Surely we are Allah's and to Him shall we return, and then said: I prayed with the Messenger of Allah (may peace be upon him) at Minā two rak'ahs of prayer. I prayed along with Abū Bakr al-Ṣiddīq two rak'ahs of prayer at Minā. I prayed along with 'Umar b. Khaṭṭāb two rak'ahs of prayer at Minā. I wish I had my share of the two rak'ahs acceptable (to God) for the four rak'ahs.

(1484) A ḥadīth like this has been transmitted by A'mash with the same chain of transmitters.

(1485) Ḥāritha b. Wahb reported: I prayed with the Messenger of Allah (may peace be upon him) two rak'ahs and most of them offered two rak'ahs only in Minā, while the people felt secure.[957]

(1486) Wahb al-Khuzā'ī reported: I prayed behind the Messenger of Allah (may peace be upon him) at Minā, and there was the greatest number of people, and they

955. Various reasons have been given for this change made by 'Uthmān. The one is that with the passage of time numerous tribes had been embracing Islam. When they saw their Caliph observing two rak'ahs they thought that the prayer was constituted of these two rak'ahs only. It was for instructing them in prayer at residence that Ḥaḍrat 'Uthmān observed complete prayer. The second reason is that Ḥaḍrat 'Uthmān had married in Mecca and the residence of in-laws is to be treated as one's own residence and one ceases to be a traveller when one goes to the residence of one's in-laws, and this was the explanation which Ḥaḍrat 'Uthmān himself gave when an objection was raised against him for offering four rak'ahs in Mecca. There is a ḥadīth narrated by Imām Aḥmad, 'Abdullah b. Zubair and Ḥumaidī to this effect: The Messenger of Allah (may peace be upon him) said: When a person marries in a town, he should observe the prayer of a resident. This is the most valid reason put forward by 'Uthmān (Ḥāfiẓ Ibn Qayyim, *Zād al-Ma'ad*, Vol. I, p. 269).

956. This shows clearly that when a resident leads the prayer, the travellers joining the congregation should follow him.

957. This ḥadīth clarifies the point that shortening of prayer is not due to fear.

prayed two rak'ahs on the occasion of the Farewell Pilgrimage. (Muslim said: Ḥāritha b. Wahb al-Khuzā'ī is the brother of 'Ubaidullah b. 'Umar son of Khaṭṭāb from the side of mother.)

Chapter CCXLVII

PRAYING IN HOUSES WHEN IT RAINS

(1487) Ibn 'Umar announced Adhān for prayer on a cold, windy night. Then added: Pray in your dwellings; and then said: When it was a cold, rainy night, the Messenger of Allah (may peace be upon him) used to command the Mu'adhdhin to say: "Pray in your dwellings."

(1488) Ibn 'Umar reported that he summoned (people) to pray on a cold, windy and rainy night, and then observed at the end of the Adhān: Pray in your dwellings, pray in your dwellings, and then said: When it was a cold night or it was raining in a journey the Messenger of Allah (may peace be upon him) used to command the Mu'adhdhin to announce: Pray in your dwellings.

(1489) Ibn 'Umar reported that he summond (people) to prayer at a place (known as) Ḍajnān, and the rest of the ḥadīth is the same, and then said: Pray in your dwellings, but he did not repeat for the second time words of Ibn 'Umar (Pray in your dwellings).

(1490) Jābir reported: We set out with the Messenger of Allah (may peace be upon him) on a journey when it began to rain. Upon this he said: He who desires may pray in his dwelling.

(1491) 'Abdullah b. 'Abbās reported that he said to the Mu'adhdhin on a rainy day: When you have announced "I testify that there is no god but Allah; I testify that Muḥammad is the Messenger of Allah," do not say: "Come to the prayer," but make this announcement: "Say prayer in your houses." He (the narrator) said that the people disapproved of it. Ibn 'Abbās said: Are you astonished at it? He (the Holy Prophet), who is better than I, did it. Jumu'a prayer is no doubt obligatory, but I do not like that I should (force you) to come out and walk in mud and slippery ground.

(1492) 'Abd-ul-Ḥamīd reported: I heard 'Abdullah b. al-Ḥārith say: 'Abdullah b. 'Abbās addressed us on a rainy day,[958] and the rest of the ḥadith is the same, but he made no mention of Jumu'a prayer, and added: He who did it (who commanded us to say prayer in our houses), i.e. the Apostle of Allah (may peace be upon him), is better than I.

(1493) This ḥadīth has been transmitted by Ayyūb and 'Āṣim al-Aḥwal with the same chain of transmitters, but in this ḥadith it is not recorded: "i.e. the Apostle of Allah (may peace be upon him)."

(1494) 'Abdullah b. Ḥārith reported that Ibn 'Abbās commanded the Mu'adhdhin to (summon the people to prayer on Friday and make announcement to say prayer in

958. Shaikh Ibn Munīr is of the opinion that this concession is not about the Jumu'a prayer, but about other prayers. Ibn 'Abbās summoned people to Jumu'a prayer and then in his address made this announcement. It implies that Jumu'a prayer was observed as usual (*vide Fatḥ al-Mulkim*, Vol. II, pp. 257, 258).

their houses) when it was rainy, and the rest of the ḥadīth is the same (except this) that he said: I do not like you should walk in muddy slippery place.

(1495) 'Abdullah b. Ḥāriṯh reported that the Mu'adhdhin of Ibn 'Abbās said Adhān on Friday (and then made the announcement to say prayer in houses) because it was a rainy day; as it has been narrated by Ma'mar and others, and in this ḥadīth it was mentioned: He who did it, i.e. the Apostle of Allah (may peace be upon him), was better than I.

(1496) A ḥadīth like this that Ibn 'Abbās ordered his Mu'adhdhin (to summon people to prayer and then make announcement to say prayer in their houses) on Friday which was a rainy day, has been transmitted by 'Abdullah b. Ḥāriṯh. Wuhaib, however, says that he did not hear it from him.

Chapter CCXLVIII

PERMISSIBILITY OF SAYING NAFL PRAYER ON A RIDING BEAST WHILE ON A JOURNEY, IN WHATEVER DIRECTION IT TURNS

(1497) Ibn 'Umar reported that the Messenger of Allah (may peace be upon him) used to say Nafl prayer on (the back of) his camel in whatever direction it took him.[959]

(1498) Ibn 'Umar reported that the Apostle (may peace be upon him) used to pray on (the back of) his camel in whatever direction it took him.

(1499) Ibn 'Umar reported that the Messenger of Allah (may peace be upon him) used to say prayer on his camel while coming from Mecca to Medina, in whatever direction his face had turned; and its was (in this context) that this verse was revealed: "So whither you turn thither is Allah's face" (ii. 115).

(1500) This ḥadīth has been transmitted by another chain of transmitters and in the one narrated by Ibn Mubārak and Ibn Abū Zā'ida (these words are narrated). Ibn 'Umar then recited: "Whither you turn thither is Allah's face," and it was revealed in this context.

(1501) Ibn 'Umar reported: I saw the Messenger of Allah (may peace be upon him) praying (Nafl prayer) on a donkey's back while his face was turned towards Khaibar.

(1502) Sa'īd b. Yasār reported: I was travelling along with Ibn 'Umar on the way to Mecca. Sa'īd said: When I apprehended dawn, I dismounted (the ride) and observed Witr prayer and then again joined him. Ibn 'Umar said to me: Where were you? I said: I apprehended the appearance of dawn,[960] so I dismounted and observed Witr prayer. Upon this 'Abdullah said: Is there not a model pattern for you in the Messenger of Allah (may peace be upon him)? I said: Yes, by Allah, and (then) he said: The Messenger of Allah (may peace be upon him) used to observe Witr prayer on the

959. Some people, on the authority of this ḥadīth, conclude that it is wrong to observe obligatory prayer in train or in aeroplanes. But this is not correct. The jurists unanimously agree that obligatory prayer can be said in a boat; therefore, it is quite logical to say that it can also be observed in train and aeroplanes, etc.

960. Witr prayer is to be observed as a part of the night prayer and it should either be observed along with 'Ishā' prayer or with Tahajjud prayer, before dawn.

camel's back.

(1503) 'Abdullah b. Dīnār reported on the authority of Ibn 'Umar that the Messenger of Allah (may peace be upon him) used to observe prayer on his ride (no matter) in which direction it had its face turned. 'Abdullah b. Dīnār said that Ibn 'Umar used to do like that.

(1504) 'Abdullah b. 'Umar reported that the Messenger of Allah (may peace be upon him) used to observe Witr prayer on his ride.

(1505) Sālim b. 'Abdullah reported on the authority of his father that the Messenger of Allah (may peace be upon him) used to observe Nafl (supererogatory) prayer on his ride no matter in what direction it turned its face, and he observed Witr too on it, but did not observe obligatory prayer on it.

(1506) 'Abdullah b. 'Āmir b. Rabī'a has reported on the authority of his father that he had seen the Messenger of Allah (may peace be upon him) observing Nafl prayer at night on a journey on the back of his ride in whichever direction it turned its face.

(1507) Anas b. Sīrīn reported: We met Anas b. Mālik as he came to Syria at a place known as 'Ain-al-Tamar[961] and saw him observing prayer on the back of his donkey with his face turned in that direction. (Hammām one of the narrators) pointed towards the left of Qibla, so I said to him: I find you observing prayer towards the side other than that of Qibla. Upon this he said: Had I not seen the Messenger of Allah (may peace be upon him) doing like this, I would not have done so at all.

Chapter CCXLIX

PERMISSIBILITY OF COMBINING TWO PRAYERS ON A JOURNEY

(1508) Ibn 'Umar reported: When the Messenger of Allah (may peace be upon him) was in a state of hurry on a journey, he combined sunset and 'Ishā' prayers.

(1509) Nāfi' reported that when Ibn 'Umar was in a state of hurry on a journey, he combined sunset and 'Ishā' prayers after the twilight had disappeared, and he would say that when the Messenger of Allah (may peace be upon him) was in a state of hurry on a journey, he combined the sunset and 'Ishā' prayers.

(1510) Sālim reported from his father to be saying: I saw the Messenger of Allah (may peace be upon him) combining the sunset and 'Ishā' prayers when he was in a hurry on a journey.

(1511) Sālim b. 'Abdullah reported that his father had said: I saw the Messenger of Allah (may peace be upon him) delaying the sunset prayer till he would combine it with the 'Ishā' prayer, when he hastened to set out on a journey.

(1512) Anas b. Mālik reported: When the Messenger of Allah (may peace be upon him) set out on a journey before the sun declined (from the meridian), he delayed the noon prayer till the afternoon prayer, and then dismounted (his ride) and combined them (noon and afternoon prayers), but if the sun had declined before his setting out on a journey, he observed noon prayer and then mounted (the ride).

(1513) Anas reported: When the Apostle of Allah (may peace be upon him) intended

961. It is a village on the way to Iraq near Syria.

to combine two prayers on a journey, he delayed the noon prayer till came the early time of the afternoon prayer, and then combined the two.

(1514) Anas reported that when the Apostle of Allah (may peace be upon him) had to set out on a journey hurriedly, he delayed the noon prayer to the earlier time for the afternoon prayer, and then he would combine them, and he would delay the sunset prayer to the time when the twilight would disappear and then combine it with the 'Ishā' prayer.[962]

Chapter CCL

COMBINATION OF PRAYERS, WHEN ONE IS RESIDENT

(1515) Ibn 'Abbās reported: The Messenger of Allah (may peace be upon him) observed the noon and afternoon prayers together, and the sunset and 'Ishā' prayers together without being in a state of fear or in a state of journey.

(1516) Ibn 'Abbās reported: The Messenger of Allah (may peace be upon him) observed the noon and afternoon prayers together in Medina without being in a state of fear or in a state of journey. (Abu Zubair said: I asked Sa'īd [one of the narrators] why he did that. He said: I asked Ibn 'Abbās as you have asked me, and he replied that he [the Holy Prophet] wanted that no one among his Ummah should be put to [unnecessary] hardship.)

(1517) Ibn 'Abbās reported that the Messenger of Allah (may peace be upon him) combined the prayers as he set on a journey in the expedition to Tabūk. He combined the noon prayer with the afternoon prayer and the sunset prayer with the 'Ishā' prayer. Sa'īd (one of the rāwīs) said to Ibn 'Abbās: What prompted him to do this? He said: He wanted that his Ummah should not be put to (unnecessary) hardship.

(1518) Mu'ādh reported: We set out with the Messenger of Allah (may peace be upon him) on the Tabūk expedition, and he observed the noon and afternoon prayers

962. This point of combining the prayers needs elucidation.

There is no difference of opinion on the point that the pilgrims should combine the prayers in 'Arafāt and Muzdalifa. The difference is on the point whether it is permissible on all occasions on a journey.

It should be borne in mind that this combination is of two kinds: real (*Ḥaqiqi*) and formal (*Ṣuwari*). In the former combination it is during the time of one prayer that the other prayer is also observed along with it. For example, in the time of Ẓuhr prayer, the afternoon prayer is observed. Similarly, at the time of the sunset prayer the 'Ishā' prayer is also combined along with it. The formal combination is that the first prayer should be delayed to the maximum extent of its time limit when the time of the second prayer also commences and it is at this time that the two prayers may be observed, the one at the latest hour of its prescribed time and the second on just at the commencement of its time.

The Shāfi'ites favour the real combination of prayers, but the Ḥanafites consider the formal combination to be permissible.

The fact is that both are permissible. The aḥādīth recorded in this section, however, lend support to the stand of the Ḥanafites. But it cannot be the final verdict as the aḥādīth recorded in the *Musnad* of Imām Aḥmad and that of Imām Shāfi'ī go in favour of the real combination. A little bit of penetration can make it clear that there is no fundamental difference between the two groups. It is only a difference of interpretation.

together and the sunset and 'Ishā' prayers together.

(1519) Mu'ādh b. Jabal reported: The Messenger of Allah (may peace be upon him) combined in the expedition to Tabūk the noon prayer with the afternoon prayer and the sunset prayer with the 'Ishā' prayer. He (one of the narrators) said: What prompted him to do that? He (Mu'ādh) replied that he (the Holy Prophet) wanted that his Ummah should not be put to (unnecessary) hardship.

(1520) Ibn 'Abbās reported that the Messenger of Allah (may peace be upon him) combined the noon prayer with the afternoon prayer and the sunset prayer with the 'Ishā' prayer in Medina without being in a state of danger or rainfall. And in the ḥadith transmitted by Wakī' (the words are): "I said to Ibn 'Abbās: What prompted him to do that? He said: So that his (Prophet's) Ummah should not be put to (unnecessary) hardship." And in the ḥadīth transmitted by Mu'āwiya (the words are): "It was said to Ibn 'Abbās: What did he intend thereby? He said he wanted that his Ummah should not be put to unnecessary hardship."

(1521) Ibn 'Abbās reported: I observed with the Apostle of Allah (may peace be upon him) eight (rak'ahs) in combination, and seven rak'ahs in combination. I (one of the narrators) said: O Abū Sha'thā', I think that he (the Holy Prophet) had delayed the noon prayer and hastened the afternoon prayer, and he delayed the sunset prayer and hastened the 'Ishā' prayer. He said: I also think so.

(1522) Ibn 'Abbās reported that the Messenger of Allah (may peace be upon him) observed in Medina seven (rak'ahs) and eight (rak'ahs), i.e. (he combined) the noon and afternoon prayers (eight rak'ahs) and the sunset and 'Ishā' prayers (seven rak'ahs).

(1523) 'Abdullah b. Shaqīq reported: Ibn 'Abbās one day addressed us in the afternoon (after the afternoon prayer) till the sun disappeared and the stars appeared, and the people began to say: Prayer, prayer. A person from Banū Tamīm came there. He neither slackened nor turned away, but (continued crying): Prayer, prayer. Ibn 'Abbās said: May you be deprived of your mother, do you teach me Sunnah? And then he said: I saw the Messenger of Allah (may peace be upon him) combining the noon and afternoon prayers and the sunset and 'Ishā' prayers. 'Abdullah b. Shaqīq said: Some doubt was created in my mind about it. So I came to Abū Huraira and asked him (about it) and he testified his assertion.

(1524) 'Abdullah b. Shaqīq al-'Uqailī reported: A person said to Ibn 'Abbās (as he delayed the prayer): Prayer. He kept silent. He again said: Prayer. He again kept silent, and he again cried: Prayer. He again kept silent and said: May you be deprived of your mother, do you teach us about prayer? We used to combine two prayers during the lifetime of the Messenger of Allah (may peace be upon him).[963]

963. This ḥadīth, i.e. of combining of two prayers, when a person is resident, and there is neither danger nor rainfall, has been explained with so many reasons. The one reason is that it was due to illness that the Holy Prophet combined the prayers. From this it has been concluded that it is permissible to combine the prayers when there is genuine need and urgency for it. But it should be remembered that it is an exception rather than a rule. The Holy Prophet seldom combined these prayers as a resident during peace time and when there was no rainfall. We should, therefore, follow this practice, but it is only in extraordinary circumstances and in exceptional cases that the prayers can be combined. This combination should in no way be made a matter of routine.

Chapter CCLI

PERMISSIBILITY OF TURNING TO THE RIGHT AND LEFT IN PRAYER

(1525) 'Abdullah reported: None of you should give a share to Satan out of your self. He should not deem that it is necessary for him to turn but to the right only (after prayer). I saw the Messenger of Allah (may peace be upon him) turning to the left.[964]

(1526) A ḥadīth like this has been transmitted by A'mash, with the same chain of transmitters.

(1527) Suddī reported: I asked Anas how I should turn—to the right or to the left—when I say my prayers. He said: I have very often seen the Messenger of Allah (may peace be upon him) turning to the right.

(1528) Anas reported: The Apostle of Allah (may peace be upon him) used to turn to the right (at the end of the prayer).

Chapter CCLII

EXCELLENCE TO BE ON THE RIGHT SIDE OF THE IMĀM

(1529) Barā' reported: When we prayed behind the Messenger of Allah (may peace be upon him) we cherished to be on his right side so that his face would turn towards us (at the end of the prayer), and he (the narrator) said: I heard him say: O my Lord! save me from Thy torment on the Day when Thou wouldst raise or gather Thy servants.

(1530) This ḥadīth has been transmitted by Mis'ar with the same chain of transmitters, but he made no mention of: "His face would turn towards us."

Chapter CCLIII

THE UNDESIRABILITY OF OBSERVING NAFL PRAYER, WHEN THE MU'ADHDHIN BEGINS ADHĀN

(1531) Abū Huraira reported the Apostle of Allah (may peace be upon him) as saying: When the prayer commences then there is no prayer (valid),[965] but the obligatory prayer. This ḥadīth has been transmitted by Warqā' with the same chain of transmitters.

964. It was a common practice with the Apostle of Allah (may peace be upon him) that at the conclusion of a prayer, he would turn his face towards the right and talk to the people or supplicated. But on this basis, it should not be taken as something obligatory. The Holy Prophet, at times, turned his face towards the left also and so we are permitted to do so.

965. It does not mean that prayer becomes completely null and void or loses its utility altogether. It implies that it stands in the way of the greater reward which one is expected to get in Farḍ rak'ahs (*Fatḥ al-Mulhim*, Vol. II, p. 270).

The scholars of Ḥadīth are agreed on the point that it is not desirable to say Nafl prayer when the Farḍ is commenced. There is, however, difference about the Sunnah of the dawn prayer.

(1532) Abū Huraira reported the Apostle of Allah (may peace be upon him) as saying : When the prayer commences, there is no prayer but the obligatory one.

(1533) A ḥadīth like this has been transmitted by Isḥāq with the same chain of transmitters.

(1534) This ḥadīth has been narrated by Abū Huraira with another chain of transmitters. Ḥammād (one of the narrators) said : I then met 'Amr (the other narrator) and he narrated it to me, but it was not transmitted directly from the Messenger of Allah (may peace be upon him).

(1535) 'Abdullah b. Mālik b. Buhaina reported : The Messenger of Allah (may peace be upon him) happened to pass by a person who was busy in praying while the (Farḍ of the) dawn prayer had commenced. He said something to him, which we do not know what it was. When we turned back we surrounded him and said : What is it that the Messenger of Allah (may peace be upon him) said to you ? He replied : He (the Holy Prophet) had said to me that he perceived as if one of them was about to observe four (rak'ahs) of the dawn prayer. Qa'nabī reported that 'Abdullah b. Mālik b. Buhaina narrated it on the authority of his father. (Abu'l-Ḥusain Muslim said) : His assertion that he has narrated this ḥadīth on the authority of his father is not correct.

(1536) Ibn Buhaina reported : The dawn prayer had commenced when the Messenger of Allah (may peace be upon him) saw a person observing prayer, whereas the Mu'adhdhin had pronounced the Iqāma. Upon this he (the Holy Prophet) remarked : Do you say four (rak'ahs) of Farḍ in the dawn prayer ?"

(1537) 'Abdullah b. Sarjis reported : A person entered the mosque, while the Messenger of Allah (may peace be upon him) was leading the dawn prayer. He observed two rak'ahs in a corner of the mosque, and then joined the Messenger of Allah (may peace be upon him) in prayer. When the Messenger of Allah (may peace be upon him) had pronounced salutations (he had concluded the prayer), he said : O, so and so, which one out of these two prayers did you count (as your Farḍ prayer), the one that you observed alone or the prayer that you observed with us ?

Chapter CCLIV

WHAT IS TO BE RECITED WHILE ENTERING THE MOSQUE

(1538) Abū Usaid reported that the Messenger of Allah (may peace be upon him) said : When any one of you enters the mosque, he should say : "O Allah ! open for me the doors of Thy mercy" ; and when he steps out he should say : "O Allah ! I beg of Thee Thy Grace." (Imām Muslim said : I heard Yaḥyā saying : I transcribed this ḥadīth from the compilation of Sulaimān b. Bilāl.)

(1539) A ḥadīth like this has been narrated from the Apostle of Allah (may peace be upon him) by Abū Usaid.

The importance of their observance has been so much stressed by the Holy Prophet that it is treated almost as Farḍ. Imām Abū Ḥanīfa and some other jurists deem it desirable to observe it even if the Farḍ are commenced, provided one is sure to join one rak'ah and not to miss it completely. Imām Abū Ḥanīfa is of the opinion that it is in this way that such a person would be able to get both the benefits, the benefit of observing the much-stressed Sunnah of the dawn prayer and the benefit of saying Farḍ along with the Imām, as it has been laid down in the ḥadīth that one who joins one rak'ah (in congregation), he in fact joins the prayer.

Chapter CCLV

EXCELLENCE OF GREETING THE MOSQUE WITH TWO RAK'AHS AND UNDESIRABILITY OF SITTING DOWN BEFORE OBSERVING THEM

(1540) Abū Qatāda (a Companion of the Prophet) reported Allah's Messenger (may peace be upon him) as saying: When any one of you enters the mosque, he should observe two rak'ahs (of Nafl prayer) before sitting.[966]

(1541) Abū Qatāda, a Companion of the Messenger of Allah (may peace be upon him), said: I entered the mosque, when the Messenger of Allah (may peace be upon him) had been sitting among people, and I also sat down among them. Upon this the Messenger of Allah (may peace be upon him) said: What prevented you from offering two raka'hs (of Nafl prayer) before sitting down? I said: Messenger of Allah, I saw you sitting and people sitting (around you and I, therefore, sat in your company). He (the Holy Prophet) then said: When anyone among you enters the mosque, he should not sit till he has observed two rak'ahs.

(1542) Jābir b. 'Abdullah reported: The Apostle of Allah (may peace be upon him) owed me a debt; he paid me back and made an addition (of this).[967] I entered the mosque and he (the Holy Prophet) said to me: Observe two rak'ahs of prayer.

Chapter CCLVI

EXCELLENCE OF OBSERVING TWO RAK'AHS IN THE MOSQUE FOR ONE WHO COMES BACK FROM A JOURNEY

(1543) Jābir b. 'Abdullah reported: The Messenger of Allah (may peace be upon him) bought a camel from me. When he came back to Medina, he ordered me to come to the mosque[968] and observe two rak'ahs of prayer.

(1544) Jābir b. 'Abdullah reported: I went with the Messenger of Allah (may peace be upon him) on an expedition and my camel delayed me and I was exhausted. The Messenger of Allah (may peace be upon him) thus came earlier than I, whereas I came on the next day and went to the mosque and found him (the Holy Prophet) at the gate of the mosque. He said: It is now that you have come. I said: Yes. He said: Leave your camel and enter (the mosque) and observe two rak'ahs. He (the narrator) said: So I entered and observed (two rak'ahs) of prayer and then went back.

966. This is meant to elevate the spiritual consciousness of man and make him realise that he is now in a new atmosphere of religious piety and devotion and nearness to Allah. Nafl prayer is a symbol of one's unbounded love for Allah. The observance of this prayer on entering the mosque transports his soul from his mundane activities to the high level of God-consciousness.

967. Along with the repayment of money, the Holy Prophet (may peace be upon him) told him an act of piety which could take him near the Lord.

968. He wanted to make him the payment for that transaction, but before this he asked him to observe two rak'ahs of prayer, since it was a symbol of devotion to Allah around which the whole life of a Muslim revolves. The Holy Prophet wanted to make God-consciousness and devotion to Him as the basis of all human activities.

(1545) Ka'b b. Mālik reported: The Messenger of Allah (may peace be upon him) did not come back from the journey but by day in the forenoon, and when he arrived, he went first to the mosque, and having prayed two rak'ahs in it he sat down in it.

Chapter CCLVII

EXCELLENCE OF THE FORENOON [969] PRAYER. TWO ARE ITS MINIMUM RAK'AHS AND EIGHT ARE ITS MAXIMUM RAK'AHS, AND AVERAGE RAK'AHS ARE FOUR OR SIX, AND EXHORTATION FOR THE OBSERVANCE OF THE PRAYER

(1546) 'Abdullah b. Shaqīq reported: I asked 'Ā'isha whether the Apostle of Allah (may peace be upon him) used to observe the forenoon prayer. She said: No, but when he came back from the journey.[970]

(1547) 'Abdullah b. Shaqīq reported: I asked 'Ā'isha whether the Apostle of Allah (may peace be upon him) used to observe forenoon prayer. She said: No, except when he came back from a journey.

(1548) 'Urwa reported 'Ā'isha to be saying: I have never seen the Messenger of Allah (may peace be upon him) observing the supererogatory prayer of the forenoon, but I observed it. And if the Messenger of Allah (may peace be upon him) abandoned any act which he in fact loved to do, it was out of fear that if the people practised it constantly, it might become obligatory for them.[971]

(1549) Mu'ādha asked 'Ā'isha (Allah be pleased with her) how many rak'ahs Allah's Messenger (may peace be upon him) prayed at the forenoon prayer.[972] She replied: Four rak'ahs, but sometimes more as he pleased.

(1550) A ḥadīth like this has been transmitted by the same chain of transmitters, but with this alteration that the transmitter said: "As Allah pleased."

969. For inculcating God-consciousness and religious devotion in people, they have been commanded to observe Nafl prayers besides obligatory prayers. Just as in the long interval between the 'Ishā' and dawn prayers, there is recommended a Nafl prayer of the Tahajjud, similarly, in the interval between the dawn and noon prayers the forenoon prayer is recommended. This prayer is of two kinds: the one is Ishrāq which is observed in the earlier hour of the morning, and the second one is Chāsht which is observed later than this. This forenoon prayer is not obligatory; it is supererogatory and is a symbol of one's keen devotion to Allah.

970. The subsequent aḥādīth make it clear that the Holy Prophet did not observe this prayer in the mosque. He used to observe Nafl prayers in his house. But when he came back from a journey which he commonly did in the forenoon, he observed prayer of gratitude in the mosque.

971. The Holy Prophet observed the forenoon prayer and that too in his house hidden from the view of men, but he abandoned it at times so that it might not be taken as an obligatory act. Now had the Holy Prophet observed it regularly and the people had followed him, it would have been treated as an obligatory prayer. The Holy Prophet did not like to put unnecessary burden upon the people and wanted that they should develop religious devotion and piety out of their own accord without any pressure. It was necessary for the elevation of their soul.

972. This proves that Ḥaḍrat 'Ā'isha did not deny the Holy Prophet's observing the forenoon prayer; what she said was that the Prophet did not observe it in the mosque.

(1551) Mu'ādha 'Adawiyya reported 'Ā'isha as saying: The Messenger of Allah (may peace be upon him) used to observe four rak'ahs in the forenoon prayer and he sometimes observed more as Allah pleased.

(1552) A ḥadīth like this has been transmitted by Qatāda with the same chain of transmitters.

(1553) 'Abd al-Raḥmān b. Abū Lailā reported: No one has ever narrated to me that he saw the Apostle of Allah (may peace be upon him) observing the forenoon prayer, except Umm Hānī. She, however, narrated that the Apostle of Allah (may peace be upon him) entered her house on the day of the Conquest of Mecca and prayed eight rak'ahs (adding): I never saw a shorter prayer than it except that he performed the bowing and prostration completely. But (one of the narrators) Ibn Bashshār in his narration made no mention of the word: "Never".

(1554) 'Abdullah b. Ḥārith b. Naufal reported: I had been asking about, as I was desirous to find one among people who should inform me, whether the Messenger of Allah (may peace be upon him) observed the forenoon prayer, but I found none to narrate that to me except Umm Hānī, daughter of Abū Ṭālib (the real sister of Ḥaḍrat 'Alī), who told me that on the day of the Conquest the Messenger of Allah (may peace be upon him) came (to our house) after the dawn had (sufficiently) arisen. A cloth was brought and privacy was provided for him (the Holy Prophet). He took a bath and then stood up and observed eight rak'ahs. I do not know whether his Qiyām (standing posture) was longer, or bending or prostration or all of them were of equal duration. She (Umm Ḥānī) further said: I never saw him saying this Nafl prayer prior to it or subsequently. (Al-Murādī narrated on the authority of Yūnus that he made no mention of the words: "He informed me.")

(1555) Abū Murra, the freed slave of Umm Ḥānī, daughter of Abū Ṭālib, reported Umm Hānī to be saying: I went to the Messenger of Allah (may peace be upon him) on the day of the Conquest of Mecca and found him taking bath, and Fāṭimah, his daughter, had provided him privacy with the help of a cloth [973] I gave him salutation and he said: Who is she? [974] I said: It is Umm Hānī, daughter of Abū Ṭālib. He (the Holy Prophet) said: Greeting for Umm Hānī. When he had completed the bath, he stood up and observed eight rak'ahs wrapped up in one cloth When he turned back (after the prayer), I said to him: Messenger of Allah, the son of my mother 'Alī b. Abū Ṭālib is going to kill a person, Fulān b. Hubaira [975] whom I have given protection Upon this the Messenger of Allah (may peace be upon him) said: We too have given protection whom you have given protection, O Umm Hānī Umm Hānī said: It was the forenoon (prayer).

(1556) Abū Murra narrated on the authority of Umm Hānī that the Messenger of Allah (may peace be upon him) on the day of the Conquest of Mecca observed in her

973. It was the common practice with the Holy Prophet to cover his private parts with the help of loin cloth even when taking a bath. And then he arranged for privacy so that even the upper part of his body was not exposed. Fāṭimah was his daughter and as such one of the members of his household. He, therefore, asked her to provide him privacy.

974. One is permitted to answer salutation while performing ablution or taking a bath.

975. His name was Ḥārith b. Hishām al-Makhzūmī, but some of the scholars assert that he was 'Abdullah b. Abū Rabī'a.

house eight rak'ahs of prayer in one cloth, its opposite corners having been tied from the opposite sides.

(1557) Abū Dharr reported Allah's Apostle (may peace be upon him) as saying: In the morning charity is due from every bone [976] in the body of every one of you. Every utterance of Allah's glorification [977] is an act of charity. Every utterance of praise [978] of Him is an act of charity, every utterance of profession of His Oneness [979] is an act of charity, every utterance of profession of His Greatness [980] is an act of charity, enjoining good is an act of charity, forbidding [981] what is disreputable is an act of charity, and two rak'ahs [982] which one prays in the forenoon will suffice.

(1558) Abū Huraira reported: My friend (the Holy Prophet, may peace be upon him) has instructed me to do three things: three fasts during every month, two rak'ahs of the forenoon prayer,[983] and observing Witr prayer before going to bed.[984]

(1559) A ḥadīth like this has been transmitted by Abū Huraira by another chain of transmitters.

(1560) Abū Huraira reported: My friend Abu'l-Qāsim (may peace be upon him) instructed me to do three things, and the rest of the ḥadīth is the same.

(1561) Abū Murra, the freed slave of Umm Hānī, narrated on the authority of Abū Dardā': My Friend (may peace be upon him) instructed me in three (acts), and I would never abandon them as long as I live. (And these three things are): Three fasts during every month, the forenoon prayer, and this that I should not sleep till I have observed the Witr prayer.

Chapter CCLVIII

EXCELLENCE OF OBSERVING TWO RAK'AHS OF SUNNAH IN THE DAWN PRAYER [985]

(1562) Ibn 'Umar reported that Ḥafṣa, the Mother of the Believers, informed him that when the Mu'adhdhin became silent after calling (people) to the dawn prayer, the Messenger of Allah (may peace be upon him) commenced the dawn (prayer) when it dawned by observing two short rak'ahs before the commencement of the (Farḍ) prayer.

976. This word "Sulāma" means digital bone or bones generally.

977. Reciting of *Subḥān Allah.*

978. *Alḥamdu Lillāh.*

979. *Lā Ilāha Illallāh.*

980. *Allāh-o-Akbar.*

981. In Islam charity or almsgiving does not mean spending of the wealth only, but it is an emblem of one's attachment and devotion to Allah and making sacrifice for His sake. Thus to abstain oneself from evil is also charity or almsgiving in Islam.

982. The words و یجزی من ذالک in the ḥadīth do not refer to the different acts of charity as described above, but as a compensation for that charity which is due from the organs, the bones and joints of a man. So the forenoon prayer is not a substitute for enjoining good or forbidding evil, but it can serve well the purpose of charity due from bones and joints.

983. This is the minimum number of the rak'ahs of the forenoon prayer.

984. When one is not used to Tahajjud prayer, one should observe Witr before going to bed.

985. Two rak'ahs of Sunnah in the dawn prayer have been greatly stressed, and these are considered to be the most important rak'ahs besides the Farḍ prayer.

(1563) This ḥadīth has been transmitted by Nāfi' with the same chain of narrators.

(1564) Ḥafṣa reported that when it was dawn, the Messenger of Allah (may peace be upon him) did not observe (any other prayers) but two short rak'ahs.

(1565) A ḥadīth like this has been transmitted by Shu'ba with the same chain of transmitters.

(1566) Ḥafṣa reported: When the dawn appeared, the Apostle of Allah (may peace be upon him) observed two rak'ahs (of Sunnah prayers).

(1567) 'Ā'isha reported: The Messenger of Allah (may peace be upon him) used to observe two rak'ahs of Sunnah (prayer) when he heard the Adhān and shortened them. (This ḥadīth has been transmitted by the same chain of transmitters and in the ḥadith narrated by Usāma the words are: "When it was dawn".)

(1568) 'Ā'isha reported that the Apostle of Allah (may peace be upon him) used to observe two (supererogatory) rak'ahs in between the call to prayer and the Iqāma of the dawn prayer.

(1569) 'Ā'isha reported that the Messenger of Allah (may peace be upon him) observed two rak'ahs of the dawn prayer and he shortened them (to the extent) that I (out of surprise) said: Did he recite in them Sūra Fātiḥa (only)?

(1570) 'Ā'isha reported: When it was dawn, the Messenger of Allah (may peace be upon him) observed two rak'ahs, and I would say: Does he recite only the opening chapter of the Qur'ān in it?

(1571) 'Ā'isha reported that the Apostle (may peace upon him) was not so much particular about observing supererogatory rak'ahs as in case of the two rak'ahs of the dawn prayer.

(1572) 'Ā'isha reported: I have never seen the Messenger of Allah (may peace be upon him) hastening as much in observing supererogatory as two rak'ahs before the (Farḍ) of the dawn prayer.

(1573) 'Ā'isha reported Allah's Messenger as saying: The two rak'ahs at dawn are better than this world and what it contains.

(1574) 'Ā'isha reported that the Apostle of Allah (may peace be upon him) said about the two (supererogatory) rak'ahs of the dawn: They are dearer to me than the whole world.

(1575) Abū Huraira reported that the Messenger of Allah (may peace be upon him) recited in the two (supererogatory) rak'ahs of the dawn (prayer): "Say: O unbelievers," (Qur'ān, cix.) and "Say: Allah is one" (cxii.).

(1576) Ibn 'Abbās reported that the Messenger of Allah (may peace be upon him) used to recite in first of the two (supererogatory) rak'ahs of the dawn: "Say: We believed in Allah and what was revealed to us . . ." verses (285-286) from Sūra Baqara, and in the second of the two: "I believe in Allah and I bear testimony that we are Muslims" (iii. 51).

(1577) Ibn 'Abbās reported that the Messenger of Allah (may peace be upon him) used to recite in the two (supererogatory) rak'ahs of the dawn prayer: "Say: We believed in Allah and what was revealed to us" and that which is found in Sūra Āl-i-'Imrān: "Come to that word (creed) which is common between you and us" (iii. 64).

(1578) This ḥadīth has been transmitted by another chain of narrators.

Chapter CCLIX

THE VIRTUE OF SUNAN[986] PRAYERS BEFORE AND AFTER THE FARḌ RAK'AHS AND THEIR NUMBER

(1579) Umm Ḥabība (the wife of the Holy Prophet) reported Allah's Messenger (may peace be upon him) as saying : A house will be built in Paradise for anyone who prays in a day and a night twelve rak'ahs ; and she added : I have never abandoned (observing them) since I heard it from the Messenger of Allah (may peace be upon him). Some of the other narrators said the same words : I have never abandoned (observing them) since I heard (from so and so).

(1580) Nu'mān b. Sālim reported with the same chain of transmitters : He who observed twelve voluntary[987] rak'ahs, a house will be built for him in Paradise.

(1581) Umm Ḥabība, the wife of the Apostle of Allah (may peace be upon him), reported Allah's Messenger (may peace be upon him) as saying : If any Muslim servant (of Allah) prays for the sake of Allah twelve rak'ahs (of Sunan) every day, over and above the obligatory ones, Allah will build for him a house in Paradise, or a house will be built for him in Paradise ; and I have not abandoned to observe them after (hearing it from the Messenger of Allah). (So said also 'Amr and Nu'mān.)

(1582) Umm Ḥabība reported the Messenger of Allah (may peace be upon him) having said : If any Muslim servant (of Allah) performed ablution, and performed it well, and then observed every day, the rest of the ḥadīth is the same.

(1583) Ibn 'Umar reported : I prayed along[988] with Allah's Messenger (may peace be upon him) two rak'ahs before[989] and two rak'ahs after the noon prayer, two rak'ahs after the sunset prayer and two rak'ahs after the 'Ishā prayer and two rak'ahs after the Friday prayer ; and so far as the sunset, 'Ishā' and Friday prayers are concerned, I observed (them) along with the Apostle of Allah (may peace be upon him) in his house.[990]

986. The Sunan prayers are of two types, Sunan al-Rātiba or Muwakkada (the stressed ones) and Ghair Muwakkad or Ghair Rawātib (not stressed). These Sunan rak'ahs are very important and are meant to make good any deficiency left in the observance of Farḍ rak'ahs. In the order of importance, the most important are the two rak'ahs of the dawn prayer (before Farḍ), then two rak'ahs of the evening prayer, then two rak'ahs of the noon prayer and two rak'ahs of the 'Ishā' prayer, all of them after the observance of Farḍ prayer and lastly four rak'ahs of the noon prayer before Farḍ rak'ahs (*Mirqāt*, Vol. III, p. 111).

987. Although *Taṭawwu'* means voluntary, but here it signifies Sunan rak'ahs and voluntary in this context means that one should observe it readily with a keen sense of devotion to Allah and without any desire for fame.

988. "Praying along" here does not mean praying behind him. It simply means : "I saw him observing those rak'ahs and I too did the same."

989. Imām Shāfi'ī, on the basis of this ḥadīth, favours the observance of two rak'ahs (of Sunan prayer in the noon) before Farḍ. The Ḥanafites are in favour of four rak'ahs which are based on the traditions transmitted by Ḥaḍrat 'Alī, Ḥaḍrat 'Ā'isha and Umm Ḥabība. The later jurists Sufyān Thaurī, 'Abdullah b. Mubārak, Isḥāq b. Rahwaih are also in favour of four. The Ḥanafites interpret these two rak'ahs as rak'ahs of greeting to the mosque as recorded in the earlier chapters. They think that the Holy Prophet observed these voluntary rak'ahs in his house and so he must be observing four in his house but, on entering the mosque, he would have observed the greeting rak'ahs. It is with four voluntary rak'ahs before the noon prayer that the twelve rak'ahs are complete.

990. Ibn 'Umar was the real brother of the Prophet's wife (Ḥaḍrat Ḥafṣa). He could, therefore, see for himself the Sunan prayer which the Holy Prophet (may peace be upon him) observed in the

Chapter CCLX

PERMISSIBILITY OF OBSERVING NAFL[991] (VOLUNTARY PRAYER) STANDING OR SITTING AND OBSERVING SOME PART OF IT STANDING OR SITTING

(1584) 'Abdullah b. Shaqīq said: I asked 'Ā'isha about the Messenger of Allah's (may peace be upon him) voluntary prayers, and she replied: Before the noon prayer, he used to pray four rak'ahs in my house; then would go out and lead the people in prayer; then come in and pray two rak'ahs. He would then lead the people in the sunset prayer; then come in and pray two rak'ahs. Then he would lead the people in the 'Ishā' prayer, and enter my house and pray two rak'ahs. He would pray nine rak'ahs during the night, including Witr. At night he would pray for a long time standing and for a long time sitting, and when he recited the Holy Qur'ān while standing, he would bow and prostrate himself from the standing position, and when he recited while sitting, he would bow and prostrate himself from the sitting position, and when it was dawn he would pray two rak'ahs.

(1585) 'Ā'isha reported that the Messenger of Allah (may peace be upon him) would pray in the night for a long time, and when he prayed standing he bowed in a standing posture, and when he prayed sitting, he bowed in a sitting posture.[992]

(1586) 'Abdullah b. Shaqīq reported: I fell ill in Persia and, therefore, prayed in a sitting posture, and I asked 'Ā'isha about it and she said: The Messenger of Allah (may peace be upon him) prayed for a long time in the night sitting.[993]

(1587) 'Abdullah b. Shaqīq al-'Uqailī reported: I asked 'Ā'isha about the prayer of the Messenger of Allah (may peace be upon him) during the night (i.e. Tahajjud prayer). She replied: He used to pray for a long time standing and for a long time sitting in the night, and when he recited the Qur'ān while standing, he would bow himself from the standing position, and when he recited while sitting, he would bow from the sitting position.

(1588) 'Abdullah b. Shaqīq al-'Uqailī reported: I asked 'Ā'isha about the prayer of the Messenger of Allah (may peace be upon him). She said: The Messenger of Allah (may peace be upon him) would observe prayer (Nafl) in a standing position as well as in a sitting position, and when he commenced the prayer in a standing position, he bowed in this very position, and when he commenced the prayer in a sitting position, he bowed in this very position.

(1589) 'Ā'isha reported: I did not see the Messenger of Allah (may peace be upon him) reciting (the Qur'ān) in the night prayer in a sitting position, till he grew old and

house. It must be remembered that the Messenger of Allah (may peace be upon him) often stressed upon his followers to observe Nafl and Sunan prayers in their houses so that they should not be seen by anyone and thus develop a keen sense of religious piety and single-minded devotion to Allah by inculcating perfect sincerity in their prayers.

991. The Nafl can be observed standing or sitting.

992. This is essential. If Nafl prayer is to be observed in a posture of standing, one should bow in this very posture and if it is observed sitting, then one should not stand up to bow and prostrate.

993. It is permitted to observe Nafl prayer either standing or sitting.

then he recited (it) in a sitting position, but when thirty or forty verses were left out of the Sūra, he would then stand up, recite them and then bowed.[994]

(1590) 'Ā'isha reported: The Messenger of Allah (may peace be upon him) used to pray while sitting (when he grew old) and he recited in this position and when the recitation equal to thirty or forty verses was left, he would then stand up and recite (for this duration) in a standing position and then bowed himself and then prostrated himself and did the same in the second rak'ah.

(1591) 'Ā'isha reported: The Messenger of Allah (may peace be upon him) used to recite in a sitting position (while observing the Tahajjud prayer) and when he intended to bow, he would stand up and recite (for the duration in which) a man (ordinarily) recites forty verses.

(1592) 'Alqama b. Waqqāṣ reported: I asked 'Ā'isha how the Messenger of Allah (may peace be upon him) did in the two rak'ahs as he (observed them) sitting. She said: He would recite (the Qur'ān) in them, and when he intended to bow, he would stand up and then bowed.[995]

(1593) 'Abdullah b. Shaqīq reported: I asked 'Ā'isha whether the Apostle of Allah (may peace be upon him) observed (Nafl) sitting. She said: Yes, when the people had made him old.[996]

(1594) 'Abdullah b. Shaqīq reported: I said to 'Ā'isha and she made a mention of that (recorded above) about the Apostle of Allah (may peace be upon him).

(1595) 'Ā'isha reported that the Messenger of Allah (may peace be upon him) died (in this very state) that he observed most of his (Nafl) prayers in a sitting position.[997]

(1596) 'Ā'isha reported: When the Messenger of Allah (may peace be upon him) grew bulky and heavy he would observe (most of his Nafl) prayers sitting.

(1597) Ḥafṣa reported: Never did I see the Messenger of Allah (may peace be upon him) observing supererogatory prayer sitting till one year before his death when he would observe Nafl prayer in a sitting position, and he would recite the Sūra (of the Qur'ān) in such a slow-measured tone (that duration of its recital) became more lengthy than the one longer than this.

(1598) Zuhrī reported this ḥadīth with the same chain of transmitters, except this that he made a mention of one year or two years.

994. This ḥadīth should not be taken as contrary to the previous ones. It has been laid down that both the positions are permissible in Nafl prayers. One can observe it sitting if one lacks strength enough to stand for longer hours or if one is ill. One is permitted to change positions even during the prayer when there is any genuine need for it. What is not preferable is that one should bow in a sitting position while one has recited the Qur'ān in a standing position and *vice versa*, without any reason.

995. Thisi s also permissible in exceptional circumstances. But it is preferable to recite some verses after standing and then bow down (*Fatḥ al-Mulhim*, Vol. II, p. 285).

996. The worries and anxieties concerning the welfare of people had burdened him and he grew old.

997. This gives an insight of Muḥammad's (may peace be upon him) devotion to Allah. He grew old not for his personal sorrows but his anxieties about Islam and the Muslims and the whole of humanity. He worked hard incessantly to lead people to the path of righteousness and underwent all kinds of suffering for this noble cause. He did this not for any worldly end but for the love and devotion of Allah and, even in broken health and old age, he would spend a major part of his time in prayer and meditation.

(1599) Jābir b. Samura reported that the Apostle of Allah (may peace be upon him) observed (Nafl) prayer sitting before his death.

(1600) 'Abdullah b. 'Amr reported: It was narrated to me that the Messenger of Allah (may peace be upon him) had said: The prayer observed by a person sitting is half of the prayer. I came to him (may peace be upon him) and found him praying in a sitting position. I placed my hand on his head. He said: O 'Abdullah b. 'Amr, what is the matter with you? I said: Messenger of Allah, it has been narrated to me that you said: The prayer of a man in a sitting position is half of the prayer, whereas you are observing prayer sitting. He (the Holy Prophet) said: Yes, it is so, but I am not like anyone amongst you.[998]

(1601) A ḥadīth like this has been narrated by Abū Yaḥyā al-A'raj with the same chain of transmitters.

Chapter CCLXI

PRAYER DURING THE NIGHT[999] AND THE NUMBER OF THE RAK'AHS WHICH THE APOSTLE (MAY PEACE BE UPON HIM) OBSERVED IN THE NIGHT AND OBSERVANCE OF ONE RAK'AH OF WITR

(1602) 'Ā'isha reported that the Messenger of Allah (may peace be upon him) used to pray eleven rak'ahs at night, observing the Witr with a single rak'ah, and

998. One interpretation is that the Holy Prophet spent most of time in meditation and prayer and he had the most heavy responsibilities upon him as the Messenger of Allah. He was, therefore, granted this special privilege that his prayer in sitting carried the same weight as prayer in standing. The second interpretation is that "I have special reason for it," i e. old age, which you do not have. The first interpretation, i.e. special privilege, seems to be more plausible.

999. Ṣalāt-ul-Lail, i.e. Tahajjud, and Qiyām-ul-Lail are generally taken to be the one and the same thing. But there is a slight distinction between them. Tahajjud is that optional prayer which is observed after sleep in the latter part of the night. Ṣalāt-ul-Lail or Qiyām-ul-Lail includes even that prayer which is recommended as a substitute for Tahajjud prayer for one who is overpowered by sleep and finds it difficult to get up at early hour of the dawn or for one who is exhausted and cannot, therefore, rise for Tahajjud.

According to Shāfi'ites, Witr prayer is a part of Ṣalāt-ul-Lail. If it is observed before Tahajjud it would be termed as Ṣalāt-ul-Lail and, if after Tahajjud, it would be called Tahajjud. The Ḥanafites, however, look upon Witr and Tahajjud as two distinct prayers.

Tahajjud prayer is optional, but it is considered to be the most effective prayer for inculcating a true religious devotion and love of God. As it is observed individually in the stillness of the latter part of the night, when most of the people enjoy sleep, it, therefore, elevates the soul of man and brings him near to God. The man experiences the Divine Presence in the depth of his own heart and in the innermost recesses of his soul and thus it creates in him a reverential and trustful consciousness of the living presence of God. The following verses of the Qur'ān make these points clear:

> O thou who is wrapped up! rise to pray in the night except a little half of it, or lessen it a little or add to it, and recite the Qur'ān well intonated. Surely the getting up by night is the firmest way to subdue (the soul) and most impressive in speech (lxxiii. 1-6).
>
> And during a part of the night, forsake sleep to offer prayer, besides what is incumbent on thee; maybe thy Lord will raise thee to a position of great glory (xvii. 79).

There are no fixed rak'ahs in the Tahajjud prayer. These vary from five to thirteen including Witr and some time in these five rak'ahs the two rak'ahs of Sunnah of the dawn prayer are also counted.

when he had finished them, he lay down on his right side, till the Mu'adhdhin came to him and he (the Holy Prophet) then observed two short rak'ahs (of Sunan of the dawn prayer).

(1603) 'Ā'isha, the wife of the Apostle of Allah (may peace be upon him), said that between the time when the Messenger of Allah (may peace be upon him) finished the 'Ishā' prayer which is called 'Atama by the people, he used to pray eleven rak'ahs, uttering the salutation at the end of every two rak'ahs, and observing the Witr with a single one. And when the Mu'adhdhin had finished the call (for the) dawn prayer and he saw the dawn clearly and the Mu'adhdhin had come to him, he stood up and prayed two short rak'ahs. Then he lay down on his right side till the Mu'adhdhin came to him for Iqāma. (This ḥadīth has been transmitted with the same chain of transmitters by Ibn Shihāb, but in it no mention has been made of Iqāma.)

(1604) 'Ā'isha reported: The Messenger of Allah (may peace be upon him) used to observe thirteen rak'ahs of the night prayer. Five out of them consisted of Witr, and he did not sit, but at the end (for salutation).[1000]

(1605) This ḥadīth has been transmitted by Hishām with the same chain of transmitters.

(1606) 'Ā'isha reported that the Messenger of Allah (may peace be upon him) used to pray thirteen rak'ahs during the night including the two rak'ahs (Sunan) of the dawn prayer.

(1607) Abū Salama b. 'Abd ul-Raḥmān asked 'Ā'isha about the (night) prayer of the Messenger of Allah (may peace be upon him) during the month of Ramaḍān.[1001] She said: The Messenger of Allah (may peace be upon him) did not observe either in Ramaḍān or in other months more than eleven rak'ahs (of the night prayer). He (in the first instance) observed four rak'ahs. Ask not about their excellence and their length (i.e. these were matchless in perfection and length). He again observed four rak'ahs, and ask not about their excellence and their length. He would then observe three rak'ahs (of the Witr prayer). 'Ā'isha again said: I said: Messenger of Allah, do you sleep before observing the Witr prayer? He said: O 'Ā'isha, my eyes sleep but my heart does not sleep.[1002]

1000. This is also permissible, but the most common practice with the Holy Prophet was that he observed two rak'ahs and then recited salutation, and again commenced the two rak'ahs and thus completed eleven or thirteen rak'ahs including the Witr. The Witr may be one or three or even five, or even seven and nine. According to the Ḥanafites, the Witr consists of three rak'ahs only, but according to the Shāfi'ites and Mālikites, and Ḥanbalites, and Ahl-i-Ḥadīth, the Witr prayer may be observed from one rak'ahs to eleven rak'ahs. The scholars of Ḥadīth are of the opinion that all these rak'ahs are not Witr but a part of the night prayer which for the sake of brevity are called Witr. These are in fact the combination of Ṣalāt-ul-Lail and Witr.

1001. It is on the basis of this ḥadīth that some of the jurists believe the prescribed rak'ahs for theTarāwīḥ prayer as eight only. The Ḥanafites differ with them and assert that it is not proper to make this deduction from the above-mentioned words of Ḥaḍrat 'Ā'isha (peace be upon her). They believe that the narrator asked 'Ā'isha explicitly about the Tahajjud prayer and she gave reply about it and it has no concern with Ṣalat-ul-Tarāwīḥ (*Fatḥ al-Mulhim*, Vol. II, p. 291).

Ḥafiẓ Ibn Qayyim, after reviewing most of the aḥādīth giving the number of the rak'ahs of the Tahajjud prayer, says: There is a sort of some agreement on eleven rak'ahs (of the Tahajjud prayer) (*Zād al-Ma'ād*, Vol. I, p. 175).

1002. This has already been discussed before ("Kitāb-ul-Īmān" and "Kitāb-us-Ṣalāt," ḥadīth No. 1448).

(1608) Abū Salama asked 'Ā'isha about the prayer of the Messenger of Allah (may peace be upon him). She said: He observed thirteen rak'ahs (in the night prayer). He observed eight rak'ahs and would then observe Witr and then observe two rak'ahs sitting,[1003] and when he wanted to bow he stood up and then bowed down, and then observed two raka'hs in between the Adhān and Iqāma of the dawn prayer.

(1609) Abū Salama reported that he asked 'Ā'isha about the prayer of the Messenger of Allah (may peace be upon him) (during the night). The rest of the ḥadīth is the same but with this exception that he (the Holy Prophet) observed nine rak'ahs including Witr.[1004]

(1610) Abū Salama is reported to have said: I came to 'Ā'isha. I said: O mother, inform me about the prayer of the Messenger of Allah (may peace be upon him). She said: His (night prayer) in Ramaḍān and (during other months) was thirteen rak'ahs at night including two rak'ahs of Fajr.

(1611) It is reported on the authority of 'Ā'isha that the prayer of Allah's Messenger (may peace be upon him) in the night consisted of ten rak'ahs. He observed a Witr and two rak'ahs (of Sunan) of the dawn prayer, and thus the total comes to thirteen rak'ahs.

(1612) 'Ā'isha thus reported about the (night prayer) of the Messenger of Allah (may peace be upon him): He used to sleep in the early part of the night, and woke up in the latter part. If he then wished intercourse with his wife, he satisfied his desire, and then went to sleep; and when the first call to prayer was made he jumped up (by Allah, she, i.e. 'Ā'isha, did not say "he stood up"), and poured water over him (by Allah she, i.e. 'Ā'isha, did not say that he took a bath but I know what she meant) and if he did not have an intercourse, he performed ablution, just as a man performs ablution for prayer and then observed two rak'ahs.[1005]

(1613) 'Ā'isha observed that the Messenger of Allah (may peace be upon him) used to observe prayer in the night and the last of his (night) prayer was Witr.

(1614) Masrūq is reported to have asked 'Ā'isha about the action (most pleasing to) the Messenger of Allah (may peace be upon him), She said: He (the Holy Prophet) loved (that action) which one keeps on doing regularly. I said (to 'Ā'isha): When did he pray (at night)? She replied: When he heard the cock crow, he got up and observed prayer.

(1615) 'Ā'isha reported: Never did the earlier part of the dawn[1006] find the Messenger of Allah (may peace be upon him) but sleeping in my house or near me.

1003. This is not a part of the regular Tahajjud prayer, but it was done by the Holy Prophet very seldom in order to tell people that one is permitted to observe Nafl after Witr.

1004. It gives the number of rak'ahs in the Tahajjud prayer as six if the Witr consists of three rak'ahs and eight if the Witr consists of one rak'ah.

1005. This ḥadīth shows how carefully the words of Ḥaḍrat 'Ā'isha (peace be upon her) were recorded and faithfully transmitted to others. This also sheds a good deal of light on the extremely modest behaviour of Ḥaḍrat 'Ā'isha. She is the Mother of the Faithful and as such it was her bounden duty to inform her sons about the personal and private life of the Holy Prophet, but at the same time she was a very shy and self-respecting lady; she, therefore, exercised utmost care in the use of words in keeping with her high dignity and honour.

1006. The Holy Prophet spent so much time in the latter part of night in devotion and prayer that he felt tired and then went to sleep before rising for the dawn prayer.

(1616) 'Ā'isha reported: When the Apostle of Allah (may peace be upon him) had prayed the two rak'ahs (Sunan) of the dawn prayer, he would talk to me if I was awake, otherwise he would lie down.

(1617) Aḥadīth like this has been narrated by 'Ā'isha by another chain of transmitters.

(1618) 'Ā'isha reported: The Messenger of Allah (may peace be upon him) used to pray in the night and when he observed Witr, he said to me: O 'Ā'isha, get up and observe Witr.[1007]

(1619) 'Ā'isha reported that the Messenger of Allah (may peace be upon him) used to offer prayer at night while she lay in front of him, and when the Witr prayer was yet to be observed, he would awaken her and she observed Witr.

(1620) 'Ā'isha reported: The Messenger of Allah (may peace be upon him) observed the Witr prayer every night and he completed Witr at the time of dawn.

(1621) Masrūq reported on the authority of 'Ā'isha that she said that the Messenger of Allah (may peace be upon him) used to observe the Witr prayer every night, maybe in the early part of night, at midnight and in the latter part, finishing his Witr at dawn.[1008]

(1622) 'Ā'isha reported that the Messenger of Allah (may peace be upon him) used to observe Witr every night, and he would (at times) complete his Witr at the end of the night.

(1623) Sa'd b. Hishām[1009] b. 'Āmir decided to participate in the expedition for the sake of Allah, so he came to Medina and he decided to dispose of his property there and buy arms and horses instead and fight against the Romans to the end of his life. When he came on Medina, he met the people of Medina. They dissuaded him to do such a thing, and informed him that a group of six men had decided to do so during the lifetime of the Apostle of Allah (may peace be upon him) and the Apostle of Allah (may peace be upon him) forbade them to do it, and said: Is there not for you a model pattern in me?[1010] And when they narrated this to him (Sa'd b. Hishām), he returned to his wife, though he had divorced her and made (people) witness to his reconciliation. He then came to Ibn 'Abbās and asked him about the Witr of the Messenger of Allah (may peace be upon him). Ibn 'Abbās said: Should I not lead you to one who knows best amongst the people of the world about the Witr of the Messenger of Allah (may peace be upon him)? He said: Who is it? He (Ibn 'Abbās) said: It is 'Ā'isha.[1011] So go to her and ask her (about Witr) and then come to me and inform me about her answer that she would give you. So I came to Ḥakīm b. Aflaḥ and requested him to

1007. This ḥadīth clearly indicates that Witr prayer is not Nafl (supererogatory) like Tahajjud, but it is Wājib (compulsory).

1008. This shows that Witr can be observed in any part of the night, but it must be observed.

1009. He was one of the eminent Successors belonging to Anṣār. He is counted as one of the reliable transmitters of Ḥadīth and has narrated many aḥādīth on the authority of Ḥadrat 'Ā'isha and Ibn 'Umar (may Allah be pleased with them). Ḥasan Baṣrī narrates on his authority. According to Zarqānī, he was one of those early Muslims who came to India.

1010. The Prophet's life is a balanced life consisting of deep religious devotion, piety, God-consciousness, prayer and meditation, but at the same time a life full of healthy social activities. The Holy Prophet did not persuade his followers to renounce the amenities of life, but he exhorted them to enjoy them with moral restraints.

1011. This gives an idea in what high esteem was 'Ā'isha (Allah be pleased with her) held by the Companions of the Holy Prophet.

take me to her. He said: I would not go to her, for I forbade her to speak anything (about the conflict) between the two groups,[1012] but she refused (to accept my advice) and went (to participate in that conflict). I (requested) him (Ḥakīm) with an oath to lead me to her. So we went to 'Ā'isha and we begged permission to meet her. She granted us permission and we went in. She said: Are you Ḥakīm? (She recognised him.) He replied: Yes. She said: Who is there with you? He said: He is Sa'd b. Hishām. She said: Which Hishām? He said: He is Hishām b. 'Āmir. She blessed him ('Āmir) with mercy from Allah and spoke good of him (Qatāda said that he died as a martyr in Uḥud). I said: Mother of the Faithful, tell me about the character[1013] of the Messenger of Allah (may peace be upon him). She said: Don't you read the Qur'ān? I said: Yes. Upon this she said: The character of the Apostle of Allah (may peace be upon him) was the Qur'ān[1014] He said: I felt inclined to get up and not ask anything (further) till death.[1015] But then I changed my mind and said: Inform me about the observance (of the night prayer) of the Messenger of Allah (may peace be upon him).[1016] She said: Did you not recite: "O thou wrapped up"?[1017] He said: Yes. She said: Allah, the Exalted and the Glorious, made the observance of the night prayer at the beginning of this Sūra obligatory.[1018] So the Apostle of Allah (may peace be upon him) and his Companions around him observed this (night prayer) for one year. Allah held

1012. It refers to the conflict between Ḥaḍrat 'Alī and Ḥaḍrat Mu'āwiya and their followers (Allah be pleased with them).

1013. The word "*khuluq*" used in the text covers a wide range of meanings. It means innate peculiarity, natural disposition, character, temper, nature and morality, qualities of head and heart.

1014. The personality of the Holy Prophet was the visible expression of all those virtues which have been described in the Qur'ān.

1015 The answer is most appropriate and good enough to lead one to the path of righteousness. Everything that is needed for the right guidance is recorded in the Qur'ān.

1016. There is highly meaningful and implied reference to the need of the Ḥadīth along with the Qur'ān. The Holy Qur'ān is a comprehensive Book and succinctly sums up all the teachings for right conduct, but for the practical details of the teachings of the Qur'ān, we have to look into the records of Ḥadīth. That is why the narrator changed his mind. He wanted to know the virtues of the Holy Prophet. 'Ā'isha's reply was that all the noble qualities found in the Holy Prophet have been described in the Holy Qur'ān. That is all true and the narrator was fully convinced of the truth of this statement. But then the idea occurred to him that there were certain practical details of the Prophet's life which have not been discussed in the Qur'ān in the form from which we can get practical guidance. This idea changed his mind and he was impelled to ask 'Ā'isha about one such thing, i.e. Witr and night prayer. The reference is no doubt there in the Qur'ān about them, but no practical detail is given. For this, he was obliged to ask 'Ā'isha to furnish him the required information.

1017. Al-Qur'ān, lxxiii. The verse begins: "O thou covering thyself up, rise to pray by night except a little half of it, or lessen it a little, or add to it, and recite the Qur'ān in a leisurely manner. Surely We shall charge you with a weighty word" (lxxiii. 6).

The tone and the style of the verse clearly reveal that it concerns the earliest period of the commencement of revelation. In receiving the first revelation, the Holy Prophet had covered himself up, as he was afraid of the great responsibilities that were going to fall on his shoulder. On this occasion he was told by Allah to be up and prepare himself through the night prayer for undertaking this great responsibility, since it is the night prayer which is the more effective means for inculcating a habit of meditation of and devotion to Allah. One is very close to Him in the stillness of the night, and one is free to pour one's heart before Him hidden from the eyes of people.

1018. The use of singular in these verses implies that it is obligatory for the Holy Prophet in order to train him for the great mission of prophethood. The other Muslims who love piety and

back the concluding portion of this Sūra for twelve months in the Heaven till (at the end of this period) Allah revealed the concluding verses of this Sūra which lightened (the burden of this prayer), and the night prayer became a supererogatory prayer after being an obligatory one. I said: Mother of the Faithful, inform me about the Witr of the Messenger of Allah (may peace be upon him). She said: I used to prepare tooth stick for him and water for his ablution, and Allah would rouse him to the extent He wished during the night. He would use the tooth stick, and perform ablution, and would offer nine rak'ahs, and would not sit but in the eighth one and would remember Allah, and praise Him and supplicate Him, then he would get up without uttering the salutation and pray the ninth rak'ah.[1019] He would then sit, remember, praise Him and supplicate Him and then utter a salutation loud enough for us to hear. He would then pray two rak'ahs sitting after uttering the salutation, and that made eleven rak'ahs. O my son, but when the Apostle of Allah (may peace be upon him) grew old and put on flesh, he observed Witr of seven, doing in the two rak'ahs as he had done formerly, and that made nine. O my son, and when the Apostle of Allah (may peace be upon him) observed prayer, he liked to keep on observing it, and when sleep or pain overpowered him and made it impossible (for him) to observe prayer in the night, he prayed twelve rak'ahs during the day.[1020] I am not aware of Allah's Prophet (may peace be upon him) having recited the whole Qur'ān during one single night, or praying through the night till morning, or fasting a complete month, except Ramaḍān. He (the narrator) said: I then went to Ibn 'Abbās and narrated to him the ḥadīth (transmitted from her), and he said: She says the truth. If I went to her and got into her presence, I whould have listened to it orally from her. He said: If I were to know that

nearness to God should also spend part of the night in meditation and prayer. But as all of them cannot bear its burden, it has been made Nafl (supererogatory) for them. The Qur'ān says:

> He knows that (all of) you are not able to do it, so He has turned to you (mercifully), so read of the Qur'ān that which is easy for you. He knows that there are sick among you, and others who travel in the land seeking of Allah's bounty, and others who fight in Allah's way (lxxiii. 20).

1019. Maulānā Shabbīr Aḥmad is of the opinion that, although Ḥaḍrat Ā'isha (may Allah be pleased with her) used the word "Witr" for all the rak'ahs of the night prayer, both Tahajjud and Witr, but while explaining the point she had in her mind exclusively the Witr prayer as the narrator had asked about it only. She said nothing about the Tahajjud prayer and informed about the Witr that the Holy Prophet sat after the second prayer but did this after sitting in the third rak'ah. As for the rak'ahs of the Tahajjud, it was clear that the Holy Prophet used to observe them by twos (*Fatḥ al-Mulhim*, Vol. II, p. 304).

1020. This gives us guidance about the compensation of Tahajjud. The man who is regular in praying Tahajjud feels an immense loss if he misses it. For his compensation an alternative has been given that he should observe twelve rak'ahs of supererogatory prayer during the daytime, particularly after the Ẓuhr prayer. Some jurists who do not believe Witr prayer to be compulsory base their claim on this ḥadīth. But their argument does not seem to be weighty. Here a substitute is suggested for Nafl prayer for those who are regular in observing it. The question of the Witr prayer does not arise in this context. We have so many other aḥādīth which give us a clear idea of the compensation of Witr prayer; for example, in Abū Dāwūd this is recorded from the Holy Prophet on the authority of Abū Sa'īd al-Khudrī: He who could not observe Witr prayer on account of sleep or who forgot to do it, he should observe it when he remembers it. It is on this ground that eminent scholars and Companions like 'Alī b. Abū Ṭālib, Sa'd b. Abī Waqqāṣ, 'Abdullah b. Mas'ūd and 'Abdullah b. 'Umar, 'Ubāda b. Sāmit, Mu'ādh b. Jabal and so many others (may Allah be pleased with all of them) are in favour of the qaḍā' (its compensation of Witr prayer.) (*Fatḥ al-Mulhim*, Vol. II, p. 305).

you do not go to her, I would not have transmitted this ḥadīth to you narrated by her.

(1624) Zurāra b. Aufā said that Sa'd b. Hishām divorced his wife, and then proceeded to Medina to sell his property, and the rest of the ḥadīth is the same.

(1625) Sa'd b. Hishām reported: I went to 'Abdullah b. 'Abbās and asked him about the Witr prayer, and the rest of the ḥadīth is the same as recorded in this event. She (Ḥaḍrat 'Ā'isha) said: Who is that Hishām? I said: Son of 'Āmir. She said: What a fine man 'Āmir was! He died as a martyr in the Battle of Uḥud.

(1626) Zurāra b. Aufā reported that Sa'd b. Hishām was his neighbour and he informed him that he had divorced his wife and he narrated the ḥadīth like the one transmitted by Sa'd. She ('Ā'isha) said: Who is Hishām? He said: The son of 'Āmir. She said: What a fine man he was; he participated in the Battle of Uḥud along with the Messenger of Allah (may peace be upon him). Ḥakīm b. Aflaḥ said: If I ever knew that you do not go to 'Ā'isha, I would not have informed you about her ḥadīth (so that you would have gone to her and heard it from her orally).

(1627) 'Ā'isha reported that when the Messenger of Allah (may peace be upon him) missed the night prayer due to pain or any other reason, he observed twelve rak'ahs during the daytime.

(1628) 'A'isha reported that when the Messenger of Allah (may peace be upon him) decided upon doing any act, he continued to do it, and when he slept at night or fell sick he observed twelve rak'ahs during the daytime. I am not aware of Allah's Messenger (may peace be upon him) observing prayer during the whole of the night till morning, or observing fast for a whole month continuously except that of Ramaḍān.[1021]

(1629) 'Umar b. Khaṭṭāb reported Allah's Messenger (may peace be upon him) as saying: Should anyone fall asleep and fail to recite his portion of the Qur'ān, or a part of it,[1022] if he recites it between the dawn prayer and the noon prayer, it will be recorded for him as though he had recited it during the night.

Chapter CCLXII

FORENOON PRAYER SHOULD BE OFFERED WHEN IT IS SUFFICIENTLY HOT

(1630) Zaid b. Arqam, on seeing some people praying in the forenoon, said: They well know that prayer at another time than this is more excellent, for Allah's Messenger (may peace be upon him) said: The prayer of those who are penitent[1023] is observed

1021. This shows that the Holy Prophet (may peace be upon him) wanted to see his followers as persons having strong will power with consistent behaviour and predictable character. He did not like men to be led by whims. He wanted that the Muslims should remain steadfast and observe their duties punctually and regularly. He, therefore, did not like them to put upon themselves burdens which they cannot easily and steadfastly shoulder.

1022. It may be recital of the Qur'ān at night which a man does regularly or may be recital of the Qur'ān in the different rak'ahs of the night prayer.

1023. *Awwābīn* is the plural of *Awwāb* and the root word (*Awaba* اوب) means to return or to be penitent. This is another name for the Chāsht prayer. It is called Awwāb prayer because it is observed at that time when the sun sufficiently rises. It is in fact the time for rest, but those who have deep love for God observe prayer. Young camels are said to feel the hot sand very much when the quarter of the day has passed. These words of the Holy Prophet give a clue by which the timing of the Chāsht prayer can be easily determined.

when your weaned camels feel the heat of the sun.

(1631) Zaid b. Arqam reported that the Messenger of Allah (may peace be upon him) went out to the people of Qubā' and saw them observing prayer; upon this he said: The prayer of the penitent should be observed when the young weaned camels feel heat of the sun.

Chapter CCLXIII

NIGHT PRAYER CONSISTS OF PAIRS OF RAK'AHS AND WITR IS A RAK'AH AT THE END OF THE NIGHT

(1632) Ibn Umar reported that a person asked the Messenger of Allah (may peace be upon him) about the night prayer. The Messenger of Allah (may peace be upon him) said: Prayer during the night should consist of pairs of rak'ahs, but if one of you fears morning is near, he should pray one rak'ah which will make his prayer an odd number for him.[1024]

(1633) Sālim reported on the authority of his father that a person asked the Apostle of Allah (may peace be upon him) about the night prayer. He said: It consists of pairs of rak'ah, but if one fears morning is near, he should make it an odd number by praying one rak'ah

(1634) 'Abdullah b. 'Umar reported: A man stood up and said: Messenger of Allah, how is the night prayer? The Messenger of Allah (may peace be upon him) said: The night prayer consists of pairs, but if you apprehend the rise of dawn, make it odd number by observing one rak'ah.

(1635) 'Abdullah b. 'Umar reported: A person asked the Apostle of Allah (may peace be upon him) as I stood between him (the Holy Prophet) and the inquirer and he said: Messenger of Allah, how is the night prayer? He (the Holy Prophet) said: It consists of pairs of rak'ahs, but if you apprehend morning, you should pray one rak'ah and make the end of your prayer as Witr.[1025] Then a person asked him (the Holy Prophet) at the end of the year and I was at that place near the Messenger of Allah (may peace be upon him); but I do not know whether he was the same person or another person, but he (the Holy Prophet) gave him the same reply.

(1636) This ḥadīth has been transmitted by Ibn 'Umar by another chain of transmitters but it does not have these words: "Then a person asked him at the end of the year," and what follows subsequently.

1024. There is a good deal of difference of opinion on the facts gathered from this ḥadīth. Imām Shāfi'ī asserts on the authority of this ḥadīth that Witr consists of one rak'ah. The Ḥanafites say that there is nothing in this ḥadīth which goes to prove that Witr is one. They interpret the ḥadīth in this way: The night prayer should be observed preferably in pairs and one who prays for such long hours that there is a fear of the approach of morning, then he should conclude the last pair as a Witr by adding one rak'ah to it (*Fatḥ al-Mulhim*, Vol. II, p. 313).

1025. Maulānā Shabbīr Aḥmad has given a very brilliant exposition of this sentence واجعل آخر صلوتک وترآ in support of his stand for three rak'ahs of Witr. He says the Holy Prophet never said: واجل الوتر آخر صلوتک (Make Witr the end of your prayer), but he said: "Make the end of your prayer as Witr," meaning thereby that by adding one rak'ah to the pair, it would become as Witr prayer.

(1637) Ibn 'Umar reported the Apostle of Allah (may peace be upon him) as saying: Hasten to pray Witr before morning.

(1638) Ibn 'Umar said: He who prayed at night should make Witr the end of his prayer, for the Messenger of Allah (may peace be upon him) ordered this.

(1639) Ibn 'Umar reported Allah's Messenger (may peace be upon him) as saying: Make Witr the end of your night prayer.

(1640) Nāfi' reported Ibn 'Umar as saying: He who observed the night prayer should make Witr the end of his prayer before dawn. The Messenger of Allah (may peace be upon him) used to order them thus.

(1641) Ibn 'Umar reported Allah's Messenger (may peace be upon him) as saying: Witr is a rak'ah at the end of the prayer.[1026]

(1642) Ibn 'Umar reported Allah's Messenger (may peace be upon him) as saying: Witr is a rak'ah at the end of the night prayer.

(1643) Abū Mijlaz reported: I asked Ibn 'Abbās about the Witr prayer. He said: I heard the Messenger of Allah (may peace be upon him) as saying: It is a rak'ah at the end of the night prayer.

(1644) Ibn 'Umar reported: A person called (the attention) of the Messenger of Allah (may peace be upon him) as he was in the mosque, and said: Messenger of Allah, how should I make the rak'ahs of the night prayer an odd number? Upon this the Messenger of Allah (may peace be upon him) said: He who prays (night prayer) he should observe it in pairs, but if he apprehends the rise of morning, he should observe one rak'ah; that would make the number odd (for the rak'ahs) observed by him. This was narrated by Abū Kuraib 'Ubaidullah b. 'Abdullah, and Ibn 'Umar did not make mention of it.

(1645) Anas b. Sīrīn reported: I asked Ibn 'Umar to tell me about the practice of the Holy Prophet (may peace be upon him) in regard to two rak'ahs before the dawn prayer: should I make lengthy recitation in them? He said: The Messenger of Allah (may peace be upon him) used to observe the night prayer in pairs and then made the number odd by observing one rak'ah. I said: I am not asking you about it. He said: You are a bulky man, will you not show me the patience to narrate to you the ḥadīth completely?[1027] The Messenger of Allah (may peace be upon him) used to observe the night prayer in pairs and then made the number odd by observing one rak'ah, and then he observed two rak'ahs before dawn quite close to the call for prayer.[1028] (Khalaf said: "Did you see [yourself the Holy Prophet observing] the two rak'ahs before the dawn?" and he made no mention of prayer.)

(1646) Anas b. Sīrīn reported: I asked Ibn 'Umar like this (as recorded in the

1026. Here is an argument in favour of one rak'ah. Maulānā Shabbīr Aḥmad says: Witr is in fact one rak'ah by which the worshipper makes his prayer an odd number, but it is not observed alone. It is observed along with the last pair of rak'ahs concluding the night prayer (*Fatḥ al-Mulhim*, Vol. II, pp. 313, 314).

1027. This was just an expression of disapproval that he was bulky and lacked brilliance of intellect and, therefore, interupted him before he completed the ḥadīth.

1028. Here call for prayer implies Iqāma. It means that the Messenger of Allah used to observe Sunan of the dawn prayer a few minutes before the commencement of the Farḍ prayer at dawn. It is, therefore, quite natural to conceive that he must have shortened the rak'ahs (Sunan) for the dawn prayer (*Fatḥ al-Mulhim*, Vol. II, p. 314).

previous ḥadīth) and he made this addition: "And he (the Holy Prophet) made the end of the night prayer as odd number by one rak'ah." And there is also (this addition): "Stop stop, you are bulky."

(1647) Ibn 'Umar reported Allah's Messenger (may peace be upon him) as saying: The night prayer consists of pairs and when you see the approach of dawn, make this number odd by one rak'ah. It was said to Ibn 'Umar: What does the (word) pair imply? He said: (It means) that salutation is uttered after every two rak'ahs.

(1648) Abū Sa'īd (al-Khudrī) reported Allah's Apostle (may peace be upon him) as saying: Observe Witr prayer before it is morning. Abū Sa'īd reported that they (the Prophet's Companions) asked the Apostle of Allah (may peace be upon him) about Witr (prayer). (In reply to their inquiry) he said: Observe Witr prayer before it is morning.

(1649) Abū Sa'īd reported that they (some of the Companions) of the Holy Prophet (may peace be upon him) asked the Apostle of Allah (may peace be upon him) about Witr. He said: Observe Witr before morning.

Chapter CCLXIV

HE WHO FEARS THAT HE WOULD NOT BE ABLE TO OBSERVE (TAHAJJUD) PRAYER AT THE END OF NIGHT SHOULD OBSERVE WITR IN THE FIRST PART OF IT

(1650) Jābir reported Allah's Messenger (may peace be upon him) as saying: If anyone is afraid that he may not get up in the latter part of the night, he should observe Witr in the first part of it; and if anyone is eager to get up in the last part of it, he should observe Witr at the end of the night, for prayer at the end of the night is witnessed (by the angels) and that is preferable.[1029]

(1651) Jābir reported Allah's Messenger (may peace be upon him) as saying: He who amongst you is afraid that he may not be able to get up at the end of the night should observe Witr (in the first part) and then sleep, and he who is confident of getting up and praying at night (i.e. Tahajjud prayer) should observe it at the end of it, for the recitation at the end of the night is visited (by angels), and that is excellent.

Chapter CCLXV

THE MOST EXCELLENT PRAYER IS ONE IN WHICH ONE STANDS FOR A LONGER TIME

(1652) Jābir reported Allah's Messenger (may peace be upon him) as saying: The most excellent prayer is that in which the duration of standing[1030] is longer.

1029. This ḥadīth provides a strong proof to the Ḥanafites in their stand to count Witr as Wājib (compulsory).

1030. According to Maulānā Shabbīr Aḥmad 'Uthmānī, the word *Qunūt* in this context implies the whole prayer including qiyām, prostration, rukū', supplication, single-minded devotion—in short all those acts which constitute the prayer.

(1653) Jābir reported : The Messenger of Allah (may peace be upon him) was asked about the prayer which was most excellent. He said : That in which the standing is longer. (This ḥadīth is narrated by another chain of transmitters too.)

(1654) Jābir said he heard Allah's Messenger (may peace be upon him) say : There is an hour during the night in which no Muslim individual will ask Allah for good in this world and the next without His giving it to him ; and that applies to every night.[1031]

(1655) Jābir reported : I heard the Apostle of Allah (may peace be upon him) as saying : There is an hour during the night in which no Muslim bondman will ask Allah for good in this world and the next but He will grant it to him.

Chapter CCLXVI

EXHORTATION TO SUPPLICATE AND MAKE MENTION (OF ALLAH) AT THE END OF THE NIGHT AND ITS ACCEPTANCE BY THE LORD

(1656) Abū Huraira reported Allah's Messenger (may peace be upon him) as saying : Our Lord, the Blessed and the Exalted, descends[1032] every night to the lowest heaven when one-third of the latter part of the night is left, and says : Who supplicates Me so that I may answer him ? Who asks Me so that I may give to him ? Who asks Me forgiveness so that I may forgive him ?

(1657) Abū Huraira reported Allah's Messenger (may peace be upon him) as saying : Allah descends every night to the lowest heaven when one-third[1033] of the first part of the night is over and says : I am the Lord ; I am the Lord ; who is there to supplicate Me so that I answer him ? Who is there to beg of Me so that I grant him ? Who is there to beg forgiveness from Me so that I forgive him ? He continues like this till the day breaks.

(1658) Abū Huraira reported Allah's Messenger (may peace be upon him) as saying : When half of the night or two-third of it is over, Allah, the Blessed and the Exalted, descends to the lowest heaven and says : Is there any begger, so that he be given ? Is

1031. The supplication never remains unresponded with Allah. Every prayer is granted, though every demand from God may not be met in the same way in which the demand is made in the very interest of the individual who makes such a demand. It is the Lord Who knows what is in the best interest of man.

1032. Some of the scholars are of the view that this descending of the Lord means descending of His Mercy and Grace. There are others who believe that descending of the Lord implies the descending of the angels with the Commands of God ; that is why some scholars read the word ينزل (Yanzil) as ينزل (Yunzil). A ḥadīth in Nasā'ī supports this which says : يا مر منا دياً يقول هل من داع ["He commands the proclaimer saying : Is there any supplicator ?"] (Qasṭalānī, *Irshād al-Sāri, Sharḥ Ṣaḥīḥ al-Bukhārī*, Vol II, p 376). There are so many other interpretations of this word "descend" used for the Lord But the most simple is that the Merciful Lord becomes more Merciful at this part of the night and showers blessings and graces upon those who get up and pray in these hours of sweet sleep.

1033. Whenever a person gets up in any part of the night after sleep, he becomes entitled to the Mercy and Grace of the Lord, because he shows by his deed that he is prepared to forgo the sweetness of the sleep for the Lord's sake.

there any supplicator so that he be answered? Is there any beggar of forgiveness so that he be forgiven? (And Allah continues it saying) till it is daybreak.

(1659) Abū Huraira reported Allah's Messenger (may peace be upon him) as saying: Allah descends to the lowest heaven at half of the night or at one-third of its latter part and says: Who is there to supplicate Me so that I answer him? Who is there to ask Me so that I grant him? And then says: Who will lend to One Who is neither indigent nor tyrant?[1034] (This ḥadīth has been narrated by Sa'd b. Sa'id with the same chain of transmitters with this addition: "Then the Blessed and the Exalted [Lord] stretches His Hands and says: Who will lend to One Who is neither indigent nor tyrant?)

(1660) Abū Sa'īd and Abū Huraira reported Allah's Messenger (may peace be upon him) as saying: Allah waits till when one-third of the first part of the night is over; He descends to the lowest heaven and says: Is there any supplicator of forgiveness? Is there any penitant? Is there any petitioner (for mercy and favour)? Is there any solicitor—till it is daybreak.

(1661) This ḥadīth is narrated by Isḥāq with the same chain of transmitters except this that the ḥadīth transmitted by Manṣūr (the above one) is more comprehensive and lengthy.

Chapter CCLXVII

ENCOURAGEMENT TO OBSERVE PRAYERS DURING RAMAḌĀN AND THAT IS TARĀWĪḤ[1035]

(1662) Abū Huraira reported Allah's Messenger (may peace be upon him) as saying: He who observed prayer at night during Ramaḍān, because of faith and seeking his reward from Allah, his previous sins would be forgiven.

(1663) Abū Huraira reported: The Messenger of Allah (may peace be upon him) used to exhort (his Companions) to pray (at night) during Ramaḍān without commanding them to observe it as an obligatory act, and say: He who observed the night prayer in Ramaḍān because of faith and seeking his reward (from Allah), all his previous sins would be forgiven. When Allah's Messenger (may peace be upon him) died, this was the practice, and it continued thus during Abū Bakr's caliphate and the early part of 'Umar's caliphate.[1036]

1034. The one who is indigent lacks means to repay the debt and the tyrant does not pay back in spite of possessing the adequate means to do so. Allah is neither indigent nor tyrant. He is the Lord of the universe and Possessor of all the treasures in the heaven and the earth. He is the Just and Merciful Lord and, therefore, gives everyone his due share and much above that.

1035. Ṣalāt-ul-Tarāwīḥ is an integral part of Ramaḍān. The Holy Prophet exhorted his followers to devote more time and attention to prayer so that the soul may be purified and elevated.

1036. It was only for three days that the Tarāwīḥ prayer was observed in congregation during the lifetime of the Holy Prophet. The people, however, observed it individually or in small groups as the conditions permitted them. Ḥadrat Abū Bakr (Allah be pleased with him) did not issue a command for the observance of congregational prayer of Tarāwīḥ. There had been so much turmoil in the country which had made the congregational prayer of Tarāwīḥ difficult. But during the caliphate of

(1664) Abū Huraira reported Allah's Messenger (may peace be upon him) as saying: He who observed the fasts of Ramaḍān with faith and seeking reward (from Allah), all his previous sins would be forgiven, and he who observed prayer on Lailat-ul-Qadr[1037] with faith and seeking reward (from Allah), all his previous sins would be forgiven.

(1665) Abū Huraira reported Allah's Apostle (may peace be upon him) as saying: He who prayed on the Lailat-ul-Qadr (the Majestic Night) knowing that it is (the same night), I (believe) that He (the Holy Prophet also) said: (He who does) it with faith and seeking reward (from Allah), his sins would be forgiven.

(1666) 'Ā'isha reported that the Messenger of Allah (may peace be upon him) prayed one night in the mosque and people also prayed along with him. He then prayed on the following night and there were many persons. Then on the third or fourth night (many people) gathered there, but the Messenger of Allah (may peace be upon him) did not come out to them (for leading the Tarāwīḥ prayer). When it was morning he said: I saw what you were doing, but I desisted to come to you (and lead the prayer) for I feared that this prayer might become obligatory for you. (He the narrator) said: It was the month of Ramaḍān.

(1667) 'Ā'isha reported: The Messenger of Allah (may peace be upon him) came out during the night and observed prayer in the mosque and some of the people prayed along with him. When it was morning the people talked about this and so a large number of people gathered there. The Messenger of Allah (may peace be upon him) went out for the second night, and they (the people) prayed along with him. When it was morning the people began to talk about it. So the mosque thronged with people on the third night. He (the Holy Prophet) came out and they prayed along with him. When it was the fourth night, the mosque was filled to its utmost capacity but the Messenger of Allah (may peace be upon him) did not come out. Some persons among them cried: "Prayer." But the Messenger of Allah (may peace be upon him) did not come to them till he came out for the morning prayer. When he had completed the morning prayer, he turned his face to the people and recited Tashahhud (I bear testimony that there is no god but Allah and I bear testimony that Muḥammad is His Messenger) and then said: Your affair was not hidden from me in the night, but I was afraid that (my observing prayer continuously) might make the night prayer obligatory for you and you might be unable to perform it.

(1668) Zirr (b. Ḥubaish) reported: I heard from Ubayy b. Ka'b a statement made by 'Abdullah b. Mas'ūd in which he said: He who gets up for prayer (every night) during the year will hit upon Lailat-ul-Qadr. Ubayy said: By Allah! there is no god

Ḥaḍrat 'Umar (Allah be pleased with him) when there was peace and order in the country, it was decided to make arrangements for observing the Tarāwīḥ prayer in congregation as was done for three days during the lifetime of the Holy Prophet (may peace be upon him), who deliberately avoided to continue this practice beyond three days so that it might not be treated as an obligatory prayer. With Ḥaḍrat 'Umar, it could not assume that position, because he is not a lawgiver from God.

1037. Lailat-ul-Qadr, literally the Night of Majesty, or Grandeur or Greatness, is a well-known night in the last ten days of the month of Ramaḍān, being more probably the 25th, 27th, or 29th night of the month. In xliv 3, it is called the Blessed Night. It is on this very night that revelation of the Qur'ān commenced. It also means the night in which things are measured out.

but He, that (Lailat-ul-Qadr) is in Ramaḍān. (He swore without reservation :) By Allah, I know the night ; it is the night on which the Messenger of Allah (may peace be upon him) commanded us to pray. It is that which precedes the morning of twenty-seventh, and its indication is that the sun rises bright on that day without rays.[1038]

(1669) Ubayy b Ka'b reported : By Allah, I know about Lailat-ul-Qadr and I know it fully well that it is the twenty-seventh night (during Ramaḍān) on which the Messenger of Allah (may peace be upon him) commanded us to observe prayer. (Shu'ba was in doubt about these words : "the night on which the Messenger of Allah [may peace be upon him] commanded us to observe the prayer." This has been transmitted to me by a friend of mine.)

(1670) Shu'ba reported this ḥadīth with the same chain of transmitters, but he made no mention that Shu'ba was in doubt and what follows subsequently.

Chapter CCLXVIII

SUPPLICATION IN THE NIGHT PRAYER

(1671) 'Ibn 'Abbās reported: I spent a night with my maternal aunt (sister of my mother) Maimūna. The Apostle of Allah (may peace be upon him) got up during the night and relieved himself, then washed his face and hands and went to sleep. He then got up again and came to the water skin and loosened its straps, then performed good ablution between the two extremes. He then stood up and observed prayer. I also stood up and stretched my body fearing that he might be under the impression that I was there to find out (what he did at night). So I also performed ablution and stood up to pray, but I stood on his left. He took hold of my hand and made me go round to his right side. The Messenger of Allah (may peace be upon him) completed thirteen rak'ahs of his night prayer. He then lay down and slept and snored (and it was his habit to snore while asleep). Then Bilāl came and he informed him about the prayer. He (the Holy Prophet) then stood up for prayer and did not perform ablution,[1039] and his supplication included these words: "O Allah, place light[1040] in my heart, light in my sight, light in my hearing, light on my right hand, light on my left hand, light above me, light below me, light in front of me, light behind me, and enhance light for me."

Kuraib (the narrator) said: There are seven (words more) which are in my heart

1038. Various interpretations have been offered for this statement. The most appropriate and appealing is that the worshipper would be so much enlightened and delighted by the spiritual light of that night that the light emanating from the sun will not be as dazzling.

1039. This explains the nature of Muḥammad's consciousness. He enjoyed sound sleep losing all contact with the material world, but even in hours of sleep he had complete awareness of himself, because at times the revelation came to him even when he was asleep. Allah kept his soul always alert and ready to receive His Commands in full consciousness. As he was fully aware of himself even in sleep, he was, therefore, not required to perform ablution after waking up. He performed it when he felt its necessity. Mere sleep did not make it obligatory for him as we find in case of other human beings.

1040. It is a light of wisdom and piety.

(but I cannot recall them) and I met some of the descendants of 'Abbās and they narrated these words to me and mentioned in them: (Light) in my sinew, in my flesh, in my blood, in my hair, in my skin, and made a mention of two more things[1041]

(1672) Kuraib, the freed slave of Ibn 'Abbās, reported that Ibn 'Abbās narrated to him that he spent a night in the house of Maimūna, the mother of the believers, who was his mother's sister. I lay down across the cushion, whereas the Messenger of Allah (may peace be upon him) and his wife lay down on it length-wise The Messenger of Allah (may peace be upon him) slept up till midnight, or a little before midnight or a litt'e after midnight, and then got up and began to cast off the effects of sleep from his face by rubbing with his hand, and then recited the ten concluding verses of Sūra 'Imrān He then stood up near a hanging water-skin and perform d ablution well, and then stood up and prayed. Ibn 'Abbās said: I also stood up and did the same, as the Messenger of Allah (may peace be upon him) had done, and then went to him and stood by his side The Messenger of Allah (may peace be upon him) placed his right hand upon my head and took hold of my right ear and twisted it,[1042] and then observed a pair of rak'ahs, again a pair of rak'ahs, again a pair of rak'ahs, again a pair of rak'ahs, again a pair of rak'ahs, again a pair of rak'ahs, and then observed Witr and then lay down till the Mu'adhdhin came to him He (the Holy Prophet) then stood up and observed two short rak'ahs, and then went out (to the mosque) and observed the dawn prayer.

(1673) Makhrama b Sulaimān narrated it with the same chain of narration and he made this addition: "He then went to the water-skin and brushed his teeth and performed ablution well He did not pour water but a little. He then awakened me and I stood up," and the rest of the ḥadīth is the same.

(1674) Ibn 'Abbās reported: I slept (one night) in the house of Maimūna, the wife of the Apostle of Allah (may peace be upon him), and the Aposlte of Allah (may peace be upon him) was with her that night. He (after sleeping for half of the night got up and) then performed ablution and then stood up and observed prayer. I too stood on his left side. He took hold of me and made me stand on his right side. He (the Holy Prophet) observed thirteen rak'ahs on that night The Messenger of Allah (may peace be upon him) then slept and snored and it was a habit with him to snore while sleeping. The Mu'adhdhin then came to him (to inform him about the prayer) He then went out and observed prayer without performing ablution. ('Amr said: Bukair b. Ashajj had narrated it to me.)

(1675) Ibn 'Abbās reported: I spent one night in the house of my mother's sister Maimūna, daughter of Ḥārith, and said to her: Awake me when the Messenger of Allah (may peace be upon him) stands to pray (at night). (She woke me up when) the Messenger of Allah (may peace be upon him) stood up for prayer. I stood on his left side He took hold of my hand and made me stand on his right side, and whenever I dozed off he took hold of my earlobe (and made me alert) He (the narrator) said: He (the Holy Prophet) observed eleven rak'ahs He then sat with his legs drawn and

1041. Two more things are: Place light in my soul and light in my tongue.

1042. The Holy Prophet did this in order to keep himself awake and alert so that he should clearly see how the night prayer is to be observed. Had there been any lapse on his part, he could not have conveyed it with perfect confidence.

wrapped in his garment and slept so that I could hear his breathing while asleep. And when the dawn appeared, he observed two short rak'ahs of (Sunan) prayer.

(1676) Ibn 'Abbās reported that he spent a night in the house of his maternal aunt, Maimūna The Messenger of Allah (may peace be upon him) got up at night and performed short ablution (taking water) from the water-skin hanging there. (Giving a description of the ablution Ibn 'Abbās said: It was short and performed with a little water) I also got up and did the same as the Apostle of Allah (may peace be upon him) had done. I then came (to him) and stood on his left. He then made me go around to his right side. He then observed prayer and went to sleep till he began to snore. Bilāl came to him and informed him about the prayer. He (the Holy Prophet) then went out and observed the dawn prayer without performing ablution. Sufyān said: It was a special (prerogative of the) Apostle of Allah may (peace be upon him) for it has been conveyed to us that the eyes of the Apostle of Allah (may peace be upon him) sleep, but his heart does not sleep.

(1677) Ibn 'Abbās said: I spent the night in the house of my mother's sister, Maimūna, and observed how the Messenger of Allah (may peace be upon him) prayed (at night) He got up and relieved himself. He then washed his face and hands and then went to sleep. He again got up and went near the water-skin and loosened its straps and then poured some water in a bowl and inclined it with his hands (towards himself) He then performed a good ablution between the two extremes and then stood up to pray. I also came and stood by his left side. He took hold of me and made me stand on his right side. It was in thirteen rak'ahs that the (night) prayer of the Messenger of Allah (may peace be upon him) was complete. He then slept till he began to snore, and we knew that he had gone to sleep by his snoring. He then went out (for the dawn prayer) and then again slept, and said while praying or prostrating himself: "O Allah! place light in my heart, light in my hearing, light in my sight, light on my right, light on my left, light in front of me, light behind me, light above me, light below me, make light for me," or he said: "Make me light."

(1678) Salama said: I met Kuraib and he reported Ibn 'Abbās as saying: I was with my mother's sister Maimūna that the Messenger of Allah (may peace be upon him) came there, and then he narrated the rest of the ḥadīth as was narrated by Ghundar and said these words: "Make me light," beyond any doubt.

(1679) Ibn 'Abbās reported: I spent a night in the house of my mother's sister, Maimūna, and then narrated (the rest of the) ḥadīth, but he made no mention of the washing of his face and two hands but he only said: He then came to the water-skin and loosened its straps and performed ablution between the two extremes, and then came to his bed and slept He then got up for the second time and came to the water-skin and loosened its straps and then performed ablution which was in fact an ablution (it was performed well), and implored (the Lord) thus: "Give me abundant light," and he made no mention of: "Make me light."

(1680) Kuraib reported that Ibn 'Abbās spent a night in the house of the Messenger of Allah (may peace be upon him) and he said: The Messenger of Allah (may peace be upon him) stood near the water-skin and poured water out of that and performed ablution in which he neither used excess of water nor too little of it, and the rest of the ḥadīth is the same, and in this mention is also made (of the fact) that on that night the Messenger of Allah (may peace be upon him) made supplication before Allah in nineteen words. Kuraib reported : I remember twelve words out of these, but have forgotten the rest. The Messenger of Allah said : "Place light in my heart, light in my tongue, light in my hearing, light in my sight, light above me, light below me, light on my right, light on my left, light in front of me, light behind me, place light in my soul, and make light abundant for me."[1043]

(1681) Ibn 'Abbās reported : I slept one night in the house of Maimūna when the Apostle of Allah (may peace be upon him) was there, with a view to seeing the prayer of the Apostle of Allah (may peace be upon him) at night. The Apostle of Allah (may peace be upon him) entered into conversation with his wife for a short while, and then went to sleep, and the rest of the ḥadīth is the same and in it mention is made of: "He then got up, performed ablution and brushed his teeth."

(1682) 'Abdullah b. 'Abbās reported : He spent (one night) in the house of the Messenger of Allah (may peace be upon him). He (the Holy Prophet) got up, brushed his teeth and performed ablution and said : "In the creation of the heavens and the earth, and the alternation of the night and the day, there are indeed signs for people of understanding" (al-Qur-ān, iii. 190), to the end of the Sūra. He then stood up and prayed two rak'ahs, standing, bowing and prostrating himself at length in them. Then he finished, went to sleep and snored. He did that three times, six rak'ahs altogether, each time cleaning his teeth, performing ablution, and reciting these verses. Then he observed three rak'ahs of Witr.[1044] The Mu'adhdhin then pronounced the Adhān and he went out for prayer and was saying : "O Allah! place light in my heart, light in my tongue, place light in my hearing, place light in my eyesight, place light behind me, and light in front of me, and place light above me, and light below me. O Allah! grant me light."

(1683) Ibn 'Abbās reported : I spent a night in the house of my mother's sister Maimūna. The Apostle of Allah (may peace be upon him) got up for observing voluntary prayer (Tahajjud) at night. The Apostle of Allah (may peace be upon him) stood by the water-skin and performed ablution and then stood up and prayed. I also got up when I saw him doing that. I also performed ablution from the water skin and then stood at his left side. He took hold of my hand from behind his back and then turned me from his back to his right side. I ('Aṭā', one of the narrators) said : Did it concern the voluntary prayer (at night) ? He ('Ibn 'Abbās) said : Yes.

(1684) Ibn 'Abbās reported : (My father) 'Abbās sent me to the Apostle of Allah (may peace be upon him) and he was in the house of my mother's sister Maimūna and I spent that night along with him. He (the Holy Prophet) got up and prayed at night, and I stood up on his left side. He caught hold of me from behind his back and made me stand on his right side.

(1685) Ibn 'Abbās reported : I spent a night in the house of my mother's sister Maimūna, and the rest of the ḥadīth is the same as narrated above.

(1686) Abū Jamra reported : I heard Ibn 'Abbās saying that the Messenger of

1043. The seven forgotten words are : Place light in my sinew, in my flesh, in my blood, in my hair, and in my skin, make me light, and grant me light.

1044. It is on the basis of this ḥadīth that Imām Abū Ḥanīfa believes Witr to be consisting of three rak'ahs.

Allah (may peace be upon him) observed thirteen rak'ahs at night.

(1687) Zaid b. Khālid al-Juhanī said : I would definitely watch at night the prayer observed by the Messenger of Allah (may peace be upon him). He prayed two short rak'ahs, then two long, long, long rak'ahs, then he prayed two rak'ahs which were shorter than the two preceding rak'ahs, then he prayed two rak'ahs which were shorter than the two preceding, then he prayed too rak'ahs which were shorter than the two preceding, then observed a single one (Witr), making a total of thirteen rak'ahs.[1045]

(1688) Jābir b. 'Abdullah reported : I accompanied the Messenger of Allah (may peace be upon him) in a journey and we reached a watering place. He said : Jābir, are you going to enter it ? I said : Yes. The Messenger of Allah (may peace be upon him) then got down and I entered it. He (the Holy Prophet) then went away to relieve himself and I placed for him water for ablution. He then came back and performed ablution, and then stood and prayed in one garment, having its ends tied from the opposite sides. I stood behind him and he caught hold of my ear and made me stand on his right side.

(1689) 'Ā'isha reported that when the Messenger of Allah (may peace be upon him) stood up at night to pray, he began his prayer with two short rak'ahs.

(1690) Abū Huraira reported Allah's Apostle (may peace be upon him) as saying: When any one of you gets up at night, he should begin the prayer with two short rak'ahs.[1046]

(1691) Ibn 'Abbās reported that when the Messenger of Allah (may peace be upon him) got up during the night to pray, he used to say : O Allah, to Thee be the praise; Thou art the light of the heavens and the earth. To Thee be the praise ; Thou art the Supporter of the heavens and the earth. To Thee be the praise ; Thou art the Lord of the heavens and the earth and whatever is therein. Thou art the Truth ; Thy promise is True, the meeting with Thee is True, Paradise is true, Hell is true, the Hour is true. O Allah, I submit to Thee ; affirm my faith in Thee ; repose my trust in Thee, and I return to Thee for repentance ; by Thy help I have disputed ; and to Thee I have come for decision, so forgive me my earlier and later sins, the sins that I committed in secret and openly. Thou art my God. There is no god but Thee.

(1692) This ḥadith has been transmitted on the authority of Ibn 'Abbās through another chain of transmitters and with slight alteration of two words. Instead of the word *Qayyām* (Supporter, as used in the above ḥadīth here the word) *Qayyim* (the Custodian) has been used, and he (further said) : "What I did in secret." And in the ḥadīth narrated by Ibn 'Uyaina there is some addition.

(1693) This ḥadīth has been transmitted by Ibn 'Abbās by another chain of transmitters and the words are nearly the same (as recorded in the above-mentioned ḥadīth).

(1694) 'Abd-ur-Raḥmān b. 'Auf reported : I asked 'Ā'isha, the mother of the believers, (to tell me) the words with which the Apostle of Allah (may peace be upon him)

1045. Zaid b. Khālid Juhanī found opportunity to watch the night prayer of the Holy Prophet because the Prophet spent that night in a tent outside his house (*Mirqāt*, Vol. III, p 126).

The total comes to thirteen only when the first two rak'ahs are not counted as a part of Tahajjud prayer. The style of these two rak'ahs indicates that these might be Tahiyyat al-Wuḍū (the two rak'ahs observed immediately after performing the ablution).

1046. Here is an implied indication that one should just lay on oneself easy task in religion and then proceed towards undertaking heavy responsibilities on oneself (*Mirqāt*, Vol. III, p. 123).

commenced the prayer when he got up at night. She said: When he got up at night he would commence his prayer with these words: O Allah, Lord of Gabriel, and Michael, and Isrāfīl, the Creator of the heavens and the earth, Who knowest the unseen and the seen; Thou decidest amongst Thy servants concerning their differences. Guide me with Thy permission[1047] in the divergent views (which the people) hold about Truth, for it is Thou Who guidest whom Thou wilt to the Straight Path [1048]

(1695) 'Alī b Abū Ṭālib reported that when the Messenger of Allah (may peace be upon him) got up at night for prayer he would say: I turn my face in complete devotion to One Who is the Originator of the heavens and the earth and I am not of the polytheists. Verily my prayer, my sacrifice, my living and my dying are for Allah, the Lord of the worlds; there is no partner with Him and this is what I have been commanded (to profess and believe) and I am of the believers. O Allah, Thou art the King, there is no god but Thee, Thou art my Lord, and I am Thy bondman. I wronged myself and make a confession of my sin.[1049] Forgive all my sins, for no one forgives the sins but Thee, and guide me in the best of conduct for none but Thee guideth anyone (in) good conduct. Remove sins from me, for none else but Thou can remove sins from me. Here I am at Thy service, and Grace is to Thee and the whole of good is in Thine hand, and one cannot get nearness to Thee through evil.[1050] My (power as well as existence) is due to Thee (Thine grace) and I turn to Thee (for supplication). Thou art blessed and Thou art exalted. I seek forgiveness from Thee and turn to Thee in repentance; and when he would bow, he would say: O Allah, it is for Thee that I bowed. I affirm my faith in Thee and I submit to Thee, and submit humbly before Thee my hearing, my eyesight, my marrow, my bone, my sinew; and when he would raise his head, he would say: O Allah, our Lord, praise is due to Thee, (the praise) with which is filled the heavens and the earth, and with which is filled that (space) which exists between them, and filled with anything that Thou desireth afterward And when he prostrated himself, he (the Holy Prophet) would say: O Allah, it is to Thee that I prostrate myself and it is in Thee that I affirm my faith, and I submit to Thee My face is submitted before One Who created it, and shaped it, and opened his faculties of hearing and seeing. Blessed is Allah, the best of Creators; and he would then say between Tashahhud and the pronouncing of salutation: Forgive me of the earlier and later

1047. "Thy permission" means 'as Thou deemest fit, for none can dictate Thee to do anything; Thou doth everything according to Thy own will."

1048. This supplication of the Holy Prophet (may peace be upon him) clearly shows that for right guidance and for acquiring correct and authentic knowledge of the Truth one has to depend upon God's help and His revelation by which He discloses His will to His Messengers and then to the people.

1049. We have explained before the nature of the sins committed by the Prophets. The Prophets never commit sins intentionally. Theirs are the minor acts of omission or commission committed inadvertently which are at once rectified by the Lord. The most delicate and sensitive consciousness of Muḥammad (may peace be upon him) was feeling with a sense of repentance even such minor omissions. This gives an idea how pure and pious the Holy Prophet was.

1050. الشر ليس اليک has been interpreted in different ways, i.e. "Evil cannot be referred to Thee". God is no doubt the creator of both evil and good, but it is man who is responsible for committing it. The second meaning is: "Nothing is evil in Thine eyes because Thou hast created everything with perfect wisdom." Anything which appears to be evil is harmful to man and not to God, for He is far beyond the effects of evil deeds and acts.

open and secret (sins) and that where I made transgression and that Thou Knowest better than I Thou art the First and the Last. There is no god, but Thee.[1051]

(1696) A'raj reported that when the Messenger of Allah (may peace be upon him) would start the prayer, he would pronounce takbir (Allah-o-Akbar) and then say : I turn my face (up to Thee), I am the first of the believers ; and when he raised his head from rukū' he said : Allah listened to him who praised Him ; O our Lord, praise be to Thee ; and he said : He shaped (man) and how fine is his shape ? And he (the narrator) said : When he pronounced salutation he said : O Allah, forgive me my earlier (sins), to the end of the ḥadīth ; and he did not say it between the Tashahhud and salutation (as mentioned above).

Chapter CCLXIX

PREFERENCE FOR PROLONGING RECITATION IN THE NIGHT PRAYER

(1697) Ḥudhaifa reported : I prayed with the Apostle of Allah (may peace be upon him) one night and he started reciting al-Baqara. I thought that he would bow at the end of one hundred verses, but he proceeded on ; I then thought that he would perhaps recite the whole (sūra) in a rak'ah, but he proceeded and I thought he would perhaps bow on completing (this sūra). He then started al-Nisā', and recited it ; he then started Āl-i-'Imrān and recited leisurely. And when he recited the verses which referred to the Glory of Allah, he Glorified (by saying *Subḥān Allah*—Glory to my Lord the Great) and when he recited the verses which tell (how the Lord) is to be begged, he (the Holy Prophet) would then beg (from Him), and when he recited the verses dealing with protection from the Lord, he sought (His) protection and would then bow and say: Glory be to my Mighty Lord; his bowing lasted about the same length of time as his standing (and then on returning to the standing posture after rukū') he would say: Allah listened to him who praised Him, and he would then stand about the same length of time as he had spent in bowing. He would then prostrate himself and say: Glory be to my Lord most High, and his prostration lasted nearly the same length of time as his standing. In the ḥadīth transmitted by Jarīr the words are: 'He (the Holy Prophet) would say: 'Allah listened to him who praised Him, our

1051. Only this single prayer is enough to give an insight into the pious and God-loving life of the Holy Prophet. He spent the whole day in observing obligatory and voluntary prayers and in attending to the multifarious responsibilities of the Divine mission and looking to the needs of his family. Then in the stillness of the night, when the animals, birds and human beings are at rest, he would get up and pray with full devotion and enter into conversation with God, begging Him most humbly to grant him His graces, forgive him his omissions. No one can read this supplication without being deeply impressed by the humility of the Apostle of Allah, his keen devotion to his Master and Creator, his consciousness of His being near to him and his implicit and never-shaking faith in His Great Power. Only a highly devoted and most sincere believer of Allah who has the most intimate relationship with Him can make such an impassioned appeal to his Lord in the stillness of the night.

Lord, to Thee is the praise."[1052]

(1698) 'Abdullah reported: I prayed with the Messenger of Allah (my peace be upon him) and he lengthened it till I entertained an evil thought. It was said to him what that thought was. He said: I thought that I should sit down and forsake him.

(1699) A ḥadīth like this has been transmitted by A'mash with the same chain of transmitters.

Chapter CCLXX

WHAT HAS BEEN RELATED (FROM THE HOLY PROPHET) ABOUT ONE WHO SLEEPS THE WHOLE NIGHT TILL MORNING

(1700) 'Abdullah (b. Mas'ūd) reported that a mention was made of a man who slept the whole night till morning. He (the Holy Prophet) remarked: That is a man in whose ears (or in whose ear) the devil urinated.[1053]

(1701) Ḥusain b. 'Alī narrated on the authority of (his father) 'Alī b. Abū Ṭālib that the Apostle of Allah (may peace be upon him) came one night to see him ('Alī) and Fāṭimah (the daughter of the Holy Prophet) and said: Don't you observe (Tahajjud) prayer? I ('Alī) said: Messenger of Allah, verily our souls are in the hands of Allah and when He wants to awaken us, He awakens us.[1054] The Messenger of Allah (may peace be upon him) went back when I said this to him[1055] He was striking his hand on his thigh[1056] while returning, and I heard him say: Verily the man disputes with many things.[1057]

1052. One is amazed to find the Prophet's devotion to prayer and his deep longing to be always in immediate contact with his Lord. A very keen sense of Godliness and a deep-rooted love for the Lord could exhort him to observe prayer in this way. Prayer is the means by which one can admit himself to the presence of the Lord. The Holy Prophet had the earnest desire to spend the maximum of his time in the presence of his Master and seek His blessings and graces. This is an unchallenging proof of the sincerity of Muḥammad (may peace be upon him) as the Messenger of Allah because he always endeavoured to be constantly in direct contact with Him.

1053. This is meaningful. It is through the ears that one hears the voice or noise which awakens one from slumber. The man who does not wake up at night is so much overpowered by the sweetness of sleep that he turns a deaf ear to the spiritual longing of his soul. He is thus overtaken by his baser self.

1054. This conversation shows that it was occasionally that Fāṭimah and 'Alī (Allah be pleased with them) missed the Tahajjud prayer. They used to observe this prayer but on occasions when they were overtaken by sleep, they missed it. It is for explaining this behaviour that 'Alī (Allah be pleased with him) put forward this plea that the soul of man is in the hand of Allah, so he wakes up when Allah so desires, otherwise he is overpowered by sleep.

1055. That the Holy Prophet silently went back without scolding his son-in-law and daughter shows that he wanted them to pray regularly at night because the night prayer elevates the soul of man, but he did not like to force them to do so as it is a voluntary prayer. This also shows that one should exercise restraint even if one is made to listen to some unpalatable words. One should not at once burst into fury on others, however closely related they are to one.

1056. This was a habit of the Arabs to express their dislike for any word or deed.

1057. The Holy Prophet did not approve of the answer given by Ḥadrat 'Alī (Allah be pleased with him) for not observing the Tahajjud prayer on that day. He did not like his idea to shift on the responsibility of his negligence to Allah. The soul is in fact in the Hand of God but one should make wilful efforts to rise for the night prayer.

(1702) Abū Huraira transmitted it from the Apostle of Allah (may peace be upon him): When any one of you goes to sleep, the devil ties three knots[1058] at the back of his neck, sealing every knot with: "You have a long night, so sleep."[1059] So if one awakes and mentions Allah, a knot will be loosened; if he performs ablution two knots are loosened; and if he prays (all) knots will be loosened, and in the morning he will be active and in good spirits; otherwise we will be in bad spirits and sluggish in the morning.

Chapter CCLXXI

PREFERENCE FOR OBSERVING NAFL PRAYER IN THE HOUSE, AND PERMISSIBILITY OF OBSERVING IT IN THE MOSQUE ALSO

(1703) Ibn 'Umar reported Allah's Apostle (may peace be upon him) as saying: Observe some of your prayers in your houses[1060] and do not make them graves[1061]

(1704) Ibn 'Umar reported Allah's Apostle (may peace be upon him) as saying: Pray in your houses, and do not make them graves.

(1705) Jābir reported Allah's Messenger (may peace be upon him) as saying: When any one of you observes prayer in the mosque he should reserve a part of his prayer for his house, for Allah would make the prayer as a means of betterment in his house.

1058. There are three stages in the night prayer: one, getting up at night, second, performing ablution, and, third, praying, and there are hindrances to all of them from the evil in man which is represented by three knots.

1059. This gives an insight into the strategy of the Satan He does not openly call a man to the path of evil, but leads him astray by false pretexts and allurements This tactic of the Satan has been exemplified in this ḥadith. The Satan does not forbid man to pray at night but tells him to sleep on as enough time is left for prayer. He makes him lethargic and indolent.

1060. The Holy Prophet (may peace be upon him) exhorted his followers to observe the obligatory prayer in the mosque in order to emphasise its social aspect, but he at the same time stressed the observance of the Nafl prayer within the four walls of the house hidden from public gaze Prayer within the house is important from different points of view. Firstly, it inculcates sincerity and single-minded devotion to Allah, because a religious act within the house cannot win a man public applause. Secondly, with prayer and devotion the atmosphere of the house is permeated with religious piety which exercises a very healthy effect on the minds of the inmates of the house. Thirdly, the members of the family, especially women and children, learn the practices of religion and imbibe the spirit of Godliness.

1061. Various explanations have been given in elucidation of this metaphor, but three are important:

(a) The dead bodies do not offer prayer in the graves, that is why the Muslims have been asked not to treat their houses as graves.

(b) It has been narrated from the Holy Prophet that he forbade to offer prayer in the graveyards and baths. Keeping in view this injunction, the Holy Prophet asked his followers not to make their houses as graves.

(c) According to metaphorical expression, the dead bodies sleep in the graves, so when the Holy Prophet asked his followers not to make their houses as graves, he in fact wanted to point out that houses should not be considered as places meant for sleeping only They should also be made as places of worship and devotion to Allah.

(1706) Abū Mūsā reported Allah's Apostle (may peace be upon him) as saying: The house in which remembrance of Allah is made and the house in which Allah is not remembered are like the living and the dead.

(1707) Abū Huraira reported Allah's Messenger (may peace be upon him) as saying: Do not make your houses as graveyards. Satan runs away from the house in which Sūra Baqara is recited.

(1708) Zaid b. Thābit reported: The Messenger of Allah (may peace be upon him) made an apartment with the help of the leaves of date trees or of mats. The Messenger of Allah (may peace be upon him) went out to pray in it. People followed him and came to pray with him. Then they again came one night and waited (for him), but the Messenger of Allah (may peace be upon him) delayed in coming out to them. And when he did not come out, they cried aloud and threw pebbles at the door The Messenger of Allah (may peace be upon him) came out in anger and said to them: By what you have been constantly doing, I was inclined to think that it (prayer) might not become obligatory for you. So you must observe prayer (optional) in your houses, for the prayer observed by a man in the house is better except an obligatory prayer.

(1709) Zaid b. Thābit reported that the Apostle of Allah (may peace be upon him) made an apartment in the mosque of mats, and he observed in it prayers for many nights till people began to gather around him, and the rest of the ḥadīth is the same but with this addition: "Had this (Nafl) prayer become obligatory for you, you would not be able to observe it."

Chapter CCLXXII

EXCELLENCE OF AN ACT (I.E. OBSERVING OF THE NIGHT PRAYER, ETC.) DONE CONSTANTLY

(1710) 'Ā'isha reported that the Messenger of Allah (may peace be upon him) had a mat and he used it for making an apartment during the night and observed prayer in it, and the people began to pray with him, and he spread it (the mat) during the day time. The people crowded round him one night. He (the Holy Prophet) then said: O people, perform such acts as you are capable of doing, for Allah does not grow weary but you will get tired. The acts most pleasing to Allah are those which are done continuously, even if they are small. And it was the habit of the members of Muḥammad's (may peace be upon him) household, that whenever they did an act they did it continuously.

(1711) 'Ā'isha is reported to have said that the Messenger of Allah (may peace be upon him) was asked about the act most pleasing to Allah. He replied: That which is done continuously, even if it is small.

(1712) 'Alqama reported: I asked 'Ā'isha, the mother of the believers, saying: O mother of the believers, how did the Messenger of Allah (may peace be upon him) act? Did he choose a particular act for a particular day? She said: No, his act was continuous, and who amongst you is capable of doing what the Messenger of Allah (may peace be upon him) did?

(1713) 'Ā'isha reported Allah's Messenger (may peace be upon him) as saying: The acts most pleasing to Allah are those which are done continuously, even if they are small, and when 'Ā'isha did any act she did it continuously.

(1714) Anas reported that the Messenger of Allah (may peace be upon him) entered the mosque (and he found) a rope tied between the two pillars; so he said: What is this? They said: It is for Zainab.[1062] She prays and when she slackens or feels tired she holds it. Upon this he (the Holy Prophet) said: Untie it. Let one pray as long as one feels fresh but when one slackens or becomes tired one must stop it.[1063] (And in the ḥadīth transmitted by Zuhair it is: "He should sit down.")

(1715) A ḥadīth like this has been narrated from the Apostle of Allah (may peace be upon him) on the authority of Anas by another chain of transmitters.

(1716) 'Urwa b. Zubair reported that 'Ā'isha, the wife of the Apostle of Allah (may peace be upon him), told him that (once) Ḥaulā' bint Tuwait b Ḥabīb b. Asad b. 'Abd al-'Uzzā passed by her (at the time) when the Messenger of Allah (may peace be upon him) was with her. I ('Ā'isha) said: It is Ḥaulā' bint Tuwait and they say that she does not sleep at night. Upon this the Messenger of Allah (may peace be upon him) said: (Oh) she does not sleep at night! Choose an act which you are capable of doing (continuously). By Allah, Allah would not grow weary, but you will grow weary.

(1717) 'Ā'isha said: The Messenger of Allah (may peace be upon him) came to me when a woman was sitting with me. He said: Who is she? I said: She is a woman who does not sleep but prays. He said: Do such acts which you are capable of doing. By Allah, Allah does not grow weary but you will grow weary. The religious act most pleasing to Him is one the doer of which does it continuously. (And in the ḥadīth transmitted by Abū Usāma [the words are]: "She was a woman from Banu Asad.")

Chapter CCLXXIII

CONCERNING DOZING OFF IN PRAYER, OR FALTERING OF ONE'S TONGUE IN THE RECITATION OF THE QUR'ĀN, OR IN MENTIONING OF ALLAH, ONE SHOULD SLEEP, OR STOP IT TILL ONE BECOMES LIVELY

(1718) 'Ā'isha reported Allah's Apostle (may peace be upon him) as saying: When anyone amongst you dozes in prayer, he should sleep, till sleep is gone, for when one of you prays while dozing he does not know whether he may be asking pardon or vilifying himself.

(1719) Abū Huraira reported Allah's Messenger (may peace be upon him) as saying: When any one of you gets up at night (for prayer) and his tongue falters in (the recitation) of the Qur'ān, and he does not know what he is reciting, he should go to sleep.

Chapter CCLXXIV

CONCERNING THE CAREFUL REMEMBERING OF THE QUR'ĀN

(1720) 'Ā'isha reported that the Apostle of Allah (may peace be upon him) heard

1062. She is Zainab bint Jahsh, the wife of the Holy Prophet (may peace be upon him).

1063. The word Qa'da (قعد) has two meanings. It implies that one should complete the Nafl prayer sitting if one feels exhausted by standing. The second meaning is that one should stop if one feels tired, which is correct and reasonable.

a person reciting the Qur'ān at night. Upon this he said: May Allah show mercy to him; he has reminded me of such and such a verse which I had missed[1064] in such and such a sūra.

(1721) 'Ā'isha reported that the Apostle of Allah (may peace be upon him) listened to the recitation of the Qur'ān by a man in the mosque. Thereupon he said: May Allah have mercy upon him; he reminded me of the verse[1065] which I had been made to forget.

(1722) 'Abdullah b. 'Umar reported Allah's Messenger (may peace be upon him) as saying: The example of a man who has memorised the Qur'ān[1066] is like that of a hobbled camel. If he remained vigilant, he would be able to retain it (with him), and if he loosened the hobbled camel it would escape.[1067]

(1723) This ḥadīth has been narrated by Ibn 'Umar from the Apostle of Allah (may peace be upon him), but in the ḥadīth transmitted by Mūsā b. 'Uqba, this addition is made: "When one who had committed the Qur'ān to memory (or who is familiar with it) gets up (for night prayer) and recites it night and day, it remains fresh in his mind, but if he does not get up (for prayer and thus does not recite it) he forgets it."

(1724) 'Abdullah reported Allah's Messenger (may peace be upon him) as saying: What a wretched person is he amongst them who says: I have forgotten such and such a verse. (He should instead of using this expression say): I have been made to forget it. Try to remember the Qur'ān for it is more apt to escape from men's minds than a hobbled camel.[1068]

(1725) 'Abdullah is reported to have said: Keep refreshing your knowledge of the sacred books (or always renew your knowledge of these sacred books) and sometimes he would mention the Qur'ān for it is more apt to escape from men's minds than animals which are hobbled, and the Messenger of Allah (may peace be upon him) said: None of you should say: I forgot such and such a verse, but he has been made to forget.

(1726) Ibn Mas'ūd reported Allah's Messenger (may peace be upon him) as

1064. In another narration the word is أنسيتها (I forgot it). Maulānā Shabbīr Aḥmad, elucidating the nature of Muḥammad's forgetfulness, says: This forgetfulness is of two kinds. The first one is natural because of the Holy Prophet (may peace be upon him) being a human being as is indicated by his words: "I am a human being like you; I forget as you forget." But it should be remembered that Allah at once reminds him what he is required to remember. He is never made to miss anything permanently on account of forgetfulness. The second type is that forgetfulness which is intended by Allah and by which Allah abrogates some of the verses, and this is supported by a verse of the Holy Qur'ān: "We shall make thee read (O Muḥammad) so that you shall not forget, save that which Allah willeth" (lxxxvii. 6, 7) (*Fatḥ al-Mulhim*, Vol. II, p. 344).

1065. It should be remembered that whenever the Apostle of Allah forgot a verse temporarily, it was done after he had read it to his Companions and they had retained it in their minds (*Fatḥ al-Mulhim*, Vol. II, p. 344).

1066. *Ṣāḥib-al-Qur'ān* may mean one who has committed the Qur'an to memory, or one who has developed a kind of proficiency in it by constantly reciting it.

1067. When the camel is constantly supervised and is kept hobbled it remains under control, otherwise it flees. Similarly, if a person recites the Qur'ān again and again and is vigilant enough as not to let it slip from his mind, it is a source of spiritual benefit to him. But when a person becomes indifferent to it, it slips out of his mind.

1068. When the recitation of the Qur'ān is neglected it is not abruptly that the Qur'ān slips out of one's mind. The process is slow like the movement of a hobbled camel which walks haltingly.

saying: Wretched is the man who says: I forgot[1069] such and such a sūra, or I forget such and such a verse, but he has been made to forget

(1727) Abū Mūsā al-Ash'arī reported Allah's Apostle (may peace be upon him) as saying: Keep refreshing your knowledge of the Qur'ān, for I swear by Him in Whose Hand is the life of Muḥammad that it is more liable to escape than camels which are hobbled.

Chapter CCLXXV

DESIRABILITY OF RECITING THE QUR'ĀN IN A SWEET VOICE

(1728) Abū Huraira reported this directly from the Messenger of Allah (may peace be upon him): God has not listened to anything as He listens to a Prophet reciting the Qur'ān in a sweet voice.

(1729) This ḥadīth has been narrated by Ibn Shihāb with the same chain of transmitters with words: "As He listens to a Prophet reciting the Qur'ān in a sweet voice."

(1730) Abū Huraira is reported to have heard Allah's Messenger (may peace be upon him) as saying: Allah does not listen to anything (more approvingly) as He listens to a Prophet reciting loudly the Qur'ān in a sweet voice.

(1731) This ḥadīth has been narrated with the same chain of transmitters by Ibn al-Hād except this that Abū Huraira reported Allah's Messenger (may peace be upon him) as saying and he did not say: "He heard it."

(1732) Abū Huraira reported Allah's Messenger (may peace be upon him) as saying: Allah has not heard anything (more pleasing) than listening to the Prophet reciting the Qur'ān in a sweet loud voice.

(1733) This ḥadīth has been narrated by another chain of transmitters but with a slight modification of words.

(1734) Buraida reported on the authority of his father that the Messenger of Allah (may peace be upon him) had said: 'Abdullah b. Qais or al-Ash'arī has been gifted with a sweet melodious voice out[1070] of the voices of the family[1071] of David.

(1735) Abū Burda narrated on the authority of Abū Mūsā that the Messenger of Allah (may peace be upon him) had said to Abū Mūsā: If you were to see me, as I was listening to your recitation (of the Qur'ān) yester night (you would have felt delighted). You are in fact endowed with a sweet voice[1072] like that of David himself.

1069. This expression—I forgot it—does not fit in with the religious responsibility of a man in regard to the Qur'ān. The Qur'ān is the most sacred treasure for a Muslim and he should not, therefore, let it slip out of his mind, and if he does it that shows his indifference to the Book of Allah which is not desirable. The second expression: "I have been made to forget it" shows that it is not due to any negligence on his part, but due to the weakness of his memory which is beyond his power.

1070. *Mizmār*, the word originally used in the text, means musical reed or pipe, now generally called a flute. But here it means not the flute, but the sweet melodious voice like that of David. *Mazāmir Dāwūd* may also mean what David used to sing or chant in the form of prayer or hymns to Allah (cf Psalms of David).

1071. According to some of the linguists آل is said to be here redundant or pleonastic, meaning the person, so the translation would be: Verily al-Ash'arī has been gifted with a sweet melodious voice like that of David himself (Lane's *Lexicon*).

1072. Islam is a natural religion in the sense that in its comprehensive system there is a reasonable arrangement for the satisfaction of every human urge. Just as man needs bread to live, similarly he

Chapter CCLXXVI

THE RECITATION BY THE APOSTLE (MAY PEACE BE UPON HIM) OF ƆŪRAT AL-FATḤ ON THE DAY OF THE CONQUEST OF MECCA

(1736) Mu'āwiya b. Qurra reported 'Abdullah b. Mughaffal al-Muzanī as saying: The Apostle of Allah (may peace be upon him) recited on his ride Sūrat al-Fatḥ [1073] during a journey in the year of the Conquest (of Mecca), and he repeated [1074] (the words) in his recitation. Mu'āwiya said: If I were not afraid that the people would crowd around me, I would have given a demonstration of (the Prophet's) recitation before you.

(1737) Mu'āwiya b. Qurra is reported to have heard 'Abdullah b. Mughaffal as saying: I saw the Messenger of Allah (may peace be upon him) reciting Sūra Fatḥ on his camel on the day of the Conquest of Mecca. He (the narrator) said: Ibn Mughaffal recited it and repeated it. Mu'āwiya said: Had there been (no crowed of) people, I would have given a practical demonstration of that which Ibn Mughaffal had mentioned from the Apostle of Allah (may peace be upon him).

(1738) This ḥadīth has been narrated bo Khālid al-Ḥārith with the same chain of transmitters (with these words:) (The Holy Prophet) was reciting Sūrat al-Fatḥ as he was travelling on his mount.

Chapter CCLXXVII

DESCENDING OF TRANQUILLITY BY THE RECITATION OF THE QUR'ĀN

(1739) Al-Barā' reported that a person was reciting Sūrat al-Kahf and there was a horse tied with two ropes at his side, a cloud overshadowed him, and as it began to come nearer and nearer his horse began to take fright from it. He went and mentioned that to the Prophet (may peace be upon him) in the morning, and he (the Holy

has a passion for sweet melodious voice, and if one is deprived of it, the harmonious development of his personality is inhibited. Sweet voice exercises a healthy effect on the minds of human beings and even that of animals. Islam recognises this basic fact of human life and it does not crush this yearning of human soul. But since its approach towards life is most healthy and balanced, it, therefore, does not allow human beings to divert their minds to unhealthy activities for satisfying their yearnings. It has, therefore, forbidden the use of musical instruments and the singing of immoral songs or such songs as make a man lethargic and rouse in him base desires. But it has at the same time encouraged the reciting of the Qur'ān in a sweet melodious voice in order to elevate the soul of man. Islam does not encourage any art, literature or music which undermines the moral fibre and the will-force of man. All that brings drowsiness and weariness in life, or which vibrates the animal lust in man, or which makes us close our eyes to the reality around us, is a message of decay and death which a dynamic religion like Islam cannot tolerate. It has sublimated the instincts of man to moral and spiritual channels. The yearning for sweet voice has found expression in Islam in the form of good Qirā'at, which is a special feature of Islamic civilisation.

1073. It is Sūra xlviii. of the Qur'ān.

1074. *Rajja'* (رجع) in recitation is repetition of short verses or portions of verses.

Prophet) said: That was tranquillity[1075] which came down at the recitation of the Qur'ān.

(1740) Ibn Isḥāq reported: I heard al Barā' as saying that a man recited al-Kahf when an animal was there in the house and it began to take fright. And as he looked around, he found a cloud overshadowing it. He mentioned that to the Apostle of Allah (may peace be upon him). Upon this he said: O so and so, recite on (the sūra) for *as-Sakina* descends at the (recitation of the Qur'ān) or on account (of the recitation) of the Qur'ān.

(1741) This ḥadīth has been narrated on the authority of al-Barā' with a slight modification of words.

(1742) Abū Sa'īd al-Khudrī told of Usaid b. Ḥuḍair saying that one night he recited the Qur'ān in his enclosure, when the horse began to jump about. He again recited and (the horse) again jumped. He again recited and it jumped as before. Usaid said: I was afraid lest it should trample (his son) Yaḥyā. I stood near it (the horse) and saw something like a canopy over my head with what seemed to be lamps in it, rising up in the sky till it disappeared. I went to the Messenger of Allah (may peace be upon him) on the next day and said: Messenger of Allah, I recited the Qur'ān during the night in my enclosure and my horse began to jump. Upon this the Messenger of Allah (may peace be upon him) said: You should have kept on reciting, Ibn Ḥuḍair. He (Ibn Ḥuḍair) said: I recited. It jumped (as before). Upon this the Messenger of Allah (may peace be upon him) again said: You should have kept on reciting, Ibn Ḥuḍair. He (Ibn Ḥuḍair) said: I recited and it again jumped (as before). The Messenger of Allah (may peace be upon him) again said: You should have kept on reciting, Ibn Ḥuḍair. He (Ibn Ḥuḍair) said: (Messenger of Allah) I finished (the recitation) for Yaḥyā was near (the horse) and I was afraid lest it should trample him. I saw something like a canopy with what seemed to be lamps in it rising up in the sky till it disappeared. Upon this the Messenger of Allah (may peace be upon him) said: Those were the angels who listened to you; and if you had continued reciting, the people would have seen them in the morning and they would not have concealed themselves from them.[1076]

Chapter CCLXXVIII

EXCELLENCE OF THE ḤĀFIẒ (ONE WHO COMMITS THE QUR'ĀN TO MEMORY) OF THE QUR'ĀN

(1743) Abū Mūsā al-Ash'arī reported Allah's Messenger (may peace be upon him) as saying: A believer who recites the Qur'ān is like an orange whose fragrance is sweet and whose taste is sweet; a believer who does not recite the Qur'ān is like a date which

1075. The word in Arabic is *as-sakina* which may be translated as tranquillity or calmness, but here it has the definite article which indicates something precise. According to Imām Nawawī this calmness is also accompanied by angels This was the reason why the horse which is not used to such spiritual sights was scared.

This shows that Divine calmness permeates the whole atmosphere with spiritual tranquillity and not only human beings but even the animals imbibe its spirit.

1076. This ḥadīth proves that it is possible for the human beings to see angels in exceptional circumstances.

has no fragrance but has a sweet taste; and the hypocrite who recites the Qur'ān is like a basil whose fragrance is sweet, but whose taste is bitter; and a hypocrite who does not recite the Qur'ān is like the colocynth which has no fragrance and has a bitter taste.

(1744) This ḥadīth has been transmitted by Qatāda with the same chain of transmitters but with one alteration that instead of the word: "hypocrite" (*munāfiq*), there it is "wicked" (*fājir*).

Chapter CCLXXIX

EXCELLENCE OF THE ONE WHO IS PROFICIENT IN THE QUR'ĀN AND ONE WHO FALTERS IN IT

(1745) 'Ā'isha reported Allah's Messenger (may peace be upon him) (as saying): One who is proficient in the Qur'ān is associated with the noble, upright, recording angels; and he who falters in it, and finds it difficult for him, will have a double reward.[1077]

(1746) This ḥadīth has been transmitted with the same chain of transmitters by Qatāda except with this change: "He who finds it hard (to recite the Qur'ān) will have a double reward."

Chapter CCLXXX

EXCELLENCE OF THE RECITING OF THE QUR'ĀN BY ONE WHO IS MORE SKILLED AND PROFICIENT BEFORE ONE WHO IS INFERIOR TO HIM

(1747) Anas reported Allah's Messenger (may peace be upon him) as saying to Ubayy b. Ka'b: Allah has commanded me to recite the Qur'ān to you. He said: Did Allah mention me to you by name? He (the Holy Prophet) said: Allah made a mention of your name to me. (On hearing this) Ubayy b. Ka'b wept.[1078]

(1748) Anas reported Allah's Messenger (may peace be upon him) as saying to Ubayy b. Ka'b: Allah has commaded me to recite to you: "Those who disbelieve were not . . ." al-Qur'ān, (xcviii. 1). He said: Did He mention me by name? He (the Holy Prophet said) Yes. Upon this he shed tears (of gratitude).

(1749) Qatāda said: I heard Anas saying that the Messenger of Allah (may peace be upon him) said to Ubayy the same thing.

Chapter CCLXXXI

EXCELLENCE OF LISTENING TO THE QUR'ĀN AND ASKING ONE WHO HAS MEMORISED IT AND TO RECITE IT FROM HIS MEMORY AND SHEDDING TEARS WHILE LISTENING TO THE RECITATION, AND DELIBERATING OVER IT

(1750) 'Abdullah (b. Mas'ūd) reported: The Messenger of Allah (may peace be upon

1077. It is because he makes more effort in learning and reciting it. This also shows the prophetic vision of the Apostle (may peace be upon him) which foresaw that many Muslims who are not Arabs or well versed in Arabic would also learn and recite the Book. Such persons have great solace and encouragement in this prophecy.

1078. These were the tears of joy for his name had been mentioned by Allah Himself.

him) asked me to recite the Qur'ān. He said: Messenger of Allah, (how) should I recite to you whereas it has been sent down to you? He (the Holy Prophet) said: I desire to hear it from someone else. So I recited Sūrat al-Nisā' till I reached the verse: "How then shall it be when We shall bring from every people a witness and bring you against them as a witness?" (verse 41).[1079] I lifted my head or a person touched me in my side, and so I lifted my head and saw his tears falling (from the Holy Prophet's eyes).

(1751) This ḥadīth has been transmitted by A'mash with the same chain of transmitters but with this addition: "The Messenger of Allah (may peace be upon him) was on the pulpit when he asked me to recite to him."

(1752) Ibrāhīm reported that the Apostle of Allah (may peace be upon him) asked 'Abdullah b Mas'ūd to recite to him (the Qur'ān). He said: Should I recite it to you while it has been sent down or revealed to you? He (the Holy Prophet) said: I love to hear it from someone else. So he ('Abdullah b. Mas'ūd) recited to him (from the beginning of Sūrat al-Nisā' up to the verse: "How shall then it be when We bring from every people a witness and bring you as a witness against them?" He (the Holy Prophet) wept (on listening to it). It is narrated on the authority of Ibn Mas'ūd through another chain of transmitters that the Apostle of Allah (may peace be upon him) also said that he had been a witness to his people as long as (said he): I lived among them[1080] or I had been among them.

(1753) 'Abdullah (b. Mas'ūd) reported: I was in Ḥimṣ[1081] when some of the people asked me to recite the Qur'ān to them. So I recited Sūra Yūsuf to them. One of the persons among the people said: By Allah, this is not how it has been sent down. I said: Woe upon you! By Allah, I recited it to the Messenger of Allah (may peace be upon him) and he said to me: You have (recited) it well. I was talking with him (the man who objected to my recitation) that I sensed the smell of wine from him. So I said to him: Do you drink wine and belie the Book (of Allah)? You would not depart till I would whip you. So I lashed him according to the prescribed punishment (for the offence of drinking wine).

(1754) This ḥadīth has been transmitted by A'mash with the same chain of transmitters but with an exception that it is not mentioned in it: "He said to me: You recited (the Qur'ān) well."

1079. The Apostles and Messengers (peace be upon all of them) of every age shall have to bear witness before God that they had faithfully delivered His message and no stone was left unturned to bring people to the path of righteousness. The last of the Holy Prophets, Muḥammad (may peace be upon him), shall have to bear this witness. Tears rolled from his eyes thinking of the heavy responsibilities of his great mission as the final dispenser of the Will of God.

1080 The Holy Prophet was reminded of the answer that Jesus Christ would give when God would question him on the Day of Judgment: "O Jesus, son of Mary! didst thou say unto men; 'Worship me and my mother as deities besides God?' and Jesus would answer: 'Glory to Thee. It is not conceivable that I would have said what I had no right (to say). Had I said it, Thou wouldst indeed have known it. Thou knowest all that is within myself, whereas I know not what is in Thy Self. Verily it is Thou alone Who fully knowest all the things that are hidden. Nothing did I tell them beyond what Thou didst bid me to (say): "Worship God (Who is my Sustainer as well as your Sustainer)." And I bore witness to them as long as I lived among them.' " (v. 119-120).

1081. It is a town in Syria.